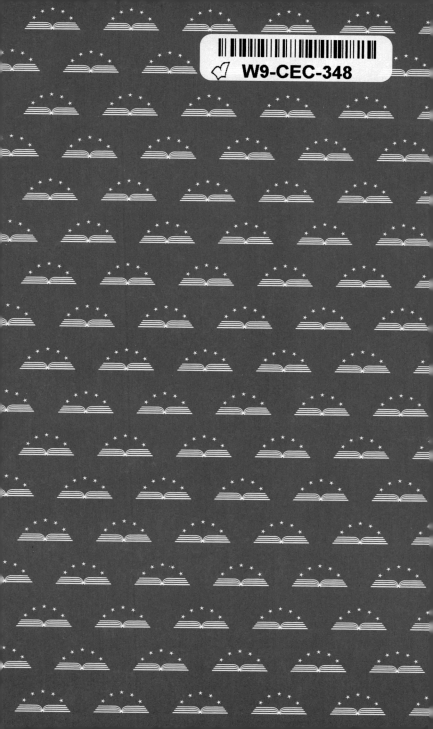

SHAKESPEARE
in AMERICA

SHAKESPEARE
in AMERICA

AN ANTHOLOGY FROM THE REVOLUTION TO NOW

JAMES SHAPIRO, EDITOR

FOREWORD BY PRESIDENT BILL CLINTON

THE LIBRARY OF AMERICA

Distributed to the trade in the United States
by Penguin Group (USA) Inc.
and in Canada by Penguin Books Canada Ltd.

Library of Congress Control Number: 2013949835

ISBN 978-1-59853-295-1

First Printing
The Library of America—251

Shakespeare in America:
An Anthology from the Revolution to Now

is published with support from

LARRY MILLER

and

DAVID PARSONS

Contents

Illustrations

(following page 352)

Foreword

BY PRESIDENT BILL CLINTON

Shakespeare only had a fleeting acquaintance with America, judging from his work, which brushed up against the New World on only a couple of occasions: in his late play, *The Tempest*, based on a story of the wreck of the Sea Venture off the coast of Bermuda in 1609 on its way to the Virginia colony, and in Henry VIII, which alludes to the visit of the Algonquin captive Epenow (the "strange Indian with the great tool come to court"), who was shown in London as a spectacle when Shakespeare was writing that play in 1613.

Nevertheless, our engagement with him has been long and sustained: generation after generation of Americans has fallen under his spell. Early American presidents felt the kinship, in ways both comfortable and uncomfortable. George Washington left the legislative haggling at the Constitutional Convention in Philadelphia on July 14, 1787, to see a production of *The Tempest*. John Adams and Thomas Jefferson visited his birthplace together while in England, and, as this volume recounts, John Quincy Adams wrote about *Othello*, finding its racial story lines disturbing. In *Democracy in America*, Alexis de Tocqueville described Shakespeare's immense popularity across the land in the 1830s: "There is hardly a pioneer hut in which the odd volume of Shakespeare cannot be found. I remember reading the feudal drama *Henry V* for the first time in a log cabin."

Abraham Lincoln, with access to so few books as a young man, did have access to Shakespeare, and the results speak for themselves. Shakespeare never stopped speaking to him, and through him. Shakespeare spoke to huge numbers of other Americans as well in the nineteenth century, including to John Wilkes Booth, who acted in Shakespeare's great drama of assassination, *Julius Caesar*, onstage before he tragically stepped out of the role and into reality. Even far from cities, out on the frontier, the bard captivated new generations of Americans. English speakers, immigrants, people of all racial backgrounds heard the rough and tumble performances, and the simple act of listening together accelerated the work of democracy.

As a high school student in one of those nineteenth century frontier towns—Hot Springs, Arkansas—I first encountered the work of Shakespeare. I was not overjoyed at first to make his acquaintance—in fact, I was required to memorize a hundred lines from *Macbeth*, including the famous soliloquy that ends:

> Life's but a walking shadow, a poor player,
> That struts and frets his hour upon the stage,
> And then is heard no more. It is a tale
> Told by an idiot, full of sound and fury,
> Signifying nothing.

That was an important early lesson about the perils of blind ambition, and the emptiness of power disconnected from higher purpose. I always cherished that early lesson—and tried never to forget it. *Macbeth* is a great play about someone whose immense ambition had an ethically inadequate object.

In 1995, my good friend Yitzhak Rabin was killed doing the work of peace in Israel. Sometimes, at moments of incomprehensible grief, Shakespeare says it for us, when we are too numb to find the words. In my eulogy for Rabin, I quoted the celebrated lines:

> The quality of mercy is not strain'd,
> It droppeth as the gentle rain from heaven
> Upon the place beneath. It is twice blest:
> It blesseth him that gives and him that takes.

—before concluding, "Let us give it, and take it."

Reading Shakespeare continues to bless us, long past the first encounter, giving much, and taking very little. I hope that all Americans enjoy their own encounter with the playwright whose work has done so much to illuminate the human condition, and to help us to understand ourselves, throughout our history.

Introduction

BY JAMES SHAPIRO

One of the more memorable episodes in the history of Shakespeare in America took place in January 1846 at Corpus Christi, Texas. Over half of the U.S. Army was gathered there, sent to provoke a war with Mexico after Congress had annexed Texas as a slave state. One of the officers described Corpus Christi at the time as "the most murderous, thieving, gambling, cut-throat, God-forsaken hole" in Texas.[1] In order to distract the idle troops, John B. Magruder oversaw the building of a theater large enough to hold eight hundred spectators. He and other officers fell to work, painting scenery and rehearsing plays, including Shakespeare's *Othello*. Admission was not cheap: a box seat cost a dollar and a place in the pit half that, but the productions played to full houses.[2] James Longstreet, who, like Magruder, later served as a distinguished Confederate general, was initially cast as Desdemona. But Longstreet, who was six feet tall, did not look right for the part, so at 5' 8" and 135 pounds, Lieutenant Ulysses S. Grant (future commander of the Union armies in the Civil War, and later the eighteenth president of the United States), was given the role instead. In later years Longstreet recalled that Grant "looked very like a girl dressed up. He really rehearsed the part of Desdemona but he did not have much sentiment." In the end, a professional actress was brought in to replace Grant after Theodoric Porter, who played Othello, objected. Longstreet recalled that "Porter said it was bad enough to play the part with a woman in the cast, and he could not pump up any sentiment with Grant dressed up as Desdemona."[3]

The story underscores the extent to which in mid-nineteenth century America Shakespeare's works were widely known, a cultural touchstone that transcended region and class. Examples abound. When, for instance, Grant had to leave the army for a while in 1854 because of drunkenness, a fellow soldier, trying to explain to a friend what had happened, compared Grant to Shakespeare's flawed but noble lieutenant in *Othello*: "like Cassio, he had a poor brain for drinking."[4] This easy familiarity with Shakespeare's works dovetails with the observation made by the French historian Alexis de Tocqueville, who after touring the United States in 1831 noted that there "is hardly a pioneer's hut which does not contain a few odd volumes of Shakespeare."[5]

The staging of *Othello* in Corpus Christi invites more questions than the few surviving details of the production can begin to answer, not least of which is, "Why *Othello* of all plays?" And since it was *Othello*, how did the production speak to its time and place? The playgoers at Corpus Christi likely responded in markedly different ways than we might today. Insofar as *Othello* is also a play about soldiers heading off to war, they were no doubt keenly interested in the play's exploration of military life, rivalry, and honor. But *Othello*, inescapably, is also about race, and the soldiers in Corpus Christi were well aware that the decision to send them there to fight (and for a sixth of them—including Porter—to die, in what Grant later called a "wicked" and "unjust" Mexican war), was driven in part by a desire to extend the reach of slavery.

Spectators throughout antebellum America, a nation hurtling toward civil war over the question of race, certainly saw *Othello* through a different lens than British audiences at the time. Parliament had formally abolished slavery in the British Empire in 1833 and black actors, including an American, Ira Aldridge, had been playing Othello on the London stage since 1825. But over a century would pass before a black man, Paul Robeson, could do the same on Broadway. We can only wonder what effect playing a woman in love with the Moor had on Grant (even as we might wonder what impact acting in a version of *The Merchant of Venice* or writing about a "broken" Shylock had on future presidents Dwight D. Eisenhower and Harry Truman).[6]

It is tempting to think that a plot about a black general eloping with a white woman would have been unpopular, if not taboo, in slave states, but the opposite was true. In the quarter-century before the Civil War, *Othello* was regularly staged in the South, twenty times, for example, in Memphis, and twice that often in Mobile, strong evidence that white Southerners could turn a blind eye toward the play's portrayal of so incendiary an issue as miscegenation (inescapable no matter how heavily edited the script or how much the hero's skin color was lightened in performance during this so-called "bronze age" of Othellos).[7] Yet in the same antebellum South it was unremarkable that a slave could be named after Shakespeare's tragic hero, as we learn from a notice of a "lusty" runaway "Negro boy" called "Othello" posted in the *South Carolina Gazette*; one wonders how many readers noted the irony that this young man's Shakespearean namesake had himself been "sold to slavery" before he was redeemed from that condition.[8] After the outbreak of war *Othello* quickly fell out of favor in the South, presumably because it was no longer possible to see the play in such blinkered ways. One of the last holdouts was Mary Preston, who in an essay published in 1869 continued to insist that "Othello *was* a *white* man!"

In a nation wrestling with great issues, Shakespeare's works allowed Americans to express views that may otherwise have been hard to articulate—or admit to. *Othello*, again, provides a case in point. One of the earliest Americans who felt compelled to write about the play was John Quincy Adams, the nation's sixth president. His credentials as an abolitionist were impeccable and he hoped to be remembered as "the acutest, the astutest, the archest enemy of southern slavery that ever existed." And yet Adams concluded that "the moral" of *Othello* is "that the intermarriage of black and white blood is a violation of the law of nature. *That* is the lesson to be learned from the play." For Adams, slavery was one thing, interracial marriage quite another.

If Adams's position on race and *Othello* sounds inconsistent, it was no more so than the laws in his native Massachusetts, which abolished slavery in 1783 but then "re-enacted its law against racial intermarriage in 1786 while eliminating legal prohibitions against interracial fornication."[9] Adams's deep discomfort with the play was shared by his mother Abigail, another strong opponent of slavery, who after seeing Sarah Siddons play Desdemona opposite John Philip Kemble in London in 1785 wrote to a friend that "my whole soul shuddered whenever I saw the sooty Moor touch fair Desdemona."[10] And she felt this revulsion even though she knew that Kemble was a white actor, playing Othello in blackface.

Eight years after John Quincy Adams wrote about *Othello*, audiences in American cities, most of them made up of white working-class men, paid to see a popular actor perform the burlesque opera *Otello*. T. D. Rice's production revisits Adams's concerns in a blackface performance that liberally uses the "N-word." His updating of Shakespeare's story provocatively brings onstage a child who is the offspring of Desdemona and Othello's union. But rather than having this boy look mixed-race, Rice mocks contemporary thinking about miscegenation by having the boy appear with one side of his face white, the other side black.[11]

The examples of Rice's outrageous burlesque and John Quincy and Abigail Adams's pained responses to *Othello* suggest that the history of Shakespeare in America is also a history of America itself, not the straightforward narrative found in textbooks, but rather one that runs parallel to the conventional story of the nation, a more sharp-edged one expressed through two-and-a-half centuries of essays, parodies, burlesques, poems, speeches, short stories, letters, musicals, novels, reviews, films, and staged performances. These works, by some of the most creative minds in America, explore the cultural fault lines that have always existed just below the surface of our national conversations, confronting us with chapters in the story of America otherwise lost or occluded.

In 1750, such an outcome would have been hard to predict. The first recorded performance of a Shakespeare play in the New World had taken place just twenty years earlier (that honor went to *Romeo and Juliet*, in New York City), and there were probably no more than five hundred performances of all of Shakespeare's plays before the Revolutionary War. The earliest professional companies to perform in the colonies were British imports, including the itinerant "London Company of Comedians" (which under new management opportunistically changed its name to the "American Company of Comedians," though its key actors remained British). In the early decades of colonial America, Shakespeare's plays and poems do not appear to have been much read either. The first volume recorded to have reached these shores was a copy of the 1685 Fourth Folio, brought to Virginia in 1696. And the first collected edition of his works was not published in America until a century after that. A major reason for these inauspicious beginnings was the Puritan values of the New England colonists. Having been staunchly anti-theatrical in the Old World, it was no surprise that the Puritans who settled the new one would view theater with suspicion. The Quaker William Penn, who founded the Pennsylvania colony, was no less hostile, attacking "the infamous plays . . . of comical wits" like Shakespeare and Ben Jonson, and enacting laws in 1682 against "stage plays . . . masques, revels . . . and the like." Even in the more tolerant Virginia there was resistance: members of the Virginia Company of London were urged not to include actors among the settlers, as they were deemed "idle persons." As late as 1774, the first Continental Congress was still admonishing colonists to shun theater and other kinds of "extravagance and dissipation." Philadelphia only ended its ban on playing in 1789 and Massachusetts, the last holdout, in 1793.[12] Until the Revolutionary War it is safe to say that in the thirteen colonies there was nothing particularly American in how Shakespeare's plays were staged, published, interpreted, or appropriated.

With the Revolution—and the growing need to redefine what it meant to be an American—that began to change. The first stirrings of a distinctively American response to Shakespeare are visible in works like Jonathan M. Sewall's "Epilogue" to a production of *Coriolanus* staged before Revolutionary troops in 1778. By the early nineteenth century, the new republic's vexed relationship with Britain had to be reconceived, and along with it its relationship to Shakespeare. Could he serve as an American no less than an English national poet? It was a question American writers wrestled with time and again in the course of the nineteenth century, from Charles Sprague's hope in 1824 that Shakespeare would bind the two countries together to Willa Cather's confident declaration at the century's end that "Shakespeare belongs to two nations now." Writers also had to confront the daunting challenge of Shakespeare's literary gifts: could America ever produce a poet to rival him? Herman Melville, half-glancing at himself, was sure it could, and believed that "men not very much inferior to Shakespeare, are this day being born upon the banks of the Ohio." If his masterpiece *Moby-Dick* bears comparison to *King Lear* and *Macbeth* it is because Melville immersed himself so deeply in these plays, leading the critic F. O. Matthiessen to conclude that "Shakespeare's conception of tragedy had so grown into the fibre of Melville's thought that much of his mature work became a re-creation of its themes in modern terms."[13]

As much as his works, Shakespeare's birthplace continued to matter for generations of Americans who no longer called England their mother country. Stratford-upon-Avon was visited by a steady stream of American tourists, including writers, American Indians, and a pair of future presidents (according to Abigail Adams, when her husband visited there with Thomas Jefferson in 1786, Jefferson "fell upon the ground and kissed it," while Adams "contented himself with cutting a relic" from a chair claimed to have belonged to Shakespeare himself).[14] For Americans, the birthplace came to matter in ways that it did not for the English themselves, and led to some of their most powerful writing about Shakespeare's legacy, including Henry James's trenchant story "The Birthplace" (1903). The greatest of American showmen, P. T. Barnum, even considered buying the run-down house in which Shakespeare was born and transporting it to America, where it could be properly displayed and venerated in what many now considered Shakespeare's adoptive home. This near-obsession with physically linking Shakespeare to America, or short of that, with reviving Shakespeare in England, continued to inform the writings and efforts of Americans, from Frederick Wadsworth Loring's poem "In the Old Churchyard at Fredericksburg" (1870) to the successful campaign led by Sam Wanamaker in the 1980s to rebuild Shakespeare's Globe Theatre close to where the original had once stood. Replicas of Shakespeare's playhouse would rise in Cleveland, Ashland, Dallas, San Diego, and elsewhere across the U.S.

The nineteenth century witnessed an explosion of interest in Shakespeare. By mid-century, as the cultural historian Laurence Levine put it, "from the large and often opulent theaters of major cities to the makeshift stages in halls, saloons, and churches of small towns and mining camps, wherever there was an audience for theater, there Shakespeare's plays were performed prominently and frequently."[15] The growing familiarity with Shakespeare can be traced in part to America's classrooms, where schoolchildren studying declamation and oratory were regularly assigned Shakespearean extracts in books like the *McGuffey's Readers*, first published in 1839. The influence of these textbooks in familiarizing the nation with Shakespeare's words was enormous: by the time that William McGuffey died in 1873, 47 million copies of his *Readers* had been sold, a number that by 1922 reached an astonishing 122 million.[16] In 1887 the German tourist Karl Knortz concluded after crisscrossing the United States that "there is certainly no land on the whole earth in which Shakespeare and the Bible are held in such high esteem."[17]

America's preoccupation with Shakespeare had its dark side as well. In 1849, friction between social classes, exacerbated by overheated patriotism, led to the bloody Astor Place riot in New York City, with Shakespeare at the heart of the conflict. The violence occurred following an attempted performance of *Macbeth* by the British actor William Charles Macready, whose appearance angered working-class supporters of a rival American actor, Edwin Forrest (who was acting in *Macbeth* at the same time at the Broadway Theatre). The controversy spilled out of the playhouse into the streets and led to the death of a score of people and the injury of perhaps a hundred others when the National Guard fired on the crowd. And in 1865, Shakespeare would figure in an even darker chapter in the nation's history: the assassination of President Lincoln by the actor John Wilkes Booth. Booth saw in Shakespeare's Brutus a kindred spirit and in a letter he wrote defending his actions justified the assassination by appealing to the authority of *Julius Caesar*: "But alas! Caesar must bleed for it."

American writers and leaders have often turned to Shakespeare in moments of national crisis. At no time in the nation's history was this truer than during the Civil War. It was during these years that Emily Dickinson wrote her great poem "Drama's Vitallest Expression is the Common Day," quietly insisting that Shakespeare had not had the last word, and that the unrecorded drama of daily life is more "vital" and lasting than the evanescent tragedies represented onstage. At the same time, in distant California, a young Mark Twain was publishing a send-up of *Julius Caesar* in a local newspaper, setting the stage for his subsequent and brilliant parody of Shakespeare in his *Adventures of Huckleberry Finn*. In Richmond, Henry Timrod, the "Laureate of the Confederacy," wrote a poem that drew on Shakespeare for the opening of a new theater in an already war-weary Virginia. And in Washington, D.C., President Lincoln sought wisdom and consolation in Shakespeare's works, reading and reciting passages from *Richard III* and from *Hamlet*, a play from which he had recently borrowed in his First Inaugural Address.

Shakespeare's words also resounded on America's battlefields. Private Sam Watkins of Tennessee described how Jefferson Davis and Robert Toombs paraphrased *Richard III* when rousing the troops, urging them to look forward to that time when "grim visaged war would smooth her wrinkled front, and when the dark clouds that had so long lowered o'er our own loved South would be in the deep bosom of the ocean buried." Another Confederate fighter, John Mosby, inspired his "Mosby's Rangers" on the eve of a raid by quoting from *The Tempest*: "we are going to mount the skies tonight or sink lower than plummet ever sounded." In the opposing camp, Shakespeare's words were also common currency. As the war ground to its conclusion, the Union General William Tecumseh Sherman quoted from *Macbeth* in describing his army's relentless march to the sea: "We have swept the country well from Savannah to here, and . . . we have captured immense stores, and destroyed machinery, guns, ammunition, and property, of inestimable value to our enemy. At all points he has fled from us, 'standing not on the order of his going.'"[18]

While Shakespeare's cultural ubiquity may have diminished in the century and a half since the end of the Civil War, his role in inspiring writers and enabling them to explore new cultural fault lines remains unchallenged. Yet the set of plays that preoccupied American writers did not change much over time: *Julius Caesar*, *Hamlet*, *Macbeth*, *Othello*, *King Lear*, *Richard III*, *The Merchant of Venice*, *Romeo and Juliet*, and *The Tempest* continued to be the mini-canon of works most frequently staged, parodied, and updated. By the 1890s, Jane Addams could discover in *King Lear* a parable of the heartless treatment of American workers by patriarchal industrialists, and Jacob Gordin could transform the same play into a tragi-comic *Jewish King Lear* that spoke with great immediacy to Yiddish-speaking immigrants. In response to the changing face of the nation, some of those anxious about the threat posed by the arrival of millions of non-English speaking immigrants to the established Anglo-Saxon culture enlisted Shakespeare to their cause. These included Henry Cabot Lodge in "Shakespeare's Americanisms" (1895) and Joseph Quincy Adams in his address at the founding of the Folger Shakespeare Library in 1932.[19]

How—or even whether—Shakespeare truly belonged to all Americans was explored in works like Toshio Mori's "Japanese Hamlet" (1939) and Langston Hughes's "Shakespeare in Harlem" (1942). By century's end, Maya Angelou, reflecting on how deeply the author of Sonnet 29 seemed to understand her plight, could provocatively declare that "Shakespeare was a Black Woman."[20] The twentieth century also ushered in the birth of that distinctively American contribution to Shakespearean adaptation, the Broadway musical, most notably *Kiss Me, Kate* (1948) and *West Side Story* (1957). It witnessed a number of major film versions of the plays as well, which in turn led influential movie critics, including James Agee and Pauline Kael, to reflect on Shakespeare in their time. And America's wars during these years generated fresh interest in Shakespeare, including Maurice Evans's performances of "G. I. Hamlet" in the Central Pacific during World War II, and Mary McCarthy's "General Macbeth" (1962), which so perfectly captures the Cold War mind-set. It is fitting that when President John F. Kennedy invited a group of American actors to the White House in 1961 to perform scenes from the plays, he referred to Shakespeare, only half in jest, as "an American playwright."[21]

Assembling a one-volume collection of American writing on Shakespeare from 1776 to the present day has led to some difficult choices—and, necessarily, omissions.[22] I have left out academic essays (already widely available) and focused on imaginative works that, while engaging Shakespeare, have also illuminated their cultural moment. A handful of them have never appeared in print and many are no longer easy to find. Some I had never encountered before working on this volume—and more than a few of these have changed the way I read the plays. Because of my misgivings about excerpting (except in the rarest of cases where a short portion is freestanding), I have reluctantly had to pass over some exceptional works that are too long to anthologize, including T. D. Rice's *Otello*, Mark Twain's *The Adventures of Huckleberry Finn*, Jacob Gordin's *Jewish King Lear*, Charles McKay's *Caliban by the Yellow Sand*, Jane Smiley's *A Thousand Acres*, John Updike's *Gertrude and Claudius*, Arthur Phillip's *The Tragedy of Arthur*, and Toni Morrison's *Desdemona*. I have also been unable to include such works as Herman Melville's *Moby-Dick* and Tony Kushner's *Angels in America*, whose Shakespearean traces are profound but less visible, as well as works by the many novelists who have ransacked Shakespeare's plays for their titles, such as Edith Wharton's *The Glimpses of the Moon*, William Faulkner's *The Sound and the Fury*, and David Foster Wallace's *Infinite Jest*. The visceral experience of seeing groundbreaking productions of the plays—on stage and on film—has been an essential part of the story of Shakespeare in America, but is impossible to convey, so I have relied on reviews by leading cultural critics to compensate for this. Above all, I have tried to bring together memorable works that speak to each other, works that taken together tell an overlooked story, one that I hope "grows to something of great constancy."

ENDNOTES

1 Thomas M. Settles, *John Bankhead Magruder: A Military Reappraisal* (Baton Rouge: Louisiana State University Press, 2009), p. 40; and Frederick Merk, *Slavery and the Annexation of Texas* (New York: Knopf, 1972).

2 Darwin Payne, "Camp Life in the Army of Occupation," *The Southwestern Historical Quarterly* 73 (July 1969–April 1970), p. 337; and James Longstreet, *From Manassas to Appomattox* (Philadelphia: J. B. Lippincott, 1896), p. 20.

3 Longstreet's unpublished remarks are preserved in the Hamlin Garland papers, Collection no. 0200, Special Collections, USC Libraries, University of Southern California. See too, Jeffrey D. Wert, *General James Longstreet* (New York: Simon and Schuster, 1993), p. 36, as well as Karl Jack Bauer, *The Mexican War, 1846–1848* (New York: Macmillan, 1974), pp. 32–43. Grant seems to have worn a beard at the time; he wrote to his fiancée the following month (on February 7, 1846): "Julia if you could see me now you would not know me, I have allowed my beard to grow two or three inches long" (*The Papers of Ulysses S. Grant*, vol. 1: 1837–1861, ed. John Y. Simon [Carbondale: Southern Illinois University Press, 1967], p. 74).

4 W. I. Reed to William C. Church, as quoted in Jean Edward Smith, *Grant* (New York: Simon and Schuster, 2001), p. 85; and Longstreet, *From Manassas to Appomattox*, p. 20.

5 As quoted in Frances Teague, *Shakespeare and the American Popular Stage* (Cambridge: Cambridge University Press, 2006), p. 1.

6 Delmar C. Homan, "Dwight Eisenhower and William Shakespeare," *Heritage of the Great Plains* 9 (1976), pp. 13–16; and Raymond H. Geselbracht, "A Boy Who Would be President: Harry Truman at School, 1892–1901, Part 2," in the National Archives's *Prologue Magazine* 36.3 (Fall 2004).

7 See, for example, Charles B. Lower, "Othello as Black on Southern Stages," in Philip C. Kolin, ed., *Shakespeare in the South: Essays on Performance* (Jackson: University Press of Mississippi, 1983), p. 201.

8 *South Carolina Gazette and General Advertiser*, July 15, 1783. I am grateful to Stacy Caffrey for bringing this to my attention.

9 Tilden G. Edelstein, "*Othello* in America: The Drama of Interracial Marriage," in *Region, Race, and Reconstruction: Essays in Honor of*

C. Vann Woodward, ed. J. Moran Kousser and James M. McPherson (New York: Oxford University Press, 1982), p. 182.

10 For how the Adams family viewed race and *Othello*, see William Jerry MacLean, "'Othello Scorned': The Racial Thought of John Quincy Adams," *Journal of the Early Republic* 4 (1984), pp. 143–60. See too Abigail Adams's letter of September 18, 1785, to William Stephens Smith in the Adams Papers, Massachusetts Historical Society.

11 T. D. Rice, "Otello, A Burlesque Opera," in *Jump Jim Crow: Lost Plays, Lyrics, and Street Prose of the First Atlantic Popular Culture*, ed. W. T. Lhamon Jr. (Cambridge, MA: Harvard University Press, 2003), p. 362 and p. 445, n. 42.

12 For this factual information, I rely heavily on the authoritative overview of "American Beginnings" in Alden T. Vaughan and Virginia Mason Vaughan, *Shakespeare in America* (Oxford: Oxford University Press, 2012), pp. 7–34; see too their catalogue of an exhibition they curated at the Folger Shakespeare Library in 2007 on *Shakespeare in American Life* (Seattle: University of Washington Press, 2007).

13 F. O. Matthiessen, *American Renaissance* (New York: Oxford University Press, 1941), p. 435.

14 As quoted in Barbara A. Mowat, "The Founders and the Bard," *Yale Review* 97 (2009), p. 1.

15 Lawrence W. Levine, *Highbrow/Lowbrow: The Emergence of Cultural Hierarchy in America* (Cambridge, MA: Harvard University Press, 1988), p. 40.

16 Vaughan and Vaughan, *Shakespeare in America*, pp. 83–84.

17 As cited in Vincent Broqua, "American Shakespeare: Introduction," p. 1, which prefaces a special issue on American Shakespeare in the French journal *Transatlantica* (2010).

18 These examples are drawn from Stephen Dickey's superb essay on "Listening to Civil War Voices" in the Folger Shakespeare Library's website on "Shakespeare in American Life."

19 For more on the ideological uses to which Shakespeare has been put in America, see Michael Bristol, *Shakespeare's America, America's Shakespeare* (New York: Routledge, 1990), and Thomas P. Cartelli, *Repositioning Shakespeare* (New York: Routledge, 1999).

20 Maya Angelou, "Journey to the Heartland," Address Delivered at

the 1985 National Assembly of Local Arts Agencies, Cedar Rapids, Iowa, June 12, 1985.

21 Helen E. Sandison, "Gentleman, You are Welcome to Elsinore," *Shakespeare Quarterly* 13 (1962), p. 81.

22 For earlier and valuable collections, see Mary R. Silsby, ed., *Tributes to Shakespeare* (New York: Harper and Brothers, 1892), and Peter Rawling, ed., *Americans on Shakespeare 1776–1914* (Aldershot, UK: Ashgate, 1999).

SHAKESPEARE
in AMERICA

Anonymous

The Pausing American Loyalist

Shakespeare's authority was enlisted by both sides during the American Revolution. The British newspaper *The Middlesex Journal, and Evening Advertiser* published this "Parody on the Soliloquy of *Hamlet*" in January 1776. The poem was most likely written by a Tory in response to the demand of the First Continental Congress of 1774 that colonists sign an "association" boycotting British goods. To sign—or not to sign—was to signal one's political and economic loyalties: for Tories, not to sign was to risk one's safety and livelihood; but to sign, for those still loyal to England, was hypocritical. This was not the first time the most famous speech in Shakespeare had been put to political ends in America: in 1770 a colonist of a more revolutionary bent had written a protest that began: "Be taxt, or not be taxt, that is the question."

A PARODY ON THE SOLILOQUY OF *HAMLET*.

To sign, or not to sign? That is the question,
Whether 'twere better for an honest Man
To sign, and so be safe; or to resolve,
Betide what will, against *Associations*,
And, by retreating, shun them. To fly—I reck
Not where: And, by that Flight, t'escape
FEATHERS and TAR, and Thousand other Ills
That *Loyalty* is Heir to: 'Tis a Consummation
Devoutly to be wished. To fly—to want—
To want? Perchance to starve: Ay, there's the rub!
For, in that Chance of Want, what Ills may come
To patriot Rage, when I have left—my All
Must give me Pause:—There's the Respect,
That makes us *trim*, and bow to Men we hate.
For, who would bear th' Indignities o'th' Times,

CONGRESS' Decrees, and wild *Convention* Plans,
The Laws controll'd, and Inj'ries unredress'd,
The Insolence of Knaves, and thousand Wrongs
Which patient *Liege men* from vile *Rebels* take,
When he, *sans* Doubt, might certain Safety find,
Only by Flying? Who would bend to Fools,
And truckle thus to mad, Mob-chosen Upstarts,
But that the Dread of something after Flight
(In that blest Country, where, yet, no moneyless
Poor Wight can live) puzzles the Will,
And makes ten Thousands rather sign—and eat,
Than fly—to starve on Loyalty.——
Thus, Dread of Want makes Rebels of us all;
And thus the native Hue of Loyalty
Is sicklied o'er with a pale Cast of *Trimming*;
And Enterprizes of great Pith and Virtue,
But unsupported, turn their Streams away,
And never come to Action.

                                    (1776)

Jonathan M. Sewall

(1748–1808)

Epilogue to Coriolanus

During the Revolutionary War Shakespeare was more often staged by British forces than by their colonial adversaries. British officers, performing in New York, Boston, Philadelphia, and elsewhere, are recorded as having staged Shakespeare's plays for the benefit of "the widows and orphans of soldiers," and their repertory tended to focus on tragedies and histories, including *Richard III*, *King Lear*, *1 Henry IV*, and *Macbeth*, all plays rooted in the British past. Lawyer and poet Jonathan M. Sewall's "Epilogue" to a performance of *Coriolanus* offers a glimpse into how Shakespeare was appropriated by the Continental army. A footnote to Sewall's "Epilogue" alludes to the "General discontent" that "prevailed in the American army when this was written and spoken," suggesting that *Coriolanus* may have been performed before (or perhaps even by) disgruntled American troops in Portsmouth, New Hampshire. The choice of play here is significant: *Coriolanus* was seen as topical and anti-authoritarian, its martial hero "a majestic Roman" who was "Driv'n" to act "by his country's base ingratitude." Written in 1778, the "Epilogue" was not published until 1801, when it was included in an edition of Sewall's *Miscellaneous Poems*.

❧

Trembling with apprehension, doubt and pain,
We have presum'd to tread this stage again.
This stage—where late, by various passions mov'd,
A Juba triumph'd, and a Marcia lov'd.
Where a Numidian, barb'rous as his clime,
Stalk'd, black with ev'ry execrable crime.
And where by demons fir'd from deepest hell,
Sempronius bellow'd, fought, blasphem'd, and fell.
Here Lucia wept with anguish torn, and love;
And there th' illustrious rival brothers strove.

Here noble Marcus bled, in youthful pride,
There Liberty, and Rome, and CATO dy'd!
    A diff'rent scene has been display'd to night;
No martyr bleeding in his country's right.
But a majestic Roman, great and good,
Driv'n by his country's base ingratitude,
From parent, wife, and offspring, whelm'd in woe,
To ask protection from a haughty foe:
To arm for those he long in arms had brav'd,
And stab that nation he so oft had sav'd.
    See him low-prostrate on the hearth! great heav'n!
Can worth so great to such extremes be driv'n?
He whom the trembling Volsci felt of late
Dart terror thro' their host, and scatter fate,
Now grov'ling at their feet! see Tullus rear
The godlike man, and answer all his pray'r.
Now crown'd joint leader of the volscian train,
And burning with revenge, he takes the plain.
What rage thy heart, what fury urg'd thy hand;
O valiant gen'ral of the volscian band!
When thou Rome's trembling legions mad'st thy prey,
And her victorious eagle bore away.
Thy vanquish'd country now astonish'd see
Their past successes owing all to thee!
Priests, augurs, senators, around thee stand,
To deprecate thy rage, and save the land.
Unmov'd thou hear'st the supplicating train,
And priests implore, and augurs sue in vain.
    Rome's weeping matrons last around thee plead,
Thy wife, thy mother, the procession lead.
What heart this tender scene unpitying bears?
What eye beholds, and melts not into tears?
VETRUVIA kneels—ah, Marcius, ah, forbear,
Thy country, parent, wife, and infant spare.
With resolution, worthy of a god,
Long the great chief inexorable stood.

By filial piety at length o'ercome,
He yields—by *nature* more subdu'd than *Rome*.
Irrevocable fate o'ertakes the deed;
By Tullus, his protector, see him bleed!
    So fell the chief whom vengeance unrestrain'd
Against his country urg'd to lift the hand.
Howe'er ungrateful Rome deserv'd to bleed,
No wrongs can justify so dire a deed.
    Learn hence, my countrymen! Rome's guilt to shun;
For honor, justice, gratitude, be known.
Nor let your unrewarded sons complain
They wield the sword, and fight, and bleed in vain.
Lest, tempted like this Roman, they rebel,
And 'gainst their country turn th' unhallow'd steel.
But keep stern CORIOLANUS still in view,
Impartial justice steadily pursue,
And to each warrior give a warrior's due!

(1778)

Peter Markoe

(c. 1752–1792)

The Tragic Genius of Shakspeare; An Ode

Peter Markoe, a poet and playwright, was educated at Oxford and Lincoln's Inn in England before coming to America around 1775. His ode was published in the year of the Constitutional Convention in Philadelphia in a volume of his *Miscellaneous Poems*. It is one of the first American poems to celebrate Shakespeare, praising him as a historian, poet, and philosopher. The poem alludes to eleven of Shakespeare's plays, reflecting Markoe's interest in a range of the dramatic works, and is notable for asserting that Shakespeare's genius is no longer confined to the "narrow bounds" of "Monopolizing Britain." In the future, Markoe writes, America will be his true home: "Shakspeare's bold spirit seeks our western shore."

✂

Is there, whose bosom *charity* inspires,
    And taste informs and genius fires?
    Is there, whose heav'n-directed soul
    Can ancient prejudice controul,
    And yield the willing, glowing heart
To nature's richest feast prepar'd by art?
    There is——Assembled here I see
    The brave, the beauteous and the free;
Who, tho' of native merit justly proud,
To genius and to Shakspeare oft have bow'd!
Shakspeare! at thy soul-harrowing name,
A pleasing horror spreads thro' all my frame!
    Offspring of genius, Shakspeare, hail!
    Youth's monitor and friend of age!
    Tho' envy frown and malice rail,
    Thy mighty genius shall prevail,
      Historian! Poet! Sage!

Born to instruct the world, from ev'ry clime
And ev'ry age his moral stores he draws;
Scorning the narrow bounds of space and time,
    Impetuous, ardent and sublime,
    He mocks the critic's colder laws,
And thundering at our breasts demands applause.
O master of the heart! I yield, I yield!
    Rapt to Pharsalia's blood-stain'd field*,
    My soul the haughty tyrant spurns,
    And with just indignation burns.
    Inflam'd by freedom's sacred zeal,
    (What laws can haughty tyrants plead?
    Virtue shall sanctify the deed.)
With Brutus I resolve and grasp the vengeful steel.
        Again obedient to his art,
        Pity assails the soften'd heart;
And see, where bending o'er his slaughter'd friend,
        In arts, in arms renown'd,
The wily chief a people's rage controuls,
        And with new fury fires their souls;
He lifts the robe, he shews each streaming wound;
With cries of vengeance earth and heav'n resound.

Guilt, from thy troubled dream awake to piercing care!
    How dar'st thou, cruel Richard†, hope to sleep?
    And thou, incestuous fratricide‡, prepare
    The harvest of thy various crimes to reap!
    A nation's woe the warlike Richmond fires;
    A father's death the gallant prince inspires.
    Yet pity 'midst the scene of terror sighs;
The virtuous youth expires; the raving virgin dies!

    And think'st thou§ yet, Ambition, that the power
    Of justice slumbers?—Mark yon tortur'd pair!
        Wildly *he* grasps the passive air;
    Th' ideal dagger haunts his midnight hour!

    *Julius Cæsar.   †Richard IIId.   ‡Hamlet.   §Macbeth.

By guilt's incessant stings pursued,
She strives to wash away the fancied blood;
Loudly proclaiming to each fear-struck breast,
    Ev'n midst the pomp of courts unblest,
    The murd'rer ne'er must hope to rest.

Ye thro' whose veins in lazy current creeps
Life's languid stream; whose hearts, unus'd to melt,
    The luxury of sorrow ne'er have felt,
When Constance* raves, or Desdemona weeps;[†]
Or when the aged fire,[‡] in accents wild,
    Mourns o'er his pious, murder'd child,
Begone, nor with your presence dare profane
The hallow'd scenes.—Yet stay—a Shakspeare's strain
    This useful lesson shall impart;
    The cruel, avaricious heart,
    Which scorns a neighbour's woes to heal,
    A Shylock's deep despair should feel.[§]

And oft, ye young and fair, for you
To nature and to virtue true,
The moral bard, with happy hand,
The beauteous, glowing portrait drew,
And bade it ev'ry breast command,
    And ev'ry heart subdue;
Sweet Imogen!—In vain her father storms;[**]
The tender wife the duteous task performs.
    With manlike step and alter'd charms,
    (Ev'n prudes her courage must approve)
    She meets her country's foes in arms,
    And almost scorns the war's alarms
        For Posthumus and love.

---

*King John.   †Othello.   ‡King Lear.   §Merchant of Venice.   **Cymbeline.

Creative Shakspeare! whither am I borne!*
   No more methinks I tread on earth;
   And see! a form of monstrous birth
Horror at once excites and hate and scorn!
   But hark! the dread magician calls;
   His airy minister appears;
   Terror no more my heart appalls,
   But sweetest notes delight my ears.
   Charming and charm'd, the tender fair
   Her toiling lover's care beguiles;
   Soft sympathy unites the pair,
   And *love*, the great enchanter, smiles.

Again I feel the dear illusive art;
I hear the melting sigh, the tender strain!†
But hatred steels each unrelenting heart;
The fix'd hereditary feuds remain,
And Romeo raves and Juliet weeps in vain.
   Ill-judging parents! to divide
   Hearts, which with genuine passion glow!
   Where youth expects a friendly guide,
   Ah! must it meet a cruel foe?
When hearts in tender sympathy combine,
The mystic union is indeed divine!
   Yet oft, with worldly wisdom curs'd,
   Parents the sacred union burst
Hence sorrow preys on many a Juliet's bloom,
And many a Romeo seeks an early tomb.

   Ye, whose nice skill to canvas gives
   Expression, symmetry and grace,
'Till all its beauties the lov'd form receives,
And boasts a Mira's shape, a Chloe's face;
   Tho' great the wonders of your art,

*The Tempest.   †Romeo and Juliet.

To Shakspeare's nobler genius yield,
　In various nature sweetly skill'd,
The moral painter of the heart
Nor thou, Philosophy! refuse
Due tribute to a Shakspeare's muse,
By passion's thunder skill'd to clear
The clouded mental atmosphere,
And guide, with unresisted art,
Conviction's lightning to the guilty heart.
Ye Patriots! for the poet's honour'd brow
The festive wreath, the laurel crown prepare,
　Which only you can well bestow,
　And he alone deserves to wear.

Monopolizing Britain! boast no more
His genius to your narrow bounds confin'd;
Shakspeare's bold spirit seeks our western shore,
A gen'ral blessing for the world design'd,
And, emulous to form the rising age,
The noblest Bard demands the noblest Stage.

(1787)

John Adams

(1735–1826)

Letter to John Quincy Adams

In early 1805 former President John Adams wrote to his son and future president, John Quincy Adams, that he had been "uncommonly engaged" of late "in Reading Shakespeare, and particularly his Historical Drama's." John Adams's diaries and correspondence with his wife, Abigail (who quoted from Shakespeare as freely and confidently as he did), confirm that he had long been immersed in Shakespeare's works. For Adams, Shakespeare was the "great Master of every Affection of the Heart and every Sentiment of the Mind as well as of all the Powers of Expression." His interest in Shakespeare's works took a more polemical edge during the 1760s, and in his political writings he would cite as examples plays as wide-ranging as *Macbeth*, *Henry VIII*, and *The Merry Wives of Windsor*. Adams's 1805 letter to his son, housed in the Massachusetts Historical Society and until now unpublished, reveals his fears for the young republic, threatened at the time by factionalism. Reading and rereading the sequence of plays that retold English history from the reign of Richard II through that of Richard III, Adams discovered in them "most instructive Examples for the perusal of this country," especially the dangers of "Treachery, Perfidy, Treason, Murder, Cruelty, Sedition and Rebellions of rival and unballanced factions." Toward the end of his letter, Adams changes Henry V's famous address to England about the dangers of traitors into a warning to his fellow countrymen: "O America! What might'est thou do" when similarly confronted by "A nest of hollow Bosoms"?

❧

Quincy Jan. 20. 1805

My dear Sir.

I received in Season, your kind Letter of the 5th and have been so very busy that I have not found time to acknowledge it, till now. When I write to you it is with no Expectation of any answer, unless it be in a bare acknowledgement to some of us, i.e. to me, your Mother or your Brother of the receipt of my Letter. I know that the public Business must as it ought to engage all your time and thoughts. The Transactions in Congress at the present Period will be of great Importance to this Country, especially the Mediterranean War, The Government of Louisiana, and the Impeachment of the Judge: and whatever part you may take in them, although at present it may appear inefficacious, may be hereafter of more consequence to your Country, than you may now imagine.

I have been uncommonly engaged and interested in Reading Shakespeare, and particularly his Historical Drama's which I have read through once with Attention, and have almost completed the Second time. During that Period of the English History, that Balance of the Constitution, from which its Liberty results, and in which its excellence consists was not formed. The commons had not an independent share in Legislation, and were not well represented, the Powers of the House of Lords were not well defined, the Prerogatives of the Crown were not exactly limited, the Judges held their Commissions durante Beneplacito the Habeas Corpus Act was not known and Magna Charta was a mere Piece of Parchment which every triumphant Faction neglected or violated at its pleasure, even much more than our national and state Constitutions are disregarded at this day. Those Plays of the great Poet if they are read by any one, with a view to the Struggles between the Red Rose and the White Rose, that is to the Treachery Perfidy Treason Murder Cruelty Sedition and Rebellions of rival and unballanced factions, if he can keep his Gravity and his attention from being diverted by the Gaiety and Drollery of Falstaff, Pistol, Nym, Peto, Fluellin and the rest of those Rakes, & Bullies he will find one of the most instructive Examples for the perusal of this Country. Hitherto we have gone no further than a few Duels, in actual Violence. In Slander we have gone as far as any nation and for any thing I know as human nature in its depravity can go. The Parties in England availed themselves of Religion, the Catholic and the Puritan, as Pretexts, and Sought the Aide and Alliances of Scotland and France, alternately, very much as ours do.—Our Presidents and Governors have not yet Wealth enough to give Dowers with their Daughters to Bonapartes Brothers or Nephews, nor are they rich enough to demand Royal or Imperial Girls for their Sons. But Suppose a Hamilton or a Burr, at the head of victorious Armies and President at the same time, and with Sons and Daughters to dispose of, and what then? Why then it will be Said

> O America! What might'est thou do, that honor
>   would thee do,
> Were all thy Children kind and natural!
> But see thy fault! France or England hath in thee found out
> A nest of hollow Bosoms, which he fills.

With regard to Judge Chace's tryal, were I in your Situation, I would read every Impeachment, that is to be found the State Tryals. So much I may say to you, without Suspecting myself of the least desire to influence your Judgment.

With regard to Mr Giles you may if you please give my Compliments to him and ask him in my name whether our Nation is now as Democratical as he wishes, or not. This jocular Question I suppose I may ask him without offence to him which is far from my Intention.

The Union of the red Rose and the white Rose, that is of the Livingstons and Clintons seems to have compleatly tryumphed over the Vice President for the present in New York. I feel much interested on the public Account in the Question what is to be his Course after the fourth of March. I am told that his Party in this State, who were very violent against him at first are changing their Language, I Suppose in consequence of Letters from Washington, and they now say that he ought to be pardoned even if upon tryal he should be found guilty.

Washington Irving
(1783–1859)

Stratford-on-Avon

By the early nineteenth century a visit to Shakespeare's birthplace was becoming part of the expected itinerary of Americans visiting England. In the spring of 1786, to cite but one example, two future U.S. presidents, John Adams and Thomas Jefferson, visited Stratford together, but were disappointed, Adams wrote, to find "nothing preserved of this great Genius," adding that the house in which Shakespeare was born was "as small and mean, as you can conceive." Washington Irving first visited Stratford in July 1815 while he was living and working in England, and his essay "Stratford-on-Avon" did much to popularize the pilgrimage site, conveying the ambivalence of American visitors at the time, a quality still visible nearly a century later in Henry James's short story "The Birthplace." The essay was first published in the United States in September 1820 in the seventh and final installment of Irving's *The Sketch Book*, a serialized collection, in which the stories and essays, including the most famous, "Rip Van Winkle," appeared under the pseudonym "Geoffrey Crayon."

Thou soft flowing Avon, by the silver stream,
Of things more than mortal sweet Shakespeare would dream;
The fairies by moonlight dance round his green bed,
For hallowed the turf is which pillowed his head.

Garrick

To a homeless man, who has no spot on this wide world which he can truly call his own, there is a momentary feeling of something like independence and territorial consequence, when, after a weary day's travel, he kicks off his boots, thrusts his feet into slippers, and stretches himself before an inn fire. Let the world without go as it may; let kingdoms rise or fall, so long as he has the wherewithal to pay his bill, he is, for the time being, the very monarch of all he surveys. The arm chair is his throne; the poker his sceptre, and the little parlour of some twelve feet square, his undisputed empire. It is a morsel of certainty, snatched from the midst of the uncertainties of life; it is a sunny moment gleaming out kindly on a cloudy day; and he who has advanced some way on the pilgrimage of existence, knows the importance of husbanding even morsels and moments of enjoyment. "Shall I not take mine ease in mine inn?" thought I, as I gave the fire a stir, lolled back in my elbow chair, and cast a complacent look about the little parlour of the Red Horse, at Stratford-on-Avon.

The words of sweet Shakespeare were just passing through my mind as the clock struck midnight from the tower of the church in which he lies buried. There was a gentle tap at the door, and a pretty chamber maid, putting in her smiling face, inquired, with a hesitating air, whether I had rung. I understood it as a modest hint that it was time to retire. My dream of absolute dominion was at an end; so abdicating my throne, like a prudent potentate, to avoid being deposed, and putting the Stratford Guide Book under my arm, as a pillow companion, I went to bed, and dreamt all night of Shakespeare, the Jubilee, and David Garrick.

The next morning was one of those quickening mornings which we sometimes have in early spring; for it was about the middle of March. The chills of a long winter had suddenly given way; the north wind had spent its last gasp; and a mild air came stealing from the west, breathing the breath of life into nature, and wooing every bud and flower to burst forth into fragrance and beauty.

I had come to Stratford on a poetical pilgrimage. My first visit was to the house where Shakespeare was born, and where, according to tradition, he was brought up to his father's craft of wool combing. It is a small mean looking edifice of wood and plaster, a true nestling place of genius, which seems to delight in hatching its offspring in bye corners. The walls of its squalid chambers are covered with names and inscriptions, in every language, by pilgrims of all nations, ranks, and conditions, from the prince to the peasant; and present a simple, but striking instance of the spontaneous and universal homage of mankind to the great poet of nature.

The house is shown by a garrulous old lady in a frosty red face, lighted up by a cold blue anxious eye, and garnished with artificial locks of flaxen hair, curling from under an exceedingly dirty cap. She was peculiarly assiduous in exhibiting the relics with which this, like all other celebrated shrines, abounds. There was the shattered stock of the very matchlock with which Shakespeare shot the deer, on his poaching exploit. There, too, was his tobacco box; which proves that he was a rival smoker of Sir Walter Raleigh; the sword also with which he played Hamlet; and the identical lanthorn with which Friar Laurence discovered Romeo and Juliet at the tomb! There was an ample supply also of Shakespeare's mulberry tree, which seems to have as extraordinary powers of self multiplication as the wood of the true cross; of which there is enough extant to build a ship of the line.

The most favourite object of curiosity, however, is Shakespeare's chair. It stands in the chimney nook of a small gloomy chamber, just behind what was his father's shop. Here he may many a time have sat when a boy, watching the slowly revolving spit with all the longing of an urchin; or of an evening, listening to the crones and gossips of Stratford, dealing forth church yard tales and legendary anecdotes of the troublesome times of England. In this chair it is the custom of every one that visits the house to sit: whether this be done with the hope of imbibing any of the inspiration of the bard I am at a loss to say, I merely mention the fact; and mine hostess privately assured me, that though built of solid oak, such was the fervent zeal of devotees, that the chair had to be new bottomed at least once in three years. It is worthy of notice also, in the history of this extraordinary chair, that it partakes something of the volatile nature of the Santa Casa of Loretto, or the flying chair of the Arabian enchanter, for though sold some few years since to a northern princess, yet, strange to tell, it has found its way back again to the old chimney corner.

I am always of easy faith in such matters, and am ever willing to be deceived, where the deceit is pleasant, and costs nothing. I am therefore a ready believer in relics, legends, and local anecdotes of goblins and great men; and would advise all travellers who travel for their gratification to be the same. What is it to us whether these stories be true or false, so long as we can persuade ourselves into the belief of them, and enjoy all the charm of the reality? There is nothing like resolute good humoured credulity in these matters; and on this occasion I went even so far as willingly to believe the claims of mine hostess to a lineal descent from the poet, when, unluckily for my faith, she put into my hands a play of her own composition, which set all belief in her consanguinity at defiance.

From the birth place of Shakespeare a few paces brought me to his grave. He lies buried in the chancel of the parish church, a large and venerable pile, mouldering with age, but richly ornamented. It stands on the banks of the Avon, on an embowered point, and separated by adjoining gardens from the suburbs of the town. Its situation is quiet and retired: the river runs murmuring at the foot of the church yard, and the elms which grow upon its banks droop their branches into its clear bosom. An avenue of limes, the boughs of which are curiously interlaced, so as to form in summer an arched way of foliage, leads up from the gate of the yard to the church porch. The graves are overgrown with grass; the grey tombstones, some of them nearly sunk into the earth, are half covered with moss, which has likewise tinted the reverend old building. Small birds have built their nests among the cornices and fissures of the walls, and keep up a continual flutter and chirping; and rooks are sailing and cawing about its lofty grey spire.

In the course of my rambles I met with the grey headed sexton, Edmonds, and accompanied him home to get the key of the church. He had lived in Stratford, man and boy, for eighty years, and seemed still to consider himself a vigorous man, with the trivial exception that he had nearly lost the use of his legs for a few years past. His dwelling was a cottage, looking out upon the Avon and its bordering meadows; and was a picture of that neatness, order, and comfort, which pervade the humblest dwellings in this country. A low white washed room, with a stone floor carefully scrubbed, served for parlour, kitchen, and hall. Rows of pewter and earthen dishes glittered along the dresser. On an old oaken table, well rubbed and polished, lay the family Bible and Prayer book, and the drawer contained the family library, composed of about half a score of well thumbed volumes. An ancient clock, that important article of cottage furniture, ticked on the opposite side of the room; with a bright warming pan hanging on one side of it, and the old man's horn handled Sunday cane on the other. The fireplace, as usual, was wide and deep enough to admit a gossip knot within its jambs. In one corner sat the old man's grand daughter sewing, a pretty blue eyed girl,—and in the opposite corner was a superannuated crony, whom he addressed by the name of John Ange, and who, I found, had been his companion from childhood. They had played together in infancy; they had worked together in manhood; they were now tottering about and gossiping away the evening of life; and in a short time they will probably be buried together in the neighbouring church yard. It is not often that we see two streams of existence running thus evenly and tranquilly side by side; it is only in such quiet "bosom scenes" of life that they are to be met with.

I had hoped to gather some traditionary anecdotes of the bard from these ancient chroniclers; but they had nothing new to impart. The long interval during which Shakespeare's writings lay in comparative neglect has spread its shadow over his history; and it is his good or evil lot that scarcely any thing remains to his biographers but a scanty handful of conjectures.

The sexton and his companion had been employed as carpenters on the preparations for the celebrated Stratford jubilee, and they remembered Garrick, the prime mover of the fête, who superintended the arrangements, and who, according to the sexton, was "a short punch man very lively and bustling." John Ange had assisted also in cutting down Shakespeare's mulberry tree, of which he had a morsel in his pocket for sale; no doubt a sovereign quickener of literary conception.

I was grieved to hear these two worthy wights speak very

dubiously of the eloquent dame who shows the Shakespeare house. John Ange shook his head when I mentioned her valuable and inexhaustible collection of relics, particularly her remains of the mulberry tree; and the old sexton even expressed a doubt as to Shakespeare having been born in her house. I soon discovered that he looked upon her mansion with an evil eye, as a rival to the poet's tomb; the latter having comparatively but few visitors. Thus it is that historians differ at the very outset, and mere pebbles make the stream of truth diverge into different channels even at the fountain head.

We approached the church through the avenue of limes, and entered by a gothic porch, highly ornamented, with carved doors of massive oak. The interior is spacious, and the architecture and embellishments superior to those of most country churches. There are several ancient monuments of nobility and gentry, over some of which hang funeral escutcheons, and banners dropping piece-meal from the walls. The tomb of Shakespeare is in the chancel. The place is solemn and sepulchral. Tall elms wave before the pointed windows, and the Avon, which runs at a short distance from the walls, keeps up a low perpetual murmur. A flat stone marks the spot where the bard is buried. There are four lines inscribed on it, said to have been written by himself, and which have in them something extremely awful. If they are indeed his own, they show that solicitude about the quiet of the grave, which seems natural to fine sensibilities and thoughtful minds:

> Good friend, for Jesus' sake, forbeare
> To dig the dust enclosed here.
> Blessed be the man that spares these stones,
> And curst be he that moves my bones.

Just over the grave, in a niche of the wall, is a bust of Shakespeare, put up shortly after his death, and considered as a resemblance. The aspect is pleasant and serene, with a finely arched forehead; and I thought I could read in it clear indications of that cheerful, social disposition, by which he was as much characterized among his cotemporaries as by the vastness of his genius. The inscription mentions his age at the time of his decease—fifty three years; an untimely death for the world: for what fruit might not have been expected from the golden autumn of such a mind, sheltered as it was from the stormy vicissitudes of life, and flourishing in the sunshine of popular and royal favour.

The inscription on the tombstone has not been without its effect. It has prevented the removal of his remains from the bosom of his native place to Westminster Abbey, which was at one time contemplated. A few years since also, as some labourers were digging to make an adjoining vault, the earth caved in, so as to leave a vacant space almost like an arch, through which one might have reached into his grave. No one, however, presumed to meddle with his remains, so awfully guarded by a malediction; and lest any of the idle or the curious, or any collector of relics, should be tempted to commit depredations, the old sexton kept watch over the place for two days, until the vault was finished and the aperture closed again. He told me that he had made bold to look in at the hole, but could see neither coffin nor bones; nothing but dust. It was something, I thought, to have seen the dust of Shakespeare.

Next to this grave are those of his wife, his favourite daughter Mrs. Hall, and others of his family. On a tomb close by, also, is a full length effigy of his old friend John Combe, of usurious memory; on whom he is said to have written a ludicrous epitaph. There are other monuments around, but the mind refuses to dwell on any thing that is not connected with Shakespeare. His idea pervades the place: the whole pile seems but as his mausoleum. The feelings, no longer checked and thwarted by doubt, here indulge in perfect confidence: other traces of him may be false or dubious, but here is palpable evidence and absolute certainty. As I trod the sounding pavement, there was something intense and thrilling in the idea, that, in very truth, the remains of Shakespeare were mouldering beneath my feet. It was a long time before I could prevail upon myself to leave the place; and as I passed through the church yard I plucked a branch from one of the yew trees, the only relic that I have brought from Stratford.

I had now visited the usual objects of a pilgrim's devotion, but I had a desire to see the old family seat of the Lucys at Charlecot, and to ramble through the park where Shakespeare, in company with some of the roysters of Stratford, committed his youthful offence of deer stealing. In this hare-brained exploit we are told that he was taken prisoner, and carried to the keeper's lodge, where he remained all night in doleful captivity. When brought into the presence of Sir Thomas Lucy, his treatment must have been galling and humiliating, for it so wrought upon his spirit as to produce a rough pasquinade, which was affixed to the park gate at Charlecot.*

This flagitious attack upon the dignity of the Knight so incensed him, that he applied to a lawyer at Warwick to put the severity of the laws in force against the rhyming deer stalker. Shakespeare did not wait to brave the united puissance of a Knight of the Shire and a country attorney. He forthwith abandoned the pleasant banks of the Avon and his paternal trade; wandered away to London; became a hanger on to the theatres; then an actor; and, finally, wrote for the stage; and thus, through the persecution of Sir Thomas Lucy, Stratford lost an indifferent wool comber and the world gained an immortal poet. He retained, however, for a long time, a sense of the harsh treatment of the Lord of Charlecot, and revenged himself in his writings; but in the sportive way of a good natured mind. Sir Thomas is said to be the original of Justice Shallow, and the satire is slyly fixed upon him by the Justice's armorial bearings, which, like those of the Knight, had white luces[†] in the quarterings.

Various attempts have been made by his biographers to soften

*The following is the only stanza extant of this lampoon:—

> A parliament member, a justice of peace,
> At home a poor scarecrow, at London an asse,
> If lowsie is Lucy, as some volke miscalle it,
> Then Lucy is lowsie, whatever befall it.
>   He thinks himself great;
>   Yet an asse in his state,
> We allow, by his ears, but with asses to mate.
> If Lucy is lowsie, as some volke miscall it,
> Then sing lowsie Lucy whatever befall it.

†The luce is a pike, or jack, and abounds in the Avon about Charlecot.

and explain away this early transgression of the poet; but I look upon it as one of those thoughtless exploits natural to his situation and turn of mind. Shakespeare, when young, had doubtless all the wildness and irregularity of an ardent, undisciplined, and undirected genius. The poetic temperament has naturally something in it of the vagabond. When left to itself it runs loosely and wildly, and delights in every thing eccentric and licentious. It is often a turn up of a die, in the gambling freaks of fate, whether a natural genius shall turn out a great rogue or a great poet; and had not Shakespeare's mind fortunately taken a literary bias, he might have as daringly transcended all civil, as he has all dramatic laws.

I have little doubt that, in early life, when running, like an unbroken colt, about the neighbourhood of Stratford, he was to be found in the company of all kinds of odd anomalous characters; that he associated with all the mad caps of the place, and was one of those unlucky urchins, at mention of whom old men shake their heads, and predict that they will one day come to the gallows. To him the poaching in Sir Thomas Lucy's park was doubtless like a foray to a Scottish Knight, and struck his eager, and as yet untamed, imagination, as something delightfully adventurous.*

The old mansion of Charlecot and its surrounding park still remain in the possession of the Lucy family, and are peculiarly interesting from being connected with this whimsical but eventful circumstance in the scanty history of the bard. As the house stood

---

*A proof of Shakespeare's random habits and associates in his youthful days, may be found in a traditionary anecdote, picked up at Stratford by the elder Ireland, and mentioned in his "Picturesque Views on the Avon."

About seven miles from Stratford lies the thirsty little market town of Bedford, famous for its ale. Two societies of the village yeomanry used to meet, under the appellation of the Bedford topers, and to challenge the lovers of good ale of the neighbouring villages, to a contest of drinking. Among others, the people of Stratford were called out to prove the strength of their heads; and in the number of the champions was Shakespeare, who, in spite of the proverb, that "they who drink beer will think beer," was as true to his ale as Falstaff to his sack. The chivalry of Stratford was staggered at the first onset, and sounded a retreat while they had yet legs to carry them off the field. They had scarcely marched a mile, when, their legs failing them, they were forced to lie down under a crab

at little more than three miles distance from Stratford, I resolved to pay it a pedestrian visit, that I might stroll leisurely through some of those scenes from which Shakespeare must have derived his earliest ideas of rural imagery.

The country was yet naked and leafless; but English scenery is always verdant, and the sudden change in the temperature of the weather was surprising in its quickening effects upon the landscape. It was inspiring and animating to witness this first awakening of spring. To feel its warm breath stealing over the senses; to see the moist mellow earth beginning to put forth the green sprout and the tender blade; and the trees and shrubs, in their reviving tints and bursting buds, giving the promise of returning foliage and flower. The cold snow drop, that little borderer on the skirts of winter, was to be seen with its chaste white blossoms in the small gardens before the cottages. The bleating of the new dropt lambs was faintly heard from the fields. The sparrow twittered about the thatched eaves and budding hedges; the robin threw a livelier note into his late querulous wintry strain; and the lark, springing up from the reeking bosom of the meadow, towered away into the bright fleecy cloud, pouring forth torrents of melody. As I watched the little songster, mounting up higher and higher, until his body was a mere speck on the white bosom of the cloud, while the ear was still filled with his music, it called to mind Shakespeare's exquisite little song in Cymbeline:

---

tree, where they passed the night. It is still standing, and goes by the name of Shakespeare's tree.

In the morning his companions awakened the bard, and proposed returning to Bedford, but he declined, saying he had had enough, having drank with

> Piping Pebworth, Dancing Marston,
> Haunted Hillbro', Hungry Grafton,
> Dudging Exhall, Papist Wicksford,
> Beggarly Broom, and Drunken Bedford.

"The villages here alluded to," says Ireland, "still bear the epithets thus given them; the people of Pebworth are still famed for their skill on the pipe and tabor: Hillborough is now called Haunted Hillborough: and Grafton is famous for the poverty of its soil."

Hark! hark! the lark at heav'n's gate sings,
  And Phœbus 'gins arise,
His steeds to water at those springs,
  On chaliced flowers that lies.

And winking mary-buds begin,
  To ope their golden eyes;
With every thing that pretty bin,
  My lady sweet arise!

Indeed the whole country about here is poetic ground: every thing is associated with the idea of Shakespeare. Every old cottage that I saw, I fancied into some resort of his boyhood, where he had acquired his intimate knowledge of rustic life and manners, and heard those legendary tales and wild superstitions which he has woven like witchcraft into his dramas. For in his time, we are told, it was a popular amusement in winter evenings "to sit round the fire, and tell merry tales of errant knights, queens, lovers, lords, ladies, giants, dwarfs, thieves, cheaters, witches, fairies, goblins, and friars." *

My route for a part of the way lay in sight of the Avon, which made a variety of the most fanciful doublings and windings through a wide and fertile valley; sometimes glittering from among willows, which fringed its borders; sometimes disappearing among groves, or beneath green banks; and sometimes rambling out into full view, and making an azure sweep round a slope of meadow land. This beautiful bosom of country is called the vale of the Red Horse. A distant line of undulating blue hills seems to be its boundary, whilst all the soft intervening landscape lies in a manner enchained in the silver links of the Avon.

---

*Scot, in his "Discoverie of Witchcraft," enumerates a host of these fireside fancies. "And they have so fraid us with bull-beggars, spirits, witches, urchins, elves, hags, fairies, satyrs, pans, faunes, syrens, kit with the can'sticke, tritons, centaurs, dwarfes, giantes, imps, calcars, conjurors, nymphes, changelings, incubus, Robin-good-fellow, the spoorne, the mare, the man in the oke, the hell-waine, the fier drake, the puckle, Tom Thombe, hobgoblins, Tom Tumbler, boneless, and such other bugs, that we were afraid of our own shadowes."

After pursuing the road for about three miles, I turned off into a footpath, which led along the borders of fields and under hedge rows to a private gate of the park; there was a style, however, for the benefit of the pedestrian; there being a public right of way through the grounds. I delight in these hospitable estates, in which every one has a kind of property—at least as far as the footpath is concerned. It in some measure reconciles a poor man to his lot, and what is more, to the better lot of his neighbour, thus to have parks and pleasure grounds thrown open for his recreation. He breathes the pure air as freely, and lolls as luxuriously under the shade, as the lord of the soil; and if he has not the privilege of calling all that he sees his own, he has not, at the same time, the trouble of paying for it, and keeping it in order.

I now found myself among noble avenues of oaks and elms, whose vast size bespoke the growth of centuries. The wind sounded solemnly among their branches, and the rooks cawed from their hereditary nests in the tree tops. The eye ranged through a long lessening vista, with nothing to interrupt the view but a distant statue; and a vagrant deer stalking like a shadow across the opening.

There is something about these stately old avenues that has the effect of gothic architecture, not merely from the pretended similarity of form, but from their bearing the evidence of long duration, and of having had their origin in a period of time with which we associate ideas of romantic grandeur. They betoken also the long settled dignity, and proudly concentrated independence of an ancient family; and I have heard a worthy but aristocratic old friend observe, when speaking of the sumptuous palaces of modern gentry, that "money could do much with stone and mortar, but thank heaven there was no such thing as suddenly building up an avenue of oaks."

It was from wandering in early life among this rich scenery, and about the romantic solitudes of the adjoining park of Fulbroke, which then formed a part of the Lucy estate, that some of Shakespeare's commentators have supposed he derived his noble forest meditations of Jaques, and the enchanting woodland pictures in

"As you like it." It is in lonely wanderings through such scenes, that the mind drinks deep but quiet draughts of inspiration, and becomes intensely sensible of the beauty and majesty of nature. The imagination kindles into reverie and rapture; vague but exquisite images and ideas keep breaking upon it; and we revel in a mute and almost incommunicable luxury of thought. It was in some such mood, and perhaps under one of those very trees before me, which threw their broad shades over the grassy banks and quivering waters of the Avon, that the poet's fancy may have sallied forth into that little song which breathes the very soul of a rural voluptuary:

> Under the green wood tree,
> Who loves to lie with me,
> And tune his merry throat
> Unto the sweet bird's note,
> Come hither, come hither, come hither,
> 　　Here shall he see
> 　　No enemy,
> But winter and rough weather.

　　I had now come in sight of the house. It is a large building of brick, with stone quoins, and is in the gothic style of Queen Elizabeth's day, having been built in the first year of her reign. The exterior remains very nearly in its original state, and may be considered a fair specimen of the residence of a wealthy country gentleman of those days. A great gateway opens from the park into a kind of court yard in front of the house, ornamented with a grass plot, shrubs, and flower beds. The gateway is in imitation of the ancient barbican; being a kind of outpost, and flanked by towers; though evidently for mere ornament, instead of defence. The front of the house is completely in the old style; with stone shafted casements, a great bow window of heavy stone work, and a portal with armorial bearings over it, carved in stone. At each corner of the building is an octagon tower, surmounted by a gilt ball and weathercock.

　　The Avon, which winds through the park, makes a bend just

at the foot of a gently sloping bank, which sweeps down from the rear of the house. Large herds of deer were feeding or reposing upon its borders; and swans were sailing majestically upon its bosom. As I contemplated the venerable old mansion, I called to mind Falstaff's encomium on Justice Shallow's abode, and the affected indifference and real vanity of the latter:

"*Falstaff.*   You have here a goodly dwelling and a rich.
  Shallow.   Barren, barren, barren; beggars all, beggars all, Sir John:—marry, good air."

Whatever may have been the joviality of the old mansion in the days of Shakespeare, it had now an air of stillness and solitude. The great iron gateway that opened into the court yard was locked; there was no show of servants bustling about the place; the deer gazed quietly at me as I passed, being no longer harried by the moss troopers of Stratford. The only sign of domestic life that I met with, was a white cat stealing with wary look and stealthy pace towards the stables, as if on some nefarious expedition. I must not omit to mention the carcass of a scoundrel crow which I saw suspended against the barn wall, as it shows that the Lucys still inherit that lordly abhorrence of poachers, and maintain that rigorous exercise of territorial power which was so strenuously manifested in the case of the bard.

After prowling about for some time, I at length found my way to a lateral portal which was the every day entrance to the mansion. I was courteously received by a worthy old housekeeper, who, with the civility and communicativeness of her order, showed me the interior of the house. The greater part has undergone alterations, and been adapted to modern tastes and modes of living: there is a fine old oaken staircase; and the great hall, that noble feature in an ancient manor house, still retains much of the appearance it must have had in the days of Shakespeare. The ceiling is arched and lofty; and at one end is a gallery, in which stands an organ. The weapons and trophies of the chace, which formerly adorned the hall of a country gentleman, have made way for family portraits. There is a wide hospitable fireplace, calculated for an ample old fashioned wood fire, formerly the rallying place of winter festivity. On the opposite side of the hall is the huge gothic bow window, with stone shafts, which looks out upon the court yard. Here are emblazoned in stained glass the armorial bearings of the Lucy family for many generations, some being dated in 1558. I was delighted to observe in the quarterings the three *white luces* by which the character of Sir Thomas was first identified with that of Justice Shallow. They are mentioned in the first scene of the Merry Wives of Windsor, where the Justice is in a rage with Falstaff for having "beaten his men, killed his deer, and broken into his lodge." The poet had no doubt the offences of himself and his comrades in mind at the time, and we may suppose the family pride and vindictive threats of the puissant Shallow to be a caricature of the pompous indignation of Sir Thomas.

"*Shallow.*   Sir Hugh, persuade me not: I will make a Star-Chamber matter of it; if he were twenty Sir John Falstaffs, he shall not abuse Robert Shallow, Esq.

Slender.   In the county of Gloster, justice of peace, and *coram*.

Shallow.   Ay, cousin Slender, and *custalorum*.

Slender.   Ay, and *ratalorum* too; and a gentleman born, master parson; who writes himself *Armigero* in any bill, warrant, quittance, or obligation, *Armigero*.

Shallow.   Ay, that I do; and have done any time these three hundred years.

Slender.   All his successors gone before him have done't, and all his ancestors that come after him may: they may give the dozen *white luces* in their coat. * * * * *

Shallow.   The council shall hear it; it is a riot.

Evans.   It is not meet the council hear of a riot; there is no fear of Got in a riot; the council, hear you, shall desire to hear the fear of Got, and not to hear a riot; take your vizaments in that.

Shallow.   Ha! o' my life, if I were young again, the sword should end it!"

Near the window thus emblazoned, hung a portrait by Sir Peter Lely of one of the Lucy family, a great beauty of the time of

Charles the Second; the old housekeeper shook her head as she pointed to the picture, and informed me that this lady had been sadly addicted to cards, and had gambled away a great portion of the family estate, among which was that part of the park where Shakespeare and his comrades had killed the deer. The lands thus lost had not been entirely regained by the family even at the present day. It is but justice to this recreant dame to confess that she had a surpassingly fine hand and arm.

The picture which most attracted my attention was a great painting over the fire place, containing likenesses of a Sir Thomas Lucy and his family who inhabited the hall in the latter part of Shakespeare's life time. I at first thought that it was the vindictive knight himself, but the housekeeper assured me that it was his son; the only likeness extant of the former being an effigy upon his tomb in the church of the neighbouring hamlet of Charlecot.*
The picture gives a lively idea of the costume and manners of the time. Sir Thomas is dressed in ruff and doublet; white shoes with roses in them; and has a peaked yellow, or, as Master Slender would say, "a cane coloured beard." His lady is seated on the opposite side of the picture in wide ruff and long stomacher, and the

*This effigy is in white marble, and represents the Knight in complete armor. Near him lies the effigy of his wife, and on her tomb is the following inscription; which, if really composed by her husband, places him quite above the intellectual level of Master Shallow:

Here lyeth the Lady Joyce Lucy wife of Sr Thomas Lucy of Charlecot in ye county of Warwick, Knight, Daughter and heir of Thomas Acton of Sutton in ye county of Worcester Esquire who departed out of this wretched world to her heavenly kingdom ye 10 day of February in ye yeare of our Lord God 1595 and of her age 60 and three. All the time of her lyfe a true and faythful servant of her good God, never detected of any cryme or vice. In religion most sounde, in love to her husband most faythful and true. In friendship most constant; to what in trust was committed unto her most secret. In wisdom excelling. In governing of her house, bringing up of youth in ye fear of God that did converse with her moste rare and singular. A great maintayner of hospitality. Greatly esteemed of her betters; misliked of none unless of the envyous. When all is spoken that can be saide a woman so garnished with virtue as not to be bettered and hardly to be equalled by any. As shee lived most virtuously so shee died most Godly. Set downe by him yt best did knowe what hath byn written to be true. Thomas Lucye.

children have a most venerable stiffness and formality of dress. Hounds and spaniels are mingled in the family group; a hawk is seated on his perch in the foreground, and one of the children holds a bow;—all intimating the knight's skill in hunting, hawking, and archery—so indispensable to an accomplished gentleman in those days.*

I regretted to find that the ancient furniture of the hall had disappeared; for I had hoped to meet with the stately elbow chair of carved oak, in which the country Squire of former days was wont to sway the sceptre of empire over his rural domains; and in which it might be presumed the redoubted Sir Thomas sat enthroned in awful state when the recreant Shakespeare was brought before him. As I like to deck out pictures for my entertainment, I pleased myself with the idea that this very hall had been the scene of the unlucky bard's examination on the morning after his captivity in the lodge. I fancied to myself the rural potentate, surrounded by his body guard of butler, pages, and blue coated serving men with their badges; while the luckless culprit was brought in, bedrooped and chapfallen; in the custody of game keepers, huntsmen and whippers in, and followed by a rabble rout of country clowns. I fancied bright faces of curious housemaids peeping from the half open doors, while from the gallery the fair daughters of the Knight leaned gracefully forward, eyeing the youthful prisoner with that pity "that dwells in womanhood."—Who would have thought that this poor varlet, thus trembling before the brief authority of a country Squire, and the sport of rustic boors, was soon to become the delight of princes; the theme of all tongues

*Bishop Earle, speaking of the country gentleman of his time, observes, "his housekeeping is seen much in the different families of dogs, and serving men attendant on their kennels; and the deepness of their throats is the depth of his discourse. A hawk he esteems the true burden of nobility, and is exceedingly ambitious to seem delighted with the sport, and have his fist gloved with his jesses." And Gilpin, in his description of a Mr. Hastings remarks, "he kept all sorts of hounds that run buck, fox, hare, otter and badger; and had hawks of all kinds both long and short winged. His great hall was commonly strewed with marrow-bones, and full of hawk perches, hounds, spaniels and terriers. On a broad hearth paved with brick, lay some of the choicest terriers, hounds and spaniels."

and ages; the dictator to the human mind; and was to confer immortality on his oppressor by a caricature and a lampoon!

I was now invited by the butler to walk into the garden, and I felt inclined to visit the orchard and arbour where the Justice treated Sir John Falstaff and Cousin Silence, "to a last year's pippen of his own graffing, with a dish of carraways;" but I had already spent so much of the day in my ramblings that I was obliged to give up any further investigations. When about to take my leave I was gratified by the civil entreaties of the housekeeper and butler, that I would take some refreshment: an instance of good old hospitality, which I grieve to say we castle hunters seldom meet with in modern days. I make no doubt it is a virtue which the present representative of the Lucys inherits from his ancestor; for Shakespeare, even in his caricature, makes Justice Shallow importunate in this respect, as witness his pressing instances to Falstaff:

> "By cock and pye, Sir, you shall not away to night * * * *. I will not excuse you; you shall not be excused; excuses shall not be admitted; there is no excuse shall serve; you shall not be excused * * * * * *. Some pigeons, Davy; a couple of shortlegged hens; a joint of mutton; and any pretty little tiny kickshaws, tell William Cook."

I now bade a reluctant farewell to the old hall. My mind had become so completely possessed by the imaginary scenes and characters connected with it, that I seemed to be actually living among them. Every thing brought them, as it were, before my eyes; and as the door of the dining room opened, I almost expected to hear the feeble voice of Master Silence quavering forth his favourite ditty:

> " 'Tis merry in hall, when beards wag all,
> And welcome merry Shrove-tide!"

On returning to my inn, I could not but reflect on the singular gift of the poet; to be able thus to spread the magic of his mind over the very face of nature; to give to things and places a charm and characters not their own, and to turn this "working day world" into a perfect fairy land. He is indeed the true enchanter, whose spell operates not upon the senses, but upon the imagination and the heart. Under the wizard influence of Shakespeare I had been walking all day in a complete delusion. I had surveyed the landscape through the prism of poetry, which tinged every object with the hues of the rainbow. I had been surrounded with fancied beings; with mere airy nothing, conjured up by poetic power; yet which, to me, had all the charm of reality. I had heard Jaques soliloquize beneath his oak; had beheld the fair Rosalind and her companion adventuring through the woodlands; and, above all, had been once more present in spirit with fat Jack Falstaff, and his contemporaries from the august Justice Shallow, down to the gentle Master Slender, and the sweet Anne Page. Ten thousand honours and blessings on the bard who has thus gilded the dull realities of life with innocent illusions; who has spread exquisite and unbought pleasures in my chequered path; and beguiled my spirit, in many a lonely hour, with the cordial and cheerful sympathies of social life!

As I crossed the bridge over the Avon on my return, I paused to contemplate the distant church in which the poet lies buried, and could not but exult in the malediction, which has kept his ashes undisturbed in its quiet and hallowed vaults. What honour could his name have derived from being mingled in dusty companionship with the epitaphs and escutcheons and venal eulogiums of a titled multitude. What would a crowded corner in Westminster Abbey have been, compared with this reverend pile, which seems to stand in beautiful loneliness as his sole mausoleum! The solicitude about the grave may be but the offspring of an overwrought sensibility; but human nature is made up of foibles and prejudices; and its best and tenderest affections are mingled with these factitious feelings. He who has sought renown about the world, and has reaped a full harvest of worldly favour, will find, after all, that there is no love, no admiration, no applause, so sweet to the soul as that which springs up in his native place. It is there that he seeks to be gathered in peace and honour among his kindred and his early friends. And when the weary heart and failing head begin to warn him that the evening of life is drawing on, he turns as fondly as does the infant to the mother's arms, to sink to sleep in the bosom of the scene of his childhood.

How would it have cheered the spirit of the youthful bard, when, wandering forth in disgrace upon a doubtful world, he cast back a heavy look upon his paternal home; could he have foreseen that, before many years, he should return to it covered with renown; that his name should become the boast and glory of his native place; that his ashes should be religiously guarded as its most precious treasure; and that its lessening spire, on which his eyes were fixed in tearful contemplation, should one day become the beacon, towering amidst the gentle landscape, to guide the literary pilgrim of every nation to his tomb.

(1820)

Charles Sprague

(1791–1875)

Prize Ode

In 1823 the manager of the Boston Theatre offered a poetry prize as part of a Shakespeare Jubilee to be celebrated on February 13, 1824. Charles Sprague's submission, which was recited at the event, won the prize, and was published in Boston later that year and subsequently reprinted in Sprague's collected works in 1841. Sprague, known as the "Banker Poet of Boston," was a descendent of some of America's founding fathers; his own father had participated in the Boston Tea Party. His formal education, like Shakespeare's, ended with grammar school. Sprague's ode on Shakespeare was widely praised: Samuel Atkins Eliot called it "unrivalled for brilliancy, variety, and power," and Ralph Waldo Emerson, who admired it greatly, wrote to Sprague asking for a copy. The poem speaks to the tension between an America that reveres Shakespeare and one that also recognizes that he was an English poet. The ending of the poem seeks to resolve this by declaring that America shall make Shakespeare its own and that his works will inspire American poets ("Thy name, thy verse, thy language shall they bear"). Though Britain lost the war of American Independence, America will be bound to her once more, through Shakespeare: "Our Roman-hearted Fathers broke / Thy parent empire's galling yoke, / But Thou, harmonious Monarch of the mind, / Around their Sons a gentler chain shall bind:— / Once more, in Thee, shall Albion's sceptre wave."

❧

God of the glorious Lyre!
Whose notes of old on lofty Pindus rang,
    While Jove's exulting quire
Caught the glad echoes and responsive sang—
    Come! bless the service and the shrine
    We consecrate to Thee and Thine!

Fierce from the frozen north,
   When Havock led his legions forth,
O'er Learning's sunny groves the dark destroyers spread:
In dust the sacred statue slept,
Fair Science round her altars wept,
   And Wisdom cowled his head.

At length, Olympian Lord of morn,
The raven veil of night was torn,
   When through golden clouds descending,
Thou didst hold thy radiant flight,
   O'er nature's lovely pageant bending,
Till Avon rolled all-sparkling to thy sight!

There, on its bank, beneath the Mulberry's shade,
Wrapped in young dreams a wild-eyed Minstrel strayed:
   Lighting there and lingering long,
   Thou didst teach the Bard his song;
      Thy fingers strung his sleeping shell;
And round his brows a garland curled,
      On his lips thy spirit fell,
And bade him wake and warm the world!

   Then *Shakspere* rose!
      Across the trembling strings
      His daring hand he flings,
   And lo! a new creation glows!
There clustering round, submissive to his will,
Fate's vassal train his high commands fulfil.
   Madness with his frightful scream,
      Vengeance leaning on his lance,
   Avarice with his blade and beam,
      Hatred blasting with a glance.
Remorse that weeps, and Rage that roars,
And Jealousy that dotes but dooms, and murders, yet adores.

Mirth, his face with sunbeams lit,
Waking Laughter's merry swell,
Arm in arm with fresh-eyed Wit,
That waves his tingling lash, while Folly shakes his bell,
From the feudal towers pale Terror rushing,
   Where the prophet bird's wail
   Dies along the dull gale,
And the sleeping monarch's blood is gushing!

Despair that haunts the gurgling stream,
Kissed by the virgin moon's cold beam,
Where some lost maid wild chaplets wreathes,
And swan-like there her own dirge breathes,
Then broken-hearted sinks to rest,
Beneath the bubbling wave that shrouds her maniac breast,

Young Love, with eye of tender gloom,
Now drooping o'er the hallowed tomb,
   Where his plighted victims lie,
   Where they met, but met to die:—
And now, when crimson buds are sleeping,
   Through the dewy arbour peeping,
Where Beauty's child, the frowning world forgot,
   To youth's devoted tale is listening,
   Rapture on her dark lash glistening,
While fairies leave their cowslip cells and guard the happy spot,
   Thus rise the phantom throng,
   Obedient to their master's song,
And lead in willing chain the wondering soul along.

For other worlds war's Great One sighed in vain,
O'er other worlds see *Shakspere* rove and reign!
The rapt Magician of his own wild lay,
Earth and her tribes his mystic wand obey,
Old ocean trembles, thunder cracks the skies,
Air teems with shapes, and tell-tale spectres rise:
Time yields his trophies up, and death restores

The mouldering victims of his voiceless shores:
Night's paltering hags their fearful orgies keep,
And faithless guilt unseals the lip of sleep;
The fireside legend, and the faded page,
The crime that cursed, the deed that blessed an age,
All, all come forth—the good to charm and cheer,
To scourge bold Vice, and start the generous tear;
With pictured Folly gazing fools to shame,
And guide young Glory's foot along the path of fame.

    Mark the sceptered Traitor slumbering!
    There flit the slaves of conscience round;
    With boding tongue foul murders numbering,
    Sleep's leaden portals catch the sound.
  In his dream of blood for mercy quaking,
  At his own dull scream behold him waking.
    Soon that dream to fate shall turn,
    For him the *living* furies burn;
For him the vulture sits on yonder misty peak,
And chides the lagging night, and whets her hungry beak.
    Hark! the trumpet's warning breath
    Echoes round the vale of death,
Where through the maddening ranks the God of slaughter rides,
And o'er their spouting trunks his reeking axle guides!
    Unhorsed, unhelmed, disdaining shield,
    The panting Tyrant scours the field,
    Vengeance! he meets thy dooming blade!
    The scourge of earth, the scorn of heaven,
    He falls, unwept and unforgiven,
    And all his guilty glories fade.
  Like a crushed reptile in the dust he lies,
  And hate's last lightning quivers from his eyes!

    Behold you crownless King—
    You whitelocked, weeping Sire;—
Where heaven's unpillared chambers ring,
And burst their streams of flood and fire;

He gave them all—the daughters of his love;—
That recreant pair!—they drive him forth to rove.
　　In such a night of wo,
　The cubless regent of the wood
　Forgets to bathe her fangs in blood,
　　　And caverns with her foe!
　　　Yet one was ever kind,
　　　Why lingers she behind?
O pity! view him by her dead form kneeling,
Even in wild frenzy holy nature feeling.
　　His aching eyeballs strain
　To see those curtained orbs unfold,
　That beauteous bosom heave again.—
　　　But all is dark and cold.
　In agony the Father shakes;
　　　Grief's choking note
　　　Swells in his throat,
　Each withered heart-string tugs and breaks!
Round her pale neck his dying arms he wreathes,
And on her marble lips his last, his death-kiss breathes.

Down! trembling wing—shall insect weakness keep,
　　　The sun-defying eagle's sweep?
　　　A mortal strike celestial strings,
　　　And feebly echo what a seraph sings?
　　　Who now shall grace the glowing throne,
　　　Where, all unrivalled, all alone,
Bold *Shakspere* sat, and looked creation through
The Minstrel-Monarch of the worlds he drew?

That throne is cold—that lyre in death unstrung,
On whose proud note delighted wonder hung.
Yet old Oblivion, as in wrath he sweeps,
One spot shall spare—the grave where *Shakspere* sleeps.
Rulers and ruled in common gloom may lie,
But nature's laureate Bards shall never die.
Art's chisselled boast, and glory's trophied shore

Must live in numbers, or can live no more.
While sculptured Jove some nameless waste may claim,
Still rolls th' Olympic Car in Pindar's fame:
Troy's doubtful walls, in ashes passed away,
Yet frown on Greece in Homer's deathless lay:
Rome, slowly sinking in her crumbling fanes,
Stands all-immortal in her Maro's strains:—
So, too, yon giant Empress of the isles,
On whose broad sway the sun forever smiles,
To time's unsparing rage one day must bend,
And all her triumphs in her *Shakspere* end!

    O Thou! to whose creative power
    We dedicate the festal hour,
While Grace and Goodness round the altar stand,
Learning's anointed train, and Beauty's rose-lipped band—
Realms yet unborn, in accents now unknown,
Thy song shall learn, and bless it for their own.
Deep in the West as Independence roves,
His banners planting round the land he loves,
Where nature sleeps in Eden's infant grace,
In time's full hour shall spring a glorious race.—
Thy name, thy verse, thy language shall they bear,
And deck for Thee, the vaulted temple there!
    Our Roman-hearted Fathers broke
    Thy parent empire's galling yoke,
But Thou, harmonious Monarch of the mind,
Around their Sons a gentler chain shall bind:—
Once more, in Thee, shall Albion's sceptre wave,
And what her mighty Lion lost, her mightier *Swan* shall save!

(1824)

John Quincy Adams

(1767–1848)

The Character of Desdemona

Born in 1767, Adams (who would serve as the sixth president of the
United States, and after that as a Massachusetts congressman) grew up
in a household steeped in Shakespeare. Late in life, Adams recalled that
he had been, "man and boy, a reader of Shakespeare at least three score
years. A pocket edition of him was among the books of my mother's
nursery-library, and at ten years of age I was as familiarly acquainted
with his lovers and his clowns, as with Robinson Crusoe, the Pilgrim's
Progress, and the Bible." Published in the December 1835 issue of *The
New England Magazine*, Adams's reflections on Desdemona's character
and what he calls her "unnatural passion" for Othello exemplify the
contradictions of antebellum views of slavery and interracial marriage.
His antislavery record was matched by few Americans: Adams famously
attacked slaveholding from the floor of the House of Representatives,
successfully defended African Americans before the Supreme Court in
the case of *United States v. The Amistad*, and opposed war with Mexico
and the annexation of Texas on the grounds that they would extend
slavery and lead to civil war. Yet Adams concludes in this essay that "the
moral" of *Othello* is "that the intermarriage of black and white blood
is a violation of the law of nature. *That* is the lesson to be learned from
the play." The Philadelphia *National Gazette* and the Georgetown *Met-
ropolitan* criticized Adams for his harsh view of Desdemona. Stung,
Adams wrote a few days later to his friend Dr. George Parkman defending his views: "The great moral lesson of the tragedy of *Othello* is, that
the black and white blood cannot be intermingled in marriage without
a gross outrage upon the law of Nature; and that, in such violations,
Nature will vindicate her laws." Adams's essay on *Othello* was collected
in James Henry Hackett's *Notes, Criticisms, and Correspondence upon
Shakespeare's Plays and Actors* in 1863, a volume that Abraham Lincoln
read (see pg. 181 of this volume).

THERE are critics who cannot bear to see the virtue and delicacy of Shakespeare's *Desdemona* called in question; who
defend her on the ground that *Othello* is not an Ethiopian, but
a Moor; that he is not black, but only tawny; and they protest
against the sable mask of *Othello* upon the stage, and against the
pictures of him in which he is always painted black. They say that
prejudices have been taken against *Desdemona* from the slanders
of *Iago*, from the railings of *Roderigo*, from the disappointed paternal rancor of *Brabantio*, and from the desponding concessions
of *Othello* himself.

I have said, that since I entered upon the third of Shakespeare's
seven ages, the first and chief capacity in which I have read and
studied him is as a *teacher of morals*; and that I had scarcely ever
seen a player of his parts who regarded him as a *moralist* at all. I
further said, that in my judgment no man could understand him
who did *not* study him pre-eminently as a teacher of morals. These
critics say they do not incline to put Shakespeare on a level with
Æsop! Sure enough *they* do not study Shakespeare as a teacher of
morals. To *them*, therefore, *Desdemona* is a perfect character; and
her love for *Othello* is not unnatural, because he is not a Congo
negro but only a sooty Moor, and has royal blood in his veins.

My objections to the character of *Desdemona* arise not from
what *Iago*, or *Roderigo*, or *Brabantio*, or *Othello* says of her; but
from what she herself *does*. She absconds from her father's house,
in the dead of night, to marry a blackamoor. She breaks a father's
heart, and covers his noble house with shame, to gratify—what?
Pure love, like that of *Juliet* or *Miranda*? No! unnatural passion;
it cannot be named with delicacy. Her admirers now say this is
criticism of 1835; that the color of *Othello* has nothing to do with
the passion of *Desdemona*. No? Why, if *Othello* had been white,
what need would there have been for her running away with
him? She could have made no better match. Her father could
have made no reasonable objection to it; and there could have
been no tragedy. If the color of *Othello* is not as vital to the whole
tragedy as the age of *Juliet* is to her character and destiny, then
have I read Shakespeare in vain. The father of *Desdemona* charges

Othello with magic arts in obtaining the affections of his daughter. Why, but because her passion for him is *unnatural*; and why is it unnatural, but because of his color? In the very first scene, in the dialogue between *Roderigo* and *Iago*, before they rouse *Brabantio* to inform him of his daughter's elopement, *Roderigo* contemptuously calls *Othello* "the thick lips." I cannot in decency quote here—but turn to the book, and see in what language *Iago* announces to her father his daughter's shameful misconduct. The language of *Roderigo* is more supportable. *He* is a Venetian gentleman, himself a rejected suitor of *Desdemona*; and who has been forbidden by her father access to his house. Roused from his repose at the dead of night by the loud cries of these two men, *Brabantio* spurns, with indignation and scorn, the insulting and beastly language of *Iago*; and sharply chides *Roderigo*, whom he supposes to be hovering about his house in defiance of his prohibitions and in a state of intoxication. He threatens him with punishment. *Roderigo* replies—

> "*Rod.* Sir, I will answer any thing.   But I beseech you,
>   If 't be your pleasure, and most wise consent,
>   (As partly, I find, it is), that your fair daughter
>   At this odd-even and dull watch o' the night,
>   Transported—with no worse nor better guard,
>   But with a knave of common hire, a gondolier,—
>   To the gross clasps of a lascivious Moor,—
>   If this be known to you, and your allowance,
>   We then have done you bold and saucy wrongs;
>   But if you know not this, my manners tell me,
>   We have your wrong rebuke. Do not believe,
>   That, from the sense of all civility,
>   I thus would play and trifle with your reverence:
>   Your daughter—if you have not given her leave,—
>   I say again, hath made a gross revolt;
>   Tying her duty, beauty, wit, and fortunes,
>   To an extravagant and wheeling stranger,
>   Of here and every where: Straight satisfy yourself:

> If she be in her chamber, or your house,
> Let loose on me the justice of the state,
> For thus deluding you."

Struck by this speech as by a clap of thunder, *Brabantio* calls up his people, remembers a portentous dream, calls for light, goes and searches with his servants, and comes back saying—

> "It is too true an evil: gone she is:
> And what's to come of my despised time,
> Is nought but bitterness."

The father's heart is broken; life is no longer of any value to him; he repeats this sentiment time after time whenever he appears in the scene; and in the last scene of the play, where *Desdemona* lies dead, her uncle Gratiano says—

> "Poor Desdemona! I am glad thy father's dead,
> Thy match was mortal to him, and pure grief
> Shore his old thread in twain."

Indeed! indeed! I must look at Shakespeare in this, as in all his pictures of human life, in the capacity of a teacher of morals. I must believe that, in exhibiting a daughter of a Venetian nobleman of the highest rank eloping in the dead of the night to marry a thick-lipped wool-headed Moor, opening a train of consequences which lead to her own destruction by her husband's hands, and to that of her father by a broken heart, he did not intend to present her as an example of the perfection of female virtue. I must look first at the action, then at the motive, then at the consequences, before I inquire in what light it is received and represented by the other persons of the drama. The first action of *Desdemona* discards all female delicacy, all filial duty, all sense of ingenuous shame. So I consider it—and so it is considered by her own father. Her offence is not a mere elopement from her father's house for a clandestine marriage. I hope it requires no unreasonable rigor or morality to consider even *that* as suited to raise a prepossession rather unfavorable to the character of a young woman of refined sensibility and elevated education. But an elopement for a clandestine marriage with a blackamoor! That is the measure of my estimation of the character of *Desdemona* from the beginning; and when I have passed my judgment upon it, and find in the play that from the first moment of her father's knowledge of the act it made him loathe his life, and that it finally broke his heart, I am then in time to inquire, what was the deadly venom which inflicted the immedicable wound:—and what is it, but the color of *Othello*?

> "Now, Roderigo,
> Where did'st thou see her?—Oh, unhappy girl!—
> *With the Moor, say'st thou?*—Who would be a father?"

These are the disjointed lamentations of the wretched parent when the first disclosure of his daughter's shame is made known to him. This scene is one of the inimitable pictures of human passion in the hands of Shakespeare, and that half line

> "With the *Moor*, say'st thou?"

comes from the deepest recesses of the soul.

Again, when *Brabantio* first meets *Othello*, he breaks out:

> "O, thou foul thief, where hast thou stow'd my daughter?
> Damn'd as thou art, thou hast enchanted her:
> For I'll refer me to all things of sense,
> If she, in chains of magic were not bound,
> Whether a maid so tender, fair, and happy,
> So opposite to marriage that she shunn'd
> The wealthy *curled* darlings of our nation,
> Would ever have to incur our general mock,
> Run from her guardage *to the sooty bosom*
> Of such a thing as thou; to fear, not to delight."

Several of the English commentators have puzzled themselves with the inquiry why the epithet "curled" is here applied to the wealthy darlings of the nation; and Dr. Johnson thinks it has no reference to the hair; but it evidently has. The *curled* hair is in antithetic contrast to the sooty bosom, the thick lips, and the woolly head.* The contrast of color is the very hinge upon which *Brabantio* founds his charge of magic, counteracting the impulse of nature.

At the close of the same scene (the second of the first act), *Brabantio*, hearing that the duke is in council upon public business of the State, determines to carry *Othello* before him for trial upon the charge of magic. "Mine," says he,

> "Mine's not a middle cause; the duke himself
> Or any of my brothers of the State
> Cannot but feel the wrong, as 'twere their own:
> For if such actions may have passage free,
> Bond slaves and Pagans shall our statesmen be."

And Steevens, in his note on this passage, says, "He alludes to the common condition of all blacks who come from their own country, both *slaves* and *pagans*; and uses the word in contempt of *Othello* and his complexion. If this Moor is now suffered to escape with impunity, it will be such an encouragement to his black countrymen, that we may expect to see all the first offices of our state filled up by the Pagans and bond-slaves of Africa." *Othello* himself in his narrative says that he had been taken by the insolent foe and sold to slavery. He *had been* a slave.

Once more—When *Desdemona* pleads to the Duke and the Council for permission to go with *Othello* to Cyprus, she says,

> "That I did love the Moor, to live with him,
> My downright violence and storm of fortune
> May trumpet to the world; *my heart's subdued,*
> *Even to the very quality of my lord;*
> I saw Othello's visage in his mind;

---

* *"Wealthy curled darlings."*

The negro's hair curled like *wool* naturally; the Venetians' locks of hair were curled artificially, and betrayed vanity and effeminacy in their desire to become the "darlings" of the *ladies*, whose curls adorn their countenance, and in many of the sex are not produced by nature, but also by the art of the toilette.— *J. H. H.*

And to his honours and his valiant parts
Did I my soul and fortunes consecrate."

In commenting upon this passage, Mr. Henley says, "That *quality* here signifies the Moorish *complexion* of Othello, and not his military profession (as Malone had supposed), is obvious from what immediately follows: 'I saw Othello's visage in his mind;' and also from what the Duke says to *Brabantio*—

"If virtue no delighted beauty lack
Your son-in-law is far more fair than black."

The characters of *Othello* and *Iago* in this play are evidently intended as contrasted pictures of human nature, each setting off the other. They are national portraits of man—the ITALIAN and the MOOR. The Italian is *white*, *crafty*, and *cruel*; a consummate villain; yet, as often happens in the realities of that description whom we occasionally meet in the intercourse of life, so vain of his own artifices that he betrays himself by boasting of them and their success. Accordingly, in the very first scene he reveals to *Roderigo* the treachery of his own character:

"For when my outward action doth demonstrate
The native act and figure of my heart
In compliment extern, 'tis not long after
But I will wear my heart upon my sleeve
For daws to peck at: I am not what I am."

There is a seeming inconsistency in the fact that a double-dealer should disclose his own secret, which must necessarily put others upon their guard against him; but the inconsistency is in human nature, and not in the poet.

The double-dealing Italian is a very intelligent man, a keen and penetrating observer, and full of ingenuity to devise and contrive base expedients. His language is coarse, rude, and obscene: his humor is caustic and bitter. Conscious of no honest principle in himself, he believes not in the existence of honesty in others. He is jealous and suspicious; quick to note every trifle light as air, and to draw from it inferences of evil as confirmed circumstances. In his dealings with the Moor, while he is even harping upon his honesty, he offers to commit any murder from extreme attachment to his person and interests. In all that *Iago* says of others, and especially of *Desdemona*, there is a mixture of truth and falsehood, blended together, in which the truth itself serves to accredit the lie; and such is the ordinary character of malicious slanders. Doctor Johnson speaks of "the soft simplicity," the "innocence," the "artlessness" of *Desdemona*. *Iago* speaks of her as a *supersubtle* Venetian; and, when kindling the sparks of jealousy in the soul of *Othello*, he says,

> "She did deceive her father, marrying you:
> And when she seemed to shake and fear your looks,
> She loved them most."

"And so she did," answers *Othello*. This charge, then, was true; and *Iago* replies:

> "Why, go to, then;
> She that so young could give out such a seeming
> To seal her father's eyes up, close as oak.—
> He thought 'twas witchcraft."

It was not witchcraft; but surely as little was it simplicity, innocence, artlessness. The effect of this suggestion upon *Othello* is terrible only because he knows it is true. *Brabantio*, on parting from him, had just given him the same warning, to which he had not then paid the slightest heed. But soon his suspicions are roused—he tries to repel them; they are fermenting in his brain: he appears vehemently moved and yet unwilling to acknowledge it. *Iago*, with fiend-like sagacity, seizes upon the paroxysm of emotion, and then comes the following dialogue:—

> "*Iago.* My lord, I see you are mov'd.
> *Othello.*   No, not much mov'd:—
>   I do not think but *Desdemona's* honest.
> *Iago.* Long live she so! and long live you to think so!

> *Othello.* And yet, how nature erring from itself,—
> *Iago.* Ay, there's the point:—As,—to be bold with you,—
>   Not to affect many proposed matches,
>   Of her own clime, complexion, or degree;
>   Whereto, we see, in all things nature tends:
>   Foh! one may smell, in such, a will most rank
>   Foul disproportion, thoughts unnatural."—

The deadly venom of these imputations, working up to frenzy the suspicions of the Moor, consist not in their falsehood but in their truth.

I have said the character of *Desdemona* was deficient in delicacy. Besides the instances to which I referred in proof of this charge, observe what she says in pleading for the restoration of *Cassio* to his office, from which he had been cashiered by *Othello* for beastly drunkenness and a consequent night-brawl, in which he had stabbed *Montano*—the predecessor of *Othello* as Governor of Cyprus—and nearly killed him; yet in urging *Othello* to restore *Cassio* to his office and to favor, *Desdemona* says—

>   "—in faith, he's penitent;
>   And yet his trespass, in our common reason,
>   (Save that, they say, the wars must make examples
>   Out of their best,) *is not almost a fault*
>   To incur a private check."

Now, to palliate the two crimes of *Cassio*—his drunken fit and his stabbing of *Montano*—the reader knows that he has been inveigled to the commission of them by the accursed artifices of *Iago*; but *Desdemona* knows nothing of this; she has no excuse for *Cassio*—nothing to plead for him but his penitence. And is this the character for a woman of delicate sentiment to give of such a complicated and heinous offence as that of which *Cassio* had been guilty, even when pleading for his pardon? No! it is not for female delicacy to extenuate the crimes of drunkenness and bloodshed, even when performing the appropriate office of raising the soul-subduing voice for mercy.

Afterwards, in the same speech, she says—

> "What! *Michael Cassio*,
> That came a-wooing with you; and many a time,
> When I have spoke of you dispraisingly,
> Hath ta'en your part; to have so much to do
> To bring *him* in!"

I will not inquire how far this avowal that she had been in the frequent habit of speaking dispraisingly of *Othello* at the very time when she was so deeply enamored with his honors and his valiant parts, was consistent with sincerity. Young ladies must be allowed a little concealment and a little disguise, even for passions of which they have no need to be ashamed. It is the rosy pudency—the irresistible charm of the sex; but the exercise of it in satirical censure upon the very object of their most ardent affections is certainly no indication of innocence, simplicity, or artlessness.

I still retain, then, the opinion—

First. That the passion of *Desdemona* for *Othello* is *unnatural*, solely and exclusively because of his color.

Second. That her elopement *to* him, and secret marriage *with* him, indicate a personal character not only very deficient in delicacy, but totally regardless of filial duty, of female modesty, and of ingenuous shame.

Third. That her deficiency in delicacy is discernible in her conduct and discourse throughout the play.

I perceive and acknowledge, indeed, the admirable address with which the part has been contrived to inspire and to warm the breast of the spectator with a deep interest in her fate; and I am well aware that my own comparative insensibility to it is not in unison with the general impression which it produces upon the stage. I shrink from the thought of slandering even a creature of the imagination. When the spectator or reader follows, on the stage or in the closet, the infernal thread of duplicity and of execrable devices with which *Iago* entangles his victims, it is the purpose of the dramatist to merge all the faults and vices of the sufferers in the overwhelming flood of their calamities, and in the unmingled detestation of the inhuman devil, their betrayer and destroyer. And in all this, I see not only the skill of the artist, but the power of the moral operator, the purifier of the spectator's heart by the agency of *terror* and *pity*.

The characters of *Othello* and *Desdemona*, like all the characters of men and women in real life, are of "mingled yarn," with qualities of good and bad—of virtues and vices in proportion differently composed. *Iago*, with a high order of intellect, is, in moral principle, the very spirit of evil. I have said the moral of the tragedy is, that the intermarriage of black and white blood is a violation of the law of nature. *That* is the lesson to be learned from the play. To exhibit all the natural consequences of their act, the poet is compelled to make the marriage secret. It must commence by an elopement, and by an outrage upon the decorum of social intercourse. He must therefore assume, for the performance of this act, persons of moral character sufficiently frail and imperfect to be capable of performing it, but in other respects endowed with pleasing and estimable qualities. Thus, the Moor is represented as of a free, and open, and generous nature; as a Christian; as a distinguished military commander in the service of the republic of Venice;—as having rendered important service to the State, and as being in the enjoyment of a splendid reputation as a warrior. The other party to the marriage is a maiden, fair, gentle, and accomplished; born and educated in the proudest rank of Venetian nobility.

Othello, setting aside his color, has every quality to fascinate and charm the female heart. *Desdemona*, apart from the grossness of her fault in being accessible to such a passion for such an object, is amiable and lovely; among the most attractive of her sex and condition. The faults of their characters are never brought into action excepting as they illustrate the moral principle of the whole story. *Othello* is not jealous by nature. On the contrary, with a strong natural understanding, and all the vigilance essential to an experienced commander, he is of a disposition so unsuspicious and confiding, that he believes in the *exceeding honesty* of

Iago long after he has ample cause to suspect and distrust him. *Desdemona, supersubtle* as she is in the management of her amour with *Othello*; deeply as she dissembles to deceive her father; and forward as she is in inviting the courtship of the Moor; discovers neither artifice nor duplicity from the moment that she is *Othello's* wife. Her innocence, in all her relations with him, is pure and spotless; her kindness for *Cassio* is mere untainted benevolence; and, though unguarded in her personal deportment towards him, it is far from the slightest soil of culpable impropriety. Guiltless of all conscious reproach in this part of her conduct, she never uses any of the artifices to which she had resorted to accomplish her marriage with *Othello*. Always feeling that she has given him no cause of suspicion, her endurance of his cruel treatment and brutal abuse of her through all its stages of violence, till he murders her in bed, is always marked with the most affecting sweetness of temper, the most perfect artlessness, and the most endearing resignation. The defects of her character have here no room for development, and the poet carefully keeps them out of sight. Hence it is that the general reader and spectator, with Dr. Johnson, give her un-qualified credit for soft simplicity, artlessness, and innocence—forgetful of the qualities of a different and opposite character, stamped upon the transactions by which she effected her marriage with the Moor. The marriage, however, is the source of all her calamities; it is the primitive cause of all the tragic incidents of the play, and of its terrible catastrophe. That the moral lesson to be learned from it is of no practical utility in England, where there are no valiant Moors to steal the affections of fair and high-born dames, may be true; the lesson, however, is not the less, couched under the form of an admirable drama; nor needs it any laborious effort of the imagination to extend the moral precept resulting from the story to a salutary admonition against all ill-assorted, clandestine, and unnatural marriages.

(*1836*)

Edgar Allan Poe

(1809–1849)

Hazlitt's Characters of Shakspeare

Poe read Shakespeare closely. His tales, poems, letters, and reviews quote or discuss twenty-eight of the plays, *Hamlet* most often. Poe was especially attuned to the way that Shakespeare makes us feel that his characters are lifelike—which, for Poe, misled critics to speak of the *dramatis personae* of the plays as if they were real people. As he suggests in this review, Shakespeare achieves this effect through his powerful identification with fictional characters like Hamlet. His observations on Hazlitt's influential study first appeared in the August 16, 1845 issue of *The Broadway Journal*, which Poe owned and edited.

✆

Wiley and Putnam's Library of Choice Reading. No. XVII.
The Characters of Shakspeare. By William Hazlitt.

THIS is one of the most interesting numbers of "The Library" yet issued. If anything *could* induce us to read anything more in the way of commentary on Shakspeare, it would be the name of Hazlitt prefixed. With his hackneyed theme he has done wonders, and those wonders well. He is emphatically a critic, brilliant, epigrammatic, startling, paradoxical, and suggestive, rather than accurate, luminous, or profound. For purposes of mere amusement, he is the best commentator who ever wrote in English. At all points, except perhaps in fancy, he is superior to Leigh Hunt, whom nevertheless he remarkably resembles. It is folly to compare him with Macaulay, for there is scarcely a single point of approximation, and Macaulay is by much the greater man. The author of "The Lays of Ancient Rome" has an intellect so well balanced and so thoroughly proportioned, as to appear, in the eyes of the multitude, much smaller than it really is. He needs a few foibles to purchase him *éclat*. Now, take away the innumerable foibles of Hunt and Hazlitt, and we should have the anomaly of finding them more diminutive than we fancy them while the foibles remain. Nevertheless, they are men of genius still.

In all commentating upon Shakspeare, there has been a radical error, never yet mentioned. It is the error of attempting to expound his characters—to account for their actions—to reconcile his inconsistencies—not as if they were the coinage of a human brain, but as if they had been actual existences upon earth. We talk of Hamlet the man, instead of Hamlet the *dramatis persona*—of Hamlet that God, in place of Hamlet that Shakspeare created. If Hamlet had really lived, and if the tragedy were an accurate record of his deeds, from this record (with some trouble) we might, it is true, reconcile his inconsistencies and settle to our satisfaction his true character. But the task becomes the purest absurdity when we deal only with a phantom. It is not (then) the inconsistencies of the acting man which we have as a subject of discussion—(although we proceed as if it were, and thus *inevitably* err,) but the whims and vacillations—the conflicting energies and indolences of the poet. It seems to us little less than a miracle, that this obvious point should have been overlooked.

While on this topic, we may as well offer an ill-considered opinion of our own as to the *intention of the poet* in the delineation of the Dane. It must have been well known to Shakspeare, that a leading feature in certain more intense classes of intoxication, (from whatever cause,) is an almost irresistible impulse to counterfeit a farther degree of excitement than actually exists. Analogy would lead any thoughtful person to suspect the same impulse in madness—where beyond doubt, it is manifest. This, Shakspeare *felt*—not thought. He felt it through his marvellous power of *identification* with humanity at large—the ultimate source of his magical influence upon mankind. He wrote of Hamlet as if Hamlet he were; and having, in the first instance, imagined his hero excited to partial insanity by the disclosures of the ghost—he (the poet) *felt* that it was natural he should be impelled to exaggerate the insanity.

(1845)

J.M.W.

First Impressions of Miss Cushman's "Romeo"

Charlotte Cushman, one of the most celebrated American actors of the nineteenth century, had initially pursued a career as an opera singer, but damaged her voice. She played her first major dramatic role—Lady Macbeth—at the age of twenty in 1836. When the English star William Charles Macready came to the States in 1843 he invited her to play opposite him as Lady Macbeth; though another actor was substituted for her, Cushman learned a great deal from closely observing Macready perform. The following year she sailed to London, where she was an immediate sensation and soon hailed by British critics "as the first actress that we have." British playgoers were both shocked by and drawn to her brashness and masculinity, which they saw as somehow queer and American, a far cry from the behavior of their demure London stage heroines. Cushman was said to have bullied her Macbeths, and, according to one contemporary, her cross-dressed Rosalind in *As You Like It* "looks in every inch a man. . . . Her mind became masculine as well as her outward semblance." Cushman, a lesbian, had to mask her sexual identity in public, though she drew on it for her powerful performances, especially in 'breeches' parts, at which she excelled. Her most memorable role was as Romeo, especially with her sister Susan playing opposite her as Juliet. According to the *Spectator*, she was "the best Romeo that has appeared on the stage these thirty years." Male critics and reviewers were largely silent about what made Cushman's gender-bending performances so compelling, and one of the only writers of the time who addresses this more or less directly was J.M.W. (just possibly the fourteen-year-old Jessie Meriton White, subsequently Jesse White Mario, journalist and activist), who saw Cushman play Romeo in London in 1846 and wrote about it shortly after for the *People's Journal*.

❧

I ASKED a lady, on her return from the Haymarket Theatre one evening, what was her opinion of Miss Cushman's performance of *Romeo*. The answer I received was, a pause, a light laugh,

and—"Oh, Miss Cushman is a very dangerous young man." The
lady's manner recalled to my mind those words of Racine—

> Car la parole est toujours supprimee
> Quand le sujet surmonte le disant.*

I felt curious to see this actress, and went to the theatre the next
time she played *Romeo*. At first I was struck by her likeness to
Macready, both in person and manner; afterwards I became convinced that this likeness was entirely the work of nature; and that
Miss Cushman does not *imitate* Macready.

Before the close of the second act the conviction was forcibly borne in upon my mind that this was not *a clever woman
merely*, but one that comes before the world in a more questionable shape—*a woman of genius*. Wanting in harmony, perhaps—
in that lowest sort of harmony which is *soothing* to the mental
faculties—but endowed with another and a far higher harmony,
which rouses them beyond their ordinary quickness, and dilates
them beyond their ordinary compass; a harmony like that in
Beethoven's wildest passages, which are a wonder and a mystery,
and a most vehement discord to the vulgar ear, but which speak
the veriest heaven-music to the "fit audience."

Judging of her as an individual from her appearance on the
stage, I should say that she is irregular, inharmonious, vehement,
awkward—thus, *in one sense*, unfeminine: that she is grand, large-
souled, and strong-passioned; a scorner of petty vanity, earnest,
unconscious, and full of rich tenderness that lies not on the
surface—thus, *in another sense*, unfeminine.

What Carlyle says of Cromwell's personal appearance may be
said of Miss Cushman's—she is not "beautiful, not at all beautiful to the man-milliner species." Her voice is deep-toned, and
with that *timbre sonore* which a high authority tells us is not the
"most excellent thing in woman." Her figure, her gait, her gestures,
are manly; at least, they are so in *Romeo*. Had I not known that
the part was played by a woman, I do not think I should have

*For our words are always suppressed
When feeling transcends expression.

suspected her sex. Whether all this be the effect of the transmuting power of genius, I know not, but am inclined to believe that it is. I should not be at all surprised to see her play *Juliet* as well as she plays *Romeo*—to see her womanised into the impassioned girl.

With regard to the character of *Romeo*, it is one that has been neglected for many years; I believe since Charles Kemble gave it up for that of *Mercutio*—when *Mercutio* became the first male character in the play. Miss Cushman has made *Romeo* a first-rate part, as Shakspeare made it, equal in interest and power to that of *Juliet*; which has always been filled by great actresses, and considered a touchstone of excellence in a peculiar department of acting.

In Miss Cushman's personation of *Romeo*, she gives all the vehemence, the warmth of passion, the melancholy, the luxuriant imagination, the glowing yet delicate vitality, the quick, lightning splendour of the Italian boy-lover. This is the *Romeo* of Shakspeare, is it not? She presents to us this youth, so graceful, fiery, and rich in tenderness; and makes us see him *beautiful* with the passionate beauty of a southern clime. But—yes, there is a *but* in my admiration of Miss Cushman's embodiment of the character which Shakspeare drew. She has not omitted anything Shakspeare created, but she has added somewhat.

To the southern temperament and its characteristics, as shown by *Romeo*, Miss Cushman unites the strong earnestness of purpose, the steadiness of will and the power to work out that will in spite of all obstacles, which belong to the northern nations. There is English or German *steadiness* below the Italian passion in every look and movement.

Hence came to my mind a perception of inconsistency. Had the real *Romeo* looked, moved, and spoken, as Miss Cushman looks, moves, and speaks, at the opening of the piece, when he is in love with *Rosaline*, there would be no play of *Romeo and Juliet*. His love for *Rosaline* would be based on surer ground than mere fairness of external form. Being thus based, he could and would strive earnestly to raise himself nearer to the excellence he adored. He would suffer during his probation, as none but passionate and affectionate natures can suffer, from "hope deferred," but he would wait—ay, years, if needful—till *Rosaline* should "grace for grace, and love for love allow," which she would do most assuredly, were she the noble being *Romeo* supposes. *Rosaline*, like all living things, must love "after her kind;" and *Romeo*, Miss Cushman's *Romeo*, is one of the best, the most noble kind—that which is gracious, loving, strong. Yes, the lady was right—"Miss Cushman is a very dangerous young man."

(1846)

Maungwudaus

(1811–1888)

"Indians of North America"

On February 5, 1848, Maungwudaus and four other "Cheppeway Indians of North America" entered their names in the visitor's book at
Shakespeare's Birthplace in Stratford-upon-Avon. Maungwudaus, meaning "great hero," was of the Ojibwa (or Chippewa) Nation. He attended
a Methodist mission school and later was a Methodist minister as well
as an interpreter and translator and took the English name George
Henry. He and his fellow American Indians visited Stratford toward
the end of a tour in which they had performed various tribal customs
through Europe. Maungwudaus subsequently recalled his experience of
visiting "Shakespeare's house and grave" in his self-published pamphlet,
*An Account of the Chippewa Indians, Who Have Been Travelling among
the Whites, in the United States, England, Ireland, Scotland, France and
Belgium* (Boston, 1848). A century or so later, James McManaway, a
scholar and former acting director of the Folger Shakespeare Library,
came across a copy of the poem that, he writes, "Maun-gwu-Daus" had
"printed in Stratford-upon-Avon" on the day of his visit. It may have
been privately printed, like his pamphlet. McManaway quoted it in full
in an essay on "Shakespeare in the United States," the only scholarly text
of the poem ever printed (and necessarily the basis of the version that appears here). It's not known how many copies of the original were printed
in 1848; despite assiduous efforts by archivists searching for it (to whom
I am deeply grateful), no original printing of Maungwudaus's poem has
been located in Stratford itself, in other British or American collections,
or in contemporary newspapers. In all likelihood, McManaway came
across a copy of this exceedingly rare publication cut-and-pasted into a
nineteenth-century scrapbook acquired by the Folger Library, perhaps
in one of the many and still uncatalogued scrapbooks assembled by the
great Shakespeare researcher and collector of the Victorian era, J. O.
Halliwell-Phillipps.

∞

Indians of North America
Heard the name that shall not decay,
They came and saw where he was born,
How great is the sound of his horn

They respect and honor his grave
As they do the grave of their brave;
Rest thou great man under these stones,
For there is yet life in thy bones.

Thy Spirit is with Mun-nid-do,
Who gave thee all thou didst do:
When we are at our native home
We shall say, "We have seen his tomb."

(1848)

Anonymous

Account of the Terrific and Fatal Riot at the New-York Astor Place Opera House

Edwin Forrest was the first great American-born tragedian; by 1849 he had been a leading Shakespeare actor for close to thirty years. William Charles Macready was at this time one of Britain's most celebrated actors. Their stage rivalry first generated controversy when Forrest hissed at a Macready performance of *Hamlet* in Edinburgh. Their enmity intensified, and when Macready toured the United States in 1848–49, scuffles broke out in the theater during his production of *Macbeth* at the new and upscale Astor Place Opera House on May 7, 1849, stopping the play. At the same time, Forrest, not to be outdone by this foreigner on his home turf, chose to perform *Macbeth* at the Broadway Theatre. The continuing antagonism between the two men was blown up by the press into a story of "the aristocracy against the people," of Englishman against American, with Shakespeare caught in the middle. When the Englishman tried to play *Macbeth* again three days later, fifteen thousand or so protesters, many of them rowdy supporters of Forrest, gathered at the Opera House and rioted. The New York State Militia was called in to disperse the crowd outside the theater and fired into it, killing more than twenty people and injuring perhaps a hundred others. Recalling the violent clash decades later, Henry James saw in it the "instinctive hostility of barbarism to culture." This anonymous pamphlet, published in the immediate aftermath of the event by H.M. Ranney, offers the most vivid surviving account of the riot.

CHAPTER FIRST

THE NIGHT OF THE 10TH. OF MAY.

On the night of the 10th of May, 1849, the Empire City, the great metropolis of the Union, was the scene of one of those horrors of civilization, which for a time make the great heart of humanity stop in its beatings. In the darkness of night, thousands of citizens were gathered in a central square of the most aristocratic quarter of New York—gathered around one of its most conspicuous and magnificent edifices, the Astor Place Opera House.

This Opera House was built expressly for the performance of the Italian Opera, but has been used at intervals for the legitimate drama, for vaudevilles, and for balls and concerts. It is fitted up and decorated with taste and magnificence, and in the opera seasons has been attended by the most wealthy and fashionable people, who have made extravagant displays of luxurious adornment. While the private boxes were taken by the season, by those who wished to enjoy the music, liked the display, and could afford the expenditure, the other seats were let at a dollar admission, and the upper tier or amphitheatre was reserved for people of humbler means or more modest pretensions, at twenty-five cents a ticket.

Around this edifice, we say, a vast crowd was gathered. On the stage the English actor Macready was trying to play the part of *Macbeth*, in which he was interrupted by hisses and hootings, and encouraged by the cheers of a large audience, who had crowded the house to sustain him. On the outside a mob was gathering, trying to force an entrance into the house, and throwing volleys of stones at the barricaded windows. In the house the police were arresting those who made the disturbance—outside they were driven back by volleys of paving stones.

In the midst of this scene of clamor and outrage, was heard the clatter of a troop of horse approaching the scene. "The military—the military are coming!" was the exclamation of the crowd. Further on was heard the quick tramp of companies of infantry, and there was seen the gleam of bayonets. A cry of rage burst from the mob. The appearance of an armed force seemed to inspire them with a sudden fury. They ceased storming the Opera House, and turned their volleys against the horsemen. Amid piercing yells and execrations, men were knocked from their horses, the untrained animals were frightened, and the force was speedily routed, and could not afterwards be rallied to perform any efficient service.

Now came the turn of the infantry. They marched down the

sidewalk in a solid column; but had no sooner taken up a position for the protection of the house, than they were assailed with volleys of missals. Soldiers were knocked down and carried off wounded. Officers were disabled. An attempt to charge with the bayonet was frustrated by the dense crowd seizing the muskets, and attempting to wrest them from the hands of the soldiers. At last the awful word was given to fire—there was a gleam of sulphurous light, a sharp quick rattle, and here and there in the crowd a man sank upon the pavement with a deep groan or a death rattle. Then came a more furious attack, and a wild yell of vengeance! Then the rattle of another death-dealing volley, far more fatal than the first. The ground was covered with killed and wounded—the pavement was stained with blood. A panic seized the multitude, which broke and scattered in every direction. In the darkness of the night yells of rage, screams of agony, and dying groans were mingled together. Groups of men took up the wounded and the dead, and conveyed them to the neighboring apothecary shops, station-houses, and the hospital.

The horrors of that night can never be described. We looked over the scene that misty midnight. The military, resting from their work of death, in stern silence were grimly guarding the Opera House. Its interior was a rendezvous and a hospital for the wounded military and police. Here and there around the building, and at the corners of the streets were crowds of men talking in deep and earnest tones of indignation. There were little processions moving off with the dead or mutilated bodies of their friends and relations. A husband, uttering frenzied curses, followed his mortally wounded wife to the hospital. An aged mother found her only son, the sole support of her declining years, in the agonies of death. Many a wife sat watching at home, in terror and alarm for her absent husband. It was an evening of dread—and it became a night of horror, which on the morrow, when the awful tragedy became more widely known, settled down upon the city like a funeral pall.

The result of that night's work was the death of twenty-two victims, either shot dead upon the spot or mortally wounded, so that they died within a few days; and the wounding of some thirty more, many of whom will be maimed for life. Into the causes which led to a result so fatal, and all the circumstances attending it, it will now be our duty to inquire.

CHAPTER SECOND.

FORREST AND MACREADY.

Mr. Edwin Forrest, the American Tragedian, was born, some forty-five years ago, in the city of Philadelphia. He was born in humble life, and worked his way up from poverty and obscurity to wealth and fame, by the power of genius. When a boy, he made his first histrionic efforts in an amateur company; afterwards, he made a professional tour at the west.

After various adventures, young Forrest found himself in the city of New-York, in the year 1826, when Gilfert was about to open the Bowery Theatre. He wanted a star of powerful attraction, and his experienced eye fell on Forrest. He was engaged—puffed in all the papers as the *Native* Tragedian—the patriotism of New-Yorkers was appealed to—Forrest used his mental gifts and great personal advantages with discretion and effect, and became a star of the first magnitude; so that, in a short time, he demanded and received two hundred dollars a night for his performances; and, with energy and temperate habits, has been able to accumulate an ample fortune.

After his first successes—determined to shine alone as a star of the first magnitude—he offered a prize of five hundred dollars for the best tragedy—suiting his powers as the hero; and the result was, Mr. Stone's "Metamora." Soon after, he secured the "Gladiator," written by Dr. Bird. These have been his most successful performances, and in them he has had no competitor, nor is it likely that he would find an equal.

Mr. William C. Macready is an English actor of great eminence. He was born in the city of Cork, (Ireland,) and must now be nearly seventy years old. In the early part of his theatrical career, he was most distinguished in such parts as "Virginius," "William

Tell," "Pierre," "Carwin," &c.; but of late, he has given his chief attention to the plays of Shakspeare—in which he has shown himself a thorough artist.

In 1827—one year after the successful commencement of Mr. Forrest's career as a star of the first magnitude—Mr. Macready visited the United States. In a fit of petulance, in which such actors are too apt to indulge, Mr. Macready came near fomenting a disturbance in Baltimore, which, but for his adroit management, might have caused him then to have been driven from the American stage. In playing "William Tell," the property-man had forgotten to furnish the arrow to be broken; and Macready was obliged to break one of his shooting arrows. In his anger at the offending party, he said—"I can't get such an arrow in your country, sir!" or, as it was reported—"I can't get wood to make such an arrow in your country!" This was construed into an insult to the country. Anonymous letters were sent to the newspapers; but, as these were sent to Mr. M., he had an opportunity to make an explanation, and avoid a row.

Macready and Forrest were starring through the country, playing alternate engagements—but not, so far as we know, developing any very decided feelings of rivalry. Their roles of characters, and spheres of action, were quite apart; and when they met each other, their intercourse—as it was many years afterward—was of the most gentlemanly character.

About the year 1835, Mr. Forrest went to Europe, and spent some time in travelling on the continent; after which, he returned to America for a short time; and then went back to England, to fulfil professional engagements—in which he was so highly successful, that on his return, he was honored with a public dinner in Philadelphia; and about this time, he was tendered a nomination to Congress by the Democracy of New-York—before whom he delivered a Fourth of July oration.

In 1844, Mr. Macready visited the United States. He and Mr. Forrest had become intimate in England; and here, Mr. F. tendered him the courtesies due to so distinguished a professional brother; but it so happened, that in most of the cities where

Macready was engaged, there were more theatres than one—and, of consequence, rival managers. Where one of these had secured Mr. Macready, the other was anxious to get the best talent to be found to run against him; and there was no one so available as Mr. Forrest—who is not the man to refuse a profitable engagement, nor did any rule of courtesy require that he should do so.

The result was, that the constant rivalry of Forrest, though carried on in the most friendly manner, could not fail to injure the success of Macready. A certain degree of partizanship was everywhere excited—for Forrest was everywhere placarded as the "*American* Tragedian,"—and the tour of Mr. Macready was comparatively a failure. A sensitive man could not but feel this; and whether he made any complaint or not, his friends saw what the difficulty was, and felt not a little chagrined about it; and when Mr. Forrest made his next and last professional visit to England, this feeling among the friends of Macready, in the theatrical press and the play-going public, found its vent. The opposition to him was, from the first, marked and fatal; and, so far as the metropolis was concerned, his tour was a failure. It was only in the provinces—away from London influence—that he met with any degree of success.

There was no need of Mr. Macready taking any active part in this matter; and there is no proof that he did so, but much to the contrary; but Mr. Forrest hastily and indignantly, and, we doubt not, sincerely, charged it upon Mr. Macready; and one night, when the latter was playing in "Hamlet," at the Theatre in Edinburgh, Mr. Forrest, who was seated in a private box, had the bad taste, as well as bad feeling, to hiss a portion of his performance in the most marked and offensive manner.

The following letter from Mr. Forrest gives his own account of this affair, which differs somewhat from the statements of Mr. Macready's friends, as will be seen hereafter.

To the Editor of the London Times,—Sir,—Having seen in your journal of the 12th instant, an article headed "Professional Jealousy," a part of which originally appeared in *The Scotsman* published in Edinburgh, I beg leave, through the medium of your columns, to state, that at the time of its publication, I addressed a letter to the Editor of *The Scotsman* upon the subject, which, as I then was in Dumfries, I sent to a friend in Edinburgh, requesting him to obtain its insertion; but as I was informed, *The Scotsman* refused to receive any communication upon the subject. I need say nothing of the injustice of this refusal. Here then I was disposed to let the matter rest, as upon more mature reflection, I did not deem it worth further attention; but now, as the matter has assumed "a questionable shape" by the appearance of the article in your journal, I feel called upon, although reluctantly, to answer it.

There are two legitimate modes of evincing approbation and disapprobation in the theatre—one expressive of approbation, by the clapping of hands, and the other by hisses to mark dissent; and as well-timed and hearty applause, is the just meed of the actor who deserves well, so also is hissing, a salutary and wholesome corrective of the abuses of the stage; and it was against one of these abuses that *my* dissent was expressed, and not, as was stated, "with a view of expressing his (my) disapproval of the manner in which Mr. Macready gave effect to a particular passage." The truth is, Mr. Macready thought fit to introduce a fancy dance into his performance of "Hamlet," which I thought, and still think, a desecration of the scene, and at which I evinced that disapprobation, for which the pseudo-critic is pleased to term me an "offender," and this was the only time during the performance that I did so, although the writer evidently seeks, in the article alluded to, to convey a different impression. It must be observed also, that I was by no means "solitary" in this expression of opinion.

That a man may manifest his pleasure or displeasure after the recognised mode, according to the best of his judgment, actuated by proper motives, and for justifiable ends, is a right, which, until now, I have never once heard questioned, and I contend, that right extends equally to an actor, in his capacity as a spectator, as to any other man; besides, from the nature of his studies, he is much more competent to judge of a theatrical performance than any *soidisant* critic, who has never himself been an actor. The writer of the article in *The Scotsman*, who has most unwarrantably singled me out for public animadversion, has carefully omitted to notice the fact, that I warmly applauded several points of Mr. Macready's performance; and more than once I regretted that the audience did not second me in so doing. As to the pitiful charge of professional jealousy preferred against me, I dismiss it with the contempt it merits, confidently relying upon all those of the profession with whom I have been associated, for a refutation of this slander.

Yours, respectfully,

EDWIN FORREST.

March, 1846. —*Times, 4th of April.*

CHAPTER THIRD.

THE QUARREL RECOMMENCED IN AMERICA.

MR. FORREST, chagrined by his failure in England, and maddened at what he imagined to be the malign influence of Macready, returned to the United States after a vain attempt to secure an engagement in Paris, in which he supposed the same influence had defeated him. He had publicly hissed Macready in Edinburgh, had avowed the act, and given his reasons. His friends here felt much as the friends of Mr. Macready had felt in England; and when the latter last year came on another professional visit to the United States, he found that a bitter feeling had been raised against him, which found its first expression, so far as we know, in the following article, that appeared in the Boston Mail on the morning of Mr. Macready's appearance at the Howard Athenæum, Boston, Monday, Oct. 30th, 1848.

[Boston Mail, Oct. 30th, 1848.]

More about Macready—His abuse of Forrest in Europe—Endeavors to put him down in Paris, London and Edinburgh—His Intrigue with Bulwer to prevent Forrest playing in Bulwer's Pieces—His Abuse of Americans.

Mr. Macready has at length arrived, and next to the grand water celebration, will create such excitement, as will emphatically mark the present epoch in time's calendar. He plays this evening at the Howard Athenæum, and refuses to show himself for less than one dollar a ticket. This was his price in New York, and with the exception of the first night, resulted in a "beggarly account of empty boxes." We repeat what we said in a former article, that Mr. Pelby, the enterprising manager of the National Theatre, deserves immortal honors for not acceding to the dictatorial terms of this actor autocrat. Although Macready saw fit on his opening night in New York, on being called out by some friends, to slur a "*certain penny paper*," that had "*dared*" to express an opinion regarding his talents and conduct, we shall not by any means give him the retort churlish; we only pity his ignorance of the institutions of this country, and hope for his own credit's sake that he will not, when he gets home, write a black book about American manners, &c., *a la* Trollope and others, but if he does, that he will spare us in the production of his brain. The reader will no doubt ask, what fault we find with Mr. Macready. Has he not the same right as other men have, to do as he pleases? We answer yes. He has a right to come to this country in the exercise of his profession; he has a right to demand a dollar from every person who witnesses his acting, and if managers of Theatres are willing to accede to his arbitrary proposals, he has certainly a right to make them. We complain not of any of these. Our charges against Macready are based upon more important grounds. It is his conduct in his own country in relation to Mr. Forrest, that we are about investigating; *his inhospitality, his crushing influence, his vindictive opposition, and his steadfast determination to ruin the prospects of that gentleman in England*, that we bring to his door. Let him deny them if he can. Every true American takes a pride in that which represents his country's interests, industry, and enterprise, and from the smallest commodity gathered from his soil to the loftiest labors of his genius, his ambition goes with it, and the strong arm of his power will protect it in every clime. Mr. Edwin Forrest is titled the American Tragedian—he is justly entitled to that honor—he has acquired it by his own labors; from a poor boy in a circus, he has arisen to be a man of fame and wealth, all of which he has lastingly gained by enterprise and talent, and secured both by economy and TEMPERANCE.

Every American-born man is willing that Mr. Forrest should wear this title, and when he visited England they were anxiously interested in his success. Macready had previously been in this country, and played engagements in every city, and made a fortune. He was extolled by the press, and treated as a gentleman by the citizens of every place he visited. But instead of returning this kindness, he acted openly towards Mr. Forrest as his determined foe. We speak by card, and write upon the very best information, viz., the highest authority. In Paris Mr. Macready and Mr. Forrest met. The latter was anxious to appear on the French boards; but Macready threw obstacles in the way, and this was the first time that the two parties were enemies. Mr. Mitchell, the enterprising lessee of St. James Theatre in London, took an English company of actors to the French capital, with Mr. Macready at the head of the list. Macready was to be the hero—the great attraction of Paris. He failed, however, to draw money to the treasury, and Mr. Mitchell lost a large sum by the speculation, or rather would have lost it, if Louis Philippe had not made him most liberal presents. Mr. Forrest had letters of introduction to Mr. Mitchell from his friends in London, but Macready was jealous, lest Forrest should prove to be *the* great star, and he cautioned Mitchell not to allow Forrest to appear. The result was that Mr. Mitchell refused to see Mr. Forrest.

The parties returned to London. The hypocrisy of Macready is apparent in his note of invitation to Mr. Forrest to dine with him. The latter, knowing the intrigue that had been carried on in Paris between Macready and Mitchell, refused, as every high-minded man should, to dine with him. This is a very different version to that recently given by some of Macready's friends—if friends he have—that Forrest was offended because he was not invited to dine; as if such a man as Mr. Forrest could take offence at such a trifle, when at the same time he was invited to dine with many of the leading nobility of England, but especially of Scotland, where he passed several months as their guest.

The next mean act towards Forrest, brought about through the influence of Macready, was when Mr. F. appeared at the Princess's Theatre in London. Mac had been endeavoring for a long time to effect an engagement with some London manager, but was unsuccessful. The success of Forrest stung him, and he resolved to "put him down." It was said at the time that he or his friends actually hired men to visit the theatre, and hiss Forrest off the stage, and Forrest was consequently received with a shower of hisses before he was heard. This mean conduct was followed up by the press, by which Forrest was most outrageously assailed, and not Forrest alone, but his country, which is proud to own him as one of her sons.

Forrest and Macready next met in Edinburgh, and from this city were sent forth the grossest calumnies against Forrest. Macready was playing at the Theatre Royal in *Hamlet*—Forrest was present. During the beginning of the piece Mr. Forrest applauded several times, and, as we are informed by an eyewitness, he started the applause when some brilliant effect had been given to a passage, so that the whole house followed him. But now comes Forrest's great sin—that giant sin which Mac will never forgive—the sin of hissing Macready for dancing and throwing up his handkerchief across the stage in the *Pas de Mouchoir*.

Mr. F. not only hissed, but the whole house hissed, and yet Macready dared to write to London, that Forrest had singly and alone attempted to hiss him from the stage.

To show that Mr. Forrest was not alone in this matter, we are able to state that two weeks afterwards *Hamlet* was repeated, when the whole house again hissed Macready's dance across the stage.

Out of this simple incident Macready contrived to create a great deal of sympathy for himself. He is, or was, part proprietor of the *London Examiner*; or if not sole owner, he possesses the body and soul of its theatrical critic, Foster, who does all kinds of dirty work for his master. Macready gave the cue to Foster, and Forrest was denounced by the *Examiner* and other papers, in which Foster or Mac had any influence. A false coloring was put on this affair, and Mac appeared to the world as a persecuted man, whereas Forrest was the one who met with persecution at every corner—in Paris, in London, in Edinburgh, and in London a second time.

But Macready's persecution did not stop here. Forrest wished to appear in London, in Bulwer's Lady of Lyons and Richelieu. To do this, permission must be obtained of the author. Forrest addressed a note to Bulwer, asking his terms for the plays. After a long delay, Bulwer replied, that he should charge Forrest £2 per night for the use of them, and he must play 40 nights! Such terms for plays, that had in a great measure lost their interest, compelled Forrest to reject them. It was ascertained that Macready and Bulwer had been much together, and that the former had prevailed on the latter not to allow Forrest the use of his compositions.

Forrest could not entertain any jealous feelings towards Mac, for he drew crowded houses during his engagement at the Princess's Theatre, whereas Macready had very slim audiences; and on one occasion we know that our own charming actress, Mrs. Barrett, on one of the off-nights, at the time Mac was playing, actually drew more money to the treasury than Macready.

We have now given a plain statement of facts, and such as cannot be controverted. It proves that actors, like Macready, Anderson, and others, find it very hard scratching in their own country, and much better pickings here. It is to be hoped, however, that we Americans will finally become awakened to the mercenary motives of such artistes, and when we have any surplus of dollars to spend, that we will be generous and just to our own home genius.

Here is displayed the feeling of the friends of Mr. Forrest, and to a great extent of Mr. Forrest himself, for the writer of this article asserts that its statements are made on the "very highest authority." On his part Mr. Macready unwisely alluded to this article in one of his before-the-curtain speeches, speaking contemptuously of the attacks of a certain penny paper. But the Bostonians are a quiet people, and Macready and Forrest played through their engagements without any popular demonstration. At New York Macready played at the Opera House, and Forrest at the Broadway Theatre. There were rumors of a disturbance, but they amounted to nothing. Both engagements were finished in peace, and both actors went to fulfil engagements at the rival theatres in Philadelphia.

Now Forrest had made some pretence of retiring from the stage—he had built himself a splendid castle on the banks of the Hudson, and had achieved a splendid fortune—but here he was, following up Macready step by step, and making no concealment of his enmity. His friends were doubtless busy, especially in

Philadelphia, his birth place. The two actors made mouths and speeches at each other. One night Macready alluded to the ungenerous treatment he had received from a rival actor. This brought Forrest out in the following

CARD.

MR. MACREADY, in his speech, last night, to the audience assembled at the Arch Street Theatre, made allusion, I understand, to "an American actor" who had the temerity, on one occasion, "*openly* to hiss him." This is true, and by the way, the *only* truth which I have been enabled to gather from the whole scope of his address. But why say "an American actor?" Why not openly charge me with the act? for I *did* it, and publicly avowed it in the Times newspaper of London, and at the same time asserted my right to do so.

On the occasion alluded to, Mr. Macready introduced a fancy dance into his performance of Hamlet, which I designated as a *pas de mouchoir*, and which I hissed, for I thought it a desecration of the scene, and the audience thought so too, for in a few nights afterwards, when Mr. Macready repeated the part of Hamlet with the same "tom-foolery," the intelligent audience of Edinburgh greeted it with a universal hiss.

Mr. Macready is stated to have said last night, that up to the time of this act on my part, he had "never entertained towards me a feeling of unkindness." I unhesitatingly pronounce this to be a wilful and unblushing falsehood. I most solemnly aver and do believe, that Mr. Macready, instigated by his narrow envious mind, and his selfish fears, did *secretly*—not *openly*—suborn several writers for the English press, to write me down. Among them was one Forster, a "toady" of the *eminent tragedian*—one who is ever ready to do his dirty work; and this Forster, at the bidding of his patron, attacked me in print even before I appeared upon the London boards, and continued his abuse at every opportunity afterwards.

I assert, also, and solemnly believe, that Mr. Macready connived, when his friends went to the theatre in London to hiss me, and did hiss me, with the purpose of driving me from the stage— and all this happened many months before the affair at Edinburgh, to which Mr. Macready refers, and in relation to which he jesuitically remarks, that "until that act, he never entertained towards me a feeling of unkindness." Bah! Mr. Macready has no feeling of kindness for any actor who is likely, by his talent, to stand in his way. His whole course as manager and as actor proves this—there is nothing in him but self—self—self—and his own countrymen, the English actors, know this well. Mr. Macready has a very lively imagination, and often draws upon it for his facts. He said in a speech at New York, that there, also, there was an "organized opposition" to him, which is likewise false. There was no opposition manifested towards him there—for I was in the city at the time, and was careful to watch every movement with regard to such a matter. Many of my friends called upon me when Mr. Macready was announced to perform, and proposed to drive him from the stage for his conduct towards me in London. My advice was, do nothing—let the superannuated driveller alone— to oppose him would be but to make him of some importance. My friends agreed with me it was, at least, the most dignified course to pursue, and it was immediately adopted. With regard to "an organized opposition to him" in Boston, this is, I believe, equally false, but perhaps in *charity* to the poor old man, I should impute these "chimeras dire," rather to the disturbed state of his guilty conscience, than to any desire on his part wilfully to misrepresent.

EDWIN FORREST.

Philadelphia, Nov. 21, 1848.

This violent and vindictive, but characteristic manifesto, as may be supposed, did not help Mr. Forrest's cause very materially, with quiet and well-judging people, but it probably found sympathy among heated partizans, and those who supposed the honor and glory of the country was at stake. Mr. Macready appears to have made up his mind at once to sue Forrest for a libel, and accordingly he issued the following:—

CARD

TO THE PUBLIC OF PHILADELPHIA.

In a card published in the Public Ledger and other morning papers of this day, Mr. Forrest having avowed himself the author of the statements, which Mr. Macready has solemnly pledged his honor to be without the least foundation, Mr. Macready cannot be wanting in self-respect so far as to bandy words upon the subject, but as the circulation of such statements is manifestly calculated to prejudice Mr. Macready in the opinion of the American Public, and affect both his professional interests and his estimation in society, Mr. Macready respectfully requests the public to suspend their judgment upon the question, until the decision of a Legal Tribunal, before which he will immediately take measures to bring it, and before which he will prove his veracity, hitherto unquestioned, shall place the truth beyond doubt.

Reluctant as he is to notice further Mr. Forrest's Card, Mr. Macready has to observe, that when Mr. Forrest appeared at the Princess's Theatre in London, he himself was absent some hundred miles from that city, and was ignorant of his engagement until after it had begun; that not one single notice on Mr. Forrest's acting appeared in the Examiner during that engagement (as its files will prove,) Mr. Forster, the distinguished Editor, whom Mr. Macready has the honor to call his friend, having been confined to his bed with a rheumatic fever during the whole period, and some weeks before and after.

For the other aspersions upon Mr. Macready, published in the Boston Mail, and now, as it is understood, avowed by Mr. Forrest, Mr. Macready will without delay appeal for legal redress.

JONES'S HOTEL, Nov. 22d, 1848.

Immediately after publishing the above, Mr. Macready committed to his counsel, Messrs. Reed & Meredith, of Philadelphia, authority to commence such legal proceedings as they might deem advisable: and, preparatory thereto, he obtained from England the documentary evidence.

As regards the charge of suborning the English press, it will be sufficient here to refer to the Times, Globe, Observer, Spectator, Morning Chronicle, Morning Post, Weekly Dispatch, Britannia, &c., &c., of dates Dec. 13, 14, 15, 16, &c., which have indignantly and emphatically denied the charge; many of which denials have already been republished in the American newspapers.

It appears, however, that when Mr. Macready came to consult

his legal advisers, two eminent Philadelphia lawyers, they wisely advised him to let the matter drop, and be satisfied with his reputation. So Macready went South, and was feted and feasted in New Orleans to his heart's content, but to the grievous discontent of Mr. Forrest and his numerous admirers.

In the meantime, Macready had written to England for evidence to prove that the statements in Mr. Forrest's Philadelphia card were libelous; and when he decided to give up his law suit, he caused these documents to be printed in a pamphlet, which however, he soon withdrew from public circulation. There were letters from Edinburgh to prove that Mr. Forrest was alone in hissing the "fancy dance" in Hamlet; letters from the proprietor and theatrical critic of the London Examiner, to show that Macready had not influenced any criticisms on Forrest in that paper; from Sir E. Bulwer Lytton, asserting that he had offered his plays to Mr. Forrest for a fair consideration, and had not withheld them at the request of Mr. Macready, with other equally pertinent documents. But what avail were these? The friends of Forrest felt sure that he had been shamefully treated in England, by the friends of Macready; and whether he was a party to the matter or not, they meant to hold him responsible, and therefore it was determined that he should never play another engagement in New York, and that determination was enforced, but oh! at what a fearful sacrifice.

CHAPTER FOURTH.

THE PLOT THICKENS—THE ENGAGEMENT AT THE OPERA HOUSE—MACREADY DRIVEN FROM THE STAGE.

It must not be supposed that this was the first manifestation of patriotic indignation on the part of the friends of Mr. Forrest, on account of his treatment in England. It was a deep and intense feeling, and was ready to burst out on any fitting occasion. It threatened Mr. Anderson, and in Philadelphia an effort was made to drive him from the stage; but a better feeling prevailed. Anderson was not charged with any ill-will to Mr. Forrest, and the opposition to him was abandoned: yet there were not wanting persons who contended that every English actor ought to be driven from the American stage, in revenge for the insult offered by England to this country, in the person of Edwin Forrest.

But when Macready, who was charged by Forrest himself with being the head and front of this offending, came to the United States, the flame of hatred was ready to burst forth, and the only wonder is, that it remained pent up so long. On his return from the South, Messrs. Niblo and Hackett, who had taken the Opera House for that purpose, announced that Mr. Macready would open an engagement on Monday night, May 7th. Mr. Forrest was playing at the Broadway Theatre. Previous to the commencement of this engagement, Mr. Macready gave a reading of a play of Shakspeare before the teachers of the public schools of New York and Brooklyn.

The announcement of this engagement was the signal for an outbreak of long-smothered indignation. It was determined that Mr. Forrest should be avenged, and that Macready should not be permitted to play before a New York audience. There was a combination of exciting causes—the feeling against England and Englishmen, handed down to us from the Revolution, and kept fresh by the insults and abuse of British writers on American manners—the injury committed against Forrest, with Macready as its presumed cause, and this was increased by the fact of Macready playing at the aristocratic, kid-glove Opera House. Far be it from us to justify these feelings—it is our duty simply to state the fact of their existence.

The public and magistrates have been accustomed to look upon theatrical disturbances, rows, and riots, as different in their character from all others. The stage is presumed to be a correction of the manners and morals of the public, and on the other hand the public has been left to correct, in its own energetic way, the manners and morals of the stage; and magistrates, looking upon it as a matter between the actors and the audience, have generally refused to interfere, unless there was a prospect of a violent breach of the peace, when they have usually ordered the house to be closed. In these theatrical disturbances, performances have been hissed, plays damned, and actors and actresses driven from the stage, with whatever degree of force has been necessary for their rejection. This has been the practice in the United States, as well as in Europe, and no actor, in any free country, has thought of acting with a posse of police at his back; much less, a file of soldiers, or a piece of artillery, to defend his rights.

On the announcement of Mr. Macready's engagement at the Opera House, it was determined that there should be a pretty forcible expression of opinion on the part of those who were indignant at the treatment of Mr. Forrest in England, and were willing, for any reason, to revenge it on Mr. Macready. There was, doubtless, some organization of forces, to bring about this result, and one person, the well-known Capt. Rynders, admits that he purchased and distributed among his friends fifty tickets, with the understanding that those who used them were to assist in hissing Macready from the stage. Other sums of money were given, and when the night arrived, it was estimated, by the Chief of Police, that not less than five hundred persons were engaged in the disturbance.

The night came—the house was crowded, and there was an ominous looking gallery. The curtain rose, and some of the actors, who were popular favorites, were received with obstreperous applause; but when Macready appeared upon the stage, in the character of Macbeth, he was assailed by a storm of hisses, yells, and a clamor that defies description. He stood his ground firmly, and the play went on, but not a word could be heard by the audience. It was in dumb show. The clamor rose higher and higher, and as hisses and threats, cat-calls and yells, were not enough to drive the obnoxious actor from the stage, less legitimate means were resorted to. Rotten eggs were thrown, pennies, and other missiles; and soon, still more outrageous demonstrations were made, and chairs were thrown from the upper part of the house, so as to peril life.

The Chief of Police was present, with a number of policemen; but the rioters boldly defied the authorities, and no arrests were attempted. It is said, in excuse, that the rioters were in overpowering numbers, that they were prepared to resist and rescue, and that they had even prepared papers of gunpowder to throw into the magnificent chandelier. A large portion of the audience consisted of ladies, whose lives might have been endangered, and there was nothing to do but to stop the performance. The curtain went down; cheers were given for Forrest, and groans for Macready, and the crowd dispersed.

Mr. Macready supposed that his engagement was terminated. He had no idea of ever making a second appearance; but his friends and the enemies of Forrest insisted upon a different course. He was assured that the public would sustain him, and the managers did not wish to lose the profits of his engagement. Mr. Hackett is a personal enemy of Forrest, and he was determined to play Macready against him at all hazards. Finally, a number of influential citizens, men of wealth and standing, with Washington Irving at their head, wrote a formal request to Mr. Macready that he should play out his engagement, and pledging themselves that the public should sustain him; and it was determined and announced that he should appear on Thursday evening, May 10th.

This announcement, as may be supposed, excited the indignation of those who had driven him from the stage. It was a combination of the aristocracy against the people, and in support of English arrogance, and it was determined that Macready should not play, and that he and his supporters should be put down at all hazards. The lessees of the Theatre were informed that the re-opening of the Theatre with Mr. Macready, would be the signal for riot; the magistrates of the city were informed of it, and were implored to avert the calamity by refusing to allow the house to be opened—for as the city authorities have the right to regulate Theatres, and to make them pay five hundred dollars a year for a license, it was presumed that they had also the right to close them. So thought the Mayor, and so he wished to act; but the lessees insisted upon their legal rights, and demanded the protection of the authorities, and the fatal decision was made which made New York, a few hours afterward, one wide scene of horror.

CHAPTER FIFTH.

THE COMBAT DEEPENS.

THE announcement that Mr. Macready would appear at the Opera House in *Macbeth* on Thursday evening produced a varied excitement throughout the community. Those who thought the city disgraced by the scenes of Monday night were anxious to have that disgrace atoned for by his successful re-appearance, while those who sympathized with the mob that drove him from the stage, looked upon his re-appearance as a new insult, and the manner in which it was brought about was as irritating to them as the act itself.

A riot was anticipated by all who were acquainted with the circumstances, except, perhaps the object of popular indignation. Mr. Macready was assured that there would be no difficulty, and he seems to have believed it—but those who so assured him well understood that those who had triumphantly driven him from the stage on Monday were not likely to submit quietly to his re-appearance.

Thursday morning, the leaders on both sides were active. The friends of Forrest were gathering their forces, and distributing tickets for the night's performance, while the lessees of the Opera House applied to the mayor and other authorities of New York for protection. Inflammatory handbills had been posted upon the walls of the city, calculated to increase the excitement. In the mayor's office, the recorder, the chief of police, the sheriff, major-general Sandford, and brigadier-general Hall, were assembled to consult on the means of protecting the Opera House, and enabling Mr. Macready to play *Macbeth*.

The mayor, Mr. Woodhull, advised Niblo and Hackett to close the house, and to avoid a riot, and the probable destruction of property and life; but these gentlemen were determined to stand upon their rights, and the city authorities decided, after consulting together, to sustain them, if necessary, with all the force at their disposal. Mr. Matsell, the chief of police, was asked if the civil force at his disposal would be sufficient for the preservation of the peace, and though he had nine hundred salaried policemen at his disposal, and the power of calling in specials at discretion, he gave it as his opinion that this force was not sufficient. It was thought necessary to call out the military.

It has been boldly questioned whether all these extraordinary preparations would have been made to protect the legal rights of humble citizens. Rich and influential men had invited Mr. Macready to play at the aristocratic Opera House. Suppose it had been some third-rate actor at the Chatham; suppose the request for him to play had come from the patrons of that establishment. The abstract question of right would have been the same; but there are many who would doubt whether the city authorities would have taken the extraordinary measure of calling out the military—and this was probably the first time such a thing was ever done under any but the most despotic governments.

The fact of the chief of police declaring that his force was not sufficient to preserve the peace—the fact that general Sandford was ordered to call out a military force sufficient for the emergency, proves that the nature and extent of the approaching riot was well understood by the authorities, and still no means were used to prevent it. It seems to have been their policy to let it gather, and come to a head, when, one would suppose, it might easily have been scattered. Had the police arrested a few of the leaders, and kept a close watch on the rioters—had they taken possession of the vicinity of the Opera House in force, and prevented the gathering of a crowd around it, it seems probable that the peace of the city, and the rights of Mr. Macready might have been maintained at a trifling sacrifice. But a different course was decided upon, and the preparations of the military and police were made accordingly. The chief detached two hundred policemen, to be stationed inside the Opera House. He also placed a detachment in the stable of Mr. Langdon, on the opposite side of Astor Place, and another body in a yard near by. General Sandford ordered out companies from several regiments, as will be more particularly stated hereafter.

And now the news spread all over the city that there was to

be a riot. The warning out of large bodies of military, was alone sufficient to excite curiosity; and yet, in all this excitement and anticipation of outrage, the mayor issued no warning proclamation. There was no one to tell hot-headed and misguided men, that it would be at the peril of their lives, if they disturbed the peace. It is evident that they thought they had a right to prevent Macready from playing. They were doing no more by him than the English had done by Forrest, and they looked upon it as a piece of retributive justice.

It must not be forgotten, that New York, for many years, has been a very quiet city. For ten years, there had not been one serious riot. The principles of law and order are habitually acknowledged, and have seldom been violated. While Philadelphia has been, for years, the scene of the most disgraceful outrages, New York has not known a more serious disturbance than could be controlled by a few policemen. But in this case, every body rushed into a fatal riot, with a mad precipitation. The calling out of the military sent thousands to the scene of conflict, who would not otherwise have gone, swelled the crowd, encouraged the rioters, and contributed to the fatal result.

It is easy to say, people had no business there; they ought to have kept away. It would be hard to show that those who were outside the house had not as good a right to gratify their curiosity as those within. But, right or wrong, we know very well what people will do in such a case. Let it be given out that there is to be a disturbance at any place, and that the military have been called out to put it down, and the consequence will be a gathering crowd, and, if there is the slightest seeming cause, a formidable riot. It seems that all the means used on the tenth of May, to preserve the peace, only helped to bring about the terrible catastrophe.

Mr. Forrest has been charged with actively fomenting these disturbances. Such a charge was made in the *Courier & Enquirer*, but it was promptly retracted, under threat of prosecution for libel, from Mr. Sedgwick, Forrest's legal counsel. It does not appear that he moved at all in the matter. He stood passive, and let the affair shape itself as it might, as there is reason to suppose Mr.

Macready had done, in England. On the night of the riot, Forrest played to a full house at the Broadway Theatre.

It would seem, after the publication of the card, signed by Washington Irving, Charles King, and about fifty others, denouncing the outrages of Monday night, and pledging themselves to sustain Macready, that the contest took on a new character. Macready was a subordinate personage, and he was to be put down less on his own account, than to spite his aristocratic supporters. The question became not only a national, but a social one. It was the rich against the poor—the aristocracy against the people; and this hatred of wealth and privilege is increasing over the world, and ready to burst out whenever there is the slightest occasion. The rich and well-bred are too apt to despise the poor and ignorant, and they must not think it strange if they are hated in return.

CHAPTER SIXTH.
THE SCENES OF THE FATAL NIGHT.

As the hour for the opening of the Opera House approached, excited crowds began to gather from all parts of the city. Hundreds of men were seen walking rapidly up Broadway. There was a great rush for tickets, and at an early hour the house was declared full, and the sale of tickets suspended. Among the audience in the house were seven ladies. The police were at their stations, and the doors and windows were strongly barricaded.

It should here be stated that the Opera House is situated midway between Broadway and the Bowery, one side fronting on Eighth Street, the other on Astor Place. The end toward Broadway is covered by buildings, but there is an open space to the Bowery.

While the crowd was gathering outside, and endeavoring to force an entrance, in which they were prevented by the police, the curtain rose, and the mock tragedy commenced. Mr. Clark, an American actor, was vociferously applauded in the part of *Macduff*. The entrance of Mr. Macready in the third scene was the signal for a storm of cheers, groans, hisses, and yells. The whole audience rose, and the greatest part, who were friendly to Macready, cheered and waved their hats and handkerchiefs; but when these cheers were spent, the noise had not subsided. A large body in the parquette, and another in the amphitheatre hissed and groaned, and the contest was kept up until a placard was displayed on the stage, on which was written—"The friends of order will remain quiet." The friends of disorder, however, kept up their noise through the first act, when the recorder and chief of police decided to quell the tumult; and in a few moments the noisiest of the rioters were arrested, and conveyed to a room in the basement, and the play went on in comparative quietness.

But by the time the tumult was suppressed in the house, it had gained its height on the outside. A vast crowd numbering ten or fifteen thousand, had gathered around the building, chiefly in Astor Place, and by the time the arrests were made in the house, and probably in consequence of some communication between the rioters in the theatre and their friends outside, the house began to be assailed with large paving stones, of which, owing to the digging of a sewer near by, there was a large supply. The stones crashed against the windows, and in some instances broke through the barricades. After the tragedy was over, the farce commenced, but it was brought to an end by the firing of the military; and the alarmed and excited audience left the theatre by the entrance in Eighth Street, under the cover of the military, while Mr. Macready got away in the disguise of an officer; and mounting a horse, escorted by a party of his friends, he left the city, and the next day took the cars for Boston, whence a few days afterward he sailed to Europe. Before leaving he expressed the deepest regret that he had not refused to appear again, in accordance with his first intention.

From the testimony of the actors and spectators of the terrible scenes which occurred that night, we have selected four accounts—that of SIDNEY H. STEWART, Esq. Clerk of the Police, a man of observation and experience in that department; that of MAJOR GENERAL SANDFORD, the Commander-in-Chief of the military; that of STEPHEN W. GAINES, Esq. and THOMAS J.

BELVIN, Esq. disinterested spectators. From the sworn testimony of these four witnesses, may be gathered a pretty correct idea of the action of the public authorities, the police, the military, the rioters, and the spectators.

TESTIMONY OF SIDNEY H. STEWART.

SIDNEY H. STEWART, Clerk of the Police, states what he saw and heard before the arrival of the military: "I left the Tombs that evening in company with Justice McGrath, and arrived at the Astor Theatre about 7 o'clock; soon after the doors were opened, the audience were assembling; on entering the house, I found the theatre filled with people and a large body of the police; most of the police magistrates were there; Judge Edmonds was there also; the understanding with the magistrates, Judge Edmonds, and the Chief of Police, and Recorder, was that no arrests should be made in the house, unless some overt act was committed, tending absolutely to a breach of the peace; the usual indulgence was to be allowed as to the hissing and applauding; that rule was observed. In the course of the evening, demonstrations were made by several in the parquette, by shaking their fists at Macready, threatening him with violence, by twelve or fifteen persons, certainly not to exceed twenty; an application was made at this time to the Chief of Police to arrest them, and remove them from the house; he delayed the order for some time, and finally sent for the Recorder to consult with him on the propriety of making arrests; after a consultation, it was concluded to make the arrests, which was done; in less than five minutes they were taken into custody, and order comparatively restored; about this time a great deal of hissing was heard in the amphitheatre, and loud applauding; the play was still going on; several arrests were made in the amphitheatre, by order of the Chief of Police and Recorder; about this time, the first breach of peace on the house was a large paving stone which came through the window into the house; the house continued to be assailed from those without; an alarm was given that a fire was below under the dress circle; it was soon extinguished; large stones were thrown at the doors on Eighth street, smashing in the panels, and doing other damage; the police were ordered into

Eighth street, say fifteen men; on my going into the street, I saw a large concourse of people, but those near the door of the theatre were mostly boys, who were apparently throwing stones; several of them were arrested by the police and brought in; I cannot say how many were aiding in the disturbance, but certainly a very small proportion to the crowd collected; the policemen arrested some six or ten of them, and the attack on the door in Eighth street ceased; the attack then, after these arrests, was made with more violence on the front of the theatre in Astor-place; a very large crowd was collected, yet I could pass in and out with ease, comparatively; this crowd did not appear to be very turbulent; a very large number appeared to be citizens looking on, and not aiding in the disturbance; the majority of those throwing stones were boys from the ages of 12 to 18 years; several of the policemen at this time complained of being struck with stones and badly hurt; the policemen kept making arrests, and bringing them in; I cannot say how many; the crowd appeared to be increasing and more dense; the mob appeared to be determined to accomplish some particular act; there seemed to be a strong determination, although they only threw stones; the force of policemen on Astor-place amounted to from fifty to seventy-five; the mob then continued to throw stones; the military then came."

TESTIMONY OF MAJOR-GENERAL SANDFORD.

I am Major General commanding the military forces of this county. On Thursday last, I received a message from the Mayor, requesting me to come to his office. I went there, and found the magistrates named by the Mayor assembled. The Mayor informed me of the object of my being sent for. The Mayor has stated correctly my reply, when I was asked in relation to the expediency of issuing an order to call out the Military. After it was decided to issue the order, it was understood by the Magistrates present, that the effort should be first made by the civil authority to preserve the peace, and that the Military should not be called out until that effort failed. I left the Mayor's office after this understanding, and then received this order:

MAYOR'S OFFICE, City Hall, May 10, 1849.

Having reason to apprehend a serious riot this evening, which will require more force to preserve the peace than is possessed by the police, Major General Sandford is requested to hold a sufficient military force in readiness to meet the apprehended emergency.   C. S. WOODHULL, Mayor.

After receiving this order, I ordered one Regiment—the 7th—of Infantry to assemble at the Artillery drill rooms, and one troop of Light Artillery with two 6 pound field pieces, to muster at the Arsenal. I directed a small detachment of Infantry to protect the pieces. The regiment, when assembled, on account of the shortness of the notice, consisted of but little over two hundred men. The regiment is known to the citizens by the title of the National Guard. I went myself, in the evening, to the Artillery drill rooms, and informed the Magistrate that I would remain there to await orders. I understood there was to be a large Police force at the Theatre. Many of the Magistrates thought this force would be sufficient without the military. The regiment was under the command of Col. Duryea. There are eight Captains in the regiment. I cannot say they were all present. Capts. Shumway, Underhill, Pond and Price, were present. We remained there until a verbal message came to me from the sheriff, the purport of which was, that a mob had attacked the house and driven in the Police force, and were assailing the building; this was between 8 and 9 o'clock, as well as I can remember. On receiving this notice, I immediately ordered the Regiment to get ready for marching, and to distribute their ammunition, which consisted of one thousand rounds of ball cartridges; I sent at the same time an order to the Arsenal yard for the horse belonging to the Regiment to come up immediately to the drill rooms, and march with us to the grounds. The horsemen carried only their sabres; the troops were put on the march, and moved rapidly up Broadway to Astor-place; the field pieces were left at the Arsenal; no order was given to the artillery. I was not aware, until I got to the ground, of the extent of the mob; I thought the force I had with me, in connection with the Police force, would be sufficient to preserve the peace. Before getting on the ground, I mounted my horse, and took charge of the cavalry, directing the Infantry to follow close after us. The horsemen, on entering Astor-place, were formed ten ahead, and advanced in that order until we got nearly opposite the corner of the Opera House; at this place, we were assailed with a shower of stones and brick bats, by which almost every man was hurt, and the horses rendered almost unmanageable; the men pushed rapidly through Astor-place, and through the whole distance were assailed with a shower of stones; the infantry followed them. The mob extended from Astor-place to the Bowery; the mounted men, being conspicuous marks, received most of the stones, and were driven off the ground. I dismounted, returned through the mob, and took charge of the Infantry. They were halted in line across the open space beyond the theatre, with a dense mob on both sides of them, who were assailing them with all sorts of opprobrious epithets, and frequent volleys of stones. I ordered Col. Duryea to form a column of division for the purpose of clearing the ground in the read of the theatre, intending afterward to go to the front. The columns were formed promptly, and moved forward through the mob, until stopped by an excavation in the ground, which I had not previously seen, on account of the darkness of the night. We filed around this broken ground, and cleared the rear of the theatre the mob retreating before us as we advanced. Two bodies of troops were stationed at each end of the theatre, extending across the street. I then sent in for the Sheriff and Chief of Police. Mr. Matsell furnished sufficient of the police to take the place of the two lines of military, and the whole were then put under march; passed through Eighth-st to Broadway, and around into Astor-place, the Sheriff at my request accompanied us. We moved down Astor-place until we got a little past the centre of the theatre. The mob partially retreated to the middle and opposite side of the street; they commenced an attack on the military by throwing paving stones. The paving in this vicinity had been taken up for the purpose, as I was informed, of laying down water pipes and building a sewer. I ordered the regiment to be divided and to form in two lines across the street; the right wing advanced toward the Bowery, and the left toward Broadway, with the view of driving the mob each way from the front of the theatre; during this period, the men were constantly assailed with showers of stones and brickbats, and many were seriously hurt; a number of men near by and Gen. Hall were struck with stones, and dangerously injured. After giving this order, I advanced toward the middle of the street to Captain Shumway, who led the first company, with Col. Duryea by his side, being outside myself next the mob; the Sheriff was behind me; at this time, we were assailed by a volley of stones, by which about eight out of eleven of the first platoon were more or less injured. Myself, Col. Duryea, and Capt. Shumway were injured. At this time, a pistol was fired by some man in the mob, by which Capt. Shumway was wounded in the leg, and, as I believe, Gen. Hall in the face. Previous to this, the crowd had been repeatedly notified by Gen. Hall and myself, and by other persons whose voices I did not recognize, that they must disperse or they would be fired upon. I was at this time partly knocked down, and when I arose, I found three or four of the front rank partly down, and the head of the column forced back toward the Opera House, the shower of stones at this time being incessant; orders were then given by myself and repeated by Col. Duryea, to charge bayonet; the attempt was made, but the crowd was so close upon the troops that there was no room for the troops to charge, and some of the men had their muskets seized by the crowd; the troops by this time were forced back to the sidewalk; I stated to the Sheriff that it was impossible to maintain our position without firing. I several times called out to the crowd that they must fall back or we would fire; after this the Sheriff gave the order to fire. Gen. Hall, who was a short distance from me, made an exclamation to fire over their heads; the order to fire was repeated by myself and Col. Duryea, and the men fired once over the heads of the crowd, against Mrs. Langdon's house. A shout then came from the mob, "They have only blank cartridges, give it to them again," and another volley of stones came instantly; the troops were then ordered to fire again; I think the order was given by myself and Gen. Hall; Gen. Hall said, "fire low;" then, for the first time, the mob began to give way; the troops then moved forward, crossing the street, and driving the crowd before them until the troops got near the corner of Lafayette-place. The mob here rallied at the corner of Lafayette-place, on one side, and at the corner of the theatre and the broken ground, on the other side, and advanced, throwing volleys of stones; several of the troops were hurt severely, and orders were given for the troops to fire—one half obliquely to the right, the other half to the left upon these two bodies of men; this was done, and the crowd fell back into Lafayette-place, and the broken ground behind the theatre. There was no firing after this; the mob kept a constant attack upon the troops for some time with stones and brickbats. The whole number of military engaged in the conflict was 210, one-half of the line toward Broadway, and the other toward Bowery; the mob has been variously estimated from ten to twenty thousand. Previously to leaving Eighth-st. to go around to the front of the theatre with the troops, I sent up the Light Artillery and the portions of the Sixth Regiment that was to support it. They arrived after the firing had ceased. One gun was placed toward the Bowery, and the other toward Broadway. The Infantry were stationed, and the mob were again told that unless they left, they would be fired upon, and the Artillery used, if necessary. The mob dispersed, and the firing ceased. Upwards of 50 men of this small detachment of 210 men, were injured, chiefly before the firing commenced. I do not believe that the troops could have withdrawn in safety when the order was given to fire, and that they could have maintained their position without firing. During a period of thirty-five years of military service, I have never seen a mob so violent as the one on that evening. I never before had occasion to give the order to fire.

TESTIMONY OF STEPHEN W. GAINES.

STEPHEN W. GAINES, sworn, says:—I am a counsellor at law, residing at No. 180 East Broadway; on Thursday evening last, I was at the corner of Astor-place and Lafayette-place; I stood upon a pile of boards; I stood there from half-past eight o'clock until after the last discharge of musketry; from the place where I stood, I had a fair view of the Opera House; when I first got there, the space between us and the theatre was filled with people, but not densely crowded at that time; I saw persons throwing stones at the principal entrance, and at the windows of the Opera House; they were nearly in front of the Opera House; sometimes a single stone, and at other times a volley; about fifty feet in front of the house was the principal scene of action; the street toward the Bowery was filled with people; there were no stones thrown from the quarter where I stood, and there were so few actually stoning the house, that it was a surprise to those witnessing it why the police did not

stop it; the first I saw of the military was the horse, and then followed the infantry; they came from Broadway, passed the Opera
House in Astor-place, and took their stand near the 4th avenue;
I saw no opposition; in about half an hour I saw the horse troops
pass up Astor-place, towards Broadway; I should have left upon
the arrival of the military, but so many coming upon the sidewalk,
I could not get out; within a short time after, the infantry passed
up in front of the house; I saw the fire from the discharge of the
muskets as it left the barrels, as the lamps were out; some of them
were fired perpendicular, some on an inclined plane towards the
house of Mrs. Langdon, and others horizontally; this was the first
discharge; we had no intimation of firing where I stood, until I
saw the flash; several other volleys were discharged immediately;
previous to firing the last volley, the street was nearly cleared;
most of the people had left the enclosure where I was; there were,
perhaps, half a dozen on the sidewalk in front of where I was; I
was still standing on the board, when the last discharge took place
up Astor-place towards the Bowery; between me and the soldiers
the space was clear; there was a small number of persons on the
corner opposite Mrs. Langdon's house; they were out of the range
of the fire; this fire was nearly in the range of where I was standing; I stepped back a pace or two, to bring myself out of the direct
line; immediately another discharge took place, that being part of
the previous discharge; upon the discharge, a man fell upon the
sidewalk in front of us; there were but a few persons near him at
the time; after he fell, he remained on the ground half a minute,
some supposed he was shamming being shot; on picking him up,
a wound was discovered in his back, by the blood running; we
took the wounded man down to the drug store corner Fourth and
Wooster street; on examining the body, we found a wound in the
lower part of his stomach; his name was Henry Otten, residing
at the corner of Hester and Orchard streets; he was standing on
the sidewalk at the time he was shot, taking no part in the disturbance; after leaving him, I learned that others had been shot; I
have been informed that he has since died.

TESTIMONY OF THOMAS J. BELVIN.

THOMAS J. BELVIN, residing at No. 133 King street, boatman:
—On Thursday evening last, I was at the disturbance at the

Astor-place Opera House; I stood on the corner of Lafayette-place, by Mrs. Langdon's house; when I got there, about half-past six o'clock, I saw a lot of half-grown boys throwing stones at the Astor Opera House; I passed on the opposite corner, and was talking to two Philadelphians; they were saying how trifling this was to some of their riots; I stayed there until the horse soldiers came, and then the infantry; then there was a rush with the boys, and we started back, and then returned again to see how the military operated; I was standing on the corner of Mrs. Langdon's house when the first firing took place; when the military left, the boys went back and commenced throwing stones again; I stood there when the first discharge took place; a man fell; I laughed, and so did others, as we thought that it was only blank cartridges to scare them; I heard a man say, "my God, look at this; he's shot;" this was at the first discharge of musketry; I heard no notice given to disperse; they might have done so; after this I started and ran down to the church on the corner of 4th street, and there I stood; I don't know how long I stood there, I was so frightened; I stood there until I heard another banging of muskets, and then I started and ran home as quick as I could; I should not have gone there, if I had known they were going to use lead; I went to see what was going on, like many others; I don't know how long I stood at the church before I heard the second firing; I was glad to get there; I jumped over several people in making my way to the church.

It is to be observed that the above accounts vary according to the position of the witnesses. Mr. Stewart confines his attention chiefly to the operations of the police; Gen. Sandford to those of the military; while others may be supposed to represent the views and feelings of the mere spectators.

On the examination of Mr. Stewart, he was asked, if, in his opinion, the riot could have been prevented or suppressed by the action of the police, without calling on the military. Though loth to give an opinion, which might be construed into a censure of the authorities, he stated his belief that the whole affair might have been differently managed.

The scene which followed the firing of the military, beggars all description. The wounded, the dying, and the dead, were scattered in every direction. There were groans of agony, cries for help, and oaths of vengeance. The dead and the wounded were borne to the drug stores at the corners of Eighth street and Broadway, and Third Avenue, and others in the vicinity, and surgeons were summoned to attend them. Some were conveyed by the police to the Fifteenth Ward Station House, and a few carried to the City Hospital. Some of the dead and wounded were laid out upon the billiard tables of Vauxhall Saloon, a large crowd gathered around, and speeches were made by excited orators.

Had none but those actively engaged in the riot been shot by the military, these details would have been sufficiently melancholy. But even then, we are to consider that the men who composed the mob, may have acted, under ordinary circumstances, like honest and respectable citizens. A mob is composed of the same men in a state of temporary insanity, and they should be treated accordingly. Sober and quiet citizens, acting under such a temporary excitement, have committed the greatest outrages. They should be restrained, but not sacrificed, unless under the most imperative necessity.

But in this case, very few of the active rioters were injured—the greater part of the killed and wounded being either spectators, or persons passing by the scene. Thus, Bridget Fagan was walking with her husband along the Bowery, shot through the leg, and died at the Hospital. Mr. Stuart, an old retired merchant, was severely wounded in the neck, while standing in the Bowery; and Mr. Collins was shot dead while getting out of a car of the Harlem Rail Road. Wm. C. Russell, a lawyer, had his arm shattered while passing around the corner of the Bowery. Mr. Livingston, standing in St. Mark's place, two blocks off, was severely wounded. There were many more such cases.

Of those who were shot down in the immediate vicinity of the Opera House, the greater portion were taking no part in the affair. Mr. George W. Gedney, a broker in Wall street, who had a wife, to whom he had been married but a little more than a year, and one child, was shot instantly dead, as he was standing inside the railing by the Langdon mansion. At the first volley, a ball pierced his brain. His wife knew he had gone to see the riot, and she had had a presentiment of some disaster. She sat watching and waiting for her husband, for it was the first time he had been out at night, without her, since their marriage. She waited until four o'clock in the morning in an agony of terror, when, unable to endure the suspense any longer, she rushed into the street, went to the house of one of her husband's friends, roused him from his slumber, and begged him to go and seek for her husband. The man went, and found poor Gedney a cold corpse. Mrs. Gedney was sitting at the window when he returned, and motioned for him to come to her, but he shook his head mournfully, and passed by in silence. She knew that her beloved husband was no more. Her neighbor, who had not the courage to tell her the awful tidings, sent his wife to comfort her. This is but one of many such cases of domestic affliction, produced by the events of that night of terror.

CHAPTER SEVENTH.

THE DAY AFTER THE RIOT—POPULAR EXCITEMENT— CORONER'S INQUEST—LIST OF THE KILLED AND WOUNDED.

The morning of the eleventh of May was one of sad excitement in the city of New York. The extent of the calamity, the number of the dead and wounded, made a deep and solemn impression. Public opinion was very much divided. The more excitable breathed threats of vengeance, and the military were kept under arms during that and the succeeding day. A meeting was called in the Park, of "Citizens opposed to the destruction of Human Life." Several thousands assembled, and resolutions were passed, thoroughly condemning the authorities for not exhausting the civil power before calling out the military, and characterizing the sacrifice of life as "the most wanton, unprovoked and murderous outrage ever perpetrated in the civilized world;" and calling upon the Grand Jury to indict the Mayor, Recorder and Sheriff, for ordering the military to fire on the citizens. Exciting and inflammatory speeches were made by Edward Strahan, Isaiah

Rynders, and Mike Walsh, but the meeting separated without disturbance.

That night, all eyes were turned toward the Opera House, for though it had been closed by the lessees, and though Macready was in Boston, it had been given out that it should be destroyed. The most efficient measures had been taken by the authorities, and a proclamation issued by the Mayor. Gen. Sandford called out four troops of horse artillery, one squadron of cavalry, four regiments of infantry, including the fifth brigade, and a detachment of the veteran artillery, with a 24 pound howitzer. The artillery was planted so as to sweep the streets around the building, and the infantry and cavalry stationed at a convenient distance. The artillery was furnished with grape, and the infantry with ball cartridge.

At dark, an immense crowd filled the streets around the Opera House, but the military took possession of the ground, dispersed the mob, and barricaded the approaches to the scene. The mob, most violent at first in Broadway, having been driven from that position, made an attack upon the troops in the Bowery, and severely injured several of the soldiers; but the police, aided by the military, arrested or dispersed the offenders. At about 9 o'clock, the mob erected a barricade across 9th street, near the Bowery, to defend themselves from the cavalry, but it was stormed by the police. At one time, the attack upon the City Guard was so severe, that they were ordered to load, and the Recorder proclaimed that another shower of stones would bring one of lead in return; but fortunately the volleys ceased. Bonfires were kindled, but these only made the leaders of the riot conspicuous, and aided the police to arrest them. About thirty arrests were made, the mob driven off in all directions, and at midnight order was restored. Half this efficiency the previous night, would have saved all bloodshed. Order was restored, and though it was reported that a large number of persons had come from Philadelphia, expressly to take part in a riot, the peace of the city was not again disturbed.

On Saturday morning, the Coroner assembled a jury, who proceeded in carriages, to view the bodies of those who were killed. After viewing them, and witnessing a surgical examination of each, the inquest was continued at the Hall of the Court of Sessions. The Mayor, Recorder, Sheriff, Chief of Police, and several military officers and citizens were examined. We have given some of the most important of the testimony.

The Jury retired at half-past six o'clock, on Sunday evening, and after being out a short time, returned the following verdict:

> We believe that Geo. A. Curtis, John McDonald, Thos. Aylwood, George Lincoln, Timothy Burns, Henry Otten, George W. Brown, Wm. Butler, George W. Taylor, Owen Burns, Thos. Belman, Neil Gray Mellis, Asa F. Collins, Wm. Harmer, Thos. Keirnan, Mathew Cahill, Geo. N. Gedney, came to their deaths by gun shot wounds, from balls fired by the Military during the riot before the Opera House, on Thursday evening, 10th May inst., by order of the civil authorities of the city of New York; and that the circumstances existing at the time justified the authorities in giving the order to fire upon the mob. We further believe that if a larger number of the Police had been ordered out, the necessity of a resort to the use of Military might have been avoided.

New York, May 14, 1849.   JAMES H. PERKINS, Foreman.

O. H. WILSON,	WM. BANTA,
LEONARD H. HEGAR,	J. C. BALDWIN,
JAMES CROPSY,	LEANDER M. SAMMIS,
SAMUEL RAYNOR,	EDWARD C. ROBINSON,
JOSEPH B. BREWSTER,	WM. S. SMITH,
GEO. W. DAWSON,	THOS. S. MILLER,

WILLIAM BALLAGH.

Five other persons, in a few days afterwards, died of their wounds. The following is believed to be a complete list of all the killed and wounded:

LIST OF THE KILLED.

GEORGE A. CURTIS,

Aged 22 years, born in Chautauque Co., printer; shot through the lungs.

JOHN Mc'DONALD,

Aged fifteen years, born in Ireland, shot through the breast.

GEORGE LINCOLN,

Aged 35 years, appeared to be a sailor; shot in the abdomen.

THOMAS AYLWOOD,

Aged 19, born in Halifax, a clerk; shot in the thigh: died after amputation of the limb.

TIMOTHY BURNS,

16 years, a printer; shot through the right lung.

HENRY OTTEN,

22 years; grocer; shot through the breast. He died in the 15th Ward station-house, in presence of his aged mother.

GEORGE W. BROWN,

From Boston; clerk; ball passed through left lung.

WILLIAM BUTLER,

24 years; ship joiner; shot through the head.

GEORGE W. TAYLOR,

21 years; house carpenter; shot through the head.

OWEN BURNS,

24 years; born in Ireland; a cartman; shot through the head.

THOMAS BELMAN,

17 years; born in Ireland; laborer; shot through the neck.

NEIL GRAY MELLIS,

27 years; the musket-ball passed directly through the heart; left a wife and one child. The deceased was a nephew to ex-Alderman Neil Gray of the 10th Ward.

ASA F. COLLINS,

45 years; born in this State; business a house agent. The deceased received a ball in the neck, as he was descending from the railroad car.

WILLIAM HARMER,

16 years; a butcher; was brought to the Bellevue Hospital early on Friday morning, having received a ball in the abdomen; he lingered until four o'clock in the afternoon, when death relieved his earthly suffering. He was a native of St. John's, New Brunswick.

THOMAS KEIRNAN,

21 years; born in Ireland; a waiter; shot in the right cheek, the ball passing into the brain.

MATHEW CAHILL,

26 years; born in Ireland; laborer; widower; shot through the right breast; one child.

TIMOTHY McGUINN,

19 years; laborer. The deceased was residing with his mother, in the rear of No. 107 West Thirteenth-street, and died soon after being brought home.

GEORGE W. GEDNEY,

34 years; born in New-York; a broker; resided at No. 82 Seventh-street. The deceased received a musket-ball directly through the brain.

JOHN DALZELL,

Was wounded in the hip, and died after amputation of the hip joint.

ROBERT MACLEURGEON,

Aged 20, a native of New York, received a wound while passing through Lafayette Place; and died at his mother's residence on Monday.

JOHN McKINSLEY,

Shot through the lungs, died on Sunday night.

HENRY BURGUIST,

Known as "Harry Bluff," lived at 410 Pearl-street. Ball grazed the neck, went into the right shoulder, coming out behind the right arm. Died of his wounds at the hospital.

BRIDGET FAGAN,

Irish; 30 years old; shot in the leg, just below the knee. She was two blocks off, walking with her husband on their way home, and fell into his arms. Died after amputation.

Thus TWENTY-THREE PERSONS were either killed on the spot, or died of their wounds shortly after.

LIST OF THE WOUNDED.

The following list is probably incomplete, as many who were not seriously wounded have not been publicly reported:

EDWARD MCCORMICK, 135 First Avenue: 19 years old; worked at 200 Mulberry-street. Shot through the side.

CONRAD BECKER, 27 Hudson-street; worked for Mahoney and Thompson, Upholsterers, Chatham-street. Ball went through the right thigh.

GEORGE N. KAY, 28 years of age; merchant; boarded at 107 Chambers-street. Ball in the right breast, going entirely through.

FREDERICK GILLESPIE, a boy; shot through the foot.

A SON of J. IRWIN, 243 Tenth-street; ball through his leg.

B. M. SEIXAS, jr.,

MATTHEW CARHART, residence First Av., corner of Twelfth-st.; shot through the breast and neck.

MR. STEWART, of the late firm of Coley, Stewart, and Co., Mobile, retired merchant; while standing in the Bowery was shot in the neck.

MR. PHILIP LIVINGSTON, a young man, who was standing in St. Mark's Place, was badly wounded, the shot entering the fore arm, and coming out near the thumb.

Lieut. J. BROWN; son of Prof. Brown; residence 42 Crosby-street; was shot as he came out of the Amphitheatre door.

Deacon A. M. COLLINS; of the Allen-street Church; was also shot.

WILLIAM SELLECK; 23 years of age; residence 227 Seventh-street; dangerously wounded by a shot; a spectator.

A young Philadelphian; name not ascertained; badly shot through the thigh.

Mr. BRAISTED; of the firm of Secor & Co.; spectator; shot through the knees.

WM. C. RUSSELL, Esq.; a lawyer of Wall-street; left his residence in Fourth-avenue, about half-past 10, and while passing the corner of Lafayette-place, had his left arm shattered by a ball.

Mr. MARSHALL LEFFERTS; of the firm of Messrs. Geo. B. Moore-wood & Co. 14 and 16 Beaver-street; while on duty as an officer, was knocked from his horse by a stone, and seriously wounded.

One of the National Guards had his jaw-bone broken by a paving-stone.

LORENZO D. SNELL, of Philadelphia; 49 Bayard-street; was shot through the thigh.

Mrs. BRENNAN, house-keeper for Mr. Kernachan, corner of Second-avenue and Ninth-street; while passing up the Bowery, on her way home, leaning upon the arm of a man, was struck by a ball in her left thigh, which passed through the fleshy part of this and the right thigh, without injuring the large vessels or the bones.

STEPHEN KEHOE.

Mr. VANDERPOOL; was wounded with a ball at the corner of the eye.

A boy, by the name of STONE.

An instance of heroism is related in one of the wounded, who, when the surgeon was about to examine his case, said, "Never mind me now, but look round and see if there is not some one who needs you more than I do!" The speech was worthy of Sir Philip Sidney. The lives of such men ought not to be lightly sacrificed.

Of the military and police, a large number were wounded, some of them severely, by paving stones. Capt. Shumway received a flesh wound with a pistol shot.

The military performed their duty, generally, with commendable coolness. Some, it is said, laid down their arms, rather than fire, and others fired into the air; but on the whole, they did quite sufficient execution, especially on those who were not actively engaged in the riot.

CHAPTER EIGHTH.

WHERE LIES THE BLAME?

THE dead are sleeping in their quiet graves. Day by day, time brings its consolations to the afflicted; but has society no lesson to learn from the horrors of which we have given as full a description as could be given, by looking at the mere surface of things? We have shown the causes which produced this dreadful sacrifice of human life—this massacre of innocent and unoffending citizens, for many of the killed were truly such. Let us endeavor to turn the terrible lesson to some useful account.

Those who were actively engaged in the scenes we have described, experience different feelings in regard to it. The mob was made up mainly of well-meaning, but ignorant, rash, and misguided men. The best feelings of our nature, when they are perverted, may produce the worst consequences. In this case, a feeling of patriotism, and a sense of justice, were the ruling motives of those who violated the laws, broke the peace of the community, defied the constituted authorities, and caused the death of twenty-three human beings. They acted in all good conscience, but an unenlightened or misguided conscience is no security against wrong. Some of the worst deeds that were ever committed, were done "in all good conscience." Thus Christ was crucified by a Jewish mob, and said, "Father, forgive them, they know not what they do." Thus, in all ages, the worst acts have been committed from the best of motives.

The authorities are probably satisfied with having maintained law and order, though at a terrible sacrifice, and the press has almost unanimously sustained them. But it should be remembered that almost all men are liable to temporary excitements. Mobs are affected with a kind of insanity. The madness of a crowd seems to be infectious. These rioters may, in their calm moments, be good and quiet citizens. We have seen some of the most sober and moral communities excited into a fury of passion. At any rate, they are brethren, and should be dealt with in love and kindness.

But law and order must be maintained; very true—it must be done at all hazards, but it should be done prudently, and with the least possible sacrifice. Humanity has its claims as well as law; and it may not be necessary to the maintenance of public order, that ignorant and misguided men, laboring under a temporary madness should be shot down like dogs, if they can be controlled by means more gentle.

The military acted naturally, under the circumstances. They were placed in an ugly position by the authorities, suffered severely for it, and obeyed their orders. No doubt, they regretted the fatal necessity. Some idea of the probable feelings of those who fired the fatal volleys, may be judged of from the fact that a brother of Mr. Gedney, who was shot dead at the first fire, was a member of one of the companies that fired the volleys. All men are brethren—but here was brother against brother, in a sense that the most unfeeling can appreciate.

A distinguished clergyman of this city, preaching on the subject of the riot, says of Macready and his right to act—"Though he had been the meanest of his kind, he should have been protected here to the conclusion of his announced engagement, if an army of ten thousand men had been required to wait upon his movements, and a ship of war chartered to convey him to his native land. We have done something to vindicate order and law, and we ought to have done more."

A zeal for the rights of Mr. Macready and his friends, and for the cause of law and order is commendable—but it must not be forgotten that other rights must have been violated, or this riot could never have taken place. Those ignorant men had a right to education, and to such conditions of cultivation, as would have made them intelligent men and good citizens. They would never have raised their hands against society, had society done its duty to them. Before they committed this wrong, they had been most deeply wronged themselves; and it would be better to provide ten thousand schoolmasters to instruct people, than ten thousand soldiers to prevent the result of their ignorance.

Men can be zealous and indignant about the rights of play actors, or their patrons—and we have no disposition to deny their rights, or to interfere with the lawful exercise of them—but they forget in how many ways the rights of our brethren are violated, and not a word is said in their behalf. Give every man the natural and social rights that belong to him and we should have few crimes and outrages to complain of, and law and order could be maintained without standing armies or ships of war.

When we go deep into the investigation of social wrongs, we shall find that society brings upon itself the very evils it attempts to subdue. Society, by an unjust distribution of the avails of industry, enables a few men to become rich, and consigns a great mass to hopeless poverty, with all its deprivations and degradations. This poverty produces ignorance, the sense of injustice, grovelling tastes, and a loss of all high ambition. The only wonder is that under such circumstances of wrong and outrage, men are so forbearing, so honest, and so orderly. The only wonder is that more crimes are not committed against both property and life. Thousands of poor people know that they are robbed and plundered every day of their lives—they feel bitterly the hardships and injustice of their lot; but how calmly do they wait God's justice to set them right! How few of them comparatively attempt to right their own wrongs, and to sieze upon a portion of what society withholds from them!

This terrible tragedy is a lesson to us all. None can escape its warning. We are all responsible, all guilty; for we make a part of a society that has permitted thousands of its members to grow up in poverty and ignorance, and exposed to the temptations of vice and crime. This mob is but a symptom of our social condition, and it points out a disease to which we should lose no time in applying a proper remedy.

THE END.

(1849)

Ralph Waldo Emerson

(1803–1882)

Shakspeare; or, the Poet

Tradition holds that Emerson knew "almost all of Shakespeare by heart" by the time he arrived at Harvard College. Whether or not that is true, his subsequent letters, essays, poems, and journals are filled with allusions to Shakespeare and his works: no other writer is mentioned by Emerson more often. The young Emerson, clearly shaped by the values of his Puritan heritage, had little patience for the "moral turpitude" of Shakespeare the playwright: "in a reformed theatre," he writes, "Shakspeare should find no place." But reading Samuel Taylor Coleridge's criticism in the late 1820s swung Emerson toward a greater appreciation of Shakespeare's singularity (though he would always prefer reading the plays to seeing them staged). Emerson's landmark essay on Shakespeare, published in his collection *Representative Men* in 1850, mixes high praise with sharp criticism, acknowledging Shakespeare's great gifts as synthesizer, thinker, and as "the type of the poet," while worrying about the dearth of information about the poet's life and famously castigating Shakespeare's immorality, belittling him as "master of the revels to mankind." Emerson's views apparently mellowed over time; when asked to deliver remarks at a tercentenary celebration of Shakespeare's birth in 1864, Emerson praised Shakespeare as "the most robust and potent thinker that ever was," one who "dwarfs all writers without a solitary exception."

⚬⚬

GREAT men are more distinguished by range and extent, than by originality. If we require the originality which consists in weaving, like a spider, their web from their own bowels; in finding clay, and making bricks, and building the house; no great men are original. Nor does valuable originality consist in unlikeness to other men. The hero is in the press of knights, and the thick of events; and, seeing what men want, and sharing their desire, he adds the needful length of sight and of arm, to come at the desired point. The greatest genius is the most indebted man. A poet is no rattlebrain, saying what comes uppermost, and, because he says every thing, saying, at last, something good; but a heart in unison with his time and country. There is nothing whimsical and fantastic in his production, but sweet and sad earnest, freighted with the weightiest convictions, and pointed with the most determined aim which any man or class knows of in his times.

The Genius of our life is jealous of individuals, and will not have any individual great, except through the general. There is no choice to genius. A great man does not wake up on some fine morning, and say, 'I am full of life, I will go to sea, and find an Antarctic continent: to-day I will square the circle: I will ransack botany, and find a new food for man: I have a new architecture in my mind: I foresee a new mechanic power:' no, but he finds himself in the river of the thoughts and events, forced onward by the ideas and necessities of his contemporaries. He stands where all the eyes of men look one way, and their hands all point in the direction in which he should go. The church has reared him amidst rites and pomps, and he carries out the advice which her music gave him, and builds a cathedral needed by her chants and processions. He finds a war raging: it educates him, by trumpet, in barracks, and he betters the instruction. He finds two counties groping to bring coal, or flour, or fish, from the place of production to the place of consumption, and he hits on a railroad. Every master has found his materials collected, and his power lay in his sympathy with his people, and in his love of the materials he wrought in. What an economy of power! and what a compensation for the shortness of life! All is done to his hand. The world has brought him thus far on his way. The human race has gone out before him, sunk the hills, filled the hollows, and bridged the rivers. Men, nations, poets, artisans, women, all have worked for him, and he enters into their labors. Choose any other thing, out of the line of tendency, out of the national feeling and history, and he would have all to do for himself: his powers would be expended in the first preparations. Great genial power, one would almost say, consists in not being original at all; in being altogether receptive; in letting the world do all, and suffering the spirit of the hour to pass unobstructed through the mind.

Shakspeare's youth fell in a time when the English people were importunate for dramatic entertainments. The court took offence easily at political allusions, and attempted to suppress them. The Puritans, a growing and energetic party, and the religious among the Anglican church, would suppress them. But the people wanted them. Inn-yards, houses without roofs, and extemporaneous enclosures at country fairs, were the ready theatres of strolling players. The people had tasted this new joy; and, as we could not hope to suppress newspapers now,—no, not by the strongest party,—neither then could king, prelate, or puritan, alone or united, suppress an organ, which was ballad, epic, newspaper, caucus, lecture, punch, and library, at the same time. Probably king, prelate, and puritan, all found their own account in it. It had become, by all causes, a national interest,—by no means conspicuous, so that some great scholar would have thought of treating it in an English history,—but not a whit less considerable, because it was cheap, and of no account, like a baker's-shop. The best proof of its vitality is the crowd of writers which suddenly broke into this field; Kyd, Marlow, Greene, Jonson, Chapman, Dekker, Webster, Heywood, Middleton, Peele, Ford, Massinger, Beaumont, and Fletcher.

The secure possession, by the stage, of the public mind, is of the first importance to the poet who works for it. He loses no time in idle experiments. Here is audience and expectation prepared. In the case of Shakspeare there is much more. At the time when he left Stratford, and went up to London, a great body of stage-plays, of all dates and writers, existed in manuscript, and were in turn produced on the boards. Here is the Tale of Troy, which the audience will bear hearing some part of every week; the Death of Julius Cæsar, and other stories out of Plutarch, which they never tire of; a shelf full of English history, from the chronicles of Brut and Arthur, down to the royal Henries, which men hear eagerly; and a string of doleful tragedies, merry Italian tales, and Spanish voyages, which all the London prentices know. All the mass has been treated, with more or less skill, by every playwright, and the prompter has the soiled and tattered manuscripts. It is now no longer possible to say who wrote them first. They have been the property of the Theatre so long, and so many rising geniuses have enlarged or altered them, inserting a speech, or a whole scene, or adding a song, that no man can any longer claim copyright on this work of numbers. Happily, no man wishes to. They are not yet desired in that way. We have few readers, many spectators and hearers. They had best lie where they are.

Shakspeare, in common with his comrades, esteemed the mass of old plays, waste stock, in which any experiment could be freely tried. Had the *prestige* which hedges about a modern tragedy existed, nothing could have been done. The rude warm blood of the living England circulated in the play, as in street-ballads, and gave body which he wanted to his airy and majestic fancy. The poet needs a ground in popular tradition on which he may work, and which, again, may restrain his art within the due temperance. It holds him to the people, supplies a foundation for his edifice; and, in furnishing so much work done to his hand, leaves him at leisure, and in full strength for the audacities of his imagination. In short, the poet owes to his legend what sculpture owed to the temple. Sculpture in Egypt, and in Greece, grew up in subordination to architecture. It was the ornament of the temple wall: at first, a rude relief carved on pediments, then the relief became bolder, and a head or arm was projected from the wall, the groups being still arranged with reference to the building, which serves also as a frame to hold the figures; and when, at last, the greatest freedom of style and treatment was reached, the prevailing genius of architecture still enforced a certain calmness and continence in the statue. As soon as the statue was begun for itself, and with no reference to the temple or palace, the art began to decline: freak, extravagance, and exhibition, took the place of the old temperance. This balance-wheel, which the sculptor found in architecture, the perilous irritability of poetic talent found in the accumulated dramatic materials to which the people were already wonted, and which had a certain excellence which no single genius, however extraordinary, could hope to create.

In point of fact, it appears that Shakspeare did owe debts in all directions, and was able to use whatever he found; and the amount of indebtedness may be inferred from Malone's laborious computations in regard to the First, Second, and Third parts of Henry VI., in which, "out of 6043 lines, 1771 were written by some author preceding Shakspeare; 2373 by him, on the foundation laid by his predecessors; and 1899 were entirely his own." And the proceeding investigation hardly leaves a single drama of his absolute invention. Malone's sentence is an important piece of external history. In Henry VIII., I think I see plainly the cropping out of the original rock on which his own finer stratum was laid. The first play was written by a superior, thoughtful man, with a vicious ear. I can mark his lines, and know well their cadence. See Wolsey's soliloquy, and the following scene with Cromwell, where,—instead of the metre of Shakspeare, whose secret is, that the thought constructs the tune, so that reading for the sense will best bring out the rhythm,—here the lines are constructed on a given tune, and the verse has even a trace of pulpit eloquence. But the play contains, through all its length, unmistakable traits of Shakspeare's hand, and some passages, as the account of the coronation, are like autographs. What is odd, the compliment to Queen Elizabeth is in the bad rhythm.

Shakspeare knew that tradition supplies a better fable than any invention can. If he lost any credit of design, he augmented his resources; and, at that day, our petulant demand for originality was not so much pressed. There was no literature for the million. The universal reading, the cheap press, were unknown. A great poet, who appears in illiterate times, absorbs into his sphere all the light which is any where radiating. Every intellectual jewel, every flower of sentiment, it is his fine office to bring to his people; and he comes to value his memory equally with his invention. He is therefore little solicitous whence his thoughts have been derived; whether through translation, whether through tradition, whether by travel in distant countries, whether by inspiration; from whatever source, they are equally welcome to his uncritical audience. Nay, he borrows very near home. Other men say wise things as well as he; only they say a good many foolish things, and do not know when they have spoken wisely. He knows the sparkle of the true stone, and puts it in high place, wherever he finds it. Such is the happy position of Homer, perhaps; of Chaucer, of Saadi. They felt that all wit was their wit. And they are librarians and historiographers, as well as poets. Each romancer was heir and dispenser of all the hundred tales of the world,—

> "Presenting Thebes' and Pelops' line
> And the tale of Troy divine."

The influence of Chaucer is conspicuous in all our early literature; and, more recently, not only Pope and Dryden have been beholden to him, but, in the whole society of English writers, a large unacknowledged debt is easily traced. One is charmed with the opulence which feeds so many pensioners. But Chaucer is a huge borrower. Chaucer, it seems, drew continually, through Lydgate and Caxton, from Guido di Colonna, whose Latin romance of the Trojan war was in turn a compilation from Dares Phrygius, Ovid, and Statius. Then Petrarch, Boccaccio, and the Provençal poets, are his benefactors: the Romaunt of the Rose is only judicious translation from William of Lorris and John of Meun: Troilus and Creseide, from Lollius of Urbino: The Cock and the Fox, from the *Lais* of Marie: The House of Fame, from the French or Italian: and poor Gower he uses as if he were only a brick-kiln or stone-quarry, out of which to build his house. He steals by this apology,—that what he takes has no worth where he finds it, and the greatest where he leaves it. It has come to be practically a sort of rule in literature, that a man, having once shown himself capable of original writing, is entitled thenceforth to steal from the writings of others at discretion. Thought is the property of him who can entertain it; and of him who can adequately place it. A certain awkwardness marks the use of borrowed thoughts; but, as soon as we have learned what to do with them, they become our own.

Thus, all originality is relative. Every thinker is retrospective. The learned member of the legislature, at Westminster, or at Washington, speaks and votes for thousands. Show us the constituency, and the now invisible channels by which the senator is made aware of their wishes, the crowd of practical and knowing men, who, by correspondence or conversation, are feeding him with evidence, anecdotes, and estimates, and it will bereave his fine attitude and resistance of something of their impressiveness. As Sir Robert Peel and Mr. Webster vote, so Locke and Rousseau think for thousands; and so there were fountains all around Homer, Menu, Saadi, or Milton, from which they drew; friends, lovers, books, traditions, proverbs,—all perished,—which, if seen, would go to reduce the wonder. Did the bard speak with authority? Did he feel himself overmatched by any companion? The appeal is to the consciousness of the writer. Is there at last in his breast a Delphi whereof to ask concerning any thought or thing, whether it be verily so, yea or nay? and to have answer, and to rely on that? All the debts which such a man could contract to other wit, would never disturb his consciousness of originality: for the ministrations of books, and of other minds, are a whiff of smoke to that most private reality with which he has conversed.

It is easy to see that what is best written or done by genius, in the world, was no man's work, but came by wide social labor, when a thousand wrought like one, sharing the same impulse. Our English Bible is a wonderful specimen of the strength and music of the English language. But it was not made by one man, or at one time; but centuries and churches brought it to perfection. There never was a time when there was not some translation existing. The Liturgy, admired for its energy and pathos, is an anthology of the piety of ages and nations, a translation of the prayers and forms of the Catholic church,—these collected, too, in long periods, from the prayers and meditations of every saint and sacred writer, all over the world. Grotius makes the like remark in respect to the Lord's Prayer, that the single clauses of which it is composed were already in use, in the time of Christ, in the rabbinical forms. He picked out the grains of gold. The nervous language of the Common Law, the impressive forms of our courts, and the precision and substantial truth of the legal distinctions, are the contribution of all the sharp-sighted, strong-minded men who have lived in the countries where these laws govern. The translation of Plutarch gets its excellence by being translation on translation. There never was a time when there was none. All the truly idiomatic and national phrases are kept, and all others successively picked out, and thrown away. Something like the same process had gone on, long before, with the originals of these books. The world takes liberties with world-books. Vedas, Æsop's Fables, Pilpay, Arabian Nights, Cid, Iliad, Robin Hood, Scottish Minstrelsy, are not the work of single men. In the composition of such works, the time thinks, the market thinks, the mason, the carpenter, the merchant, the farmer, the fop, all think for us. Every book supplies its time with one good word; every municipal law, every trade, every folly of the day, and the generic catholic genius who is not afraid or ashamed to owe his originality to the originality of all, stands with the next age as the recorder and embodiment of his own.

We have to thank the researches of antiquaries, and the Shakspeare Society, for ascertaining the steps of the English drama, from the Mysteries celebrated in churches and by churchmen, and the final detachment from the church, and the completion of secular plays, from Ferrex and Porrex, and Gammer Gurton's Needle, down to the possession of the stage by the very pieces which Shakspeare altered, remodelled, and finally made his own. Elated with success, and piqued by the growing interest of the problem, they have left no book-stall unsearched, no chest in a garret unopened, no file of old yellow accounts to decompose in damp and worms, so keen was the hope to discover whether the boy Shakspeare poached or not, whether he held horses at the theatre door, whether he kept school, and why he left in his will only his second-best bed to Ann Hathaway, his wife.

There is somewhat touching in the madness with which the passing age mischooses the object on which all candles shine, and all eyes are turned; the care with which it registers every trifle touching Queen Elizabeth, and King James, and the Essexes, Leicesters, Burleighs, and Buckinghams; and lets pass without a single valuable note the founder of another dynasty, which alone will cause the Tudor dynasty to be remembered,—the man who carries the Saxon race in him by the inspiration which feeds him, and on whose thoughts the foremost people of the world are now for some ages to be nourished, and minds to receive this and not another bias. A popular player,—nobody suspected he was the poet of the human race; and the secret was kept as faithfully from poets and intellectual men, as from courtiers and frivolous people. Bacon, who took the inventory of the human understanding for his times, never mentioned his name. Ben Jonson, though we have strained his few words of regard and panegyric, had no suspicion of the elastic fame whose first vibrations he was attempting. He no doubt thought the praise he has conceded to him generous, and esteemed himself, out of all question, the better poet of the two.

If it need wit to know wit, according to the proverb, Shakspeare's time should be capable of recognizing it. Sir Henry Wotton was born four years after Shakspeare, and died twenty-three years after him; and I find, among his correspondents and acquaintances, the following persons: Theodore Beza, Isaac Casaubon, Sir Philip Sidney, Earl of Essex, Lord Bacon, Sir Walter Raleigh, John Milton, Sir Henry Vane, Isaac Walton, Dr. Donne, Abraham Cowley, Bellarmine, Charles Cotton, John Pym, John Hales, Kepler, Vieta, Albericus Gentilis, Paul Sarpi, Arminius; with all of whom exists some token of his having communicated, without enumerating many others, whom doubtless he saw,—Shakspeare, Spenser, Jonson, Beaumont, Massinger, two Herberts, Marlow, Chapman, and the rest. Since the constellation of great men who appeared in Greece in the time of Pericles, there was never any such society;—yet their genius failed them to find out the best head in the universe. Our poet's mask was impenetrable. You cannot see the mountain near. It took a century to make it suspected; and not until two centuries had passed, after his death, did any criticism which we think adequate begin to appear. It was not possible to write the history of Shakspeare till now; for he is the father of German literature: it was on the introduction of Shakspeare into German, by Lessing, and the translation of his works by Wieland and Schlegel, that the rapid burst of German literature was most intimately connected. It was not until

the nineteenth century, whose speculative genius is a sort of living
Hamlet, that the tragedy of Hamlet could find such wondering
readers. Now, literature, philosophy, and thought, are Shakspear-
ized. His mind is the horizon beyond which, at present, we do not
see. Our ears are educated to music by his rhythm. Coleridge and
Goethe are the only critics who have expressed our convictions
with any adequate fidelity: but there is in all cultivated minds a
silent appreciation of his superlative power and beauty, which, like
Christianity, qualifies the period.

The Shakspeare Society have inquired in all directions, advertised the missing facts, offered money for any information that
will lead to proof; and with what result? Beside some important
illustration of the history of the English stage, to which I have
adverted, they have gleaned a few facts touching the property, and
dealings in regard to property, of the poet. It appears that, from
year to year, he owned a larger share in the Blackfriars' Theatre:
its wardrobe and other appurtenances were his: that he bought an
estate in his native village, with his earnings, as writer and share-
holder; that he lived in the best house in Stratford; was intrusted
by his neighbors with their commissions in London, as of borrowing money, and the like; that he was a veritable farmer. About the
time when he was writing Macbeth, he sues Philip Rogers, in the
borough-court of Stratford, for thirty-five shillings, ten pence,
for corn delivered to him at different times; and, in all respects,
appears as a good husband, with no reputation for eccentricity or
excess. He was a good-natured sort of man, an actor and share-
holder in the theatre, not in any striking manner distinguished
from other actors and managers. I admit the importance of this
information. It was well worth the pains that have been taken to
procure it.

But whatever scraps of information concerning his condition these researches may have rescued, they can shed no light
upon that infinite invention which is the concealed magnet of
his attraction for us. We are very clumsy writers of history. We tell
the chronicle of parentage, birth, birth-place, schooling, school-
mates, earning of money, marriage, publication of books, celebrity,

death; and when we have come to an end of this gossip, no ray of
relation appears between it and the goddess-born; and it seems
as if, had we dipped at random into the "Modern Plutarch," and
read any other life there, it would have fitted the poems as well.
It is the essence of poetry to spring, like the rainbow daughter
of Wonder, from the invisible, to abolish the past, and refuse all
history. Malone, Warburton, Dyce, and Collier, have wasted their
oil. The famed theatres, Covent Garden, Drury Lane, the Park,
and Tremont, have vainly assisted. Betterton, Garrick, Kemble,
Kean, and Macready, dedicate their lives to this genius; him they
crown, elucidate, obey, and express. The genius knows them not.
The recitation begins; one golden word leaps out immortal from
all this painted pedantry, and sweetly torments us with invitations
to its own inaccessible homes. I remember, I went once to see the
Hamlet of a famed performer, the pride of the English stage; and
all I then heard, and all I now remember, of the tragedian, was that
in which the tragedian had no part; simply, Hamlet's question to
the ghost,—

> "What may this mean,
> That thou, dead corse, again in complete steel
> Revisit'st thus the glimpses of the moon?"

That imagination which dilates the closet he writes in to the
world's dimension, crowds it with agents in rank and order, as
quickly reduces the big reality to be the glimpses of the moon.
These tricks of his magic spoil for us the illusions of the green-
room. Can any biography shed light on the localities into which
the Midsummer Night's Dream admits me? Did Shakspeare
confide to any notary or parish recorder, sacristan, or surrogate,
in Stratford, the genesis of that delicate creation? The forest of
Arden, the nimble air of Scone Castle, the moonlight of Portia's
villa, "the antres vast and desarts idle," of Othello's captivity,—
where is the third cousin, or grand-nephew, the chancellor's file
of accounts, or private letter, that has kept one word of those
transcendent secrets? In fine, in this drama, as in all great works
of art,—in the Cyclopæn architecture of Egypt and India; in the

Phidian sculpture; the Gothic ministers; the Italian painting; the Ballads of Spain and Scotland,—the Genius draws up the ladder after him, when the creative age goes up to heaven, and gives way to a new, who see the works, and ask in vain for a history.

Shakspeare is the only biographer of Shakspeare; and even he can tell nothing, except to the Shakspeare in us; that is, to our most apprehensive and sympathetic hour. He cannot step from off his tripod, and give us anecdotes of his inspirations. Read the antique documents extricated, analyzed, and compared, by the assiduous Dyce and Collier; and now read one of those skiey sentences,—aerolites,—which seem to have fallen out of heaven, and which, not your experience, but the man within the breast, has accepted as words of fate; and tell me if they match; if the former account in any manner for the latter; or, which gives the most historical insight into the man.

Hence, though our external history is so meagre, yet, with Shakspeare for biographer, instead of Aubrey and Rowe, we have really the information which is material, that which describes character and fortune, that which, if we were about to meet the man and deal with him, would most import us to know. We have his recorded convictions on those questions which knock for answer at every heart,—on life and death, on love, on wealth and poverty, on the prizes of life, and the ways whereby we come at them; on the characters of men, and the influences, occult and open, which affect their fortunes; and on those mysterious and demoniacal powers which defy our science, and which yet interweave their malice and their gift in our brightest hours. Who ever read the volume of the Sonnets, without finding that the poet had there revealed, under masks that are no masks to the intelligent, the lore of friendship and of love; the confusion of sentiments in the most susceptible, and, at the same time, the most intellectual of men? What trait of his private mind has he hidden in his dramas? One can discern, in his ample pictures of the gentleman and the king, what forms and humanities pleased him; his delight in troops of friends, in large hospitality, in cheerful giving. Let Timon, let Warwick, let Antonio the merchant, answer for his great heart. So far from Shakspeare's being the least known, he is the one person, in all modern history, known to us. What point of morals, of manners, of economy, of philosophy, of religion, of taste, of the conduct of life, has he not settled? What mystery has he not signified his knowledge of? What office, or function, or district of man's work, has he not remembered? What king has he not taught state, as Talma taught Napoleon? What maiden has not found him finer than her delicacy? What lover has he not outloved? What sage has he not outseen? What gentleman has he not instructed in the rudeness of his behavior?

Some able and appreciating critics think no criticism on Shakspeare valuable, that does not rest purely on the dramatic merit; that he is falsely judged as poet and philosopher. I think as highly as these critics of his dramatic merit, but still think it secondary. He was a full man, who liked to talk; a brain exhaling thoughts and images, which, seeking vent, found the drama next at hand. Had he been less, we should have had to consider how well he filled his place, how good a dramatist he was,—and he is the best in the world. But it turns out, that what he has to say is of that weight, as to withdraw some attention from the vehicle; and he is like some saint whose history is to be rendered into all languages, into verse and prose, into songs and pictures, and cut up into proverbs; so that the occasion which gave the saint's meaning the form of a conversation, or of a prayer, or of a code of laws, is immaterial, compared with the universality of its application. So it fares with the wise Shakspeare and his book of life. He wrote the airs for all our modern music: he wrote the text of modern life; the text of manners: he drew the man of England and Europe; the father of the man in America: he drew the man, and described the day, and what is done in it: he read the hearts of men and women, their probity, and their second thought, and wiles; the wiles of innocence, and the transitions by which virtues and vices slide into their contraries: he could divide the mother's part from the father's part in the face of the child, or draw the fine demarcations of freedom and of fate: he knew the laws of repression which make the police of nature: and all the sweets and all the terrors of human lot lay in his mind as truly but as softly as the landscape lies on the eye. And the importance of this wisdom of life sinks the form, as of Drama or Epic, out of notice. 'Tis like making a question concerning the paper on which a king's message is written.

Shakspeare is as much out of the category of eminent authors, as he is out of the crowd. He is inconceivably wise; the others, conceivably. A good reader can, in a sort, nestle into Plato's brain, and think from thence; but not into Shakspeare's. We are still out of doors. For executive faculty, for creation, Shakspeare is unique. No man can imagine it better. He was the farthest reach of subtlety compatible with an individual self,—the subtilest of authors, and only just within the possibility of authorship. With this wisdom of life, is the equal endowment of imaginative and of lyric power. He clothed the creatures of his legend with form and sentiments, as if they were people who had lived under his roof; and few real men have left such distinct characters as these fictions. And they spoke in language as sweet as it was fit. Yet his talents never seduced him into an ostentation, nor did he harp on one string. An omnipresent humanity coördinates all his faculties. Give a man of talents a story to tell, and his partiality will presently appear. He has certain observations, opinions, topics, which have some accidental prominence, and which he disposes all to exhibit. He crams this part, and starves that other part, consulting not the fitness of the thing, but his fitness and strength. But Shakspeare has no peculiarity, no importunate topic; but all is duly given; no veins, no curiosities: no cow-painter, no bird-fancier, no mannerist is he: he has no discoverable egotism: the great he tells greatly; the small, subordinately. He is wise without emphasis or assertion; he is strong, as nature is strong, who lifts the land into mountain slopes without effort, and by the same rule as she floats a bubble in the air, and likes as well to do the one as the other. This makes that equality of power in farce, tragedy, narrative, and love-songs; a merit so incessant, that each reader is incredulous of the perception of other readers.

This power of expression, or of transferring the inmost truth of things into music and verse, makes him the type of the poet, and has added a new problem to metaphysics. This is that which throws him into natural history, as a main production of the globe, and as announcing new eras and ameliorations. Things were mirrored in his poetry without loss or blur: he could paint the fine with precision, the great with compass; the tragic and the comic indifferently, and without any distortion or favor. He carried his powerful execution into minute details, to a hair point; finishes an eyelash or a dimple as firmly as he draws a mountain; and yet these, like nature's, will bear the scrutiny of the solar microscope.

In short, he is the chief example to prove that more or less of production, more or fewer pictures, is a thing indifferent. He had the power to make one picture. Daguerre learned how to let one flower etch its image on his plate of iodine; and then proceeds at leisure to etch a million. There are always objects; but there was never representation. Here is perfect representation, at last; and now let the world of figures sit for their portraits. No recipe can be given for the making of a Shakspeare; but the possibility of the translation of things into song in demonstrated.

His lyric power lies in the genius of the piece. The sonnets, though their excellence is lost in the splendor of the dramas, are as inimitable as they: and it is not a merit of lines, but a total merit of the piece; like the tone of voice of some incomparable person, so is this a speech of poetic beings, and any clause as unproducible now as a whole poem.

Though the speeches in the plays, and single lines, have a beauty which tempts the ear to pause on them for their euphuism, yet the sentence is so loaded with meaning, and so linked with its foregoers and followers, that the logician is satisfied. His means are as admirable as his ends; every subordinate invention, by which he helps himself to connect some irreconcilable opposites, is a poem too. He is not reduced to dismount and walk, because his horses are running off with him in some distant direction: he always rides.

The finest poetry was first experience: but the thought has suffered a transformation since it was an experience. Cultivated men often attain a good degree of skill in writing verses; but it is easy

to read, through their poems, their personal history: any one acquainted with parties can name every figure: this is Andrew, and
that is Rachel. The sense thus remains prosaic. It is a caterpillar
with wings, and not yet a butterfly. In the poet's mind, the fact
has gone quite over into the new element of thought, and has lost
all that is exuvial. This generosity abides with Shakspeare. We say,
from the truth and closeness of his pictures, that he knows the
lesson by heart. Yet there is not a trace of egotism.

One more royal trait properly belongs to the poet. I mean his
cheerfulness, without which no man can be a poet,—for beauty is
his aim. He loves virtue, not for its obligation, but for its grace: he
delights in the world, in man, in woman, for the lovely light that
sparkles from them. Beauty, the spirit of joy and hilarity, he sheds
over the universe. Epicurus relates, that poetry hath such charms
that a lover might forsake his mistress to partake of them. And
the true bards have been noted for their firm and cheerful temper.
Homer lies in sunshine; Chaucer is glad and erect; and Saadi says,
"It was rumored abroad that I was penitent; but what had I to
do with repentance?" Not less sovereign and cheerful,—much
more sovereign and cheerful, is the tone of Shakspeare. His name
suggests joy and emancipation to the heart of men. If he should
appear in any company of human souls, who would not march in
his troop? He touches nothing that does not borrow health and
longevity from his festal style.

And now, how stands the account of man with this bard and benefactor, when in solitude, shutting our ears to the reverberations
of his fame, we seek to strike the balance? Solitude has austere
lessons; it can teach us to spare both heroes and poets; and it
weighs Shakspeare also, and finds him to share the halfness and
imperfection of humanity.

Shakspeare, Homer, Dante, Chaucer, saw the splendor of
meaning that plays over the visible world; knew that a tree had
another use than for apples, and corn another than for meal, and
the ball of the earth, than for tillage and roads: that these things
bore a second and finer harvest to the mind, being emblems of its

thoughts, and conveying in all their natural history a certain mute commentary on human life. Shakspeare employed them as colors to compose his picture. He rested in their beauty; and never took the step which seemed inevitable to such genius, namely, to explore the virtue which resides in these symbols, and imparts this power,—what is that which they themselves say? He converted the elements, which waited on his command, into entertainments. He was master of the revels to mankind. Is it not as if one should have, through majestic powers of science, the comets given into his hand, or the planets and their moons, and should draw them from their orbits to glare with the municipal fireworks on a holiday night, and advertise in all towns, "very superior pyrotechny this evening!" Are the agents of nature, and the power to understand them, worth no more than a street serenade, or the breath of a cigar? One remembers again the trumpet-text in the Koran,— "The heavens and the earth, and all that is between them, think ye we have created them in jest?" As long as the question is of talent and mental power, the world of men has not his equal to show. But when the question is to life, and its materials, and its auxiliaries, how does he profit me? What does it signify? It is but a Twelfth Night, or Midsummer-Night's Dream, or a Winter Evening's Tale: what signifies another picture more or less? The Egyptian verdict of the Shakspeare Societies comes to mind, that he was a jovial actor and manager. I can not marry this fact to his verse. Other admirable men have led lives in some sort of keeping with their thought; but this man, in wide contrast. Had he been less, had he reached only the common measure of great authors, of Bacon, Milton, Tasso, Cervantes, we might leave the fact in the twilight of human fate: but, that this man of men, he who gave to the science of mind a new and larger subject than had ever existed, and planted the standard of humanity some furlongs forward into Chaos,—that he should not be wise for himself,—it must even go into the world's history, that the best poet led an obscure and profane life, using his genius for the public amusement.

Well, other men, priest and prophet, Israelite, German, and Swede, beheld the same objects: they also saw through them that which was contained. And to what purpose? The beauty straight-way vanished; they read commandments, all-excluding mountainous duty; an obligation, a sadness, as of piled mountains, fell on them, and life became ghastly, joyless, a pilgrim's progress, a probation, beleaguered round with doleful histories of Adam's fall and curse, behind us; with doomsdays and purgatorial and penal fires before us; and the heart of the seer and the heart of the listener sank in them.

It must be conceded that these are half-views of half-men. The world still wants its poet-priest, a reconciler, who shall not trifle with Shakspeare the player, nor shall grope in graves with Swedenborg the mourner; but who shall see, speak, and act, with equal inspiration. For knowledge will brighten the sunshine; right is more beautiful than private affection; and love is compatible with universal wisdom.

(1850)

Herman Melville

(1809–1891)

Hawthorne and His Mosses

Melville most likely wrote "Hawthorne and His Mosses" after visiting Nathaniel Hawthorne in Vermont in the summer of 1850; this review of *Mosses from an Old Manse* was published shortly thereafter, and anonymously, in the *Literary World*. Melville, while a native New Yorker, adopts the narrative persona of a "Virginian" in this essay and addresses an increasingly sensitive nationalist question: how was an American writer to rival Shakespeare? Melville is clearly thinking as much about his own literary struggles and promise as he is of Hawthorne's when he concludes that "Shakespeares are this day being born on the banks of the Ohio." He published this review while in the midst of writing his greatest work, *Moby-Dick*, a novel deeply indebted to Shakespeare, especially to the playwright's dark and tragic vision. His engagement with Shakespeare is confirmed in the nearly five hundred passages Melville marked in the edition of Shakespeare's works that he had recently acquired and was deeply immersed in at this time.

❧

BY A VIRGINIAN SPENDING JULY IN VERMONT

A PAPERED chamber in a fine old farm-house—a mile from any other dwelling, and dipped to the eaves in foliage—surrounded by mountains, old woods, and Indian ponds,—this, surely, is the place to write of Hawthorne. Some charm is in this northern air, for love and duty seem both impelling to the task. A man of a deep and noble nature has seized me in this seclusion. His wild, witch voice rings through me; or, in softer cadences, I seem to hear it in the songs of the hill-side birds, that sing in the larch trees at my window.

Would that all excellent books were foundlings, without father or mother, that so it might be, we could glorify them, without including their ostensible authors. Nor would any true man take exception to this;—least of all, he who writes,—"When the Artist rises high enough to achieve the Beautiful, the symbol by which he makes it perceptible to mortal senses becomes of little value in his eyes, while his spirit possesses itself in the enjoyment of the reality."

But more than this. I know not what would be the right name to put on the title-page of an excellent book, but this I feel, that the names of all fine authors are fictitious ones, far more so than that of Junius,—simply standing, as they do, for the mystical, ever-eluding Spirit of all Beauty, which ubiquitously possesses men of genius. Purely imaginative as this fancy may appear, it nevertheless seems to receive some warranty from the fact, that on a personal interview no great author has ever come up to the idea of his reader. But that dust of which our bodies are composed, how can it fitly express the nobler intelligences among us? With reverence be it spoken, that not even in the case of one deemed more than man, not even in our Saviour, did his visible frame betoken anything of the augustness of the nature within. Else, how could those Jewish eyewitnesses fail to see heaven in his glance.

It is curious, how a man may travel along a country road, and yet miss the grandest, or sweetest of prospects, by reason of an intervening hedge, so like all other hedges, as in no way to hint of the wide landscape beyond. So has it been with me concerning the enchanting landscape in the soul of this Hawthorne, this most excellent Man of Mosses. His "Old Manse" has been written now four years, but I never read it till a day or two since. I had seen it in the book-stores—heard of it often—even had it recommended to me by a tasteful friend, as a rare, quiet book, perhaps too deserving of popularity to be popular. But there are so many books called "excellent," and so much unpopular merit, that amid the thick stir of other things, the hint of my tasteful friend was disregarded; and for four years the Mosses on the old Manse never refreshed me with their perennial green. It may be, however, that all this while, the book, like wine, was only improving in flavor and body. At any rate, it so chanced that this long procrastination eventuated in a happy result. At breakfast the other day, a mountain girl, a cousin of mine, who for the last two weeks has every morning helped me to strawberries and raspberries,—which, like the roses and pearls in the fairy-tale, seemed to fall into the saucer from those strawberry-beds her cheeks,—this delightful creature, this charming Cherry says to me—"I see you spend your mornings in the hay-mow; and yesterday I found there 'Dwight's Travels in New England'. Now I have something far better than that,—something more congenial to our summer on these hills. Take these raspberries, and then I will give you some moss."—"Moss!" said I.—"Yes, and you must take it to the barn with you, and good-bye to 'Dwight'".

With that she left me, and soon returned with a volume, verdantly bound, and garnished with a curious frontispiece in green,—nothing less, than a fragment of real moss cunningly pressed to a fly-leaf.—"Why this," said I spilling my raspberries, "this is the 'Mosses from an Old Manse'". "Yes" said cousin Cherry "yes, it is that flowery Hawthorne."—"Hawthorne and Mosses" said I "no more: it is morning: it is July in the country: and I am off for the barn".

Stretched on that new mown clover, the hill-side breeze blowing over me through the wide barn door, and soothed by the hum of the bees in the meadows around, how magically stole over me this Mossy Man! and how amply, how bountifully, did he redeem that delicious promise to his guests in the Old Manse, of whom it is written—"Others could give them pleasure, or amusement, or instruction—these could be picked up anywhere—but it was for me to give them rest. Rest, in a life of trouble! What better could be done for weary and world-worn spirits? what better could be done for anybody, who came within our magic circle, than to throw the spell of a magic spirit over him?"—So all that day, half-buried in the new clover, I watched this Hawthorne's "Assyrian dawn, and Paphian sunset and moonrise, from the summit of our Eastern Hill."

The soft ravishments of the man spun me round about in a web of dreams, and when the book was closed, when the spell was over, this wizard "dismissed me with but misty reminiscences, as if I had been dreaming of him".

What a mild moonlight of contemplative humor bathes that Old Manse!—the rich and rare distilment of a spicy and slowly-oozing heart. No rollicking rudeness, no gross fun fed on fat dinners, and bred in the lees of wine,—but a humor so spiritually gentle, so high, so deep, and yet so richly relishable, that it were hardly inappropriate in an angel. It is the very religion of mirth; for nothing so human but it may be advanced to that. The orchard of the Old Manse seems the visible type of the fine mind that has described it. Those twisted, and contorted old trees, "that stretch out their crooked branches, and take such hold of the imagination, that we remember them as humorists, and odd-fellows." And then, as surrounded by these grotesque forms, and hushed in the noon-day repose of this Hawthorne's spell, how aptly might the still fall of his ruddy thoughts into your soul be symbolized by "the thump of a great apple, in the stillest afternoon, falling without a breath of wind, from the mere necessity of perfect ripeness"! For no less ripe than ruddy are the apples of the thoughts and fancies in this sweet Man of Mosses.

"Buds and Bird-voices"—What a delicious thing is that!— "Will the world ever be so decayed, that Spring may not renew its greenness?"—And the "Fire-Worship". Was ever the hearth so glorified into an altar before? The mere title of that piece is better than any common work in fifty folio volumes. How exquisite is this:—"Nor did it lessen the charm of his soft, familiar courtesy and helpfulness, that the mighty spirit, were opportunity offered him, would run riot through the peaceful house, wrap its inmates in his terrible embrace, and leave nothing of them save their whitened bones. This possibility of mad destruction only made his domestic kindness the more beautiful and touching. It was so sweet of him, being endowed with such power, to dwell, day after day, and one long, lonesome night after another, on the dusky hearth, only now and then betraying his wild nature, by thrusting his red tongue out of the chimney-top! True, he had done much mischief in the world, and was pretty certain to do more, but his warm heart atoned for all. He was kindly to the race of man."

But he has still other apples, not quite so ruddy, though full as ripe;—apples, that have been left to wither on the tree, after the pleasant autumn gathering is past. The sketch of "The Old Apple Dealer" is conceived in the subtlest spirit of sadness; he whose "subdued and nerveless boyhood prefigured his abortive prime, which, likewise, contained within itself the prophecy and image of his lean and torpid age". Such touches as are in this piece can not proceed from any common heart. They argue such a depth of tenderness, such a boundless sympathy with all forms of being, such an omnipresent love, that we must needs say, that this Hawthorne is here almost alone in his generation,—at least, in the artistic manifestation of these things. Still more. Such touches as these,—and many, very many similar ones, all through his chapters—furnish clews, whereby we enter a little way into the intricate, profound heart where they originated. And we see, that suffering, some time or other and in some shape or other,—this only can enable any man to depict it in others. All over him, Hawthorne's melancholy rests like an Indian Summer, which though bathing a whole country in one softness, still reveals the distinctive hue of every towering hill, and each far-winding vale.

But it is the least part of genius that attracts admiration. Where Hawthorne is known, he seems to be deemed a pleasant writer, with a pleasant style,—a sequestered, harmless man, from whom any deep and weighty thing would hardly be anticipated:—a man who means no meanings. But there is no man, in whom humor and love, like mountain peaks, soar to such a rapt height, as to receive the irradiations of the upper skies;—there is no man in whom humor and love are developed in that high form called genius; no such man can exist without also possessing, as the indispensable complement of these, a great, deep intellect, which drops down into the universe like a plummet. Or, love and humor are only the eyes, through which such an intellect views this world. The great beauty in such a mind is but the product of its strength. What, to all readers, can be more charming than the piece entitled

"Monsieur du Miroir"; and to a reader at all capable of fully fathoming it, what, at the same time, can possess more mystical depth of meaning?—Yes, there he sits, and looks at me,—this "shape of mystery", this "identical Monsieur du Miroir".—"Methinks I should tremble now, were his wizard power of gliding through all impediments in search of me, to place him suddenly before my eyes".

How profound, nay appalling, is the moral evolved by the "Earth's Holocaust"; where—beginning with the hollow follies and affectations of the world,—all vanities and empty theories and forms, are, one after another, and by an admirably graduated, growing comprehensiveness, thrown into the allegorical fire, till, at length, nothing is left but the all-engendering heart of man; which remaining still unconsumed, the great conflagration is nought.

Of a piece with this, is the "Intelligence Office", a wondrous symbolizing of the secret workings in men's souls. There are other sketches, still more charged with ponderous import.

"The Christmas Banquet", and "The Bosom Serpent" would be fine subjects for a curious and elaborate analysis, touching the conjectural parts of the mind that produced them. For spite of all the Indian-summer sunlight on the hither side of Hawthorne's soul, the other side—like the dark half of the physical sphere—is shrouded in a blackness, ten times black. But this darkness but gives more effect to the ever-moving dawn, that forever advances through it, and circumnavigates his world. Whether Hawthorne has simply availed himself of this mystical blackness as a means to the wondrous effects he makes it to produce in his lights and shades; or whether there really lurks in him, perhaps unknown to himself, a touch of Puritanic gloom,—this, I cannot altogether tell. Certain it is, however, that this great power of blackness in him derives its force from its appeals to that Calvinistic sense of Innate Depravity and Original Sin, from whose visitations, in some shape or other, no deeply thinking mind is always and wholly free. For, in certain moods, no man can weigh this world, without throwing in something, somehow like Original Sin, to strike the uneven balance. At all events, perhaps no writer has ever wielded this terrific thought with greater terror than this same harmless Hawthorne. Still more: this black conceit pervades him, through and through. You may be witched by his sunlight,—transported by the bright gildings in the skies he builds over you;—but there is the blackness of darkness beyond; and even his bright gildings but fringe, and play upon the edges of thunder-clouds.—In one word, the world is mistaken in this Nathaniel Hawthorne. He himself must often have smiled at its absurd misconception of him. He is immeasurably deeper than the plummet of the mere critic. For it is not the brain that can test such a man; it is only the heart. You cannot come to know greatness by inspecting it; there is no glimpse to be caught of it, except by intuition; you need not ring it, you but touch it, and you find it is gold.

Now it is that blackness in Hawthorne, of which I have spoken, that so fixes and fascinates me. It may be, nevertheless, that it is too largely developed in him. Perhaps he does not give us a ray of his light for every shade of his dark. But however this may be, this blackness it is that furnishes the infinite obscure of his back-ground,— that back-ground, against which Shakespeare plays his grandest conceits, the things that have made for Shakespeare his loftiest, but most circumscribed renown, as the profoundest of thinkers. For by philosophers Shakespeare is not adored as the great man of tragedy and comedy.—"Off with his head! so much for Bucking-ham!" this sort of rant, interlined by another hand, brings down the house,—those mistaken souls, who dream of Shakespeare as a mere man of Richard-the-Third humps, and Macbeth daggers. But it is those deep far-away things in him; those occasional flashings-forth of the intuitive Truth in him; those short, quick probings at the very axis of reality;—these are the things that make Shakespeare, Shakespeare. Through the mouths of the dark characters of Hamlet, Timon, Lear, and Iago, he craftily says, or sometimes insinuates the things, which we feel to be so terrifically true, that it were all but madness for any good man, in his own proper character, to utter, or even hint of them. Tormented into desperation, Lear the frantic King tears off the mask, and speaks the sane madness of vital truth. But, as I before said, it is the least part of genius that attracts admiration. And so, much of the blind, unbridled admiration that has been heaped upon Shakespeare, has been lavished upon the least part of him. And few of his endless commentators and critics seem to have remembered, or even perceived, that the immediate products of a great mind are not so great, as that undeveloped, (and sometimes undevelopable) yet dimly-discernable greatness, to which these immediate products are but the infallible indices. In Shakespeare's tomb lies infinitely more than Shakspeare ever wrote. And if I magnify Shakespeare, it is not so much for what he did do, as for what he did not do, or refrained from doing. For in this world of lies, Truth is forced to fly like a scared white doe in the woodlands; and only by cunning glimpses will she reveal herself, as in Shakespeare and other masters of the great Art of Telling the Truth,—even though it be covertly, and by snatches.

But if this view of the all-popular Shakespeare be seldom taken by his readers, and if very few who extol him, have ever read him deeply, or, perhaps, only have seen him on the tricky stage, (which alone made, and is still making him his mere mob renown)—if few men have time, or patience, or palate, for the spiritual truth as it is in that great genius;—it is, then, no matter of surprise that in a contemporaneous age, Nathaniel Hawthorne is a man, as yet, almost utterly mistaken among men. Here and there, in some quiet arm-chair in the noisy town, or some deep nook among the noiseless mountains, he may be appreciated for something of what he is. But unlike Shakespeare, who was forced to the contrary course by circumstances, Hawthorne (either from simple disinclination, or else from inaptitude) refrains from all the popularizing noise and show of broad farce, and blood-besmeared tragedy; content with the still, rich utterances of a great intellect in repose, and which sends few thoughts into circulation, except they be arterialized at his large warm lungs, and expanded in his honest heart.

Nor need you fix upon that blackness in him, if it suit you not. Nor, indeed, will all readers discern it, for it is, mostly, insinuated to those who may best understand it, and account for it; it is not obtruded upon every one alike.

Some may start to read of Shakespeare and Hawthorne on the same page. They may say, that if an illustration were needed, a lesser light might have sufficed to elucidate this Hawthorne, this small man of yesterday. But I am not, willingly, one of those, who, as touching Shakespeare at least, exemplify the maxim of Rochefoucault, that "we exalt the reputation of some, in order to depress that of others";—who, to teach all noble-souled aspirants that there is no hope for them, pronounce Shakespeare absolutely unapproachable. But Shakespeare has been approached. There are minds that have gone as far as Shakespeare into the universe. And hardly a mortal man, who, at some time or other, has not felt as great thoughts in him as any you will find in Hamlet. We must not inferentially malign mankind for the sake of any one man, whoever he may be. This is too cheap a purchase of contentment for conscious mediocrity to make. Besides, this absolute and un-conditional adoration of Shakespeare has grown to be a part of our Anglo Saxon superstitions. The Thirty Nine articles are now Forty. Intolerance has come to exist in this matter. You must be-lieve in Shakespeare's unapproachability, or quit the country. But what sort of a belief is this for an American, a man who is bound to carry republican progressiveness into Literature, as well as into Life? Believe me, my friends, that Shakespeares are this day being born on the banks of the Ohio. And the day will come, when you shall say who reads a book by an Englishman that is a modern? The great mistake seems to be, that even with those Americans who look forward to the coming of a great literary genius among us, they somehow fancy he will come in the costume of Queen Elizabeth's day,—be a writer of dramas founded upon old English history, or the tales of Boccaccio. Whereas, great geniuses are parts of the times; they themselves are the times; and possess a correspondent coloring. It is of a piece with the Jews, who while their Shiloh was meekly walking in their streets, were still praying for his magnificent coming; looking for him in a chariot, who was already among them on an ass. Nor must we forget, that, in his own lifetime, Shakespeare was not Shakespeare, but only Master William Shakespeare of the shrewd, thriving, business firm of Condell, Shakespeare & Co., proprietors of the Globe Theatre in London; and by a courtly author, of the name of Greene, was hooted at, as an "upstart crow" beautified "with other birds' feathers". For, mark it well, imitation is often the first charge brought against real originality. Why this is so, there is not space to set forth here. You must have plenty of sea-room to tell the Truth in; especially, when it seems to have an aspect of newness, as America did in 1492, though it was then just as old, and perhaps older than Asia, only those sagacious philosophers, the common sailors, had never seen it before; swearing it was all water and moonshine there.

Now, I do not say that Nathaniel of Salem is a greater than William of Avon, or as great. But the difference between the two men is by no means immeasurable. Not a very great deal more, and Nathaniel were verily William.

This, too, I mean, that if Shakespeare has not been equalled, he is sure to be surpassed, and surpassed by an American born now or yet to be born. For it will never do for us who in most other things out-do as well as out-brag the world, it will not do for us to fold our hands and say, In the highest department advance there is none. Nor will it at all do to say, that the world is getting grey and grizzled now, and has lost that fresh charm which she wore of old, and by virtue of which the great poets of past times made themselves what we esteem them to be. Not so. The world is as young today, as when it was created; and this Vermont morning dew is as wet to my feet, as Eden's dew to Adam's. Nor has Nature been all over ransacked by our progenitors, so that no new charms and mysteries remain for this latter generation to find. Far from it. The trillionth part has not yet been said; and all that has been said, but multiplies the avenues to what remains to be said. It is not so much paucity, as superabundance of material that seems to incapacitate modern authors.

Let America then prize and cherish her writers; yea, let her glorify them. They are not so many in number, as to exhaust her good-will. And while she has good kith and kin of her own, to take to her bosom, let her not lavish her embraces upon the household of an alien. For believe it or not England, after all, is, in many things, an alien to us. China has more bowels of real love for us than she. But even were there no Hawthorne, no Emerson, no Whittier, no Irving, no Bryant, no Dana, no Cooper, no Willis (not the author of the "Dashes," but the author of the "Belfry Pigeon")—were there none of these, and others of like calibre among us, nevertheless, let America first praise mediocrity even, in her own children, before she praises (for everywhere, merit demands acknowledgment from every one) the best excellence in the children of any other land. Let her own authors, I say, have the priority of appreciation. I was much pleased with a hot-headed Carolina cousin of mine, who once said,—"If there were no other American to stand by, in Literature,—why, then, I would stand by Pop Emmons and his 'Fredoniad,' and till a better epic came along, swear it was not very far behind the Iliad." Take away the words, and in spirit he was sound.

Not that American genius needs patronage in order to expand. For that explosive sort of stuff will expand though screwed up in a vice, and burst it, though it were triple steel. It is for the nation's sake, and not for her authors' sake, that I would have America be heedful of the increasing greatness among her writers. For how great the shame, if other nations should be before her, in crowning her heroes of the pen. But this is almost the case now. American authors have received more just and discriminating praise (however loftily and ridiculously given, in certain cases) even from some Englishmen, than from their own countrymen. There are hardly five critics in America; and several of them are asleep. As for patronage, it is the American author who now patronizes his country, and not his country him. And if at times some among them appeal to the people for more recognition, it is not always with selfish motives, but patriotic ones.

It is true, that but few of them as yet have evinced that decided originality which merits great praise. But that graceful writer, who perhaps of all Americans has received the most plaudits from his own country for his productions,—that very popular and amiable writer, however good, and self-reliant in many things, perhaps owes his chief reputation to the self-acknowledged imitation of a foreign model, and to the studied avoidance of all topics but smooth ones. But it is better to fail in originality, than to succeed in imitation. He who has never failed somewhere, that man can not be great. Failure is the true test of greatness. And if it be said, that continual success is a proof that a man wisely knows his powers,—it is only to be added, that, in that case, he knows them to be small. Let us believe it, then, once for all, that there is no hope for us in these smooth pleasing writers that know their powers. Without malice, but to speak the plain fact, they but furnish an appendix to Goldsmith, and other English authors. And we want no American Goldsmiths; nay, we want no American Miltons. It were the vilest thing you could say of a true American author, that he were an American Tompkins. Call him an American, and have done; for you can not say a nobler thing of him.—But it is not meant that all American writers should studiously cleave to nationality in their writings; only this, no American writer should write like an Englishman, or a Frenchman; let him write like a man, for then he will be sure to write like an American. Let us away with this Bostonian leaven of literary flunkeyism towards England. If either must play the flunkey in this thing, let England do it, not us. And the time is not far off when circumstances may force her to it. While we are rapidly preparing for that political supremacy among the nations, which prophetically awaits us at the close of the present century; in a literary point of view, we are deplorably unprepared for it; and we seem studious to remain so. Hitherto, reasons might have existed why this should be; but no good reason exists now. And all that is requisite to amendment in this matter, is simply this: that, while freely acknowledging all excellence, everywhere, we should refrain from unduly lauding foreign writers and, at the same time, duly recognize the meritorious writers that are our own;—those writers, who breathe that unshackled, democratic spirit of Christianity in all things, which now takes the practical lead in this world, though at the same time led by ourselves—us Americans. Let us boldly contemn all imitation, though it comes to us graceful and fragrant as the morning; and foster all originality, though, at first, it be crabbed and ugly as our own pine knots. And if any of our authors fail, or seem to fail, then, in the words of my enthusiastic Carolina cousin, let us clap him on the shoulder, and back him against all Europe for his second round. The truth is, that in our point of view, this matter of a national literature has come to such a pass with us, that in some sense we must turn bullies, else the day is lost, or superiority so far beyond us, that we can hardly say it will ever be ours.

And now, my countrymen, as an excellent author, of your own flesh and blood,—an unimitating, and, perhaps, in his way, an inimitable man—whom better can I commend to you, in the first place, than Nathaniel Hawthorne. He is one of the new, and far better generation of your writers. The smell of your beeches and hemlocks is upon him; your own broad praries are in his soul; and if you travel away inland into his deep and noble nature, you will hear the far roar of his Niagara. Give not over to future generations the glad duty of acknowledging him for what he is. Take that joy to your self, in your own generation; and so shall he feel those grateful impulses in him, that may possibly prompt him to the full flower of some still greater achievement in your eyes. And by confessing him, you thereby confess others; you brace the whole brotherhood. For genius, all over the world, stands hand in hand, and one shock of recognition runs the whole circle round.

In treating of Hawthorne, or rather of Hawthorne in his writings (for I never saw the man; and in the chances of a quiet plantation life, remote from his haunts, perhaps never shall) in treating of his works, I say, I have thus far omitted all mention of his "Twice Told Tales", and "Scarlet Letter". Both are excellent; but full of such manifold, strange and diffusive beauties, that time would all but fail me, to point the half of them out. But there are things in those two books, which, had they been written in England a century ago, Nathaniel Hawthorne had utterly displaced many of the bright names we now revere on authority. But

I am content to leave Hawthorne to himself, and to the infallible finding of posterity; and however great may be the praise I have bestowed upon him, I feel, that in so doing, I have more served and honored myself, than him. For, at bottom, great excellence is praise enough to itself; but the feeling of a sincere and appreciative love and admiration towards it, this is relieved by utterance; and warm, honest praise ever leaves a pleasant flavor in the mouth; and it is an honorable thing to confess to what is honorable in others.

But I cannot leave my subject yet. No man can read a fine author, and relish him to his very bones, while he reads, without subsequently fancying to himself some ideal image of the man and his mind. And if you rightly look for it, you will almost always find that the author himself has somewhere furnished you with his own picture.—For poets (whether in prose or verse), being painters of Nature, are like their brethren of the pencil, the true portrait-painters, who, in the multitude of likenesses to be sketched, do not invariably omit their own; and in all high instances, they paint them without any vanity, though, at times, with a lurking something, that would take several pages to properly define.

I submit it, then, to those best acquainted with the man personally, whether the following is not Nathaniel Hawthorne;—and to himself, whether something involved in it does not express the temper of his mind,—that lasting temper of all true, candid men—a seeker, not a finder yet:—

> "A man now entered, in neglected attire, with the aspect of a thinker, but somewhat too rough-hewn and brawny for a scholar. His face was full of sturdy vigor, with some finer and keener attribute beneath; though harsh at first, it was tempered with the glow of a large, warm heart, which had force enough to heat his powerful intellect through and through. He advanced to the Intelligencer, and looked at him with a glance of such stern sincerity, that perhaps few secrets were beyond its scope.
>
> "'I seek for Truth', said he."

*   *   *

Twenty four hours have elapsed since writing the foregoing. I have just returned from the hay mow, charged more and more with love and admiration of Hawthorne. For I have just been gleaning through the Mosses, picking up many things here and there that had previously escaped me. And I found that but to glean after this man, is better than to be in at the harvest of others. To be frank (though, perhaps, rather foolish) notwithstanding what I wrote yesterday of these Mosses, I had not then culled them all; but had, nevertheless, been sufficiently sensible of the subtle essence, in them, as to write as I did. To what infinite height of loving wonder and admiration I may yet be borne, when by repeatedly banqueting on these Mosses, I shall have thoroughly incorporated their whole stuff into my being,—that, I can not tell. But already I feel that this Hawthorne has dropped germinous seeds into my soul. He expands and deepens down, the more I contemplate him; and further, and further, shoots his strong New-England roots into the hot soil of my Southern soul.

By careful reference to the "Table of Contents", I now find, that I have gone through all the sketches; but that when I yesterday wrote, I had not at all read two particular pieces, to which I now desire to call special attention,—"A Select Party", and "Young Goodman Brown". Here, be it said to all those whom this poor fugitive scrawl of mine may tempt to the perusal of the "Mosses," that they must on no account suffer themselves to be trifled with, disappointed, or deceived by the triviality of many of the titles to these Sketches. For in more than one instance, the title utterly belies the piece. It is as if rustic demijohns containing the very best and costliest of Falernian and Tokay, were labelled "Cider", "Perry," and "Elderberry wine". The truth seems to be, that like many other geniuses, this Man of Mosses takes great delight in hoodwinking the world,—at least, with respect to himself. Personally, I doubt not, that he rather prefers to be generally esteemed but a so-so sort of author; being willing to reserve the thorough and acute appreciation of what he is, to that party most qualified to judge—that is, to himself. Besides, at the bottom of their natures, men like Hawthorne, in many things, deem the plaudits of the public such strong presumptive evidence of mediocrity in the object of them, that it would in some degree render them doubtful of their own powers, did they hear much and vociferous braying concerning them in the public pastures. True, I have been braying myself (if you please to be witty enough, to have it so) but then I claim to be the first that has so brayed in this particular matter; and therefore, while pleading guilty to the charge still claim all the merit due to originality.

But with whatever motive, playful or profound, Nathaniel Hawthorne has chosen to entitle his pieces in the manner he has, it is certain, that some of them are directly calculated to deceive—egregiously deceive, the superficial skimmer of pages. To be downright and candid once more, let me cheerfully say, that two of these titles did dolefully dupe no less an eagle-eyed reader than myself; and that, too, after I had been impressed with a sense of the great depth and breadth of this American man. "Who in the name of thunder" (as the country-people say in this neighborhood) "who in the name of thunder", would anticipate any marvel in a piece entitled "Young Goodman Brown"? You would of course suppose that it was a simple little tale, intended as a supplement to "Goody Two Shoes". Whereas, it is deep as Dante; nor can you finish it, without addressing the author in his own words—"It is yours to penetrate, in every bosom, the deep mystery of sin." And with Young Goodman, too, in allegorical pursuit of his Puritan wife, you cry out in your anguish,—

> "'Faith!' shouted Goodman Brown, in a voice of agony and desperation; and the echoes of the forest mocked him, crying— 'Faith! Faith!' as if bewildered wretches were seeking her all through the wilderness."

Now this same piece, entitled "Young Goodman Brown", is one of the two that I had not all read yesterday; and I allude to it now, because it is, in itself, such a strong positive illustration of that blackness in Hawthorne, which I had assumed from the mere occasional shadows of it, as revealed in several of the other sketches. But had I previously perused "Young Goodman Brown",

I should have been at no pains to draw the conclusion, which I came to, at a time, when I was ignorant that the book contained one such direct and unqualified manifestation of it.

The other piece of the two referred to, is entitled "A Select Party", which, in my first simplicity upon originally taking hold of the book, I fancied must treat of some pumpkin-pie party in Old Salem, or some chowder party on Cape Cod. Whereas, by all the gods of Peedee! it is the sweetest and sublimest thing that has been written since Spencer wrote. Nay, there is nothing in Spencer that surpasses it, perhaps, nothing that equals it. And the test is this: read any canto in "The Faery Queen", and then read "A Select Party", and decide which pleases you the most,—that is, if you are qualified to judge. Do not be frightened at this; for when Spencer was alive, he was thought of very much as Hawthorne is now,— was generally accounted just such a "gentle" harmless man. It may be, that to common eyes, the sublimity of Hawthorne seems lost in his sweetness,—as perhaps in this same "Select Party" of his; for whom, he has builded so august a dome of sunset clouds, and served them on richer plate, than Belshazzar's when he banquetted his lords in Babylon.

But my chief business now, is to point out a particular page in this piece, having reference to an honored guest, who under the name of "The Master Genius" but in the guise of "a young man of poor attire, with no insignia of rank or acknowledged eminence", is introduced to the Man of Fancy, who is the giver of the feast. Now the page having reference to this "Master Genius", so happily expresses much of what I yesterday wrote, touching the coming of the literary Shiloh of America, that I cannot but be charmed by the coincidence; especially, when it shows such a parity of ideas, at least in this one point, between a man like Hawthorne and a man like me.

And here, let me throw out another conceit of mine touching this American Shiloh, or "Master Genius", as Hawthorne calls him. May it not be, that this commanding mind has not been, is not, and never will be, individually developed in any one man? And would it, indeed, appear so unreasonable to suppose, that this great fullness and overflowing may be, or may be destined to be, shared by a plurality of men of genius? Surely, to take the very greatest example on record, Shakespeare cannot be regarded as in himself the concretion of all the genius of his time; nor as so immeasurably beyond Marlow, Webster, Ford, Beaumont, Jonson, that those great men can be said to share none of his power? For one, I conceive that there were dramatists in Elizabeth's day, between whom and Shakespeare the distance was by no means great. Let anyone, hitherto little acquainted with those neglected old authors, for the first time read them thoroughly, or even read Charles Lamb's Specimens of them, and he will be amazed at the wondrous ability of those Anaks of men, and shocked at this renewed example of the fact, that Fortune has more to do with fame than merit,—though, without merit, lasting fame there can be none.

Nevertheless, it would argue too illy of my country were this maxim to hold good concerning Nathaniel Hawthorne, a man, who already, in some few minds, has shed "such a light, as never illuminates the earth, save when a great heart burns as the household fire of a grand intellect."

The words are his,—in the "Select Party"; and they are a magnificent setting to a coincident sentiment of my own, but ramblingly expressed yesterday, in reference to himself. Gainsay it who will, as I now write, I am Posterity speaking by proxy—and after times will make it more than good, when I declare—that the American, who up to the present day, has evinced, in Literature, the largest brain with the largest heart, that man is Nathaniel Hawthorne. Moreover, that whatever Nathaniel Hawthorne may hereafter write, "The Mosses from an Old Manse" will be ultimately accounted his masterpiece. For there is a sure, though a secret sign in some works which prove the culmination of the powers (only the developable ones, however) that produced them. But I am by no means desirous of the glory of a prophet. I pray Heaven that Hawthorne may *yet* prove me an impostor in this prediction. Especially, as I somehow cling to the strange fancy, that, in all men, hiddenly reside certain wondrous, occult properties—as in some plants and minerals—which by some happy but very rare accident (as bronze was discovered by the melting of the iron and brass in the burning of Corinth) may chance to be called forth here on earth; not entirely waiting for their better discovery in the more congenial, blessed atmosphere of heaven.

Once more—for it is hard to be finite upon an infinite subject, and all subjects are infinite. By some people, this entire scrawl of mine may be esteemed altogether unnecessary, inasmuch, "as years ago" (they may say) "we found out the rich and rare stuff in this Hawthorne, whom you now parade forth, as if only *yourself* were the discoverer of this Portuguese diamond in our Literature".— But even granting all this; and adding to it, the assumption that the books of Hawthorne have sold by the five-thousand,— what does that signify?—They should be sold by the hundred-thousand; and read by the million; and admired by every one who is capable of admiration.

(1850)

William Wells Brown
(1814–1884)

Ira Aldridge

Born into slavery in Kentucky in 1814, William Wells Brown escaped to freedom at age twenty and went on to become a leading abolitionist, historian, travel writer, and novelist (his *Clotel* was the first novel published by an African American). Brown traveled to Britain in 1849 and, after the passage of the Fugitive Slave Law the following year, which put him at risk of capture and re-enslavement, remained there writing and lecturing until 1854 (when his freedom was purchased). While there, he saw the great black actor, Ira Aldridge, play both Othello and Hamlet. Brown recalled that experience a decade later in *The Black Man: His Antecedents, His Genius, and His Achievements* (1862). Ira Aldridge, who was born and educated in New York City, left for England as a teenager to pursue opportunities denied to black actors in America. He thought it useful there to promote himself as African-born (a fabrication, along with a few other invented biographical anecdotes that appeared in Aldridge's ghostwritten *Memoir* and are repeated in Brown's sketch). Aldridge first played Othello on the London stage in 1825. Some British critics had difficulty with the idea of a black man playing Shakespeare (a reviewer for the *Times* complained that it was "utterly impossible" for Aldridge to pronounce the language correctly "owing to the shape of his lips," while one for the *Athenaeum* objected to a white Desdemona "being pawed about" onstage by a black actor). Aldridge soon established himself as a popular Shakespeare actor in Britain and on the Continent, adding to his repertory the parts of Richard III, King Lear, Macbeth, and Shylock (which, a Russian critic noted, he performed sympathetically as "an exploited, despised Jew" who was "the bearer of the sorrow and tragedy of his hunted people"). Aldridge died in 1867, shortly before he was to return to the United States and finally play Othello there.

✌

O N looking over the columns of *The Times*, one morning, I
saw it announced under the head of "Amusements," that
"Ira Aldridge, the African Roscius," was to appear in the character
of Othello, in Shakspeare's celebrated tragedy of that name, and,
having long wished to see my sable countryman, I resolved at once
to attend. Though the doors had been open but a short time when
I reached the Royal Haymarket, the theatre where the performance was to take place, the house was well filled, and among the
audience I recognized the faces of several distinguished persons
of the nobility, the most noted of whom was Sir Edward Bulwer
Lytton, the renowned novelist—his figure neat, trim, hair done up
in the latest fashion—looking as if he had just come out of a band-
box. He is a great lover of the drama, and has a private theatre at
one of his country seats, to which he often invites his friends, and
presses them into the different characters.

As the time approached for the curtain to rise, it was evident
that the house was to be "jammed." Stuart, the best Iago since the
days of Young, in company with Roderigo, came upon the stage
as soon as the green curtain went up. Iago looked the villain, and
acted it to the highest conception of the character. The scene is
changed, all eyes are turned to the right door, and thunders of
applause greet the appearance of Othello. Mr. Aldridge is of the
middle size, and appeared to be about three quarters African; has
a pleasant countenance, frame well knit, and seemed to me the
best Othello that I had ever seen. As Iago began to work upon his
feelings, the Moor's eyes flashed fire, and, further on in the play,
he looked the very demon of despair. When he seized the deceiver
by the throat, and exclaimed, "Villain! be sure thou prove my love
false: be sure of it—give me the ocular proof—or, by the worth
of my eternal soul, thou hadst better have been born a dog, Iago,
than answer my waked wrath," the audience, with one impulse,
rose to their feet amid the wildest enthusiasm. At the end of the
third act, Othello was called before the curtain, and received the
applause of the delighted multitude. I watched the countenance
and every motion of Bulwer Lytton with almost as much interest
as I did that of the Moor of Venice, and saw that none appeared

to be better pleased than he. The following evening I went to witness his Hamlet, and was surprised to find him as perfect in that as he had been in Othello; for I had been led to believe that the latter was his greatest character. The whole court of Denmark was before us; but till the words, "'Tis not alone my inky cloak, good mother," fell from the lips of Mr. Aldridge, was the general ear charmed, or the general tongue arrested. The voice was so low, and sad, and sweet, the modulation so tender, the dignity so natural, the grace so consummate, that all yielded themselves silently to the delicious enchantment. When Horatio told him that he had come to see his father's funeral, the deep melancholy that took possession of his face showed the great dramatic power of Mr. Aldridge. "I pray thee do not mock me, fellow-student," seemed to come from his inmost soul. The animation with which his countenance was lighted up, during Horatio's recital of the visits that the ghost had paid him and his companions, was beyond description. "Angels and ministers of grace defend us," as the ghost appeared in the fourth scene, sent a thrill through the whole assembly. His rendering of the "Soliloquy on Death," which Edmund Kean, Charles Kemble, and William C. Macready have reaped such unfading laurels from, was one of his best efforts. He read it infinitely better than Charles Kean, whom I had heard at the "Princess," but a few nights previous. The vigorous starts of thought, which in the midst of his personal sorrows rise with such beautiful and striking suddenness from the ever-wakeful mind of the humanitarian philosopher, are delivered with that varying emphasis that characterizes the truthful delineator, when he exclaims, "Frailty, thy name is woman!" In the second scene of the second act, when revealing to Guildenstern the melancholy which preys upon his mind, the beautiful and powerful words in which Hamlet explains his feelings are made very effective in Mr. Aldridge's rendering: "This most excellent canopy, the air, the brave o'erchanging firmament, this majestical roof fretted with golden fire. . . . What a piece of work is a man! How noble in reason! how infinite in faculties! in form and moving how express and admirable! in action how like an angel! in apprehension how like a God!" In the last scene of the second act, when Hamlet's imagination, influenced by the interview with the actors, suggests to his rich mind so many eloquent reflections, Mr. Aldridge enters fully into the spirit of the scene, warms up, and when he exclaims, "He would drown the stage with tears, and cleave the general ear with horrid speech,—make mad the guilty, and appall the free," he is very effective; and when this warmth mounts into a paroxysm of rage, and he calls the King "Bloody, bawdy villain! Remorseless, treacherous, lecherous, kindless villain!" he sweeps the audience with him, and brings down deserved applause. The fervent soul and restless imagination, which are ever stirring at the bottom of the fountain, and sending bright bubbles to the top, find a glowing reflection on the animated surface of Mr. Aldridge's colored face. I thought Hamlet one of his best characters, though I saw him afterwards in several others.

Mr. Aldridge is a native of Senegal, in Africa. His forefathers were princes of the Foulah tribe, whose dominions were in Senegal, on the banks of the river of that name, on the west coast of Africa. To this shore one of our early missionaries found his way, and took charge of Ira's father, Daniel Aldridge, in order to qualify him for the work of civilizing and evangelizing his countrymen. Daniel's father, the reigning prince, was more enlightened than his subjects, probably through the instruction of the missionary, and proposed that his prisoners taken in battle should be exchanged, and not, as was the custom, sold as slaves. This wish interfered with the notions and perquisites of his tribe, especially his principal chiefs; and a civil war raged among the people. During these differences, Daniel, then a promising youth, was brought to the United States by the missionary, and sent to Schenectady College to receive the advantages of a Christian education. Three days after his departure, the revolutionary storm, which was brewing, broke out openly, and the reigning prince, the advocate of humanity, was killed.

Daniel Aldridge remained in America till the death of the rebellious chief, who had heeded the conspiracy, and reigned instead of the murdered prince. During the interval, Daniel had become a minister of the gospel, and was regarded by all classes as a man of uncommon abilities. He was, however, desirous to establish himself at the head of his tribe, possess himself of his birthright, and advance the cause of Christianity among his countrymen. For this purpose he returned to his native country, taking with him a young wife, one of his own color, whom he had but just married in America. Daniel no sooner appeared among the people of his slaughtered father, than old disagreements revived, civil war broke out, the enlightened African was defeated, barely escaping from the scene of strife with his life, and for some time unable to quit the country, which was watched by numerous enemies anxious for his capture. Nine years elapsed before the proscribed family escaped to America, during the whole of which time they were concealed in the neighborhood of their foes, enduring vicissitudes and hardships that can well be imagined, but need not be described.

Ira Aldridge was born soon after his father's arrival in Senegal, and on their return to America, was intended by the latter for the church. Many a white parent has "chalked out" in vain for his son a similar calling, and the best intentions have been thwarted by an early predilection quite in an opposite direction. We can well account for the father's choice in this instance, as in keeping with his own aspirations; and we can easily imagine his disappointment upon abandoning all hope of seeing one of his blood and color following specially in the service of his great Master. The son, however, began betimes to show his early preference and ultimate passion. At school he was awarded prizes for declamation, in which he excelled; and there his curiosity was excited by what he heard of theatrical representations, which he was told *embodied* all the fine ideas *shadowed forth* in the language he read and committed to memory. It became the wish of his heart to witness one of these performances, and that wish he soon contrived to gratify, and finally he became a candidate for histrionic fame.

Notwithstanding the progress Ira had made in learning, no qualities of the mind could compensate, in the eyes of the Americans, for the dark hue of his skin. The prevailing prejudice, so strong among all classes, was against him. This induced his removal to England, where he entered at the Glasgow University, and, under Professor Sandford, obtained several premiums, and the medal for Latin composition.

On leaving college, Mr. Aldridge at once commenced preparing for the stage, and shortly after appeared in a number of Shaksperian characters, in Edinburgh, Glasgow, Manchester, and other provincial cities, and soon after appeared on the boards of Drury Lane and Covent Garden, where he was stamped the "African Roscius." The *London Weekly Times* said of him, "Mr. Ira Aldridge is a dark mulatto, with woolly hair. His features are capable of great expression, his action is unrestrained and picturesque, and his voice clear, full, and resonant. His powers of energetic declamation are very marked, and the whole of his acting appears impulsed by a current of feeling of no inconsiderable weight and vigor, yet controlled and guided in a manner that clearly shows the actor to be a person of much study and great stage ability." The *Morning Chronicle* recorded his "Shylock" as among the "finest pieces of acting that a London audience had witnessed since the days of the elder Kean."

(1862)

Nathaniel Hawthorne

(1804–1864)

Recollections of a Gifted Woman

Delia Bacon was one of the first to propose that William Shakespeare of Stratford was not the true author of the plays long attributed to him—and that the plays, written by Sir Francis Bacon and others, reflected deeply republican values. She first committed her theory to print in an essay that appeared in *Putnam's Monthly* in 1856 after Ralph Waldo Emerson, who had befriended her, persuaded its publishers to serialize her work. The following year she published a dense book, *The Philosophy of the Plays of Shakspere Unfolded*. Hawthorne first met and befriended her while serving as a United States consul in England in the late 1850s. Bacon shared with him her theories of Shakespearean authorship and he was struck by how her ideas ran "counter to the religious doctrines in which she had been educated." Though skeptical about Bacon's claims that Shakespeare didn't write his plays (and convinced, as he wrote in his journal, that "she is a monomaniac"), Hawthorne showed, in the words of Delia Bacon's nephew Theodore Bacon, an "inexhaustible patience, gentleness, and generosity" toward her, helping her see her book into print and even paying out of pocket to cover the costs of its publication. Hawthorne embellished upon a letter that Delia Bacon had sent to him in October 1856 describing her nocturnal visit to Shakespeare's grave. It formed the basis of this powerful and sympathetic portrait in which she also comes across as a character straight out of Hawthorne's Gothic fiction. This essay first appeared in the January 1863 issue of *The Atlantic Monthly*, four years after Delia Bacon went mad, then died; it was reprinted in *Our Old Home: A Series of English Sketches* in 1863.

❦

FROM Leamington to Stratford-on-Avon the distance is eight or nine miles, over a road that seemed to me most beautiful. Not that I can recall any memorable peculiarities; for the country, most of the way, is a succession of the gentlest swells

RECOLLECTIONS OF A GIFTED WOMAN

and subsidences, affording wide and far glimpses of champaign scenery, here and there, and sinking almost to a dead level as we draw near Stratford. Any landscape in New England, even the tamest, has a more striking outline, and besides would have its blue eyes open in those lakelets that we encounter almost from mile to mile at home, but of which the Old Country is utterly destitute; or it would smile in our faces through the medium of the wayside brooks that vanish under a low stone arch, on one side of the road, and sparkle out again on the other. Neither of these pretty features is often to be found in an English scene. The charm of the latter consists in the rich verdure of the fields, in the stately wayside trees and carefully kept plantations of wood, and in the old and high cultivation that has humanized the very sods by mingling so much of man's toil and care among them. To an American there is a kind of sanctity even in an English turnip-field, when he thinks how long that small square of ground has been known and recognized as a possession, transmitted from father to son, trodden often by memorable feet, and utterly redeemed from savagery by old acquaintanceship with civilized eyes. The wildest things in England are more than half tame. The trees, for instance, whether in hedge-row, park, or what they call forest, have nothing wild about them. They are never ragged; there is a certain decorous restraint in the freest outspread of their branches, though they spread wider than any self-nurturing tree; they are tall, vigorous, bulky, with a look of age-long life, and a promise of more years to come, all of which will bring them into closer kindred with the race of man. Somebody or other has known them from the sapling upward; and if they endure long enough, they grow to be traditionally observed and honored, and connected with the fortunes of old families, till, like Tennyson's Talking Oak, they babble with a thousand leafy tongues to ears that can understand them.

An American tree, however, if it could grow in fair competition with an English one of similar species, would probably be the more picturesque object of the two. The Warwickshire elm has not so beautiful a shape as those that overhang our village streets; and as for the redoubtable English oak, there is a certain

John Bullism in its figure, a compact rotundity of foliage, a lack of irregular and various outline, that make it look wonderfully like a gigantic cauliflower. Its leaf, too, is much smaller than that of most varieties of American oak; nor do I mean to doubt that the latter, with free leave to grow, reverent care and cultivation, and immunity from the axe, would live out its centuries as sturdily as its English brother, and prove far the nobler and more majestic specimen of a tree at the end of them. Still, however one's Yankee patriotism may struggle against the admission, it must be owned that the trees and other objects of an English landscape take hold of the observer by numberless minute tendrils, as it were, which, look as closely as we choose, we never find in an American scene. The parasitic growth is so luxuriant, that the trunk of the tree, so gray and dry in our climate, is better worth observing than the boughs and foliage; a verdant mossiness coats it all over so that it looks almost as green as the leaves; and often, moreover, the stately stem is clustered about, high upward, with creeping and twining shrubs, the ivy, and sometimes the mistletoe, close-clinging friends, nurtured by the moisture and never too fervid sunshine, and supporting themselves by the old tree's abundant strength. We call it a parasitical vegetation; but if the phrase imply any reproach, it is unkind to bestow it on this beautiful affection and relationship which exist in England between one order of plants and another: the strong tree being always ready to give support to the trailing shrub, lift it to the sun, and feed it out of its own heart, if it crave such food; and the shrub, on its part, repaying its foster-father with an ample luxuriance of beauty, and adding Corinthian grace to the tree's lofty strength. No bitter winter nips these tender little sympathies, no hot sun burns the life out of them; and therefore they outlast the longevity of the oak, and, if the woodman permitted, would bury it in a green grave, when all is over.

Should there be nothing else along the road to look at, an English hedge might well suffice to occupy the eyes, and, to a depth beyond what he would suppose, the heart of an American. We often set out hedges in our own soil, but might as well set out figs or pine-apples and expect to gather fruit of them. Something grows, to be sure, which we choose to call a hedge; but it lacks the dense, luxuriant variety of vegetation that is accumulated into the English original, in which a botanist would find a thousand shrubs and gracious herbs that the hedge-maker never thought of planting there. Among them, growing wild, are many of the kindred blossoms of the very flowers which our pilgrim fathers brought from England, for the sake of their simple beauty and home-like associations, and which we have ever since been cultivating in gardens. There is not a softer trait to be found in the character of those stern men than that they should have been sensible of these flower-roots clinging among the fibres of their rugged hearts, and have felt the necessity of bringing them over sea and making them hereditary in the new land, instead of trusting to what rarer beauty the wilderness might have in store for them.

Or, if the roadside has no hedge, the ugliest stone fence (such as, in America, would keep itself bare and unsympathizing till the end of time) is sure to be covered with the small handiwork of Nature; that careful mother lets nothing go naked there, and, if she cannot provide clothing, gives at least embroidery. No sooner is the fence built than she adopts and adorns it as a part of her original plan, treating the hard, uncomely construction as if it had all along been a favorite idea of her own. A little sprig of ivy may be seen creeping up the side of the low wall and clinging fast with its many feet to the rough surface; a tuft of grass roots itself between two of the stones, where a pinch or two of wayside dust has been moistened into nutritious soil for it; a small bunch of fern grows in another crevice; a deep, soft, verdant moss spreads itself along the top and over all the available inequalities of the fence; and where nothing else will grow, lichens stick tenaciously to the bare stones and variegate the monotonous gray with hues of yellow and red. Finally, a great deal of shrubbery clusters along the base of the stone wall, and takes away the hardness of its outline; and in due time, as the upshot of these apparently aimless or sportive touches, we recognize that the beneficent Creator of all things, working through His handmaiden whom we call Nature, has deigned to mingle a charm of divine gracefulness even with so earthly an institution as a boundary fence. The clown who wrought at it little dreamed what fellow-laborer he had.

The English should send us photographs of portions of the trunks of trees, the tangled and various products of a hedge, and a square foot of an old wall. They can hardly send anything else so characteristic. Their artists, especially of the later school, sometimes toil to depict such subjects, but are apt to stiffen the lithe tendrils in the process. The poets succeed better, with Tennyson at their head, and often produce ravishing effects by dint of a tender minuteness of touch, to which the genius of the soil and climate artfully impels them: for, as regards grandeur, there are loftier scenes in many countries than the best that England can show; but, for the picturesqueness of the smallest object that lies under its gentle gloom and sunshine, there is no scenery like it anywhere.

In the foregoing paragraphs I have strayed away to a long distance from the road to Stratford-on-Avon; for I remember no such stone fences as I have been speaking of in Warwickshire, nor elsewhere in England, except among the Lakes, or in Yorkshire, and the rough and hilly counties to the north of it. Hedges there were along my road, however, and broad, level fields, rustic hamlets, and cottages of ancient date,—from the roof of one of which the occupant was tearing away the thatch, and showing what an accumulation of dust, dirt, mouldiness, roots of weeds, families of mice, swallows' nests, and hordes of insects, had been deposited there since that old straw was new. Estimating its antiquity from these tokens, Shakspeare himself, in one of his morning rambles out of his native town, might have seen the thatch laid on; at all events, the cottage-walls were old enough to have known him as a guest. A few modern villas were also to be seen, and perhaps there were mansions of old gentility at no great distance, but hidden among trees; for it is a point of English pride that such houses seldom allow themselves to be visible from the high-road. In short, I recollect nothing specially remarkable along the way, nor in the immediate approach to Stratford; and yet the picture of that June morning has a glory in my memory, owing chiefly, I believe, to the charm of the English summer-weather, the really good days of which are the most delightful that mortal man can ever hope to be favored with. Such a genial warmth! A little too warm, it might be, yet only to such a degree as to assure an American (a certainty to which he seldom attains till attempered to the customary austerity of an English summer-day) that he was quite warm enough. And after all, there was an unconquerable freshness in the atmosphere, which every little movement of a breeze shook over me like a dash of the ocean-spray. Such days need bring us no other happiness than their own light and temperature. No doubt, I could not have enjoyed it so exquisitely, except that there must be still latent in us Western wanderers (even after an absence of two centuries and more) an adaptation to the English climate which makes us sensible of a motherly kindness in its scantiest sunshine, and overflows us with delight at its more lavish smiles.

The spire of Shakspere's church—the Church of the Holy Trinity—begins to show itself among the trees at a little distance from Stratford. Next we see the shabby old dwellings, intermixed with mean-looking houses of modern date; and the streets being quite level, you are struck and surprised by nothing so much as the tameness of the general scene; as if Shakspeare's genius were vivid enough to have wrought pictorial splendors in the town where he was born. Here and there, however, a queer edifice meets your eye, endowed with the individuality that belongs only to the domestic architecture of times gone by; the house seems to have grown out of some odd quality in its inhabitant, as a sea-shell is moulded from within by the character of its inmate; and having been built in a strange fashion, generations ago, it has ever since been growing stranger and quainter, as old humorists are apt to do. Here, too, (as so often impressed me in decayed English towns,) there appeared to be a greater abundance of aged people wearing small-clothes, and leaning on sticks, than you could assemble on our side of the water by sounding a trumpet and proclaiming a reward for the most venerable. I tried to account for this phenomenon by several theories: as, for example, that our new towns are unwholesome for age and kill it off unseasonably; or that our old men have a subtile sense of fitness, and die of their own accord rather than live in an unseemly contrast with youth and novelty: but the secret may be, after all, that hair-dyes, false teeth, modern arts of dress, and other contrivances of a skin-deep youthfulness, have not crept into these antiquated English towns, and so people grow old without the weary necessity of seeming younger than they are.

After wandering through two or three streets, I found my way to Shakspeare's birthplace, which is almost a smaller and humbler house than any description can prepare the visitor to expect; so inevitably does an august inhabitant make his abode palatial to our imaginations, receiving his guests, indeed, in a castle in the air, until we unwisely insist on meeting him among the sordid lanes and alleys of lower earth. The portion of the edifice with which Shakspeare had anything to do is hardly large enough, in the basement, to contain the butcher's stall that one of his descendants kept, and that still remains there, windowless, with the cleaver-cuts in its hacked counter, which projects into the street under a little penthouse-roof, as if waiting for a new occupant.

The upper half of the door was open, and, on my rapping at it, a young person in black made her appearance and admitted me: she was not a menial, but remarkably genteel (an American characteristic) for an English girl, and was probably the daughter of the old gentlewoman who takes care of the house. This lower room has a pavement of gray slabs of stone, which may have been rudely squared when the house was new, but are now all cracked, broken, and disarranged in a most unaccountable way. One does not see how any ordinary usage, for whatever length of time, should have so smashed these heavy stones; it is as if an earthquake had burst up through the floor, which afterwards had been imperfectly trodden down again. The room is whitewashed and very clean, but wofully shabby and dingy, coarsely built, and such as the most poetical imagination would find it difficult to idealize. In the rear of this apartment is the kitchen, a still smaller room, of a similar rude aspect; it has a great, rough fireplace, with space for a large family under the blackened opening of the chimney, and an immense passage-way for the smoke, through which Shakspeare may have seen the blue sky by day and the stars glimmering down at him by night. It is now a dreary spot where the long-extinguished embers used to be. A glowing fire, even if it covered only a quarter part of the hearth, might still do much towards making the old kitchen cheerful. But we get a depressing idea of the stifled, poor, sombre kind of life that could have been lived in such a dwelling, where this room seems to have been the gathering-place of the family, with no breadth or scope, no good retirement, but old and young huddling together cheek by jowl. What a hardy plant was Shakspeare's genius, how fatal its development, since it could not be blighted in such an atmosphere! It only brought human nature the closer to him, and put more unctuous earth about his roots.

Thence I was ushered up-stairs to the room in which Shakspeare is supposed to have been born; though, if you peep too curiously into the matter, you may find the shadow of an ugly doubt on this, as well as most other points of his mysterious life. It is the chamber over the butcher's shop, and is lighted by one broad window containing a great many small, irregular panes of glass. The floor is made of planks, very rudely hewn, and fitting together with little neatness; the naked beams and rafters, at the sides of the room and overhead, bear the original marks of the builder's broad-axe, with no evidence of an attempt to smooth off the job. Again we have to reconcile ourselves to the smallness of the space enclosed by these illustrious walls—a circumstance more difficult to accept, as regards places that we have heard, read, thought, and dreamed much about, than any other disenchanting particular of a mistaken ideal. A few paces—perhaps seven or eight—take us from end to end of it. So low it is, that I could easily touch the ceiling, and might have done so without a tiptoe-stretch, had it been a good deal higher; and this humility of the chamber has tempted a vast multitude of people to write their names overhead in pencil. Every inch of the side-walls, even into the obscurest nooks and corners, is covered with a similar record; all the window-panes, moreover, are scrawled with diamond signatures, among which is said to be that of Walter Scott; but so many persons have sought to immortalize themselves in close vicinity to his name that I really could not trace him out. Methinks it is strange that people do not strive to forget their forlorn little identities, in such situations, instead of thrusting them forward into the dazzle of a great renown, where, if noticed, they cannot but be deemed impertinent.

This room, and the entire house, so far as I saw it, are white-washed and exceedingly clean; nor is there the aged, musty smell with which old Chester first made me acquainted, and which goes far to cure an American of his excessive predilection for antique residences. An old lady, who took charge of me up-stairs, had the manners and aspect of a gentlewoman, and talked with some-what formidable knowledge and appreciative intelligence about Shakspeare. Arranged on a table and in chairs were various prints, views of houses and scenes connected with Shakspeare's memory, together with editions of his works and local publications about his home and haunts, from the sale of which this respectable lady perhaps realizes a handsome profit. At any rate, I bought a good many of them, conceiving that it might be the civillest way of requiting her for her instructive conversation and the trouble she took in showing me the house. It cost me a pang (not a curmud-geonly, but a gentlemanly one) to offer a downright fee to the ladylike girl who had admitted me; but I swallowed my delicate scruples with some little difficulty, and she digested hers, so far as I could observe, with no difficulty at all. In fact, nobody need fear to hold out half a crown to any person with whom he has occasion to speak a word in England.

I should consider it unfair to quit Shakspeare's house without the frank acknowledgment that I was conscious of not the slight-est emotion while viewing it, nor any quickening of the imagina-tion. This has often happened to me in my visits to memorable places. Whatever pretty and apposite reflections I may have made upon the subject had either occurred to me before I ever saw Strat-ford, or have been elaborated since. It is pleasant, nevertheless, to think that I have seen the place; and I believe that I can form a more sensible and vivid idea of Shakspeare as a flesh-and-blood individual now that I have stood on the kitchen-hearth and in the birth-chamber; but I am not quite certain that this power of realization is altogether desirable in reference to a great poet. The Shakspeare whom I met there took various guises, but had not his laurel on. He was successively the roguish boy,—the youthful deer-stealer—the comrade of players,—the too familiar friend of Davenant's mother,—the careful, thrifty, thriven man of property who came back from London to lend money on bond, and occupy the best house in Stratford,—the mellow, red-nosed, autumnal boon-companion of John a' Combe—and finally, (or else the Stratford gossips belied him,) the victim of convivial habits who met his death by tumbling into a ditch on his way home from a drinking-bout, and left his second-best bed to his poor wife.

I feel, as sensibly as the reader can, what horrible impiety it is to remember these things, be they true or false. In either case, they ought to vanish out of sight on the distant ocean-line of the past, leaving a pure, white memory, even as a sail, though perhaps darkened with many stains, looks snowy white on the far horizon. But I draw a moral from these unworthy reminiscences and this embodiment of the poet, as suggested by some of the grimy actualities of his life. It is for the high interests of the world not to insist upon finding out that its greatest men are, in a certain lower sense, very much the same kind of men as the rest of us, and often a little worse; because a common mind cannot properly digest such a discovery, nor ever know the true proportion of the great man's good and evil, nor how small a part of him it was that touched our muddy or dusty earth. Thence comes moral bewilderment, and even intellectual loss, in regard to what is best of him. When Shakspeare invoked a curse on the man who should stir his bones, he perhaps meant the larger share of it for him or them who should pry into his perishing earthliness, the defects or even the merits of the character that he wore in Stratford, when he had left mankind so much to muse upon that was imperishable and divine. Heaven keep me from incurring any part of the anathema in requital for the irreverent sentences above written!

From Shakspeare's house, the next step, of course, is to visit his burial-place. The appearance of the church is most venerable and beautiful, standing amid a great green shadow of lime-trees, above which rises the spire, while the Gothic battlements and buttresses and vast arched windows are obscurely seen through the boughs. The Avon loiters past the churchyard, an exceedingly sluggish river, which might seem to have been considering which way it should flow ever since Shakspeare left off paddling in it, and gathering the large forget-me-nots that grow among its flags and water-weeds.

An old man in small-clothes was waiting at the gate; and inquiring whether I wished to go in, he preceded me to the church-porch, and rapped. I could have done it quite as effectually for myself; but it seems, the old people of the neighborhood haunt about the churchyard, in spite of the frowns and remonstrances of the sexton, who grudges them the half-eleemosynary sixpence which they sometimes get from visitors. I was admitted into the church by a respectable-looking and intelligent man in black, the parish-clerk, I suppose, and probably holding a richer incumbency than his vicar, if all the fees which he handles remain in his own pocket. He was already exhibiting the Shakspere monuments to two or three visitors, and several other parties came in while I was there.

The poet and his family are in possession of what may be considered the very best burial-places that the church affords. They lie in a row, right across the breadth of the chancel, the foot of each gravestone being close to the elevated floor on which the altar stands. Nearest to the side-wall, beneath Shakspeare's bust, is a slab bearing a Latin inscription addressed to his wife, and covering her remains; then his own slab, with the old anathematizing stanza upon it; then that of Thomas Nash, who married his grand-daughter; then that of Dr. Hall, the husband of his daughter Susannah; and, lastly Susannah's own. Shakspeare's is the commonest-looking slab of all, being just such a flag-stone as Essex street in Salem used to be paved with, when I was a boy. Moreover, unless my eyes or recollection deceive me, there is a crack across it, as if it had already undergone some such violence as the inscription deprecates. Unlike the other monuments of the family, it bears no name, nor am I acquainted with the grounds or authority on which it is absolutely determined to be Shakspeare's; although, being in a range with those of his wife and children, it might naturally be attributed to him. But, then why does his wife, who died afterwards, take precedence of him and occupy the place next to his bust? And where are the graves of another daughter and a son, who have a better right in the family-row than Thomas Nash, his grandson-in-law? Might not one or both of them have been laid under the nameless stone? But it is dangerous trifling with Shakspeare's dust; so I forbear to meddle further with the grave, (though the prohibition makes it tempting,) and shall let whatever bones be in it rest in peace. Yet I must needs add that the inscription on the bust seems to imply that Shakspeare's grave was directly underneath it.

The poet's bust is affixed to the northern wall of the church, the base of it being about a man's height, or rather more, above the floor of the chancel. The features of this piece of sculpture are entirely unlike any portrait of Shakspeare that I have ever seen, and compel me to take down the beautiful, lofty-browed, and noble picture of him which has hitherto hung in my mental portrait gallery. The bust cannot be said to represent a beautiful face or an eminently noble head; but it clutches firmly hold of one's sense of reality and insists upon your accepting it, if not as Shakspeare the poet, yet as the wealthy burgher of Stratford, the friend of John a' Combe, who lies yonder in the corner. I know not what the phrenologists say to the bust. The forehead is but moderately developed, and retreats somewhat, the upper part of the skull rising pyramidally; the eyes are prominent almost beyond the penthouse of the brow; the upper lip is so long that it must have been almost a deformity, unless the sculptor artistically exaggerated its length, in consideration, that, on the pedestal, it must be foreshortened by being looked at from below. On the whole, Shakspeare must have had a singular rather than a prepossessing face; and it is wonderful how, with this bust before its eyes, the world has persisted in maintaining an erroneous notion of his appearance, allowing painters and sculptors to foist their idealized nonsense on us all, instead of the genuine man. For my part, the Shakspeare of my mind's eye is henceforth to be a personage of a ruddy English complexion, with a reasonably capacious brow, intelligent and quickly observant eyes, a nose curved slightly outward, a long, queer upper-lip, with the mouth a little unclosed beneath it, and cheeks considerably developed in the lower part and beneath the chin. But when Shakspeare was himself, (for nine-tenths of the time, according to all appearances, he was but the burgher of Stratford,) he doubtless shone through this dull mask and transfigured it into the face of an angel.

Fifteen or twenty feet behind the row of Shakspeare gravestones is the great east-window of the church, now brilliant with stained glass of recent manufacture. On one side of this window, under a sculptured arch of marble, lies a full-length marble figure of John a' Combe, clad in what I take to be a robe of municipal dignity, and holding its hands devoutly clasped. It is a sturdy English figure, with coarse features, a type of ordinary man whom we smile to see immortalized in the sculpturesque material of poets and heroes; but the prayerful attitude encourages us to believe that the old usurer may not, after all, have had that grim reception in the other world which Shakspeare's squib foreboded for him. By-the-by, till I grew somewhat familiar with Warwickshire pronunciation, I never understood that the point of those ill-natured lines was a pun. "'Oho!' quoth the Devil, ''tis my John a' Combe!'"—that is, "'My John has come!'"

Close to the poet's bust is a nameless, oblong, cubic tomb, supposed to be that of a clerical dignitary of the fourteenth century. The church has other mural monuments and altar tombs, one or two of the latter upholding the recumbent figures of knights in armor and their dames, very eminent and worshipful personages in their day, no doubt, but doomed to appear forever intrusive and impertinent within the precincts which Shakspeare has made his own. His renown is tyrannous, and suffers nothing else to be recognized within the scope of its material presence, unless illuminated by some side-ray from himself. The clerk informed me that interments no longer take place in any part of the church. And it is better so; for methinks a person of delicate individuality, curious about his burial-place, and desirous of six feet of earth for himself alone, could never endure to lie buried near Shakspeare, but would rise up at midnight and grope his way out of the church-door, rather than sleep in the shadow of so stupendous a memory.

I should hardly have dared to add another to the innumerable descriptions of Stratford-on-Avon, if it had not seemed to me that this would form a fitting framework to some reminiscences of a very remarkable woman. Her labor, while she lived, was of a nature and purpose outwardly irreverent to the name of Shakspeare, yet, by its actual tendency, entitling her to the distinction of being that one of all his worshippers who sought, though she knew it not, to place the richest and stateliest diadem upon his brow. We Americans, at least, in the scanty annals of our literature, cannot afford to forget her high and conscientious exercise of noble faculties, which, indeed, if you look at the matter in one way, evolved only a miserable error, but, more fairly considered, produced a result worth almost what it cost her. Her faith in her own ideas was so genuine, that, erroneous as they were, it transmuted them to gold, or, at all events, interfused a large proportion of that precious and indestructible substance among the waste material from which it can readily be sifted.

The only time I ever saw Miss Bacon was in London, where she had lodgings in Spring Street, Sussex Gardens, at the house of a grocer, a portly, middle-aged, civil, and friendly man, who, as well as his wife, appeared to feel a personal kindness towards their lodger. I was ushered up two (and I rather believe three) pair of stairs into a parlor somewhat humbly furnished, and told that Miss Bacon would come soon. There were a number of books on the table, and, looking into them, I found that every one had some reference, more or less immediate, to her Shakspearian theory—a volume of Raleigh's "History of the World," a volume of Montaigne, a volume of Lord Bacon's letters, a volume of Shakspeare's plays; and on another table lay a large roll of manuscript, which I presume to have been a portion of her work. To be sure, there was a pocket-Bible among the books, but everything else referred to the one despotic idea that had got possession of her mind; and as it had engrossed her whole soul as well as her intellect, I have no doubt that she had established subtle connections between it and the Bible likewise. As is apt to be the case with solitary students, Miss Bacon probably read late and rose late; for I took up Montaigne (it was Hazlitt's translation) and had been reading his Journey to Italy a good while before she appeared.

I had expected (the more shame for me, having no other ground of such expectation than that she was a literary woman) to see a very homely, uncouth, elderly personage, and was quite agreeably disappointed by her aspect. She was rather uncommonly tall, and had a striking and expressive face, dark hair, dark eyes, which shone with an inward light as soon as she began to speak, and by-and-by a color came into her cheeks and made her look almost young. Not that she really was so; she must have been beyond middle-age: and there was no unkindness in coming to that conclusion, because, making allowance for years and ill-health, I could suppose her to have been handsome and exceedingly attractive once. Though wholly estranged from society, there was little or no restraint or embarrassment in her manner: lonely people are generally glad to give utterance to their pent-up ideas, and often bubble over with them as freely as children with their new-found syllables. I cannot tell how it came about, but we immediately found ourselves taking a friendly and familiar tone together, and began to talk as if we had known one another a very long while. A little preliminary correspondence had indeed smoothed the way, and we had a definite topic in the contemplated publication of her book.

She was very communicative about her theory, and would have been much more so had I desired it; but, being conscious within myself of a sturdy unbelief, I deemed it fair and honest rather to repress than draw her out upon the subject. Unquestionably, she was a monomaniac; these overmastering ideas about the authorship of Shakspeare's plays, and the deep political philosophy concealed beneath the surface of them, had completely thrown her off her balance; but at the same time they had wonderfully developed her intellect, and made her what she could not otherwise have become. It was a very singular phenomenon: a system of philosophy growing up in this woman's mind without her volition,—contrary, in fact, to the determined resistance of her volition,—and substituting itself in the place of everything that originally grew there. To have based such a system on fancy, and unconsciously elaborated it for herself, was almost as wonderful as really to have found it in the plays. But, in a certain sense, she did actually find it there. Shakspeare has surface beneath surface, to an immeasurable depth, adapted to the plummet-line of every reader; his works present many phases of truth, each with scope large enough to fill a contemplative mind. Whatever you seek in him you will surely discover, provided you seek truth. There is no exhausting the various interpretation of his symbols; and a thousand years hence, a world of new readers will possess a whole library of new books, as we ourselves do, in these volumes old already. I had half a mind to suggest to Miss Bacon this explanation of her theory, but forbore, because (as I could readily perceive) she had as princely a spirit as Queen Elizabeth herself, and would at once have motioned me from the room.

I had heard, long ago, that she believed that the material evidences of her dogma as to the authorship, together with the key of the new philosophy, would be found buried in Shakspeare's grave. Recently, as I understood her, this notion had been somewhat modified, and was now accurately defined and fully developed in her mind, with a result of perfect certainty. In Lord Bacon's letters, on which she laid her finger as she spoke, she had discovered the key and clue to the whole mystery. There were definite and minute instructions how to find a will and other documents relating to the conclave of Elizabethan philosophers, which were concealed (when and by whom she did not inform me) in a hollow space in the under surface of Shakspeare's gravestone. Thus the terrible prohibition to remove the stone was accounted for. The directions, she intimated, went completely and precisely to the point, obviating all difficulties in the way of coming at the treasure, and even, if I remember right, were so contrived as to ward off any troublesome consequences likely to ensue from the interference of the parish-officers. All that Miss Bacon now remained in England for—indeed, the object for which she had come hither, and which had kept her here for three years past—was to obtain possession of these material and unquestionable proofs of the authenticity of her theory.

She communicated all this strange matter in a low, quiet tone; while, on my part, I listened as quietly, and without any expression of dissent. Controversy against a faith so settled would have shut her up at once, and that, too, without in the least weakening her belief in the existence of those treasures of the tomb; and had it been possible to convince her of their intangible nature, I apprehend that there would have been nothing left for the poor enthusiast save to collapse and die. She frankly confessed that she could no longer bear the society of those who did not at least lend a certain sympathy to her views, if not fully share in them; and meeting little sympathy or none, she had now entirely secluded herself from the world. In all these years, she had seen Mrs. Farrar a few times, but had long ago given her up,—Carlyle once or twice, but not of late, although he had received her kindly; Mr. Buchanan, while minister in England, had once called on her, and General Campbell, our Consul in London, had met her two or three times on business. With these exceptions which she marked so scrupulously that it was perceptible what epochs they were in the monotonous passage of her days, she had lived in the profoundest solitude. She never walked out; she suffered much from ill-health; and yet, she assured me, she was perfectly happy.

I could well conceive it; for Miss Bacon imagined herself to have received (what is certainly the greatest boon ever assigned to mortals) a high mission in the world, with adequate powers for its accomplishment; and lest even these should prove insufficient, she had faith that special interpositions of Providence were forwarding her human efforts. This idea was continually coming to the surface, during our interview. She believed, for example, that she had been providentially led to her lodging-house and put in relations with the good-natured grocer and his family; and, to say the truth, considering what a savage and stealthy tribe the London lodging-house keepers usually are, the honest kindness of this man and his household appeared to have been little less than miraculous. Evidently, too, she thought that Providence had brought me forward—a man somewhat connected with literature —at the critical juncture when she needed a negotiator with the booksellers; and, on my part, though little accustomed to regard myself as a divine minister, and though I might even have preferred that Providence should select some other instrument, I had no scruple in undertaking to do what I could for her. Her book, as I could see by turning it over, was a very remarkable one, and worthy of being offered to the public, which, if wise enough to appreciate it, would be thankful for what was good in it and merciful to its faults. It was founded on a prodigious error, but was built up from that foundation with a good many prodigious truths. And, at all events, whether I could aid her literary views or no, it would have been both rash and impertinent in me to attempt drawing poor Miss Bacon out of her delusions, which were the condition on which she lived in comfort and joy, and in the exercise of great intellectual power. So I left her to dream as she pleased about the treasures of Shakspeare's tombstone, and to form whatever designs might seem good to herself for obtaining possession of them. I was sensible of a ladylike feeling of propriety in Miss Bacon, and a New-England orderliness in her character, and, in spite of her bewilderment, a sturdy common-sense, which I trusted would begin to operate at the right time, and keep her from any actual extravagance. And as regarded this matter of the tombstone, so it proved.

The interview lasted above an hour, during which she flowed out freely, as to the sole auditor, capable of any degree of intelligent sympathy, whom she had met with in a very long while. Her conversation was remarkably suggestive, alluring forth one's own ideas and fantasies from the shy places where they usually haunt. She was indeed an admirable talker, considering how long she had held her tongue for lack of a listener—pleasant, sunny and shadowy, often piquant, and giving glimpses of all a woman's various and readily changeable moods and humors; and beneath them all there ran a deep and powerful under-current of earnestness, which did not fail to produce in the listener's mind something like a temporary faith in what she herself believed so fervently. But the streets of London are not favorable to enthusiasms of this kind, nor, in fact, are they likely to flourish anywhere in the English atmosphere; so that, long before reaching Paternoster Row, I felt that it would be a difficult and doubtful matter to advocate the publication of Miss Bacon's book. Nevertheless, it did finally get published.

Months before that happened, however, Miss Bacon had taken up her residence at Stratford-on-Avon, drawn thither by the magnetism of those rich secrets which she supposed to have been hidden by Raleigh, or Bacon, or I know not whom, in Shakspeare's grave, and protected there by a curse, as pirates used to bury their gold in the guardianship of a fiend. She took a humble lodging and began to haunt the church like a ghost. But she did not condescend to any stratagem or underhand attempt to violate the grave, which, had she been capable of admitting such an idea, might possibly have been accomplished by the aid of a resurrection-man. As her first step, she made acquaintance with the clerk, and began to sound him as to the feasibility of her enterprise and his own willingness to engage in it. The clerk apparently listened with not unfavorable ears; but, as his situation (which the fees of pilgrims, more numerous than at any Catholic shrine, render lucrative) would have been forfeited by any malfeasance in office, he stipulated for liberty to consult the vicar. Miss Bacon requested to tell her own story to the reverend gentleman, and seems to have been received by him with the utmost kindness, and even to have succeeded in making a certain impression on his mind as to the desirability of the search. As their interview had been under the seal of secrecy, he asked permission to consult a friend, who, as Miss Bacon either found out or surmised, was a practitioner of the law. What the legal friend advised she did not learn; but the negotiation continued, and certainly was never broken off by an absolute refusal on the vicar's part. He, perhaps, was kindly temporizing with our poor countrywoman, whom an Englishman of ordinary mould would have sent to a lunatic asylum at once. I cannot help fancying, however, that her familiarity with the events of Shakspeare's life, and of his death and burial, (of which she would speak as if she had been present at the edge of the grave,) and all the history, literature, and personalities of the Elizabethan age, together with the prevailing power of her own belief, and the eloquence with which she knew how to enforce it, had really gone some little way toward making a convert of the good clergyman. If so, I honor him above all the hierarchy of England.

The affair certainly looked very hopeful. However erroneously, Miss Bacon had understood from the vicar that no obstacles would be interposed to the investigation, and that he himself would sanction it with his presence. It was to take place after nightfall; and all preliminary arrangements being made, the vicar and clerk professed to wait only her word in order to set about lifting the awful stone from the sepulchre. So, at least, Miss Bacon believed; and as her bewilderment was entirely in her own thoughts, and never disturbed her perception or accurate remembrance of external things, I see no reason to doubt it, except it be the tinge of absurdity in the fact. But, in this apparently prosperous state of things, her own convictions began to falter. A doubt stole into her mind whether she might not have mistaken the depository and mode of concealment of those historic treasures; and after once admitting the doubt, she was afraid to hazard the shock of uplifting the stone and finding nothing. She examined the surface of the gravestone, and endeavored, without stirring it, to estimate whether it were of such thickness as to be capable of containing the archives of the Elizabethan club. She went over anew the proofs, the clues, the enigmas, the pregnant sentences, which she had discovered in Bacon's letters and elsewhere, and now was frightened to perceive that they did not point so definitely to Shakspeare's tomb as she had heretofore supposed. There was an unmistakably distinct reference to a tomb, but it might be Bacon's, or Raleigh's, or Spenser's; and instead of the "Old Player," as she profanely called him, it might be either of those three illustrious dead, poet, warrior, or statesman, whose ashes, in Westminster Abbey, or the Tower burial-ground, or wherever they sleep, it was her mission to disturb. It is very possible, moreover, that her acute mind may always have had a lurking and deeply latent distrust of its own fantasies, and that this now became strong enough to restrain her from a decisive step.

But she continued to hover around the church, and seems to have had full freedom of entrance in the daytime, and special license, on one occasion at least, at a late hour of the night. She went thither with a dark-lantern, which could but twinkle like a glow-worm through the volume of obscurity that filled the great dusky edifice. Groping her way up the aisle and towards the chancel, she sat down on the elevated part of the pavement above Shakspeare's grave. If the divine poet really wrote the inscription there, and cared as much about the quiet of his bones as its deprecatory earnestness would imply, it was time for those crumbling relics to bestir themselves under her sacrilegious feet. But they were safe. She made no attempt to disturb them; though, I believe, she looked narrowly into the crevices between Shakspeare's and the two adjacent stones, and in some way satisfied herself that her single strength would suffice to lift the former, in case of need. She threw the feeble ray of her lantern up towards the bust, but could not make it visible beneath the darkness of the vaulted roof. Had she been subject to superstitious terrors, it is impossible to conceive of a situation that could better entitle her to feel them, for, if Shakspeare's ghost would rise at any provocation, it must have shown itself then; but it is my sincere belief, that, if his figure had appeared within the scope of her dark-lantern, in his slashed doublet and gown, and with his eyes bent on her beneath the high, bald forehead, just as we see him in the bust, she would have met him fearlessly and controverted his claims to the authorship of the plays, to his very face. She had taught herself to contemn "Lord Leicester's groom" (it was one of her disdainful epithets for the world's incomparable poet) so thoroughly, that even his disembodied spirit would hardly have found civil treatment at Miss Bacon's hands.

Her vigil, though it appears to have had no definite object, continued far into the night. Several times she heard a low movement in the aisles: a stealthy, dubious foot-fall prowling about in the darkness, now here, now there, among the pillars and ancient tombs, as if some restless inhabitant of the latter had crept forth to peep at the intruder. By-and-by the clerk made his appearance, and confessed that he had been watching her ever since she entered the church.

About this time it was that a strange sort of weariness seems to have fallen upon her: her toil was all but done, her great purpose, as she believed, on the very point of accomplishment, when she began to regret that so stupendous a mission had been imposed on the fragility of a woman. Her faith in the new philosophy was as mighty as ever, and so was her confidence in her own adequate development of it, now about to be given to the world; yet she wished, or fancied so, that it might never have been her duty to achieve this unparalleled task, and to stagger feebly forward under her immense burden of responsibility and renown. So far as her personal concern in the matter went, she would gladly have forfeited the reward of her patient study and labor for so many years, her exile from her country and estrangement from her family and friends, her sacrifice of health and all other interests to this one pursuit, if she could only find herself free to dwell in Stratford and be forgotten. She liked the old slumberous town, and awarded the only praise that ever I knew her to bestow on Shakspeare, the individual man, by acknowledging that his taste in a residence was good, and that he knew how to choose a suitable retirement for a person of shy, but genial temperament. And at this point, I cease to possess the means of tracing her vicissitudes of feeling any farther. In consequence of some advice which I fancied it my duty to tender, as being the only confidant whom she now had in the world, I fell under Miss Bacon's most severe and passionate displeasure, and was cast off by her in the twinkling of an eye. It was a misfortune to which her friends were always particularly liable; but I think that none of them ever loved, or even respected, her most ingenuous and noble, but likewise most sensitive and tumultuous character, the less for it.

At that time her book was passing through the press. Without prejudice to her literary ability, it must be allowed that Miss Bacon was wholly unfit to prepare her own work for publication, because, among many other reasons, she was too thoroughly in earnest to know what to leave out. Every leaf and line was sacred, for all had been written under so deep a conviction of truth as to assume, in her eyes, the aspect of inspiration. A practised book-maker, with entire control of her materials, would have shaped out a duodecimo volume full of eloquent and ingenious dissertation, —criticisms which quite take the color and pungency out of other people's critical remarks on Shakspeare,—philosophic truths which she imagined herself to have found at the roots of his conceptions, and which certainly come from no inconsiderable depth somewhere. There was a great amount of rubbish, which any competent editor would have shovelled out of the way. But Miss Bacon thrust the whole bulk of inspiration and nonsense into the press in a lump, and there tumbled out a ponderous octavo volume, which fell with a dead thump at the feet of the public, and has never been picked up. A few persons turned over one or two of the leaves, as it lay there, and essayed to kick the volume deeper into the mud; for they were the hack critics of the minor periodical press in London, than whom, I suppose, though excellent fellows in their way, there are no gentlemen in the world less sensible of any sanctity in a book, or less likely to recognize an author's heart in it, or more utterly careless about bruising, if they do recognize it. It is their trade. They could not do otherwise. I never thought of blaming them. It was not for such an Englishman as one of these to get beyond the idea that an assault was meditated on England's greatest poet. From the scholars and critics of her own country, indeed, Miss Bacon might have looked for a worthier appreciation, because many of the best of them have higher cultivation, and finer and deeper literary sensibilities than all but the very profoundest and brightest of Englishmen. But they are not a courageous body of men; they dare not think a truth that has an odor of absurdity, lest they should feel themselves bound to speak it out. If any American ever wrote a word in her behalf, Miss Bacon never knew it, nor did I. Our journalists at once republished some of the most brutal vituperations of the English press, thus pelting their poor countrywoman with stolen mud, without even waiting to know whether the ignominy was deserved. And they never have known it, to this day, nor ever will.

The next intelligence that I had of Miss Bacon was by a letter from the mayor of Stratford-on-Avon. He was a medical man, and wrote both in his official and professional character, telling me that an American lady, who had recently published what the mayor called a "Shakspeare book," was afflicted with insanity. In a lucid interval she had referred to me, as a person who had some knowledge of her family and affairs. What she may have suffered before her intellect gave way, we had better not try to imagine. No author had ever hoped so confidently as she; none ever failed more utterly. A superstitious fancy might suggest that the anathema on Shakspeare's tombstone had fallen heavily on her head in requital of even the unaccomplished purpose of disturbing the dust beneath, and that the "Old Player" had kept so quietly in his grave, on the night of her vigil, because he foresaw how soon and terribly he would be avenged. But if that benign spirit takes any care or cognizance of such things now, he has surely requited the injustice that she sought to do him—the high justice that she really did—by a tenderness of love and pity of which only he could be capable. What matters it, though she called him by some other name? He had wrought a greater miracle on her than on all the world besides. This bewildered enthusiast had recognized a depth in the man whom she decried, which scholars, critics, and learned societies, devoted to the elucidation of his unrivalled scenes, had never imagined to exist there. She had paid him the loftiest honor that all these ages of renown have been able to accumulate upon his memory. And when, not many months after the outward failure of her lifelong object, she passed into the better world, I know not why we should hesitate to believe that the immortal poet may have met her on the threshold and led her in, reassuring her with friendly and comfortable words, and thanking her (yet with a smile of gentle humor in his eyes at the thought of certain mistaken speculations) for having interpreted him to mankind so well.

I believe that it has been the fate of this remarkable book never to have had more than a single reader. I myself am acquainted with it only in insulated chapters and scattered pages and paragraphs. But, since my return to America, a young man of genius and enthusiasm has assured me that he has positively read the book from beginning to end, and is completely a convert to its doctrines. It belongs to him, therefore, and not to me,—whom, in almost the last letter that I received from her, she declared unworthy to meddle with her work,—it belongs surely to this one individual, who has done her so much justice as to know what she wrote, to place Miss Bacon in her due position before the public and posterity.

This has been too sad a story. To lighten the recollection of it, I will think of my stroll homeward past Charlecote Park, where I beheld the most stately elms, singly, in clumps, and in groves, scattered all about in the sunniest, shadiest, sleepiest fashion; so that I could not but believe in a lengthened, loitering, drowsy enjoyment which these trees must have in their existence. Diffused over slow-paced centuries, it need not be keen nor bubble into thrills and ecstasies, like the momentary delights of short-lived human beings. They were civilized trees, known to man and befriended by him for ages past. There is an indescribable difference—as I believe I have heretofore endeavored to express —between the tamed, but by no means effete (on the contrary, the richer and more luxuriant) Nature of England, and the rude, shaggy, barbarous Nature which offers us its racier companionship in America. No less a change has been wrought among the wildest creatures that inhabit what the English call their forests. By-and-by, among those refined and venerable trees, I saw a large herd of deer, mostly reclining, but some standing in picturesque groups, while the stags threw their large antlers aloft, as if they had been taught to make themselves tributary to the scenic effect. Some were running fleetly about, vanishing from light into shadow and glancing forth again, with here and there a little fawn careering at its mother's heels. These deer are almost in the same relation to the wild, natural state of their kind that the trees of an English park hold to the rugged growth of an American forest. They have held a certain intercourse with man for immemorial years; and, most probably, the stag that Shakspeare killed was one of the progenitors of this very herd, and may himself have been a partly civilized and humanized deer, though in a less degree than these remote posterity. They are a little wilder than sheep, but they do not snuff the air at the approach of human beings, nor evince much alarm at their pretty close proximity; although if you continue to advance, they toss their heads and take to their heels in a kind of mimic terror, or something akin to feminine skittishness, with a dim remembrance or tradition, as it were, of their having come of a wild stock. They have so long been fed and protected by man, that they must have lost many of their native instincts, and, I suppose, could not live comfortably through even an English winter without human help. One is sensible of a gentle scorn at them for such dependency, but feels none the less kindly disposed towards the half-domesticated race; and it may have been his observation of these tamer characteristics in the Charlecote herd that suggested to Shakspeare the tender and pitiful description of a wounded stag, in "As You Like It."

At a distance of some hundreds of yards from Charlecote Hall, and almost hidden by the trees between it and the roadside, is an old brick archway and porter's lodge. In connection with this entrance there appears to have been a wall and an ancient moat, the latter of which is still visible, a shallow, grassy scoop along the base of an embankment of the lawn. About fifty yards within the gateway stands the house, forming three sides of a square, with three gables in a row on the front and on each of the two wings; and there are several towers and turrets at the angles, together with projecting windows, antique balconies, and other quaint ornaments suitable to the half-Gothic taste in which the edifice was built. Over the gateway is the Lucy coat-of-arms, emblazoned in its proper colors. The mansion dates from the early days of Elizabeth, and probably looked very much the same as now when

Shakspeare was brought before Sir Thomas Lucy for outrages among his deer. The impression is not that of gray antiquity, but of stable and time-honored gentility, still as vital as ever.

It is a most delightful place. All about the house and domain there is a perfection of comfort and domestic taste, an amplitude of convenience, which could have been brought about only by the slow ingenuity and labor of many successive generations, intent upon adding all possible improvement to the home where years gone by and years to come give a sort of permanence to the intangible present. An American is sometimes tempted to fancy that only by this long process can real homes be produced. One man's lifetime is not enough for the accomplishment of such a work of Art and Nature, almost the greatest merely temporary one that is confided to him; too little, at any rate,—yet perhaps too long when he is discouraged by the idea that he must make his house warm and delightful for a miscellaneous race of successors, of whom the one thing certain is, that his own grandchildren will not be among them. Such repinings as are here suggested, however, come only from the fact, that, bred in English habits of thought, as most of us are, we have not yet modified our instincts to the necessities of our new forms of life. A lodging in a wigwam or under a tent has really as many advantages, when we come to know them, as a home beneath the roof-tree of Charlecote Hall. But, alas! our philosophers have not yet taught us what is best, nor have our poets sung us what is beautifullest, in the kind of life that we must lead; and therefore we still read the old English wisdom, and harp upon the ancient strings. And thence it happens, that, when we look at a time-honored hall, it seems more possible for men who inherit such a home, than for ourselves, to lead noble and graceful lives, quietly doing good and lovely things as their daily work, and achieving deeds of simple greatness when circumstances require them. I sometimes apprehend that our institutions may perish before we shall have discovered the most precious of the possibilities which they involve.

(1863)

Emily Dickinson

(1830–1886)

Drama's Vitallest Expression is the Common Day

While her letters quote from Shakespeare's works (and her family's copy of the *Works*, a Boston edition of Charles Knight's eight-volume set published in 1853, may bear her penciled markings), "Drama's Vitallest Expression" is the only one of Emily Dickinson's poems that explicitly mentions Shakespeare. In her insistence that the mostly unrecorded drama of daily life is more "vital" than the evanescent tragedies represented onstage, Dickinson clears room for those writing after Shakespeare, women writers in particular. At the same time, her poem partakes of the lingering anti-theatrical prejudices of nineteenth-century New England culture. "Drama's Vitallest Expression" was written in Amherst in the midst of the Civil War. It would not be published until 1929.

∽

Drama's Vitallest Expression is the Common Day
That arise and set about Us -
Other Tragedy
Perish in the Recitation -
This - the best enact
When the Audience is scattered
And the Boxes shut -

"Hamlet" to Himself were Hamlet -
Had not Shakespeare wrote -
Though the "Romeo" left no Record
Of his Juliet,

It were infinite enacted
In the Human Heart -
Only Theatre recorded
Owner cannot shut -

(1863)

Henry Timrod

(1828–1867)

Address Delivered at the Opening of the New Theatre at Richmond

Henry Timrod was born in Charleston, South Carolina, in 1828. He studied at the University of Georgia, passed over a career in the law, and taught privately before enlisting in the Confederate army (first in the infantry, for which his failing health was unsuited, then as a war correspondent). Timrod's first book of poetry came out in 1860 and his *Complete Poems* was published posthumously thirteen years later. Timrod, who was regarded as "the Laureate of the Confederacy," died at age thirty-nine of tuberculosis shortly after the war ended; he described his last year as marked by "beggary, starvation, death, bitter grief, utter want of hope." His "Address Delivered at the Opening of the New Theatre at Richmond" was to be included in a British edition of his poems to be published in London, but that volume never materialized due to the naval blockade of the South. He wrote this poem in 1863, submitting it in the hopes of winning a $100 prize (which another leading Southern poet, Paul Hayne, won). The competition was part of the celebration marking the opening of the New Richmond Theatre in February 1863, which featured *As You Like It* as its first production. Timrod's inspiring poem soon circulated widely in the Confederacy, appearing in *The Southern Literary Messenger*, *The Charleston Daily Courier*, *The Southern Illustrated News*, and *The Magnolia Weekly*. Through Shakespeare's characters, Timrod traces a trajectory (from the innocent Miranda to the brave, idealistic, and ultimately doomed Hamlet) that mirrored the experiences of his war-weary Southern readers.

A PRIZE POEM.

A fairy ring
Drawn in the crimson of a battle-plain—
From whose weird circle every loathsome thing
    And sight and sound of pain
Are banished, while about it in the air,
And from the ground, and from the low-hung skies,
    Throng, in a vision fair
As ever lit a prophet's dying eyes,
    Gleams of that unseen world
That lies about us, rainbow-tinted shapes
    With starry wings unfurled,
Poised for a moment on such airy capes
    As pierce the golden foam
    Of sunset's silent main—
Would image what in this enchanted dome,
    Amid the night of war and death
In which the armed city draws its breath,
    We have built up!
For though no wizard wand or magic cup
    The spell hath wrought,
Within this charmed fane, we ope the gates
    Of that divinest Fairy-land,
    Where under loftier fates
Than rule the vulgar earth on which we stand,
Move the bright creatures of the realm of thought.
Shut for one happy evening from the flood
That roars around us, here you may behold—
    As if a desert way
    Could blossom and unfold
    A garden fresh with May—
Substantialized in breathing flesh and blood,
    Souls that upon the poet's page
    Have lived from age to age,
And yet have never donned this mortal clay.

A golden strand
Shall sometimes spread before you like the isle
        Where fair Miranda's smile
Met the sweet stranger whom the father's art
        Had led unto her heart,
Which, like a bud that waited for the light,
        Burst into bloom at sight!
Love shall grow softer in each maiden's eyes
As Juliet leans her cheek upon her hand,
        And prattles to the night.
        Anon, a reverend form,
        With tattered robe and forehead bare,
That challenge all the torments of the air,
                Goes by!
And the pent feelings choke in one long sigh,
While, as the mimic thunder rolls, you hear
        The noble wreck of Lear
Reproach like things of life the ancient skies,
        And commune with the storm!
Lo! next a dim and silent chamber where,
Wrapt in glad dreams in which, perchance, the Moor
        Tells his strange story o'er,
The gentle Desdemona chastely lies,
Unconscious of the loving murderer nigh.
        Then through a hush like death
        Stalks Denmark's mailëd ghost!
And Hamlet enters with that thoughtful breath
Which is the trumpet to a countless host
Of reasons, but which wakes no deed from sleep;
        For while it calls to strife,
He pauses on the very brink of fact
To toy as with the shadow of an act,
And utter those wise saws that cut so deep
        Into the core of life!

Nor shall be wanting many a scene
Where forms of more familiar mien,
Moving through lowlier pathways, shall present
The world of every day,
Such as it whirls along the busy quay,
Or sits beneath a rustic orchard wall,
Or floats about a fashion-freighted hall,
Or toils in attics dark the night away.
Love, hate, grief, joy, gain, glory, shame, shall meet,
As in the round wherein our lives are pent;
Chance for a while shall seem to reign,
While Goodness roves like Guilt about the street,
And Guilt looks innocent.
But all at last shall vindicate the right,
Crime shall be meted with its proper pain,
Motes shall be takes from the doubter's sight,
And Fortune's general justice rendered plain.
Of honest laughter there shall be no dearth,
Wit shall shake hands with humor grave and sweet,
Our wisdom shall not be too wise for mirth,
Nor kindred follies want a fool to greet.
As sometimes from the meanest spot of earth
A sudden beauty unexpected starts,
So you shall find some germs of hidden worth
Within the vilest hearts;
And now and then, when in those moods that turn
To the cold Muse that whips a fault with sneers,
You shall, perchance, be strangely touched to learn
You've struck a spring of tears!

But while we lead you thus from change to change,
Shall we not find within our ample range
Some type to elevate a people's heart—
Some hero who shall teach a hero's part
In this distracted time?

Rise from thy sleep of ages, noble Tell!
And, with the Alpine thunders of thy voice,
As if across the billows unenthralled
Thy Alps unto the Alleghanies called,
    Bid Liberty rejoice!
Proclaim upon this trans-Atlantic strand
The deeds which, more than their own awful mien
Make every crag of Switzerland sublime!
And say to those whose feeble souls would lean,
Not on themselves, but on some outstretched hand,
That once a single mind sufficed to quell
The malice of a tyrant; let them know
That each may crowd in every well-aimed blow,
Not the poor strength alone of arm and brand,
But the whole spirit of a mighty land!

Bid Liberty rejoice! Aye, though its day
Be far or near, these clouds shall yet be red
With the large promise of the coming ray.
Meanwhile, with that calm courage which can smile
Amid the terrors of the wildest fray,
Let us among the charms of Art awhile
    Fleet the deep gloom away;
Nor yet forget that on each hand and head
Rest the dear rights for which we fight and pray.

(1863)

Abraham Lincoln

(1809–1865)

Letter to James H. Hackett

Abraham Lincoln read and valued the works of Shakespeare through-out his life. His son Robert recalled that Lincoln would carry a copy of Shakespeare's works around the White House (even as he had carried it about earlier in his career on the judicial circuit), and the president's secretary, John Hay, reported how Lincoln would read aloud from the plays late at night. We catch a glimpse of Lincoln's deep familiarity with the plays from the recollections of the artist Francis Carpenter, who remembered how Lincoln, when he grew bored sitting for a painting, recited Richard III's opening soliloquy ("Now is the winter of our dis-content") "with a degree of force and power that made it seem like a new creation." To Carpenter's further surprise, Lincoln also quoted from memory Claudius's long soliloquy in *Hamlet* ("O, my offense is rank"). Before becoming president, and even in his first years in office, Lincoln didn't have many opportunities to see Shakespeare's plays performed, but he managed to do so on March 13, 1863, when, in the company of one of his secretaries, William O. Stoddard, he saw the great American Falstaff of the day, James Henry Hackett, in *Henry IV, Part 1*. Stoddard reported that Lincoln seemed "to be studying the character and its rendering criti-cally, as if to ascertain the correctness of his own conception as compared with that of the professional artist." Hackett soon after sent Lincoln a copy of his recent book on Shakespeare (which included an essay by John Quincy Adams on *Othello*, for which see pg. 42 in this volume), and Lincoln sent back the following unusually revealing letter. He clearly loved *Macbeth* (historians note how rarely Lincoln used superlatives like "wonderful"), but was also impatient with the gap between the Shake-speare he had read and knew intimately and the radically altered and often debased versions—adaptations, really—that he saw performed by Hackett and others, and that critical view is visible in this letter.

❧

                                        Executive Mansion,
My dear Sir: Washington, August 17, 1863.

Months ago I should have acknowledged the receipt of your book, and accompanying kind note; and I now have to beg your pardon for not having done so.

For one of my age, I have seen very little of the drama. The first presentation of Falstaff I ever saw was yours here, last winter or spring. Perhaps the best compliment I can pay is to say, as I truly can, I am very anxious to see it again. Some of Shakspeare's plays I have never read; while others I have gone over perhaps as frequently as any unprofessional reader. Among the latter are Lear, Richard Third, Henry Eighth, Hamlet, and especially Macbeth. I think nothing equals Macbeth. It is wonderful. Unlike you gentlemen of the profession, I think the soliloquy in Hamlet commencing "O, my offence is rank" surpasses that commencing "To be, or not to be." But pardon this small attempt at criticism. I should like to hear you pronounce the opening speech of Richard the Third. Will you not soon visit Washington again? If you do, please call and let me make your personal acquaintance.

                                            Yours truly

Mark Twain

(1835–1910)

The Killing of Julius Cæsar "Localized"

This sketch first ran in a new literary magazine, *The Californian*, on November 12, 1864. It was Twain's seventh freelance contribution to this San Francisco journal, and he liked the story well enough to reprint it three years later in *The Celebrated Jumping Frog of Calaveras County*. A Boston reviewer of that collection singled out the story and punningly praised it as "a capital rendering" of Caesar's death. Twain's parody cuts two ways: knocking Shakespeare down to size and at the same time imitating the kind of sensationalist newspaper coverage of murders so popular at the time (and to which he himself had contributed when writing for another San Francisco paper, the *Morning Call*). Twain had been toying with Shakespeare parodies from the outset of his writing career. One of his earliest publications (which appeared in the *Keokuk Saturday Post* on October 18, 1856) was a burlesque of *Julius Caesar*, written from the perspective of a country bumpkin, under the name "Thomas Jefferson Snodgrass." While in London in 1873, Twain had seen the American actor Edwin Booth play Hamlet, and spoke with him after the performance, suggesting that *Hamlet* be updated for the times by adding a modern-day comic commentator. Twain soon tried his hand at this addition to Shakespeare's play, didn't like what he had written, and burned it. In 1881 he tried again, making his way through Act I and part of Act II. But this too remained unpublished in his lifetime. His most memorable and accomplished Shakespeare parody is the pastiche of the soliloquies of Hamlet and Macbeth that appeared in Chapters 21 and 22 of his *Adventures of Huckleberry Finn* in 1885.

[BEING THE ONLY TRUE AND RELIABLE ACCOUNT EVER
PUBLISHED, AND TAKEN FROM THE ROMAN "DAILY
EVENING FASCES," OF THE DATE OF THAT TREMENDOUS
OCCURRENCE.]

NOTHING in the world affords a newspaper reporter so much satisfaction as gathering up the details of a bloody and mysterious murder, and writing them up with aggravated circumstantiality. He takes a living delight in this labor of love—for such it is to him—especially if he knows that all the other papers have gone to press and his will be the only one that will contain the dreadful intelligence. A feeling of regret has often come over me that I was not reporting in Rome when Cæsar was killed—reporting on an evening paper and the only one in the city, and getting at least twelve hours ahead of the morning paper boys with this most magnificent "item" that ever fell to the lot of the craft. Other events have happened as startling as this, but none that possessed so peculiarly all the characteristics of the favorite "item" of the present day, magnified into grandeur and sublimity by the high rank, fame, and social and political standing of the actors in it. In imagination I have seen myself skirmishing around old Rome, button-holing soldiers, senators and citizens by turns, and transferring "all the particulars" from them to my note-book; and, better still, arriving "at the base of Pompey's statue" in time to say persuasively to the dying Cæsar: "O, come now, you ain't so far gone, you know, but what you could stir yourself up a little and tell a fellow just how this thing happened, if you was a mind to, couldn't you—now do!" and get the "straight of it" from his own lips. And be envied by the morning paper hounds!

Ah! if I had lived in those days I would have written up that item gloatingly, and spiced it with a little moralizing here and plenty of blood there; and some dark, shuddering mystery; and praise and pity for some, and misrepresentation and abuse for others, (who didn't patronize the paper,) and gory gashes, and notes of warning as to the tendency of the times, and extravagant descriptions of the excitement in the Senate-house and the street, and all that sort of thing.

However, as I was not permitted to report Cæsar's assassination in the regular way, it has at least afforded me rare satisfaction to translate the following able account of it from the original Latin of the *Roman Daily Evening Fasces* of that date—second edition:

Our usually quiet city of Rome was thrown into a state of wild excitement, yesterday, by the occurrence of one of those bloody affrays which sicken the heart and fill the soul with fear, while they inspire all thinking men with forebodings for the future of a city where human life is held so cheaply, and the gravest laws are so openly set at defiance. As the result of that affray, it is our painful duty, as public journalists, to record the death of one of our most esteemed citizens—a man whose name is known wherever this paper circulates, and whose fame it has been our pleasure and our privilege to extend, and also to protect from the tongue of slander and falsehood, to the best of our poor ability. We refer to Mr. J. Cæsar, the Emperor elect.

The facts of the case, as nearly as our reporter could determine them from the conflicting statements of eye-witnesses, were about as follows: The affair was an election row, of course. Nine-tenths of the ghastly butcheries that disgrace the city now-a-days, grow out of the bickerings and jealousies and animosities engendered by these accursed elections. Rome would be the gainer by it if her very constables were elected to serve a century, for in our experience we have never even been able to choose a dog-pelter without celebrating the event with a dozen knock-downs and a general cramming of the station-house with drunken vagabonds over night. It is said that when the immense majority for Cæsar at the polls in the market was declared the other day, and the crown was offered to that gentleman, even his amazing unselfishness in refusing it three times, was not sufficient to save him from the whispered insults of such men as Casca, of the Tenth Ward, and other hirelings of the disappointed candidate, hailing mostly from the Eleventh and Thirteenth, and other outside districts, who were overheard speaking ironically and contemptuously of Mr. Cæsar's conduct upon that occasion.

We are further informed that there are many among us who think they are justified in believing that the assassination of Julius Cæsar was a put-up thing—a cut-and-dried arrangement, hatched by Marcus Brutus and a lot of his hired roughs, and carried out only too faithfully according to the programme. Whether there be good grounds for this suspicion or not, we leave to the people to judge for themselves, only asking that they will read the following account of the sad occurrence carefully and dispassionately before they render that judgment:

The Senate was already in session, and Cæsar was coming down the street toward the capitol, conversing with some personal friends, and followed, as usual, by a large number of citizens. Just as he was passing in front of Demosthenes and Thucydides' drug-store, he was observing casually to a gentleman who, our informant thinks, is a fortune-teller, that the Ides of March were come. The reply was, Yes, they were come, but not gone yet. At this moment Artemidorus stepped up and passed the time of day, and asked Cæsar to read a schedule or a tract, or something of the kind, which he had brought for his perusal. Mr. Decius Brutus also said something about an "humble suit" which *he* wanted read. Artemidorus begged that attention might be paid to his first, because it was of personal consequence to Cæsar. The latter replied that what concerned himself should be read last, or words to that effect. Artemidorus begged and beseeched him to read the paper instantly. [Mark that; it is hinted by William Shakspeare, who saw the beginning and the end of the unfortunate affray, that this "schedule" was simply a note discovering to Cæsar that a plot was brewing to take his life.] However, Cæsar shook him off, and refused to read any petition in the street. He then entered the capitol, and the crowd followed him.

About this time, the following conversation was overheard, and we consider that, taken in connection with the events which succeeded it, it bears an appalling significance: Mr. Popilius Lena remarked to George W. Cassius (commonly known as the "Nobby Boy of the Third Ward,") a bruiser in the pay of the Opposition, that he hoped his enterprise to-day might thrive; and when Cassius asked, "What enterprise?" he only closed his left eye temporarily, and said with simulated indifference, "Fare you well," and sauntered toward Cæsar. Marcus Brutus, who is suspected of being the ringleader of the band that killed Cæsar, asked what it was that Lena had said; Cassius told him, and added in a low tone, "*I fear our purpose is discovered.*"

Brutus told his wretched accomplice to keep an eye on Lena, and a moment after, Cassius urged that lean and hungry vagrant, Casca, whose reputation here is none of the best, to be sudden, for *he feared prevention.* He then turned to Brutus, apparently much excited, and asked what should be done, and swore that either he or Cæsar *should never turn back*—he would kill himself first. At this time, Cæsar was talking to some of the back-country members about the approaching fall elections, and paying little attention to what was going on around him. Billy Trebonius got into conversation with the people's friend and Cæsar's—Mark Antony—and under some pretence or other, got him away, and Brutus, Decius, Casca, Cinna, Metellus Cimber, and others of the gang of infamous desperadoes that infest Rome at present, closed around the doomed Cæsar. Then Metellus Cimber knelt down and begged that his brother might be recalled from banishment, but Cæsar rebuked him for his fawning, sneaking conduct, and refused to grant his petition. Immediately, at Cimber's request, first Brutus and then Cassius begged for the return of the banished Publius; but Cæsar still refused. He said he could not be moved; that he was as fixed as the North Star, and proceeded to speak in the most complimentary terms of the firmness of that star, and its steady character. Then he said he was like it, and he believed he was the only man in the country that was; therefore, since he was "constant" that Cimber should be banished, he was also "constant" that he should stay banished, and he'd be d—d if he didn't keep him so!

Instantly seizing upon this shallow pretext for a fight, Casca sprang at Cæsar and struck him with a dirk, Cæsar grabbing him by the arm with his right hand, and launching a blow straight from the shoulder with his left, that sent the reptile bleeding to the earth. He then backed up against Pompey's statue, and squared himself to receive his assailants. Cassius and Cimber and Cinna rushed upon him with their daggers drawn, and the former succeeded in inflicting a wound upon his body, but before he could strike again, and before either of the others could strike at all, Cæsar stretched the three miscreants at his feet with as many blows of his powerful fist. By this time the Senate was in an indescribable uproar; the throng of citizens in the lobbies had blockaded the doors in their frantic efforts to escape from the building, the Sergeant-at-Arms and his assistants were struggling with the assassins, venerable Senators had cast aside their encumbering robes and were leaping over benches and flying down the aisles in wild confusion toward the shelter of the Committee-rooms, and a thousand voices were shouting "PO-LICE! PO-LICE!" in discordant tones that rose above the frightful din like shrieking winds above the roaring of a tempest. And amid it all, great Cæsar stood with his back against the statue, like a lion at bay, and fought his assailants weaponless and hand-to-hand, with the defiant bearing and the unwavering courage which he had shown before on many a bloody field. Billy Trebonius and Caius Ligarius struck him with their daggers and fell, as their brother-conspirators before them had fallen. But at last, when Cæsar saw his old friend Brutus step forward, armed with a murderous knife, it is said he seemed utterly overpowered with grief and amazement, and dropping his invincible left arm by his side, he hid his face in the folds of his mantle and received the treacherous blow without an effort to stay the hand that gave it. He only said "*Et tu, Brute?*" and fell lifeless on the marble pavement.

We learn that the coat deceased had on when he was killed was the same he wore in his tent on the afternoon of the day he overcame the Nervii, and that when it was removed from the corpse it was found to be cut and gashed in no less than seven different places. There was nothing in the pockets. It will be exhibited at the Coroner's inquest, and will be damning proof of the fact of the killing. These latter facts may be relied on, as we get them from Mark Antony, whose position enables him to learn every item of news connected with the one subject of absorbing interest of to-day.

LATER.—While the Coroner was summoning a jury, Mark Antony and other friends of the late Cæsar got hold of the body and lugged it off to the Forum, and at last accounts Antony and Brutus were making speeches over it and raising such a row among the people that, as we go to press, the Chief of Police is satisfied there is going to be a riot, and is taking measures accordingly.

(1864)

Oliver Wendell Holmes

(1809–1894)

Shakespeare. Tercentennial Celebration. April 23, 1864

On April 24, 1864, Ralph Waldo Emerson recorded in his journal that "Yesterday the Saturday Club met to keep the birthnight of Shakspeare, at the end of the third century." To honor the three hundredth anniversary of Shakespeare's birth, Emerson asked many of the great American men of letters (no women were invited) to join his regular literary circle, the Saturday Club, and celebrate at Revere House in Boston, and thirty-two of them attended. Among them was Oliver Wendell Holmes, who, Emerson noted, recited "a fine poem . . . read so admirably well, that I could not tell whether in itself it were one of his best or not." Shakespeare's anniversary coincided with some of the bloodiest days of the Civil War (the battle at Gettysburg had been fought the previous summer and shortly after this literary gathering in Boston, Grant would launch the Wilderness Campaign, in which Holmes's son, the future supreme court justice, would fight). No wonder, then, that Holmes's occasional poem betrays a fierce awareness of the ongoing war that was raging, and from which Shakespeare could provide only a brief respite: "War-wasted, haggard, panting from the strife, / We turn to other days and far-off lands," for it is a time, he writes, "while our martyrs fall, our heroes bleed." Holmes, a much-admired poet, essayist, novelist, and medical reformer, first published his poem eleven years later in *Songs of Many Seasons* (1875).

∽

"Who claims our Shakespeare from that realm unknown,
   Beyond the storm-vexed islands of the deep,
Where Genoa's roving mariner was blown?
   Her twofold Saint's-day let our England keep;
Shall warring aliens share her holy task?"
      The Old World echoes ask.

O land of Shakespeare! ours with all thy past,
  Till these last years that make the sea so wide,
Think not the jar of battle's trumpet-blast
  Has dulled our aching sense to joyous pride
In every noble word thy sons bequeathed
    The air our fathers breathed!

War-wasted, haggard, panting from the strife,
  We turn to other days and far-off lands,
Live o'er in dreams the Poet's faded life,
  Come with fresh lilies in our fevered hands
To wreathe his bust, and scatter purple flowers,—
    Not his the need, but ours!

We call those poets who are first to mark
  Through earth's dull mist the coming of the dawn,—
Who see in twilight's gloom the first pale spark,
  While others only note that day is gone;
For him the Lord of light the curtain rent
    That veils the firmament.

The greatest for its greatness is half known,
  Stretching beyond our narrow quadrant-lines,—
As in that world of Nature all outgrown
  Where Calaveras lifts his awful pines,
And cast from Mariposa's mountain-wall
    Nevada's cataracts fall.

Yet heaven's remotest orb is partly ours,
  Throbbing its radiance like a beating heart;
In the wide compass of angelic powers
  The instinct of the blindworm has its part;
So in God's kingliest creature we behold
    The flower our buds infold.

With no vain praise we mock the stone-carved name
  Stamped once on dust that moved with pulse and breath,
As thinking to enlarge that amplest fame
  Whose undimmed glories gild the night of death:
We praise not star or sun; in these we see
      Thee, Father, only thee!

Thy gifts are beauty, wisdom, power, and love:
  We read, we reverence on this human soul,—
Earth's clearest mirror of the light above,—
  Plain as the record on thy prophet's scroll,
When o'er his page the effluent splendors poured,
      Thine own, "Thus saith the Lord!"

This player was a prophet from on high,
  Thine own elected. Statesman, poet, sage,
For him thy sovereign pleasure passed them by;
  Sidney's fair youth, and Raleigh's ripened age,
Spenser's chaste soul, and his imperial mind
      Who taught and shamed mankind.

Therefore we bid our hearts' Te Deum rise,
  Nor fear to make thy worship less divine,
And hear the shouted choral shake the skies,
  Counting all glory, power, and wisdom thine;
For thy great gift thy greater name adore,
      And praise thee evermore!

In this dread hour of Nature's utmost need,
  Thanks for these unstained drops of freshening dew!
O, while our martyrs fall, our heroes bleed,
  Keep us to every sweet remembrance true,
Till from this blood-red sunset springs new-born
      Our Nation's second morn!

John Wilkes Booth

(1838–1865)

Letter to the National Intelligencer

John Wilkes Booth, a committed anti-abolitionist and Confederate sympathizer, assassinated President Abraham Lincoln at Ford's Theatre in Washington, D.C., on April 14, 1865. Earlier that day, at the National Hotel, he wrote and sealed a three-page letter intended for publication in the *National Intelligencer*, justifying his actions. Apparently, the only other person who saw this letter was Booth's fellow actor, John Matthews, who knew of Booth's plot. Matthews later testified that Booth had turned the letter over to him, requesting that he deliver it to the publishers. After the president was shot Matthews realized that the incriminating letter was still in his possession and feared being "lynched on the spot" if caught with it. So, after reading it through "a couple of times," he "burned it." Booth was bitterly disappointed that his letter was not published in the immediate aftermath of the assassination. The text of the letter was subsequently reconstructed by Matthews (relying on his actor's memory and most likely access to Booth's other writings), and published in the *Washington Evening Star* on December 7, 1881. The letter concludes with a quotation from Act 2 of *Julius Caesar* underscoring Booth's close identification with the leading conspirator, Brutus. Booth, an accomplished Shakespeare actor (highly praised for his roles as Hamlet, Romeo, and Richard III) had performed the part of Antony in *Julius Caesar* on November 25, 1864, alongside his brothers, Junius and Edwin (who played Brutus), in a performance hailed at the time as "the greatest theatrical event in New York history," and whose proceeds went toward the erection of the statue of Shakespeare that still stands in Central Park.

❧

Washington, D. C., April 14, 1865.

To My Countrymen:

For years I have devoted my time, my energies and every dollar I possessed in the world to the furtherance of an object. I have been baffled and disappointed. The hour has come when I must change my plan. Many, I know—the vulgar herd—will blame me for what I am about to do, but posterity I am sure will justify me. Right or wrong, God judge me, not man. Be my motive good or bad, of one thing I am sure—the lasting condemnation of the North. I love peace more than life. Have loved the Union beyond expression. For four years have I waited, hoped and prayed for the dark clouds to break and for a restoration of our former sunshine. To wait longer would be a crime. My prayers have proved as idle as my hope. God's will be done. I go to see and share the bitter end. This war is at war with the Constitution and the reserved rights of the states. It is a war upon southern rights and institutions. The nomination of Abraham Lincoln four years ago bespoke war. His election forced it. I have ever held the south were right. In a foreign war I too could say 'country, right or wrong.' But in a struggle such as ours (where the brother tries to pierce the brother's heart) for God's sake choose the right. When a country like this spurns justice from her side she forfeits the allegiance of every honest freeman, and should leave him untrammeled by any fealty soever to act as his conscience may approve.

People of the north, to hate tyranny, to love liberty and justice, to strike at wrong and oppression was the teaching of our fathers. The study of our early history will not let me forget it, and may it never!

I do not want to forget the heroic patriotism of our fathers who rebelled against the oppression of the mother country.

This country was formed for the white, not the black man. And looking upon African slavery from the same standpoint held by the noble framers of our constitution, I, for one, have ever considered it one of the greatest blessings, both for themselves and us, that God ever bestowed upon a favored nation. Witness heretofore our wealth and power; witness their elevation and enlightenment above their race elsewhere. I have lived among it most of my life and have seen less harsh treatment from master to man than I have beheld in the north from father to son. Yet, Heaven knows no one would be willing to do more for the negro race than I, could I but see a way to still better their condition.

But Lincoln's policy is only preparing the way for their total annihilation. The south are not, nor have they been, fighting for the continuance of slavery. The first battle of Bull Run did away with that idea. Their causes since for war have been as noble and greater far than those that urged our fathers on. Even should we allow they were wrong at the beginning of this contest, cruelty and injustice have made the wrong become the right, and they stand now before the wonder and admiration of the world as a noble band of patriotic heroes. Hereafter, reading of their deeds, Thermopylæ will be forgotten.

When I aided in the capture and execution of John Brown (who was a murderer on our western boarder, and who was fairly tried and convicted before an impartial judge and jury of treason, and who, by the way, has since been made a god), I was proud of my little share in the transaction, for I deemed it my duty, and that I was helping our common country to perform an act of justice. But what was a crime in poor John Brown is now considered (by themselves) as the greatest and only virtue of the whole republican party.

Strange transmigration! Vice to become a virtue, simply because more indulge in it. I thought then, as now, that the abolitionists were the only traitors in the land, and that the entire party deserved the same fate as poor old Brown. Not because they wished to abolish slavery, but on account of the means they have ever endeavored to use to effect that abolition. If Brown were living I doubt whether he himself would set slavery against the Union. Most, or nearly all the North, do openly curse the Union if the South are to return and retain a single right guaranteed to them by every tie which we once revered as sacred. The South can make no choice. It is either extermination or slavery for themselves (worse than death) to draw from. I know my choice and hasten to accept it. I have studied hard to discover upon what grounds the right of a state to secede has been denied, when our very name, United States, and the Declaration of Independence provide for secession. But there is now no time for words. I know how foolish I shall be deemed for undertaking such a step as this, where, on the one side, I have many friends and everything to make me happy, where my profession alone has gained me an income of more than $20,000 a year, and where my great personal ambition in my profession has such a great field for labor. On the other hand, the south have never bestowed upon me one kind word; a place now where I have no friends, except beneath the sod; a place where I must either become a private soldier or a beggar. To give up all of the former for the latter, besides my mother and sister whom I love so dearly, (although they so widely differ from me in opinion), seems insane: but God is my judge. I love justice more than I do a country that disowns it; more than fame and wealth, more (Heaven pardon me if wrong) more than a happy home. I have never been upon a battle-field, but oh! my countrymen, could you all but see the reality or effects of this horrid war, as I have seen them, in every state save Virginia, I know you would think like me, and pray the Almighty to create in the northern mind a sense of right and justice (even should it possess no seasoning of mercy) and He would dry up the sea of blood between us which is daily growing wider. Alas! I have no longer a country. She is fast approaching her threatened doom. Four years ago I would have given a thousand lives to see her remain (as I had always known her) powerful and unbroken, and now I would hold my life as naught to see her what she was. Oh! my friends, if the fearful scenes of the past four years had never been enacted, or if what has been had been a frightful dream, from which we could now awake, with what overflowing hearts could we bless our God and pray for His continued favor.

How I have loved the old flag can never now be known. A few years since and the entire world could boast of none so pure and spotless. But I have of late been seeing and hearing of the bloody deeds of which she had been made the emblem, and shudder to think how changed she has grown. Oh! how I have longed to see her break from the mist of blood and death so circled, around her folds, spoiling her beauty, and tarnishing her honor. But no: day by day has she been dragged deeper and deeper into cruelty and oppression, till now (in my eyes) her once bright red stripes look like bloody gashes on the face of heaven. I look now upon my early admiration of her glories as a dream. My love is now for the south alone, and to her side I go penniless. Her success has been near my heart, and I have labored faithfully to further an object which would have more than proved my unselfish devotion. Heart sick and disappointed I turn from the path which I had been following into a bolder and more perilous one. Without malice I make the change. I have nothing in my heart except a sense of duty to my choice. If the south is to be aided it must be done quickly. It may already be too late. When Cæsar had conquered the enemies of Rome and the power that was his menaced the liberties of the people, Brutus arose and slew him. The stroke of his dagger was guided by his love for Rome. It was the spirit and ambition of Cæsar that Brutus struck at.

> "O then that we could come by Cæsar's spirit,
> And not dismember Cæsar! But alas!
> Cæsar must bleed for it!"

I answer with Brutus.

> He who loves his country better than gold or life,
>   JOHN W. BOOTH.

Herman Melville

(1809–1891)

The Coming Storm

The picture that Melville describes here, "A Coming Storm," was painted in 1863 in the midst of the Civil War by Sanford R. Gifford, who captured the interplay of light and water and weather on the shores of Lake George in upstate New York. Melville, who first saw this haunting landscape at a National Academy exhibition in Manhattan, shortly after the assassination of President Lincoln in April 1865, was struck by the fact that the painting was owned by the Shakespeare actor Edwin Booth, brother of Lincoln's murderer. Melville's poem (whose title changes the painting's "A" to "The") explores the possibility that Edwin Booth grasped, consciously or unconsciously, that something of the impending national (and for Booth familial) tragedy was prefigured in the painting. The poem was first published in *Battle-Pieces and Aspects of the War* in 1866 and the painting is now in the collection of the Philadelphia Museum of Art.

*A Picture by S. R. Gifford, and owned by E. B.
Included in the N. A. Exhibition, April, 1865*

All feeling hearts must feel for him
    Who felt this picture. Presage dim—
Dim inklings from the shadowy sphere
    Fixed him and fascinated here.

A demon-cloud like the mountain one
    Burst on a spirit as mild
As this urned lake, the home of shades.
    But Shakspeare's pensive child

Never the lines had lightly scanned,
    Steeped in fable, steeped in fate;
The Hamlet in his heart was 'ware,
    Such hearts can antedate.

No utter surprise can come to him
    Who reaches Shakspeare's core;
That which we seek and shun is there—
    Man's final lore.

(1866)

Sanford Gifford, *A Coming Storm* (1863).

G.W.H. Griffin

(1829–1879)

"Shylock," A Burlesque

Burlesques of Shakespeare's plays, which had their heyday between the 1840s and 1870s, first began to appear around 1800. But it wasn't until the 1830s that *The Merchant of Venice* began to be parodied. The portraits of Shylock as "Dealer in Old Clothes" and those of his "hooked-nose" friends who speak English with Yiddish-inflected accents, owe less to Shakespeare's moneylender than to nineteenth-century caricatures of Jews. This burlesque clearly responds to the soaring number of Jewish immigrants to the United States, especially to urban areas, where these minstrels were typically staged (the number of Jews in America had increased a hundredfold from 1820 to 1880, from roughly 3,000 to as many as 300,000). G.W.H. Griffin, born in 1829, was one of the leading minstrel and blackface performers of his day. He wrote many of the scripts for his company, Christy's Minstrels, played Shylock, Othello, and other lead roles, and toured widely, from New York to Chicago to San Francisco. Based on topical references in the burlesque to the recent sparring between New York political figures, Griffin probably wrote this piece as early as 1867. When it was published a few years later it was listed among the company's "Ethiopian" dramas. While there is no indication that Griffin played Shylock in blackface (and the title page only identifies it as a burlesque rather than an "Ethiopian" burlesque) the ambiguous classification suggests that Jews at this time were imagined not only in religious terms but also in racial ones.

※

CHARACTERS.—[SHYLOCK.]

Shylock [*Dealer in Old Clothes.*]. . . . Mr. G. W. H. GRIFFIN.
Dook . . . . " Geo. CHRISTY.
Antonio . . . . " Geo. PERCIVAL.
Bassanio . . . . " R. HUGHES.
Lorenzo . . . . " Otto BURBANK.
Portia . . . . " Fred ABBOTT.
Jessica . . . . " W. W. HODGKIN.

SCENE I.—*The Rialto in Chatham-street.—Two hooked-nose gentlemen discovered* R., *walking up and down before a clothing-store.*

Enter SHYLOCK, L. U. E., *to the air of "Old clo', Old clo',"*
from the Orchestra.

Shylock   Aha! my frients; how's pishness dis cold day?
          I've brought you vun pair pants, and lettle veskit, eh!
First hooked-nose gent   Ah! Shylock, you are faulty with the rest,
          You mustn't call it "veskit," call it "west!"
Second ditto   And "vun pair pants," too, how it sounds,
          Whoever saw a *clown* in pantaloons?
          You should say *trousers*, if you wish, my pet,
          To rouse us from a breach of etiquette.
                    Band strikes up an air from "Faust."
Shylock [*Advancing.*]   Sirs, I will not put up with it,
               Sirs, I will not put up with it,
               Sirs, I will not put up with it,
               And if you don't shut up pretty quick,
               I shall give you your notice to quit.
Hooked-nose gents [*Repeat.*]
               And if we don't shut up pretty quick,
               He'll give us our notice to quit.
                    [*They all break out in a perspiration.*

Enter ANTONIO, *in haste.—He advances toward* SHYLOCK.
Antonio   Oh, She-ylock! dearest, best of men,
          Oh, gentle Jew, pray lend me two pun ten?

	To be without a cent is deep disgrace.
	At Crooks' I cannot even "run my face."
	At Simpson's, too, to-day, I left my "ticker."
Shylock	That's *watch* 'are up to! all for liquor!
Antonio	Not so, my friend; this printed ticket means
	I popped my watch to get some pork and beans;
Shylock	Faugh! how nasty *pork* must be!
Antonio	*Porquoi?* But, *bein's*, you say so, why, it be,
	But still it is a change; these hotels make
	A dinner out a *martyr* to the *stake*;
	Potato, too, as hard as any wood—
	Peut-etre, they think that, so they do you good;
Shylock	You asked for cash, but you'll not get *assent* from me,
Antonio	Be *decent*, Jew! if you *dissent*,
	Why take my bond at ten per cent.;
	So now, good Shylock, how about the cash?
	To have it I'm *itching*.
Shylock	Don't be rash!
	My landlord says he's bound to raise my rent,
	And if I lend it, why its shent-per-shent!
Antonio	Oh, hang the terms, the money have I *must*,
	I'm bound to-night to spend it on a *bust*,
	Sculptures, you see, induce my taste to roam,
	I'll pay you, Shylock, when my ship comes home.

Enter BASSANIO.—*He advances to* SHYLOCK *and* ANTONIO.

Bassanio	Say, Tony! have yer raised the wind?
	Who's that old Bluebeard—how he grinned!
Antonio	And well he may, he's made a precious haul,
	If I raised the *wind*, he'll raise a squall.
Shylock [*Aside.*]	Oh, how these *squalid* Christians talk of gold—
	In *my* opinion Tony's "badly sold!"
	If at the time he doesn't come and pay—
	I'll cut his *liver out*, the very day!
	If he's a liver then, he shall not prate,
	He must *die early*, so he shan't *di-late!*

[*Orchestra plays* "Tapioca."—*The trio advance to the front and sing*

Shylock [*Impressively.*]   Whack fol de riddle rol de ri do,
Antonio [*Mysteriously.*]   Whack fol de riddle lol de day!
Shylock   Whack fol de riddle rol de ri do,
Antonio   Whack fol de riddle lol de day!
Bassanio [*Joyfully.*]   Oh, me! Oh, my!
All [*With a will.*] Whack fol de riddle lol de diddle lol de day!
                        All dance off.—Scene closes.

SCENE II—PORTIA's *Room.—A lounge—table—and two chairs.*

Enter PORTIA, R.U.F., *in a blue dress and a melancholy frame of*
mind.—She is reading a letter from ANTONIO.
                Music.—"The last rose of summer."
Portia   'Tis the last note from that bummer,
                    And I can't say I like its tone;
                 For his boozy companions—
                    Will not grant him a loan;
                 I'm dead broke, too, oh, how dreadful,
                    To be wanting in cash—
                 I must get some, or there will be
                    A-a-bad-fi-i-nancial crash!   [*Crash outside.*
                 With my tiddy fol lol de lol de li do, &c.
                    [*Goes to lounge and sinks into a sweet sleep.*
                 Enter ANTONIO, *by the window* C.
Antonio [*Looking at her.*]
                 Her eye-lids both completely closed she keeps—
                 And as they say in melo drama "she sul-leeps."
Portia [*Rising.*]   Don't be too sure of that my friend—
Antonio   Well, did you get my *note of hand?*
Portia   Your *note off hands* me very much—
                 I'm deeply grieved that you should write me such a
                 letter Tony—
Antonio   *Now let a* feller speak,
                 I want the *spons* the middle of next week
Portia   You want the *spons, sir*? And you think
                 I must stand *sponser* for your nasty drink!

Go to that table, there, uns*table* man,
And bury that big head in that big can;
You say you're thirsty—and you have good reason,
That table what you *sees on*, you may *sieze on*;
Drink, drink your fill, and fill your drink to me,
Get drunk at home, and baulk old Kennedy.

Antonio   Aha! hast heard the news? The Sunday News, I mean.

Portia   Five cents? sold by all dealers,

Antonio   Yes, they're Keen on *Keno*, and they say just now
That Kennedy to Connolly must bow!
The Judge has ta'en him by the *beard*, d'ye see!

Portia   Oh, don't *be-ard* with that *felo-dye-se*;

Antonio   But soft! I'll tell you of this serious wrong,
In verse, inversing an old song.

[*They advance to front.—Music—*"Wearing of the Green."]

Antonio   Oh, Portia, dear, and did you hear,
The news that's going around:
Another flaw in the Excise law,
Judge Conolly has found!
Old Superintendent Kennedy,
Of New York he was king:
Until the big Judge floor'd him flat—
And thus broke up his ring.

[PORTIA *leaves him singing—and exits softly.*

Antonio   I'm left *alone*, but still without *a loan*,
I really feel quite *lonely* that *I'll own*;
There are *two doors* to this room I conjecture,
'Tis in the *Tu-dor* style of architecture;
Or rather say the *Doric*, since I see
That leading to the pantry there makes three;
I wonder *who's in* this one, for I feel
My courage *oozing* out; I'll softly steal
Up to the door—Oh, goodness as I live!
There is Nerissa!—

Enter NERISSA.

Nerissa   Don't be so inquisitive!

How dare you seek, mischievous blade
The *Mysteries* of your Mistress' waiting maid?

Antonio   Well, I'll to t'other door—

Nerissa   I think you'd better,
For Shylock's hunting for his recreant debtor;

Antonio   Oh, lor! Oh, lor! That horrid *two-pun-ten*,
I shan't wish oft *to pun* with him again;
Oh, wretched *punster*, I'm indeed undone,
For he makes *pun stir* well as any one!

                    Enter SHYLOCK, *door* R.

Shylock   Aha! my frient, this week your bond is *dew*,
Will it be missed?—

Antonio   You can't sue
I'm under age, you villain of a Jew;
At all events pray wait until the day,
And then your dastardly demands I'll pay;

[*Aside.*]   What shall I do? I have no bonds at home,
I think I'll take some from my friend Jerome.

Shylock   If you don't pay, my knife I'll sharpen keen,
Upon my soul—

Antonio   Upon your *sole* you mean,
Your *mien* is haughty—but your soul is *mean*

                    Enter BASSANIO, R.U.E.

Bassanio   Hallo, my tulips, *at it* once again!

Antonio   His *at it tude* on your part gives me pain,
We are not common-councilmen pray understand,
So at our heads pray throw no vile ink-stand.

Shylock   Give me an *ink*-ling of it, it is quite *ink*-redulous!

Bassanio   *Ink-redulous?* You surely mean *red-ink-ulous*;

Nerissa   Here, stop this *chaffing*, I am *chafing* nigh,
You quite forget a lady's standing by;
This *badinage* is simply my *aversion*,
I don't *a verse shun*, but I make assersion
That if you find *a verse 'un* than the one I sing,
Why you shall take the *Medal*.

Antonio   This *meddling*

In our affairs, I don't half like—
To leader of Orchestra] Pray give the cue—strike upper C. good
					Mike.
    Orchestra plays "Dudah!" *and characters sing* "That's So."

Nerissa	The yacht race now has all cooled down,
	The thing was really done up brown;
	That's so, that's so too!
Chorus	We're bound to sail all day, to sail till all is blue,
	I'll bet my money on the *Henrietta*
	That's so, that's so too!
Antonio	Old Barnum run for Congress once,
	I never thought he'd be such a dunce,
	That's so, that's so too!
	He'd run some other day, but he thinks it will not do,
	He'd better stick to his menagerie,
	That's so, that's so too!
Shylock	Oh, Wall-street is a tick'lish place,
	There's ruin in the golden race,
	That's so, that's so too!
	When gold goes up all day, oh, that's the time to do,
Chorus	I bets my monish on the bulls and bears,
	That's so, that's so too!
Bassanio	Woman's rights are all the rage,
	Girls want to vote when they come of age
	That's so, that's so too!
Chorus	And then they'll vote all day—
	Oh! Lord, help me and you,
	I'll bet my money on the crinoline,
	That's so, that's so too!
Ensemble	Then come, let us all take a "tod" or two,
	We'll drink in spite of the Excise hue,
	That's so, that's so too!
	We're bound to drink all day, hang old Kennedy's crew,
	We'll drink bad health to the excise board,
	That's so, that's so too!

    [*While they are singing Chorus, scene closes in to*

SCENE III.— *Shylock's House—Three "Golden Balls" hanging in front*—JESSICA *discovered in the doorway.*
Music—"Naughty, Naughty Men."

Jessica [*Sings.*]

> Your pantaloons are gorgeous, your coat it fits, oh, Lord, yes,
> Your vest is brilliant moleskin, oh, you naughty, naughty man!
> Your boots with blacking glimmer, than you no one is slimmer,
> Your hat is Knox's patent, oh, you natty, natty man!
> But ah, when we're united, my fond hopes may be blighted,
> Your hair is all your care now, oh, you natty, natty man!
> You'll beat your wife and curse her, or else you'll treat her worser,
> Your clothes are all you think of, oh, you natty, natty, stupid
> blockhead man!

[*Musing.*] Oh, dear Lorenzo, why are you not here?

Enter LORENZO.

Lorenzo	I'm out of *breath*, my *breth*ren want me dear,
	But I escaped them, and you see I'm here.
Jessica	Your *ear*, Lorenzo—
Lorenzo	Well, I said I was,
Jessica	Oh, bosh! don't bandy words, because
	My father's out, *let's seize* the day, and go!
Lorenzo	*Let's see*, my dear, have we now a good show?
	'Twere cruelty to animals to fail, you know.
Jessica	Oh, bother cruelty, you surely quite forget,
	That the humane society has met!
	Wherever *Harvy* or *Van-am-Burgh* go,
	We poor beasts surely have *the best of show*!
Lorenzo	Then, come, your father's ducats we must thieve,
	My *ducat diamonds*! let's make haste and leave,
	I've got a few five-twenties in my pocket—
	Come, close the door, put up your *chain and locket*
Jessica	Suppose we should be caught, my dear Lorenzy?
	I've *caught his eye* a gleaming in a frenzy!
Lorenzo	Come on, I say, you *cauterised* my heart.

[*As they are going*

Enter SHYLOCK.

Shylock [*Shaking fist.*]

    Tief! murder! robbery! my daughter and my mart!

Lorenzo Will you shut up your head? we wasn't going,

    We were merely stepping out to hear the rooster

    crowing.

      Music—"Gipsy's Warning."

Shylock [*Sings.*]

Trust him not, oh, gentle lady, for he *owes* me many stamps;

 Heed him not, he will ill-treat you, like the other Christian

  scamps.

Of your money he will beat you, better men can sure be got;

 Come back to my house and seat you, gentle lady, trust him not.

Jessica You're a stupid, you were *trusting* to a reed with rotten core;

 As he swindled you I love him better, far, than e'er before!

Lorenzo Yes, I'll be a *little mother.*

Jessica You dry up! or I shall wish

    That you were a *little father.*

Shylock Give me back my dear monish.

[*Exeunt* JESSICA *and* LORENZO. SHYLOCK *dances off frantically.*]

SCENE IV.— *Trial of* ANTONIO —*The Dook discovered at a table,*
 with a pint pot and a stack of clay pipes before him—SHYLOCK
 L., *with a large knife*—ANTONIO *with the mumps*—PRINCE OF
 ARAGON *in full armor.*

Antonio [*Musing.*]

    I'm quite *down-hearted*, if I ain't I'm *dashed*,

    My money's gone, and all my hopes are smashed;

    Of Winslow's Soothing Syrup I will take,

    And see what changed condition that will make.

Shylock What means this talk? Be certain that

    No *Syrup-titious* grumbling you be at,

    And if again I hear you hoot,

    I'll fix your case with a little *boot.*

P. of Aragon Now by my halidome, whatever that may be

    This crafty Jew is full of *Jeux d'esprit*!

The Dook	Right, right, good Prince, but come, let's get to work,
	I think poor Tony finds the *Jew* a *Turk*.
To Shylock	What is your plaint, come, spit it out at once,
	This Christian owes you two-pun-ten? The dunce
	To borrow from a Jew—
Shylock	What! revile my claim,
	Oh, mighty *Khan*, oh, sweet *a merry Khan*,
	Don't bubble over in your righteous wrath,
	A *Khan*, you know, should hold some else than *froth*.
The Dook	Well, what say you, Jew, will you consent
	To take it from his hide? the cash you lent
	Is clearly lost, so do what you think better,
	To rid yourself of an insolvent debtor.

> [SHYLOCK *advances flourishing knife.*
> *Enter* PORTIA *and attendants.*

Portia	Hold you willain! I'm not *willin* yet
	Antonio's buzzum shall be upset;
	But, now wade in! like a duck in the mud,
	But remember, you *draw not one drop of blood*!
Shylock [*Shrinking back.*]	
	The game is up, I cannot solve this riddle,
	I'm trembling like a cat-gut on a fiddle;
	I've lost my *flesh*, my *monish*, and my *daughter*,
	Now I'll sneak out like a lamb to the slaughter;
Omnes	No you don't.

[*They all rush after him, bring him back, crying out,* "Toss him in a
blanket." *They get large canvas and toss him in air until*

CURTAIN.

(c. 1867)

Mary Preston

Othello

Little is known about Mary Preston, of Harford County, Maryland, who published *Studies in Shakspeare*, a book of fourteen essays shortly after the defeat of the Confederacy. Her collection is marked throughout by the powerful impact that the Civil War, and the issues that gave rise to it, had on her reading of Shakespeare. Preston's sympathies are clearly with the South—and she is especially alert to the contemporary resonance of the plays, which lurks just below the surface of her essays and sometimes breaks that surface. So, for example, *Macbeth* triggers a recollection of the courageous action of "a Confederate general on the bloody field of Manassas," while *Julius Caesar* holds lessons regarding "how best to reconcile foes" and how to honor Brutus as "the chief of a lost cause." The recent war made Shakespeare's plays about civil strife especially poignant for her, as her account of the ending of *Richard III* makes clear, which leads her to imagine "the conquerors of this battle-field look[ing] over its sickening scenes of carnage among the wounded and the slain, among the noble and the brave, among those who fell, sword in hand, battling bravely for what they esteemed the right, among the dying and the dead, whose voices shall never again fall, like sweetest music, upon the ears of loved ones waiting, watching for the well-known footsteps." Preston is best remembered today for her insistent plea at the end of the following essay that "Othello *was* a *white* man!"

❧

MOORE tells us, in his "Life of Lord Byron,"—one of the *few readable biographies*,—that this unhappy nobleman had a morbid craving after a knowledge of all the mental struggles through which humanity wades to another life. That Lord Byron's *morbid* characteristic is common to us all, in a more *healthy* form, is made apparent to us by the strange *pleasure* we take in *Tragedy!*—in the fact that *pathos* is a necessary ingredient—however brightly overshadowed or cast in the background,—of all we esteem as *truly* beautiful or as *really* interesting. Our sweetest songs are our saddest. Our most popular scenery has ever a ruined castle or a fallen tower to whisper to the mind of *departed* greatness. But Lord Byron had, as we have in Shakespeare's plays, a *medicine* for his *diseased* fancy. Here, he, as we do, could have studied the passions that agitate man's heart, and make it like a troubled sea, whose waves of feeling know no calm or rest. Here he had, as we have, a clear mirror in which to find a true reflection of the mysteries of human motive and conduct.

These plays are, when properly studied, epitomes of practical learning, containing examples to warn and to comfort. The *reader* need not *experience crime to understand it.* What we know of the author of these plays does not lead us to regard him as *worse* for his familiarity with the vicious and depraved workings of the human heart. He was an artist delineating the features of vice, without practicing the vices he portrayed. Do not let us forget this definition. It may be instructive to learn which are the footsteps of crime; but it can only be to us an irreparable injury to *walk in them.* Our author is always careful to enforce this precaution.

Of all the great tumultuous passions which dominate in the heart of man, none is more cruel in its effects on the subject, or on his victims, none is more powerful, none more deaf to the voice of reason, than jealousy. If it made its approach decked out in its true colors, the true, the noble, and the good would flee its approach. But jealousy advances upon its victim by a series of *unexpected* attacks. It takes the citadel of the heart by a path unknown to its garrison. The conquest is won while the besieged is slumbering in the confidence of perfect security. The captive is fettered while singing of freedom. Jealousy is found intrenched where men are still strong in their belief of knowing its advances, and exulting in the hope of repelling its attacks.

Jealousy grows, too, on a tree whose blossoms are of such a lovely form and color, that it is difficult to persuade ourselves that a fatal poison is often found to lurk in their fragrance, and, eventually, to destroy the fair promise of their beauty. It is strange, too, to observe the shallow, the fallacious foundations on which jealousy rears its disproportionate edifice. Looks, words, actions, nay, *conjectured thoughts*, "trifles light as air," and *as insubstantial*, are, to the jealous, symbols of feeling that have no existence, save in the visionary conceptions of the jealous.

In the character of Othello we trace all these *distinctive* and *peculiar* badges of jealousy. Othello is a man whom the casual reader of human nature might deem an *improbable* subject of jealousy. The more discerning see that this vice oftentimes fastens itself on the best of men. Like the vampire, it feeds on human life without considering the worth of its victim. Wherever love gains the ascendancy over reason, jealousy follows with its stealthy step.

Othello, then, it is not surprising to learn, was a frank, *brave* man; not rashly, not thoughtlessly brave. This freedom from the bravery of a mere *prize-fighter* is shown by Othello during the sudden attack on him at night by the enraged father of Desdemona and his friends. It was no boast, but the expression of a true courage, when the gallant soldier said on this occasion:

> "Hold your hands,
> Both you of my inclining and the rest;
> *Were it my cue to fight*, I should have known it."

Bravery in Othello was a principle, not a mere impulse. Othello was a *just* man. Iago alleges as his reason of dislike of Othello, that no outside influence could sway him from a determination he had once made; for though "three great ones" sued to Othello, to make Iago his lieutenant instead of Cassio, Othello still retained the latter as his choice. There is no trait more pleasing (save to an unjust person, who has no patience or consideration for any one who differs with him) than that of the man who perseveres in his sense of duty, unmoved by the seductive voices that would beguile him from honor's path. Othello's frankness and truthfulness are shown in the readiness he expresses to meet the consequences of his elopement with a powerful nobleman's daughter, in his frank and manly avowal to the Duke and his council, of his (Othello's) marriage with Desdemona.

How *natural* is the origin of *this love-match*. Othello and

Desdemona are entirely opposite in character. The histories of "the course of true love" teach us this apparent opposition of feeling is often the bond of union. Two streams rushing from different directions find, at last, the same outlet—the ocean. Two hearts, impelled by different motives, unite together in love. Othello is brave; Desdemona is timid. Othello is a plain, artless soldier; Desdemona is a beautiful, accomplished lady. Othello is obstinate; Desdemona is yielding, where no great principle is at stake. Notice the foundations of their intimacy, and let it be a warning to fathers. Othello and Desdemona "are thrown together." "Her father oft invited me;" thus giving Othello an opportunity of knowing Desdemona, and of being known by her. How well the whole story of this courtship is summed up by Othello, as he concludes its simple narrative:

> "*She loved me* for the *dangers* I had pass'd,
> And *I loved her* that she did *pity* them."

How striking the Duke's commentary on all this:

> "I think this tale would win my daughter too."

We learn, then, from Shakspeare's great exemplar of jealousy, that it is a vice that may fasten upon a man of a great and of a generous heart, capable of winning the affections of a fascinating and virtuous woman. This instructs us, that jealousy often lodges in a fair temple, and accounts for many speeches and many actions in those from whom we hoped better things. An insidious and powerful agent of evil has, unconsciously to the owner, become the tenant of the heart.

Let us now *briefly* dissect the character of Iago. It is one worthy of a more skilful anatomist. Macaulay informs us, in his essay on "Machiavelli," that the *Italian* people would admire Iago's character more than Othello's, because this latter was *deceived* by the former. I do not think any but a degraded people would have *such a preference*. In Iago, Shakspeare has given us the lineaments of *envy*. It is a *meaner* vice than jealousy; hence, he represents it as dwelling in the heart of a man, in every respect Othello's inferior.

For, while a brave, magnanimous, generous, great man may be jealous, it is *impossible* that he should ever become envious. His *love* might, in its excess, impel him into a jealous state of mind, but his generosity would lead him to rejoice *always* in the merit of even his enemy. Envy is the desire of detracting from worth, or, debasing that which is in itself a proper object of praise. Envy is an uneasy and unhappy feeling, at the sight of either intrinsic or adventitious *superiority* in other men. The *faintest* whispers of such a degrading vice are detected by the honest heart and repudiated.

Iago, therefore, is Othello's *inferior* in position, in attainments, in reputation, in all that makes a man either respectable or great. And it is this sense of Othello's superiority that preys upon Iago's mind; not to excite him to a noble emulation in those characteristics of superiority, but to fill him with an envy—a desire to reduce Othello to his own base level.

Iago is entirely the reverse of the frank Othello. He is a *cunning* fellow; this is his degree of knowledge. He is a hypocrite, apparently zealous in the service of his employer; *this is his frankness*. Iago is never any one's tool. No indeed! Iago is always on guard. *His mean spirit teaches him* the wisdom of vigilance, and stands sentinel over him. Iago is suspicious even of his faithful wife. How can such a man have faith in anything resembling his own nature? He knows himself too well for *any nonsense of this kind*. Iago's intelligence—it is proverbial "that it takes more sense to make a knave than a fool"—is only of the *crafty* order: it is not capable of soaring to any height of wisdom, but it is amply sufficient to grovel in the dirt of envy.

Hence, we find, Iago chooses a *proper* instrument to stir up jealousy in Othello's heart. He selects for his vile purpose Cassio, whose *freedom* from a guilty thought will lead to pay his friend's wife those attentions prompted by sincere respect, which jealousy can exaggerate into evidences of criminal affection; Cassio, whose unaffected and frankly avowed admiration for Desdemona might have been dwelt on by a happy husband with pride and with pleasure; Cassio, who is brave, charitable, young, and handsome, on whom a woman with a free heart might have gladly bestowed it.

As a proof of Cassio and of Desdemona's freedom from entertaining for each other any guilty feeling, notice how the dramatist represents them, as never suspecting Othello's altered manner, is in consequence of their mutual friendship. Desdemona persists to the last moment in entreating her husband's kind offices for Cassio, unconscious that in so doing, she is adding fuel to his jealousy. Cassio still entreats Desdemona to act as peace-maker between him and Othello, little knowing that he is doing the woman he so honors a serious injury. Desdemona feels secure from unworthy suspicions in the breastplate of her truth, to the very last moment. Cassio is blundering, through the sense of honor he cherishes for his friend, and that friend's wife.

The misery of the man, tormented by jealous surmises, fears, doubts!—the mental agonies of doubting where a man has placed his all of hope, and it must either live there, or die forevermore!—the tortures of jealousy, when it attaches itself to a gallant spirit, which struggles against what it feels unworthy of itself, and yet cannot shake it off;—these premonitions of this awful passion are shadowed forth by the exulting Iago, as he marks the fiend usurping sovereignty in Othello's breast:

> "Look where he comes! not poppy, nor mandragora,
> Nor all the drowsy syrups of the world
> Shall ever medicine thee to that sweet sleep
> Which thou ow'dst yesterday."

It is worthy of remark, that under the sway of jealousy, Othello loses all his interest in his old pursuits:

> "Othello's occupation's gone."

The man's mind becomes a chaos of wild, conflicting thoughts. Reason's voice is stifled in this "tempest of the heart." The *will* itself is fettered, and the man is a helpless wreck, driven by the storms of suspicion upon a dreary ocean stretching out before him, with no lighthouse to direct his course. Poor, lost Othello! He says:—

"I think my wife be honest, and think she is not;
I think that thou art just [Iago], and think thou art not."

Though the tragical close of Othello's *jealousy* may not be an *every-day* consequence, still it may with truth be affirmed of jealousy, that it is a passion whose baleful effects may be traced in lives, in characters, worthy of a poet's pen. But as the choicest flowers, when "bit by the envious worm" wither, and their freshness of color dies away, so the lives of our best, the *flowers* of the *human race*, when blasted by jealousy, bring forth no fruits worthy of the blossom.

In conclusion, let me add a word of explanation to my reader. In studying the play of Othello, I have always *imagined* its hero *a white* man. It is true the dramatist paints him black, but this shade does not suit the man. It is a stage decoration, which *my taste* discards,—a fault of color, from an artistic point of view. I have, therefore, as I before state in *my readings* of this play, dispensed with it. Shakspeare was too correct a delineator of human nature to have colored Othello *black*, if he had personally acquainted himself with the idiosyncrasies of the African race.

We may regard, then, the daub of black upon Othello's portrait as an *ebullition* of fancy, a *freak* of imagination,—the visionary conception of an ideal figure,—one of the few erroneous strokes of the great master's brush, the *single* blemish on a faultless work.

Othello *was* a *white* man!

(1869)

Frederick Wadsworth Loring

(1848–1871)

In the Old Churchyard at Fredericksburg

During the Civil War an unknown journalist circulated a story that an Englishman who had known Shakespeare personally and subsequently emigrated to America was buried in an old cemetery in Fredericksburg, Virginia. The long inscription on his tombstone read:

> Here lies the body of Edward Heldon, Practitioner in Physics and Chirurgery. Born in Bedfordshire, England, in the year of our Lord, 1542. Was contemporary with and one of the pall-bearers of William Shakespeare of the Avon. After a brief illness his spirit ascended in the year of our Lord 1618—aged 76.

Frederick Wadsworth Loring was a Boston-born, Harvard-educated poet, journalist, and novelist. According to Mrs. Annie Sawyer Downs, a friend of Loring's, "I well remember his writing and then reading to us the verses afterwards published in *The Atlantic Monthly* of September 1870. We all saw the item in a bit of newspaper used for wrapping; and it took such hold of his imagination that he talked of it all day, and the next morning brought the poem as a result." The alleged tombstone turned out to be a myth (and its story is wonderfully told by Moncure D. Conway in "Hunting a Mythical Pall-Bearer," which appeared in *Harper's* in 1886). Loring died at the age of twenty-three while working as a correspondent in Arizona for *Appleton's Journal*. He and others in his stagecoach were killed by a band of Yavapai Indians at what came to be known as the Wickenburg Massacre. Contemporary readers of Loring's poem would have remembered how many lives were destroyed in the battle at Fredericksburg in December 1862, where the Confederacy suffered over 5,000 casualties and the Union troops over 12,000.

In the old churchyard at Fredericksburg
    A gravestone stands to-day,
Marking the place where a grave has been,
Though many and many a year has it seen
    Since its tenant mouldered away.
      And that quaintly carved old stone
       Tells its simple tale to all:—
      "Here lies a bearer of the pall
       At the funeral of Shakespeare."

There in the churchyard at Fredericksburg
    I wandered all alone,
Thinking sadly on empty fame,
How the great dead are but a name,—
    To few are they really known.
      Then upon this battered stone
       My listless eye did fall,
      Where lay the bearer of the pall
       At the funeral of Shakespeare.

Then in the churchyard at Fredericksburg
    It seemed as though the air
Were peopled with phantoms that swept by,
Flitting along before my eye,
    So sad, so sweet, so fair;
      Hovering about this stone,
       By some strange spirit's call,
      Where lay a bearer of the pall
       At the funeral of Shakespeare.

For in the churchyard at Fredericksburg
    Juliet seemed to love,
Hamlet mused, and the old Lear fell,
Beatrice laughed, and Ariel
    Gleamed through the skies above,
      As here, beneath this stone,

Lay in his narrow hall
He who before had borne the pall
At the funeral of Shakespeare.

And I left the old churchyard at Fredericksburg;
Still did the tall grass wave,
With a strange and beautiful grace,
Over the sad and lonely place,
Where hidden lay the grave;
And still did the quaint old stone
Tell its wonderful tale to all:—
"Here lies a bearer of the pall
At the funeral of Shakespeare."

(1870)

Walt Whitman

(1819–1892)

What Lurks behind Shakspere's Historical Plays?

Walt Whitman's lifelong love of Shakespeare is well documented. He himself recalled that as "boy or young man I had seen, (reading them carefully the day beforehand,) quite all Shakspere's acting dramas, play'd wonderfully well," as well as how while living in Brooklyn, "I went regularly every week in the mild seasons down to Coney island, at that time a long, bare unfrequented shore, which I had all to myself, and where I loved, after bathing, to race up and down the hard sand, and declaim Homer or Shakspere to the surf and sea-gulls." He closely read Shakespeare criticism and frequently alluded to the plays and poetry in his work. Yet Whitman struggled to find a place for Shakespeare in democratic America and was especially troubled with what he considered to be an anti-democratic strain in a writer deemed "monarchical or aristocratic." In his 1884 essay "What Lurks behind Shakspere's Historical Plays?" Whitman modified his view expressed thirteen years earlier in his *Democratic Vistas* (1871) that the "great poems, Shakspere included, are poisonous to the idea of the pride and dignity of the common people, the life-blood of democracy." The new essay also underscored the extent to which Whitman searched for something deeper and veiled in Shakespeare's works, not only in the politics of the plays but also in the possibility that they were written by someone else. His *Leaves of Grass* includes a poem, "Shakspere-Bacon's Cipher" that elaborates on this idea of a hidden meaning, unseen by the rigid and doctrinaire (he had first called the poem "A Hint to Scientists"):

> I doubt it not—then more, far more;
> In each old song bequeath'd—in every noble page or text,
> (Different—something unreck'd before—some unsuspected author,)
> In every object, mountain, tree, and star—in every birth and life,
> As part of each—evolv'd from each—meaning, behind the ostent,
> A mystic cipher waits infolded.

WE all know how much *mythus* there is in the Shakspere question as it stands to-day. Beneath a few foundations of proved facts are certainly engulf'd far more dim and elusive ones, of deepest importance—tantalizing and half suspected—suggesting explanations that one dare not put in plain statement. But coming at once to the point, the English historical plays are to me not only the most eminent as dramatic performances (my maturest judgment confirming the impressions of my early years, that the distinctiveness and glory of the Poet reside not in his vaunted dramas of the passions, but those founded on the contests of English dynasties, and the French wars,) but form, as we get it all, the chief in a complexity of puzzles. Conceiv'd out of the fullest heat and pulse of European feudalism—personifying in unparallel'd ways the mediæval aristocracy, its towering spirit of ruthless and gigantic caste, with its own peculiar air and arrogance (no mere imitation)—only one of the "wolfish earls" so plenteous in the plays themselves, or some born descendant and knower, might seem to be the true author of those amazing works—works in some respects greater than anything else in recorded literature.

The start and germ-stock of the pieces on which the present speculation is founded are undoubtedly (with, at the outset, no small amount of bungling work) in "Henry VI." It is plain to me that as profound and forecasting a brain and pen as ever appear'd in literature, after floundering somewhat in the first part of that trilogy—or perhaps draughting it more or less experimentally or by accident—afterward developed and defined his plan in the Second and Third Parts, and from time to time, thenceforward, systematically enlarged it to majestic and mature proportions in "Richard II," "Richard III," "King John," "Henry IV," "Henry V," and even in "Macbeth," "Coriolanus" and "Lear." For it is impossible to grasp the whole cluster of those plays, however wide the intervals and different circumstances of their composition, without thinking of them as, in a free sense, the result of an *essentially controling plan*. What was that plan? Or, rather, what was veil'd behind it?—for to me there was certainly something so veil'd. Even the episodes of Cade, Joan of Arc, and the like (which sometimes seem to me like interpolations allow'd,) may be meant to foil the possible sleuth, and throw any too 'cute pursuer off the scent. In the whole matter I should specially dwell on, and make much of, that inexplicable element of every highest poetic nature which causes it to cover up and involve its real purpose and meanings in folded removes and far recesses. Of this trait—hiding the nest where common seekers may never find it—the Shaksperean works afford the most numerous and mark'd illustrations known to me. I would even call that trait the leading one through the whole of those works.

All the foregoing to premise a brief statement of how and where I get my new light on Shakspere. Speaking of the special English plays, my friend William O'Connor says:

> They seem simply and rudely historical in their motive, as aiming to give in the rough a tableau of warring dynasties,—and carry to me a lurking sense of being in aid of some ulterior design, probably well enough understood in that age, which perhaps time and criticism will reveal. . . . . Their atmosphere is one of barbarous and tumultuous gloom,—they do not make us love the times they limn, ... and it is impossible to believe that the greatest of the Elizabethan men could have sought to indoctrinate the age with the love of feudalism which his own drama in its entirety, if the view taken of it herein be true, certainly and subtly saps and mines.

Reading the just-specified plays in the light of Mr. O'Connor's suggestion, I defy any one to escape such new and deep utterance-meanings, like magic ink, warm'd by the fire, and previously invisible. Will it not indeed be strange if the author of "Othello" and "Hamlet" is destin'd to live in America, in a generation or two, less as the cunning draughtsman of the passions, and more as putting on record the first full exposé—and by far the most vivid one, immeasurably ahead of doctrinaires and economists—of the political theory and results, or the reason-why and necessity for them which America has come on earth to abnegate and replace?

The summary of my suggestion would be, therefore, that while the more the rich and tangled jungle of the Shaksperean area is travers'd and studied, and the more baffled and mix'd, as so far appears, becomes the exploring student (who at last surmises everything, and remains certain of nothing,) it is possible a future age of criticism, diving deeper, mapping the land and lines freer, completer than hitherto, may discover in the plays named the scientific (Baconian?) inauguration of modern Democracy—furnishing realistic and first-class artistic portraitures of the mediæval world, the feudal personalities, institutes, in their morbid accumulations, deposits, upon politics and sociology,—may penetrate to that hard-pan, far down and back of the ostent of to-day, on which (and on which only) the progressism of the last two centuries has built this Democracy which now holds secure lodgment over the whole civilized world.

Whether such was the unconscious, or (as I think likely) the more or less conscious, purpose of him who fashion'd those marvellous architectonics, is a secondary question.

(1884)

William Winter

(1836–1917)

The Art of Edwin Booth: Hamlet

In 1821 a British actor named Junius Brutus Booth abandoned his wife and son and moved to the United States, starting a new family and spending the next three decades on tour, performing major Shakespeare roles. He would also establish a Shakespeare dynasty, for three of his sons from his second family followed him onto the stage: Junius Brutus Jr., John Wilkes, and Edwin. Edwin Booth was by many accounts the finest American actor of his day (and certainly the best loved), celebrated for his cerebral and naturalistic portrayals of Richard III, Iago, and especially Hamlet, a role he first played in 1853 and continued to perform until his retirement from the stage in 1891. Booth famously played the part a hundred times at New York's Winter Garden during the 1864–65 season, hailed as "the great Shakespearean event of the century" (one that Booth himself grew weary of). Shortly after, his career almost came to an end when his brother John Wilkes Booth assassinated President Lincoln and the entire Booth family came under suspicion. Edwin Booth also built one of the greatest American theaters. It stood on the corner of Sixth Avenue and 23rd Street in Manhattan and was adorned with a statue of Shakespeare. But Booth was unable to sustain his vision for it as a cutting-edge theatrical space where a resident company would attract America's leading actors; a decade after the 1873 financial crash and Booth's subsequent declaration of bankruptcy, Booth's Theatre was torn down and replaced by a department store. In 1876 Booth invited William Winter, the distinguished drama critic for the New York *Tribune*, to collaborate on a set of Shakespeare promptbooks, with Winter doing the editing and providing introductory essays. Shortly after Booth died in 1893, Winter published *The Life and Art of Edwin Booth*, in which he recalled Booth's particular gifts in each of his major roles—most notably his Hamlet, which Winter, like many others of the day, considered his greatest.

✎

B ooth's impersonation of Hamlet was one of the best known works of the dramatic age. In many minds the actor and the character had become identical, and it is not to be doubted that Booth's performance of Hamlet will live, in commemorative dramatic history, with great representative embodiments of the stage—with Garrick's Lear, Kemble's Coriolanus, Edmund Kean's Richard, Macready's Macbeth, Forrest's Othello, and Irving's Mathias, and Becket. That it deserved historic permanence is the conviction of a great body of thoughtful students of Shakespeare and of the art of acting, in Great Britain and Germany as well as in America. In the elements of intellect, imagination, sublimity, mystery, tenderness, incipient delirium, and morbid passion, it was exactly consonant with what the best analysis has determined as to the conception of Shakespeare; while in sustained vigour, picturesque variety, and beautiful grace of execution, it was a model of executive art,—of demeanour, as the atmosphere of the soul,—facial play, gesticulation, and fluent and spontaneous delivery of the text; a delivery that made the blank verse as natural in its effect as blank verse ought to be, or can be, without ever dropping it to the level of colloquialism and commonplace.

In each of Booth's performances a distinguishing attribute was simplicity of treatment, and that was significantly prominent in his portrayal of Hamlet. The rejection of all singularity and the avoidance of all meretricious ornament resulted in a sturdy artistic honesty, which could not be too much admired. The figure stood forth, distinct and stately, in a clear light. The attitudes, movements, gestures, and facial play combined in a fabric of symmetry and of always adequate expression. The text was spoken with ample vocal power and fine flexibility. The illustrative "business" was strictly accordant with the wonderful dignity and high intellectual worth of Shakespeare's creation. The illusion of the part was created with an almost magical sincerity, and was perfectly preserved. Booth's Hamlet was—as Hamlet on the stage should always be—an imaginative and poetic figure; and yet it was natural. To walk upon the stage with the blank verse stored in memory, with every particle of the business pre-arranged, with every emotion aroused yet controlled, and every effect considered, known, and preordained, and yet to make the execution of a design seem involuntary and spontaneous,—that is the task set for the actor, and that task was accomplished by Booth.

Much is heard about "nature" in acting, and about the necessity of "feeling," on the part of an actor. The point has been too often obscured by ignorant or careless reasoning. An actor who abdicates intellectual supremacy ceases to be an actor, for he never can present a consistent and harmonious work. To yield to unchecked feeling is to go to pieces. The actor who makes his audience weep is not he who himself weeps, but he who seems to weep. He will have the feeling, but he will control it and use it, and he will not show it in the manner of actual life. Mrs. Siddons said of herself that she had got credit for the truth and feeling of her acting, when she was only relieving her own heart of its grief; but Mrs. Siddons knew how to act, whatever were her personal emotions,—for it was she who admonished a young actor, saying, "You feel too much." Besides, every artist has a characteristic, individual way. If the representative of Hamlet will express the feelings of Hamlet, will convey them to his audience, and will make the poetic ideal an actual person, it makes no difference whether he is excited or quiescent. Feeling did not usually run away with Dion Boucicault: yet he could act Daddy O'Dowd so as to convulse an audience with sympathy and grief. Jefferson, the quintessence of tenderness, has often accomplished the same result with Rip Van Winkle. In one case the feeling was assumed and controlled; in the other, it is experienced and controlled. Acting is an art, and not a spasm; and when you saw Booth as Hamlet you saw a noble exemplification of that art,—the ideal of a poet, supplied with a physical investiture and made actual and natural, yet not lowered to the level of common life.

The tenderness of Hamlet toward Ophelia—or, rather, toward his ideal of Ophelia—was always set in a strong light, in Booth's acting of the part. He likewise gave felicitous expression to a deeper view of that subject—to Hamlet's pathetic realisation that Ophelia is but a fragile nature, upon which his love has been wasted, and that, in such a world as this, love can find no anchor and no security. The forlorn desolation of the prince was thus made emphatic. One of the saddest things in Hamlet's experience is his baffled impulse to find rest in love—the crushing lesson, not only that Ophelia is incompetent to understand him, but that the stronger and finer a nature is, whether man or woman, the more inevitably it must stand alone. That hope by which so many fine spirits have been lured and baffled, of finding another heart upon which to repose when the burden of life becomes too heavy to be borne alone, is, of all hopes, the most delusive. Loneliness is the penalty of greatness. Booth was definite, also, as to the "madness" of Hamlet.* He was not absolutely mad, but substantially sane,—guarding himself, his secrets, and his purposes by assumed wildness; yet the awful loneliness of existence to which Hamlet has been sequestered by his vast, profound, all-embracing, contemplative intellect, and by the mental shock and wrench that he has sustained, was allowed to colour his temperament. That idea might, in its practical application, be advantageously carried much further than it ever was by any actor; for, after the ghost-scene, the spiritual disease of the Dane would augment its ravages, and his

---

* In reply to a question on this subject, Booth wrote the following letter, which was printed by its recipient, in the *Nashville* (Tenn.) *Banner.*—

DEAR SIR: The subject to which you refer is, as you well know, one of endless controversy among the learned heads, and I dare say they will "war" over it "till time fades into eternity." I think I am asked the same question nearly three hundred and sixty-five times a year, and I usually find it safest to side with both parties in dispute, being one of those, perhaps, referred to in the last line of the following verse:—

> "Genius, the Pythian of the beautiful,
> Leaves her large truths a riddle to the dull;
> From eyes profane a veil the Isis screens,
> And fools on fools still ask what Hamlet means."

Yet, I will confess that I do not consider Hamlet mad,—except in "craft." My opinion may be of little value, but 'tis the result of many weary walks with him, "for hours together, here in the lobby."

Truly yours,
EDWIN BOOTH.

figure should then appear in blight, disorder, dishevelment, and hopeless misery. Poetic gain, however, may sometimes be dramatic loss. To Hamlet the dreamer, Booth usually gave more emphasis than to Hamlet the sufferer—wisely remembering therein the value of stage effect for an audience. His Hamlet was a man to whom thoughts are things and actions are shadows, and who is defeated and overwhelmed by spiritual perceptions too vast for his haunted spirit, by griefs and shocks too great for his endurance, by wicked and compelling environments too strong for his nerveless opposition, and by duties too practical and onerous for his diseased and irresolute will. That was as near to the truth of Shakespeare as acting can reach, and it made Hamlet as intelligible as Hamlet can ever be.

To a man possessing the great intellect and the infinitely tender sensibility of Hamlet, grief does not come in the form of dejection, but in the form of a restless, turbulent, incessant agonising fever of vital agitation. He is never at rest. The grip that misery has fastened upon his soul is inexorable. Contemplation of the action and reaction of his spirit and his anguish is, to a thoughtful observer, kindred with observance of the hopeless suffering of a noble and beloved friend who is striving in vain against the slow, insidious, fatal advance of wasting disease, which intends death, and which will certainly accomplish what it intends. The spirit of Hamlet is indomitable. It may be quenched, but it cannot be conquered. The freedom into which it has entered is the awful freedom that misery alone can give. Beautiful, desolate, harrowed with pain, but ever tremulous with the life of perception and feeling, it moves among phantom shapes and ghastly and hideous images, through wrecks of happiness and the glimmering waste of desolation. It is a distracted and irresolute spirit, made so by innate gloom and by the grandeur of its own vast perceptions. But it is never supine.

That pathetic condition of agonised unrest, that vitality of exquisite torture in the nature and experience of Hamlet, was indicated by Booth. He moved with grace; he spoke the text with ease, polish, spontaneous fluency, and rich and strong significance.

The noble ideal and the clear-cut execution were obvious. But he crowned all by denoting, with incisive distinctness and with woful beauty, the pathetic vitality of the Hamlet experience. His impersonation had wealth of emotion, exalted poetry of treatment, and a dream-like quality that could not fail to fascinate; but, above all, when at its best, it had the terrible reality of suffering. There was no "realism" in it, no fantastic stage business, no laboured strangeness of new readings: it was a presentment of the spiritual state of a gifted man, whom nature and circumstance have made so clear-sighted and yet so wretchedly dubious that his surroundings overwhelm him, and life becomes to him a burden and a curse. Hamlet is a mystery. But, seeing that personation, the thinker saw what Shakespeare meant. Many a human soul has had, or is now enduring, this experience, confronted with the duty of fulfilling a rational life, yet heartbroken with personal affliction, and bewildered with a sense of the awful mysteries of spiritual destiny and the supernal world. This is the great subject that Booth's performance of Hamlet presented—and presented in an entirely great manner. His scenes with the Ghost had a startling weirdness. His parting from Ophelia had the desolate and afflicting and therefore right effect of a parting from love, no less than from its object. His sudden delirium, in the killing of the concealed spy upon Hamlet's interview with the Queen, was wonderfully fine, and it always evoked a prodigious enthusiasm.

Booth's Hamlet did not love Ophelia. He had left behind not only that special love, but love itself—which was something that he remembered but could no longer feel. His Hamlet retained, under all the shocks of spiritual affliction, and through all the blight of physical suffering, a potent intellectual concentration and a princely investiture of decorous elegance: it was not a Hamlet of collapse and ruin: it was neither "fat" nor "scant of breath"—neither lethargic with the languor of misery, nor heavy with the fleshly grossness of supine sloth and abject prostration. The heart was corroded with sorrow, but the brain stood firm. Yet there were moments when the sanity of Booth's Hamlet lapsed into transient frenzy. A pathetic, involuntary tenderness played through his manner toward Ophelia, whom once he has loved and trusted, but whom he now knows to be a frail nature, however lovely and sweet. The pervasive tone of the embodiment was that of a sad isolation from humanity, a dream-like vagueness of condition,—as of one who wanders upon the dusky confines of another world,—and a drifting incertitude, very eloquent of the ravages of a terrible spiritual experience. The latter attribute was the poetic charm of Booth's Hamlet, and the poetic charm, the fine intellectuality, and the graceful execution of the work gave it at once extraordinary beauty and remarkable influence.

Acting, at its best, is the union of perfect expression with a true ideal. Booth's ideal of Hamlet satisfied the imagination more especially in this respect, that it left Hamlet substantially undefined. The character, or rather the temperament, was deeply felt, was imparted with flashes of great energy, and at moments was made exceedingly brilliant; but, for the most part, it was lived out in a dream, and was left to make its own way. There was no insistence on special views or on being specifically understood. And this mood mellowed the execution and gave it flexibility and warmth. Booth was an actor of uncertain impulses and conditions, and he was rightly understood only by those who saw him often, in any specified character. Like all persons of acute sensibility, he had his good moments and his bad ones—moments when the genial fire of the soul was liberated, and moments when the artistic faculties could only operate in the hard, cold mechanism of professional routine. Sometimes he seemed lethargic and indifferent. At other times he would put forth uncommon power, and in the ghost scenes and the great third act, would create a thrilling illusion and lift his audience into noble excitement. At its best his performance of Hamlet exalted the appreciative spectator by arousing a sense of the pathos of our mortal condition as contrasted with the grandeur of the human mind and the vast possibilities of spiritual destiny; and therein it was a performance of great public benefit and importance.

Booth's Hamlet was poetic. The person whom he represented was not an ancient Dane, fair, blue-eyed, yellow-haired, stout, and lymphatic, but was the dark, sad, dreamy, mysterious hero of a poem. The actor did not go behind the tragedy, in quest of historical realism, but, dealing with an ideal subject, treated it in an ideal manner, as far removed as possible from the plane of actual life. Readers of the play of Hamlet are aware that interest in the Prince of Denmark is not, to any considerable extent, inspired by the circumstances that surround him, but depends upon the quality of the man—his spirit and the fragrance of his character. There is an element in Hamlet no less elusive than beautiful, which lifts the mind to a sublime height, fills the heart with a nameless grief, and haunts the soul like the remembered music of a gentle voice that will speak no more. It might be called sorrowful grandeur, sad majesty, ineffable mournfulness, grief-stricken isolation, or patient spiritual anguish. Whatever called, the name would probably be inadequate; but the power of the attribute itself can never fail to be felt. Hamlet fascinates by his personality; and no man can succeed in presenting him who does not possess in himself that peculiar quality of fascination. It is something that cannot be drawn from the library, or poured from the flagon, or bought in the shops. Booth possessed it—and that was the first cause of his great success in the character.

Booth's Hamlet was likewise spiritual. Therein the actor manifested not alone the highest quality that can characterise acting, but a perfectly adequate intuitive knowledge of the Shakespearian conception. It is not enough, in the presentation of this part, that an actor should make known the fact that Hamlet's soul is haunted by supernatural powers: he must also make it felt that Hamlet possesses a soul such as it is possible for supernatural powers to haunt. In Shakespeare's pages it may be seen that—at the beginning, and before his mind has been shocked and unsettled by the awful apparition of his father's spirit in arms—Hamlet is a man darkly prone to sombre thought upon the nothingness of this world and the solemn mysteries of the world beyond the grave; and this mental drift does not flow from the student's fancy, but is the spontaneous, passionate tendency of his soul—for, in the very first self-communing passage that he utters, he is found to have been brooding on the expediency of suicide; and not long afterwards he is found avowing the belief that the powers of hell have great control over spirits as weak and melancholy as his own. A hint suffices. The soul of Hamlet must be felt to have been—in its original essence and condition, before grief, shame, and terror arrived, to burden and distract it—intensely sensitive to the miseries that are in this world; to the fact that it is an evanescent pageant, passing, on a thin tissue, over what Shakespeare himself has greatly called "the blind cave of eternal night;" and to all the vague, strange influences, sometimes beautiful, sometimes terrible, that are wafted out of the great unknown. Booth's embodiment of Hamlet was so thoroughly saturated with this feeling that often it seemed to be more a spirit than a man.

The statement of those felicities indicates Booth's natural adaptability and qualification for the character. Nature made it in him "a property of easiness" to be poetic and spiritual, according to the mood in which Hamlet is depicted. Hence the ideal of Shakespeare was the more easily within his grasp, and he stood abundantly justified—as few other actors have ever been—in undertaking to present it. The spiritualised intellect, the masculine strength, the feminine softness, the over-imaginative reason, the lassitude of thought, the autumnal gloom, the lovable temperament, the piteous, tear-freighted humour, the princely grace of condition, the brooding melancholy, the philosophic mind, and the deep heart, which are commingled in the poet's conception, found their roots and springs in the being of the man. Booth seemed to live Hamlet rather than to act it. His ideal presented a man whose nature is everything lovable; who is placed upon a pinnacle of earthly greatness; who is afflicted with a grief that breaks his heart and a shock that disorders his mind; who is charged with a solemn and dreadful duty, to the fulfillment of which his will is inadequate; who sees so widely and understands so little the nature of things in the universe that his sense of moral responsibility is overwhelmed, and his power of action arrested; who thinks greatly, but to no purpose; who wanders darkly in the borderland between reason and madness, haunted now with sweet strains and majestic images of heaven, and now with terrific, uncertain shapes of hell; and who drifts aimlessly, on a sea of misery, into the oblivion of death. This man is a type of beings upon the earth to whom life is a dream, all its surroundings too vast and awful for endurance, all its facts sad, action impossible or fitful and fruitless, and of whom it can never be said that they are happy till the grass is growing on their graves. That type Booth displayed, with symmetry and grace of method, in an artistic form which was harmony itself. If to be true to Shakespeare, in that vast, complex, and difficult creation, and to interpret the truth with beautiful action, is to attain to greatness in the dramatic art, then surely Booth was a great actor.

Booth's method in the scenes with the Ghost would endure the severest examination, and in those sublime situations he fully deserved the tribute that Cibber pays to the Hamlet of Betterton. Those are the test scenes, and Booth left his spectators entirely satisfied with the acting of them.

If I were to pause upon special points in the execution,—which, since they illumine the actor's ideal and vindicate his genius, are representative and deeply significant,—I should indicate the subtlety with which, almost from the first, the sense of being haunted was conveyed to the imagination; the perfection with which the weird and awful atmosphere of the ghost-scenes was preserved, by the actor's transfiguration into tremulous suspense and horror; the human tenderness and heartbreaking pathos of the scene with Ophelia; the shrill, terrific cry and fate-like swiftness and fury that electrified the moment of the killing of Polonius; and the desolate calm of despairing surrender to bleak and cruel fate, with which Hamlet, as he stood beside the grave of Ophelia, was made so pitiable an object that no man with a heart in his bosom could see him without tears. Those were peaks of majesty in Booth's impersonation.

Thought is not compelled, in remembering Booth's Hamlet, to stop short with the statement that the thing was well done. It may go further than that, and rejoice in the conviction that the thing itself was right. There are in the nature of Hamlet—which is grace,

sweetness, and grandeur corroded by grief and warped by incipient insanity—depths below depths of misery and self-conflict;
and doubtless it was a sense of this that made Kemble say that an
actor of the part is always finding something new in it; but Booth's
ideal of Hamlet possessed the indescribable poetic element which
fascinates, and the spiritual quality which made it the ready instrument of "airs from heaven or blasts from hell." The heart had
been broken by grief. The mind had been disordered by a terrible
shock. The soul,—so predisposed to brooding upon the hollow-
ness of this fragile life and the darkness of futurity that already it
counsels suicide before the great blow has fallen and the prince
confronts his father's wandering ghost,—was full of vast, fantastic
shapes, and was swayed by strange forces of an unknown world.
The condition was princely, the manner exalted, the humour full
of tears, the thought weighed down with a wide and wandering
sense of the mysteries of the universe; and the power of action was
completely benumbed. That is Shakespeare's Hamlet, and that
nature Booth revealed;—in aspect, as sombre as the midnight sky;
in spirit, as lovely as the midnight stars. That nature, furthermore,
he portrayed brilliantly, knowing that sorrow, however powerful
in the element of oppression, cannot fascinate. The Hamlet that is
merely sorrowful, though he might arouse pity, would not inspire
affection. It is the personality beneath the anguish that makes the
anguish so stately, so awful, so majestic. By itself the infinite grief
of Hamlet would overwhelm with the monotony of gray despair;
but, since the nature that shines through it is invested with the
mysterious and fascinating glamour of beauty in ruin, the grief becomes an active pathos, and the sufferer is loved as well as pitied.
Nor does it detract from the loveliness of the ideal, that it is cursed
with incipient and fitful insanity. Thought is shocked by the word
and not the thing, when it rejects this needful attribute of a character otherwise eternally obscure. No one means that Hamlet
needs a strait-jacket. The insanity is a cloud only, and only now
and then present—as with many sane men whom thought, passion, and suffering urge at times into the border-land between
reason and madness. That lurid gleam was the first conspicuously

evident in Booth's Hamlet after the first apparition of the Ghost, and again after the climax of the play scene; but, flowing out of an art-instinct too spontaneous always to have direct intention, it played intermittently along the whole line of the personation, and added weight and weirdness and pathos to remediless misery.

Booth's embodiment of Hamlet was a pleasure to the eye, a delight to the sense of artistic form and moving, a thrilling presence to the imagination, and a sadly significant emblem to the spiritual consciousness. Booth was never at any time inclined, when impersonating Hamlet, to employ those theatrical expedients that startle an audience and diffuse nervous excitement. Except at the delirious moment when the prince rushes upon the arras, and stabs through it the hidden spy whom he wildly hopes is the king, his acting was never diverted from that mood of intellectual concentration which essentially is the condition of Hamlet. In that moment his burst of frensied eagerness—half horror, and half-exultant delight—liberated the passion that smoulders beneath Hamlet's calm, and it was irresistibly enthralling. There were indications of the same passion, in the delivery of the soliloquy upon the artificial grief of the player, at the climax of the play scene, and in the half-lunatic rant over Ophelia's grave. But those variations only served to deepen the darkness of misery with which his embodiment of Hamlet was saturated, and the gloomy grandeur of the haunted atmosphere in which it was swathed.

Booth's ideal of Hamlet was a noble person overwhelmed with a fatal grief, which he endures, for the most part with a patient sweetness that is deeply pathetic, but which sometimes drives him into delirium and must inevitably cause his death. In the expression of that ideal, which is true to Shakespeare, he never went as far as Shakespeare's text would warrant. He never allowed his votaries to see Hamlet as Ophelia saw him, in that hour of eloquent revelation when,—without artifice and in the unpremeditated candour of involuntary sincerity,—his ravaged and blighted figure stood before her, in all the pitiable disorder of self-abandoned sorrow. To show Hamlet in that way would be to show him exactly as he is in Shakespeare; but in a theatrical representation that expedient, while it might gratify the few, would certainly repel the many. Real grief is not attractive, and the grief of Hamlet is real; it is not simply a filial sorrow for the death of his beloved father; a mournful shame at his mother's hasty marriage with his uncle; an affliction of the haunted soul because it knows that his father's spirit is condemned to fast in fires and to walk the night. It is deeper still. It is an elemental misery, coexistent with his being; coincident with his conviction of the utter fatuity of this world and with his mental paralysis of comprehension,—awe-stricken and half insane,—in presence of the unfathomable mystery that environs man's spiritual life. Entirely and literally to embody the man whose nature is convulsed in that way would be to oppress an audience with what few persons understand, and most persons deem intolerable, the reality of sorrow. Hamlet upon the stage must be interesting, and, in a certain sense, he must be brilliant; and Booth always made him so. But that noble actor—so fine in his intuitions, so just in his methods—could not be otherwise than true to his artistic conscience. He embodied Hamlet not simply as the picturesque and interesting central figure in a story of intrigue, half amatory and half political, in an ancient royal court, but as the representative type of man at his highest point of development, vainly confronting the darkness and doubt that enshroud him in this pain-stricken, transitory mortal state, and—because his vision is too comprehensive, his heart too tender, and his will too weak for the circumstances of human life—going to his death at last, broken, defeated, baffled, a mystery among mysteries, a disastrous failure, but glorious through it all, and infinitely more precious, to those who even vaguely comprehend his drift, than the most successful man that ever was created.

Treating Hamlet in that spirit Booth was not content merely to invest him with symmetry of form, poetry of motion, statuesque grace of pose, and the exquisite beauty of musical elocution, and to blend those gracious attributes with dignity of mind and spontaneous, unerring refinement of temperament and manner. He went further, because he illumined the whole figure with a tremulous light of agonised vitality. That was the true ideal of

Hamlet—in whose bosom burns the fire that is not quenched. Students of Shakespeare,—who are, of course, students of human life and of themselves, and who think that perhaps they are in this world for some higher purpose than the consumption of food and the display of raiment,—could think upon it, and gather strength from it. Booth's art, in the acting of Hamlet, was art applied to its highest purpose, and invested with dignity, power, and truth.

(1893)

William Dean Howells

(1837–1920)

Shakespeare

William Dean Howells, one of the leading men of letters in late nineteenth-century America, was a prolific novelist, critic, and influential editor of the *Atlantic Monthly*. He was also an accomplished dramatist. Howells's formal schooling ended at an early age. His first exposure to Shakespeare came around 1850, after his family moved to Dayton, Ohio, where he had a chance to see a touring company perform *Macbeth*, *Othello*, and *Richard III*. After his family moved again a few years later, this time to Jefferson, Ohio, Howells's familiarity with Shakespeare deepened, thanks in part to a free library in town that stocked the plays. This essay recalls with great affection his formative experience in Jefferson, where he memorized and recited long sections of Shakespeare's plays with his boyhood friend Jim Williams. These nostalgic recollections, written nearly a half-century after his boyhood in Ohio, captures the extent to which, in mid-nineteenth-century America, Shakespeare was part of the fabric of small-town life, where, as Howells writes, "Printers in the old-time offices were always spouting Shakespeare more or less," and where a young and aspiring writer could fall in love with the character of Falstaff and begin to make his own "imitations of Shakespeare." Looking back on a lifetime of reading Shakespeare and seeing his plays staged, Howells acknowledges his considerable debt to Shakespeare, concludes that Shakespeare's plays "are neither worse nor better because of the theatre," is not ashamed to admit that there is still one of his plays (unnamed) that he hasn't yet read, and adds that he doesn't think that he would have missed much had he "never read Pericles and Winter's Tale."

❦

THE establishment of our paper in the village where there had been none before, and its enlargement from four to eight pages, were events so filling that they left little room for any other excitement but that of getting acquainted with the young people of the village, and going to parties, and sleigh rides, and walks, and drives, and picnics, and dances, and all the other pleasures which that community seemed to indulge beyond any other we had known. The village was smaller than the one we had just left, but it was by no means less lively, and I think that for its size and time and place it had an uncommon share of what has since been called culture. The intellectual experience of the people was mainly theological and political, as it was everywhere in that day, but there were several among them who had a real love for books, and when they met at the druggist's, as they did every night, to dispute of the inspiration of the scriptures and the principles of the Free Soil party, the talk sometimes turned upon the respective merits of Dickens and Thackeray, Gibbon and Macaulay, Wordsworth and Byron. There were law students who read Noctes Ambrosianæ, the Age of Reason, and Bailey's Festus, as well as Blackstone's Commentaries; and there was a public library in that village of six hundred people, small but very well selected, which was kept in one of the lawyers' offices, and was free to all. It seems to me now that the people met there oftener than they do in most country places, and rubbed their wits together more, but this may be one of those pleasing illusions of memory which men in later life are subject to.

I insist upon nothing, but certainly the air was friendlier to the tastes I had formed than any I had yet known, and I found a wider if not deeper sympathy with them. There was one of our printers who liked books, and we went through Don Quixote together again, and through the Conquest of Granada, and we began to read other things of Irving's. There was a very good little stock of books at the village drugstore, and among those that began to come into my hands were the poems of Dr. Holmes, stray volumes of De Quincey, and here and there minor works of Thackeray's. I believe I had no money to buy them, but there was an open account, or a comity, between the printer and the bookseller, and I must have been allowed a certain discretion in regard to getting books.

Still, I do not think I went far in the more modern authors, or gave my heart to any of them. Suddenly, it was now given to Shakespeare, without notice or reason, that I can recall, except that my friend liked him too, and that we found it a double pleasure to read him together. Printers in the old-time offices were always spouting Shakespeare more or less, and I suppose I could not have kept away from him much longer in the nature of things. I cannot fix the time or place when my friend and I began to read him, but it was in the fine print of that unhallowed edition of ours, and presently we had great lengths of him by heart, out of Hamlet, out of the Tempest, out of Macbeth, out of Richard III., out of Midsummer-Night's Dream, out of the Comedy of Errors, out of Julius Cæsar, out of Measure for Measure, out of Romeo and Juliet, out of Two Gentlemen of Verona.

These were the plays that we loved, and must have read in common, or at least at the same time: but others that I more especially liked were the Histories, and among them particularly the Henrys, where Falstaff appeared. This gross and palpable reprobate greatly took my fancy. I delighted in him immensely, and in his comrades, Pistol, and Bardolph, and Nym. I could not read of his death without emotion, and it was a personal pang to me when the prince, crowned king, denied him: blackguard for blackguard, I still think the prince the worse blackguard. Perhaps I flatter myself, but I believe that even then, as a boy of sixteen, I fully conceived of Falstaff's character, and entered into the author's wonderfully humorous conception of him. There is no such perfect conception of the selfish sensualist in literature, and the conception is all the more perfect because of the wit that lights up the vice of Falstaff, a cold light without tenderness, for he was not a good fellow, though a merry companion. I am not sure but I should put him beside Hamlet, and on the same level, for the merit of his artistic completeness, and at one time I much preferred him, or at least his humor.

As to Falstaff personally, or his like, I was rather fastidious, and would not have made friends with him in the flesh, much or little. I reveled in all his appearances in the Histories, and I tried to be as happy where a factitious and perfunctory Falstaff comes to life again in the Merry Wives of Windsor, though at the bottom of my heart I felt the difference. I began to make my imitations of Shakespeare, and I wrote out passages where Falstaff and Pistol and Bardolph talked together, in that Ercles vein which is so easily caught. This was after a year or two of the irregular and interrupted acquaintance with the author which has been my mode of friendship with all the authors I have loved. My worship of Shakespeare went to heights and lengths that it had reached with no earlier idol, and there was a supreme moment, once, when I found myself saying that the creation of Shakespeare was as great as the creation of a planet.

There ought certainly to be some bound beyond which the cult of favorite authors should not be suffered to go. I should keep well within the limit of that early excess now, and should not liken the creation of Shakespeare to the creation of any heavenly body bigger, say, than one of the nameless asteroids that revolve between Mars and Jupiter. Even this I do not feel to be a true means of comparison, and I think that in the case of all great men we like to let our wonder mount and mount, till it leaves the truth behind, and honesty is pretty much cast out for ballast. A wise criticism will no more magnify Shakespeare because he is already great than it will magnify any less man. But we are loaded down with the responsibility of finding him all we have been told he is, and we must do this or suspect ourselves of a want of taste, a want of sensibility. At the same time, we may really be honester than those who have led us to expect this or that of him, and more truly his friends. I wish the time might come when we could read Shakespeare, and Dante, and Homer, as sincerely and as fairly as we read any new book by the least known of our contemporaries. The course of criticism is toward this, but when I began to read Shakespeare I should not have ventured to think that he was not at every moment great. I should no more have thought of questioning the poetry of any passage in him than of questioning the proofs of holy writ. All the same, I knew very well that much which I read was really poor stuff, and the persons and positions were often preposterous. It is a great pity that the ardent youth should not be permitted and even encouraged to say this to himself, instead of falling slavishly before a great author and accepting him at all points as infallible. Shakespeare is fine enough and great enough when all the possible detractions are made, and I have no fear of saying now that he would be finer and greater for the loss of half his work, though if I had heard any one say such a thing then I should have held him as little better than one of the wicked.

Upon the whole it was well that I had not found my way to Shakespeare earlier, though it is rather strange that I had not. I knew him on the stage in most of the plays that used to be given. I had shared the conscience of Macbeth, the passion of Othello, the doubt of Hamlet; many times, in my natural affinity for villains, I had mocked and suffered with Richard III.

Probably no dramatist ever needed the stage less, and none ever brought more to it. There have been few joys for me in life comparable to that of seeing the curtain rise on Hamlet, and hearing the guards begin to talk about the ghost; and yet how fully this joy imparts itself without any material embodiment! It is the same in the whole range of his plays: they fill the scene, but if there is no scene they fill the soul. They are neither worse nor better because of the theatre. They are so great that it cannot hamper them; they are so vital that they enlarge it to their own proportions and endue it with something of their own living force. They make it the size of life, and yet they retire it so wholly that you think no more of it than you think of the physiognomy of one who talks importantly to you. I have heard people say that they would rather not see Shakespeare played than to see him played ill, but I cannot agree with them. He can better afford to be played ill than any other man that ever wrote. Whoever is on the stage it is always Shakespeare who is speaking to me, and perhaps this is the reason why in the past I can trace no discrepancy between reading his plays and seeing them.

The effect is so equal from either experience that I am not sure as to some plays whether I read them or saw them first, though as to most of them I am aware that I never saw them at all; and if the whole truth must be told there is still one of his plays that I have not read, and I believe it is esteemed one of his greatest. There are several, with all my reading of others, that I had not read till within a few years; and I do not think I should have lost much if I had never read Pericles and Winter's Tale.

In those early days I had no philosophized preference for reality in literature, and I dare say if I had been asked, I should have said that the plays of Shakespeare where reality is least felt were the most imaginative; that is the belief of the puerile critics still; but I suppose it was my instinctive liking for reality that made the great Histories so delightful to me, and that rendered Macbeth and Hamlet vital in their very ghosts and witches. There I found a world appreciable to experience, a world inexpressibly vaster and grander than the poor little affair that I had only known a small obscure corner of, and yet of one quality with it, so that I could be as much at home and citizen in it as where I actually lived. There I found joy and sorrow mixed, and nothing abstract or typical, but everything standing for itself, and not for some other thing. Then, I suppose it was the interfusion of humor through so much of it, that made it all precious and friendly. I think I had a native love of laughing, which was fostered in me by my father's way of looking at life, and had certainly been flattered by my intimacy with Cervantes; but whether this was so or not, I know that I liked best and felt deepest those plays and passages in Shakespeare where the alliance of the tragic and the comic was closest. Perhaps in a time when self-consciousness is so widespread, it is the only thing that saves us from ourselves. I am sure that without it I should not have been naturalized to that world of Shakespeare's Histories, where I used to spend so much of my leisure, with such a sense of his own intimate companionship there as I had nowhere else. I felt that he must somehow like my being in the joke of it all, and that in his great heart he had room for a boy willing absolutely to lose himself in him, and be as one of his creations.

It was the time of life with me when a boy begins to be in love with the pretty faces that then peopled this world so thickly, and I did not fail to fall in love with the ladies of that Shakespeare-world where I lived equally. I cannot tell whether it was because I found them like my ideals here, or whether my ideals acquired merit because of their likeness to the realities there; they appeared to be all of one degree of enchanting loveliness; but upon the whole I must have preferred them in the plays, because it was so much easier to get on with them there; I was always much better dressed there; I was vastly handsomer; I was not bashful or afraid, and I had some defects of these advantages to contend with here.

That friend of mine, the printer whom I have mentioned, was one with me in a sense of the Shakesperean humor, and he dwelt with me in the sort of double being I had in those two worlds. We took the book into the woods at the ends of the long summer afternoons that remained to us when we had finished our work, and on the shining Sundays of the warm, late spring, the early, warm autumn, and we read it there on grassy slopes or heaps of fallen leaves; so that much of the poetry is mixed for me with a rapturous sense of the out-door beauty of this lovely natural world. We read turn about, one taking the story up as the other tired, and as we read the drama played itself under the open sky and in the free air with such orchestral effects as the soughing woods, or some rippling stream afforded. It was not interrupted when a squirrel dropped a nut on us from the top of a tall hickory; and the plaint of a meadow-lark prolonged itself with unbroken sweetness from one world to the other.

But I think it takes two to read in the open air. The pressure of walls is wanted to keep the mind within itself when one reads alone; otherwise it wanders and disperses itself through nature. When my friend left us for want of work in the office, or from the vagarious impulse which is so strong in our craft, I took my Shakespeare no longer to the woods and fields, but pored upon him mostly by night, in the narrow little space which I had for my study, under the stairs at home. There was a desk pushed back against the wall, which the irregular ceiling sloped down to meet behind it, and at my left was a window, which gave a good light on the writing-leaf of my desk. This was my workshop for six or seven years, and it was not at all a bad one; I have had many since that were not so much to the purpose; and though I would not live my life over, I would willingly enough have that little study mine again. But it is gone as utterly as the faces and voices that made home around it, and that I was fierce to shut out of it, so that no sound or sight should molest me in the pursuit of the end which I sought gropingly, blindly, with every little hope, but with an intense ambition, and a courage that gave way under no burden, before no obstacle. Long ago changes were made in the low, rambling house which threw my little closet into a larger room; but this was not until after I had left it many years; and as long as I remained a part of that dear and simple home it was my place to read, to write, to muse, to dream.

I sometimes wish in these later years that I had spent less time in it, or that world of books which it opened into; that I had seen more of the actual world, and had learned to know my brethren in it better. I might so have amassed more material for after use in literature, but I had to fit myself to use it, and I suppose that this was what I was doing, in my own way, and by such light as I had. I often toiled wrongly and foolishly; but certainly I toiled, and I suppose no work is wasted. Some strength I hope was coming to me, even from my mistakes, and though I went over ground that I need not have traversed, if I had not been left so much to find the way alone, yet I was not standing still, and some of the things that I then wished to do I have done. I do not mind owning that in others I have failed. For instance, I have never surpassed Shakespeare as a poet, though I once firmly meant to do so; but then, it is to be remembered that very few other people have surpassed him, and that it would not have been easy.

(1895)

Willa Cather

(1873–1947)

FROM *Between the Acts; Antony and Cleopatra*

While Willa Cather is best known for her novels of frontier life on the Great Plains, early on in her career she was an accomplished and witty drama critic. She began reviewing for the *Nebraska State Journal* and the *Lincoln Courier* while an undergraduate at the University of Nebraska, and published an essay on "Shakespeare and Hamlet" in the *Journal* during her first year of college in 1891, two months after enrolling in a Shakespeare course. Her *Journal* column, Between the Acts, on Shakespeare's birthday—in which she writes that "Shakespeare belongs to two nations now"—appeared on April 29, 1894. The following year Cather reviewed a touring production of *Antony and Cleopatra* twice, first, briefly, in the *Journal* on October 23, 1895, then at greater length and more seriously three days later in the *Lincoln Courier*. She was particularly unforgiving of Lillian Lewis's Cleopatra. In her earlier and more cutting review of that production Cather writes of how "a barge drew up and from it descended a large, limp, lachrymose, 'Kleo-paw-tra,' with an Iowa accent, a St. Louis air and the robust physique of a West England's farmer's wife." As her later review (printed here) demonstrates, her closely observed accounts of local productions capture the feel of the many traveling productions of Shakespeare's plays crisscrossing the nation at this time.

∽

THE twenty-third of April has come and gone again, just as it has done for three hundred and thirty years since it was made hallowed to the world. I wonder how many people know or care that it has come again. Perhaps some few Shakespearian scholars who are scholars rejoiced that morning, and a great many professional people, and perhaps the stars that mete out human fate, and the angels, if there are any. But the people of the world, who call themselves society, and the people of the schools, who call themselves culture, knew little and cared less. We have a Thanks-giving day in memory of blessings we never get, a Fourth of July in memory of a document that is largely a dead letter, a George Washington's day, a Saint Patrick's day, a Decoration day, a St. Valentin's day in memory of nonsense and an Arbor day in memory of nothing whatever, but the day of William Shakespeare's birth passes without honor or recognition, except among the faithful hearts of a despised profession. Even the light opera and comedy people know and reverence that day which pastors and professors do not recognize. Julia Marlowe, with that womanly sweetness and delicacy characteristic of her, spent the day and night in solitude, in contemplation and adoration of Mary Arden, who, as a Chicago critic beautifully puts it, is almost as much to be envied among women as that other Mary of holy memory.

*   *   *

There was one year when that day was fittingly observed, and that was when Mary Anderson, that good queen of art, left her crowded London houses and went down to Stratford, and on the night of the 28d played "Rosalind" to dedicate the great theatre that the people of Stratford built in the memory of Shakespeare. It was more fitting perhaps that an American woman play there that night than an English woman because Shakespeare belongs to two nations now. Then one always fancies if he had been born just a few centuries later he would have been an American. That night must have been one to remember, when even the stolid English country folk were moved to their depths, and the crowds that went down from London sat breathless, and the actress, who herself was so like Shakespeare's great woman, between the acts was on her knees in her dressing room with her crucifix in her hands. Mary Anderson said afterward that in all her professional career she never enjoyed and suffered and hoped and feared as she did that night.

Perhaps some day the Anglo-Saxon races will realize what Shakespeare did for them, how he dignified their language, exalted their literature and letters above that of all people, and gave them their place among the nations of the earth. If I were asked for the answer of the riddle of things, I would as lief say "Shakespeare" as anything. For him alone it was worth while that a planet should be called out of Chaos and a race formed out of nothingness. He justified all history before him, sanctified all history after him.

(1894)

———————————

WHEN Homer wished for a tongue of iron and a throat of brass that he might tell the ships and the number of them that came from distant Argos, he should have saved time and eloquence and merely wished to be an advance man. Advance men can talk till the town clock stops, till the cows come home, till the grass on your grave grows green. And of all advance men I never met no one who could out-talk Mr. Lawrence Marston, the husband and playwright of Lillian Lewis. A good share of his conversation Mr. Marston devoted to Cleopatra, and to clearing Cleopatra's record, which latter was kind and considerate of him. Mr. Marston is very sure that Antony and Cleopatra were married. I think he even has theories as to who performed the ceremony and knows who were the bridesmaids and best men. "Of course she was married to Antony," quoth he. "Why, just think how that affair would have hurt her social standing in Egypt if she had not been!" Truly. Then Mr. Marston thinks that Cleopatra was married to Julius Cæsar also, despite the fact that Julius was no longer young and had a wife in Rome. When humbly asked as to whether this much married queen were Pompey's wife also, Mr. Marston hedged and said he thought that little story about Pompey and the languid lily of the Nile was all gossip. And the numerous slave stories he is sure were all slander. He thinks, too, that Cleopatra was very domestic, that she used to butter Antony's toast and patch his tunic and darn the stockings of the numerous little Antonys.

I feel that I am not at all able to do justice to Lillian Lewis as the Egyptian lotus bud. I shall see her in my dreams, that coy, kittenish matron, bunched up on a moth-eaten tiger stroking Mark

Antony's double chin. I never saw a less regal figure and carriage. I have seen waiters in restaurants who were ten times more queenly. Her movements were exactly like those of the women who give you Turkish baths in Chicago. And ah! the giddy manner in which she buckled on his armor and the fulsome way in which she gurgled,

> but, since my lord
> Is Antony again, I will be Cleopatra.

I suppose that is what the learned Malaprop of the *Evening News* would call "cloyish abandon." And the queer little motions she made when she put that imaginary snake in her bosom, it was so suggestive of fleas. And her resounding faint when she saw a vision of Mark Antony in his cunning little pink wedding tunic being married to *Octavia*.

There was just one good thing about Lillian Lewis' *Cleopatra*, and that was that, as hunger makes one dream of banquets, it recalled the only Cleopatra on earth worth the seeing, the royal Egyptian of Sarah Bernhardt. I could see it all again, that royal creature with the face of flame, every inch a queen and always a woman. The bewildering reality of that first scene with *Mark Antony* in which her caresses are few, fitful, unexpected, light as air and hot as fire. The regal queenliness with which she sends him from her back to Rome, when she touches his sword with her lips and invokes the god of victory, and one feels that in her veins there flows the blood of a hundred centuries of kings. And the restlessness of her when he is gone. How she beats the heated pillows with feverish impatience and strains her eyes out across the glowing desert and the sleepy Nile. The madness of her fury when the messenger delivers his news, how her face became famished and hungry and her eyes burned like a tiger's and her very flesh seemed to cleave to her bones. How, but bah! it is not possible to describe it. It was like the lightning which flashes and terrifies and is gone. Through it all she keeps doing little things that you do not expect to see on the stage, things that make you feel within yourself how she loves and how she hates. She gives you those moments of absolute reality of experience, of positive knowledge that are the test of all great art. The thing itself is in her, the absolute quality that all books write of, all songs sing of, all men dream of, that only one in hundreds ever knows or realizes. It leaps up and strikes you between the eyes, makes you hold your breath and tremble. And this reminds me of what Plutarch says, that Cleopatra's chiefest charm was not in her beautiful face, nor her keen wit, nor her wealth of wisdom, but "in the immensity of what she had to give," in her versatility, her intensity, her sensitiveness to every emotion, her whole luxuriant personality.

I wish it had been Sardou's Cleopatra that Miss Lewis played, for, compared to Shakespeare's it is cheap and tawdry, it has less beauty to mar, less dignity to lose. There have been innumerable attempts to dramatize that greatest love story of the ages. They began with Virgil, who tried to do it in that dramatic fourth book of the Aeneid in the person of the *infelix Dido*. Since then poets and dramatists and novelists galore have struggled with it. But among them all the great William is the only man who has made a possible character of the Egyptian queen. Some wise men say, indeed, that he had a living model for it, and that his Cleopatra "with Phœbus' amorous pinches black and wrinkled deep in time" was none other than the Dark Lady of the sonnets. The more one reads the sonnets the more probable that seems, and yet I think he was great enough to have done it without a model. He had no model for Caesar or Brutus or Antony and certainly none for Juliet. His mind worked independently of any romances or tragedies in his own life. It, in itself, had loved all loves, suffered all sorrow, known all tragedies. I sometimes think that if there is anything in the theory of re-incarnation he must have been them all, Troilus, Antony, Romeo, Hamlet. No personal experience in fog-clouded England, no love in dusky Elizabethan London could have brought to him the sun and langor of the south, the beauty and luxury and abundant life of the lotus land. It was amusing even while it was painful to see the childish way in which they played with his great purposes and mangled his great art the other night. "Father, forgive them, for they knew not what they did."

The gleeful, irresponsible way in which they went through that first scene where Antony is down in Egypt kissing away kingdoms and provinces. But Cleopatra was one woman of the ages, one unique product of the centuries, she had more than mortal resources and the love she inspired was almost more than mortal. No ordinary woman could be expected to enact it. As Antony said, if she would set a limit to the love she made men feel she "must needs find out new heaven, new earth." Well, she found them. She was more than a woman, she was a realization of things dreamed. As that shrewd philosopher, Enobarbus, said to Antony when a repentant mood was on him,

> "O, sir, you had then left unseen
> A wonderful piece of work,
> Which not to have been blest withal
> Would have discredited your travel"

To know Cleopatra was then a sort of finishing touch to a great man's education. If a man was to be traveled and experienced he must see her, as today, he must see the pyramids. All the greatest Romans took post graduate work in Egypt.

The finest drinking scene in literature was cut out the other night, while a dozen trivial scenes were left in. The talk about the serpents of Egypt which takes place between *Lepidus* and *Antony* Miss Lewis and her versatile husband saw fit to have spoken by Lepidus and Enobarbus. Now the only purpose of that scene is to recall to Antony Egypt and that one queen of serpents, recall them until he drinks and drinks again, till his foot steps are unsteady and he finally goes out flushed and reeling, leaning on the steady arm of Caesar, the beginning to the end. They failed utterly to bring out the meaning of that scene where the fight is declared by sea, where the gods have first made mad he whom they would destroy and Antony cries, "By sea, by sea!"

I wonder if any other poet could have given to Antony the dignity and majesty that Shakespeare gives him in defeat. After Actium, when Antony meets the queen he says,

O, whither hast thou led me, Egypt?
. . . .
Thy full supremacy thou knewest,
And that thy beck might from the bidding of the Gods
Command me.

It is said with a simplicity and pathos that dignify even its weakness. And O, the greatness of him after the last defeat. Well does
Enobarbus call him an old lion dying. When they tell him that
the queen is dead, all the simple manliness in him comes out.
"The long day's task is done, and we must sleep." When the ruse
is confessed he is not angry, he is beyond all that now. The key
note of the whole tragedy, the grand motif rounds once again.
He does what he has always done. He has always gone back to her,
after every wrong, after every treachery. He has left kingdoms and
principalities to go to her, thrown away half the world to seek her,
and now of his old captain, he asks one last favor, that they carry
him to her now that he cannot go himself anymore, and he goes,
for the last time.

That last meeting, that awful scene in which Antony, bleeding and dying, is dragged up to the sides of the monument, Miss
Lewis omits. Possibly because it is almost impossible to represent
it on the stage, possibly because the play is long and something
must be cut to give time to the barefoot ballet. At any rate to cut
it is to divest the play of half its greatness. For the "moral" of the
play, if there be one, is in the last line that Antony speaks before
the mists cloud over him and he begins to wander back to the old
days of empire and delight.

One word, sweet queen:
Of Caesar seek your honor, with your safety.

That he should have lived for her and died for her, lost the
world for her and yet should have had to say that at the end! There
is a tragedy for you, in its darkest melancholy. The tragedy of all
such love and such relations, of everything on earth that hides
shame at its heart, that is without honor and absolute respect. All

the hundreds of French novels that have been written upon the *union libre* have told us nothing new about it after that. That one line has in it all the doubt and dark tragedy of the whole thing. We Anglo-Saxons have no need of a "Sapho" or of the numerous and monotonous works of M. Paul Bourget. That story has all been written for us once as it never can be again, by a master whose like no one world can bear twice, whose ashes one planet can carry but once in its bosom.

(1895)

Henry Cabot Lodge

(1850–1924)

Shakespeare's Americanisms

Henry Cabot Lodge's essay, published in *Harper's Magazine*, offered a riposte to English critics who mocked "Americanisms" as a debasement of the mother-tongue, while at the same time reflecting his concerns about America's linguistic legacy and identity. Lodge notes here that the earliest English settlers, both in Virginia and the New England colonies, had brought Shakespeare's language with them and that expressions London snobs now deride as "Americanisms" can be found in Shakespeare. Paradoxically, then, these so-called Americanisms are arguably more authentic than current English usage. Lodge's conclusion—that "it is much better for all who speak [English] to give their best strength to defending it and keeping it pure and vigorous, so that it may go on spreading and conquering"—may usefully be read in light of his larger political goals, which Lodge pressed for as a United States Senator for over three decades: restricting large-scale immigration and advocating an imperialist American foreign policy. Lodge had strong views about what it meant to be American and considered education and the English language as essential to "Americanizing" immigrants, which for him was crucial to the well-being of the nation. Four years before he wrote "Shakespeare's Americanisms" he argued that "the immigration of the people who have settled and built up the nation during the last 250 years, and who have been, with trifling exceptions, kindred either in race or language, or both, is declining, while the immigration of people who are not kindred either in race or language, and who represent the most ignorant classes and the lowest labor of Europe, is increasing with frightful rapidity."

❧

MUCH has been written first and last about certain English words and phrases which are commonly called "Americanisms." That they are so classified is due to our brethren of England, who seem to think that in this way they not only relieve themselves of all responsibility for the existence of these offending parts of speech, but that they also in some mysterious manner make them things apart and put them outside the pale of the English language. No one would be hard-hearted enough to grudge to our island kindred any comfort they may take in this mental operation, but that any one should cherish such a belief shows a curious ignorance, not merely as to many of the words in question, but as to the history and present standing of the language itself. To describe an English word or phrase as American or British or Australian or Indian or South African may be convenient if we wish to define that portion of the English-speaking people among whom it originated or by whom it has been kept or revived from the usage of an earlier day. But it is worse than useless to do so if an attempt to exclude the word from English speech is thereby intended. It is no longer possible in any such fashion as this to set up arbitrary metes and bounds to the great language which has spread over the world with the march of the people who use it. The "Queen's English" was a phrase correct enough in the days of Elizabeth or Anne, but it is an absurdity in those of Victoria. In the time of the last Tudor or the last Stuart every one whose native tongue was English could be properly set down as a subject of the English Queen. No such proposition is possible now. The English-speaking people who owe no allegiance to England's Queen are to-day more numerous than those who do.

In the face of facts like these it is just as impossible to set limits to the language or to establish a proprietorship in it in any given place as it would be to fetter the growth of the people who speak it. This it is also which makes it out of the question to have any fixed standard of English in the narrow sense not uncommon in other languages. It is quite possible to have Tuscan Italian or Castilian Spanish or Parisian French as the standard of correctness, but no one ever heard of "London English" used in that sense. The reason is simple. These nations have ceased to spread and colonize. They are practically stationary. But English is the language of a conquering, colonizing race, which in the last three centuries has subdued and possessed ancient civilizations and virgin continents alike, and whose speech is now heard in the remotest corners of the earth.

It is not the least of the many glories of the English tongue that it has proved equal to the task which its possessors have imposed upon it. Like the race, it has shown itself capable of assimilating new elements without degeneration. It has met new conditions, adapted itself to them, and prevailed over them. It has proved itself flexible without weakness, and strong without rigidity. With all its vast spread it still remains unchanged in essence and in all its great qualities.

For such a language with such a history no standard of a province or a city can be fixed in order to make a narrow rule from which no appeal is possible. The usage of the best writers for the written, and of the best-educated and most highly trained men for the spoken word, without regard to where they may have been born or to where they live, is the only possible standard for English speech. Such a test may not be very sharply defined, but it is the only one practicable for a language which has done so much, and which is constantly growing and advancing. As a rule of conduct in writing or speaking it is true that this kind of standard may be in unessential points a little vague. But this defect, if it be one, is outweighed a thousand times by the fact that the language is thus freed from the stiffness and narrowness which denote that the race has ceased to march, and that expansion for people and speech alike is at an end.

Yet the changes made during this worldwide extension, with all the infinite variety of new conditions which accompanied it, are, after all, more apparent than real. That they should be so few and at the same time so all-sufficient for every fresh need that has arisen demonstrates better than anything else the marvellous strength and richness inherent in the English language. In some cases new words have been invented or added to express new facts or new things, and these are both valuable and necessary. In other cases old words, both in the mother-country and elsewhere, have, in the processes of time and of altered conditions, been changed in meaning and usage, sometimes for the better and sometimes for the worse. In still other instances old words and old meanings have lived on or been revived by one branch of the race, when given up or modified elsewhere.

It is this last fact which makes it so futile to try to read out of the language and its literature words and phrases merely because they are not used in the island whence people and speech started on their career of conquest. It does not in the least follow, because a word is not used to-day in England, that it is either new or bad. It may be both, as is the case with many words which have never travelled outside the mother-country, and with many others which have never been heard in the parent-land. On the other hand, it may equally well be neither. The mere fact that a word exists in one place and not in another, of itself proves nothing. That those of the English-speaking people who have remained in Great Britain should condemn as pestilent innovations words which they do not use themselves is very natural, but quite un-scientific. It is the same attitude as that of the Tory reviewer who condemns some of James Russell Lowell's letters as "provincial." They are different in tone and thought from that to which he is accustomed, and hence he asserts that they must be bad. The real trouble is merely that the letters are American and not English, continental and not insular. They are not in the language or the spirit of the critic's own parish, that is all. They jar on his habits of thought because they differ from his standard, and so he sets them down as provincial, failing hopelessly to see that mere difference proves nothing either way as to merits or defects. So a word used in the United States and not in England may be good or bad, but the mere fact that it is in use in one place and not in the other has no bearing as to either its goodness or the reverse. Its virtues or its defects must be determined on grounds more relative than this.

The best proof of the propositions just advanced can be found by examining some of the words which exist here and not in Great Britain, or which are used here with a meaning differing from that of British usage. It is well to remember at the outset that the English speech was planted in this country by English emigrants, who settled Virginia and New England at the beginning of the seventeenth century. To Virginia came many educated men, who became the planters, land-owners, and leaders of the infant State, and although they did little for nearly a century in behalf of general education, the sons of the governing class were either taught at home by English tutors or sent across the water to English colleges. In New England the average education among the first settlers was high, and they showed their love of learning by their immediate foundation of a college and of a public-school system. The Puritan leaders and their powerful clergy were, as a rule, college-bred men, with all the traditions of Oxford and Cambridge fresh in their minds and dear to their hearts. They would have been the last men to corrupt or abuse the mother-tongue, which they cherished more than ever in the new and distant land. The language which these people brought with them to Virginia and Massachusetts, moreover, was, as Mr. Lowell has remarked, the language of Shakespeare, who lived and wrote and died just at the period when these countrymen of his were taking their way to the New World. In view of these latter-day criticisms it might seem as if these emigrants should have brought some other English with them than that of Shakespeare's England, but luckily or unluckily that was the only mode of speech they had. It followed very naturally that some of the words thus brought over the water, and then common to the English on both sides of the Atlantic, survived only in the New World, to which they were transplanted. This is not remarkable, but it is passing strange that words not only used in Shakespeare's time, but used by Shakespeare himself, should have lived to be disdainfully called "Americanisms" by people now living in Shakespeare's own country. It is well, therefore, to look at a few of these words occasionally, if only to refresh our memories. No single example, perhaps, is new, but when we bring several into a little group they make a picturesque illustration of the futility of undertaking to shut out a word from good society because it is used in one place where English-speaking people dwell and not in another.

What Mr. Bartlett in his dictionary of Americanisms calls justly one of "the most marked peculiarities of American speech" is the constant use of the word "well" as an interjection, especially at the beginning of sentences. Mr. Bartlett also says, "Englishmen have told me that they could always detect an American by this use of the word." Here perhaps is a clew to the true nationality of the Danish soldiers with Italian names and idiomatic English speech who appear in the first scene of *Hamlet*:

> *Bernardo.* Have you had quiet guard?
> *Francisco.* Not a mouse stirring.
> *Bernardo.* Well, good-night.

This is as excellent and precise an example of the every-day American use of the word "well" as could possibly be found. The fact is that the use of "well" as an interjection is so common in Shakespeare that Mrs. Clarke omits the word used in that capacity from her concordance, and explains its omission on the ground of its constant repetition, like "come," "look," "marry," and so on. Thus has it come to pass that an American betrays his nationality to an Englishman because he uses the word "well" interjectionally, as Shakespeare used it. I have seen more than once patronizing criticisms of this peculiarity of American speech, but have never suffered at the sight, because I have always been able to take to myself the consolation of Lord Byron, that it is

"Better to err with Pope than shine with Pye."

Our English brethren, again, use the word "ill" in speaking of a person "afflicted with disease"—to take Johnson's definition of the word "sick." They restrict the word "sick" to "nausea," and regard our employment of it, as applicable to any kind of disease, or to a person out of health from any cause, as an "Americanism." And yet this "Americanism" is Elizabethan and Shakespearian. For example, in *Midsummer-Night's Dream* (Act I., Scene I.), Helena says, "Sickness is catching," which is not the chief characteristic of the ailment to which modern English usage confines the word. In *Cymbeline*, again (Act V., Scene IV.), we find the phrase, "one that's sick o' the gout." Examples might be multiplied, for Shakespeare rarely uses the word "ill," but constantly the word "sick" in the general sense. In the Bible the use of "sick" is, I believe, unbroken. The marriage service says, "in sickness and in health," and Johnson's definition, as Mr. Bartlett points out, conforms to the usage of Chaucer, Milton, Dryden, and Cowper. Even the Englishman who starts with surprise at our general application of "sick" and "sickness," and who is nothing if not logical, would not think of describing an officer of the army as absent on "ill-leave" or as placed upon the "ill-list." The English restriction of the use of these two words is, in truth, wholly unwarranted, and should be given up in favor of the better and older American usage, which is that of all the highest standards of English literature.

The conditions of travelling have changed so much during this century, and all the methods of travel are so new, that most of the words connected with it are of necessity new also, either in form or application. In some cases the same phrases have come in both England and the United States. In others different words have been chosen by the two nations to express the same thing, and, so far as merit goes, there is little to choose between them. But there are a few words in this department which are as old as travelling itself, and which were as necessary in the days of the galley and the pack-horse as they are in those of the steamship and the railroad. One of them is the comprehensive term for the things which travellers carry with them. Englishmen commonly use the word "luggage"; we Americans the word "baggage." In this we agree with Touchstone, who, using a phrase which has become part of our daily speech, says (Act III., Scene II.), "though not with bag and baggage, yet with scrip and scrippage." Leontes also, in the *Winter's Tale* (Act I., Scene II.), uses the same phrase as Touchstone. It may be argued that both allusions are drawn from military language, in which "baggage" is always used. But this will not avail, for "luggage" occurs twice at least in Shakespeare referring solely to the effects of an army. In *Henry V.* (Act V., Scene IV.) we find "the luggage of our camp"; and Fluellen says, in the same play (Act IV., Scene VII.), "Kill the poys and the luggage!" Shakespeare used both words indifferently in the same sense, and the "Americanism" was as familiar to him as the "Briticism."

In this same connection it may be added that the word "trunk," which we use where the English say "box," is, like "baggage," Shakespearian. It occurs in *Lear* (Act II., Scene II.), where Kent calls Oswald a "one-trunk-inheriting slave." Johnson interpreted this to mean "trunk-hose," which makes no sense. Steevens said "trunk" here meant "coffer," and that all his property was in one "coffer" or "trunk." This seems to have been the accepted version ever since, as it is certainly the obvious and sensible one.

Almost always the preservation or revival of a Shakespearian word is something deserving profound gratitude, but the great master of English gives some authority for one thoroughly distasteful phrase. This is the use of the word "stage" as a verb in the sense of to put upon the stage, a habit which has become of late sadly common. So the Duke, in the first scene of *Measure for Measure*, says,

> "I love the people,
> But do not like to stage me to their eyes."

Again, in *Antony and Cleopatra* (Act III., Scene XI.), "be stag'd to the show, against a sworder." And again, later in the same play (Act V., Scene II.), Cleopatra says,

> "the quick comedians
> Extemp'rally will stage us."

It is true that these examples all refer to persons and not to "staging plays," as the phrase runs to-day, but the use of the word, especially in the last case, seems identically the same.

Among characteristic American words none is more so than "to guess," in the sense of "to think." The word is old and good, but the significance that we give it is charged against us as an innovation of our own, and wholly without warrant. One sees it continually in English comic papers and in books also put into the mouths of Americans as a discreditable but unmistakable badge of nationality. Shakespeare uses the word constantly, generally in the stricter and narrower sense where it implies conjecture. Yet he also uses it in the broader American sense of thinking. For example, in

Measure for Measure (Act IV., Scene IV.), Angelo says, "And why
meet him at the gates, and redeliver our authorities there?" To
which Escalus replies, in a most emphatically American fashion,
"I guess not." There is no questioning, no conjecture here. It is
simply our common American form of "I think not." Again, in
the *Winter's Tale* (Act IV., Scene III.), Camillo says, "Which, I
do guess, you do not purpose to him." This is the same use of the
word in the sense of to think, and other instances might be added.
In view of this it seems not a little curious that a bit of Shakespeare's English in the use of an excellent Saxon word should be
selected above all others by Englishmen of the nineteenth century
to brand an American, not merely with his nationality, but with
the misuse of his mother-tongue. Be it said also in passing that
"guess" is a far better word than "fancy," which the British are fond
of putting to a similar service.

Leaving now legitimate words, and turning to the children of
the street and the market-place, we find some curious examples,
not only of American slang, but of slang which is regarded as
extremely fresh and modern. Mr. Brander Matthews, in his most
interesting article on that subject, has already pointed out that a
"deck of cards" is Shakespearian. In *Henry VI.* (Third Part, Act V.,
Scene I.), Gloucester says,

> "But while he thought to steal the single ten,
> The king was slyly fingered from the deck."

Mr. Matthews has also cited a still more remarkable example of
recent slang from the Sonnets, of all places in the world, where
"fire out" is used in the exact colloquial sense of to-day. It occurs
in the 144th Sonnet,

> "Yet this shall I ne'er know, but live in doubt
> Till my bad angel fire my good one out."

"Square," in the sense of fair or honest, and the verb "to be
square," in the sense of to be fair or honest, are thought modern,
and are now so constantly used that they have wellnigh passed

beyond the boundaries of slang. If they do so, it is but a return to their old place, for Shakespeare has this use of the word, and in serious passages. In *Timon of Athens* (Act V., Scene V.) the First Senator says,

> "All have not offended;
> For those that were, it is not square to take
> On those that are, revenges."

In *Antony and Cleopatra* (Act II., Scene II.) Mecænas says, "She's a most triumphant lady, if report be square to her."

"In the soup," to express defeat and disaster, is apparently very recent, and yet it is singularly like the language of Pompey in *Measure for Measure* (Act III., Scene II.), when he says, "Troth, sir, she hath eaten up all her beef, and she is herself in the tub."

Even more recent than "in the soup" is the use of the word "stuffed," to denote contemptuously what may be most nearly described as large and ineffective pretentiousness. But in *Much Ado about Nothing* (Act I., Scene I.) the Messenger says, "A lord to a lord, a man to a man; stuffed with all honorable virtues." To which Beatrice replies, "It is so, indeed; he is no less than a *stuffed man*: but for the stuffing,—Well, we are all mortal." Here Beatrice uses the phrase "stuffed man" in contempt, catching up the word of the messenger.

"Flapjack," perhaps, is hardly to be called slang, but it is certainly an American phrase for a griddle-cake. We must have brought it with us, however, from Shakespeare's England, for there it is in *Pericles* (Act II., Scene I.), where the Grecian—very Grecian—fisherman says, "Come, thou shalt go home, and we'll have flesh for holidays, fish for fasting days, and moreo'er puddings and flapjacks; and thou shalt be welcome."

I will close this little collection of Shakespeare's Americanisms with a word that is not slang, but the use of which in this country shows the tenacity with which our people have held to the Elizabethan phrases that their ancestors brought with them. In *As You Like It* (Act I., Scene I.), Charles the Wrestler says, "They say many young gentlemen flock to him every day, and fleet the time carelessly, as they did in the golden world." "Fleet," as a verb in the sense of "to pass" or "to move," may yet survive in some parts of England, but it has certainly disappeared from the literature and the ordinary speech of both England and the United States. It is still in use, however, in this exact Shakespearian sense in the daily speech of people on the island of Nantucket, in the State of Massachusetts. I have heard it there frequently, and it is owing no doubt to the isolation of the inhabitants that it still lingers, as it does, an echo of the Elizabethan days, among American fishermen in the closing years of the nineteenth century.

In tracing a few Americanisms, as they are called, to the land whence they emigrated so many years ago, I have not gone beyond the greatest master of the language. A little wider range, with excursions into other fields, would furnish us with pedigrees almost as good, if not quite so lofty, for many other words and phrases which are set down by the British guardians of our language as "Americanisms," generally with some adjective of an uncomplimentary character. But such further collection would be merely cumulative. These few examples from Shakespeare are quite sufficient to show that because a word is used by one branch of the English-speaking people and not by another, it does not therefore follow that the word in question is not both good and ancient. They prove also that words which some persons frown upon and condemn, merely because their own parish does not use them, may have served well the greatest men who ever wrote or spoke the language, and that they have a place and a title which the criticisms upon them can never hope to claim.

It is a little lesson which is worth taking to heart, for the English speech is too great an inheritance to be trifled with or wrangled over. It is much better for all who speak it to give their best strength to defending it and keeping it pure and vigorous, so that it may go on spreading and conquering, as in the centuries which have already closed. The true doctrine, which may well be taken home to our hearts on both sides of the water, has never been better put than in Lord Houghton's fine lines:

"Beyond the vague Atlantic deep,
Far as the farthest prairies sweep,
Where forest glooms the nerve appall,
Where burns the radiant Western fall,
One duty lies on old and young—
With filial piety to guard,
As on its greenest native sward,
The glory of the English tongue.

"That ample speech! That subtle speech!
Apt for the need of all and each:
Strong to endure, yet prompt to bend
Wherever human feelings tend.
Preserve its force; expand its powers;
And through the maze of civic life,
In Letters, Commerce, even in Strife,
Forget not it is yours and ours."

(1895)

Jane Addams

(1860–1935)

A Modern Lear

Jane Addams was a political and social reformer, anti-war activist, feminist, author, and the first American woman to be awarded the Nobel Peace Prize. Her engagement with Shakespeare began early on: she published a perceptive college essay on *Macbeth* in *Rockford Seminary Magazine* in 1880 and her class established a Shakespeare club the following year. In "A Modern Lear" Addams reads Shakespeare's tragedy against the recent and bloody Pullman Strike that had far-reaching consequences for American industry, labor, and government. The industrialist George Pullman had built and closely controlled a company town (which he had named after himself) where workers who built railcars at his Chicago factory lived. Conflict broke out when Pullman cut wages and laid off workers yet refused to lower their rents. Arbitration failed to end the conflict since Pullman refused to negotiate. A government injunction against the boycott and a massive strike that threatened the national mail and transportation systems soon followed. The strike collapsed after President Grover Cleveland sent in federal troops. Addams probably finished writing "A Modern Lear" in late 1895 before delivering it in March 1896 to an audience of five hundred at the Chicago Woman's Club (and subsequently before other groups around the country). Addams explores the ways in which industrial ties resemble family ones and imagines the labor conflict in light of the relationship of Lear and Cordelia. While her sharpest criticism is reserved for the blind and willful feudal king, Cordelia too, Addams writes, "does not escape our censure" (nor, by implication, did the workers). Pullman reportedly resented her speech "bitterly" and nine editors turned it down in 1896; Addams shared it at the time with John Dewey, who called it "one of the greatest things I ever read both as to its form and its ethical philosophy." "A Modern Lear" was belatedly published in *The Survey* in 1912.

THOSE of us who lived in Chicago during the summer of 1894 were confronted by a drama which epitomized and, at the same time, challenged the code of social ethics under which we live, for a quick series of unusual events had dispelled the good nature which in happier times envelops the ugliness of the industrial situation. It sometimes seems as if the shocking experiences of that summer, the barbaric instinct to kill, roused on both sides, the sharp division into class lines, with the resultant distrust and bitterness, can only be endured if we learn from it all a great ethical lesson. To endure is all we can hope for. It is impossible to justify such a course of rage and riot in a civilized community to whom the methods of conciliation and control were open. Every public-spirited citizen in Chicago during that summer felt the stress and perplexity of the situation and asked himself, "How far am I responsible for this social disorder? What can be done to prevent such outrageous manifestations of ill-will?"

If the responsibility of tolerance lies with those of the widest vision, it behooves us to consider this great social disaster, not alone in its legal aspect nor in its sociological bearings, but from those deep human motives, which, after all, determine events.

During the discussions which followed the Pullman strike, the defenders of the situation were broadly divided between the people pleading for individual benevolence and those insisting upon social righteousness; between those who held that the philanthropy of the president of the Pullman company had been most ungratefully received and those who maintained that the situation was the inevitable outcome of the social consciousness developing among working people.

In the midst of these discussions the writer found her mind dwelling upon a comparison which modified and softened all her judgments. Her attention was caught by the similarity of ingratitude suffered by an indulgent employer and an indulgent parent. King Lear came often to her mind. We have all shared the family relationship and our code of ethics concerning it is somewhat settled. We also bear a part in the industrial relationship, but our ethics concerning that are still uncertain. A comparative study of these two relationships presents an advantage, in that it enables us to consider the situation from the known experience toward the unknown. The minds of all of us reach back to our early struggles, as we emerged from the state of self-willed childhood to a recognition of the family claim.

We have all had glimpses of what it might be to blaspheme against family ties; to ignore the elemental claim they make upon us, but on the whole we have recognized them, and it does not occur to us to throw them over. The industrial claim is so difficult; the ties are so intangible that we are constantly ignoring them and shirking the duties which they impose. It will probably be easier to treat of the tragedy of the Pullman strike as if it were already long past when we compare it to the family tragedy of Lear which has already become historic to our minds and which we discuss without personal feeling.

Historically considered, the relation of Lear to his children was archaic and barbaric, holding in it merely the beginnings of a family life, since developed. We may in later years learn to look back upon the industrial relationships in which we are now placed as quite as incomprehensible and selfish, quite as barbaric and undeveloped, as was the family relationship between Lear and his daughters. We may then take the relationship of this unusually generous employer at Pullman to his own townful of employees as at least a fair one, because so exceptionally liberal in many of its aspects. King Lear doubtless held the same notion of a father's duty that was held by the other fathers of his time; but he alone was a king and had kingdoms to bestow upon his children. He was unique, therefore, in the magnitude of his indulgence, and in the magnitude of the disaster which followed it. The sense of duty held by the president of the Pullman company doubtless represents the ideal in the minds of the best of the present employers as to their obligations toward their employes, but he projected this ideal more magnificently than the others. He alone gave his men so model a town, such perfect surroundings. The magnitude of his indulgence and failure corresponded and we are forced to challenge the ideal itself: the same ideal which, more or less clearly defined, is floating in the minds of all philanthropic employers.

This older tragedy implied mal-adjustment between individuals; the forces of the tragedy were personal and passionate. This modern tragedy in its inception is a mal-adjustment between two large bodies of men, an employing company and a mass of employes. It deals not with personal relationships, but with industrial relationships.

Owing, however, to the unusual part played in it by the will of one man, we find that it closely approaches Lear in motif. The relation of the British King to his family is very like the relation of the president of the Pullman company to his town; the denouement of a daughter's break with her father suggests the break of the employes with their benefactor. If we call one an example of the domestic tragedy, the other of the industrial tragedy, it is possible to make them illuminate each other.

It is easy to discover striking points of similarity in the tragedies of the royal father and the philanthropic president of the Pullman company. The like quality of ingratitude they both suffered is at once apparent. It may be said that the ingratitude which Lear received was poignant and bitter to him in proportion as he recalled the extraordinary benefits he had heaped upon his daughters, and that he found his fate harder to bear because he had so far exceeded the measure of a father's duty, as he himself says. What, then, would be the bitterness of a man who had heaped extraordinary benefits upon those toward whom he had no duty recognized by common consent; who had not only exceeded the righteousness of the employer, but who had worked out original and striking methods for lavishing goodness and generosity? More than that, the president had been almost persecuted for this goodness by the more utilitarian members of his company and had at one time imperiled his business reputation for the sake of the benefactions to his town, and he had thus reached the height of sacrifice for it. This model town embodied not only his hopes and ambitions, but stood for the peculiar effort which a man makes for that which is misunderstood.*

* While the town of Pullman was in process of construction the Pullman stock was sometimes called out on the New York Exchange: "How much for flowerbeds and fountains?" To which the company naturally objected.

It is easy to see that although the heart of Lear was cut by ingratitude and by misfortune, it was cut deepest of all by the public pity of his people, in that they should remember him no longer as a king and benefactor, but as a defeated man who had blundered through over-softness. So the heart of the Chicago man was cut by the unparalleled publicity which brought him to the minds of thousands as a type of oppression and injustice, and to many others as an example of the evil of an irregulated sympathy for the "lower classes." He who had been dined and feted throughout Europe as the creator of a model town, as the friend and benefactor of workingmen, was now execrated by workingmen throughout the entire country. He had not only been good to those who were now basely ungrateful to him, but he felt himself deserted by the admiration of his people.

In shops such as those at Pullman, indeed, in all manufacturing affairs since the industrial revolution, industry is organized into a vast social operation. The shops are managed, however, not for the development of the workman thus socialized, but for the interests of the company owning the capital. The divergence between the social form and the individual aim becomes greater as the employes are more highly socialized and dependent, just as the clash in a family is more vital in proportion to the development and closeness of the family tie. The president of the Pullman company went further than the usual employer does. He socialized not only the factory but the form in which his workmen were living. He built and, in a great measure, regulated an entire town. This again might have worked out into a successful associated effort, if he had had in view the sole good of the inhabitants thus socialized, if he had called upon them for self-expression and had made the town a growth and manifestation of their wants and needs. But, unfortunately, the end to be obtained became ultimately commercial and not social, having in view the payment to the company of at least 4 per cent on the money invested, so that with this rigid requirement there could be no adaptation of rent to wages, much less to needs. The rents became statical and the wages competitive, shifting inevitably with the demands of trade. The president assumed that he himself knew the needs of his men, and so far from wishing them to express their needs he denied to them the simple rights of trade organization, which would have been, of course, the merest preliminary to an attempt at associated expression. If we may take the dictatorial relation of Lear to Cordelia as a typical and most dramatic example of the distinctively family tragedy, one will asserting its authority through all the entanglement of wounded affection, and insisting upon its selfish ends at all costs, may we not consider the absolute authority of this employer over his town as a typical and dramatic example of the industrial tragedy? One will directing the energies of many others, without regard to their desires, and having in view in the last analysis only commercial results?

It shocks our ideal of family life that a man should fail to know his daughter's heart because she awkwardly expressed her love, that he should refuse to comfort and advise her through all difference of opinion and clashing of will. That a man should be so absorbed in his own indignation as to fail to apprehend his child's thought; that he should lose his affection in his anger, is really no more unnatural than that the man who spent a million of dollars on a swamp to make it sanitary for his employes, should refuse to speak to them for ten minutes, whether they were in the right or wrong; or that a man who had given them his time and thought for twenty years should withdraw from them his guidance when he believed them misled by ill-advisers and wandering in a mental fog; or that he should grow hard and angry when they needed tenderness and help.

Lear ignored the common ancestry of Cordelia and himself. He forgot her royal inheritance of magnanimity, and also the power of obstinacy which he shared with her. So long had he thought of himself as the noble and indulgent father that he had lost the faculty by which he might perceive himself in the wrong. Even when his spirit was broken by the storm he declared himself more sinned against than sinning. He could believe any amount of kindness and goodness of himself, but could imagine no fidelity on the part of Cordelia unless she gave him the sign he demanded.

The president of the Pullman company doubtless began to build his town from an honest desire to give his employes the best surroundings. As it developed it became a source of pride and an exponent of power, that he cared most for when it gave him a glow of benevolence. Gradually, what the outside world thought of it became of importance to him and he ceased to measure its usefulness by the standard of the men's needs. The theater was complete in equipment and beautiful in design, but too costly for a troupe who depended upon the patronage of mechanics, as the church was too expensive to be rented continuously. We can imagine the founder of the town slowly darkening his glints of memory and forgetting the common stock of experience which he held with his men. He cultivated the great and noble impulses of the benefactor, until the power of attaining a simple human relationship with his employes, that of frank equality with them, was gone from him. He, too, lost the faculty of affectionate in-terpretation, and demanded a sign. He and his employes had no mutual interest in a common cause.

Was not the grotesque situation of the royal father and the philanthropic employer to perform so many good deeds that they lost the power of recognizing good in beneficiaries? Were not both so absorbed in carrying out a personal plan of improvement that they failed to catch the great moral lesson which their times offered them? This is the crucial point of the tragedies and may be further elucidated.

Lear had doubtless swung a bauble before Cordelia's baby eyes that he might have the pleasure of seeing the little pink and tender hands stretched for it. A few years later he had given jewels to the young princess, and felt an exquisite pleasure when she stood before him, delighted with her gaud and grateful to her father. He demanded the same kind of response for his gift of the kingdom, but the gratitude must be larger and more carefully expressed, as befitted such a gift. At the opening of the drama he sat upon his throne ready for this enjoyment, but instead of delight and gratitude he found the first dawn of character. His daughter made the awkward attempt of an untrained soul to be honest, to be scrupulous in the expressions of its feelings. It was new to him that his child should be moved by a principle outside of himself, which even his imagination could not follow; that she had caught the notion of an existence so vast that her relationship as a daughter was but part of it.

Perhaps her suitors, the King of France or the Duke of Burgundy, had first hinted to the young Cordelia that there was a fuller life beyond the seas. Certain it is that someone had shaken her from the quiet measure of her insular existence and that she had at last felt the thrill of the world's life. She was transformed by a dignity which recast her speech and made it self-contained, as is becoming a citizen of the world. She found herself in the sweep of a notion of justice so large that the immediate loss of a kingdom seemed of little consequence to her. Even an act which might be construed as disrespect to her father was justified in her eyes because she was vainly striving to fill out this larger conception of duty.

The test which comes sooner or later to many parents had come to Lear, to maintain the tenderness of the relation between father and child, after that relation had become one between adults; to be contented with the responses which this adult made to the family claim, while, at the same time, she felt the tug upon her motions and faculties of the larger life, the life which surrounds and completes the individual and family life, and which shares and widens her attention. He was not sufficiently wise to see that only that child can fulfill the family claim in its sweetness and strength who also fulfills the larger claim, that the adjustment of the lesser and larger implies no conflict. The mind of Lear was not big enough for this test. He failed to see anything but the personal slight involved; the ingratitude alone reached him. It was impossible for him to calmly watch his child developing beyond the strength of his own mind and sympathy.

Without pressing the analogy too hard may we not compare the indulgent relation of this employer to his town to the relation which existed between Lear and Cordelia? He fostered his employes for many years, gave them sanitary houses and beautiful parks, but in their extreme need, when they were struggling with the most difficult question which the times could present to them, when, if ever, they required the assistance of a trained mind and a comprehensive outlook, he lost his touch and had nothing wherewith to help them. He did not see the situation. He had been ignorant of their gropings toward justice. His conception of goodness for them had been cleanliness, decency of living, and above all, thrift and temperance. He had provided them means for all this; had gone further, and given them opportunities for enjoyment and comradeship. But he suddenly found his town in the sweep of a world-wide moral impulse. A movement had been going on about him and through the souls of his workingmen of which he had been unconscious. He had only heard of this movement by rumor. The men who consorted with him at his club and in his business had spoken but little of it, and when they had discussed it had contemptuously called it the "Labor Move- ment," headed by deadbeats and agitators. Of the force and power of this movement, of all the vitality within it, of that conception of duty which induces men to go without food and to see their wives and children suffer for the sake of securing better wages for fellow-workmen whom they have never seen, this president had dreamed absolutely nothing. But his town had at last become swept into this larger movement, so that the giving up of comfort- able homes, of beautiful surroundings, seemed as naught to the men within its grasp.

Outside the ken of this philanthropist, the proletariat had learned to say in many languages that "the injury of one is the concern of all." Their watchwords were brotherhood, sacrifice, the subordination of individual and trade interests to the good of the working class; and their persistent strivings were toward the ultimate freedom of that class from the conditions under which they now labor.

Compared to these watchwords the old ones which the philan- thropic employer had given his town were negative and inadequate.

When this movement finally swept in his own town, or, to speak more fairly, when in their distress and perplexity his own

employes appealed to the organized manifestation of this movement, they were quite sure that simply because they were workmen in distress they would not be deserted by it. This loyalty on
the part of a widely ramified and well organized union toward
the workmen in a "scab shop," who had contributed nothing to its
cause, was certainly a manifestation of moral power.

That the movement was ill-directed, that it was ill-timed and
disastrous in results, that it stirred up and became confused in
the minds of the public with the elements of riot and bloodshed,
can never touch the fact that it started from an unselfish impulse.

In none of his utterances or correspondence did the president
of the company for an instant recognize this touch of nobility, although one would imagine that he would gladly point out this bit
of virtue, in what he must have considered the moral ruin about
him. He stood throughout pleading for the individual virtues,
those which had distinguished the model workman of his youth,
those which had enabled him and so many of his contemporaries
to rise in life, when "rising in life" was urged upon every promising boy as the goal of his efforts. Of the new code of ethics he had
caught absolutely nothing. The morals he had taught his men did
not fail them in their hour of confusion. They were self-controlled
and destroyed no property.* They were sober and exhibited no
drunkenness, even though obliged to hold their meetings in the
saloon hall of a neighboring town. They repaid their employer in
kind, but he had given them no rule for the higher fellowship and
life of association into which they were plunged.

The virtues of one generation are not sufficient for the next,
any more than the accumulations of knowledge possessed by one
age are adequate to the needs of another.

Of the virtues received from our fathers we can afford to lose
none. We accept as a precious trust those principles and precepts
which the race has worked out for its highest safeguard and protection. But merely to preserve those is not enough. A task is laid

---

* The bill presented to the city of Chicago by the Pullman company for damages
received during the strike was $26—the result only of petty accidents.

upon each generation to enlarge their application, to ennoble their conception, and, above all, to apply and adapt them to the peculiar problems presented to it for solution.

The president of this company desired that his employes should possess the individual and family virtues, but did nothing to cherish in them those social virtues which his own age demanded. He rather substituted for that sense of responsibility to the community, a feeling of gratitude to himself, who had provided them with public buildings, and had laid out for them a simulacrum of public life.

Is it strange that when the genuine feeling of the age struck his town this belated and almost feudal virtue of personal gratitude fell before it?

Day after day during that horrible suspense, when the wires constantly reported the same message, "The president of the company holds that there is nothing to arbitrate," one longed to find out what was in the mind of this man, to unfold his ultimate motive. One concludes that he must have been sustained by the consciousness of being in the right. Only that could have held him against the great desire for fair play which swept over the country. Only the training which an arbitrary will receives by years of consulting first its own personal and commercial ends could have made it strong enough to withstand the demands for social adjustment. He felt himself right from the *commercial* standpoint, and could not see the situation from the *social* standpoint. For years he had gradually accustomed himself to the thought that his motive was beyond reproach; that his attitude to his town was always righteous and philanthropic. Habit held him persistent in this view of the case through all the changing conditions.

The diffused and subtle notion of dignity held by the modern philanthropist bears a curious analogy to the personal barbaric notion of dignity held by Lear. The man who persistently paced the seashore, while the interior of his country was racked with a strife which he alone might have arbitrated, lived out within himself the tragedy of King Lear. The shock of disaster upon egotism is apt to produce self-pity. It is possible that his self-pity and loneliness may have been so great and absorbing as to completely shut out from his mind a compunction of derelict duty. He may have been unconscious that men were charging him with a shirking of the issue.

Lack of perception is the besetting danger of the egoist, from whatever cause his egoism arises and envelopes him. But, doubtless, philanthropists are more exposed to this danger than any other class of people within the community. Partly because their efforts are overestimated, as no standard of attainment has yet been established, and partly because they are the exponents of a large amount of altruistic feeling with which the community has become equipped and which has not yet found adequate expression, they are therefore easily idealized.

Long ago Hawthorne called our attention to the fact that "philanthropy ruins, or is fearfully apt to ruin, the heart, the rich juices of which God never meant should be pressed violently out, and distilled into alcoholic liquor by an unnatural process; but it should render life sweet, bland and gently beneficent."

One might add to this observation that the muscles of this same heart may be stretched and strained until they lose the rhythm of the common heart-beat of the rest of the world.

Modern philanthropists need to remind themselves of the old definition of greatness: that it consists in the possession of the largest share of the common human qualities and experiences, not in the acquirements of peculiarities and excessive virtues. Popular opinion calls him the greatest of Americans who gathered to himself the largest amount of American experience, and who never forgot when he was in Washington how the "crackers" in Kentucky and the pioneers of Illinois thought and felt, striving to retain their thoughts and feelings, and to embody only the mighty will of the "common people." The danger of professionally attaining to the power of the righteous man, of yielding to the ambition "for doing good," compared to which the ambitions for political position, learning, or wealth are vulgar and commonplace, ramifies throughout our modern life, and is a constant and settled danger in philanthropy.

In so far as philanthropists are cut off from the influence of the *Zeit-Geist*, from the code of ethics which rule the body of men, from the great moral life springing from our common experiences, so long as they are "good to people," rather than "with them," they are bound to accomplish a large amount of harm. They are outside of the influence of that great faith which perennially springs up in the hearts of the people, and re-creates the world.

In spite of the danger of overloading the tragedies with moral reflections, a point ought to be made on the other side. It is the weakness in the relation of the employes to the employer, the fatal lack of generosity in the attitude of workmen toward the company under whose exactions they feel themselves wronged.

In reading the tragedy of King Lear, Cordelia does not escape our censure. Her first words are cold, and we are shocked by her lack of tenderness. Why should she ignore her father's need for indulgence, and be so unwilling to give him what he so obviously craved? We see in the old king "the overmastering desire of being beloved, which is selfish, and yet characteristic of the selfishness of a loving and kindly nature alone." His eagerness produces in us a strange pity for him, and we are impatient that his youngest and best-beloved child cannot feel this, even in the midst of her search for truth and her newly acquired sense of a higher duty. It seems to us a narrow conception that would break thus abruptly with the past, and would assume that her father had no part in her new life. We want to remind her that "pity, memory and faithfulness are natural ties," and surely as much to be prized as is the development of her own soul. We do not admire the Cordelia "who loves according to her bond" as we later admire the same Cordelia who comes back from France that she may include in her happiness and freer life the father whom she had deserted through her self-absorption. She is aroused to her affection through her pity, but when the floodgates are once open she acknowledges all. It sometimes seems as if only hardship and sorrow could arouse our tenderness, whether in our personal or social relations; that the king, the prosperous man, was the last to receive the justice which can come only through affectionate interpretation. We feel less pity for Lear on his throne than in the storm, although he is the same man, bound up in the same self-righteousness, and exhibiting the same lack of self-control.

As the vision of the life of Europe caught the sight and quickened the pulses of Cordelia, so a vision of the wider life has caught the sight of workingmen. After the vision has once been seen it is impossible to do aught but to press toward its fulfillment. We have all seen it. We are all practically agreed that the social passion of the age is directed toward the emancipation of the wage-worker; that a great accumulation of moral force is overmastering men and making for this emancipation as in another time it has made for the emancipation of the slave; that nothing will satisfy the aroused conscience of men short of the complete participation of the working classes in the spiritual, intellectual and material inheritance of the human race. But just as Cordelia failed to include her father in the scope of her salvation and selfishly took it for herself alone, so workingmen in the dawn of the vision are inclined to claim it for themselves, putting out of their thoughts the old relationships; and just as surely as Cordelia's conscience developed in the new life and later drove her back to her father, where she perished, drawn into the cruelty and wrath which had now become objective and tragic, so the emancipation of working people will have to be inclusive of the employer from the first or it will encounter many failures, cruelties and reactions. It will result not in the position of the repentant Cordelia but in that of King Lear's two older daughters.

If the workingmen's narrow conception of emancipation was fully acted upon, they would hold much the same relationship to their expropriated employer that the two elder daughters held to their abdicated father. When the kingdom was given to them they received it as altogether their own, and were dominated by a sense of possession; "it is ours not yours" was never absent from their consciousness. When Lear ruled the kingdom he had never been without this sense of possession, although he expressed it in indulgence and condescending kindness. His older daughters expressed it in cruelty, but the motive of father and children was not unlike. They did not wish to be reminded by the state and retinue of the old King that he had been the former possessor. Finally, his mere presence alone reminded them too much of that and they banished him from the palace. That a newly acquired sense of possession should result in the barbaric, the incredible scenes of bitterness and murder, which were King Lear's portion, is not without a reminder of the barbaric scenes in our political and industrial relationships, when the sense of possession, to obtain and to hold, is aroused on both sides. The scenes in Paris during the political revolution or the more familiar scenes at the mouths of the mines and the terminals of railways occur to all of us.

The doctrine of emancipation preached to the wage-workers alone runs an awful risk of being accepted for what it offers them, for the sake of the fleshpots, rather than for the human affection and social justice which it involves. This doctrine must be strong enough in its fusing power to touch those who think they lose, as well as those who think they gain. Only thus can it become the doctrine of a universal movement.

The new claim on the part of the toiling multitude, the new sense of responsibility on the part of the well-to-do, arise in reality from the same source. They are in fact the same "social compunction," and, in spite of their widely varying manifestations, logically converge into the same movement. Mazzini once preached, "the consent of men and your own conscience are two wings given you whereby you may rise to God." It is so easy for the good and powerful to think that they can rise by following the dictates of conscience by pursuing their own ideals, leaving those ideals unconnected with the consent of their fellow-men. The president of the Pullman company thought out within his own mind a beautiful town. He had power with which to build this town, but he did not appeal to nor obtain the consent of the men who were living in it. The most unambitious reform, recognizing the necessity for this consent, makes for slow but sane and strenuous progress, while the most ambitious of social plans and experiments, ignoring this, is prone to the failure of the model town of Pullman.

The man who insists upon consent, who moves with the people, is bound to consult the feasible right as well as the absolute right. He is often obliged to attain only Mr. Lincoln's "best possible," and often have the sickening sense of compromising with his best convictions. He has to move along with those whom he rules toward a goal that neither he nor they see very clearly till they come to it. He has to discover what people really want, and then "provide the channels in which the growing moral forces of their lives shall flow." What he does attain, however, is not the result of his individual striving, as a solitary mountain climber beyond the sight of the valley multitude, but it is underpinned and upheld by the sentiments and aspirations of many others. Progress has been slower perpendicularly, but incomparably greater because lateral.

He has not taught his contemporaries to climb mountains, but he has persuaded the villagers to move up a few feet higher. It is doubtful if personal ambition, whatever may have been its commercial results, has ever been of any value as a motive power in social reform. But whatever it may have done in the past, it is certainly too archaic to accomplish anything now. Our thoughts, at least for this generation, cannot be too much directed from mutual relationships and responsibilities. They will be warped, unless we look all men in the face, as if a community of interests lay between, unless we hold the mind open, to take strength and cheer from a hundred connections.

To touch to vibrating response the noble fibre in each man, to pull these many fibres, fragile, impalpable and constantly breaking, as they are, into one impulse, to develop that mere impulse through its feeble and tentative stages into action, is no easy task, but lateral progress is impossible without it.

If only a few families of the English speaking race had profited by the dramatic failure of Lear, much heart-breaking and domestic friction might have been spared. Is it too much to hope that some of us will carefully consider this modern tragedy, if perchance it may contain a warning for the troublous times in which we live? By considering the dramatic failure of the liberal employer's plans for his employes we may possibly be spared useless industrial tragedies in the uncertain future which lies ahead of us.

(1895)

Belle Marshall Locke

(1867–1933)

The Hiartville Shakespeare Club

Belle Marshall Locke, a New Hampshire native, was already writing for popular publications as a teenager. Though she married young, she continued to write ballads, operas, and comedies, including "A Modern Desdemona," studied under Edna Chaffee Noble (famous for her Detroit Training School of Elocution and English Literature), taught drama and speech, directed plays and operas, and published her work, including *The Hiartville Shakespeare Club* (regrettably, "A Modern Desdemona" does not appear to have survived). In the two decades before Locke wrote this farce about a women's reading and acting group, set in an imaginary Hiartville, Shakespeare clubs, most of them run by and for women, had begun to spread across the country. Her skit, for performance by seven young women, depended on her female readers' easy familiarity with these groups and, no doubt, with the pretensions of some of them (signaled in the pun on "High Art" in her title and the name she gives to the club's president, Maria Knowitall). By the early twentieth century there were more than five hundred Shakespeare clubs across the country, in rural as well as urban areas, and they played a significant role in the popularization of Shakespeare in middle-class America. These clubs forged intellectual communities, promoted self-education, supported libraries, encouraged performance, and often chronicled their activities (gently parodied in Locke's story when Maria mistakenly reads from a cookbook instead of the "secretary's book"). By the end of World War II, as more women entered the workplace and universities, the clubs' cultural moment had passed and, until recently, when scholars like Katherine West Scheil turned their attention to it, their part in the story of Shakespeare in America had been largely forgotten.

✤

A FARCE IN ONE ACT FOR GIRLS.

CHARACTERS.

CAROLINE GUSHINGTON, the hostess.

MARIA KNOWITALL, president of the club.

DAISY LIGHTHEART,

MERRIE WEATHERVANE, } members of the club.

ROSE BUDD,

NAN GIDDY,

NORA O'BRIEN, a servant

SCENE.—*Miss Gushington's parlor. Small table with pictures and books upon it; larger table with writing materials; couch with pillows and afghan; large and small screen, chairs, etc. Nora discovered with carpet-sweeper. sweeping.*

NORA O'BRIEN.   Sure the Shak-a-spear class is comin' here to-day and Miss Caroline says for me to fix the room. (*Sets carpet-sweeper off the stage.*) "Don't set the chairs back stiff," says she, "but kind o' careless loike." (*Takes two chairs from up stage, and arranges at center, backs together.*) I wonder will that suit her. "Give the room an air of aise and comfort," says she. Faith, I don't know what that manes, but I'll thry an' toss things up in an aisy-lookin' fashion. (*Throws two books on floor and pulls table-cover awry.*) Maybe this Shak-a-spear class wants their room to luk as if there had been a scrimmage. (*Turns chair over, at larger table, and throws sofa-pillow on floor.*)

Enter Caroline Gushington.

CAROLINE.   For mercy's sake, Nora, what are you doing?

NORA.   Fixin' things careless loike, miss (*pushing couch out*).

CAROLINE.   Stop, instantly! You are the stupidest girl I ever knew. Re-arrange everything in place. You do not understand me; (*sentimentally*) so few do! I wanted an air of unstudied grace about the room, not a Pandemonium effect.

NORA (*aside*).   Phat's that she's sayin' (*arranging furniture*)!

CAROLINE.   But you have no soul!

NORA (*dropping chair*).   Oh, my!

CAROLINE.   Figuratively speaking, I mean.

NORA (*helplessly, aside*).   She'll drive me clane mad wid those big words. No soul, is it?

CAROLINE.   Do not stand there, conversing with yourself! It is a bad fashion. I would rid myself of it.

NORA (*aside*).   There she goes agin!

CAROLINE.   *Will* you cease? My nerves are sensitive to-day and your voice has a discordant tone that grates upon them horribly. You may go now. I would be alone.

NORA (*looking at her pityingly, aside*).   She's losin' her wits, poor thing!   [*Exit.*

CAROLINE (*sitting at larger table*).   What a world we live in! If I could create a place for mortals to abide, I'd set apart a little corner for the delicate, highly-organized beings like myself, where they could dwell in an intellectual atmosphere, undisturbed by the common herd. (*Looks at watch.*) Two o'clock; quite time for the Shakspeare class to arrive.

NORA (*looking in at door*).   Miss Knowitall is here, miss!

CAROLINE.   Show her in.

  Enter Maria Knowitall preceded by Nora. Exit Nora.

CAROLINE (*rising and extending hand*).   My dear Marie! how do you do?

MARIA (*shaking hands heartily*).   In perfect health, Caroline, but I do wish you would drop that absurd fashion of calling me Marie! M-a-r-i-a spells Maria.

CAROLINE.   But the French is so much softer, chérie.

MARIA.   I haven't the slightest idea what that last word means and, as there is nothing soft in my nature, the English language is quite good enough for me.

CAROLINE.   Ah! you are such a practical girl!

MARIA (*seating herself at table*).   Yes, practical to the ends of my fingers! (*Looks at watch.*) *I* am exactly on time, the *others* are late. 'Tis a detestable habit to keep people waiting! Don't you think so?

CAROLINE (*seating herself as before*).   Detestable is a harsh word, my dear!

MARIA.   Well, it means something, and I detest many people!

CAROLINE.   I could never do that. It must be very fatiguing.

NORA (*at door*).   The rist of the Shak-a-spear class is come, miss.

CAROLINE.   Bid them enter, Nora, and assist the young ladies to remove their wraps.

NORA.   Yis, miss.   [*Exit.*

MARIA (*looking at Caroline*).   I wish I could shake some life into that girl!

Enter Daisy Lightheart, Merrie Weathervane, Rose Budd and Nan Giddy.

CAROLINE (*rising and shaking hands*).   Welcome, ladies, to our intellectual feast! (*Girls go up stage arranging hair, looking about, chatting etc.*)

DAISY.   Are we late? You see the girls called for me and we met Dick Generous at the corner, and he treated us to soda. Now there being two s's awaiting us, namely, Shakspeare, and soda, I took the soda first, as that wouldn't keep, and I knew Shakspeare would. Hope we haven't kept you waiting.

MARIA.   Indeed you have!

DAISY.   So sorry, but couldn't help it, you see. (*Maria starts to speak, Daisy interrupting.*) Now don't scold, but let's to work! We are in downright earnest, to-day, aren't we girls? (*Girls coming down exclaim in chorus: "Yes!" "Yes indeed!" "Just try us!"*)

CAROLINE.   Pray be seated.

Caroline, as before, at table. Girls bring chairs down near couch and exclaim in chorus: "Let me sit next you!" "Come over here!" "Don't pull my dress so!" Rose Budd and Nan Giddy, in chairs, right of couch. Merrie Weathervane and Daisy Lightheart, on couch.

MARIA (*rapping on table*).   Will the meeting please come to order! We will first listen to the reading of the secretary's report.

MERRIE (*going to table with book, opening it*).   Angel Cake— good gracious! I've brought my cook-book. (*Girls giggle.*)

MARIA (*rapping on table*).   Order! As none of us are ambitious to become dyspeptics, we will not take time to listen to your receipts.

MERRIE.   They're better than yours! My cake was just lovely at the fair, the other night.

DAISY.   That's so, Merrie! I ate two pieces and——

MARIA (*rapping*).   Order! (*Merrie resumes seat.*) As this is to be an informal meeting, we shall enter at once into the discussion of the Shakspearean entertainment that we are to produce for the benefit of crippled foot-ball players. Those who have selected their scenes will demonstrate the fact by raising the right hand. (*All raise hands.*) That enables us to make out the programme (*taking pencil and paper*). Miss Lightheart, what is your selection?

DAISY.   Miss Weathervane and myself are to do the balcony scene from "Romeo and Juliet." (*Maria writes.*)

MARIA.   Miss Budd?

ROSE.   Miss Giddy and myself have arranged a scene from the "Taming of the Shrew." (*Maria writes.*)

MARIA.   And you, Miss Gushington?

CAROLINE.   I have culled and arranged a few of Ophelia's mad sayings and shall endeavor to render them. (*M. writes.*)

MARIA.   Which, with a selection by myself, will make quite a neat Shakspearean programme. And now that we are together, I propose that we have an impromptu rehearsal. What do you say?

    Girls clap hands and exclaim in chorus: "Oh, lovely! How nice!
                    By all means!"

MARIA (*rapping on table*).   Order! Miss Budd, you and Miss Giddy may begin by rehearsing your scene.

NAN (*rising*).   I am to impersonate Katharine, the shrew, and Miss Budd, my sister Bianca. We begin with *Act II. Scene I.* where Katharine has tied Bianca's hands.

ROSE (*rising*).   I think, Miss Giddy, that you should explain that Bianca was a handsome, generous girl, and Katharine ugly in mind and body, else the motive for tying Bianca's hands might be misconstrued.

NAN.   I shall do nothing of the sort. I do not intend to play Katharine in that manner; I shall make her a handsome, spirited young woman, or I shall not play the part.

ROSE.   But Shakspeare represents her——

NAN.   That has nothing to do with the case! *I* am to represent her this time, and if you think I am going on the stage looking old and wrinkled, you are mistaken!

MARIA (*rapping on table*).   Order! Go on with your scene.

ROSE.   Of course if you intend to make a guy of yourself——

NAN.   Excuse me, that is just what I refuse to do.

MARIA.   *Will* you proceed? (*Girls come center.*)

NAN.   Hold out your hands (*taking handkerchief*).

ROSE.   Now don't tie them so tight that they will look red as beets!

NAN.   If you thought less of how you look, you'd get on much better with your part.

MARIA.   Order! Go on with your selection.

NAN (*to Rose*).   You begin.

ROSE (*as Bianca*).   "Good sister, wrong me not, nor wrong yourself, to make a bondmaid and a slave of me. Unbind my hands!"

NAN (*as Katharine*).   "Of all thy suitors, here I charge thee, tell whom thou lovest best: see thou dissemble not."

ROSE (*as Bianca*).   "Believe me, sister, of all the men alive I never yet beheld that special face which I could fancy more than any other."

NAN (*as Katharine, seizing her by the shoulders*).   "Minion, thou liest!"

ROSE.   Hark (*turning head quickly*)! Oh, oh, dear! I've got a crick in my neck! This is terrible! (*Holds side of neck with both hands.*) I can't move my head an inch.

NAN.   That's a pretty thing for you to do! You cut me out of my best speech. What if you had done that on the stage? Here, let me straighten it for you. (*Reaches out right arm, Rose throws out left arm quickly, hitting Nan in the face.*)

ROSE.   Get away!

NAN (*holding on to nose*).   Oh, you've hurt my nose! you've made it bleed! (*Takes handkerchief from pocket, on which has been put something to imitate blood, and holds it to nose.*) Oh! oh! oh!

MARIA (*rapping*).   Order! As you both seem disabled, you had better retire and give some one else a chance.

Caroline pushes chair from table up right, and assists Rose into it then rings bell. Enter Nora.

CAROLINE.   Bring some liniment and a roll of cotton, that you will find on my bureau, and bathe Miss Budd's neck.

NAN.   No matter about my nose, I presume. (*Sits left.*)

NORA.   Faith, I'll bathe that, too! (*Exit Nora, returning at once, with liniment and cotton. Nora runs from one to the other, bathes Rose's neck, and wets a large bunch of cotton, placing it on Nan's nose.*

MARIA.   It seems rather unfortunate that our first number should end in this way.

ROSE.   It all came about in striving to be true to nature. The sentiment required the pose of listening. I gave a quick turn of the head, as I should, and I got a crick in my neck. Oh! Oh!

NAN.   And your arm being muscular, which is not required, I got a bloody nose.

CAROLINE.   But we must not mind such trifles when we are pursuing the road to high art. We must expect to meet obstacles and to overcome them. We should revel in the fact that we are students of nature and that we are studying the only true system. All others are base impositions and we must not hesitate to proclaim the fact.

MARIA.   Stop talking and let us proceed with our programme. Miss Lightheart your number is next.

DAISY.   But what will I do for a balcony?

MERRIE.   I have an idea!

MARIA.   Is it possible!

MERRIE.   We will put a chair on the table and a screen around it, and another screen on the floor, and lo, you have your balcony! (*Arranges table, at which Maria has been seated, up L. C. with small screen around chair, which she places on table, and larger screen in front of table, or one large screen on floor can be used.*) But I can never do Romeo in this costume!

DAISY.   I brought your moustache (*Gives box to her*).

CAROLINE.   Nora, bring my brother's mackintosh and the military hat he left in the hall.   [*Exit Nora.*

DAISY.   Oh, Caroline, you're a genius!

CAROLINE.   So I've oft been told.

Enter Nora, with hat and coat, Merrie takes them and retires.

DAISY.   Now for the balcony! (*Mounts to chair assisted by Caroline.*) Oh, this is real cosy! Where is Merrie? (*Calls.*) I say, Romey!

MERRIE (*outside.*)   Wait until I get fixed, can't you?

DAISY.   Well, make haste! You must not keep your audience waiting.

Enter Merrie with mackintosh, hat and moustache on. She carries a good-sized dry-goods box; placing it a short distance from table, she mounts it.

MERRIE.   Here I am, begin!

DAISY.   You begin first, you know.

MERRIE.   Oh, yes! (*as Romeo.*) "But soft, what light through yonder window breaks! It is the east and Juliet is the sun!"

DAISY (*as Juliet*).   "Oh, Romeo! Romeo! wherefore art thou Romeo?"

MERRIE (*as Romeo*).   "Shall I hear more, or shall I speak at this?"

DAISY (*as Juliet*).   "'Tis but thy name that is my enemy thou are thyself though, not a Montague. Oh, be some other name! What's in a name? that which we call a rose, by any other name would smell as sweet; so Romeo would, were he not Romeo called. Romeo, doff thy name and for that name, which is no part of thee, take all myself." Your moustache is crooked.

MERRIE (*as Romeo*).   "I take thee at thy word." (*Fixes moustache.*) Bother the thing! "Call me but love, and I'll be new baptized. Henceforth I never will be Romeo." I tell you I won't wear this moustache!

DAISY (*as Juliet*).   "What man art thou, that, thus bescreened in night, so stumblest on my counsel?"

MERRIE (*as Romeo*).   "By a name I know not how to tell thee who I am. My name, dear saint, is hateful to myself, because it is an enemy to thee. Had I it written, I would tear the word."

DAISY (*as Juliet*).   "My ears have not yet drunk a hundred words of that tongue's utterance, yet I know the sound. Art thou not Romeo and a Montague?"

MERRIE (*as Romeo*).   "Neither, fair saint, if either thee dislike."

DAISY (*as Juliet*).   "How cam'st thou hither, tell me? and wherefore? The orchard walls are high and hard to climb, and the place death, considering who thou art, if any of my kinsmen find thee here."

*Daisy rises, looks back, pushes chair off table and falls behind it,
    being hidden by screen. She screams violently. Merrie jumps off
    box to assist her and falls.*

MERRIE (*holding foot with both hands*).   Oh, I've sprained
my ankle! Oh, dear! Oh, dear!

DAISY.   Oh! Oh! Oh!

*Maria pulls away screen and discovers Daisy on floor; her fore head
    has a red mark, made with grease-paint, while she was behind
    screen. She is crying hysterically. Caroline and Maria assist her
    to rise.*

CAROLINE.   Place her on the couch. (*They do so.*)

NORA.   Niver moind, there's plinty of liniment. (*She bathes
Daisy's head, and goes from one to another as they groan, attending
them.*)

MERRIE (*on floor*).   Somebody pick me up! A sprained ankle
is more serious than a scratched face!

DAISY.   You hit the table!

MERRIE.   I did not!

ROSE.   If you had a neck like mine——

NAN.   Or a nose like mine——

MARIA.   Silence! all of you.

*Nora and Caroline assist Merrie into chair. Nora removes her boot,
    placing foot in chair, and bathes it. The girls are all at back of
    stage; Rose at right, Merrie next, Nan next, and Daisy on couch,
    left.*

MARIA (*solemnly, after a pause*).   There are only a few of us left!

CAROLINE (*surprised*).   Is that slang?

MARIA.   Certainly not! It is the plain, unvarnished truth.

CAROLINE.   As we have made the injured as comfortable as
possible, let us hear your selection, Maria.

MARIA.   I had thought of giving an impersonation of Lady
Macbeth. I have arranged a little scene but——

CAROLINE.   Try it.

MARIA (*rising and reciting tragically*).   "That which hath
made them (*nods left*) drunk——

DAISY.   Excuse me, Miss Knowitall, but do not nod towards
me; it is too suggestive.

MARIA (*resuming*). "That which hath made them (*nods right*) drunk——"

ROSE.   Don't call attention to me, please!

MARIA (*impatiently*).   Will some one suggest a way?

CAROLINE.   Excuse me, Maria, but I would suggest that you nod front. The football boys will sit there and they will not object to such a trifling allusion.

MARIA (*again reciting*).   "That which hath made them (*nods front*) drunk hath made me bold. What hath quenched them hath given me fire. Hark! (*Listens. Nora strikes same attitude with bottle in one hand.*) Peace! it was the owl, that shrieked! Hark! I laid their daggers ready. (*Nora drops in fright behind Merrie's chair, who reassures her and Nora rises touching her forehead and pointing to Maria, as if she were mad.*) He could not miss them. Had he not resembled my father as he slept, I had done 't!" Macbeth did show a sickly womanish fear of blood; and when at last he nerved his hand to do the deed, horror took possession of his soul and, frenzied, he cried out: "Whence is that knocking? (*Nora tip-toes down and looks off.*) How is't with me when every noise appalls me? What hands are here? Ha! they pluck out mine eyes! (*Nora stands near with open mouth shaking bottle and listening.*) Will all great Neptune's ocean wash this blood clean from off my hand?" And then the feast that followed, when Banquo's spirit—— Banquo's spirit——(*Strikes attitude of fear, Nora the same pose.*)

CAROLINE (*excitedly*).   Go on! Go on!

MARIA.   I don't believe I'll give that. (*Girls groan.*) I think I'll costume my brother's little boy and let him play Prince Arthur to my Hubert. Nora, you stand there and be the attendant. I want to see how it begins. What can we use for irons? You know we must be realistic.

CAROLINE.   Nora, get my curling-tongs.

NORA (*aside*).   Sure I'm goin' to be a member of the Shak-a-spear class, too! (*Exit, and returns with curling-irons.*)

MARIA (*as Hubert*).   "Heat me these irons hot, and look you, stand within the arras and when I strike my foot upon the bosom of the ground, rush forth and bind the boy which you will find with me, fast to the chair."

NORA.   Which b'y?

MARIA.   Never mind! Now you can exit with the irons.

NORA.   I can phwat?

MARIA.   Exit! disappear! fly! and when I strike my foot so, you can return with the irons. (*Exit Nora.*) I wonder if we could fix Nora up and let her do the attendant. Let me see if she knows enough to come in when I give the cue. After Arthur says, "If an angel should have come to me and told me Hubert should put out mine eyes, I would not have believed him; no tongue, but Hubert's." (*Stamps.*) "Come forth!"

> *Enter, Nora, with curling-irons.*

MARIA.   "Do as I bid you do!"

NORA.   Sure I have.

MARIA.   Then Arthur says, "Oh, save me, Hubert! my eyes are out even with the fierce looks of these bloody men." Then my words are, "Give me the irons, I say!" (*Takes irons, drops them and screams.*) Heavens! they are red-hot! (*Girls giggle.*)

NORA.   Sure, you told me to hate thim!

MARIA.   Fool! you have burned my fingers to a blister! (*Walks, blowing fingers, etc.*)

CAROLINE.   Nora, how could you be so stupid!

NORA.   Niver moind! there's plinty of liniment. (*Assists Maria to seat at table, and wraps her fingers in cotton, putting liniment on them.*)

CAROLINE.   It's a burning shame!

MARIA.   Don't try to say funny things! If *you* had this hand——

ROSE.   Or my neck——

NAN.   Or my nose——

DAISY.   Or my head——

MERRIE.   Or my foot——

MARIA.   You would be unconscious!

CAROLINE.   Indeed, I am very sorry!

MARIA.   You are dying to laugh! but go on with the programme. We'll finish it, or die. (*Sits.*)

CAROLINE.   Do you mean it?

MARIA.   Certainly. (*Holds hand up blowing it, etc.*)
NORA (*aside*).   It's the finest scrimmage I ever saw!

[*Exit.*

MARIA.   Begin, Caroline.
CAROLINE (*as Ophelia, reciting*).   "Where is the beauteous
majesty of Denmark (*saluting*)?"

(*Sings.*) "How should I your true love know
                    From another one?
                By his cockle hat and staff,
                    And his sandal shoon."

"Say you? nay, pray you, mark."

                "He is dead and gone, lady,
                    He is dead and gone;
                At his head, a grass-green turf,
                    At his heels a stone."

"I hope all will be well. We must be patient; but I cannot
choose but weep, to think they should lay him i' the cold ground."

                "They bore him bare faced on the bier:
                    Hey no nonny, nonny, hey nonny;
                And in his grave rained many a tear——"

(*Takes bunch of flowers from table.*) "There's rosemary, that's for
remembrance; pray you, love, remember; and there are pansies,
that's for thoughts. There's fennel for you and columbines; there's
rue, for you; and here's some for me. There's a daisy, I would give
you some violets, but they withered all, when my father died. They
say he made a good end."

                "For bonny, sweet Robin is all my joy—"

(*Changing air.*) "And will he not come again?
                And will he not come again?
                No, no he is dead,
                Go to thy death-bed,
                He will never come again."

NORA (*entering, screaming*).   Oh, dear, oh, dear, phwat will I do! phwat will I do!

CAROLINE.   What is it?

NORA.   Sure while I was puttin' on the liniment, some burglar walked in an' stole all the spoons!

Girls scream in chorus: "A burglar!"

CAROLINE (*tragically*).   Ye gods, the spoons! my grandma's spoons (*fainting*)!

Caroline falls on floor. Nora rushes to her with liniment and in a confused manner bathes the soles of her boots, then bathes her head, places liniment to her nose, etc.

MARIA (*rapping*).   Order! Ladies, I move that this meeting be adjourned, sine die; those in favor of the motion may signify it by saying, aye. (*Girls feebly say: "Aye."*)

MARIA.   'Tis a vote. Nora! (*Nora steps over Caroline.*) Call the ambulance and see that the members of the Shakspeare Club are conveyed to their respective homes. (*Nora steps over Caroline again, and exits.*) Football may be dangerous, but it is a baby's game compared with Shakspeare (*rising*). But, ladies, we should feel proud (*gesticulating with hand wrapped in cotton*), for, in spite of disaster we have finished our programme! (*Girls try to rise but drop into chairs exclaiming, "Oh! Oh!"*)

CURTAIN.

(*1896*)

Henry James

(1843–1916)

The Birthplace

When in 1844 the great American showman P. T. Barnum visited Stratford-upon-Avon and saw the house in which Shakespeare was born, he considered buying and transporting this wonder of the world to his American Museum in New York. But his plans, if they were more than bluster, were thwarted. He writes in his autobiographical *The Life of P. T. Barnum* (1855) that news of his "project leaked out, British pride was touched, and several English gentlemen interfered and purchased the premises for a Shakspearian Association." A half-century later, Shakespeare's birthplace—and all it signified—continued to exercise a powerful hold on the imagination of American tourists and writers. In June 1901 Henry James recorded in his notebook a story idea—"a little *donnée*"—inspired by an anecdote he had heard about a couple who had been put "in charge of the Shakespeare house—the Birthplace," who grew disgusted by their job and quit after six months, having, James surmised, found their office "full of humbug, full of lies and superstition *imposed* upon them by the great body of visitors, who want the positive impressive story about every object, every feature of the house, every dubious thing." James at first imagined that his story would climax with his fictional protagonists "denying Shakespeare—say they do it on the spot itself—one day—in the presence of a big, gaping, admiring batch." In the end, the story takes a different turn, Shakespeare himself is never named, and a pair of fictional American tourists play a decisive role in the narrative. James worked on "The Birthplace" the following summer and autumn before publishing it in his 1903 short story collection, *The Better Sort*.

❧

I T seemed to them at first, the offer, too good to be true, and their friend's letter, addressed to them to feel, as he said, the ground, to sound them as to inclinations and possibilities, had almost the effect of a brave joke at their expense. Their friend, Mr. Grant-Jackson, a highly preponderant, pushing person, great in discussion and arrangement, abrupt in overture, unexpected, if not perverse, in attitude, and almost equally acclaimed and objected to in the wide midland region to which he had taught, as the phrase was, the size of his foot—their friend had launched his bolt quite out of the blue and had thereby so shaken them as to make them fear almost more than hope. The place had fallen vacant by the death of one of the two ladies, mother and daughter, who had discharged its duties for fifteen years; the daughter was staying on alone, to accommodate, but had found, though extremely mature, an opportunity of marriage that involved retirement, and the question of the new incumbents was not a little pressing. The want thus determined was of a united couple of some sort, of the right sort, a pair of educated and competent sisters possibly preferred, but a married pair having its advantages if other qualifications were marked. Applicants, candidates, besiegers of the door of everyone supposed to have a voice in the matter, were already beyond counting, and Mr. Grant-Jackson, who was in his way diplomatic and whose voice, though not perhaps of the loudest, possessed notes of insistence, had found his preference fixing itself on some person or brace of persons who had been decent and dumb. The Gedges appeared to have struck him as waiting in silence—though absolutely, as happened, no busybody had brought them, far away in the north, a hint either of bliss or of danger; and the happy spell, for the rest, had obviously been wrought in him by a remembrance which, though now scarcely fresh, had never before borne any such fruit.

Morris Gedge had for a few years, as a young man, carried on a small private school of the order known as preparatory, and had happened then to receive under his roof the small son of the great man, who was not at that time so great. The little boy, during an absence of his parents from England, had been dangerously ill, so dangerously that they had been recalled in haste, though with inevitable delays, from a far country—they had gone to America, with the whole continent and the great sea to cross again—and

had got back to find the child saved, but saved, as couldn't help
coming to light, by the extreme devotion and perfect judgment
of Mrs. Gedge. Without children of her own, she had particularly attached herself to this tiniest and tenderest of her husband's
pupils, and they had both dreaded as a dire disaster the injury to
their little enterprise that would be caused by their losing him.
Nervous, anxious, sensitive persons, with a pride—as they were
for that matter well aware—above their position, never, at the
best, to be anything but dingy, they had nursed him in terror and
had brought him through in exhaustion. Exhaustion, as befell, had
thus overtaken them early and had for one reason and another
managed to assert itself as their permanent portion. The little
boy's death would, as they said, have done for them, yet his recov-
ery hadn't saved them; with which it was doubtless also part of a
shy but stiff candour in them that they didn't regard themselves
as having in a more indirect manner laid up treasure. Treasure was
not to be, in any form whatever, of their dreams or of their waking
sense; and the years that followed had limped under the weight,
had now and then rather grievously stumbled, had even barely escaped laying them in the dust. The school had not prospered, had
but dwindled to a close. Gedge's health had failed, and, still more,
every sign in him of a capacity to publish himself as practical. He
had tried several things, he had tried many, but the final appearance was of their having tried him not less. They mostly, at the
time I speak of, were trying his successors, while he found himself,
with an effect of dull felicity that had come in this case from the
mere postponement of change, in charge of the grey town-library
of Blackport-on-Dwindle, all granite, fog and female fiction. This
was a situation in which his general intelligence—acknowledged
as his strong point—was doubtless conceived, around him, as feeling less of a strain than that mastery of particulars in which he was
recognised as weak.

It was at Blackport-on-Dwindle that the silver shaft reached
and pierced him; it was as an alternative to dispensing dog's-eared
volumes the very titles of which, on the lips of innumerable glib
girls, were a challenge to his temper, that the wardenship of so

different a temple presented itself. The stipend named differed
little from the slim wage at present paid him, but even had it been
less the interest and the honour would have struck him as deter-
minant. The shrine at which he was to preside—though he had
always lacked occasion to approach it—figured to him as the most
sacred known to the steps of men, the early home of the supreme
poet, the Mecca of the English-speaking race. The tears came into
his eyes sooner still than into his wife's while he looked about
with her at their actual narrow prison, so grim with enlightenment, so ugly with industry, so turned away from any dream, so
intolerable to any taste. He felt as if a window had opened into
a great green woodland, a woodland that had a name, glorious,
immortal, that was peopled with vivid figures, each of them renowned, and that gave out a murmur, deep as the sound of the sea,
which was the rustle in forest shade of all the poetry, the beauty,
the colour of life. It would be prodigious that of this transfigured
world *he* should keep the key. No—he couldn't believe it, not even
when Isabel, at sight of his face, came and helpfully kissed him.
He shook his head with a strange smile. "We shan't get it. Why
should we? It's perfect."

"If we don't he'll simply have been cruel; which is impossible
when he has waited all this time to be kind." Mrs. Gedge did believe—she *would*; since the wide doors of the world of poetry had
suddenly pushed back for them it was in the form of poetic justice
that they were first to know it. She had her faith in their patron;
it was sudden, but it was not complete. "He remembers—that's
all; and that's our strength."

"And what's *his*?" Gedge asked. "He may *want* to put us
through, but that's a different thing from being able. What are
our special advantages?"

"Well, that we're just the thing." Her knowledge of the needs
of the case was, as yet, thanks to scant information, of the vaguest,
and she had never, more than her husband, stood on the sacred
spot; but she saw herself waving a nicely-gloved hand over a collection of remarkable objects and saying to a compact crowd of

gaping, awe-struck persons: "And now, please, *this* way." She even heard herself meeting with promptness and decision an occasional inquiry from a visitor in whom audacity had prevailed over awe. She had been once, with a cousin, years before, to a great northern castle, and that was the way the housekeeper had taken them round. And it was not moreoever, either, that she thought of herself as a housekeeper: she was well above that, and the wave of her hand wouldn't fail to be such as to show it. This, and much else, she summed up as she answered her mate. "Our special advantages are that you're a gentleman."

"Oh!" said Gedge, as if he had never thought of it, and yet as if too it were scarce worth thinking of.

"I see it all," she went on; "they've *had* the vulgar—they find they don't do. We're poor and we're modest, but anyone can see what we are."

Gedge wondered. "Do you mean——?" More modest than she, he didn't know quite what she meant.

"We're refined. We know how to speak."

"Do we?"—he still, suddenly, wondered.

But she was, from the first, surer of everything than he; so that when a few weeks more had elapsed and the shade of uncertainty—though it was only a shade—had grown almost to sicken him, her triumph was to come with the news that they were fairly named. "We're on poor pay, though we manage"—she had on the present occasion insisted on her point. "But we're highly cultivated, and for them to get *that*, don't you see? without getting too much with it in the way of pretensions and demands, must be precisely their dream. We've no social position, but we don't *mind* that we haven't, do we? a bit; which is because we know the difference between realities and shams. We hold to reality, and that gives us common sense, which the vulgar have less than anything, and which yet must be wanted there, after all, as well as anywhere else."

Her companion followed her, but musingly, as if his horizon had within a few moments grown so great that he was almost

lost in it and required a new orientation. The shining spaces surrounded him; the association alone gave a nobler arch to the sky.
"Allow that we hold also a little to the romance. It seems to me
that that's the beauty. We've missed it all our life, and now it's
come. We shall be at head-quarters for it. We shall have our fill
of it."

She looked at his face, at the effect in it of these prospects,
and her own lighted as if he had suddenly grown handsome.
"Certainly—we shall live as in a fairy-tale. But what I mean is that
we shall give, in a way—and so gladly—quite as much as we get.
With all the rest of it we're, for instance, neat." Their letter had
come to them at breakfast, and she picked a fly out of the butter-
dish. "It's the way we'll *keep* the place"—with which she removed
from the sofa to the top of the cottage-piano a tin of biscuits that
had refused to squeeze into the cupboard. At Blackport they were
in lodgings—of the lowest description, she had been known, with
a freedom felt by Blackport to be slightly invidious, to declare.
The Birthplace—and that itself, after such a life, was exaltation—
wouldn't be lodgings, since a house close beside it was set apart
for the warden, a house joining on to it as a sweet old parsonage
is often annexed to a quaint old church. It would all together be
their home, and such a home as would make a little world that
they would never want to leave. She dwelt on the gain, for that
matter, to their income; as, obviously, though the salary was not
a change for the better, the house, given them, would make all the
difference. He assented to this, but absently, and she was almost
impatient at the range of his thoughts. It was as if something, for
him—the very swarm of them—veiled the view; and he presently,
of himself, showed what it was.

"What I can't get over is its being such a man——!" He almost,
from inward emotion, broke down.

"Such a man——?"

"Him, *him*, HIM——!" It was too much.

"Grant-Jackson? Yes, it's a surprise, but one sees how he has
been meaning, all the while, the right thing by us."

"I mean *Him*," Gedge returned more coldly; "our becoming

familiar and intimate—for that's what it will come to. We shall just live with Him."

"Of course—it *is* the beauty." And she added quite gaily: "The more we do the more we shall love Him."

"No doubt—but it's rather awful. The more we *know* Him," Gedge reflected, "the more we shall love Him. We don't as yet, you see, know Him so very tremendously."

"We do so quite as well, I imagine, as the sort of people they've had. And that probably isn't—unless you care, as we do—so awfully necessary. For there are the facts."

"Yes—there are the facts."

"I mean the principal ones. They're all that the people—the people who come—want."

"Yes—they must be all *they* want."

"So that they're all that those who've been in charge have needed to know."

"Ah," he said as if it were a question of honour, "*we* must know everything."

She cheerfully acceded: she had the merit, he felt, of keeping the case within bounds. "Everything. But about him personally," she added, "there isn't, is there? so very, very much."

"More, I believe, than there used to be. They've made discoveries."

It was a grand thought. "Perhaps *we* shall make some!"

"Oh, I shall be content to be a little better up in what has been done." And his eyes rested on a shelf of books, half of which, little worn but much faded, were of the florid "gift" order and belonged to the house. Of those among them that were his own most were common specimens of the reference sort, not excluding an old Bradshaw and a catalogue of the town-library. "We've not even a Set of our own. Of the Works," he explained in quick repudiation of the sense, perhaps more obvious, in which she might have taken it.

As a proof of their scant range of possessions this sounded almost abject, till the painful flush with which they met on the admission melted presently into a different glow. It was just for that kind of poorness that their new situation was, by its intrinsic charm, to console them. And Mrs. Gedge had a happy thought. "Wouldn't the Library more or less have them?"

"Oh no, we've nothing of that sort: for what do you take us?" This, however, was but the play of Gedge's high spirits: the form both depression and exhilaration most frequently took with him being a bitterness on the subject of the literary taste of Blackport. No one was so deeply acquainted with it. It acted with him in fact as so lurid a sign of the future that the charm of the thought of removal was sharply enhanced by the prospect of escape from it. The institution he served didn't of course deserve the particular reproach into which his irony had flowered; and indeed if the several Sets in which the Works were present were a trifle dusty, the dust was a little his own fault. To make up for that now he had the vision of immediately giving his time to the study of them; he saw himself indeed, inflamed with a new passion, earnestly commenting and collating. Mrs. Gedge, who had suggested that they ought, till their move should come, to read Him regularly of an evening—certain as they were to do it still more when in closer quarters with Him—Mrs. Gedge felt also, in her degree, the spell; so that the very happiest time of their anxious life was perhaps to have been the series of lamplight hours, after supper, in which, alternately taking the book, they declaimed, they almost performed, their beneficent author. He became speedily more than their author—their personal friend, their universal light, their final authority and divinity. Where in the world, they were already asking themselves, would they have been without him? By the time their appointment arrived in form their relation to him had immensely developed. It was amusing to Morris Gedge that he had so lately blushed for his ignorance, and he made this re-mark to his wife during the last hour they were able to give to their study, before proceeding, across half the country, to the scene of their romantic future. It was as if, in deep, close throbs, in cool after-waves that broke of a sudden and bathed his mind, all pos-session and comprehension and sympathy, all the truth and the life and the story, had come to him, and come, as the newspapers said, to stay. "It's absurd," he didn't hesitate to say, "to talk of our not 'knowing.' So far as we don't it's because we're donkeys. He's *in* the thing, over His ears, and the more we get into it the more we're with Him. I seem to myself at any rate," he declared, "to *see* Him in it as if He were painted on the wall."

"Oh, *doesn't* one rather, the dear thing? And don't you feel where it is?" Mrs. Gedge finely asked. "We see Him because we love Him—that's what we do. How can we not, the old darling—with what He's doing for us? There's no light"—she had a sententious turn—"like true affection."

"Yes, I suppose that's it. And yet," her husband mused, "I see, confound me, the faults."

"That's because you're so critical. You see them, but you don't mind them. You see them, but you forgive them. You mustn't mention them *there*. We shan't, you know, be there for *that*."

"Dear no!" he laughed: "we'll chuck out anyone who hints at them."

II

If the sweetness of the preliminary months had been great, great too, though almost excessive as agitation, was the wonder of fairly being housed with Him, of treading day and night in the footsteps He had worn, of touching the objects, or at all events the surfaces, the substances, over which His hands had played, which his arms, his shoulders had rubbed, of breathing the air—or something not too unlike it—in which His voice had sounded. They had had a little at first their bewilderments, their disconcertedness; the place was both humbler and grander than they had exactly prefigured, more at once of a cottage and of a museum, a little more archaically bare and yet a little more richly official. But the sense was strong with them that the point of view, for the inevitable ease of the connection, patiently, indulgently awaited them; in addition to which, from the first evening, after closing-hour, when the last blank pilgrim had gone, the mere spell, the mystic presence—as if they had had it quite to themselves—were all they could have desired. They had received, by Grant-Jackson's care and in addition to a table of instructions and admonitions by the number, and in some particulars by the nature, of which they found themselves slightly depressed, various little guides, handbooks, travellers' tributes, literary memorials and other catch-penny publications, which, however, were to be for the moment swallowed up in the interesting episode of the induction or initiation appointed for them in advance at the hands of several persons whose connection with the establishment was, as superior to their own, still more official, and at those in especial of one of the ladies who had for so many years borne the brunt. About the instructions from above, about the shilling books and the well-known facts and the full-blown legend, the supervision, the subjection, the submission, the view as of a cage in which he should circulate and a groove in which he should slide, Gedge had preserved a certain play of mind; but all power of reaction appeared suddenly to desert him in the presence of his so visibly competent predecessor and as an effect of her good offices. He had not the resource, enjoyed by his wife, of seeing himself, with impatience, attired in black silk of a make characterised by just the right shade of austerity; so that this firm, smooth, expert and consummately respectable middle-aged person had him somehow, on the whole ground, completely at her mercy.

It was evidently something of a rueful moment when, as a lesson—she being for the day or two still in the field—he accepted Miss Putchin's suggestion of "going round" with her and with the successive squads of visitors she was there to deal with. He appreciated her method—he saw there had to *be* one; he admired her as succinct and definite; for there were the facts, as his wife had said at Blackport, and they were to be disposed of in the time; yet he felt like a very little boy as he dangled, more than once, with Mrs. Gedge, at the tail of the human comet. The idea had been that they should, by this attendance, more fully embrace the possible accidents and incidents, as it were, of the relation to the great public in which they were to find themselves; and the poor man's excited perception of the great public rapidly became such as to resist any diversion meaner than that of the admirable manner of their guide. It wandered from his gaping companions to that of the priestess in black silk, whom he kept asking himself if either he or Isabel could hope by any possibility ever remotely to resemble; then it bounded restlessly back to the numerous persons who revealed to him, as it had never yet been revealed, the happy power of the simple to hang upon the lips of the wise. The great thing seemed to be—and quite surprisingly— that the business was easy and the strain, which as a strain they had feared, moderate; so that he might have been puzzled, had he fairly caught himself in the act, by his recognising as the last effect of the impression an odd absence of the ability to rest in it, an agitation deep within him that vaguely threatened to grow. "It isn't, you see, so very complicated," the black silk lady seemed to throw off, with everything else, in her neat, crisp, cheerful way; in spite of which he already, the very first time—that is after several parties had been in and out and up and down—went so far as to wonder if there weren't more in it than she imagined. She was, so to speak, kindness itself—was all encouragement and reassurance; but it was just her slightly coarse redolence of these very things that, on repetition, before they parted, dimmed a little, as he felt, the light of his acknowledging smile. That, again, she took for a symptom of some pleading weakness in him—he could never be as brave as she; so that she wound up with a few pleasant words from the very depth of her experience. "You'll get into it, never fear—it will *come*; and then you'll feel as if you had never done anything else." He was afterwards to know that, on the spot, at this moment, he must have begun to wince a little at such a menace; that he might come to feel as if he had never done anything but what Miss Putchin did loomed for him, in germ, as a penalty to pay. The support she offered, none the less, continued to strike him; she put the whole thing on so sound a basis when she said: "You see they're so nice about it—they take such an interest. And they never do a thing they shouldn't. That was always everything to mother and me." "They," Gedge had already noticed, referred constantly and hugely, in the good woman's talk, to the millions who shuffled through the house; the pronoun in question was

forever on her lips, the hordes it represented filled her consciousness, the addition of their numbers ministered to her glory. Mrs.
Gedge promptly met her. "It must be indeed delightful to see the
effect on so many, and to feel that one may perhaps do something
to make it—well, permanent." But he was kept silent by his becoming more sharply aware that this was a new view, for him, of
the reference made, that he had never thought of the quality of
the place as derived from Them, but from Somebody Else, and
that They, in short, seemed to have got into the way of crowding
out Him. He found himself even a little resenting this for Him,
which perhaps had something to do with the slightly invidious
cast of his next inquiry.

"And are They always, as one might say—a—stupid?"

"Stupid!" She stared, looking as if no one *could* be such a thing
in such a connection. No one had ever been anything but neat and
cheerful and fluent, except to be attentive and unobjectionable
and, so far as was possible, American.

"What I mean is," he explained, "is there any perceptible proportion that take an interest in Him?"

His wife stepped on his toe; she deprecated irony. But his mistake fortunately was lost on their friend. "That's just why they
come, that they take such an interest. I sometimes think they
take more than about anything else in the world." With which
Miss Putchin looked about at the place. "It *is* pretty, don't you
think, the way they've got it now?" This, Gedge saw, was a different "They"; it applied to the powers that were—the people
who had appointed him, the governing, visiting Body, in respect to which he was afterwards to remark to Mrs. Gedge that a
fellow—it was the difficulty—didn't know "where to have her."
His wife, at a loss, questioned at that moment the necessity of
having her anywhere, and he said, good-humouredly, "Of course;
it's all right." He was in fact content enough with the last touches
their friend had given the picture. "There are many who know all
about it when they come, and the Americans often are tremendously up. Mother and me really enjoyed"—it was her only slip—
"the interest of the Americans. We've sometimes had ninety a day,

and all wanting to see and hear everything. But you'll work them off; you'll see the way—it's all experience." She came back, for his comfort, to that. She came back also to other things: she did justice to the considerable class who arrived positive and primed. "There are those who know more about it than you do. But *that* only comes from their interest."

"Who know more about what?" Gedge inquired.

"Why, about the place. I mean they have their ideas—of what everything is, and *where* it is, and what it isn't, and where it *should* be. They do ask questions," she said, yet not so much in warning as in the complacency of being seasoned and sound; "and they're down on you when they think you go wrong. As if you ever could! You know too much," she sagaciously smiled; "or you *will*."

"Oh, you mustn't know *too* much, must you?" And Gedge now smiled as well. He knew, he thought, what he meant.

"Well, you must know as much as anybody else. I claim, at any rate, that I do," Miss Putchin declared. "They never really caught me."

"I'm very sure of *that*," Mrs. Gedge said with an elation almost personal.

"Certainly," he added, "I don't want to be caught." She rejoined that, in such a case, he would have *Them* down on him, and he saw that this time she meant the powers above. It quickened his sense of all the elements that were to reckon with, yet he felt at the same time that the powers above were not what he should most fear. "I'm glad," he observed, "that they ever ask questions; but I happened to notice, you know, that no one did to-day."

"Then you missed several—and no loss. There were three or four put to me too silly to remember. But of course they mostly *are* silly."

"You mean the questions?"

She laughed with all her cheer. "Yes, sir; I don't mean the answers."

Whereupon, for a moment snubbed and silent, he felt like one of the crowd. Then it made him slightly vicious. "I didn't know but you meant the people in general—till I remembered that I'm to understand from you that *they're* wise, only occasionally breaking down."

It was not really till then, he thought, that she lost patience; and he had had, much more than he meant no doubt, a cross-questioning air. "You'll see for yourself." Of which he was sure enough. He was in fact so ready to take this that she came round to full accommodation, put it frankly that every now and then they broke out—not the silly, oh no, the intensely inquiring. "We've had quite lively discussions, don't you know, about well-known points. They want it all *their* way, and I know the sort that are going to as soon as I see them. That's one of the things you do—you get to know the sorts. And if it's what you're afraid of—their taking you up," she was further gracious enough to say, "you needn't mind a bit. What *do* they know, after all, when for us it's our life? I've never moved an inch, because, you see, I shouldn't have been here if I didn't know where I was. No more will *you* be a year hence—you know what I mean, putting it impossibly—if *you* don't. I expect you do, in spite of your fancies." And she dropped once more to bed-rock. "There are the facts. Otherwise where would any of us be? That's all you've got to go upon. A person, however cheeky, can't have them *his* way just because he takes it into his head. There can only be *one* way, and," she gaily added as she took leave of them, "I'm sure it's quite enough!"

III

Gedge not only assented eagerly—one way *was* quite enough if it were the right one—but repeated it, after this conversation, at odd moments, several times over to his wife. "There can only be one way, one way," he continued to remark—though indeed much as if it were a joke; till she asked him how many more he supposed she wanted. He failed to answer this question, but resorted to another repetition, "There are the facts, the facts," which, perhaps, however, he kept a little more to himself, sounding it at intervals in different parts of the house. Mrs. Gedge was full of comment on their clever introductress, though not restrictively save in the matter of her speech, "Me and mother," and a general tone—which certainly was not their sort of thing. "I don't know," he said, "perhaps it comes with the place, since speaking in immortal verse doesn't seem to come. It must be, one seems to see, one thing or the other. I dare say that in a few months I shall also be at it—'me and the wife.'"

"Why not me and the missus at once?" Mrs. Gedge resentfully inquired. "I don't think," she observed at another time, "that I quite know what's the matter with you."

"It's only that I'm excited, awfully excited—as I don't see how one can not be. You wouldn't have a fellow drop into this berth as into an appointment at the Post Office. Here on the spot it goes to my head; how can that be helped? But we shall live into it, and perhaps," he said with an implication of the other possibility that was doubtless but part of his fine ecstasy, "we shall live through it." The place acted on his imagination—how, surely, shouldn't it? And his imagination acted on his nerves, and these things together, with the general vividness and the new and complete immersion, made rest for him almost impossible, so that he could scarce go to bed at night and even during the first week more than once rose in the small hours to move about, up and down, with his lamp, standing, sitting, listening, wondering, in the stillness, as if positively to recover some echo, to surprise some secret, of the *genius loci*. He couldn't have explained it—and didn't in fact need to explain it, at least to himself, since the impulse simply held him and shook him; but the time after closing, the time above all after the people—Them, as he felt himself on the way to think of them, predominant, insistent, all in the foreground—brought him, or ought to have brought him, he seemed to see, nearer to the enshrined Presence, enlarged the opportunity for communion and intensified the sense of it. These nightly prowls, as he called them, were disquieting to his wife, who had no disposition to share in them, speaking with decision of the whole place as just the place to be forbidding after dark. She rejoiced in the distinctness, contiguous though it was, of their own little residence, where she trimmed the lamp and stirred the fire and heard the kettle sing, repairing the while the omissions of the small domestic who slept out; she foresaw herself with some promptness, draw-ing rather sharply the line between her own precinct and that in which the great spirit might walk. It would be with them, the great spirit, all day—even if indeed on her making that remark, and in just that form, to her husband, he replied with a queer "But will he though?" And she vaguely imaged the development of a domestic antidote after a while, precisely, in the shape of curtains more markedly drawn and everything most modern and lively, tea, "patterns," the newspapers, the female fiction itself that they had reacted against at Blackport, quite defiantly cultivated.

These possibilities, however, were all right, as her companion said it was, all the first autumn—they had arrived at summer's end; as if he were more than content with a special set of his own that he had access to from behind, passing out of their low door for the few steps between it and the Birthplace. With his lamp ever so carefully guarded, and his nursed keys that made him free of treasures, he crossed the dusky interval so often that she began to qualify it as a habit that "grew." She spoke of it almost as if he had taken to drink, and he humoured that view of it by confess-ing that the cup was strong. This had been in truth, altogether, his immediate sense of it; strange and deep for him the spell of silent sessions before familiarity and, to some small extent, disap-pointment had set in. The exhibitional side of the establishment had struck him, even on arrival, as qualifying too much its char-acter; he scarce knew what he might best have looked for, but the three or four rooms bristled overmuch, in the garish light of day, with busts and relics, not even ostensibly always *His*, old prints and old editions, old objects fashioned in His likeness, furniture "of the time" and autographs of celebrated worshippers. In the quiet hours and the deep dusk, none the less, under the play of the shifted lamp and that of his own emotion, these things too recov-ered their advantage, ministered to the mystery, or at all events to the impression, seemed consciously to offer themselves as personal to the poet. Not one of them was really or unchallengeably so, but they had somehow, through long association, got, as Gedge always phrased it, into the secret, and it was about the secret he asked them while he restlessly wandered. It was not till months had elapsed that he found how little they had to tell him, and he was quite at his ease with them when he knew they were by no means where his sensibility had first placed them. They were as out of it as he; only, to do them justice, they had made him immensely feel. And still, too, it was not they who had done that most, since his sentiment had gradually cleared itself to deep, to deeper refinements.

The Holy of Holies of the Birthplace was the low, the sublime Chamber of Birth, sublime because, as the Americans usually said—unlike the natives they mostly found words—it was so pathetic; and pathetic because it was—well, really nothing else in the world that one could name, number or measure. It was as empty as a shell of which the kernel has withered, and contained neither busts nor prints nor early copies; it contained only the Fact—*the* Fact itself—which, as he stood sentient there at midnight, our friend, holding his breath, allowed to sink into him. He *had* to take it as the place where the spirit would most walk and where he would therefore be most to be met, with possibilities of recognition and reciprocity. He hadn't, most probably—*He* hadn't—much inhabited the room, as men weren't apt, as a rule, to convert to their later use and involve in their wider fortune the scene itself of their nativity. But as there were moments when, in the conflict of theories, the sole certainty surviving for the critic threatened to be that He had not—unlike other successful men— *not* been born, so Gedge, though little of a critic, clung to the square feet of space that connected themselves, however feebly, with the positive appearance. He was little of a critic—he was nothing of one; he hadn't pretended to the character before coming, nor come to pretend to it; also, luckily for him, he was seeing day by day how little use he could possibly have for it. It would be to him, the attitude of a high expert, distinctly a stumblingblock, and that he rejoiced, as the winter waned, in his ignorance, was one of the propositions he betook himself, in his odd manner, to enunciating to his wife. She denied it, for hadn't she, in the first place, been present, wasn't she still present, at his pious, his tireless study of everything connected with the subject?—so present that she had herself learned more about it than had ever seemed likely. Then, in the second place, he was not to proclaim on the housetops any point at which he might be weak, for who knew, if it should get abroad that they were ignorant, what effect might be produced——?

"On the attraction"—he took her up—"of the Show?"

He had fallen into the harmless habit of speaking of the place as the "Show"; but she didn't mind this so much as to be diverted by it. "No; on the attitude of the Body. You know they're pleased with us, and I don't see why you should want to spoil it. We got in by a tight squeeze—you know we've had evidence of that, and that it was about as much as our backers could manage. But we're proving a comfort to them, and it's absurd of you to question your suitability to people who were content with the Putchins."

"I don't, my dear," he returned, "question anything; but if I should do so it would be precisely because of the greater advantage constituted for the Putchins by the simplicity of their spirit. They were kept straight by the quality of their ignorance—which was denser even than mine. It was a mistake in us, from the first, to have attempted to correct or to disguise ours. We should have waited simply to become good parrots, to learn our lesson—all on the spot here, so little of it is wanted—and squawk it off."

"Ah, 'squawk,' love—what a word to use about Him!"

"It isn't about Him—nothing's about Him. None of Them care tuppence about Him. The only thing They care about is this empty shell—or rather, for it isn't empty, the extraneous, preposterous stuffing of it."

"Preposterous?"—he made her stare with this as he had not yet done.

At sight of her look, however—the gleam, as it might have been, of a queer suspicion—he bent to her kindly and tapped her cheek. "Oh, it's all right. We *must* fall back on the Putchins. Do you remember what she said?—'They've made it so pretty now.' They *have* made it pretty, and it's a first-rate show. It's a first-rate show and a first-rate billet, and He was a first-rate poet, and you're a first-rate woman—to put up so sweetly, I mean, with my nonsense."

She appreciated his domestic charm and she justified that part of his tribute which concerned herself. "I don't care how much of your nonsense you talk to me, so long as you *keep* it all for me and don't treat *Them* to it."

"The pilgrims? No," he conceded—"it isn't fair to Them. They mean well."

"What complaint have we, after all, to make of Them so long as They don't break off bits—as They used, Miss Putchin told us, so awfully—to conceal about Their Persons? She broke them at least of that."

"Yes," Gedge mused again; "I wish awfully she hadn't!"

"You would like the relics destroyed, removed? That's all that's wanted!"

"There *are* no relics."

"There won't be any soon, unless you take care." But he was already laughing, and the talk was not dropped without his having patted her once more. An impression or two, however, remained with her from it, as he saw from a question she asked him on the morrow. "What did you mean yesterday about Miss Putchin's simplicity—its keeping her 'straight'? Do you mean mentally?"

Her "mentally" was rather portentous, but he practically confessed. "Well, it kept her up. I mean," he amended, laughing, "it kept her down."

It was really as if she had been a little uneasy. "You consider there's a danger of your being affected? You know what I mean. Of its going to your head. You do know," she insisted as he said nothing. "Through your caring for him so. You'd certainly be right in that case about its having been a mistake for you to plunge so deep." And then as his listening without reply, though with his look a little sad for her, might have denoted that, allowing for extravagance of statement, he saw there was something in it: "Give up your prowls. Keep it for daylight. Keep it for *Them*."

"Ah," he smiled, "if one could! My prowls," he added, "are what I most enjoy. They're the only time, as I've told you before, that I'm really with *Him*. Then I don't see the place. He isn't the place."

"I don't care for what you 'don't' see," she replied with vivacity; "the question is of what you do see."

Well, if it was, he waited before meeting it. "Do you know what I sometimes do?" And then as she waited too: "In the Birthroom there, when I look in late, I often put out my light. That makes it better."

"Makes what——?"

"Everything."

"What is it then you see in the dark?"

"Nothing!" said Morris Gedge.

"And what's the pleasure of that?"

"Well, what the American ladies say. It's so fascinating."

IV

The autumn was brisk, as Miss Putchin had told them it would be, but business naturally fell off with the winter months and the short days. There was rarely an hour indeed without a call of some sort, and they were never allowed to forget that they kept the shop in all the world, as they might say, where custom was least fluctuating. The seasons told on it, as they tell upon travel, but no other influence, consideration or convulsion to which the population of the globe is exposed. This population, never exactly in simultaneous hordes, but in a full, swift and steady stream, passed through the smoothly-working mill and went, in its variety of degrees duly impressed and edified, on its artless way. Gedge gave himself up, with much ingenuity of spirit, to trying to keep in relation with it; having even at moments, in the early time, glimpses of the chance that the impressions gathered from so rare an opportunity for contact with the general mind might prove as interesting as anything else in the connection. Types, classes, nationalities, manners, diversities of behaviour, modes of seeing, feeling, of expression, would pass before him and become for him, after a fashion, the experience of an untravelled man. His journeys had been short and saving, but poetic justice again seemed inclined to work for him in placing him just at the point in all Europe perhaps where the confluence of races was thickest. The theory, at any rate, carried him on, operating helpfully for the term of his anxious beginnings and gilding in a manner—it was the way he characterised the case to his wife—the somewhat stodgy gingerbread of their daily routine. They had not known many people, and their visiting-list was small—which made it again poetic justice that they should be visited on such a scale. They dressed and were at home, they were under arms and received, and except for the offer of refreshment—and Gedge had his view that there would eventually be a *buffet* farmed out to a great firm—their hospitality would have made them princely if mere hospitality ever did. Thus they were launched, and it was interesting, and from having been ready to drop, originally, with fatigue, they emerged even-winded and strong in the legs, as if they had had an Alpine holiday. This experience, Gedge opined, also represented, as a gain, a like seasoning of the spirit—by which he meant a certain command of impenetrable patience.

The patience was needed for the particular feature of the ordeal that, by the time the lively season was with them again, had disengaged itself as the sharpest—the immense assumption of veracities and sanctities, of the general soundness of the legend with which everyone arrived. He was well provided, certainly, for meeting it, and he gave all he had, yet he had sometimes the sense of a vague resentment on the part of his pilgrims at his not ladling out their fare with a bigger spoon. An irritation had begun to grumble in him during the comparatively idle months of winter when a pilgrim would turn up singly. The pious individual, entertained for the half-hour, had occasionally seemed to offer him the promise of beguilement or the semblance of a personal relation; it came back again to the few pleasant calls he had received in the course of a life almost void of social amenity. Sometimes he liked the person, the face, the speech: an educated man, a gentleman, not one of the herd; a graceful woman, vague, accidental, unconscious of him, but making him wonder, while he hovered, who she was. These chances represented for him light yearnings and faint flutters;

they acted indeed, within him, in a special, an extraordinary way. He would have liked to talk with such stray companions, to talk with them *really*, to talk with them as he might have talked if he had met them where he couldn't meet them—at dinner, in the "world," on a visit at a country-house. Then he could have said—and about the shrine and the idol always—things he couldn't say now. The form in which his irritation first came to him was that of his feeling obliged to say to them—to the single visitor, even when sympathetic, quite as to the gaping group—the particular things, a dreadful dozen or so, that they expected. If he had thus arrived at characterising these things as dreadful the reason touches the very point that, for a while turning everything over, he kept dodging, not facing, trying to ignore. The point was that he was on his way to become two quite different persons, the public and the private, and yet that it would somehow have to be managed that these persons should live together. He was splitting into halves, unmistakeably—he who, whatever else he had been, had at least always been so entire and, in his way, so solid. One of the halves, or perhaps even, since the split promised to be rather unequal, one of the quarters, was the keeper, the showman, the priest of the idol; the other piece was the poor unsuccessful honest man he had always been.

There were moments when he recognised this primary character as he had never done before; when he in fact quite shook in his shoes at the idea that it perhaps had in reserve some supreme assertion of its identity. It was honest, verily, just by reason of the possibility. It was poor and unsuccessful because here it was just on the verge of quarrelling with its bread and butter. Salvation would be of course—the salvation of the showman—rigidly to *keep* it on the verge; not to let it, in other words, overpass by an inch. He might count on this, he said to himself, if there weren't any public—if there weren't thousands of people demanding of him what he was paid for. He saw the approach of the stage at which they would affect him, the thousands of people—and perhaps even more the earnest individual—as coming really to see if he were earning his wage. Wouldn't he soon begin to fancy them in league with the Body, practically deputed by it—given, no doubt, a kindled suspicion—to look in and report observations? It was the way he broke down with the lonely pilgrim that led to his first heart-searchings—broke down as to the courage required for damping an uncritical faith. What they all most wanted was to feel that everything was "just as it was"; only the shock of having to part with that vision was greater than any individual could bear unsupported. The bad moments were upstairs in the Birthroom, for here the forces pressing on the very edge assumed a dire intensity. The mere expression of eye, all-credulous, omnivorous and fairly moistening in the act, with which many persons gazed about, might eventually make it difficult for him to remain fairly civil. Often they came in pairs—sometimes one had come before—and then they explained to each other. He never in that case corrected; he listened, for the lesson of listening: after which he would remark to his wife that there was no end to what he was learning. He saw that if he should really ever break down it would be with her he would begin. He had given her hints and digs enough, but she was so inflamed with appreciation that she either didn't feel them or pretended not to understand.

This was the greater complication that, with the return of the spring and the increase of the public, her services were more required. She took the field with him, from an early hour; she was present with the party above while he kept an eye, and still more an ear, on the party below; and how could he know, he asked himself, what she might say to them and what she might suffer *Them* to say—or in other words, poor wretches, to believe—while removed from his control? Some day or other, and before too long, he couldn't but think, he must have the matter out with her—the matter, namely, of the *morality* of their position. The morality of women was special—he was getting lights on that. Isabel's conception of her office was to cherish and enrich the legend. It was already, the legend, very taking, but what was she there for but to make it more so? She certainly wasn't there to chill any natural piety. If it was all in the air—all in their "eye," as the vulgar might say—that He *had* been born in the Birthroom, where was the value of the sixpences they took? where the equivalent they had engaged to supply? "Oh dear, yes—just about *here*"; and she must tap the place with her foot. "Altered? Oh dear, no—save in a few trifling particulars; you see the place—and isn't that just the charm of it?—quite as *He* saw it. Very poor and homely, no doubt; but that's just what's so wonderful." He didn't want to hear her, and yet he didn't want to give her her head; he didn't want to make difficulties or to snatch the bread from her mouth. But he must none the less give her a warning before they had gone *too* far. That was the way, one evening in June, he put it to her; the affluence, with the finest weather, having lately been of the largest, and the crowd, all day, fairly gorged with the story. "We mustn't, you know, go *too* far."

The odd thing was that she had now ceased to be even conscious of what troubled him—she was so launched in her own career. "Too far for what?"

"To save our immortal souls. We mustn't, love, tell too many lies."

She looked at him with dire reproach. "Ah now, are you going to begin again?"

"I never *have* begun; I haven't wanted to worry you. But, you know, we don't know anything about it." And then as she stared, flushing: "About His having been born up there. About anything, really. Not the least little scrap that would weigh, in any other connection, as evidence. So don't rub it in so."

"Rub it in how?"

"That He *was* born——" But at sight of her face he only sighed. "Oh dear, oh dear!"

"Don't you think," she replied cuttingly, "that He was born anywhere?"

He hesitated—it was such an edifice to shake. "Well, we don't know. There's very little *to* know. He covered His tracks as no other human being has ever done."

She was still in her public costume and had not taken off the gloves that she made a point of wearing as a part of that uniform; she remembered how the rustling housekeeper in the Border castle, on whom she had begun by modelling herself, had worn them. She seemed official and slightly distant. "To cover His tracks. He must have had to exist. Have we got to give *that* up?"

"No, I don't ask you to give it up *yet*. But there's very little to go upon."

"And is that what I'm to tell Them in return for everything?"

Gedge waited—he walked about. The place was doubly still after the bustle of the day, and the summer evening rested on it as a blessing, making it, in its small state and anciently, mellow and sweet. It was good to be there, and it would be good to stay. At the same time there was something incalculable in the effect on one's nerves of the great gregarious density. That was an attitude that had nothing to do with degrees and shades, the attitude of wanting all or nothing. And you couldn't talk things over with it. You could only do this with friends, and then but in cases where you were sure the friends wouldn't betray you. "Couldn't you adopt," he replied at last, "a slightly more discreet method? What we can say is that things have been *said*; that's all *we* have to do with. 'And is this really'—when they jam their umbrellas into the floor—'the very *spot* where He was born?' 'So it has, from a long time back, been described as being.' Couldn't one meet Them, to be decent a little, in some such way as that?"

She looked at him very hard. "Is that the way *you* meet them?"

"No; I've kept on lying—without scruple, without shame."

"Then why do you haul me up?"

"Because it has seemed to me that we might, like true companions, work it out a little together."

This was not strong, he felt, as, pausing with his hands in his pockets, he stood before her; and he knew it as weaker still after she had looked at him a minute. "Morris Gedge, I propose to be *your* true companion, and I've come here to stay. That's all I've got to say." It was not, however, for "You had better try yourself and see," she presently added. "Give the place, give the story away, by so much as a look, and—well, I'd allow you about nine days. Then you'd see."

He feigned, to gain time, an innocence. "They'd take it so ill?"

And then, as she said nothing: "They'd turn and rend me? They'd tear me to pieces?"

But she wouldn't make a joke of it. "They wouldn't *have* it, simply."

"No—they wouldn't. That's what I say. They won't."

"You had better," she went on, "begin with Grant-Jackson. But even that isn't necessary. It would get to him, it would get to the Body, like wildfire."

"I see," said poor Gedge. And indeed for the moment he did see, while his companion followed up what she believed her advantage.

"Do you consider it's *all* a fraud?"

"Well, I grant you there was somebody. But the details are naught. The links are missing. The evidence—in particular about that room upstairs, in itself our Casa Santa—is *nil*. It was so awfully long ago." Which he knew again sounded weak.

"Of course it was awfully long ago—that's just the beauty and the interest. Tell Them, *tell* Them," she continued, "that the evidence is *nil*, and I'll tell them something else." She spoke it with such meaning that his face seemed to show a question, to which she was on the spot of replying "I'll tell them that you're a——" She stopped, however, changing it. "I'll tell them exactly the opposite. And I'll find out what you say—it won't take long—to do it. If we tell different stories, *that* possibly may save us."

"I see what you mean. It would perhaps, as an oddity, have a success of curiosity. It might become a draw. Still, they but want broad masses." And he looked at her sadly. "You're no more than one of Them."

"If it's being no more than one of them to love it," she answered, "then I certainly am. And I am not ashamed of my company."

"To love *what*?" said Morris Gedge.

"To love to think He was born there."

"You think too much. It's bad for you." He turned away with his chronic moan. But it was without losing what she called after him.

"I decline to let the place down." And what was there indeed to say? They *were* there to keep it up.

V

He kept it up through the summer, but with the queerest consciousness, at times, of the want of proportion between his secret rage and the spirit of those from whom the friction came. He said to himself—so sore as his sensibility had grown—that They were gregariously ferocious at the very time he was seeing Them as individually mild. He said to himself that They were mild only because *he* was—he flattered himself that he was divinely so, considering what he might be; and that he should, as his wife had warned him, soon enough have news of it were he to deflect by a hair's breadth from the line traced for him. *That* was the collective fatuity—that it was capable of turning, on the instant, both to a general and to a particular resentment. Since the least breath of discrimination would get him the sack without mercy, it was absurd, he reflected, to speak of his discomfort as light. He was gagged, he was goaded, as in omnivorous companies he doubtless sometimes showed by a strange silent glare. They would get him the sack for that as well, if he didn't look out; therefore wasn't it in effect ferocity when you mightn't even hold your tongue? They wouldn't let you off with silence—They insisted on your committing yourself. It was the pound of flesh—They would have it; so under his coat he bled. But a wondrous peace, by exception, dropped on him one afternoon at the end of August. The pressure had, as usual, been high, but it had diminished with the fall of day, and the place was empty before the hour for closing. Then it was that, within a few minutes of this hour, there presented themselves a pair of pilgrims to whom in the ordinary course he would have remarked that they were, to his regret, too late. He was to wonder afterwards why the course had, at sight of the visitors—a gentleman and a lady, appealing and fairly young—shown for him as other than ordinary; the consequence sprang doubtless from something rather fine and unnameable, something, for instance, in the tone of the young man, or in the light of his eye, after hearing the statement on the subject of the hour. "Yes, we know it's late; but it's just, I'm afraid, *because* of that. We've had rather a notion of escaping the crowd—as, I suppose, you mostly have one now; and it was really on the chance of finding you alone——!"

These things the young man said before being quite admitted, and they were words that any one might have spoken who
had not taken the trouble to be punctual or who desired, a little
ingratiatingly, to force the door. Gedge even guessed at the sense
that might lurk in them, the hint of a special tip if the point were
stretched. There were no tips, he had often thanked his stars, at
the Birthplace; there was the charged fee and nothing more;
everything else was out of order, to the relief of a palm not formed
by nature for a scoop. Yet in spite of everything, in spite especially
of the almost audible chink of the gentleman's sovereigns, which
might in another case exactly have put him out, he presently
found himself, in the Birthroom, access to which he had gracefully
enough granted, almost treating the visit as personal and private.
The reason—well, the reason would have been, if anywhere, in
something naturally persuasive on the part of the couple, unless
it had been, rather, again, in the way the young man, once he was
in the place, met the caretaker's expression of face, held it a moment and seemed to wish to sound it. That they were Americans
was promptly clear, and Gedge could very nearly have told what
kind; he had arrived at the point of distinguishing kinds, though
the difficulty might have been with him now that the case before
him was rare. He saw it, in fact, suddenly, in the light of the golden
midland evening, which reached them through low old windows,
saw it with a rush of feeling, unexpected and smothered, that
made him wish for a moment to keep it before him as a case of
inordinate happiness. It made him feel old, shabby, poor, but he
watched it no less intensely for its doing so. They were children
of fortune, of the greatest, as it might seem to Morris Gedge, and
they were of course lately married; the husband, smooth-faced
and soft, but resolute and fine, several years older than the wife,
and the wife vaguely, delicately, irregularly, but mercilessly pretty.
Somehow, the world was theirs; they gave the person who took
the sixpences at the Birthplace such a sense of the high luxury
of freedom as he had never had. The thing was that the world
was theirs not simply because they had money—he had seen rich
people enough—but because they could in a supreme degree

think and feel and say what they liked. They had a nature and a culture, a tradition, a facility of some sort—and all producing in them an effect of positive beauty—that gave a light to their liberty and an ease to their tone. These things moreover suffered nothing from the fact that they happened to be in mourning; this was probably worn for some lately-deceased opulent father, or some delicate mother who would be sure to have been a part of the source of the beauty, and it affected Gedge, in the gathered twilight and at his odd crisis, as the very uniform of their distinction.

He couldn't quite have said afterwards by what steps the point had been reached, but it had become at the end of five minutes a part of their presence in the Birthroom, a part of the young man's look, a part of the charm of the moment, and a part, above all, of a strange sense within him of "Now or never!" that Gedge had suddenly, thrillingly, let himself go. He had not been definitely conscious of drifting to it; he had been, for that, too conscious merely of thinking how different, in all their range, were such a united couple from another united couple that he knew. They were everything he and his wife were not; this was more than anything else the lesson at first of their talk. Thousands of couples of whom the same was true certainly had passed before him, but none of whom it was true with just that engaging intensity. This was *because* of their transcendent freedom; that was what, at the end of five minutes, he saw it all come back to. The husband had been there at some earlier time, and he had his impression, which he wished now to make his wife share. But he already, Gedge could see, had not concealed it from her. A pleasant irony, in fine, our friend seemed to taste in the air—he who had not yet felt free to taste his own.

"I think you weren't here four years ago"—that was what the young man had almost begun by remarking. Gedge liked his remembering it, liked his frankly speaking to him; all the more that he had given him, as it were, no opening. He had let them look about below, and then had taken them up, but without words, without the usual showman's song, of which he would have been afraid. The visitors didn't ask for it; the young man had taken

the matter out of his hands by himself dropping for the benefit
of the young woman a few detached remarks. What Gedge felt,
oddly, was that these remarks were not inconsiderate of him; he
had heard others, both of the priggish order and the crude, that
might have been called so. And as the young man had not been
aided to this cognition of him as new, it already began to make
for them a certain common ground. The ground became immense
when the visitor presently added with a smile: "There was a good
lady, I recollect, who had a great deal to say."

It was the gentleman's smile that had done it; the irony *was*
there. "Ah, there has been a great deal said." And Gedge's look at
his interlocutor doubtless showed his sense of being sounded. It
was extraordinary of course that a perfect stranger should have
guessed the travail of his spirit, should have caught the gleam
of his inner commentary. That probably, in spite of him, leaked
out of his poor old eyes. "Much of it, in such places as this," he
heard himself adding, "is of course said very irresponsibly." *Such
places as this!*—he winced at the words as soon as he had uttered
them.

There was no wincing, however, on the part of his pleasant
companions. "Exactly so; the whole thing becomes a sort of
stiff, smug convention, like a dressed-up sacred doll in a Spanish
church—which you're a monster if you touch."

"A monster," said Gedge, meeting his eyes.

The young man smiled, but he thought he looked at him a little
harder. "A blasphemer."

"A blasphemer."

It seemed to do his visitor good—he certainly *was* looking
at him harder. Detached as he was he was interested—he was
at least amused. "Then you don't claim, or at any rate you don't
insist——? I mean you personally."

He had an identity for him, Gedge felt, that he couldn't have
had for a Briton, and the impulse was quick in our friend to testify
to this perception. "I don't insist to *you*."

The young man laughed. "It really—I assure you if I may—
wouldn't do any good. I'm too awfully interested."

"Do you mean," his wife lightly inquired, "in—a—pulling it down? That is in what you've said to me."

"Has he said to you," Gedge intervened, though quaking a little, "that he would like to pull it down?"

She met, in her free sweetness, this directness with such a charm! "Oh, perhaps not quite the *house*——!"

"Good. You see we live on it—I mean *we* people."

The husband had laughed, but had now so completely ceased to look about him that there seemed nothing left for him but to talk avowedly with the caretaker. "I'm interested," he explained, "in what, I think, is *the* interesting thing—or at all events the eternally tormenting one. The fact of the abysmally little that, in proportion, we know."

"In proportion to what?" his companion asked.

"Well, to what there must have been—to what in fact there *is*—to wonder about. That's the interest; it's immense. He escapes us like a thief at night, carrying off—well, carrying off everything. And people pretend to catch Him like a flown canary, over whom you can close your hand and put Him back. He won't *go* back; he won't *come* back. He's not"—the young man laughed—"such a fool! It makes Him the happiest of all great men."

He had begun by speaking to his wife, but had ended, with his friendly, his easy, his indescribable competence, for Gedge— poor Gedge who quite held his breath and who felt, in the most unexpected way, that he had somehow never been in such good society. The young wife, who for herself meanwhile had continued to look about, sighed out, smiled out—Gedge couldn't have told which—her little answer to these remarks. "It's rather a pity, you know, that He *isn't* here. I mean as Goethe's at Weimar. For Goethe *is* at Weimar."

"Yes, my dear; that's Goethe's bad luck. There he sticks. *This* man isn't anywhere. I defy you to catch Him."

"Why not say, beautifully," the young woman laughed, "that, like the wind, He's everywhere?"

It wasn't of course the tone of discussion, it was the tone of joking, though of better joking, Gedge seemed to feel, and more within his own appreciation, than he had ever listened to; and this was precisely why the young man could go on without the effect of irritation, answering his wife but still with eyes for their companion. "I'll be hanged if He's *here*!"

It was almost as if he were taken—that is, struck and rather held—by their companion's unruffled state, which they hadn't meant to ruffle, but which suddenly presented its interest, perhaps even projected its light. The gentleman didn't know, Gedge was afterwards to say to himself, how that hypocrite was inwardly all of a tremble, how it seemed to him that his fate was being literally pulled down on his head. He was trembling for the moment certainly too much to speak; abject he might be, but he didn't want his voice to have the absurdity of a quaver. And the young woman—charming creature!—still had another word. It was for the guardian of the spot, and she made it, in her way, delightful. They had remained in the Holy of Holies, and she had been looking for a minute, with a ruefulness just marked enough to be pretty, at the queer old floor. "Then if you say it *wasn't* in this room He was born—well, what's the use?"

"What's the use of what?" her husband asked. "The use, you mean, of our coming here? Why, the place is charming in itself. And it's also interesting," he added to Gedge, "to know how you get on."

Gedge looked at him a moment in silence, but he answered the young woman first. If poor Isabel, he was thinking, could only have been like that!—not as to youth, beauty, arrangement of hair or picturesque grace of hat—these things he didn't mind; but as to sympathy, facility, light perceptive, and yet not cheap, detachment! "I don't say it wasn't—but I don't say it *was*."

"Ah, but doesn't that," she returned, "come very much to the same thing? And don't They want also to see where He had His dinner and where He had His tea?"

"They want everything," said Morris Gedge. "They want to see where He hung up His hat and where He kept His boots and where His mother boiled her pot."

"But if you don't show them——?"

"They show *me*. It's in all their little books."

"You mean," the husband asked, "that you've only to hold your tongue?"

"I try to," said Gedge.

"Well," his visitor smiled, "I see you *can*."

Gedge hesitated. "I can't."

"Oh, well," said his friend, "what does it matter?"

"I do speak," he continued. "I can't sometimes not."

"Then how do you get on?"

Gedge looked at him more abjectly, to his own sense, than he had ever looked at anyone—even at Isabel when she frightened him. "I don't get on. I speak," he said, "since I've spoken to *you*."

"Oh, *we* shan't hurt you!" the young man reassuringly laughed.

The twilight meanwhile had sensibly thickened; the end of the visit was indicated. They turned together out of the upper room, and came down the narrow stair. The words just exchanged might have been felt as producing an awkwardness which the young woman gracefully felt the impulse to dissipate. "You must rather wonder why we've come." And it was the first note, for Gedge, of a further awkwardness—as if he had definitely heard it make the husband's hand, in a full pocket, begin to fumble.

It was even a little awkwardly that the husband still held off. "Oh, we like it as it is. There's always *something*." With which they had approached the door of egress.

"What is there, please?" asked Morris Gedge, not yet opening the door, as he would fain have kept the pair on, and conscious only for a moment after he had spoken that his question was just having, for the young man, too dreadfully wrong a sound. This personage wondered, yet feared, had evidently for some minutes been asking himself; so that, with his preoccupation, the caretaker's words had represented to him, inevitably, "What is there, please, for *me*?" Gedge already knew, with it, moreover, that he wasn't stopping him in time. He had put his question, to show he himself wasn't afraid, and he must have had in consequence, he was subsequently to reflect, a lamentable air of waiting.

The visitor's hand came out. "I hope I may take the liberty

——?" What afterwards happened our friend scarcely knew, for
it fell into a slight confusion, the confusion of a queer gleam of
gold—a sovereign fairly thrust at him; of a quick, almost violent
motion on his own part, which, to make the matter worse, might
well have sent the money rolling on the floor; and then of marked
blushes all round, and a sensible embarrassment; producing indeed, in turn, rather oddly, and ever so quickly, an increase of
communion. It was as if the young man had offered him money
to make up to him for having, as it were, led him on, and then,
perceiving the mistake, but liking him the better for his refusal,
had wanted to obliterate this aggravation of his original wrong.
He had done so, presently, while Gedge got the door open, by
saying the best thing he could, and by saying it frankly and gaily.
"Luckily it doesn't at all affect the *work*!"

The small town-street, quiet and empty in the summer even-
tide, stretched to right and left, with a gabled and timbered house
or two, and fairly seemed to have cleared itself to congruity with
the historic void over which our friends, lingering an instant to
converse, looked at each other. The young wife, rather, looked
about a moment at all there wasn't to be seen, and then, before
Gedge had found a reply to her husband's remark, uttered, evidently in the interest of conciliation, a little question of her own
that she tried to make earnest. "It's our unfortunate ignorance,
you mean, that doesn't?"

"Unfortunate or fortunate. I like it so," said the husband. "'The
play's the thing.' Let the author alone."

Gedge, with his key on his forefinger, leaned against the doorpost, took in the stupid little street, and was sorry to see them
go—they seemed so to abandon him. "That's just what They
won't do—not let *me* do. It's all I want—to let the author alone.
Practically"—he felt himself getting the last of his chance—"there
is no author; that is for us to deal with. There are all the immortal
people—*in* the work; but there's nobody else."

"Yes," said the young man—"that's what it comes to. There
should really, to clear the matter up, be no such Person."

"As you say," Gedge returned, "it's what it comes to. There *is*
no such Person."

The evening air listened, in the warm, thick midland stillness, while the wife's little cry rang out. "But *wasn't* there——?"

"There was somebody," said Gedge, against the doorpost. "But They've killed Him. And, dead as He is, They keep it up, They do it over again, They kill Him every day."

He was aware of saying this so grimly—more grimly than he wished—that his companions exchanged a glance and even perhaps looked as if they felt him extravagant. That was the way, really, Isabel had warned him all the others would be looking if he should talk to Them as he talked to *her*. He liked, however, for that matter, to hear how he should sound when pronounced incapable through deterioration of the brain. "Then if there's no author, if there's nothing to be said but that there isn't anybody," the young woman smilingly asked, "why in the world should there be a house?"

"There shouldn't," said Morris Gedge.

Decidedly, yes, he affected the young man. "Oh, I don't say, mind you, that you should pull it down!"

"Then where would you *go*?" their companion sweetly inquired.

"That's what my wife asks," Gedge replied.

"Then keep it up, keep it up!" And the husband held out his hand.

"That's what my wife says," Gedge went on as he shook it.

The young woman, charming creature, emulated the other visitor; she offered their remarkable friend her handshake. "Then mind your wife."

The poor man faced her gravely. "I would if she were such a wife as you!"

VI

It had made for him, all the same, an immense difference; it had given him an extraordinary lift, so that a certain sweet after-taste of his freedom might, a couple of months later, have been suspected of aiding to produce for him another, and really a more considerable, adventure. It was an odd way to think of it, but he had been, to his imagination, for twenty minutes in good society—that being the term that best described for him the company of people to whom he hadn't to talk, as he further phrased it, rot. It was his title to society that he had, in his doubtless awkward way, affirmed; and the difficulty was just that, having affirmed it, he couldn't take back the affirmation. Few things had happened to him in life, that is few that were agreeable, but at least *this* had, and he wasn't so constructed that he could go on as if it hadn't. It was going on as if it had, however, that landed him, alas! in the situation unmistakeably marked by a visit from Grant-Jackson, late one afternoon toward the end of October. This had been the hour of the call of the young Americans. Every day that hour had come round something of the deep throb of it, the successful secret, woke up; but the two occasions were, of a truth, related only by being so intensely opposed. The secret had been successful in that he had said nothing of it to Isabel, who, occupied in their own quarter while the incident lasted, had neither heard the visitors arrive nor seen them depart. It was on the other hand scarcely successful in guarding itself from indirect betrayals. There were two persons in the world, at least, who felt as he did; they were persons, also, who had treated him, benignly, as feeling as *they* did, who had been ready in fact to overflow in gifts as a sign of it, and though they were now off in space they were still with him sufficiently in spirit to make him play, as it were, with the sense of their sympathy. This in turn made him, as he was perfectly aware, more than a shade or two reckless, so that, in his reaction from that gluttony of the public for false facts which had from the first tormented him, he fell into the habit of sailing, as he would have said, too near the wind, or in other words—all in presence of the people—of washing his hands of the legend. He had crossed the line—he knew it; he had struck wild—They drove him to it; he had substituted, by a succession of uncontrollable profanities, an attitude that couldn't be understood for an attitude that but too evidently *had* been.

This was of course the franker line, only he hadn't taken it, alas! for frankness—hadn't in the least, really, *taken* it, but had been simply himself caught up and disposed of by it, hurled by his fate against the bedizened walls of the temple, quite in the way of a priest possessed to excess of the god, or, more vulgarly, that of a blind bull in a china-shop—an animal to which he often compared himself. He had let himself fatally go, in fine, just for irritation, for rage, having, in his predicament, nothing at all to do with frankness—a luxury reserved for quite other situations. It had always been his sentiment that one lived to learn; he had learned something every hour of his life, though people mostly never knew what, in spite of its having generally been—hadn't it?—at somebody's expense. What he was at present continually learning was the sense of a form of words heretofore so vain—the famous "false position" that had so often helped out a phrase. One used names in that way without knowing what they were worth; then of a sudden, one fine day, their meaning was bitter in the mouth. This was a truth with the relish of which his fireside hours were occupied, and he was quite conscious that a man was exposed who looked so perpetually as if something had disagreed with him. The look to be worn at the Birthplace was properly the beatific, and when once it had fairly been missed by those who took it for granted, who, indeed, paid sixpence for it—like the table-wine in provincial France, it was *compris*—one would be sure to have news of the remark.

News accordingly was what Gedge had been expecting—and what he knew, above all, had been expected by his wife, who had a way of sitting at present as with an ear for a certain knock. She didn't watch him, didn't follow him about the house, at the public hours, to spy upon his treachery; and that could touch him even though her averted eyes went through him more than her fixed. Her mistrust was so perfectly expressed by her manner of showing she trusted that he never felt so nervous, never so tried to keep straight, as when she most let him alone. When the crowd thickened and they had of necessity to receive together he tried himself to get off by allowing her as much as possible the word. When people appealed to him he turned to her—and with more of ceremony than their relation warranted: he couldn't help *this* either, if it seemed ironic—as to the person most concerned or most competent. He flattered himself at these moments that no one would have guessed her being his wife; especially as, to do her justice, she met his manner with a wonderful grim bravado—grim, so to say, for himself, grim by its outrageous cheerfulness for the simple-minded. The lore she *did* produce for them, the associations of the sacred spot that she developed, multiplied, embroidered; the things in short she said and the stupendous way she said them! She wasn't a bit ashamed; for why need virtue be ever ashamed? It *was* virtue, for it put bread into his mouth—he meanwhile, on his side, taking it out of hers. He had seen Grant-Jackson, on the October day, in the Birthplace itself—the right setting of course for such an interview; and what occurred was that, precisely, when the scene had ended and he had come back to their own sitting-room, the question she put to him for information was: "Have you settled it that I'm to starve?"

She had for a long time said nothing to him so straight—which was but a proof of her real anxiety; the straightness of Grant-Jackson's visit, following on the very slight sinuosity of a note shortly before received from him, made tension show for what it was. By this time, really, however, his decision had been taken; the minutes elapsing between his reappearance at the domestic fireside and his having, from the other threshold, seen Grant-Jackson's broad, well-fitted back, the back of a banker and a patriot, move away, had, though few, presented themselves to him as supremely critical. They formed, as it were, the hinge of his door, that door actually ajar so as to show him a possible fate beyond it, but which, with his hand, in a spasm, thus tightening on the knob, he might either open wide or close partly and altogether. He stood, in the autumn dusk, in the little museum that constituted the vestibule of the temple, and there, as with a concentrated push at a crank of a windlass, he brought himself round. The portraits on the walls seemed vaguely to watch for it; it was in their august presence—kept dimly august, for the moment, by Grant-Jackson's impressive check of his application of a match to the vulgar gas—that the great man had uttered, as if it said all, his "You know, my dear fellow, really——!" He had managed it with the special tact of a fat man, always, when there *was* any, very fine; he had got the most out of the time, the place, the setting, all the little massed admonitions and symbols; confronted there with his victim on the spot that he took occasion to name to him afresh as, to *his* piety and patriotism, the most sacred on earth, he had given it to be understood that in the first place he was lost in amazement and that in the second he expected a single warning now to suffice. Not to insist too much moreover on the question of gratitude, he would let his remonstrance rest, if need be, solely on the question of taste. *As* a matter of taste alone——! But he was surely not to be obliged to follow that up. Poor Gedge indeed would have been sorry to oblige him, for he saw it was precisely to the atrocious taste of unthankfulness that the allusion was made. When he said he wouldn't dwell on what the fortunate occupant of the post owed him for the stout battle originally fought on his behalf, he simply meant he *would*. That was his tact—which, with everything else that had been mentioned, in the scene, to help, really had the ground to itself. The day *had* been when Gedge couldn't have thanked him enough—though he had thanked him, he considered, almost fulsomely—and nothing, nothing that he could coherently or reputably name, had happened since then. From the moment he was pulled up, in short, he had no case, and if he exhibited, instead of one, only hot tears in his eyes, the mystic gloom of the temple either prevented his friend from see-ing them or rendered it possible that they stood for remorse. He had dried them, with the pads formed by the base of his bony thumbs, before he went in to Isabel. This was the more fortunate as, in spite of her inquiry, prompt and pointed, he but moved about the room looking at her hard. Then he stood before the fire a little with his hands behind him and his coat-tails divided, quite as the person in permanent possession. It was an indication his wife appeared to take in; but she put nevertheless presently another question. "You object to telling me what he said?"

"He said 'You know, my dear fellow, really——?'"

"And is that all?"

"Practically. Except that I'm a thankless beast."

"Well!" she responded, not with dissent.

"You mean that I *am*?"

"Are those the words he used?" she asked with a scruple.

Gedge continued to think. "The words he used were that I give away the Show and that, from several sources, it has come round to Them."

"As of course a baby would have known!" And then as her husband said nothing: "Were *those* the words he used?"

"Absolutely. He couldn't have used better ones."

"Did he call it," Mrs. Gedge inquired, "the 'Show'?"

"Of course he did. The Biggest on Earth."

She winced, looking at him hard—she wondered, but only for a moment. "Well, it *is*."

"Then it's something," Gedge went on, "to have given *that* away. But," he added, "I've taken it back."

"You mean you've been convinced?"

"I mean I've been scared."

"At last, at last!" she gratefully breathed.

"Oh, it was easily done. It was only two words. But here I am."

Her face was now less hard for him. "And what two words?"

"'You know, Mr. Gedge, that it simply won't do.' That was all. But it was the way such a man says them."

"I'm glad, then," Mrs. Gedge frankly averred, "that he *is* such a man. How did you ever think it *could* do?"

"Well, it was my critical sense. I didn't ever know I had one— till They came and (by putting me here) waked it up in me. Then I had, somehow, don't you see? to live with it; and I seemed to feel that, somehow or other, giving it time and in the long run, it might, it *ought* to, come out on top of the heap. Now that's where, he says, it simply won't do. So I must put it—I *have* put it—at the bottom."

"A very good place, then, for a critical sense!" And Isabel, more placidly now, folded her work. "*If*, that is, you can only keep it there. If it doesn't struggle up again."

"It can't struggle." He was still before the fire, looking round at the warm, low room, peaceful in the lamplight, with the hum of the kettle for the ear, with the curtain drawn over the leaded casement, a short moreen curtain artfully chosen by Isabel for the effect of the olden time, its virtue of letting the light within show ruddy to the street. "It's dead," he went on; "I killed it just now."

He spoke, really, so that she wondered. "Just now?"

"There in the other place—I strangled it, poor thing, in the dark. If you'll go out and see, there must be blood. Which, indeed," he added, "on an altar of sacrifice, is all right. But the place is forever spattered."

"I don't want to go out and see." She rested her locked hands on the needlework folded on her knee, and he knew, with her eyes on him, that a look he had seen before was in her face. "You're off your head you know, my dear, in a way." Then however, more cheeringly: "It's a good job it hasn't been too late."

"Too late to get it under?"

"Too late for Them to give you the second chance that I thank God you accept."

"Yes, if it *had* been——!" And he looked away as through the ruddy curtain and into the chill street. Then he faced her again. "I've scarcely got over my fight yet. I mean," he went on, "for you."

"And I mean for *you*. Suppose what you had come to announce to me now were that we had *got* the sack. How should I enjoy, do you think, seeing you turn out? Yes, out *there*!" she added as his eyes again moved from their little warm circle to the night of early winter on the other side of the pane, to the rare, quick footsteps, to the closed doors, to the curtains drawn like their own, behind which the small flat town, intrinsically dull, was sitting down to supper.

He stiffened himself as he warmed his back; he held up his head, shaking himself a little as if to shake the stoop out of his shoulders, but he had to allow she was right. "What would have become of us?"

"What indeed? We should have begged our bread—or I should be taking in washing."

He was silent a little. "I'm too old. I should have begun sooner."

"Oh, God forbid!" she cried.

"The pinch," he pursued, "is that I can do nothing else."

"Nothing whatever!" she agreed with elation.

"Whereas here—if I cultivate it—I perhaps *can* still lie. But I must cultivate it."

"Oh, you old dear!" And she got up to kiss him.

"I'll do my best," he said.

VII

"Do you remember us?" the gentleman asked and smiled—with the lady beside him smiling too; speaking so much less as an earnest pilgrim or as a tiresome tourist than as an old acquaintance. It was history repeating itself as Gedge had somehow never expected, with almost everything the same except that the evening was now a mild April-end, except that the visitors had put off mourning and showed all their bravery—besides showing, as he doubtless did himself, though so differently, for a little older; except, above all, that—oh, seeing them again suddenly affected him as not a bit the thing he would have thought it. "We're in England again, and we were near; I've a brother at Oxford with whom we've been spending a day, and we thought we'd come over." So the young man pleasantly said while our friend took in the queer fact that he must himself seem to them rather coldly to gape. They had come in the same way, at the quiet close; another August had passed, and this was the second spring; the Birthplace, given the hour, was about to suspend operations till the morrow; the last lingerer had gone, and the fancy of the visitors was, once more, for a look round by themselves. This represented surely no greater presumption than the terms on which they had last parted with him seemed to warrant; so that if he did inconsequently stare it was just in fact because he was so supremely far from having forgotten them. But the sight of the pair luckily had a double effect, and the first precipitated the second—the second being really his sudden vision that everything perhaps depended for him on his recognising no complication. He must go straight on, since it was what had for more than a year now so handsomely answered; he must brazen it out consistently, since that only was what his dignity was at last reduced to. He mustn't be afraid in one way any more than he had been in another; besides which it came over him with a force that made him flush that their visit, in its essence, must have been for himself. It was good society again, and *they* were the same. It wasn't for him therefore to behave as if he couldn't meet them.

These deep vibrations, on Gedge's part, were as quick as they were deep; they came in fact all at once, so that his response, his declaration that it was all right—"Oh, *rather*, the hour doesn't matter for *you*!"—had hung fire but an instant; and when they were within and the door closed behind them, within the twilight of the temple, where, as before, the votive offerings glimmered on the walls, he drew the long breath of one who might, by a self-betrayal, have done something too dreadful. For what had brought them back was not, indubitably, the sentiment of the shrine itself—since he knew their sentiment; but their intelligent interest in the queer case of the priest. Their call was the tribute of curiosity, of sympathy, of a compassion really, as such things went, exquisite—a tribute *to* that queerness which entitled them to the frankest welcome. They had wanted, for the generous wonder of it, to see how he was getting on, how such a man in such a place *could*; and they had doubtless more than half expected to see the door opened by somebody who had succeeded him. Well, somebody *had*—only with a strange equivocation; as they would have, poor things, to make out for themselves, an embarrassment as to which he pitied them. Nothing could have been more odd, but verily it was this troubled vision of their possible bewilderment, and this compunctious view of such a return for their amenity, that practically determined for him his tone. The lapse of the months had but made their name familiar to him; they had on the other occasion inscribed it, among the thousand names, in the current public register, and he had since then, for reasons of his own, reasons of feeling, again and again turned back to it. It was nothing in itself; it told him nothing—"Mr. and Mrs. B. D. Hayes, New York"—one of those American labels that were just like every other American label and that were, precisely, the most remarkable thing about people reduced to achieving an identity in such other ways. They could be Mr. and Mrs. B. D. Hayes and yet they could be, with all presumptions missing—well, what these callers were. It had quickly enough indeed cleared the situation a little further that his friends had absolutely, the other time, as it came back to him, warned him of his original danger, their anxiety about which had been the last note sounded between them. What he was afraid of, with this reminiscence, was that, finding him still safe, they would, the next thing, definitely congratulate him and perhaps even, no less candidly, ask him how he had managed. It was with the sense of nipping some such inquiry in the bud that, losing no time and holding himself with a firm grip, he began, on the spot, downstairs, to make plain to them how he had managed. He averted the question in short by the assurance of his answer. "Yes, yes, I'm still here; I suppose it *is* in a manner to one's profit that one does, such as it is, one's best." He did his best on the present occasion, did it with the gravest face he had ever worn and a soft serenity that was like a large damp sponge passed over their previous meeting—over everything in it, that is, but the fact of its pleasantness.

"We stand here, you see, in the old living-room, happily still to be reconstructed in the mind's eye, in spite of the havoc of time, which we have fortunately, of late years, been able to arrest. It was of course rude and humble, but it must have been snug and quaint, and we have at least the pleasure of knowing that the tradition in respect to the features that do remain is delightfully uninterrupted. Across that threshold He habitually passed; through those low windows, in childhood, He peered out into the world that He was to make so much happier by the gift to it of His genius; over the boards of this floor—that is over *some* of them, for we mustn't be carried away!—his little feet often pattered; and the beams of this ceiling (we must really in some places take care of *our* heads!) he endeavoured, in boyish strife, to jump up and touch. It's not often that in the early home of genius and renown the whole tenor of existence is laid so bare, not often that we are able to retrace, from point to point and from step to step, its connection with

objects, with influences—to build it round again with the little
solid facts out of which it sprang. This, therefore, I need scarcely
remind you, is what makes the small space between these walls—
so modest to measurement, so insignificant of aspect—unique
on all the earth. *There is nothing like it*," Morris Gedge went on,
insisting as solemnly and softly, for his bewildered hearers, as over
a pulpit-edge; "there is nothing at all like it anywhere in the world.
There is nothing, only reflect, for the combination of greatness,
and, as we venture to say, of intimacy. You may find elsewhere perhaps absolutely fewer changes, but where shall you find a *presence*
equally diffused, uncontested and undisturbed? Where in particular shall you find, on the part of the abiding spirit, an equally
towering eminence? You may find elsewhere eminence of a considerable order, but where shall you find *with* it, don't you see,
changes, after all, so few, and the contemporary element caught so,
as it were, in the very fact?" His visitors, at first confounded, but
gradually spellbound, were still gaping with the universal gape—
wondering, he judged, into what strange pleasantry he had been
suddenly moved to break out, and yet beginning to see in him an
intention beyond a joke, so that they started, at this point, almost
jumped, when, by as rapid a transition, he made, toward the old
fireplace, a dash that seemed to illustrate, precisely, the act of eager
catching. "It is in this old chimney corner, the quaint inglenook
of our ancestors—just there in the far angle, where His little stool
was placed, and where, I dare say, if we could look close enough,
we should find the hearthstone scraped with His little feet—that
we see the inconceivable child gazing into the blaze of the old
oaken logs and making out there pictures and stories, see Him
conning, with curly bent head, His well-worn hornbook, or por-
ing over some scrap of an ancient ballad, some page of some such
rudely bound volume of chronicles as lay, we may be sure, in His
father's window-seat."

It was, he even himself felt at this moment, wonderfully
done; no auditors, for all his thousands, had ever yet so inspired him. The odd, slightly alarmed shyness in the two faces,
as if in a drawing-room, in their "good society," exactly, some act

incongruous, something grazing the indecent, had abruptly been perpetrated, the painful reality of which faltered before coming home—the visible effect on his friends, in fine, wound him up as to the sense that *they* were worth the trick. It came of itself now— he had got it so by heart; but perhaps really it had never come so well, with the staleness so disguised, the interest so renewed and the clerical unction, demanded by the priestly character, so successfully distilled. Mr. Hayes of New York had more than once looked at his wife, and Mrs. Hayes of New York had more than once looked at her husband—only, up to now, with a stolen glance, with eyes it had not been easy to detach from the remarkable countenance by the aid of which their entertainer held them. At present, however, after an exchange less furtive, they ventured on a sign that they had not been appealed to in vain. "Charming, charming, Mr. Gedge!" Mr. Hayes broke out; "we feel that we've caught you in the mood."

His wife hastened to assent—it eased the tension. "It *would* be quite the way; except," she smiled, "that you'd be too dangerous. You've really a genius!"

Gedge looked at her hard, but yielding no inch, even though she touched him there at a point of consciousness that quivered. This was the prodigy for him, and had been, the year through— that he did it all, he found, easily, did it better than he had done anything else in his life; with so high and broad an effect, in truth, an inspiration so rich and free, that his poor wife now, lit- erally, had been moved more than once to fresh fear. She had had her bad moments, he knew, after taking the measure of his new direction—moments of readjusted suspicion in which she won- dered if he had not simply embraced another, a different perversity. There would be more than one fashion of giving away the show, and wasn't *this* perhaps a question of giving it away by excess? He could dish them by too much romance as well as by too little; she had not hitherto fairly apprehended that there might *be* too much. It was a way like another, at any rate, of reducing the place to the absurd; which reduction, if he didn't look out, would re- duce *them* again to the prospect of the streets, and this time surely without an appeal. It all depended, indeed—he knew she knew that—on how much Grant-Jackson and the others, how much the Body, in a word, would take. He knew she knew what he himself held it would take—that he considered no limit could be drawn to the quantity. They simply wanted it piled up, and so did everybody else; wherefore, if no one reported him, as before, why were They to be uneasy? It was in consequence of idiots brought to reason that he had been dealt with before; but as there was now no form of idiocy that he didn't systematically flatter, goading it on really to its *own* private doom, who was ever to pull the string of the guillotine? The axe was in the air—yes; but in a world gorged to satiety there were no revolutions. And it had been vain for Isabel to ask if the other thunder-growl also hadn't come out of the blue. There was actually proof positive that the winds were now at rest. How could they be more so?—he appealed to the receipts. These were golden days—the show had never so flourished. So he had argued, so he was arguing still—and, it had to be owned, with every appearance in his favour. Yet if he inwardly winced at the tribute to his plausibility rendered by his flushed friends, this was because he felt in it the real ground of his optimism. The charming woman before him acknowledged his "genius" as he himself had had to do. He had been surprised at his facility until he had grown used to it. Whether or no he had, as a fresh menace to his future, found a new perversity, he had found a vocation much older, evidently, than he had at first been prepared to recognise. He had done himself injustice. He liked to be brave because it came so easy; he could measure it off by the yard. It was in the Birthroom, above all, that he continued to do this, having ushered up his companions without, as he was still more elated to feel, the turn of a hair. She might take it as she liked, but he had had the lucidity—all, that is, for his own safety—to meet without the grace of an answer the homage of her beautiful smile. She took it apparently, and her husband took it, but as a part of his odd humour, and they followed him aloft with faces now a little more responsive to the manner in which, on *that* spot, he would naturally come out. He came out, according to the word of his assured private receipt, "strong." He missed a little, in truth, the usual round-eyed question from them—the inveterate artless cue with which, from moment to moment, clustered troops had, for a year, obliged him. Mr. and Mrs. Hayes were from New York, but it was a little like singing, as he had heard one of his Americans once say about something, to a Boston audience. He did none the less what he could, and it was ever his practice to stop still at a certain spot in the room and, after having secured attention by look and gesture, suddenly shoot off: "Here!"

They always understood, the good people—he could fairly love them now for it; they always said, breathlessly and unanimously, "There?" and stared down at the designated point quite as if some trace of the grand event were still to be made out. This movement produced, he again looked round. "Consider it well: *the* spot of earth——!" "Oh, but it isn't *earth*!" the boldest spirit—there was always a boldest—would generally pipe out. Then the guardian of the Birthplace would be truly superior—as if the unfortunate had figured the Immortal coming up, like a potato, through the soil. "I'm not suggesting that He was born on the bare ground. He was born *here*!"—with an uncompromising dig of his heel. "There ought to be a brass, with an inscription, let in." "Into the floor?"—it always came. "Birth and burial: seedtime, summer, autumn!"—that always, with its special, right cadence, thanks to his unfailing spring, came too. "Why not as well as into the pavement of the church?—you've *seen* our grand old church?" The former of which questions nobody ever answered—abounding, on the other hand, to make up, in relation to the latter. Mr. and Mrs. Hayes even were at first left dumb by it—not indeed, to do them justice, having uttered the word that produced it. They had uttered no word while he kept the game up, and (though that made it a little more difficult) he could yet stand triumphant before them after he had finished with his flourish. Then it was only that Mr. Hayes of New York broke silence.

"Well, if we wanted to see, I think I may say we're quite satisfied. As my wife says, it *would* seem to be your line." He spoke now, visibly, with more ease, as if a light had come: though he made no joke of it, for a reason that presently appeared. They were coming down the little stair, and it was on the descent that his companion added her word.

"Do you know what we half *did* think——?" And then to her husband: "Is it dreadful to tell him?" They were in the room below, and the young woman, also relieved, expressed the feeling with gaiety. She smiled, as before, at Morris Gedge, treating him as a person with whom relations were possible, yet remaining just uncertain enough to invoke Mr. Hayes's opinion. "We *have* awfully wanted—from what we had heard." But she met her husband's graver face; he was not quite out of the wood. At this she was slightly flurried—but she cut it short. "You must know—don't you?—that, with the crowds who listen to you, we'd have heard."

He looked from one to the other, and once more again, with force, something came over him. They had kept him in mind, they were neither ashamed nor afraid to show it, and it was positively an interest, on the part of this charming creature and this keen, cautious gentleman, an interest resisting oblivion and surviving separation, that had governed their return. Their other visit had been the brightest thing that had ever happened to him, but this was the gravest; so that at the end of a minute something broke in him and his mask, of itself, fell off. He chucked, as he would have said, consistency; which, in its extinction, left the tears in his eyes. His smile was therefore queer. "Heard how I'm going it?"

The young man, though still looking at him hard, felt sure, with this, of his own ground. "Of course, you're tremendously talked about. You've gone round the world."

"You've heard of me in America?"

"Why, almost of nothing else!"

"That was what made us feel——!" Mrs. Hayes contributed.

"That you must see for yourselves?" Again he compared, poor Gedge, their faces. "Do you mean I excite—a—scandal?"

"Dear no! Admiration. You renew so," the young man observed, "the interest."

"Ah, there it is!" said Gedge with eyes of adventure that seemed to rest beyond the Atlantic.

"They listen, month after month, when they're out here, as you must have seen; and they go home and talk. But they sing your praise."

Our friend could scarce take it in. "Over *there*?"

"Over there. I think you must be even in the papers."

"Without abuse?"

"Oh, we don't abuse everyone."

Mrs. Hayes, in her beauty, it was clear, stretched the point. "They rave about you."

"Then they *don't* know?"

"Nobody knows," the young man declared; "it wasn't anyone's knowledge, at any rate, that made us uneasy."

"It was your own? I mean your own sense?"

"Well, call it that. We remembered, and we wondered what had happened. So," Mr. Hayes now frankly laughed, "we came to see."

Gedge stared through his film of tears. "Came from America to see *me*?"

"Oh, a part of the way. But we wouldn't, in England, not have seen you."

"And now we *have*!" the young woman soothingly added.

Gedge still could only gape at the candour of the tribute. But he tried to meet them—it was what was least poor for him—in their own key. "Well, how do you like it?"

Mrs. Hayes, he thought—if their answer were important—laughed a little nervously. "Oh, you see."

Once more he looked from one to the other. "It's too beastly easy, you know."

Her husband raised his eyebrows. "You conceal your art. The emotion—yes; that must be easy; the general tone must flow. But about your facts—you've so many: how do you get *them* through?"

Gedge wondered. "You think I get too many——?"

At this they were amused together. "That's just what we came to see!"

"Well, you know, I've felt my way; I've gone step by step; you wouldn't believe how I've tried it on. *This*—where you see me—is where I've come out." After which, as they said nothing: "You hadn't thought I *could* come out?"

Again they just waited, but the husband spoke: "Are you so awfully sure you *are* out?"

Gedge drew himself up in the manner of his moments of emotion, almost conscious even that, with his sloping shoulders, his long lean neck and his nose so prominent in proportion to other matters, he looked the more like a giraffe. It was now at last that he really caught on. "I *may* be in danger again—and the danger is what has moved you? Oh!" the poor man fairly moaned. His appreciation of it quite weakened him, yet he pulled himself together. "You've your view of my danger?"

It was wondrous how, with that note definitely sounded, the air was cleared. Lucid Mr. Hayes, at the end of a minute, had put the thing in a nutshell. "I don't know what you'll think of us—for being so beastly curious."

"I think," poor Gedge grimaced, "you're only too beastly kind."

"It's all your own fault," his friend returned, "for presenting us (who are not idiots, say) with so striking a picture of a crisis. At our other visit, you remember," he smiled, "you created an anxiety for the opposite reason. Therefore if *this* should again be a crisis for you, you'd really give us the case with an ideal completeness."

"You make me wish," said Morris Gedge, "that it might be one."

"Well, don't try—for our amusement—to bring one on. I don't see, you know, how you can have much margin. Take care—take care."

Gedge took it pensively in. "Yes, that was what you said a year ago. You did me the honour to be uneasy as my wife was."

Which determined on the young woman's part an immediate question. "May I ask, then, if Mrs. Gedge is now at rest?"

"No; since you do ask. *She* fears, at least, that I go too far; *she* doesn't believe in my margin. You see, we *had* our scare after your visit. They came down."

His friends were all interest. "Ah! They came down?"

"Heavy. They brought *me* down. That's *why*——"

"Why are you down?" Mrs. Hayes sweetly demanded.

"Ah, but my dear man," her husband interposed, "you're not down; you're *up*! You're only up a different tree, but you're up at the tip-top."

"You mean I take it too high?"

"That's exactly the question," the young man answered; "and the possibility, as matching your first danger, is just what we felt we couldn't, if you didn't mind, miss the measure of."

Gedge looked at him. "I feel that I know what you at bottom *hoped*."

"We at bottom 'hope,' surely, that you're all right."

"In spite of the fool it makes of everyone?"

Mr. Hayes of New York smiled. "Say *because* of that. We only ask to believe that everyone *is* a fool!"

"Only you haven't been, without reassurance, able to imagine fools of the size that my case demands?" And Gedge had a pause, while, as if on the chance of some proof, his companion waited. "Well, I won't pretend to you that your anxiety hasn't made me, doesn't threaten to make me, a bit nervous; though I don't quite understand it if, as you say, people but rave about me."

"Oh, *that* report was from the other side; people in our country so very easily rave. You've seen small children laugh to shrieks when tickled in a new place. So there are amiable millions with us who are but small children. They perpetually present new places for the tickler. What we've seen in further lights," Mr. Hayes good-humouredly pursued, "is your people *here*—the Committee, the Board, or whatever the powers to whom you're responsible."

"Call them my friend Grant-Jackson then—my original backer, though I admit, for that reason, perhaps my most formidable critic. It's with him, practically, I deal; or rather it's by him I'm dealt with—*was* dealth with before I stand or fall by him. But he has given me my head."

"Mayn't he then want you," Mrs. Hayes inquired, "just to show as flagrantly running away?"

"Of course—I see what you mean. I'm riding, blindly, for a fall, and They're watching (to be tender of me!) for the smash that may come of itself. It's Machiavellic—but everything's possible. And what did you just now mean," Gedge asked—"especially if you've only heard of my prosperity—by your 'further lights'?"

His friends for an instant looked embarrassed, but Mr. Hayes came to the point. "We've heard of your prosperity, but we've also, remember, within a few minutes, heard *you*."

"I was determined you *should*," said Gedge. "I'm good then—but I overdo?" His strained grin was still sceptical.

Thus challenged, at any rate, his visitor pronounced. "Well, if you don't; if at the end of six months more it's clear that you haven't overdone; then, *then*——"

"Then what?"

"Then it's great."

"But it *is* great—greater than anything of the sort ever was. I overdo, thank goodness, yes; or I would if it were a thing you *could*."

"Oh, well, if there's *proof* that you can't——!" With which, and an expressive gesture, Mr. Hayes threw up his fears.

His wife, however, for a moment, seemed unable to let them go. "Don't They want then *any* truth?—none even for the mere look of it?"

"The look of it," said Morris Gedge, "is what I give!"

It made them, the others, exchange a look of their own. Then she smiled. "Oh, well, if they think so——!"

"You at least don't? You're like my wife—which indeed, I remember," Gedge added, "is a similarity I expressed a year ago the wish for! At any rate I frighten *her*."

The young husband, with an "Ah, wives are terrible!" smoothed it over, and their visit would have failed of further excuse had not, at this instant, a movement at the other end of the room suddenly engaged them. The evening had so nearly closed in, though Gedge, in the course of their talk, had lighted the lamp nearest them, that they had not distinguished, in connection with the opening of the door of communication to the warden's lodge, the appearance of another person, an eager woman, who, in her impatience, had barely paused before advancing. Mrs. Gedge—her identity took but a few seconds to become vivid—was upon them, and she had not been too late for Mr. Hayes's last remark. Gedge saw at once that she had come with news; no need even, for that certitude, of her quick retort to the words in the air—"You may say as well, sir, that they're often, poor wives, terrified!" She knew nothing of the friends whom, at so unnatural an hour, he was showing about; but there was no livelier sign for him that this didn't matter than the possibility with which she intensely charged her "Grant-Jackson, to see you at once!"—letting it, so to speak, fly in his face.

"He has been with you?"

"Only a minute—he's there. But it's you he wants to see."

He looked at the others. "And what does he want, dear?"

"God knows! There it is. It's his horrid hour—it *was* that other time."

She had nervously turned to the others, overflowing to them, in her dismay, for all their strangeness—quite, as he said to himself, like a woman of the people. She was the bare-headed goodwife talking in the street about the row in the house, and it was in this character that he instantly introduced her: "My dear doubting wife, who will do her best to entertain you while I wait upon our friend." And he explained to her as he could his now protesting companions—"Mr. and Mrs. Hayes of New York, who have been here before." He knew, without knowing why, that her announcement chilled him; he failed at least to see why it should chill him so much. His good friends had themselves been visibly affected by it, and heaven knew that the depths of brooding fancy in him were easily stirred by contact. If they had wanted a crisis they accordingly had found one, albeit they had already asked leave to retire before it. This he wouldn't have. "Ah no, you must really see!"

"But we shan't be able to bear it, you know," said the young woman, "if it *is* to turn you out."

Her crudity attested her sincerity, and it was the latter, doubtless, that instantly held Mrs. Gedge. "It *is* to turn us out."

"Has he told you that, madam?" Mr. Hayes inquired of her—it being wondrous how the breath of doom had drawn them together.

"No, not told me; but there's something in him there—I mean in his awful manner—that matches too well with other things. We've seen," said the poor pale lady, "other things enough."

The young woman almost clutched her. "Is his manner very awful?"

"It's simply the manner," Gedge interposed, "of a very great man."

"Well, very great men," said his wife, "are very awful things."

"It's exactly," he laughed, "what we're finding out! But I mustn't keep him waiting. Our friends here," he went on, "are directly interested. You mustn't, mind you, let them go until we know."

Mr. Hayes, however, held him; he found himself stayed. "We're so directly interested that I want you to understand this. If anything happens——"

"Yes?" said Gedge, all gentle as he faltered.

"Well, *we* must set you up."

Mrs. Hayes quickly abounded. "Oh, *do* come to us!"

Again he could but look at them. They were really wonderful folk. And but Mr. and Mrs. Hayes! It affected even Isabel, through her alarm; though the balm, in a manner, seemed to foretell the wound. He had reached the threshold of his own quarters; he stood there as at the door of the chamber of judgment. But he laughed; at least he could be gallant in going up for sentence. "Very good then—I'll come to you!"

This was very well, but it didn't prevent his heart, a minute later, at the end of the passage, from thumping with beats he could count. He had paused again before going in; on the other side of this second door his poor future was to be let loose at him. It was broken, at best, and spiritless, but wasn't Grant-Jackson there, like a beast-tamer in a cage, all tights and spangles and circus attitudes, to give it a cut with the smart official whip and make it spring at him? It was during this moment that he fully measured the effect for his nerves of the impression made on his so oddly earnest friends—whose earnestness he in fact, in the spasm of this last effort, came within an ace of resenting. They had upset him by contact; he was afraid, literally, of meeting his doom on his knees; it wouldn't have taken much more, he absolutely felt, to make him approach with his forehead in the dust the great man whose wrath was to be averted. Mr. and Mrs. Hayes of New York had brought tears to his eyes; but was it to be reserved for Grant-Jackson to make him cry like a baby? He wished, yes, while he palpitated, that Mr. and Mrs. Hayes of New York hadn't had such an eccentricity of interest, for it seemed somehow to come from *them* that he was going so fast to pieces. Before he turned the knob of the door, however, he had another queer instant; making out that it had been, strictly, his case that was interesting, his funny power, however accidental, to show as in a picture the attitude of others—not his poor, dingy personality. It was this latter quantity, none the less, that was marching to execution. It is to our friend's credit that he *believed*, as he prepared to turn the knob, that he was going to be hanged; and it is certainly not less to his credit that his wife, on the chance, had his supreme thought. Here it was that—possibly with his last articulate breath—he thanked his stars, such as they were, for Mr. and Mrs. Hayes of New York. At least they would take care of her.

They were doing that certainly with some success when, ten minutes later, he returned to them. She sat between them in the beautified Birthplace, and he couldn't have been sure afterwards that each wasn't holding her hand. The three together, at any rate, had the effect of recalling to him—it was too whimsical—some picture, a sentimental print, seen and admired in his youth, a "Waiting for the Verdict," a "Counting the Hours," or something of that sort; humble respectability in suspense about humble innocence. He didn't know how he himself looked, and he didn't care; the great thing was that he wasn't crying—though he might have been; the glitter in his eyes was assuredly dry, though that there *was* a glitter, or something slightly to bewilder, the faces of the others, as they rose to meet him, sufficiently proved. His wife's eyes pierced his own, but it was Mrs. Hayes of New York who spoke. "*Was* it then for that——?"

He only looked at them at first—he felt he might now enjoy it.

"Yes, it was for 'that.' I mean it was about the way I've been going on. He came to speak of it."

"And he's gone?" Mr. Hayes permitted himself to inquire.

"He's gone."

"It's over?" Isabel hoarsely asked.

"It's over."

"Then we go?"

This it was that he enjoyed. "No, my dear; we stay."

There was fairly a triple gasp; relief took time to operate. "Then why did he come?"

"In the fulness of his kind heart and of *Their* discussed and decreed satisfaction. To express Their sense——!"

Mr. Hayes broke into a laugh, but his wife wanted to know. "Of the grand work you're doing?"

"Of the way I polish it off. They're most handsome about it. The receipts, it appears, speak——"

He was nursing his effect; Isabel intently watched him, and the others hung on his lips. "Yes, speak——?"

"Well, volumes. They tell the truth."

At this Mr. Hayes laughed again. "Oh, *they* at least do?"

Near him thus, once more, Gedge knew their intelligence as one—which was so good a consciousness to get back that his tension now relaxed as by the snap of a spring and he felt his old face at ease. "So you can't say," he continued, "that we don't want it."

"I bow to it," the young man smiled. "It's what I said then. It's *great*."

"It's great," said Morris Gedge. "It couldn't be greater."

His wife still watched him; her irony hung behind. "Then we're just as we were?"

"No, not as we were."

She jumped at it. "Better?"

"Better. They give us a rise."

"Of income?"

"Of our sweet little stipend—by a vote of the Committee. That's what, as Chairman, he came to announce."

The very echoes of the Birthplace were themselves, for the instant, hushed; the warden's three companions showed, in the conscious air, a struggle for their own breath. But Isabel, with almost a shriek, was the first to recover hers. "They double us?"

"Well—call it that. 'In recognition.' There you are." Isabel uttered another sound—but this time inarticulate; partly because Mrs. Hayes of New York had already jumped at her to kiss her. Mr. Hayes meanwhile, as with too much to say, but put out his hand, which our friend took in silence. So Gedge had the last word. "And there *you* are!"

(1903)

1. Ira Aldridge as Othello, circa 1854.

DR. MAUNGWUDAUS

2. Maungwudaus, a member of the Chippewa Nation, visited Stratford-upon-Avon in 1848 and wrote a poem in honor of Shakespeare.

3. Charlotte Cushman as Romeo, with her sister Susan as Juliet, circa 1846.

GREAT RIOT AT THE ASTOR PLACE OPERA HOUSE, NEW YORK.
ON THURSDAY EVENING MAY 10TH 1849.

4. Troops fire on rioters protesting William Charles Macready's *Macbeth* at New York's Astor Place Opera House in 1849.

5. John Wilkes Booth, left, with his brothers Edwin and Junius Brutus Jr., in a benefit performance of *Julius Caesar* in 1864.

6. Jacob Adler, star of New York's Yiddish stage, as Shylock, with Jessica and Lancelot, in a late nineteenth- or early twentieth-century production of *The Merchant of Venice*.

7. John Barrymore in 1922 as Hamlet.

8. "Voodoo Macbeth" at Harlem's Lafayette Theatre in 1936.

9. Cinna the Poet with the mob that attacks him in Orson Welles's 1937 production of *Julius Caesar* at the Mercury Theatre.

10. Paul Robeson as Othello and Uta Hagen as Desdemona in the 1943 Theatre Guild production of *Othello*.

11. Patricia Morison, as Kate, in the musical *Kiss Me, Kate*, which opened on Broadway in 1948.

12. Marlon Brando as Antony in Joseph L. Mankiewicz's
1953 film of *Julius Caesar*.

PLAYBILL

a weekly magazine for theatregoers

WEST SIDE STORY

13. Playbill from the 1957 Broadway production of *West Side Story*.

14. Orson Welles as Falstaff in his 1966 film *Chimes at Midnight*.

15. A reconstruction of the Globe Theatre at the Great Lakes Exposition in Cleveland, 1936–37.

16. Joseph Papp, founder of the Public Theater, at the Delacorte, under construction in New York City's Central Park in 1961.

Mark Twain

(1835–1910)

Autobiographical Dictation

The aging Mark Twain dictated a half-million words in two hundred and fifty sessions from 1906 to 1909, hoping the material that would emerge from this would "become a model for all future autobiographies." The following dictation, typed, then marked up in Twain's hand, was part of the autobiographical dictations that were never published. Twain claims to have become interested in the authorship controversy as far back as his time as a young man steering steamboats on the Mississippi River in 1857, and when he visited Shakespeare's birthplace in 1872 his skepticism was reinforced. His last book, published later in 1909, *Is Shakespeare Dead?* (subtitled *From My Autobiography*), made this case wittily and at length, and was grounded in Twain's conviction that great fiction was necessarily autobiographical: you could only write believably about what you knew or experienced firsthand. The evidence of the plays confirmed for Twain that Shakespeare of Stratford could not have known enough about the law in particular to have written them. Twain's autobiographical dictation of January 11, 1909, was prompted by a visit of weekend guests to his home in Redding, Connecticut: Helen Keller, her teacher and companion Anne Sullivan, and Sullivan's husband, William Macy (a confirmed Baconian, who had brought with him galleys of a forthcoming book, *Some Acrostic Signatures of Francis Bacon*, by William Stone Booth, which claimed that Bacon had hidden proof of his authorship of Shakespeare's plays). Twain's secretary, Isabel Lyon, who was there that weekend as well, recalled how Twain "seized upon" this evidence with "a destroying zeal. . . . and you'd think that both men had Shakespeare by the throat righteously strangling him for some hideous crime." Booth's book is the "bombshell" Twain alludes to in his dictation. Helen Keller, who was also convinced by the acrostics, immersed herself in the literature of the authorship question and completed a thirty-four-page manuscript, "A Concealed Poet Disclosed," but was unable to get it published.

❦

Dᴵᴄᴛᴀᴛᴇᴅ at Stormfield, January 11th, 1909.

From away back towards the very beginning of the Shakspeare-Bacon controversy I have been on the Bacon side, and have wanted to see our majestic Shakspeare unhorsed. My reasons for this attitude may have been good, they may have been bad, but such as they were, they strongly influenced me. It always seemed unaccountable to me that a man could be so prominent in Elizabeth's little London as historians and biographers claim that Shakspeare was, and yet leave behind him hardly an incident for people to remember him by; leave behind him nothing much but trivialities; leave behind him little or nothing but the happenings of an utterly commonplace life, happenings that could happen to the butcher and the grocer, the candlestickmaker and the undertaker, and there an end—deep, solemn, sepulchral silence. It always seemed to me that not even a distinguished horse could die and leave such biographical poverty behind him. His biographers did their best, I have to concede it, they took his attendance at the grammar-school; they took his holding of horses at sixpenny tips; they took his play-acting on the other side of the river; they took his picturesque deer-stealing; they took his diligent and profitable Stratford wool-staplings, they took his too-previous relations with his subsequent wife; they took his will—that monumental will!—with its solemnly comic second-best bed incident; they took his couple of reverently preserved and solely existant signatures in the which he revealed the fact that he didn't know how to spell his own name; they took this poor half-handful of inconsequential odds and ends, and spun it out, and economized it, and inflated it to bursting, and made a biography with a capital B out of it. It seemed incomprehensibly odd to me, that a man situated as Shakspeare apparently was, could live to be fifty-two years old and never a thing happen to him.

When Ignatius Donnelly's book came out, eighteen or twenty years ago, I not only published it, but read it. It was an ingenious piece of work and it interested me. The world made all sorts of fun of it, but it seemed to me that there were things in it which the thoughtful could hardly afford to laugh at. They have passed out of my mind now, or have grown vague with time and wear, but I still remember one of those smart details of Donnelly's. According to my recollection he remarked that it is quite natural for writers, when painting pictures with their pens, to use scenery that they are familiar with in place of using scenery that they only know about by hearsay. In this connection he called attention to the striking fact that Shakspeare does not use Stratford surroundings and Stratford names when he wants to localize an event, but uses scenes familiar to Lord Bacon instead; hardly even mentioning Stratford, but mentioning St. Albans three-and-twenty times!

Ignatius Donnelly believed he had found Bacon's name acrostified—or acrosticised—I don't know which is right—cryptically concealed all through the Shaksperean plays. I think his acrostics were not altogether convincing; I believe a person had to work his imagination rather hard sometimes if he wanted to believe in the acrostics. Donnelly's book fell pretty flat, and from that day to this the notion that Bacon wrote Shakspeare has been dying a slow death. Nowadays one hardly ever sees even a passing reference to it, and when such references have occurred they have uniformly been accompanied by a gentle sneer.

Well, two or three weeks from now a bombshell will fall upon us which may possibly woundily astonish the human race! For there is secretly and privately a book in press in Boston, by an English clergyman, which may unhorse Shakspeare permanently and put Bacon in the saddle. Once more the acrostic will be in the ascendant, and this time it may be that some people will think twice before they laugh at it. That wonder of wonders, Helen Keller, has been here on a three days' visit with her devoted teachers and protectors Mr. and Mrs. John Macy, and Macy has told me about the clergyman's book and bound me to secrecy. I am divulging the secret to my autobiography for distant future revealment, but shall keep the matter to myself in conversation. The clergyman has found Bacon's name concealed in acrostics in more than a hundred places in the plays and sonnets. I have examined a couple of the examples and I feel that just these two examples all by themselves are almost sufficient to discrown Shakspeare and enthrone Bacon. One of the examples is the Epilogue to "The Tempest." In this acrostic Bacon's name is concealed in its Latin form—Francisco Bacono. You take the last word of the Epilogue (free) and move your finger to the left to the beginning of that last line, then to the right along the next line above, then to the left again to the beginning of the third line and so on and so on, going left then right then left until you find a word which begins with R. You will find it in the fifth line from the bottom; your finger will then be moving to the left; it will encounter an A at the beginning of the sixth line and will thence move to the right; it will move to the left through the seventh line and to the right again along the eighth line and will encounter an N in that line. Nine lines above, it will find C and I; two lines above that it will find S. In this acrostic no letters are used that occur within a word or at the right-hand end of it; continue the process and you find the C and the O properly placed; only letters that *begin* words and letters that stand *by themselves* are used.

"Bacono" begins with the word "be" at the end of the next to the last line, and proceeds right and left as before, picking up initial letters as it goes along until it reaches the first line of the Epilogue, and that line furnishes the close of the name "Bacono."

Through the last page of "King Lear" is scattered the acrostic "Verulam", spelt backwards. It begins with the last word of the last line, which is a stage direction ("*Exeunt with a dead march*"). That line, furnishes two of the letters, M and A, the line immediately above furnishes the L; you travel upward nine lines before you come to a word beginning with U; four lines higher up you find a word beginning with R; twenty-one lines above that you find a word beginning with E, and you do not find it any earlier; you find the V in the line immediately above that and the acrostic stands completed.

One may examine those two examples until he is tired, hoping that these two names got distributed in this orderly and system-atic way without a hitch anywhere, by *accident*, and he will have only his interesting labor for his pains. If he had only one example he might, by clever and possibly specious reasoning, convince himself that the thing was an accident; but when he finds two examples strictly following the law of the system he will know, for sure, that not both of them are accidents; and he will probably end by conceding that nineteen-twentieths of the probabilities are that both are results of design and neither of them a miracle. For he will know that nothing short of a miracle could produce a couple of such elaborate and extraordinary accidents as these.

Mr. Macy says that there are between 100 and 150 examples in the plays and sonnets that are the match of these two. This being so, the likelihood that Shakspeare riddled his works with Bacon's name and Bacon's titles and forgot to acrosticise his own anywhere is exceedingly remote—much remoter than any distance measurable on this planet, indeed remoter than that new planet of Professor Pickering's which is so far outside Neptune's orbit that it makes Neptune seem sort of close to us and sociably situated.

These acrostics have been dug out of the earliest and least doctored editions of Shakspeare. Sometimes in the much-edited editions of our day changes in the text break up the acrostic. The general reader will not have access to the folio of 1623 and its brethren, therefore photographic facsimiles will be made from those early editions and placed before the reader of the clergyman's book, so that he can trace out the acrostics for himself. I am to have proof sheets as fast as they issue from the galleys, and am to behave myself and keep still. I shall live in a heaven of excited anticipation for a while now. I have allowed myself for so many many years the offensive privilege of laughing at people who believed in Shakspeare that I shall perish with shame if the clergyman's book fails to unseat that grossly commercial wool-stapler. However, we shall see. I shan't order my monument yet.

George Santayana

(1863–1952)

Shakespeare: Made in America

The philosopher, essayist, novelist, and poet George Santayana—his full name was Jorge Agustín Nicolás Ruiz de Santayana y Borrás—was born in Spain and moved to America as a child. He was educated at Boston Latin School and then Harvard, where he later joined the illustrious philosophy department. His upbringing and training—not so much *of* America as *in* it—allowed Santayana to view American culture from a unique perspective, one that he brings to bear in this essay on the value of Shakespeare in early twentieth-century American culture. A great deal is going on in what appears to be a playful essay, first published in *The New Republic*. Santayana wrestles here with his ambivalence toward America as well as with his limitations as a poet, while struggling to come to grips with his disappointment with Shakespeare as philosopher and moralist (what he later called the "strange absence of religion" in Shakespeare, that kept Santayana from fully approving of him). Santayana's aphorism in *The Last Puritan*—"America is the greatest of opportunities and the worst of influences"—offers a clue to his "experiment" here, a translation into contemporary American idiom of Shakespeare's great sonnet "When in Disgrace with Fortune and Men's Eyes." His was not a Shakespeare "for all time," but one, rather, whose language is now anachronistic if not obsolete, the cultural legacy of his words and world largely unavailable to modern American culture—a conclusion that underscores the challenges facing truly original modern poets.

❧

Custom blinds us to the costume of thought. Not until the fashion has entirely changed do we see how extravagant the old costume was. The late middle ages and the renaissance, when modern languages took shape, had a very elaborate and modish dress for the mind as well as for the body. Notice, for instance, how Shakespeare can deck out a Hock sentiment, proper to any schoolboy:

When in disgrace with fortune and men's eyes
I all alone beweep my outcast state
And trouble deaf heaven with my bootless cries
And look upon myself and curse my fate,
Wishing me like to one more rich in hope,
Featur'd like him, like him with friends possess'd,
Desiring this man's art and that man's scope,
With what I most enjoy contented least,
Yet in these thoughts myself almost despising,—
Haply I think on thee; and then my state,
Like to the lark at break of day arising
From sullen earth, sings hymns at heaven's gate:
For thy sweet love remember'd such wealth brings
That then I scorn to change my state with kings.

For Shakespeare this sonnet is comparatively plain and direct, yet it is simply encrusted with old-fashioned jewels and embroideries. How much so will become clear if we venture to paraphrase it, scrupulously leaving out every suggestion that could not have had its origin in the twentieth century and in America.

In the first few lines almost every connotation is obsolete and will have to be abandoned. So the idea of falling out of favor at a court where the capricious monarch is Fortune. This mythological Fortune was rather a verbal deity from the beginning and had become merely rhetorical even in Shakespeare's time; for us it is worse, and the unrepublican image is inadmissible. To *beweep* anything is also contrary to our manners; if tears ever escape us it is not ceremoniously nor as a fit accompaniment to magnificent lamentations. As to *men's eyes*, we look through our eyes, but seldom talk through them; and if we wish to shake off an objectionable friend we do not cast withering glances upon him, like the noble savage. We simply avoid the man; or if we are inclined to be offensively demonstrative, we cut him. The word *outcast* is still current; but the background which gave poignancy to that metaphor belongs to a bygone age. No one can be easily excommunicated in our tolerant society. If one circle disowns him he will slip into another, perhaps with relief, and find it no less self-respecting, even in jail; and if he makes bold to flaunt his crime or his heresy, he will excite more interest than loathing, and a party of sympathizers will probably flock to his side.

No less obsolete is the habit of troubling heaven with one's bootless cries. Even the lover in the sonnet, though he might have prayed, would hardly have emitted cries; only in remote antiquity his predecessors in the art of troubling heaven may actually have wailed. Nowadays hardly anybody would pray in the hope of recovering his friends or his property by divine interposition. People certainly have recourse to religion, and often in a more desperate need than ever; but to modern feeling religion opens a second sphere of interest and hope, without being expected to further our worldly hopes and interests.

In the body of the sonnet there are a number of phrases which, without being in the least archaic, have a certain grand sweeping air and *panache* about them quite foreign to our experience. The word *art*, for instance, to most Americans suggests the profession of painting; the intended faculty of doing all things easily and well would have to be called ability or skill, or more pungently and characteristically, *brains*. This single transition from art to brains speaks volumes. Again, while no nation was ever more hopeful than America or more optimistic, to say *rich in hope* is to give the matter a different twist. You are optimistic when you take for granted or religiously assure yourself that the future, whatever it may be, will be all right, and will somehow grow better and better. You are rich in hope when you have great and definite expectations, are heir or aspirant to an exalted position, and can picture in a concrete form the happy future before you. So a bridegroom is rich in hope on his wedding morning, or an expectant mother when making bibs for her first-born; but the optimist may be as poor in hope as in experience.

Similarly the phrase *I look upon myself* expresses something different from our self-consciousness. It describes the shock of suddenly seeing yourself as others see you, as when you unexpectedly come upon yourself in a mirror. The poet is borrowing men's eyes in order to consider and pity himself; he is not retreating into a psychological observation of what is hidden from others in his consciousness.

The eleventh and twelfth lines will have to be sacrificed in their entirety. There are no larks in America. There is no heaven in modern cosmology such that the blue sky in which larks sing should be called the gate of it. And what hymns could the poet have been thinking of? Christmas carols, perhaps, or such as the choir of Magdalen College in Oxford greet the sunrise with on May morning from the top of their lovely tower. In any case they were pre-Puritan hymns, hymns of joyful familiarity with a religion sweetly and humanly miraculous, hymns not associated with drawling tunes, funerals, or a vague sense of constraint and edification. For these two lines, therefore, we must substitute something wholly different, yet as nearly equivalent as possible. I can think of nothing domesticated in America nearer to larks and to bright religion than music is. So orchestral strains shall take the place of larks, with profound apologies; and in speaking of music we may perhaps slightly inflate the poetic bellows, since modern shyness does not attack our souls so much in that invisible wilderness.

As to the final couplet, we may still talk occasionally of being as happy as a king or as drunk as a lord, but whatever seduction there may once have been in those images, they have paled. Something of far greater moment, however, lies submerged here. The unsophisticated reader may pass approvingly over the phrase *thy sweet love*, as if the poet might just as well have written *our sweet love* instead, meaning that mutual, complete, hearty, happy, plebeian love which alone should figure in our revised American version. Yet as a matter of fact the sentiment and pathos of the original are profoundly different, being charged with the most exotic metaphysical overtones. If we compare this sonnet with the rest of Shakespeare's, and consider the W. H. to whom at least by a poetic fiction they were addressed, it becomes evident that *thy sweet love* can only mean *the sweet love of thee*, a love which the poet did not and could not aspire to see returned. That ornate and exuberant age had so much passion to spare that it could think it but graceful adulation for a poet to address the intensest and richest effusions of love to some insipid youth in a high station. And behind that lavish play of expression (for perhaps it was nothing more) we must not ignore the possibility that the passion expressed may sometimes have been real, at least in those who first set this literary fashion; and in that case, seeing that even if graciously tolerated, such adoration could not possibly be mutual, we are at once transported into the dim sanctuary of Platonic love, where youth and beauty, at an aesthetic remove and because of their intrinsic virtue, are reputed to communicate a supreme and sufficient bliss to the worshipper, with all those moral and saving effects which this sonnet, for instance, celebrates. The lover in his infatuation, and in the religious chastening of it, is said somehow to find God. Humbug or philosophy, this Platonic mysticism has long been a classic refuge of hopeless emotion, and Shakespeare's sonnets march conventionally in the devout procession. Such ambiguous mysteries, however, are alien to modern sentiment and to the plain man's experience, and we may shut them out without further parlance.

Plucked of all its Elizabethan feathers, our sonnet might then present somewhat the following appearance:

> When times are hard and old friends fall away
> And all alone I lose my hope and pluck,
> Doubting if God can hear me when I pray,
> And brood upon myself and curse my luck,
> Envying some stranger for his handsome face,
> His wit, his wealth, his chances, or his friends,
> Desiring this man's brains and that man's place,
> And vexed with all I have that makes amends,
> Yet in these thoughts myself almost despising,—
> By chance I think of you; and then my mind,
> Like music from deep sullen murmurs rising
> To peals and raptures, leaves the earth behind:
> For if you care for me, what need I care
> To own the world or be a millionaire?

The reader may laugh, but I have not made the sonnet absurd on purpose; on the contrary I have tried to keep it as good as possible under the conditions imposed. The experiment is not intended to show how an American poet would actually feel or treat Shakespeare's subject, for he would either compose fine imitative literature, with a lapse here and there which he might not be conscious of, or else he would give birth to something entirely novel. The experiment is meant only to make evident how much old finery there is in our literary baggage, and how original an original poet would have to be. Any wise man of Shakespeare's time might have prophesied that ruffs would no longer be worn in three hundred years, but only a genius could have foretold our trousers. So any critic may unfrock Shakespeare, but to dress his thought up again in the costume of a future poetry can be given only to the future poets themselves.

(1915)

Robert Frost

(1874–1963)

'Out, Out—'

'Out, Out—' appeared in Frost's second volume of poems, *Mountain Interval*. The event it describes was likely inspired by an article that ran in March 1910 in a local New Hampshire newspaper, *The Littleton Courier*, describing the death of Raymond Tracy Fitzgerald, a young man who died of shock after his hand was badly injured in a sawing accident. Frost took his title from Macbeth's world-weary and dispassionate speech upon hearing of the death of his wife: "Out, out, brief candle! / Life's but a walking shadow, a poor player, / That struts and frets his hour upon the stage, / And then is heard no more." Macbeth's words echo those of Lady Macbeth's earlier in the play—"Out, damn'd spot! out, I say!"—recalling a bloody, fatal deed that cannot be undone.

The buzz saw snarled and rattled in the yard
And made dust and dropped stove-length sticks of wood,
Sweet-scented stuff when the breeze drew across it.
And from there those that lifted eyes could count
Five mountain ranges one behind the other
Under the sunset far into Vermont.
And the saw snarled and rattled, snarled and rattled,
As it ran light, or had to bear a load.
And nothing happened: day was all but done.
Call it a day, I wish they might have said
To please the boy by giving him the half hour
That a boy counts so much when saved from work.
His sister stood beside them in her apron
To tell them 'Supper.' At the word, the saw,
As if to prove saws knew what supper meant,
Leaped out at the boy's hand, or seemed to leap—

He must have given the hand. However it was,
Neither refused the meeting. But the hand!
The boy's first outcry was a rueful laugh,
As he swung toward them holding up the hand
Half in appeal, but half as if to keep
The life from spilling. Then the boy saw all—
Since he was old enough to know, big boy
Doing a man's work, though a child at heart—
He saw all spoiled. 'Don't let him cut my hand off—
The doctor, when he comes. Don't let him, sister!'
So. But the hand was gone already.
The doctor put him in the dark of ether.
He lay and puffed his lips out with his breath.
And then—the watcher at his pulse took fright.
No one believed. They listened at his heart.
Little—less—nothing!—and that ended it.
No more to build on there. And they, since they
Were not the one dead, turned to their affairs.

(1916)

Charlotte Perkins Gilman

(1860–1935)

Shakespeare's Heroines as Human Beings

In 1916, as part of the events celebrating the anniversary of Shakespeare's death, *The New York Times* published a series of essays about Shakespeare, including one by the leading social critic and feminist Charlotte Perkins Gilman, best known today as the author of the much-anthologized story "The Yellow Wall Paper." In her essay, subtitled "Others Gave Only Femininity to Their Women Characters," Gilman breaks from the long-established tradition of extolling Shakespeare's heroines as exemplars of proper feminine decorum, arguing instead that the plays record "not only the womanly virtues of these Heroines, but their broad humanness, that preponderant quality to which we are still so generally oblivious." It was a view that dovetailed with her larger intellectual project of challenging the ways in which women were defined through men, and were defined as well (and constrained both socially and economically) by the tendency to exaggerate what were imagined to be characteristics peculiar to their gender. In one of her most telling examples in this essay she questions these assumptions—taken for granted in Shakespeare criticism no less than in the broader culture of her day—wryly noting of Portia, celebrated for saving Antonio's life in the trial scene of *The Merchant of Venice*: "had she, naturally pleased by her successful excursion into the law, chosen to remain a lawyer, this we should have unsparingly condemned as unwomanly."

∞

I N so large a picture of life as opens to the reader of Shakespeare we may look with confidence for the facts, even as we should look for them in studying the vast original.

Indeed, as the artist sees more than an ordinary observer, and, by virtue of his art, makes the ordinary observer see what he would not otherwise have noticed, we find the characteristics of humanity more plainly to be studied through the great dramatist than as they push and tumble confusedly before us in living persons.

To point out, as shown by Shakespeare, that all men were cowards—if he had so presented them—would be a heavy charge against manhood: and if he had represented women as all fools, or all liars, or all unchaste, it would either have to be taken as heavy testimony that they were so, or as proving the poet himself a fool or liar, and acquainted only with the vicious among women.

Among the immense literature of comment on this master there are books and to spare about his presentation of women— their nobility, their wit, their virtue, their wisdom, their courage, their devoted love, and, to admit all sides, their weakness and criminality.

The special point here chosen to illustrate is that in this great array of womanhood the depicter of character, by virtue of his truth in observance, has shown far more than was intended. In these many pages there stand recorded not only the womanly virtues of these heroines, but their broad humanness, that preponderant quality to which we are still so generally oblivious.

In our whole previous world view we have overlooked this quality in women, attributing it perforce to men, as types of race, but seeing in women only feminine qualities. Always we have fixed our eyes on "the true woman," seeing only her womanliness, and, if she did not agree with the specifications already in mind, she was branded as "unwomanly," as being like a man.

To give a conspicuous instance from another source, even more widely studied than Shakespeare, note the characteristics set forth in that long-standing Ideal Woman, whose price was above rubies, and our interpretation of them. She has been preached about for centuries, and held up from a thousand pulpits as a model to be imitated, but how many preachers and commentators have dwelt upon the really remarkable human qualities of that Virtuous Woman? Always they dilate on her domestic devotion, her care for that scarlet-clothed household of hers, her kind words and charity; but never on the conspicuous fact that she earned her own living, and possibly supported her family—her husband had "no need for spoil." Indeed, so universal is the masculine preconception that small notice is taken of the fact that the immortal description is by a woman, by the mother of King Lemuel. It will refresh many memories to look at that last chapter of "Proverbs"—to realize the humanness of her, and see what a good manufacturer, merchant, viticulturist, and real estate dealer that lady was.

So, in our Shakespeare, we have dwelt long and lovingly on the pronounced—and premature—passion of the child Juliet; on the superb chastity of Isabel; on the husband-dominating criminality of Lady Macbeth or of Queen Dionyza. We have enjoyed the ruthless repartee of Beatrice, and admired the daring flight and merry play of Rosalind; even recognized, as we must, the wisdom of Portia; but in the whole brilliant procession, good, bad, and indifferent, it is the qualities we call womanly that we look for, and what we look for we see.

Even Portia, while traversing all the traditions of her sex, did so at the behest of love, to save the life of her lover's friend and win a happy marriage—quite womanly this. Had she, naturally pleased by her successful excursion into the law, chosen to remain a lawyer, this we should have unsparingly condemned as unwomanly.

Before going further, let us clearly and without offense define what is this Humanness here discussed.

All living creatures, above the early tentative stages of asexualism and of hermaphroditism, are male and female. As such, they have their several qualities, pertaining to each sex, and found, throughout nature, so distinguishing each. The males, in all species, have their masculine qualities—predominant desire for the female, the impulse to combat, and self-expression or pride. The females, in all species, have their power of attraction for the male, and the instincts of motherhood, that widening flow of tenderness, patience, protective care, and ingenious industry, out of which has grown so much of our later development. But quite aside from these sex qualities, belonging to all kinds of males and females, each kind has its race qualities, common to both, peculiar only to that species.

Humanness is our distinguishing race quality. It is that which differentiates us from all other animals, and which develops in us as we evolve to higher social stages; we grow more human as we progress.

The human qualities outnumber and outweigh the sex qualities so preponderantly that they cannot escape notice; but we have failed to recognize their nature because of misnaming them in the beginning. We called them "masculine." We thought all the widening powers of the human intellect, the breadth and depth of human feeling, the accumulating wonders of human invention and execution, were masculine qualities, peculiar to men as such. Having this conviction firmly in mind, no array of facts could move us from it, and when, without dogmatism, a great artist paints us women by scores, differing as men differ, showing, as men do, all shades of character, all grades of power, we see them still only as women, and call this wide variety of humanness just "womanly."

Yet, with the new conception held in mind, how clearly we may see the difference.

Let us allow Juliet to be purely feminine, a precociously passionate young thing—poor baby, coming out at 14!—and her mother boasting that she bore her daughter at about the same age. No wonder that she showed small human distinction—she might, perhaps, had she lived to grow up.

Strange that these amorous young things should stand so high in our estimation as "lovers," when Romeo was so swift in the transfer of his light affection that even the good Friar must cry out on him. Let Juliet pass—she was a beautiful and over-ardent child.

Yet even at that age, another damsel, one Marina, stands out as sharply different as marble from moonshine. Not Shakespeare's, some say, this Marina? Never mind, she makes a good contrast. She was but 14, and while inevitably described as beautiful, the marvel of her was in her human attributes—"trained in music, letters; who hath gained of education all the grace which makes her both the heart and place of general wonder."

Neither music nor letters pertain to sex. This proficiency was quite human. But note further:

This youthful paragon is stolen by pirates and sold to a most evil madam in a strange city. In Elizabeth Robins's piteous and too true story of "My Little Sister" there is no help for the child. She was but a helpless young female and sank to utter ruin. But Marina, instead of succumbing, used her human faculties. She so preached to the gentlemen who approached her that they went away resolved on virtue. She persuaded the Governor himself to forego his desires, and when the hardened menial of the house was sent to compass her downfall she outreasoned him and persuaded him to get her pupils instead of customers.

So we have her, at Juliet's age, earning honest money by the use of human faculties, and thereby preserving her feminine honor so above approach that the aforesaid Governor marries her—after assuring himself that she is of suitable lineage.

Let us turn to Volumnia, that noblest Roman of them all. She was a type of the honor worshipper, military honor at that; not herself "seeking the bubble reputation at the cannon's mouth," or at the sword's point, but joyfully desiring it for her son.

Virgilia is but a wife, a timid, affectionate thing, weeping sadly in her husband's absence and refusing to go and make calls with Valeria. A nicely touched person, Valeria, with her Usher—a good talker and none too patient of housewifery. Virgilia remains in dolorous femininity, but Volumnia—she was a Person, an able and determined human being. See how she reasons with that crazy-tempered son of hers, the heroic, brave, insolent, and injudicious Caius Martius Coriolanus: he who would not refrain from insulting the citizens long enough to get himself elected; he who talked so loudly of his "country" and evidently thought of nothing further in it than the first families.

His mother was proud enough, but she was also reasonable, human. She explains to him that he thinks nothing of lying, cheating in course of active warfare; why stick at a little flattery—or even mere self-restraint (surely he might have gone that far)—when so much is at stake. Does he follow her advice? By no means.

He says he will—agrees to do it—starts out in that mind, but changes said mind at the first touch on that insensate pride of his.

The humanness of Volumnia was so apparent that when Sicinius demands, "Are you mankind?" she answers: "Ay, fool, is that a shame?" And finally, when by wise words she once more changes her son's mind and saves the city from his vengeance, listen to Menenius:

> This Volumnia
> Is worth of Consuls, Senators, patricians,
> A city full: of tribunes, such as you,
> A sea and land full.

An able person this, and valued not for feminine chastity and maternity, but for human ability.

The idea of feminine chastity and how to test it, as shown in this Elizabethan age, was crude enough. Instead of setting ardent love against high principle, we find the mischievous proposals made, as Angelo makes his, as a price for a boon desired—a price which Isabel very rightly refused to pay. Note here another sudden change of "the masculine mind," where Claudio first lauds his sister's decision as noble and just, and then, on second thought, begs her to save his life by her shame—which she again quite properly refuses.

But Isabel stands forth not only for so steadfastly refusing what she did not want, but for the very able plea she made to Angelo for mercy. Further, when it came her turn, she showed mercy to him at the request of Marianna. Note this carefully. The man had not only insulted her, but sought to coerce her through her affection for her brother. Then, doubly perfidious, after—as he supposed—she had paid the price, he had sent to have poor Claudio killed. The sister, still supposing he is killed, is so moved by the grief of Marianna that she forgets the evident justice of punishing Angelo, and asks the Duke to have mercy upon him. This is by no means what is called "feminine." It is human, and most nobly so.

Again, when the peerless Imogen is approached by the smooth Italian villain, he makes no slightest effort to win her affection, but slanders her husband, and suggests that she revenge herself through adultery, which she naturally refuses. One feels as if there was not much faith in this same chastity if it was supposed likely to give way on such attack.

The bad human qualities we find in both men and women, but in this world of drama, as in our common life, there is more wickedness, and baser, among men. In many cases the women do their mischief to promote the interests of those they love. For her daughter, Philoten, does Dionyza order Marina's destruction. She was jealous for her own child's advancement. For her son, Cloten, does Cymbeline's Queen plot and poison. For her husband does Lady Macbeth urge murder.

Now, the men villains are villains on their own account, light-minded at times, at others profoundly evil. We may call the evil characteristics human, shared by men and women; but the saving grace of doing it for the good of others seems feminine.

There is no lack of instances of the feminine, the ultra-feminine, the super-feminine, and, alas! of that poor wreck and ruin of femininity, the victim and victimizer of men. Anything more painfully exhibiting woman's weakness could hardly be devised than the scene where Lady Anne, in the full height of her grief and fury, mourning her husband, Prince Edward, and his father, King Henry, both killed by the unspeakable Richard, yet gives way to his suit under no other pressure than the sheer force of compliment.

Yet in spite of all the too-evident proof of arrested human development in women, reared as they then were in an atmosphere calculated to bring out and intensify every feminine attribute, and in spite of the world tradition, recognizing only those attributes, this Seer, looking at life open-eyed, observes and reproduces the human qualities which will manifest themselves in spite of all neglect.

That any woman should show courage in an age when they were utter dependents on the favor of men—when a girl was told:

> To you your father should be as a God,
> One that composed your beauties: yea—and one
> To whom you are but as a form in wax,
> By him imprinted, and within his power
> To leave the figure, or disfigure it—

shows a braver spirit than was needed by men.

See, then, the magnificent humanness of Cordelia—no "feminine weakness," no "feminine flattery," no "feminine timidity"; in the face of offending the parent she did love so dearly, and losing her rightful share in the division of the country, Cordelia tells the truth.

This high courage no one will say is characteristic of women as such; their very sympathy and tenderness militate against it; nor is it in the least to be confounded with the belligerent bravery of men. It is a human quality, one of the noblest.

Neither is the sordid flattery and double dealing of the weaker sisters feminine; the drama and all history show such conduct frequently in men.

It is true, from the limitations of women's estate, and the further limitations of "the heart interest" in drama, that most of these ladies are introduced as daughter of this man, wife of that one, or "beloved of Proteus," "beloved by Valentine," or "in love with the Duke." The only human distinctions allowed them are those of rank—the Queens seem fully as conscious of their power and as able to use it as the Kings; and the serving women of the servile positions they share with serving men. Their dignity and pride are human; their loyalty and devotion are human; and while registering perforce the inevitable emphasis upon their feminine relationships, it surely seems as if the great poet delighted in bringing out these characteristics of our common race, wherever he found them.

Intelligent, clever creatures! How they read the facts as far as visible! Listen to the chaste Diana planning with her mother and Helena how that lady may secure her rights as Bertram's wife: "My mother told me just how he would woo, as if she sat in his heart.

She says, all men have the like oaths. He had sworn to marry me when his wife died; therefore I'll lie with him, when I am buried." Wise Diana!

As we review them all, from best-known Rosalind, through all the fair ladies, wise and pure or too gayly disposed, it is their wit, wisdom, courage, ingenuity, perseverance, nobility, cheerfulness, devotion; and high duty that we love—in a word, their humanness.

(1916)

Charles Mills Gayley

(1858–1932)

Heart of the Race

On April 21, 1916, "Heart of the Race" was read aloud on the Berkeley campus of the University of California, where Charles Mills Gayley taught Shakespeare, as part of the Shakespeare Tercentenary celebrations. It was published that same day in the *Oakland Tribune*, then read by Gayley at various American campuses, and subsequently reprinted in the international collection, *A Book of Homage to Shakespeare* (1916). The poem did double duty: implicitly urging Americans to enter the Great War on England's side and, in marshalling a cultural argument for that military intervention, portraying Shakespeare as poet of both the English and American race (by which Gayley meant, quite specifically, the Anglo-Saxon "race" that could be traced back—as he could trace his own lineage—to those on the *Mayflower* and to the first English settlers in America). Gayley would elaborate on his arguments linking Shakespeare to the roots of American democracy in his book, *Shakespeare and the Founders of Liberty in America*, published in 1917.

※

Not in marble or bronze, the sum of thy lineaments;
   Not in colour or line that painter or graver may trace.
Out of the kingdom of vision, gleaming, transcendent, immortal,
   Issue thy creatures and step into vesture of time and place—
Each with passion and pulse of thy heart; but, passing the portal,
      Each in likeness of us. And listening, wondering,
   Lo, from the lips of each we gather a thought of thy Face!

Nature walleth her womb with wreckage of history:
   Touch, O Poet, thy lyre, and heart-beats frozen in stone
Tremble to life once more—to the towers of pain and of pity—
   Build themselves into thee, thy ramparts of rapture and moan,

Cry with a human voice from the passioning walls of thy city—
    Hamlets, Richards, Cordelias, prisoned, oblivious,
  Dateless minions of death, till summoned by thee alone.

    Fortune maketh of men pipes for her fingering;
  Thou hast made of thine England music of nobler employ:
Men whose souls are their own; whose breastplate, honour untainted;
    Of promise precise, God-fearing, abhorring the dreams that destroy—
The Moloch of Force ensky'd, the ape of Necessity sainted;—
    To country and freedom true; merciful, generous,
  Valiant to merit in Fate the heart's-ease mortals enjoy.

    Shaper, thou, of the tongue! Under the Pleiades,
  Under the Southern Cross, under the Boreal Crown,
Where there's a mother's lap and a little one seeking a story,
    Where there's a teacher or parson, or player come to the town—
Mage of the opaline phrase, meteoric, dissolving in glory,
    Splendid lord of the word predestined, immutable—
  Children are learning thy English and handing the heritage down.

    Who but opens thy book: odorous memories
  Breathe of the dear, dear land, sceptred and set in the sea.
Her primrose pale, her sweet o' the year, have savour and semblance
    For Perditas woo'd in the tropics and Florizels tutored by thee.
The rue of her sea-wallèd garden, the rosemary, wake to remembrance
    Where furrowed exiles from home, wintered with pilgriming,
  Yearn for the white-faced shores, and turn thy page on the knee.

    No philosopher, thou: best of philosophers!
  Blood and judgement commingled are masters of self-control.
Poet of common sense, reality, weeping, and laughter:
    Not in the caverns of Time, not in the tides that roll
On the high shore of this world, not in the dim hereafter—
    In reason and sorrow, the hope; in mercy, the mystery:
  By selling hours of dross we enrich the moment of soul.

Poet, thou, of the Blood: of states and of nations
Passing thy utmost dream, in the uttermost corners of space!
Poet, thou, of my countrymen—born to the speech, O Brother,
Born to the law and freedom, proud of the old embrace,
Born of the *Mayflower*, born of Virginia—born of the Mother!
Poet, thou of the Mother! the blood of America,
Turning in tribute to thee, revisits the Heart of the Race.

(1916)

T. S. Eliot

(1888–1965)

Hamlet and His Problems

Born into a family with deep roots in New England, Thomas Sterns Eliot was raised in the Midwest and later wrote that "it is self-evident that St. Louis affected me more deeply than any other environment has ever done." When he enrolled at the Milton Academy for a year in 1905 before attending Harvard, his mother wrote to the headmaster there that her son "has read practically all of Shakespeare, whom he admires, and retains much in memory." Eliot himself later confessed that "the only pleasure that I got from Shakespeare was the pleasure of being commended for reading him; had I been a child of more independent mind I should have refused to read him at all." Yet his works, most famously his poem "Marina," are steeped in Shakespeare and reflect a profound and lifelong engagement with his plays. At the time that Eliot wrote "Hamlet and His Problems" he had been living in England for four years, since the outbreak of World War I. During these years Shakespeare was much invoked in England for nationalistic purposes, a bardolatry intensified by the celebrations that took place on the three-hundredth anniversary of Shakespeare's death in 1916. Eliot's review can be read in part as a repudiation of this by an aspiring young American who a year earlier had declared in the *Egoist* his intention to "disturb and alarm the public: to upset its reliance upon Shakespeare, Nelson, Wellington, and Sir Isaac Newton." "Hamlet and His Problems" proved to be one of the landmark works of Shakespeare criticism, one that broke with both the influential Romantic readings of Coleridge as well as with more recent Freudian interpretations. Eliot heretically declares in this essay that *Hamlet* is "most certainly an artistic failure"; where others found an enigma, he spied a fault. In later years Eliot, who by then had taken British citizenship, admitted that his attack may have been a bit "jaundiced," a young poet's self-criticism redirected at Shakespeare.

❧

THE PROBLEM OF "HAMLET." By the Right Hon. J. M. Robertson. (Allen & Unwin. 5s. net.)

WE are very glad to find Hamlet in the hands of so learned
and scrupulous a critic as Mr. Robertson. Few critics have
even admitted that "Hamlet" the play is the primary problem, and
Hamlet the character only secondary. And Hamlet the character
has had an especial temptation for that most dangerous type of
critic: the critic with a mind which is naturally of the creative
order, but which through some weakness in creative power exer-
cises itself in criticism instead. These minds often find in Hamlet
a vicarious existence for their own artistic realization. Such a
mind had Goethe, who made of Hamlet a Werther; and such
had Coleridge, who made of Hamlet a Coleridge; and probably
neither of these men in writing about Hamlet remembered that
his first business was to study a work of art. The kind of criticism
that Goethe and Coleridge produced, in writing of Hamlet, is the
most misleading kind possible. For they both possessed unquestionable critical insight, and both make their critical aberrations
the more plausible by the substitution—of their own Hamlet for
Shakespeare's—which their creative gift effects. We should be
thankful that Walter Pater did not fix his attention on this play.

Qua work of art, the work of art cannot be interpreted; there
is nothing to interpret; we can only criticize it according to standards, in comparison to other works of art; and for "interpretation" the chief task is the presentation of relevant historical facts
which the reader is not assumed to know. Mr. Robertson points
out, very pertinently, how critics have failed in their "interpretation" of "Hamlet" by ignoring what ought to be very obvious:
that "Hamlet" is a stratification, that it represents the efforts of
a series of men, each making what he could out of the work of
his predecessors. The "Hamlet" of Shakespeare will appear to us
very differently if, instead of treating the whole action of the play
as due to Shakespeare's design, we perceive his "Hamlet" to be
superposed upon much cruder material which persists even in
the final form.

We know that there was an older play by Thomas Kyd, that extraordinary dramatic (if not poetic) genius who was in all probability the author of two plays so dissimilar as the "Spanish Tragedy" and "Arden of Feversham"; and what this play was like we can guess from three clues: from the "Spanish Tragedy" itself, from the tale of Belleforest upon which Kyd's "Hamlet" must have been based, and from a version acted in Germany in Shakespeare's lifetime which bears strong evidence of having been adapted from the earlier, not from the later play. From these three sources it is clear that in the earlier play the motive was a revenge-motive simply; that the action or delay is caused, as in the "Spanish Tragedy," solely by the difficulty of assassinating a monarch surrounded by guards, and that the "madness" of Hamlet was feigned in order to escape suspicion, and successfully. In the final play of Shakespeare, on the other hand, there is a motive which is more important than that of revenge, and which explicitly "blunts" the latter; the delay in revenge is unexplained on grounds of necessity or expediency; and the effect of the "madness" is not to lull but to arouse the king's suspicion. The alteration is not complete enough, however, to be convincing. Furthermore, there are verbal parallels so close to the "Spanish Tragedy" as to leave no doubt that in places Shakespeare was merely *revising* the text of Kyd. And finally there are unexplained scenes—the Polonius-Laertes and the Polonius-Reynaldo scenes—for which there is little excuse; these scenes are not in the verse style of Kyd, and not beyond doubt in the style of Shakespeare. These Mr. Robertson believes to be scenes in the original play of Kyd reworked by a third hand, perhaps Chapman, before Shakespeare touched the play. And he concludes, with very strong show of reason, that the original play of Kyd was, like certain other revenge-plays, in two parts of five acts each. The upshot of Mr. Robertson's examination is, we believe, irrefragable: that Shakespeare's "Hamlet," so far as it is Shakespeare's, is a play dealing with the effect of a mother's guilt upon her son, and that Shakespeare was unable to impose this motive successfully upon the "intractable" material of the old play.

Of the intractability there can be no doubt. So far from being

Shakespeare's masterpiece, the play is most certainly an artistic failure. In several ways the play is puzzling, and disquieting as is none of the others. Of all the plays it is the longest and is possibly the one on which Shakespeare spent most pains; and yet he has left in it superfluous and inconsistent scenes which even hasty revision should have noticed. The versification is variable. Lines like

> Look, the morn, in russet mantle clad,—
> Walks o'er the dew of yon high eastern hill,

are of the Shakespeare of "Romeo and Juliet." The lines in Act V. sc. ii.,

> Sir, in my heart there was a kind of fighting
> That would not let me sleep . . . .
> Up from my cabin,
> My sea-gown scarf'd about me, in the dark
> Grop'd I to find out them: had my desire;
> Finger'd their packet;

are of his quite mature. Both workmanship and thought are in an unstable condition. We are surely justified in attributing the play, with that other profoundly interesting play of "intractable" material and astonishing versification, "Measure for Measure," to a period of crisis, after which follow the tragic successes which culminate in "Coriolanus." "Coriolanus" may be not as "interesting" as "Hamlet," but it is, with "Antony and Cleopatra," Shakespeare's most assured artistic success. And probably more people have thought "Hamlet" a work of art because they found it interesting, than have found it interesting because it is a work of art. It is the "Mona Lisa" of literature.

The grounds of "Hamlet's" failure are not immediately obvious. Mr. Robertson is undoubtedly correct in concluding that the essential emotion of the play is the feeling of a son towards a guilty mother:

> [Hamlet's] tone is that of one who has suffered tortures on the score of his mother's degradation . . . The guilt of a mother is an

almost intolerable motive for drama, but it had to be maintained and emphasized to supply a psychological solution, or rather a hint of one.

This, however, is by no means the whole story. It is not merely the "guilt of a mother" that cannot be handled as Shakespeare handled the suspicion of Othello, the infatuation of Antony, or the pride of Coriolanus. The subject might conceivably have expanded into a tragedy like these, intelligible, self-complete, in the sunlight. "Hamlet," like the sonnets, is full of some stuff that the writer could not drag to light, contemplate, or manipulate into art. And when we search for this feeling, we find it, as in the sonnets, very difficult to localize. You cannot point to it in the speeches; indeed, if you examine the two famous soliloquies you see the versification of Shakespeare, but a content which might be claimed by another, perhaps by the author of the "Revenge of Bussy d'Ambois," Act V. sc. i. We find Shakespeare's "Hamlet" not in the action, not in any quotations that we might select, so much as in an unmistakable tone which is unmistakably not in the earlier play.

The only way of expressing emotion in the form of art is by finding an "objective correlative"; in other words, a set of objects, a situation, a chain of events which shall be the formula of that *particular* emotion; such that when the external facts, which must terminate in sensory experience, are given, the emotion is immediately evoked. If you examine any of Shakespeare's more successful tragedies, you will find this exact equivalence; you will find that the state of mind of Lady Macbeth walking in her sleep has been communicated to you by a skilful accumulation of imagined sensory impressions; the words of Macbeth on hearing of his wife's death strike us as if, given the sequence of events, these words were automatically released by the last event in the series. The artistic "inevitability" lies in this complete adequacy of the external to the emotion; and this is precisely what is deficient in "Hamlet." Hamlet (the man) is dominated by an emotion which is inexpressible, because it is in *excess* of the facts as they appear. And the supposed identity of Hamlet with his author is genuine to this point; that Hamlet's bafflement at the absence of objective equivalent to his feelings is a prolongation of the bafflement of his creator in the face of his artistic problem. Hamlet is up against the difficulty that his disgust is occasioned by his mother, but that his mother is not an adequate equivalent for it; his disgust envelops and exceeds her. It is thus a feeling which he cannot understand; he cannot objectify it, and it therefore remains to poison life and obstruct action. None of the possible actions can satisfy it; and nothing that Shakespeare can do with the plot can express Hamlet for him. And it must be noticed that the very nature of the *données* of the problem precludes objective equivalence. To have heightened the criminality of Gertrude would have been to provide the formula for a totally different emotion in Hamlet; it is just *because* her character is so negative and insignificant that she arouses in Hamlet the feeling which she is incapable of representing.

The "madness" of Hamlet lay to Shakespeare's hand; in the earlier play a simple ruse, and to the end, we may presume, understood as a ruse by the audience. For Shakespeare it is less than madness and more than feigned. The levity of Hamlet, his repetition of phrase, his puns, are not part of a deliberate plan of dissimulation, but a form of emotional relief. In the character Hamlet it is the buffoonery of an emotion which can find no outlet in action; in the dramatist it is the buffoonery of an emotion which he cannot express in art. The intense feeling, ecstatic or terrible, without an object or exceeding its object, is something which every person of sensibility has known; it is doubtless a study to pathologists. It often occurs in adolescence; the ordinary person puts these feelings to sleep, or trims down his feeling to fit the business world; the artist keeps it alive by his ability to intensify the world to his emotions. The Hamlet of Laforgue is an adolescent; the Hamlet of Shakespeare is not, he has not that explanation and excuse. We must simply admit that here Shakespeare tackled a problem which proved too much for him. Why he attempted it at all is an insoluble puzzle; under compulsion of what experience he attempted to express the inexpressibly horrible, we cannot ever know. We need a great many facts in his biography; and we should like to know whether, and when, and after or at the same time as what personal experience, he read Montaigne, II., xii.: "Apologie de Raimond Sebond." We should have, finally, to know something which is by hypothesis unknowable, for we assume it to be an experience which, in the manner indicated, exceeded the facts. We should have to understand things which Shakespeare did not understand himself. In the Storm in "Lear," and in the last scene of "Othello," Shakespeare triumphed in tearing art from the impossible: "Hamlet" is a failure. The material proved intractable in a deeper sense than that intended by Mr. Robertson in his admirable essay.

(1919)

William Carlos Williams

(1883–1963)

To Mark Anthony in Heaven

In 1943 William Carlos Williams corresponded with his fellow poet (and Shakespeare admirer) Louis Zukofsky about writing a "book on Shakespeare": "The amusing thing is that I've always wanted to do such a book. . . . The man is constantly in my mind, more than his writing—which is the wrong way about for a writer." Williams never wrote such a book; the most expansive he would ever be in print about Shakespeare was in his brief but powerful remarks in *The Embodiment of Knowledge* (1974), where Williams writes that "Shakespeare is misunderstood if he is made a great figure, a bighead, a colossus of learning," and argues that he "is the effect of a kind of thing which has been unique in the world, a namelessness of unprecedented freedom, permeable and bulk—a dumbness as of a tree, river, sky, nation, peasant—recording almost mindlessly, greatness." Williams's exposure to Shakespeare began at an early age. His father, he recalled in a *Paris Review* interview, "used to read poetry to me. Shakespeare. He had a group who used to come to our house, a Shakespeare club. They did dramatic readings. So I was always interested in Shakespeare." Though clearly fascinated with the man and his works, "To Mark Anthony in Heaven" is the only poem Williams published on a Shakespearean subject. The poem's speaker reflects on Mark Antony's seemingly shameful decision to flee from the battle of Actium, pursuing Cleopatra rather than his foes. Antony's followers consider this flight disgraceful and describe how Antony "claps on his sea-wing, and (like a doting mallard), / Leaving the fight in heighth, flies after her." But Williams, like Shakespeare, allows for an alternative interpretation: that Antony saw something extraordinary in Cleopatra—saw it "above the battle's fury"—that determined his fatal choice. The poem first appeared in the January 1920 issue of *The Little Review*.

❧

This quiet morning light
reflected, how many times
from grass and trees and clouds
enters my north room
touching the walls with
grass and clouds and trees.
Anthony,
trees and grass and clouds.
Why did you follow
that beloved body
with your ships at Actium?
I hope it was because
you knew her inch by inch
from slanting feet upward to the roots of her hair
and down again and that
you saw her
above the battle's fury—
clouds and trees and grass—

For then you are
listening in heaven.

(1920)

Lorenz Hart

(1895–1943)

and **Morrie Ryskind**

(1895–1985)

Shakespeares of 1922

Before his premature death at age forty-eight, the lyricist Lorenz Hart teamed up with Richard Rodgers on twenty-six Broadway musicals, including the first adaptation of a Shakespeare play for musical theater: *The Boys from Syracuse* (1938). Morrie Ryskind, who recalls in his memoirs that by the age of ten he had read all of Shakespeare's works, is best known for the scripts and screenplays he wrote for the Marx Brothers, including *Animal Crackers* (1929) and *A Night at the Opera* (1935). Before either of them had achieved fame independently, Hart and Ryskind collaborated on a vaudeville sketch for the actor Georgie Price. Their skit consisted of an opening song—"Broadway has a Shakespeare fad"— followed by five refrains: in each, Price would introduce himself as a famous Shakespeare character (but modernized, so that Antony is a baseball fan and Hamlet the son of a bootlegger), then launch into a witty and parodic speech, before ending with a brief song. Its sophisticated humor and lyrics were intended to flatter the audience's familiarity with the plays (including the "Julius Caesar that we studied at school"). "Shakespeares of 1922" stands midway between the nineteenth-century minstrel shows and the as yet unborn Shakespeare musical.

⚘

VERSE
Broadway has a Shakespeare fad,
Actors all are Shakespeare mad,
And I'd like to do
His great plays for you.
But I'll bring them up to date,

387

Five acts you won't have to wait
Till you hear the best scenes of the dramas.
And the plays will look like new
When I add a song or two.
I'll make Shakespeare seem the cat's pajamas!

REFRAIN I
First I'll play Shylock for he's Spanish like me—
Shylock's from Arverne by the Sea, Long Island.
He'll be the star of my new Shakespeare revue,
Shylocks of 1922.

SPEECH
He hath disgraced me, he hath cost me half a million. Laughed at
my losses, mocked at my gains. If I sell for four dollars a dozen, he
sells for three seventy-five. And what's his reason? I'm a Jehuda!
Hath not a Jehuda eyes? Hath not a Jehuda hands, organs, dimensions, broadcloth, velveteen, sateen, tricolette, and different-
quality serges? If you gyp us, do we not bleed? If you do not pay
us, do we not sue? And if you cancel our orders, shall we not revenge? Revenge! Revenge on Antonio!

FINISH
If I catch Antonio Spagoni the toreador!
He shall die! Ach ai vei!
He shall die diddy diddy ei, die, die, die
Ach oy vei!
He shall die! He shall die!
I soon will be takin'
A pound of his bacon
If I catch him bending tonight.

REFRAIN 2
Hamlet, the Prince of Denmark, can't make me wince,
I'll play the Danish pastry Prince.

He wasn't crazy at all,
But I am crazy to do
Hamlets of 1922.

SPEECH

To be or not to be, that is the question! Whether 'tis nobler to buy
your Gordon's gin, and pay the prices of outrageous bootleggers,
or to take arms against this sea of highwaymen, and make your
own home brew! To drink, to die (to dream, perchance). Alcohol,
aye, there's the rub! Home brew does make cowards of us all.

Mother, you have my father much offended. You made him
drink shellac. You are toy queen. Your husband's brother's wife.
And, would it were not so, so you my mother.

FINISH

Mammy! Mammy!
The sun will rise, and the sun will drop,
But the sun won't shine where you sent my pop!
Mammy! Mammy! If you make one more drop
I'll call in a cop,
My mammy!

REFRAIN 3

Poor old King Lear, who was bearded and gray,
Without the whiskers I will play.
How he went mad in the rainstorm,
I'll show in my revue,
Lears of 1922.

SPEECH

Blow winds, chap these hands, what care I. They have turned me
out. Ah, foul rain, thou art good for crops, but tough on an old
bird like me. Alas, O Jupiter, why didn't I get a five years' lease?
Here I stand, King Lear, I was raised by the King, my father, I
was raised by the Queen, my mother, and now, O ye Gods, now

I've been raised by the landlord. Here I stand in the storm! Ah, daughters, this is a hell of a night to kick thy poor old father out. My landlord. I had to sell my icebox to pay him. I had to sell my flivver to pay him. I belong to the landlord! Even my clothes are rent! I saved and saved. I had to give up my shaving, but I didn't raise my beard to pay a landlord! Blow, winds! Spit! I think I'm going cuckoo! He rents more flats every day. Last week he made an apartment out of the elevator. Next week there'll be no closets. Let fall the rain, Lear should worry!

FINISH
Though April showers may come my way
They can't grow flowers in bales of hay.
And when it's raining, I just reflect,
Because it isn't raining rain at all,
It's just a stage effect!
I see a rainbow, and life's worthwhile,
For I'm insane, bo, that's why I smile.
I haven't even got a bathtub,
So I hope the rain is strong
Whenever April showers come along.

REFRAIN 4
In Julius Caesar that we studied at school,
Mark Ant'ny knocked 'em for a gool.
But I don't need hungry supers in my modern revue,
Caesars of 1922.

SPEECH
Friends, buyers and countrymen! Lend me your ears. I come to bury Babe Ruth, not to praise him! The strikeouts men make live after them, the homers are oft interr'd with their bones. So let it be with Baby. Rest these noble bones, for he hath pulled the biggest bone since Merkel forgot to touch second base. Aye, a base bone! Judge Landis, as you know, was Baby's angel. Judge O

ye Gods, when he cut Babe Ruth's salary, that was the unkindest
cut of all. For when the noble Babe Ruth saw him stab, he cried,
"Et tu, Landis! The Vaudeville for Baby!" So he went to work for
Keith. And at the portals of the Palace, great Babe Ruth fell flat!
Oh, what a fall there was, my countrymen! But last year, the bat
of Babe Ruth would have swung against the world. Now, he makes
all his home runs at night!

FINISH

After the ball went over,
Bambino swung, that's all.
All he could hit was the umpire,
After the ball.

REFRAIN 5

All the world loves a lover like Romeo,
They named a cigar for him, you know.
That's why I must find some other name to call my revue,
Dumbbells of 1922.

SPEECH

Ah, there she sits, my Juliet, on the fire escape! Burning up with a
tender passion. See how she rests her chins upon her hand. Would
that I were a glove upon that hand, then I would be a happy kid!
Juliet, our love will be famous forever. They named a cigar after us.
Romeo and Juliet. Twenty-five cents. Us for two bits, while Robert Burns for a dime, and Prince Hamlet chokes you for a nickel.
What's in a name? Sir Walter Scott had a medicine named after
him—Scott's Emulsion! Nellie Melba, she's a peach, Wilson is a
whiskey, and Napoleon is a cream cake! They named a vegetable
for a baseball player, Corn on Cobb! And the best they can do for
Lincoln is to name a penny after him. Mary Garden's only a scent.
What's in a name? A rose by any other name would smell as sweet.
A Limburger by any other name would smell! Juliet, when I come
to you beneath your balcony . . .

FINISH

You'll hear me calling Yoo-hoo
'Neath your window ev'ry night!
You sweetly answer Yoo-hoo
As you're standing in the light.
While I'm climbing up the ladder
And I get a worm's-eye view,
Love may be blind, so Yoo-hoo
Means I love you.

(1922)

Stark Young

(1881–1963)

John Barrymore's Hamlet

The critic Heywood Broun spoke for many at the time when he said that John Barrymore's was "the clearest, the most interesting, intelligent and exciting Hamlet of our generation." In the aftermath of World War I a different kind of art was called for, a departure from the stale and inhibiting traditions of the past. The same year, 1922, that Barrymore was breaking with what Stark Young calls here the "dead husks of forms," so too were Joyce in *Ulysses*, Woolf in *Jacob's Room*, and T. S. Eliot in *The Waste Land*. In rendering nineteenth-century theatrical traditions anachronistic, it was a Hamlet both of and for its times. The novelist Ludwig Lewisohn found Barrymore's performance to be in "the key of fine modern poetry," conveying the "restrained but intense expressiveness of the bearing of modern men who live with their nerves and woes in narrow rooms." Barrymore's directors, Arthur Hopkins and Robert Edmond Jones, shared a strong interest in psychoanalysis and there is little doubt that the production was brushed by Freud's Oedipal theory. Barrymore himself imagined Hamlet as "tortured and outraged from the very opening of the action," a man with "the vibrant, highly sensitized and beautiful nature of an artist," who "has his hysterical outbursts, but he has too much charm, too much humanity, to be gloomy or lugubrious when he is in control." It ran for 101 performances in its first season (one more, deliberately, than Edwin Booth's *Hamlet* had), followed by a road tour, then a London engagement. Stark Young's review, which first ran in *The New Republic* in December 1922, acknowledged both the originality and technical limitations of Barrymore's Hamlet. The Mississippi-born Young was more than just a theater critic: he trained with Brander Matthews (one of the finest theater scholars of the day), taught at Amherst College, wrote plays, and had developed, as this essay confirms, a strong point of view.

❧

The Tragedy of Hamlet.
Sam H. Harris Theatre. November 20, 1922.

Mr. JOHN BARRYMORE seemed to gather together in himself all the Hamlets of his generation, to simplify and direct everyone's theory of the part. To me his Hamlet was the most satisfying that I have seen, not yet as a finished creation, but a foundation, a continuous outline. Mounet-Sully's Hamlet was richer and more sonorous; Forbes-Robertson's at times more sublimated; Irving's more sharply devised and Sothern's, so far as we are concerned strictly with the verse pattern, was more securely read. But there is nothing in Mr. Barrymore's Hamlet to get in the way of these accomplishments also, with time and study. And in what he has done there is no inherent quality that need prevent his achieving the thing most needed to perfect, in its own kind, his Hamlet; I mean a certain dilation and abundance in all his reactions. This Hamlet of Mr. Barrymore's must give us—and already promises— the sense of a larger inner tumult and indeed of a certain cerebral and passionate ecstasy, pressing against the external restraint of him. He needs the suggestion of more vitality, ungovernable and deep, of more complex suffering, of not only intellectual subtlety but intellectual power as well, all this added to the continuity of distinction that he already has, the shy and humorous mystery, the proud irony, the terrible storms of pain. Mr. Barrymore brings to the part what is ultimately as necessary to a fine actor as to a fine singer, the physical gifts that enable him to express his idea. He has a beautiful presence, a profound magnetism. His English, much of which is but recently acquired through the teaching of the remarkable Mrs. Margaret Carrington, is almost wholly reborn from what it once was, and is now almost pure, even and exact, though not yet wholly flexible. His voice, also to a considerable extent Mrs. Carrington's production, is not supreme. It is not a rich and sonorous volume such as Mansfield had, but is capable of high, intelligent training, and is already in the middle tones highly admirable.

With such an artist as Mr. Barrymore has risen to be, one cannot escape the matter of the technical means by which he fills out and develops the kind of truth that he sees in his role, or confuses and prevents its realization. His chief technical triumph, I think, lies in the absence from his work of all essentially theatrical faults. There are no idle tricks of the voice, no empty display of actor vanity and professional virtuosity, no foolish strutting, none of the actor idol's way of feeling his oats. There is no egotistical intrusion on the play, no capricious distortion of the truth in the service of histrionic exhibitionism. Throughout the performance the technical method is invariably derived from the conception of the part and never allowed to run ahead of it.

Mr. Barrymore's important technical limitations at this stage of his achievement seem to me to be two. The first concerns the verse. The "resistant flexibility," to use an old phrase, that is the soul of fine reading, he has not yet completely acquired. Much of his reading is excellent; but now and again in his effort to keep the verse true to its inner meaning and to the spiritual naturalness that underlies it—and because, too, of a lack of concentration on his projection at times—Mr. Barrymore seems to be afraid to admit the line for what it is, verse. Sometimes he allows the phrases to fall apart in such a way that the essential musical pattern of the verse—which is a portion of the idea itself—is lost. In the line—to take an example—

> Why, she would hang on him,

he put a heavy stress on the word "hang" and almost let the "him" disappear; a useless naturalism, for the same effect of sense emphasis can be secured and yet the verse pattern of the lines preserved, by sustaining the nasals in "on" and "him" with no more actual stress on them than Mr. Barrymore used.

For one more instance out of a good many, take the line

> Must, like a whore, unpack my heart with words.

Mr. Barrymore let the phrase "like a whore" fall out solid from the verse, which then began anew with "unpack." But there is a certain sustained unity to the line; "must" and "unpack" have a resistant connection together—to be secured by the tone—which the intervening phrase does not break off. And, as a matter of fact, everywhere in Shakespeare the long, difficult, elaborate and complex passages depend above everything on their musical unity to recreate out of their many details that first profound unity of emotion from which they sprang. Without this unity these details appear to be—as in fact they often are, in the earlier plays especially—mere images and ornaments thrown in, whose artificiality is only embarrassing.

The other technical limitation that I feel in Mr. Barrymore is in his rendering of decreasing emotion. To be able to rise successfully to emotional heights is one measure of an actor's art; but this declining gradation is a no less sure test of it. For an illustration of what I mean, take the passage in the closet scene where the Ghost vanishes.

> HAMLET: Why, look you there! look how it steals away!
>   My father in his habit as he lived!
>   Look, where he goes, even now, out at the portal!
> QUEEN: This is the very coinage of your brain;
>   This bodiless creation ecstasy
>   Is very cunning in.
> HAMLET: Ecstasy!
>   My pulse as yours doth temperately keep time,—

Mr. Barrymore repeats the word and goes on with the speech in a reasonable and almost even tone. But in such places a part of the effect of preceding emotion appears in the gradual lessening of it in the actor's manner and voice. This speech of Hamlet's is reasonable, yes, but the calm in the thought precedes the calm in the state of emotion; the will and the idea are to rule but only after conflict with the emotion.

I cannot admire too much Mr. Barrymore's tact in the scenes with Polonius. Most actors for the applause they get play up for all it is worth Hamlet's seemingly rude wit at the old man's expense. But Mr. Barrymore gave you only Hamlet's sense of the world grown empty and life turned to rubbish in this old counselor. And, without seeming to do so he made you feel that Polonius stood for the kind of thing in life that had taken Ophelia from him. How finely—even in that last entreaty to Laertes for fair usage—Mr. Barrymore maintained an absence of self-pity in Hamlet, and thus enlarged the tragic pity of the play! What a fine vocal economy he exercised in the scene where Horatio tells him of his father's ghost! And what a stroke of genius it was, when by Ophelia's grave Hamlet had rushed through those mad lines, piling one wild image on another, and comes to the

> Nay, and thou'lt mouth,
> I'll rant as well as thou

to drop on that last, on the "I'll rant as well as thou," into an aspirate tone, hoarse, broken with grief and with the consciousness of his words' excess and the excess of irony in all things!

And I must admire the economy of business—not all Mr. Barrymore's, of course, but partly due to Mr. Hopkins, Mrs. Carrington and Mr. Jones—all through the part. The nunnery scene with Ophelia was done with a reaching out of the hands almost; the relation of Hamlet to his mother and through her to the ghost was achieved by his moving toward the ghost on his knees and being caught in his mother's arms, weaving together the bodies of those two, who, whatever their sins might be, must belong to each other at such terrible cost. There were no portraits on the wall with a ghost stepping out, as Hackett used to do it in the sixties. There was no crawling forward on the floor to watch the King during the play, as so many actors have done; and none of Ophelia's peacock fan for Hamlet to tap his breast with and fling into the air, as Irving used to do. About all this production there were none of those accessories in invented business; there was for the most part, and always in intention, only that action proceeding from the inner necessity of the moment and leaning on life, not on stage expedients. The inner limitations of Mr. John Barrymore's Hamlet are both less tangible and less amendable perhaps. They are in the direction of the poetic and human. With time, meditation and repetition it will gain in these respects no doubt; but it needs now more warmth, more abundance in all the reactions, more dilation of spirit. It takes too much for granted, makes

Hamlet too easy to understand, and so lacks mystery and scope. It needs a larger inner tumult, more of a cerebral and passionate ecstasy pressing against the outward restraint of the whole pattern. It needs more of the sense of an ungovernable vitality, more complex subtlety and power. It needs more tenderness and, above all, more, if you like generosity.

Miss Fuller's Ophelia could not dominate the longer speeches in her first scenes. But in the mad scenes she sang her ballads with unheard-of poignancy; and the mere slip of her white, flitting body was itself the image of pathos. Miss Fuller sharpened the effect of madness by putting into it a hint of that last betrayal that insanity brings to Ophelia: indecency. Miss Yurka, though she subsided at times out of the part when she had nothing to do, read her lines admirably; and contrived to suggest without overstating it the loose quality in this woman that subjected her to the King. Mr. O'Brien's Polonius was good, simplified rather far, perhaps, but with a certain force of truth that rendered what Polonius, despite his fatuity, has: a kind of grotesque distinction. Mr. Reginald Pole brought to the Ghost's lines a fine ear and an exact method of reading the verse that you gratefully detect before he is three lines under way. The Laertes of Mr. Sidney Mather is the only very bad performance in the company. The role is extra difficult because of its Renaissance approach, through character and reality, to the flowery gallantry and lyric expedition required; though the bases of Laertes' feelings and actions seem to me fresh, accessible and human. The fact remains, nevertheless, that unless the actor gets the manner and flourish of Laertes, the expression of his vivid, poignant and decorative meaning cannot find its due outlet. Mr. Tyrone Power's King—superb in voice and metre— was admirable. He suggested not mere villainy but rather a tragic figure of force and heavy will. Mr. Power's King gave us also the sense of great charm exerted upon those around him that is attributed to the character in the play.

It is in the scene where Hamlet catches the King praying and does not kill him—the climax of the play—that the method of production employed by Mr. Hopkins and Mr. Jones is reduced, it seemed to me, to its most characteristic terms. The King enters through the curtain, already used a number of times, with the saints on it. He kneels, facing the audience. He lifts his hands and speaks to heaven. Hamlet enters through the same curtain. He debates the fitness of the time for the King's murder, decides against it, withdraws. The King says

> My words fly up, my thoughts remain below;
> Words without thoughts never to heaven go.

and rises and goes out. One man is here, one is there. Here are the uplifted hands, there the sword drawn. Here, sick conscience, power, and tormented ambition; there, the torture of conflicting thoughts, the irony, the resolution. Two bodies and their relation to each other, the words, the essential drama, the eternal content of the scene. No tricks, no plausible business, no palace chapel. And no tradition.

Tradition of conception there is now and again, of course; but throughout the entire production there is very little concern about external tradition. And what of it? If we had some kind of Théâtre Français, a conservatory where a classic like *Hamlet* would be seen from time to time as a star returns on its course; or if in our theatre we had a succession of rival Hamlets, as was once the case, the question of tradition would be more important. Under such conditions a certain symbolism of stage business might develop, full of deep significance, familiar and accepted, and not to be abandoned too readily. But in the American theatre today the disregard of Shakespearean tradition is easy and commendable. To pursue it doggedly is to block the way with dead husks of forms once full of meaning. It only thwarts the audience and Shakespeare's living matter with a kind of academic archaism and, even, with a certain fanaticism; which consists, as Santayana says, in redoubling your effort when you have forgotten your aim. Messrs. Hopkins and Jones and Barrymore have, for the most part, let sleeping dogs lie. Nothing could be easier than not to do so; hence their eminence.

Mr. Robert Edmond Jones has created a permanent setting

of architectural forms and spaces, bounded across the stage, and down two-thirds to the front line of it, with a play of steps. Within this, easy variations are possible to indicate the changes of scene. The design of the setting cannot be conveyed in words, of course, but it is princely, austere and monumental. It has no clutter of costumes or elaborate variations in apartments, but instead a central rhythm of images, of light and shade innate to the dramatic moment. The shortcoming of this bold and eloquent setting is that it either goes too far or does not go far enough. In this respect the limit was reached when the time came for the scene of Ophelia's burial, where the setting was at least enough like a palace to make the grave toward the front of the stage—and therefore the whole scene—appear to be incongruous if not absurd. A greater vastness of imagination was thus required of the designer. In his defense it should be said, however, that our theatre does not easily allow for repeated experiment, with the discarding and choosing and the expense involved.

This production of *Hamlet* is important and is out of class with Shakespeare production from other sources. This is not through any perfection in the field of the Shakespearean so called; but because it works toward the discovery of the essential and dramatic elements that from the day it was written have underlain this play. The usual Shakespeare production, however eminent, goes in precisely the opposite direction. It does not reveal the essential so much as it dresses up the scene at every conceivable angle, with trappings, research, scenery, business.

Such a production as this of *Hamlet* could not hope to be uniformly successful. But in its best passages, without any affectation of the primitive or archaic, it achieved what primitive art can achieve: a fundamental pattern so simple and so revealing that it appeared to be mystical; and so direct and strong that it restored to the dramatic scene its primary truth and magnificence. For a long time to come this *Hamlet* will be remembered as one of the glories of our theatre.

(1922)

George F. Whicher

(1889–1954)

Shakespeare for America

By the late nineteenth century the fantasy of transporting to America the home in which Shakespeare had been born had given way to the desire to bring Shakespeare's literary riches to the New World. Along with Gilded Age industrialists J. P. Morgan and Henry E. Huntington, Henry Clay Folger (president of Standard Oil Company of New York) was one of the major book collectors of the early twentieth century, his interest in Shakespeare first sparked by hearing Emerson lecture in 1879. Huntington's and Morgan's tastes were eclectic; Folger narrowed his collecting to Shakespeare and his world. Not long after his marriage to Emily Clara Jordan, in 1885, he purchased a 1685 Fourth Folio of Shakespeare's works at auction for $107.50. It would be the first of many such acquisitions. Over the course of the next four decades the Folgers purchased seventy-nine First Folios, along with some of the rarest of quartos and manuscripts and thousands of Elizabethan rare books and prints, forming the backbone of the finest Shakespeare collection in the world. The Folgers flirted with the idea of creating a permanent home for this collection in England or in New York City before determining that an edifice should be built to house these works in Washington, D.C. The site, a block from the Capitol, had been earmarked for an extension of the Library of Congress, but in 1928 a congressional resolution secured for the Folgers the right to build there. Initially conceived as the "Folger Shakespeare Memorial," the building was ultimately called the Folger Shakespeare Library, intended "for promoting and diffusing knowledge of the writings and history of Shakespeare." George F. Whicher, who taught at Amherst College (under whose auspices the Folger Shakespeare Library has been administered), published this essay in *The Atlantic Monthly* shortly before the building opened in 1932.

❧

I

THE founding of libraries, not for the circulation of books among general readers, but as repositories of rare editions and other literary treasures, is a comparatively recent development in the United States. Though university and college libraries have often been enriched by special gifts or purchases of early printed books or manuscript materials, and two large collections of Americana, the John Carter Brown Library at Providence and the William L. Clements Library at Ann Arbor, have been separately housed on university campuses, the establishing of such independent institutions as the Pierpont Morgan Library in New York and the Henry E. Huntington Library in San Marino, California, is significant of a new departure in American cultural life.

Each of the two collections last named makes accessible to scholars a wealth of material ranging over the whole extent of English literature and including books of particular interest to the student of Shakespeare. In this latter respect the Huntington Library, where the famous Devonshire collection is now lodged, is especially notable for the number and rarity of the items it contains. Mr. Morgan, however, was a collector of rare books in general, while Mr. Huntington's interests were so widely diversified as to include Americana, incunabula, and English books printed before 1640; in both instances the early editions of Shakespeare now in their libraries were acquired as part of a larger buying programme.

The gathering of books and other objects of interest with the sole aim of illustrating the life and works of Shakespeare was the consistent avocation of another American collector, Mr. Henry Clay Folger, one-time president and later chairman of the board of the Standard Oil Company of New York, whose library, suitably housed and endowed with ample funds for its maintenance and expansion, is soon to be permanently established and opened to public use in Washington. With quiet intensity and scholarly concentration, Mr. Folger made it his life work to bring together all the books and other materials that might be serviceable to a student of Shakespeare, and he succeeded even beyond his hopes in forming what is undoubtedly the largest and richest collection of its kind that the world has seen or will ever see again. When the great mass of books, manuscripts, documents, playbills, costumes, prints, paintings, musical scores, and objects of historical interest assembled by Mr. Folger are installed in the building now approaching completion across the street from the Library of Congress, the United States will have at each side of the continent a centre for advanced scholarship in English studies whose resources in certain fields will be comparable to those of the British Museum and the Bodleian libraries. The cultural consequences, though not easy to assess in advance, may be very considerable.

Meanwhile the fact that the executive head of one of the country's leading industries should have spent nearly all his leisure time, during years when he was burdened with heavy responsibilities, in the study of Shakespeare's text,—for Mr. Folger was both a reader and an expert bibliographer,—and in gathering books for the proper study of Shakespeare, is a circumstance not to be overlooked in making up America's cultural account. In the social history of our times such representative avocations of leading business men deserve at least as much emphasis as the occasional titanisms more conspicuously featured by the press, caricatured in popular fiction, and accepted by uncritical foreigners as characteristically American.

Thanks largely to Mr. Folger's single-minded and single-handed efforts, with due respect also to Mr. Huntington's, the United States has come abreast of Great Britain in establishing important Shakespeare collections for scholarly use; this after years of lagging behind. The British Museum received by the bequest of David Garrick in 1779 the nucleus of its Shakespeare library; in the same year a second important collection formed by Edward Capell was presented to Trinity College, Cambridge; and in 1812 the Bodleian received by bequest the books of Edmund Malone, the Shakespearean editor. For more than half a century thereafter British libraries were able to acquire Shakespeareana with little competition from America. Then the collecting of rare books became a favorite pastime of American millionaires, and little by little nearly all the early editions of Shakespeare privately owned in England passed into the hands of collectors in this country.

The transfer was of no immediate benefit to Shakespeare scholars, because books in private ownership, whether in British country houses or in the libraries of American men of wealth, could not readily be consulted. Even as late as the time of Shakespeare's tercentennial in 1916, Miss Henrietta C. Bartlett, who catalogued the exhibition arranged by the New York Public Library, was able to say: 'Unfortunately there are in America but three public institutions which contain original editions of Shakespeare's works of sufficient value to form the basis for an exhibition.' Since these words were written, however, the most important private collections of Shakespeare in the United States have become, in effect if not strictly in fact, public possessions under conditions that make them permanently available to scholars. The amassing of a nearly complete series of texts under one roof, wherever that roof is situated, is a great improvement on having them scattered in many places, and students of Shakespeare on both sides of the Atlantic may find reason for satisfaction in the bringing together of such collections by Mr. Huntington and Mr. Folger. 'It is a very fine achievement,' writes Dr. Alfred W. Pollard of the British Museum, 'and one which every wise Englishman will view not merely without jealousy, but with the greatest possible pleasure that they have thought it worth accomplishing, and have accomplished it.'

It was characteristic of Mr. Folger, indeed a part of his business training, never to announce his plans until he was ready to carry them into effect. He always conducted his buying of Shakespearean rarities alone, except for the devoted and competent assistance of Mrs. Folger, who helped him to keep a manuscript record of his purchases. His books were stored in bank vaults and storage rooms, never assembled in one place, and rarely shown. Consequently few persons in this country, even among bookmen, realized the magnitude of his achievement. In England, where the importance of his work was better appreciated, he was repeatedly urged to leave his collection as a Shakespeare memorial at Stratford-on-Avon. This he declined to do. His final intention, as expressed in a letter of January 19, 1928, was 'to help make the United States a centre for literary study and progress.'

In an even more practical way his design to promote the study of Shakespeare in the United States appears in another provision for the ultimate disposal of his collection. By the terms of his will the administration of the Folger Shakespeare Library and of the fund for its support is entrusted to the trustees of Amherst College, who in compensation for their services are instructed to apply to the purposes of the college approximately one quarter of the annual income from the Shakespeare fund. The material benefit to the college of this generous arrangement does not need to be emphasized, though at first glance it may seem incongruous to place a library in Washington under the control of the trustees of a small undergraduate college in New England. But in making this disposition of his property Mr. Folger was presumably not actuated merely by affectionate loyalty to the college where he received his education. It would have been a simple matter for him to have benefited the college and founded the library by separate bequests, if he had wished to do so. His intention rather was to place the continuation of the most cherished personal interest of his life in the hands of men aware of educational values and in immediate contact with a scholarly enterprise. Under such direction the Folger Shakespeare Library might be expected to develop into something more than a mausoleum for rare books or a shrine to a venerated name; it might be made to exercise a living influence throughout the United States as a centre of literature and learning dedicated to the spirit of a master poet.

II

A Shakespeare library conceived as a national institution is of particular significance to scholars, teachers of literature, and writers. Let us first consider the opportunities of scholarship that the opening of the Folger Library will make available.

Through the courtesy of Mr. William Adams Slade, the director for the time being on appointment by Mrs. Folger, I have before me a condensed survey of the main features of the Folger collection. It extends to some fifteen typewritten pages, single-spaced. Very little of the information so generously supplied can be given within the limits of this paper, but by a selection of statistics and specific details I may be able to suggest the extent and richness of the library's resources. It should be said, however, that Mr. Slade has as yet had no opportunity to examine the books and that the information here given is compiled from Mr. Folger's manuscript catalogue.

Though Shakespeare's writings are the nucleus around which the entire library has been built, not all the seventy thousand books in the collection are by or about Shakespeare. Early editions of other Elizabethan and Jacobean authors are liberally represented, particularly those from which the dramatist drew plots or quotations, or which he is supposed to have read, or which contain allusions to his works. But we may well begin with editions of Shakespeare.

On this subject Mr. Slade writes: 'The Folger Shakespeare Library contains upward of 1400 different copies of the collected works (different editions and duplicate copies both included) in a total of about 9700 volumes. In addition, besides numerous copies of the sonnets and poems, it has, as one would expect, a very great number of the separate editions of the plays, *Hamlet* leading, with over 800 copies; *Macbeth* next, with over 500; *Romeo and Juliet* and the *Merchant of Venice* next, each with over 400; and the others following. For historical, literary, or critical study it will obviously be of great service to have at hand such a collection of different editions, so largely supplied as they are with introductions, notes, essays, and critical apparatus. Moreover, a large number of the copies contain MS. notes by editors, men of letters, and others, giving the volumes added value and interest.'

Practising a resolute synecdoche, I cull from the list that illustrates this last statement only these items: Rowe's First Edition, 1709, John Dennis's own copy, with full notes in his handwriting, regarded as the earliest annotated copy known; Theobald's Second Edition, 1750, MS. notes by the poet Gray; Hanmer's

Second Edition, 1770–1771, Sarah Siddon's copy, with her notes for Shakespeare readings; Charles Lamb's copy; S. T. Coleridge's copy, with his MS. notes; First American Edition, eight volumes, 1795, President John Adams's copy; Bell Edition, 1774, Volume I only, George Washington's copy; Abraham Lincoln's copy, edition of 1835, autograph and MS. notes.

Of all the collected editions the most interesting to both laymen and special students is, of course, the First Folio of 1623, containing the earliest printed versions of twenty of the thirty-seven plays included in the Shakespeare canon. Only a few more than two hundred copies of this book have been preserved, and of these seventy-nine, including six fragments, are in the Folger collection. Among them are: the Daniel Folio, once owned by the Baroness Burdett-Coutts, and listed by Sir Sidney Lee as one of fourteen copies in a perfect state of preservation; three others also regarded as perfect, though apparently not so listed by Lee; six of twenty-seven copies placed by Lee in the second division of the first class because of minute defects; and perhaps most interesting of all, though not perfect, the Vincent Folio, the tallest known copy and one of the first to come from the press, bearing on its title-page an inscription recording its presentation by William Jaggard, the printer of the volume, to Augustine Vincent, the herald who had been instrumental in securing the grant of Shakespeare's arms. This last First Folio was the first copy that Mr. Folger acquired, and, though it was not the most expensive book in his library, he was accustomed to refer to it as 'the most precious book in the world.' Among the less distinguished copies in a company where all are of high distinction is one that Mr. Folger must have regarded with special affection, the Roberts Folio, used by Chatto and Windus in the production of the reduced facsimile edited by J. O. Halliwell-Phillips in 1876. It was with the purchase of this facsimile for one dollar and twenty-five cents that Mr. Folger commenced his career as a student of Shakespeare's text and a collector of Shakespearean books.

The folios succeeding the first are also generously represented, the Second Folio by at least fifty copies, the Third Folio by at least twenty-four (including both issues), and the Fourth Folio by at least thirty. (Only approximate figures can be given.)

Next to the folios, which stand foremost among the glories of the Folger Library, come the plays in quarto, of which the earliest printed are among the rarest of rare books. Not infrequently an edition is known by only three to six surviving copies, and in some instances a single copy is all that remains. Seventeen plays were printed in quarto form before the issue of the First Folio, fourteen of them, as is now maintained, from fairly reliable manuscripts, and five (counting *Romeo and Juliet* and *Hamlet* once in each group) from 'stolne and surreptitious copies' irregularly secured by catchpenny publishers. Of the five 'bad' quartos Mr. Folger was able to obtain all but the 1603 *Hamlet*, and of the fourteen 'good' first quartos twelve, the missing items being *Richard II* (1597) and the *First Part of Henry IV* (1598). To compensate for these gaps his library includes a unique fragment (four leaves) regarded by Halliwell-Phillipps as a 'portion of the first and hitherto unknown edition of the *First Part of Henry IV*, published by Wise early in the year 1598,' and a unique third edition of *Richard II* (1598) which has been the object of much bibliographical attention. Mr. Folger also possessed the only known copy of *Titus Andronicus* (1594), the earliest printed of all Shakespeare's plays; one of the three known copies of *Hamlet* (1604), the first issue of the revised play; and the rare second edition of *Pericles* (1611), besides both states of the first edition. Out of a large and representative collection of later quartos, from which only three of those issued prior to 1623 appear to be missing, the item that most insistently demands recognition is the bound set of the Jaggard-Pavier quartos of 1619, the only complete set known to have survived in seventeenth-century binding. A second but incomplete copy of the same curious book is noted in Mr. Folger's record of his purchases and will be eagerly examined when his library is catalogued.

Plays that Shakespeare revised and plays wrongfully attributed to him by enterprising publishers are well represented, nearly always in the form of first quartos, but there is no room to list them here. We must pass on to the poems. Of the very scarce early issues of *Venus and Adonis* the Folger Library holds a unique fragment of the third edition, one of two known copies of the sixth edition, and one of two known copies of the thirteenth. There are two of the ten recorded copies of the *Rape of Lucrece*, first edition, and single examples of the third, sixth, seventh, and eighth editions. The *Sonnets* are represented by two copies of the first printing (1609). Finally, there are ten copies of the first collected edition of the *Poems* (1640), at least one of which has the rare portrait by William Marshall, the second likeness of Shakespeare to be engraved.

Rare original issues of works by other Elizabethan authors abound, but I must pass them over except to remark that the library is especially rich in materials, both manuscripts and printed, relating to Ben Jonson and Francis Bacon. So also I must dismiss cursorily the works of adapters, imitators, and 'improvers' of Shakespeare; the writings of editors, critics, and commentators, much of them in the form of marginal notes; and the great mass of manuscript materials, beginning with the original diary of the Reverend John Ward, vicar of Stratford-on-Avon from 1662 to 1681, and including hundreds of autograph letters from famous authors—Voltaire, Goethe, the Brownings, Tennyson, and Swinburne among others. A final word must be said of the materials illustrating stage history, and here again I quote Mr. Slade:—

The leading exponents of Shakespeare on the stage, especially from the age of Cibber, are the subject of a series of special groups containing printed books, prompt books, autograph letters, original manuscripts, portraits, playbills, programmes, clippings, scrapbooks, costumes, stage properties, association objects, etc., etc. The Garrick material would give distinction to any library. The Cibbers, Macklin, Mrs. Clive, Mrs. Siddons, Mrs. Jordan, the Kembles, Macready, the Keans, Phelps, Forrest, Helen Faucit (afterwards Lady Martin), Charlotte Cushman, the Booths, the Barretts, Helena Modjeska, Mary Anderson, Sir Henry Irving, Ellen Terry, Ada Rehan, John Drew, Forbes-Robertson, E. H. Sothern, Julia Marlowe, Beerbohm Tree, these and others all figure. The entries under William Winter's name, representing not only Winter's writings but also the items collected by him, fill nearly six pages of the catalogue. The playbills are so many that they may actually number anywhere from fifty thousand to half a million. The Augustin Daly material includes about 6000 letters covering the period from 1860 to 1900.

Portraits, statues, prints, drawings, water colors, oil paintings, medals—it is useless to try to particularize further. Even Walt Whitman's appetite for 'auctioneer's catalogues' of details would be glutted. Sufficient to say that there will be a museum in connection with the Folger Library with thousands of objects to fill it.

Even an abbreviated and inadequate survey of the contents of the Folger Library may suggest how much it holds for the study and delight of investigators in many fields of English literature. Though its chief distinction rests upon its Elizabethan and seventeenth-century books, yet there is abundant material also to interest the student of eighteenth- and nineteenth-century letters. Countless special studies might be based on its rare volumes and manuscripts, or on particular collections illustrating some minor point in regard to Shakespeare, but worthy of attention on their own account. The nature of the library as a whole, however, makes it preëminently the place where certain kinds of investigation may be most conveniently carried on and where indeed some organized effort might profitably be made to utilize the extraordinary resources of the collection.

Mr. Folger's main interest in Shakespeare lay in textual and bibliographical problems, and accordingly the 'fine kit of tools for the proper study of Shakespeare' (as he called his library) was assembled with an eye to this type of investigation. This intention explains what might otherwise seem its unnecessary richness in First Folios. Between the various copies of this book there are minute but possibly significant differences. Had Mr. Folger lived to make use of his library, it was his design to supervise such a collation of First Folios as has never before been possible. This remains for others to perform. It is but one step, however, in the bibliographical study of Shakespeare for which his collection provides the means. To Shakespeare's earliest editors an error in the printing of quartos and folios was merely a blemish to be removed by the readiest means at hand. To a modern editor, on the contrary, an error may be a significant indication of some stage in the process that Shakespeare's plays went through between the time when they left his hand and the time when the better-authorized but not entirely accurate versions appeared in the First Folio. The problem is not in the first instance to eliminate mistakes, but to interpret them in order that corrections of the text may be intelligently made. Presumably no absolute certainty will ever be reached concerning every word that Shakespeare wrote, but that is no reason why all the available information should not be collected and used for what it may be worth in the formation of as sound a text as can be made.

An association of Shakespeare scholars brought together for a limited object could do much to utilize the remarkable resources of the Folger collection, but it might be possible to organize under the direction of the library a scholarly enterprise of a more permanent and systematic kind. In the American Academies at Rome and Athens we have a type of institution founded for the study of a subject at points where the richness of the material justifies the continued maintenance of a body of experts. The Folger Library will create in Washington a centre for the study of the literature of Elizabethan England comparable to the best that can be found in Great Britain. It would be easy to conceive there an American Academy for English Studies that might, like its prototypes abroad, bring into profitable cooperation a permanent staff of experts attached to the library, visiting scholars of distinction, and younger men appointed to fellowships. From such a centre of scholarship might be issued a series of publications that would quicken the advance of knowledge in the most important field of literary investigation, while young men trained there and occasionally returning for periods of research might exercise a salutary influence on the teaching of English in American colleges.

III

So far we have considered the Folger Library simply as a collection of books, a tool whereby scholars may increase the general store of learning. The rare volumes assembled by Mr. Folger, however, will occupy only a part of the building designed to hold them. The beautiful structure conceived by the architect, Mr. Paul P. Cret, in consultation with Mr. Alexander B. Trowbridge, is planned both without and within to express a larger purpose than that of being only a kind of sanctuary for Shakespeare students.

Outwardly the building is classic in spirit, though not an archæological imitation of any particular period of classic architecture, and in certain details is suggestive of a restrained modernism. The simplicity of the marble façade is emphasized by the introduction of sculptured panels, one at the foot of each of the nine bays, representing scenes from the best-known Shakespearean plays; these will stand at a point where they may easily be studied by visitors. Within this classic shell the architect has very boldly conceived the idea of producing a Tudor interior. The transition is made gradually, since the long exhibition gallery which runs parallel to the main façade is designed in the spirit of English work of the early Renaissance. The large reading room or library proper, which lies behind the gallery, will be carried out in the architectural manner of Shakespeare's time, though with some mixture, because at one end of the room there will stand a window with Gothic tracery which in its stonework is a copy of the principal window in the church at Stratford where Shakespeare lies buried. The left wing of the building will contain a small auditorium modeled on the pattern of an Elizabethan theatre, about which a whole story might be written. The many elements of form combined in the design of the library building appropriately suggest the richness and variety of the tradition gathered up in Shakespeare's works and through them handed down to our own day. So, too, by means of architectural masses and sculptured figures speaking to the passer-by, and more directly by means of its museum and stage, the Folger Shakespeare Library will be enabled to impress the public mind, enlighten the uninformed, and help those already interested to fuller knowledge.

Of the stage included in the Folger Library a word more should be said. It will be one of the few places in the world where Shakespeare's plays may be acted under conditions like those for which they were originally written. One may confidently suppose that it will be used not only for lectures and readings, but for occasional performances by our greatest actors in the Shakespearean tradition and for the instruction of school and college groups in methods of staging and acting Elizabethan dramas. Though the auditorium will seat less than three hundred people, its productions may reach a wider audience through talking pictures and radio. By this means the stage of the Folger Library may be made a centre for the cultivation of the spoken language as a thing of beauty and may contribute in no small degree to revive a sense of dramatic verse as a noble equivalent to operatic music. Anyone who has heard a performance of French classical drama in France will understand how much English-speaking audiences have yet to learn in this respect.

The reading room of the Folger Library will, of course, not be open to the public at large. A place where rare volumes are treasured and where literary research is to be carried on cannot be used directly as an instrument for general education. But, in addition to the educational work forwarded by its museum and theatre, the Folger Library may as a research institution exercise an indirect but notable influence upon formal education in schools and colleges. It is not too optimistic to suppose that the creation of a permanent centre for Shakespeare study will tend to accentuate the teaching of Shakespeare and gradually help to bring about a new emphasis in the study of literature. In considering the possible effects of such a library on the great academic industry that the teaching of English has become, however, we are entering a field of speculation where consummations devoutly to be wished will not necessarily come to pass unless belief in them and desire for them bring them into being.

English literature as a part of formal education is still comparatively new and its character is far from settled. Courses in English literature may be studies in æsthetic appreciation, in social history, in illustrations of a favorite 'philosophy of life,' in textual or linguistic problems, or in the biography of authors. Nearly all these types of courses are given at any point in the educational programme where it happens to be convenient or locally traditional to place them. There is no controlling conviction as to what aspects of the subject should come first or what aspects are central. College announcements are stuffed with far too many courses in English, a large number of them dealing with side issues and fringes of the subject. In one large university recently thirteen courses were simultaneously being given in the short story alone. It is time that English departments were de-upholstered. So far as the Folger Library may serve to focus attention on the central figure in English literature, its influence will be entirely wholesome.

Opportunities to engage in research at the Folger Library and reports of the work being carried on there may also help to spread among the smaller colleges an idea of English as a subject of advanced study, and so bring them some of the advantages that a college at a university derives from its association with the graduate schools. These advantages do not consist in the introduction into the college of courses of graduate-school type, but in the permeation through the college community of a mature attitude toward learning. The most obvious defects of the detached college are its absorption in its own affairs, its tendency to conceive of classroom teaching as the whole duty of its faculty, and its readiness to define learning as something to be given students to 'prepare them for life.' Even a distant or occasional contact with a different type of institution, where learning is cultivated, not for the sake of adolescent learners, but for the sake of a subject to be pursued, can hardly fail to have a tonic effect on the college. It may assist in establishing there a conception of learning as a way of life that some men instinctively prefer to all other careers, and thereby enable the college to give its students the greatest of all educational experiences, that of association with older minds moving steadily in their own orbits.

IV

The Folger Shakespeare Library is already a property of no in-considerable value. Its building will soon be one of the sights of the national capital; its book collection is obviously destined to become a Mecca for scholars, and its museum and theatre instru-ments of public instruction. But there is one more question to be asked. Can an institution so dedicated, and supported by the most munificent bequest ever made for the purpose of literary study and progress, be directed to the encouragement of contemporary letters as well as to the stimulation of research and criticism? Can it serve to make evident that the spirit of Shakespeare is continued down to our own day by the work of original writers no less than by the activities of actors, editors, and commentators?

We are dealing now with a conception for which there is no precedent, with an ideal that may be realized more through sub-tleties of emphasis and the spirit in which things are done than through any specific acts. It would be easy to cut off a Shakespeare memorial from the living current of literature, to close the circuit and consider it a monument to what has been rather than to what may be again. When books become precious possessions, it is pos-sible for the curators to forget that the values they are guarding are not implicit in the volumes as physical objects, that to preserve paper and bindings is not all that is required in treasuring up the life-blood of a master spirit.

If it is hard to go beyond the idea of a Shakespeare library as a repository of priceless possessions, it is even more difficult to avoid making it the preserve of an unmellowed, fiercely special-ized scholarship which views literature merely as an excuse for historical fact finding, textual emendation, and critical footnotes. All these things should, of course, be done, but with a sense that they are not more than preliminaries and appendages to literary study, that the task of scientific investigation is always secondary to the work of original creation. An institution founded for the promotion and diffusion of knowledge in regard to Shakespeare, and with the line 'For wisedomes sake, a word that all men love' written upon its frieze, should not be unmindful of the noble aims of scholarship as defined for the Elizabethan age by Sidney: 'This purifying of wit, this enriching of memory, enabling of judgment, and enlarging of conceit, which commonly we call learning, under what name soever it come forth, or to what end soever it be directed, the final end is to lead and draw us to as high a perfection as our degenerate souls, made worse by their clayey lodging, can be capable of.' The clarification of judgment and direction of sympathies which supreme poetry effects should not be lost sight of in a concern for remedying the defects of Elizabethan printing. It was through Emerson that Mr. Folger learned to honor Shakespeare above all other writers, and no words of Emerson's could more suitably be inscribed in the paradise of 'the restorers of readings, the emendators, the bibliomaniacs of all degrees' than his saying, 'Shakespeare was not made by the study of Shakespeare.'

One who loves books according to the letter may readily retort: 'True, but since by no conceivable alchemy can I be made like Shakespeare, I take it that the work I am fitted to do is other than his. My purpose is to discover what the poet actually wrote and what his words mean. I command the texts and firmly believe that I can tell what lines he set down, and how they were probably punctuated, better than he could do himself if he were here to-day and had to trust his memory. This library provides me with the tools appropriate to my trade; just as the scientist belongs in the laboratory, so I belong here.'

The research scholar has his rights, even when he puts them low, and there is no danger that the importance of his work will not be appreciated at the Folger Library. The danger is rather that the business of technical scholarship will be overdone and the claims of contemporary letters ignored. But in a large sense the writer of imaginative literature is the true inheritor of the Shakespearean tradition, while the textual and critical student is perpetuating the tradition of Scaliger. It would not be inappropriate if recent poetry, discriminatingly chosen, were sometimes read in the Folger Theatre and thus given the prestige of association with Shakespeare's memory.

We are inheritors both of what Shakespeare accomplished and

of what he left undone. In the long gallery of his characters, beside those whose names and natures are as familiar to us as our closest friends', are figures that he merely touched upon in passing, whose names are mentioned but who never appear bodily upon his scene: that fellow of infinite jest and merriment whose bones lie in the graveyard at Elsinore; the Lady Rosaline who so keenly discerned the shallowness of Romeo's infatuation for her; Kate, the tough girl of the rollicking catch, who would n't love a sailor; old Double, who drew a good bow, as Justice Shallow tells us, until time drew a better against him; Mariana's brother Frederick, the great soldier who miscarried at sea; the maid called Barbara from whom Desdemona learned her 'willow' song; and

> Stephen Sly, and old John Naps of Greece,
> And Peter Turph, and Henry Pimpernell.

We know what insights into the paradox of life the poet revealed through his Hamlet, Lear, Falstaff, Brutus, Prospero; but what he might have added through these whose faces flicker for but a moment in the lucid mirror of his mind, whose stories are hinted but untold, is forever lost to us save as poetry recovers it. To forward the work of imagination in interpreting human nature from age to age would be the worthiest function of a Shakespeare memorial. If that can be done, the Folger Library may come to be a kind of embassy to the people of the United States from the 'realms of gold' where others besides Shakespeare have traveled.

(1931)

Joseph Quincy Adams

(1881–1946)

Shakespeare and American Culture

John Quincy Adams Jr., a leading Shakespeare scholar (and no relation to the American presidents who had written about Shakespeare), served as the first director of research at the Folger Shakespeare Library. He delivered this inaugural lecture on the day that the building was officially opened on April 23, 1932, and chose to speak about "Shakespeare and American Culture." According to the *Washington Post*, it was "as distinguished an audience as ever has gathered in Washington for any cultural event," and included President and Mrs. Hoover, ambassadors, cabinet members, justices, congressmen, and leading educators. England's King George V sent a message welcoming the event "as forming another bond of friendship between our two nations." Echoing some of the arguments Henry Cabot Lodge had made about immigration in 1895 in "Shakespeare's Americanisms," Adams described what he saw as Shakespeare's decisive role in ensuring that "a homogeneous nation" retained a culture "that is still essentially English." When "America seemed destined to become a babel of tongues and cultures," Adams argued, the required teaching of Shakespeare's works in American classrooms helped combat "the forces of immigration" that had become "a menace to the preservation of our long-established English civilization."

IN its capital city a nation is accustomed to rear monuments to those persons who most have contributed to its well-being. And hence Washington has become a city of monuments. Varied in kind, and almost countless in number, they proclaim from every street, park and circle the affection of a grateful American people. Yet, amid them all, three memorials stand out, in size, dignity and beauty, conspicuous above the rest: the memorials to Washington, Lincoln, and Shakespeare. Do we not feel that this is right? Professor Ashley Thorndike, in an address before the

British Academy in London, recently said: "Washington, Lincoln, Shakespeare, they are the three whom Americans universally worship; and you will not find a fourth, of ours or any other nation to add to this trinity." The assertion is true. And in keeping with that truth, to the members of this trinity there stand in our capital city imposing memorials that are not only superior in magnitude, but are, each in its kind, supremely fitting.

The monument to Washington is a majestic granite shaft reaching into the heavens. In triumph it points to a hero, forever enshrined in history among those who have gloriously achieved for their country. And, as it leaps upward from earth, it seems to become, in visible representation, a mighty paean of praise continually rising from the hearts of a people to whom he gave freedom and national existence. The monument to Lincoln, in contrast, is a quiet marble shrine. Like the Greek temples of old, which it copies in form, it encloses the statue of, as it were, a god—the god, indeed, of our idolatry. There, hushed in awe, we venerate the simple man who walked among us in charity, and who, after a martyr's death, lives as an inspiration to the higher life of our people. The monument to Shakespeare is equally appropriate, a noble library, housed in a building as lovely as a poem itself. Here are stored the priceless treasures of the master's works, and here are to come the men and women of our land to study anew his thoughts and his matchless art, and then to go out to quicken abroad the influence of his keen and gentle mind.

The three monuments thus stand as memorials, and as symbols, of the three great personal forces that have molded the political, the spiritual, and the intellectual life of our nation.

Washington and Lincoln are indisputably Americans; no one could ever think of them as otherwise. We produced them. Nor, I venture to assert, is our claim to Shakespeare, though divided, less strong. Before the British colonists left their ancestral home in England they had already done their share to bring forth this poet-seer—the culminating genius of their race. Subsequently they shifted the place of their residence, but not to a foreign country. Was not Elizabeth, in the words of the poet Spenser, "Queen of Virginia?" Did not Sir Walter Raleigh, another poet, proudly style himself "Lord of Virginia?" They were, then, in a certain sense, Americans; and so was Shakespeare; so was every Elizabethan, for all, from the Virgin Queen herself in Whitehall to the humblest apprentice in the Strand, had a proprietary interest in that new portion of their empire beyond the sea where the red cross flag had boldly been planted. The deep personal concern which every Elizabethan felt in America was eloquently expressed by Shakespeare's Warwickshire friend and fellow-poet, Michael Drayton, in his "Ode to the Virginia Voyage":

> You brave, heroic minds,
> Worthy your country's name,
>   That honour still pursue,
>   Go, and subdue,
> Whilst loit'ring hinds
> Lurke here at home with shame.
> Britons, you stay too long!
> Quickly aboard bestow you!
>   And with a merry gale,
>   Swell your stretch'd sail
> With vows as strong
> As the winds that blow you.

And what were the vows that, in the hopes of all patriotic Elizabethans, were to swell the sails of those early voyagers? Drayton tells us: vows to keep this half of the New World English—forever "ours to hold, Virginia."

Thus urged by their far-seeing poets and statesmen, who were dreaming dreams of a mighty empire of British civilization and ideals in the north to offset the mighty empire of Spanish civilization and deals in the south, the voyagers came. They established a newer England beyond the sea. And with them they brought the language and the culture which after centuries of effort they had helped to produce. Shakespeare, as the finest flower of that language and culture, was their birthright. Nothing could rob them of him. And being theirs, he is ours, is of us, their descendants.

We may claim him with as much justice as do the modern descendants of those Elizabethans who, in the words of Drayton, lurked at home. It is not without profound significance that year after year Englishmen and Americans, as members of one family, journey in devout pilgrimage to the same humble birthplace on the quiet Avon; nor is it without significance that on this hallowed day of April, in the far twentieth century, Englishmen are assembling at Stratford and Americans at Washington to dedicate national memorials to the same poet. Do not these things mean that Shakespeare is the common possession of both branches of the Anglo-Saxon race?

But I will not labor a point that needs no stressing. Rather, I desire to show the influence which Shakespeare has exerted upon American life, and the importance of that influence in preserving English culture among a people who now occupy a domain vaster than the Elizabethans dreamed of. And, in order to make the story clear, I shall deal successively with the three periods in our history which, it seems to me, have exercised a determining force in molding our civilization: first, the period of the British settlement of the colonies, when the foundations of our racial stock and of our American culture were laid; secondly, the period of territorial expansion, when frontier conditions came to modify the character of our nation as a whole; and thirdly, the period of foreign immigration, when the ethnic texture of our population was seriously altered. And I shall try to show that in all three periods Shakespeare played no small part in fulfilling the patriotic wish of the Elizabethans, "ours to hold, Virginia"—not, to be sure, in political bonds, but, what is more important, in bonds of a common Anglo-Saxon culture.

Those British voyagers who originally came to the shores of America needed to have, as Drayton declared, "brave, heroic minds," for they faced almost superhuman difficulties before they could establish in the New World something like the social order of their native land. Their energies at first were necessarily expended in mere physical effort—in driving back hostile savages, in felling primeval forests, in building homes, in persuading a stubborn soil to yield crops, in bridging streams, in hewing roads through the wilderness, in initiating trade, and, in general, in making life for the white man possible on a wild and totally uncivilized continent. They had little time for intellectual activity, and what little time they had they devoted—such was their nature—to religion and theology. We commonly think of the early colonists as lustily wielding the axe on six days, and then on the seventh walking solemnly to church with a musket on the shoulder and a Bible under the arm.

Yet this period of hardships was transitory, a necessary preparation for better things. It was inevitable that in the course of years, as the task of subduing nature eased, as increasing wealth brought material comfort and leisure, and as a growing commerce established ever closer contact with the home land, a cultivation of the liberal arts should emerge. Schools arose by the side of churches; colleges and universities were founded—Harvard in 1638, William and Mary in 1693, Yale in 1701, Princeton in 1746, to mention the earliest; and, before 1750, beginning with a Boston Library established in 1656, more than a score of public subscription libraries were opened along the seacoast all the way from Georgia to Maine. At last that love for the literature of the imagination, a love inherited from the golden age of Elizabeth, could assert itself; and shortly there spread throughout the colonies a reading of books other than the Bible, the almanac, and treatises on theology and law.

In the field of "belles-lettres" the taste of the provinces, as might be expected, was largely determined by that then prevailing in the mother country. In England, Shakespeare, who long had been praised by the higher critics as a "natural" though not a "correct" or "artful" poet, was at the beginning of the eighteenth century gradually being elevated in popular esteem to the lofty eminence he since has enjoyed; and this enthronement of the dramatist as the "King of Poets" naturally found an echo across the Atlantic. In Massachusetts we discover—not, perhaps, without surprise—no other person than the austere minister of God, the Reverend Cotton Mather, purchasing a copy of the precious First

Folio. In Virginia, somewhat later, another Folio, we learn, was in the beautiful Westover mansion of Colonel William Byrd. These facts show that the works of Shakespeare, though they did not, with the Bible, cross on the Mayflower, soon followed; and that the poet, hospitably received in the Western home of his countrymen, was already beginning his gentle sway over puritans and cavaliers alike.

How many copies of his plays made their way into the colonies before the close of the seventeenth century we can only guess; but they could not have been numerous. Even in England copies were far from common. It was not until 1709 that a practical set of his works, other than the rare and ponderous folios, was rendered available to general readers, when Rowe published his handy octavo edition in six volumes. That edition, we know, was at once imported for sale in America. In Massachusetts we find a set in the Harvard University Library, and in Virginia, a set in the home of the Washington family. Other editions, issued now in quick succession as the poet's fame rapidly mounted—in 1714, 1723, 1725, 1726, 1728, 1731, 1733, 1734, 1735, etc.—followed to take their place on American bookstalls. As a result, by the middle of the century Shakespeare's plays were available to readers in almost every library of importance, public or private, from Charleston to Boston. Benjamin Franklin was able to read them as a youth. George Washington could find them in his early home at Wakefield; and a volume from his set at Mount Vernon is now in the Folger collection. Thomas Jefferson, at Monticello, acquired the rarest of all Shakespearean items, a complete copy of the 1619 issue of the quartos. That copy, which he presented to the University of Virginia, was early destroyed by fire; the only other copy known is today ranked among the most treasured possessions of the Folger Library. So fast, indeed, did the reading of Shakespeare grow, that before the close of the century there was evoked a handsome American edition of his works in eight volumes.

Yet the mere reading of Shakespeare's dramas as literature left much to be desired; for, as his friend Marston reminds us, "the life of these things consists in action." Neither a full appreciation of his genius, nor a full exercise of his influence, was possible without the public representation of his plays. Fortunately the establishment of the American theatre was not long to be delayed, though almost everywhere opposed by puritanical sentiment. Both religious and political leaders were likely to raise some objection to sporadic performances by amateurs or semi-amateurs in university halls or private rooms; they were sure to raise strong objection to regular performances by professional troupes in buildings converted into theatres—"temples of Satan," as they called them. Yet two factors aided in the ultimate institution of the American stage: in the first place, the people at large, not always careful of their souls, were eager to have the monotony of their provincial lives broken by dramatic amusements; in the second place, the most straitlaced authorities were forced to admit that Shakespeare represented literary art in its highest form. Accordingly, in response to public demand, theatrical entertainments of a professional nature were finally introduced into the colonies; and the venturesome actors, when threatened by puritan forces, sought protection under the aegis of the divine bard.

Let us observe the beginnings. Late in 1749 a professional troupe attempted to act in Philadelphia, but its members were promptly arrested and their performances suppressed. Whereupon they transferred their effort to the city of New York. The "Weekly Post-Boy" of February 26, 1750, carried to its readers the interesting news that this "company of comedians," recently arrived, had "taken a convenient room for their purpose, in one of the buildings lately belonging to the Honorable Rip Van Dam, . . . in Nassau Street, where they intend to perform as long as the season lasts." The more god-fearing citizens were greatly disturbed by this foray of the Devil in their midst; and Massachusetts, taking alarm, as already had Philadelphia, at once passed "An Act to Prevent Plays." Nevertheless, on March 5, the actors distributed play-bills at the doors of every home in the city, running as follows: "By his Excellency's permission, at the Theatre in Nassau Street . . . will be presented the historical tragedy of King Richard III, wrote originally by Shakespeare." And so, amid rumblings of hostility, Shakespeare made his first recorded bow on the American stage. Apparently he was not denied appreciative audiences, for in 1751 a second troupe, described as "a new company of comedians," opened the little Nassau Street theatre with "Othello," which soon was followed by "Richard III." Plays by Shakespeare, of course, did not constitute all or even a majority of the attractions presented by these early actors; in a town so small as New York—with fewer than 10,000 inhabitants—a variety of shows was necessary to entertain a limited public, and numerous works by lesser dramatists then popular in London were offered to theatregoers. But the name "Shakespeare" lent respectability, if not dignity, to the struggling troupes, and served as a protecting shield against the slings and arrows of outraged morality.

Before another year had passed, the professional actors, in their endeavor to establish the drama in America, were ably reinforced. In 1752 an English troupe, headed by Lewis and Beatrice Hallam, with Rigby and Malone, all well-known on the boards of London, came to tour the colonies. Landing at Williamsburg, the capital of Virginia, they opened their American venture with a Shakespearean performance, selecting for the purpose "The Merchant of Venice." And, in explanation of their crossing the sea, they devised a special Prologue in which they represented Thespis as having called in clarion tones to British actors:

> "Haste to Virginia's plains, my sons! Repair!"
> The Goddess said, "Go, confident to find
> An audience sensible, polite, and kind."

After performing for some months in the South, the English actors traveled to New York, where, however, they met such serious opposition that they were forced to address an open letter to the public. "We little imagined," they declare, that "in a city so polite as this the Muses would be banish'd, the works of the immortal Shakespeare, and other of the greatest geniuses England ever produc'd, deny'd admittance among them." The shrewd appeal to "the immortal Shakespeare," we may suspect, did them yeoman's service; at any rate, they were shortly permitted to open the little improvised theatre in Nassau Street, where, among other plays, they presented "King Lear," "Romeo and Juliet," and "Richard III," with general applause. So appreciative, indeed, did these English professionals find audiences, both North and South, that they made America their home; and during the next twenty years they toured the chief towns of the Atlantic seaboard, giving, in their varied repertory, "Hamlet," "Macbeth," "Romeo and Juliet," "King John," "Henry IV," "The Taming of the Shrew," "The Merchant of Venice," "Richard III," "Cymbeline," "Othello," "The Tempest," and "King Lear."

Soon other companies, budding from this English troupe, or entirely recruited from native talent, arose in response to the growing demand for dramatic entertainment, and plays, good or bad, were presented even in the remoter villages and hamlets. The strollers at first encountered much puritanical opposition; yet in the fame of Shakespeare, whom they were fond of crying up as "the immortal," "the divine," they could usually find protection. Thus, for instance, when in Newport, Rhode Island, some hostility to their coming arose, the actors promptly announced a performance of the poet's great tragedy, "Othello," which they advertised as: "A series of moral dialogues, in five parts, depicting the evil effects of jealousy and other bad passions, and proving that happiness can only spring from VIRTUE." Again, when the famous John Street Theatre, the first permanent home of the drama in New York City, was erected in spite of howls of protest, the actors presented during the first season no fewer than ten different plays by Shakespeare, including "King Lear," "Othello," "Hamlet," "Macbeth," "Romeo and Juliet" among the tragedies, "The Merchant of Venice," "The Taming of the Shrew" among the comedies, "Henry IV" among the histories, and "Cymbeline" and "The Tempest" among the romances. What more could be asked for by a polite and cultivated community?

Thus Shakespeare played his part in the New World in helping to establish the drama on a firm foundation; and from the very beginning he took his seat upon the throne of the American stage, a position from which he has since ruled our theatres, inspired our actors, and exercised upon our public an influence for that which is good in taste, in manners, and in art.

I have dwelt at some length on the colonial period of our history, for then were laid the bases of our national culture; and one of the main stones upon which that culture has since been reared was the clear recognition and appreciation of Shakespeare's greatness.

So far, obviously, the colonists had been attempting merely to transplant from overseas the civilization of their former home. But there came a time, near the close of the eighteenth century, when, with intense bitterness of feeling, they severed the ties that held them to England, and constituted themselves into an independent nation. From now on, as Americans, they were to pursue their own way in the spacious New World, relatively free from European influences, and to develop in accordance with forces originating from within.

Those forces drove them at once into an astonishing era of territorial expansion. Men, dissatisfied for one reason or another with society as existing in the original state hugging the Atlantic seaboard, moved in steady stream across the mountains into the wilderness that lay beyond. With their wives and children they pushed ever westward, over the Appalachian range, over the river-valleys, over the prairies, and, finally, over the Rocky Mountain range even to the shore of a new ocean. But, as these restless spirits marched toward the setting sun, they left behind them settlements. Villages, towns, cities sprang up in their wake; social life was organized; and behind the constantly retreating frontier the task of creating a civilization was undertaken.

To a certain extent the earlier history of the colonies was now repeated. In the covered wagon of the pioneers, as in the Mayflower of the Pilgrims, the Bible had traveled westward; and promptly churches were everywhere erected to minister to the religious and social needs of the people. Later, in the more favored regions, as population increased, wealth and leisure emerged, and society became self-conscious, a desire for the finer things of life began to asset itself, and the effort was made to import the culture of the older and more opulent East. This could most readily be done through the cultivation of letters; and the spirit of Shakespeare, acknowledged by all as the greatest of poets, was invoked. In the towns and cities along the Ohio and Mississippi, and then further west, wherever civilization took root, we find him exerting his potent influence.

Copies of his works were purchased and set in homes by the side of the family Bible; children studied him at school; men and women read him in the evenings by the light of the open fire; itinerant elocutionists gave recitals from his more famous plays; traveling troupes of actors, seedy in worn costumes, yet trailing the glory of the Eastern theatre, came to present the ever-popular "Hamlet," "Othello," and "Richard III"; public lecturers, flaunting the weeds of scholarship, delivered orations on his mind and art; preachers quoted him in their sermons, lawyers and politicians in their speeches; even manufacturers of patent medicines, of which there seemed to be no end, issued what they called "Shakespearean Almanacs," adorned with elegant extracts from his works.

Thus Shakespeare, bearing the sceptre of cultivation, moved in the dusty trail of the pioneers, and thus the elements of British culture were preserved in the hearts of a far-flung people who in race were still essentially English. However shallow in places that culture might be, as shallow it inevitably was in a frontier life, it retained, like gold beaten to airy thinness, its original virtue; and from ocean to ocean it served to give to American civilization something like homogeneity.

I am not, I believe, overemphasizing the influence of Shakespeare in America during this awkward—we might say adolescent—period of growth. The truth is, one of the astonishing manifestations of our intellectual life at this time was the rise in the first half of the nineteenth century of what has been fitly called "Shakespeare idolatry." Among the middle as well as the higher classes, admiration for the poet grew into a passionate worship, a worship which in its universality and extravagance has had no counterpart in England or any other country. How are we to explain this remarkable phenomenon? The sheer excellence of Shakespeare as an artist cannot be regarded as adequate to account for the veneration accorded him by the very rank and file of a not over-cultivated folk; another reason must be sought, more tangible in kind, and springing from some fundamental characteristic of the people as a whole.

Perhaps we shall find that reason issuing from the most potent and universal trait of Americans of the nineteenth century, namely, that they were deeply religious, and, further, intensely puritanical in their outlook upon life. The dominating sects—Congregationalists, Baptists, Presbyterians, Methodists, and the like—all held, in accordance with puritanism from which they were derived, that secular amusements, as theatergoing, card-playing, the reading of novels, dancing and similar frivolities, interfered with one's spiritual progress. Accordingly, worldly pleasures were frowned upon, and a release of the aesthetic emotions, when such did not relate to righteousness, was curbed. The free expression of man's nature was "cabin'd, cribb'd, bound in" by a narrow conception of the Kingdom of Heaven. Americans had originally sought in the New World the opportunity to establish a religion according to their own ideals; in this they had succeeded. And with that religion they were entirely satisfied; confident, indeed, that in their spiritual culture they were superior to the nations of Europe. Yet these same Americans realized that in their secular culture they were deficient, that their provincial civilization lacked elements of beauty which in the Old World made for a richer and more fruitful existence. Possessed thus with a sense of inferiority, they were pathetically eager to acquire some part of the refinement which cast a glamor over life in countries beyond the Atlantic.

For this refinement naturally they looked to England; and naturally they first turned to literature. In England Shakespeare, at the beginning of the nineteenth century, under the influence of Coleridge, Lamb, Hazlitt, and other romanticists, had entered upon an era of super-idolatry. With unbounded enthusiasm he was being acclaimed as the greatest genius produced by the human race, the wisest and noblest of all who had thought and had left an artistic record of their thought. Americans promptly seized upon him. If they could not have many heroes of letters, at least they could have the best. They made him the very symbol of culture. As such, he stood apart, clothed with a special virtue; and the reading of his plays was freed from the ban normally set upon the pleasures of Vanity Fair. To study him became a duty. And, starved as Americans were in their intellectual and aesthetic natures, they were overcome by the richness and beauty of his offerings. In his poetry they found art in its loveliest aspects. In his exposition of men and deeds they found a wisdom so profound, yet clear, that their minds were stimulated to a fresh and grateful activity. In the brave world that he flashed before their eyes they found a courtly display of life, a refinement of taste, and a politeness of manners that gave them a new conception of courtesy and of disciplined character. Finally, in his revelation of the essential beauty and truth that lie at the heart of all things, they found a lofty moral philosophy that harmonized with their deeply religious instincts. Emerson merely expressed the opinion of his fellows when in 1844 he wrote:

"What point of morals, of manners, of economy, of philosophy, of religion, of taste, of the conduct of life, has he not settled? What mystery has he not signified his knowledge of? What office or function, or district of man's work, has he not remembered? What king has he not taught state? What maiden has not found him finer than her delicacy? What lover has he not outloved? What sage has he not outseen? What gentleman has he not instructed in the rudeness of his behavior?"

Believing thus, it is not surprising that Americans, learned and lay, North, South, and West began to give to the Sweet Swan of Avon a place of eminence with the Holy Scriptures themselves, holding the one to be supreme in the field of spiritual, the other in the field of secular culture. "Shakespeare and the Bible"—so the common phrase ran, linking the two in a superlative evaluation; and no man was regarded as complete who failed to know both.

How important this idolatry of Shakespeare was for preserving in America a homogeneity of English culture when our territory was being rapidly expanded, and our civilization stretched across a wilderness almost to the breaking point, I have already noted. Even greater was its importance when foreign immigration, in floodgate fashion, poured into our land to threaten the continued existence of that homogeneity.

The first great wave of immigration came about the middle of the nineteenth century. In the rich river-valleys of the Mississippi and the Ohio, men were needed to develop the resources of a virgin soil; and to the beckoning of opportunity aliens came, by thousands and hundreds of thousands, mainly from Germany, Norway, Sweden, and other north-European countries. They labored hard, readily acquired a competence, and multiplied with astonishing rapidity. Though honest, thrifty, and altogether admirable as citizens, they began in the big Middle West seriously to alter the solid Anglo-Saxon character of the people. A little later, after the Civil War, and with the beginning of the great era of industrialism, there swept in a second wave of immigration, vaster in scope, and far more threatening in kind. Factories, mines, railroads, lumber-camps, all phases of American industrial activity, needed laborers. On every ship they came, by millions now, instead of thousands, and not only Germans and Scandinavians, but Italians, Poles, Slavs, Hungarians, Czechs, Greeks, Lithuanians, Rumanians, Armenians—from almost every clime under the sun. They swarmed into the land like the locust in Egypt; and everywhere, in an alarming way, they tended to keep to themselves, in the larger cities, in mining towns, in manufacturing centres, where they maintained their group solidarity. Foreign in their background and alien in their outlook upon life, they exhibited varied racial characteristics, varied ideals, and varied types of civilization. America seemed destined to become a babel of tongues and cultures.

Fortunately, about the time the forces of immigration became a menace to the preservation of our long-established English civilization, there was initiated throughout the country a system of free and compulsory education for youth. In a spirit of efficiency, that education was made stereotyped in form; and in a spirit of democracy, every child was forced by law to submit to its discipline. The discipline devised was not, perhaps, ideal; but it was virtually the same in every state and territory, and had the merit of giving one training to the heterogeneous population which now filled our land. As a result, whatever the racial antecedents, out of the portals of the schools emerged, in the second or third generation, a homogeneous people, speaking the same language, inspired by the same ideals, exemplifying the same culture. Indeed, to the European mind, Americans possess a likeness that borders on fatal monotony; they dress alike, behave alike, speak alike, think alike, throughout the length and breadth of our vast territory. Yet, I venture to believe, that sameness, if it constitutes our weakness, constitutes also our strength; and it was achieved, in the face of adverse conditions, by the simple but effective device of giving to our children, at their most impressionable age, the stamp of a common schooling.

On the side of the humanities, that schooling concerned itself mainly with the English language and literature—a choice, of course, dictated by practical considerations; not only did the child of American parentage need to learn how to express himself with force and precision, but the child of foreign parentage needed to be taught the tongue of the country of his adoption. The so-called "dead languages," Greek and Latin, which in Europe constituted the basis of elementary training, were not entirely ignored, yet were regarded as less practical, and hence less necessary. The emphasis was all on English grammar and composition, fortified by a study of English literature.

And here Shakespeare, the object of general idolatry, was again called upon to play a part in American national life, this time on the stage of education. In our fixed plan of elementary schooling, he was made the corner-stone of cultural discipline. A study of his works was required in successive grades extending over a period of years. Elaborately annotated texts of his plays were devised, and sold in editions running into millions. Everywhere pupils were set to the task of memorizing his lines, of reciting on platforms his more eloquent passages, of composing innumerable essays on his art, his technique, his ideals of life, his conceptions of character, of presenting his plays in amateur theatricals. What American child, during the last half-century, could not repeat Portia's speech on the quality of mercy, or Mark Antony's orations over the dead body of Caesar? What boy or girl did not know the story of "Romeo and Juliet," of "As You Like It," of "King Lear?" or was not familiar with Falstaff, Macbeth, Shylock, or the melancholy Dane? To their young and receptive minds the great English dramatist was held up as the supreme thinker, artist, poet. Not Homer, nor Dante, nor Goethe, not Chaucer, nor Spenser, nor even Milton, but Shakespeare was made the chief object of their study and veneration.

This study and veneration did not stop with the grammar and high schools; it was carried into the colleges and universities, and there pursued with still more intensity. Nor did it stop with the end of formal education. Americans, who from early youth had been trained in the cult of the divine poet, when they passed into the distractions of a busy life, continued to worship at his shrine. Audiences flocked to see him on the stage. Ladies in almost every town organized literary clubs, in which they read his plays through the winter months. Men of business and of the professions founded Shakespeare Societies—as The Shakespeare Society of Philadelphia, or the Shakespeare Society of Washington—for spiritual quickening after arduous labor.

Persons of wealth developed the mania for collecting Shakespeareana, and the steady flow of Folios and Quartos across the Atlantic began, until the majority of such treasures rested in America. Exegeses on the text, the language, the verse arose, and such men as Verplanck, Hudson, White, Corson, Alden, and, above all, Furness, placed our country in the front rank of Shakespearean scholarship. The worship extended even to the contemporaries of the poet, and the whole age of Elizabeth became the object of study, reverence, and collection. We may confidently say that today Americans at large are more familiar with the dramatist than are any other people on the globe. From the grammar-school boy with shining morning face, to great captains of industry harassed by responsibilities, they are all lovers of Shakespeare. The beautiful building which we are here gathered to dedicate stands as a product of that love—most beautiful, perhaps, in that point of view.

If out of America, unwieldy in size, and commonly called the melting-pot of races, there has been evolved a homogeneous nation, with a culture that is still essentially English, we must acknowledge that in the process Shakespeare has played a major part.

Will he not, in the future, play yet another part; namely, to bind together more and more the two great branches of the Anglo-Saxon people? The tie will not be political, will not rest on treaties, which too often, when tested, prove to be scraps of paper; rather it will be spiritual. Theodore Watts Dunton, viewing the endless stream of American pilgrims—eastward flowing this time—to the poet's home in Stratford, expressed this desire on behalf of England:

> Let the breath of Avon, rich in meadow's bloom,
> Bind her to that great daughter, sever'd long—
> To near and far-off children young and strong—
> With fetters woven of Avon's flower perfume.

And Thomas Carlyle expressed a confident faith in the reality and permanence of that bond in words that may fittingly close my address:

> America is parted from us, so far as parliament could part it. Call it not fantastic, for there is much reality in it:—Here, I say, is an English King, whom no time or chance, parliament or combination of parliaments, can dethrone! This King Shakespeare, does he not shine, in crowned sovereignty, over us all, as the noblest, gentlest, yet strongest of rallying-signs; indestructible; really more valuable in that point of view than any other means or appliance whatsoever? We can fancy him as radiant aloft over all the nations

of Englishmen a thousand years hence. From Paramatta, from New York, wheresoever, under what sort of Parish-Constable so-ever, English men and women are, they will say to one another: "Yes, this Shakespeare is ours: we produced him; we speak and think by him; we are of one blood and kind with him."

(1932)

James Thurber

(1894–1961)

The Macbeth Murder Mystery

Humorist James Thurber was as celebrated for his cartoons as he was for his short fiction. He published nearly forty books in all. He became a member of the staff of *The New Yorker* in 1927 and this send-up of crime fiction (and of Shakespeare) ran in the October 2, 1937, issue. The story, set at an English hotel in the Lake District, turns on an American woman who picks up a paperback copy of *Macbeth*, mistakenly thinking it was a detective story—and who then analyzes it as a whodunit. It was reprinted in *My World—And Welcome To It* (1942) and was subsequently adapted as part of a revue, *A Thurber Carnival*, which opened on Broadway in February 1960.

"IT was a stupid mistake to make," said the American woman I had met at my hotel in the English lake country, "but it was on the counter with the other Penguin books—the little sixpenny ones, you know, with the paper covers—and I supposed of course it was a detective story. All the others were detective stories. I'd read all the others, so I bought this one without really looking at it carefully. You can imagine how mad I was when I found it was Shakespeare." I murmured something sympathetically. "I don't see why the Penguin-books people had to get out Shakespeare's plays in the same size and everything as the detective stories," went on my companion. "I think they have different-colored jackets," I said. "Well, I didn't notice that," she said. "Anyway, I got real comfy in bed that night and all ready to read a good mystery story and here I had 'The Tragedy of Macbeth'—a book for high-school students. Like 'Ivanhoe.'" "Or 'Lorna Doone,'" I said. "Exactly," said the American lady. "And I was just crazy for a good Agatha Christie, or something. Hercule Poirot is my favorite detective."

"Is he the rabbity one?" I asked. "Oh, no," said my crime-fiction expert. "He's the Belgian one. You're thinking of Mr. Pinkerton, the one that helps Inspector Bull. He's good, too."

Over her second cup of tea my companion began to tell the plot of a detective story that had fooled her completely—it seems it was the old family doctor all the time. But I cut in on her. "Tell me," I said. "Did you read 'Macbeth'?" "I *had* to read it," she said. "There wasn't a scrap of anything else to read in the whole room." "Did you like it?" I asked. "No, I did not," she said, decisively. "In the first place, I don't think for a moment that Macbeth did it." I looked at her blankly. "Did what?" I asked. "I don't think for a moment that he killed the King," she said. "I don't think the Macbeth woman was mixed up in it, either. You suspect them the most, of course, but those are the ones that are never guilty—or shouldn't be, anyway." "I'm afraid," I began, "that I—" "But don't you see?" said the American lady. "It would spoil everything if you could figure out right away who did it. Shakespeare was too smart for that. I've read that people never *have* figured out 'Hamlet,' so it isn't likely Shakespeare would have made 'Macbeth' as simple as it seems." I thought this over while I filled my pipe. "Who do you suspect?" I asked, suddenly. "Macduff," she said, promptly. "Good God!" I whispered, softly.

"Oh, Macduff did it, all right," said the murder specialist. "Hercule Poirot would have got him easily." "How did you figure it out?" I demanded. "Well," she said, "I didn't right away. At first I suspected Banquo. And then, of course, he was the second person killed. That was good right in there, that part. The person you suspect of the first murder should always be the second victim." "Is that so?" I murmured. "Oh, yes," said my informant. "They have to keep surprising you. Well, after the second murder I didn't know *who* the killer was for a while." "How about Malcolm and Donalbain, the King's sons?" I asked. "As I remember it, they fled right after the first murder. That looks suspicious." "Too suspicious," said the American lady. "Much too suspicious. When they flee, they're never guilty. You can count on that." "I believe," I said, "I'll have a brandy," and I summoned the waiter. My companion leaned toward me, her eyes bright, her teacup quivering. "Do you know who discovered Duncan's body?" she demanded. I said I was sorry, but I had forgotten. "Macduff discovers it," she said, slipping into the historical present. "Then he comes running downstairs and shouts, 'Confusion has broke open the Lord's anointed temple' and 'Sacrilegious murder has made his masterpiece' and on and on like that." The good lady tapped me on the knee. "All that stuff was *rehearsed*," she said. "You wouldn't say a lot of stuff like that, offhand, would you—if you had found a body?" She fixed me with a glittering eye. "I—" I began. "You're right!" she said. "You wouldn't! Unless you had practiced it in advance. 'My God, there's a body in here!' is what an innocent man would say." She sat back with a confident glare.

I thought for a while. "But what do you make of the Third Murderer?" I asked. "You know, the Third Murderer has puzzled 'Macbeth' scholars for three hundred years." "That's because they never thought of Macduff," said the American lady. "It was Macduff, I'm certain. You couldn't have one of the victims murdered by two ordinary thugs—the murderer always has to be somebody important." "But what about the banquet scene?" I asked, after a moment. "How do you account for Macbeth's guilty actions there, when Banquo's ghost came in and sat in his chair?" The lady leaned forward and tapped me on the knee again. "There wasn't any ghost," she said. "A big, strong man like that doesn't go around seeing ghosts—especially in a brightly lighted banquet hall with dozens of people around. Macbeth was *shielding somebody*!" "Who was he shielding?" I asked. "Mrs. Macbeth, of course," she said. "He thought she did it and he was going to take the rap himself. The husband always does that when the wife is suspected." "But what," I demanded, "about the sleep-walking scene, then?" "The same thing, only the other way around," said my companion. "That time *she* was shielding *him*. She wasn't asleep at all. Do you remember where it says, 'Enter Lady Macbeth with a taper'?" "Yes," I said. "Well, people who walk in their sleep *never carry lights*!" said my fellow-traveler. "They have a second sight. Did you ever hear of a sleepwalker carrying a light?" "No," I said, "I never did." "Well, then, she wasn't asleep. She was acting guilty to shield Macbeth." "I think," I said, "I'll have another brandy," and I called the waiter. When he brought it, I drank it rapidly and rose to go. "I believe," I said, "that you have got hold of something. Would you lend me that 'Macbeth'? I'd like to look it over tonight. I don't feel, somehow, as if I'd ever really read it." "I'll get it for you," she said. "But you'll find that I am right."

I read the play over carefully that night, and the next morning, after breakfast, I sought out the American woman. She was on the putting green, and I came up behind her silently and took her arm. She gave an exclamation. "Could I see you alone?" I asked, in a low voice. She nodded cautiously and followed me to a secluded spot. "You've found out something?" she breathed. "I've found out," I said triumphantly, "the name of the murderer!" "You mean it wasn't Macduff?" she said. "Macduff is as innocent of those murders," I said, "as Macbeth and the Macbeth woman." I opened the copy of the play, which I had with me, and turned to Act II, Scene 2. "Here," I said, "you will see where Lady Macbeth says, 'I laid their daggers ready. He could not miss 'em. Had he not resembled my father as he slept, I had done it.' Do you see?" "No," said the American woman, bluntly, "I don't." "But it's simple!" I exclaimed. "I wonder I didn't see it years ago. The reason Duncan resembled Lady Macbeth's father as he slept is that *it actually was her father*!" "Good God!" breathed my companion, softly. "Lady Macbeth's father killed the King," I said, "and, hearing someone coming, thrust the body under the bed and crawled into the bed himself." "But," said the lady, "you can't have a murderer who only appears in the story once. You can't have that." "I know that," I said, and I turned to Act II, Scene 4. "It says here, 'Enter Ross with an old Man.' Now, that old man is never identified and it is my contention he was old Mr. Macbeth, whose ambition was to make his daughter Queen. There you have your motive." "But even then," cried the American lady, "he's still a minor character!" "Not," I said, gleefully, "when you realize that he was also *one of the weird sisters in disguise*!" "You mean one of the three witches?"

"Precisely," I said. "Listen to this speech of the old man's. 'On Tuesday last, a falcon towering in her pride of place, was by a mousing owl hawk'd at and kill'd.' Who does that sound like?" "It sounds like the way the three witches talk," said my companion, reluctantly. "Precisely!" I said again. "Well," said the American woman, "maybe you're right, but—" "I'm sure I am," I said. "And do you know what I'm going to do now?" "No," she said. "What?" "Buy a copy of 'Hamlet,'" I said, "and solve *that*!" My companion's eyes brightened. "Then," she said, "you don't think Hamlet did it?" "I am," I said, "absolutely positive he didn't." "But who," she demanded, "do you suspect?" I looked at her cryptically. "Everybody," I said, and disappeared into a small grove of trees as silently as I had come.

(1937)

Sidney B. Whipple

(1888–1975)

Orson Welles's Julius Caesar

Twenty-two-year-old Orson Welles's modern-dress staging of *Julius Caesar* in 1937 at the Mercury Theatre is widely regarded as one of the defining productions of that play in its four-hundred-year history. It spoke to the moment, with Hitler on the rise and the Anti-Comintern Pact (in which the Axis powers, Germany, Italy, and Japan, formed a military alliance) signed one year before the production opened. Welles, who subtitled the play "The Death of a Dictator," cut Shakespeare's script drastically, though his focus on fascism and mob violence led him to stage in full, for the first time in America, the scene in which Cinna the Poet is attacked in the street; for Welles it was "a lynching mob, the kind of mob that gives you a Hitler or Mussolini." Welles put Brutus (whose part he took for himself) at the center of the play, and described him as a "fellow who thinks the times are out of joint but who is really out of joint with his time," one who "under a modern dictatorship, would be the first to be put up against a wall and shot." The production, with its powerful message and innovative lighting, music, and design, had a broad impact through glowing reviews, both locally and nationally. A pair of them were written by one of New York's leading drama critics, Sidney B. Whipple, who so admired this "startling" production that he twice wrote about it in the *New York World-Telegram* during the opening week of the run. In his second piece Whipple captures for posterity the powerful effect of a single scene, the death of Cinna the Poet. Schoolchildren from around the New York area were brought to performances, and for those who couldn't see it, Columbia Records sold a recording of the complete performance, mob cries and all—a first for a professional theater production in America.

❦

New *"Julius Caesar" at Mercury Theater*

ORSON WELLES and the Mercury Theater group have remade Shakespeare's "Julius Caesar," molding it into a modern tragedy of dictatorship that is one of the most interesting dramatic episodes to be seen on the New York stage today.

They have dared to throw off every past convention, to work with words and lights rather than with costumes and scenery, and yet they have kept vividly alive the spirit of the drama and have maintained intact its rugged vitality.

This performance, which had its premiere last night at the Mercury Theater (once known as the Comedy), is as different from the Shakespeare now playing at the Mansfield as day is from night. It is startling, yet absorbing. It is marked by some of the most restrained acting and some of the most effective elocution we have seen this season. We feel that William Shakespeare himself might have been astonished—but he would have felt rather pleased with it because of its sincerity.

SHOCK WHEN CURTAIN RISES.

You are apt to be shocked when the curtain rises to disclose in the dim gray light that shades rather than illuminates the blood-red brick wall at the back, a modern Caesar in the type of military uniform affected by a Mussolini or a Hitler, his head thrown back in characteristic arrogance to receive the hails of the populace. But when you have recovered from this first surprise (which is as soon as the first words are uttered) you accept the situation and continue to accept it to the end.

Mr. Welles, the Brutus of this novel presentation, gives us an honest man, an almost saintly man, a man ever fixed in principle and faithful to his conscience. The conspirators surrounding him, even to the lean and hungry ones, are made for a time to appear heroic in the light of the honesty that inspires his decision. You are never in doubt as to the purity of a movement that must encompass the assassination of the dictator.

It is almost impossible to speak too graciously about some of the acting that abounds in this play. Mr. Welles considers every speech, weighs it well and delivers it with purposeful enunciation. If at times some of the rhythm may seem to disappear because of the numerous pauses, it may be said that even his nuances are eloquent. The dispassionate tone of his utterances carries great weight.

FINE PERFORMANCE OF ANTONY.

George Coulouris, seen last season as the munitions manufacturer in "Ten Million Ghosts," is Antony. His performance borders on perfection and good taste marks his delivery of the funeral oration over Caesar's bier.

Martin Gabel's Cassius also lives and breathes. Here is a forceful Cassius dominant in a secondary part, and making wholly understandable his effective power as the prime organizer of the conspiracy.

Joseph Holland's Caesar is as arrogant and defiant as necessary, though he seems to be a symbol rather than a man. There is in it the reckless, swaggering self-confidence of dictatorship, the brutality of speech, the thunderous stride of importance.

As we have indicated, this "Julius Caesar" is in modern dress. Yet it is in costume, for the military uniforms, the Sam Browne belts, the shoulder ornaments and boots dominate the street dress worn by the minor actors and the "crowds" on the streets of Rome.

NO EMBELLISHMENT NEEDED.

No scenic embellishment exists whatsoever, and none is needed. The red brick wall at the rear forms a back drop for many of the scenes. It can be "painted" out at will by the use of lights. Frequently spot lights illuminate the speaker who holds the center of the stage and the little knot of people around him. Actors do not disappear into wings or through doors. They are merely blotted out by darkness.

Because the play has been shortened by elision of everything but essentials, the curtain rises (in the evening) at 9 o'clock, and there is no intermission. It may be said here, as a tribute to the acting, that none is needed.

The "Julius Caesar" of the Mercury Theater is a splendid

experiment by a group of serious and unusually competent actors. If you would experience a new and engrossing adventure see it by all means.

Beauties of "Caesar" Impressive

Once in a long while there comes to the New York stage a performance so inspiring that the trance which it induces persists for days, and your mind's eye reviews, again and again, those scenes which have so captured your imagination.

The "Julius Caesar" of the Mercury Theater group is such a production, and because nothing has happened since last Thursday night to turn a playgoer's thought elsewhere, an enthusiast may be pardoned for saying a few more words about it.

As is generally known by now, Orson Welles and his sturdy band of Fascist and Liberal conspirators perform the amazing feat of holding an audience in the spell of their acting for nearly two hours, without the aid of stage furniture, scenery, settings or (except for a few uniforms) costumes. They do it with three priceless ingredients—the beauty of William Shakespeare's words, the beauty of elocution, and the beauty of light.

NOT ALL IN ONE SCENE.

Now, it is to the credit of the Mercurians that all this beauty is not reserved for one scene, the scene they hope to make "tremendous." As much loving thought and direction is lavished upon the most minor episodes as upon some climax in which the individual actor has an opportunity to rise to the heights. The movement of masses on this unencumbered stage, advancing or retreating in the darkness, gliding by in the shadows or filling the black streets of Rome with the thunder of mob hysteria—all these manifestations assail your emotions as deeply as the funeral oration of Mark Antony.

The scene dealing with the tragedy of Cinna the Poet, for example, is a triumph for the direction of Mr. Welles and the playing of Norman Lloyd. Never has the ruthless and brutal terrorism of mob action been more finely pictured on the stage.

SEEN IN HALF-LIGHT.

In the half-light of the stage the slender figure of the poet is picked out against the red background of the brick wall. He is whistling a little carefree air, wandering bemused in the street. Suddenly he is confronted with a little knot of man hunters, obviously trying to mop up the conspirators and any suspects who come in their way. There are questions.

"But I am Cinna, the poet," he says, mildly, repeating over and over the words, "Cinna, the poet," and handing out his scribblings with polite bewilderment, to prove his identity.

For several moments not a hand is laid on him. He starts to move away, but out of the darkness another group of men appear to block him. He turns and turns again, and each time a new force moves in to face him.

"But I am Cinna, the poet; Cinna, the poet," he protests. The mob becomes more dense. Around him is a small ring of light, and in the shadows an ever-tightening, pincer-like mass movement. Then in one awful moment of madness the jaws of the mob come together on him and he is swallowed up and rushed into black oblivion.

A DYNAMIC SCENE.

Mr. Lloyd's gently comic bewilderment, his pathetic innocence and the crushing climax as the human juggernaut rolls down upon him make this one of the most dynamic scenes in today's theater.

Those who have seen this "Julius Caesar" are now anxious to see Thomas Dekker's "merrie-conceited comedy," "The Shoemaker's Holiday," which is promised for December. But, in all fairness to the Mercury Theater, they could not find fault with Mr. Welles and his companions if they should decide to play the present production on and on and on and on.

(1937)

Toshio Mori

(1910–1980)

Japanese Hamlet

Born in Oakland, California, in 1910, Toshio Mori is one of the earliest Japanese American writers, best known for his short stories. This poignant story, apparently written in 1939 but not published until after the war, appeared in the August 17, 1946 issue of the *Pacific Citizen* (the leading paper of the Pacific Asian American community) under the title "The School Boy Hamlet." It ran there alongside columns such as "Two-Thirds of the U. S. Citizens Believe False Reports of Espionage by U. S. Japanese." Mori spent most of the war years imprisoned in Utah at the Topaz War Relocation Center before he was allowed to return to his home in California. The story, which so powerfully explores issues of identification and exclusion, was reprinted under the title "Japanese Hamlet" in Mori's collection *The Chauvinist and Other Stories* in 1979.

❧

H E used to come to the house and ask me to hear him recite. Each time he handed me a volume of *The Complete Works of William Shakespeare*. He never forgot to do that. He wanted me to sit in front of him, open the book, and follow him as he recited his lines. I did willingly. There was little for me to do in the evenings so when Tom Fukunaga came over I was ready to help out almost any time. And as his love for Shakespeare's plays grew with the years he did not want anything else in the world but to be a Shakespearean actor.

Tom Fukunaga was a schoolboy in a Piedmont home. He had been one since his freshman days in high school. When he was thirty-one he was still a schoolboy. Nobody knew his age but he and the relatives. Every time his relatives came to the city they put up a roar and said he was a good-for-nothing loafer and ought to be ashamed of himself for being a schoolboy at this age.

"I am not loafing," he told his relatives. "I am studying very hard."

One of his uncles came often to the city to see him. He tried a number of times to persuade Tom to quit stage hopes and schoolboy attitude. "Your parents have already disowned you. Come to your senses," he said. "You should go out and earn a man's salary. You are alone now. Pretty soon even your relatives will drop you."

"That's all right," Tom Fukunaga said. He kept shaking his head until his uncle went away.

When Tom Fukunaga came over to the house he used to tell me about his parents and relatives in the country. He told me in particular about the uncle who kept coming back to warn and persuade him. Tom said he really was sorry for Uncle Bill to take the trouble to see him.

"Why don't you work for someone in the daytime and study at night?" I said to Tom.

"I cannot be bothered with such a change at this time," he said. "Besides, I get five dollars a week plus room and board. That is enough for me. If I should go out and work for someone I would have to pay for room and board besides carfare so I would not be richer. And even if I should save a little more it would not help me become a better Shakespearean actor."

When we came down to the business of recitation there was no recess. Tom Fukunaga wanted none of it. He would place a cup of water before him and never touch it. "Tonight we'll begin with Hamlet," he said many times during the years. *Hamlet* was his favorite play. When he talked about Shakespeare to anyone he began by mentioning Hamlet. He played parts in other plays but always he came back to Hamlet. This was his special role, the role which would establish him in Shakespearean history.

There were moments when I was afraid that Tom's energy and time were wasted and I helped along to waste it. We were miles away from the stage world. Tom Fukunaga had not seen a backstage. He was just as far from the stagedoor in his thirties as he was in his high school days. Sometimes as I sat holding Shakespeare's book and listening to Tom I must have looked worried and discouraged.

"Come on, come on!" he said. "Have you got the blues?"

One day I told him the truth: I was afraid we were not getting anywhere, that perhaps we were attempting the impossible. "If you could contact the stage people it might help," I said. "Otherwise we are wasting our lives."

"I don't think so," Tom said. "I am improving every day. That is what counts. Our time will come later."

That night we took up Macbeth. He went through his parts smoothly. This made him feel good. "Some day I'll be the ranking Shakespearean actor," he said.

Sometimes I told him I liked best to hear him recite the sonnets. I thought he was better with the sonnets than in the parts of Macbeth or Hamlet.

"I'd much rather hear you recite his sonnets, Tom," I said.

"Perhaps you like his sonnets best of all," he said. "Hamlet is my forte. I know I am at my best playing Hamlet."

For a year Tom Fukunaga did not miss a week coming to the house. Each time he brought a copy of Shakespeare's complete works and asked me to hear him say the lines. For better or worse he was not a bit down-hearted. He still had no contact with the stage people. He did not talk about his uncle who kept coming back urging him to quit. I found out later that his uncle did not come to see him any more.

In the meantime Tom stayed at the Piedmont home as a schoolboy. He accepted his five dollars a week just as he had done years ago when he was a freshman at Piedmont High. This fact did not bother Tom at all when I mentioned it to him. "What are you worrying for?" he said. "I know I am taking chances. I went into this with my eyes open, so don't worry."

But I could not get over worrying about Tom Fukunaga's chances. Every time he came over I felt bad for he was wasting his life and for the fact that I was mixed in it. Several times I told him to go somewhere and find a job. He laughed. He kept coming to the house and asked me to sit and hear him recite Hamlet.

The longer I came to know Tom the more I wished to see him well off in business or with a job. I got so I could not stand his coming to the house and asking me to sit while he recited. I began to dread his presence in the house as if his figure reminded me of my part in the mock play that his life was, and the prominence that my house and attention played.

One night I became desperate. "That book is destroying you, Tom. Why don't you give this up for a while?"

He looked at me curiously without a word. He recited several pages and left early that evening.

Tom did not come to the house again. I guess it got so that Tom could not stand me any more than his uncle and parents. When he quit coming I felt bad. I knew he would never abandon his ambition. I was equally sure that Tom would never rank with the great Shakespearean actors, but I could not forget his simple persistence.

One day, years later, I saw him on the Piedmont car at Fourteenth and Broadway. He was sitting with his head buried in a book and I was sure it was a copy of Shakespeare's. For a moment he looked up and stared at me as if I were a stranger. Then his face broke into a smile and he raised his hand. I waved back eagerly.

"How are you, Tom" I shouted.

He waved his hand politely again but did not get off, and the car started up Broadway.

(1939)

Langston Hughes

(1902–1967)

Shakespeare in Harlem

Langston Hughes was a leading African American playwright, novelist, and poet. Born in 1902 in Joplin, Missouri, Hughes grew up in the Midwest and traveled widely in the United States and abroad. By the time that his collection *Shakespeare in Harlem* appeared during World War II, he had relocated to Harlem and had shifted away from the radical politics that had defined much of his earlier writing. The bold title of his poem "Shakespeare in Harlem," after which the collection is named, confronts readers with some fundamental questions: is it simply a Shakespearean lyric updated and relocated to Harlem? Or should we read it primarily as an act of translation, rendered into contemporary language, inflected by the rhythms of jazz and the blues, of the kind of Shakespeare verse we find in *As You Like It* ("It was a lover and his lass, / With a hey, and a ho, and a hey nonino")? Or does its title suggest that whatever it is that Shakespeare represents, Harlem has its own indigenous version of it—forcing us to look a little harder at what we mean by both "Shakespeare" and "Harlem"? A short, lyrical play by Hughes, also called "Shakespeare in Harlem," and which also riffs on *As You Like It* (taking as its frame the famous speech about the Seven Ages of Man but turning it into "a man's blues have seven ages") was staged in New York in 1960.

❧

Hey ninny neigh!
And a hey nonny noe!
Where, oh, where
Did my sweet mama go?

Hey ninny neigh
With a tra-la-la-la!
They say your sweet mama
Went home to her ma.

(1942)

Samuel Sillen

(1910–1973)

Paul Robeson's Othello

October 19, 1943—the night Paul Robeson became the first black actor to play *Othello* on Broadway—was widely recognized not only as a landmark event for the American stage but also as one in American race relations. W.E.B. Du Bois wondered in an editorial if a white actor would ever play Shakespeare's Moor again. Critical praise was near universal and the production ran for a record-breaking 296 performances on Broadway. Its director, Margaret Webster, played Emilia, Uta Hagen was Desdemona, and a Puerto Rican actor, José Ferrer, was Iago. The integration onstage was mirrored in the audiences. At a time when separate seating for blacks and whites was still the norm in many northern cities as well as throughout the South, Robeson contractually stipulated that during the national tour (which ran from September 1944 to April 1945) he would refuse to perform in any segregated theater. In playing Othello, Robeson was deeply aware of his link to his great predecessor, Ira Aldridge. Years earlier, Robeson had taken voice lessons from Aldridge's daughter, Amanda, and she had given him the gold earrings her father had worn as Othello. Robeson had long been a political activist, and FBI informants reported that he was making political appearances while performing *Othello* on tour. His political advocacy endeared him to those on the left, including Samuel Sillen, a prominent figure in the Communist literary movement of the 1930s and 1940s, who reviewed *Othello* effusively for *The New Masses*—an influential magazine of the cultural left that ran from 1926 to 1948 and published such writers as Richard Wright, Dorothy Parker, John Dos Passos, Ralph Ellison, and Ernest Hemingway. Sillen, who had a doctorate in English literature, was as attuned to what was fresh interpretively about the production (with its emphasis on race rather than sexual jealousy) as he was to the extent to which the production resonated with its cultural moment.

∞

PAUL ROBESON's Othello is indescribably magnificent. He is the authentic Moor of Shakespeare's towering vision, a colossus among men, a figure of epic grandeur and of transcendent nobility and force. In his bearing, his tone, his look, Robeson invests the character with incomparable tragic dignity. He bursts through the petty dimensions of the contemporary stage, exalting the imagination, sending a profound shock of discovery through the mind. He involves us in the coils of human suffering. He reanimates a great tradition of significant and resonant speech. No artist in our lifetime has so triumphantly gripped us and torn us and raised us to the uttermost peak of awareness and compassion.

It is more than a personal triumph, it is a historic triumph that we have been privileged to witness. The deeply shaken audience that could not stop cheering the greatest people's artist of America was at the same time proclaiming an epochal event in the history of our culture. For the first time on the professional stage in America we have seen a Negro Othello. The theater that in the last century exiled Ira Aldridge has at last embraced Aldridge's successor. Shakespeare wrote about a black man, and the dramatic crux of the play is incomprehensible unless we recognize that Othello is different in color and cultural conditioning from the Venetians whose army he leads. Yet the oppressive hand of bigotry has forcibly kept black men from playing the role. October 19, 1943, is an emancipation date for the American theater. With almost unqualified unanimity and enthusiasm the critics declare that Robeson's Othello has been unsurpassed in their experience. Not only are we seeing our first Negro Othello, but perhaps our greatest Othello.

Let us not fail to note the circumstances that surround this great event. It takes place near the end of our second year of war against a national enemy who commits his savageries under the banner of racial superiority. It takes place at a time when in our own country schoolhouses are being closed to colored children. But the people are beginning to raise their own banners. Robeson's Othello is a glorious standard raised by democratic America in defiance of Nazism, just as it is a shattering rebuke, a creative challenge to Jim-Crow, the helpmate of Nazism in this land. If the glad tidings were relayed by the OWI to Asia, Africa, and the other continents, they would evoke more joy and confidence than libraries of abstractions. In the bleak hamlet of a poll-tax state the news rekindles aspiration. Among our thoughtful troops at the front it stimulates a new sense of fraternity. For this event, the fruit of long struggle, is an assertion that victory is no longer beyond men's sight. It foreshadows the more civilized future.

Of all Shakespeare's plays, *Othello* has been most abused by later interpreters, whether on the stage or in the study. It is therefore most fortunate that this production has been conceived and directed by the most intelligent Shakespearean student of our theater, Margaret Webster. She has repudiated the timidities and distortions that have muffled the essential meaning of the play. In her version she has brilliantly illustrated the ideas treated in her recent volume *Shakespeare Without Tears*. She has utilized all the resources of Shakespearean scholarship at the same time that she has directed her appeal to the living audience in the theater today. Miss Webster's somewhat condensed two-act version is authoritative without being pedantic, and it is excellent theater without resorting to frivolous tampering for the sake of trivial effects. The production has great integrity. It is dominated by an idea, and it achieves a sense of dedication to an idea.

This idea has nothing in common with the conventional and utterly erroneous idea that *Othello* is primarily a play of sexual jealousy. The fact is that Othello is by nature the least jealous of men. To him it is quite incredible that one should "follow still the changes of the moon with fresh suspicions." He is generous, magnanimous. He is easy prey for "honest" Iago, for his is a trusting nature which cannot easily ascribe to others the ignoble sentiments which he has not himself experienced. He resists Iago's insinuations of Desdemona's infidelity until, as it seems to him, clear proof has been produced. And when he is convinced, he does not nurse any emotion resembling jealousy. For critics to quote Shakespeare's alleged views on the green-eyed monster jealousy is like the schoolmaster's question in Joyce's *Ulysses* to the effect that Shakespeare said "Put money in thy purse." In both instances it is not Shakespeare talking but the least scrupulous villain in all literature, Iago.

Othello's torment is rather that of a man who, far from doubting, has great faith in those he loves. He suffers the shock of a profound disillusionment. Chaos is indeed come again when the woman who alone could persuade him to give up his "unhoused free condition," the woman whose love had become the meaning of his whole life proves unfaithful. It is of course a terrible irony that he, who could smother a life that was dearer than his own, acted under the illusion of deceit—an illusion shrewdly manufactured by the shrewdest of deceivers. His soul and body had been ensnared. Even at the very end he finds the perfidy of "that demi-devil" scarcely comprehensible, and before dying he cannot resist asking "Why?"

What Iago appeals to in Othello is not so much sexual jealousy as his consciousness of difference in color. Othello had known the true worth of a Desdemona who was willing to "trumpet to the world" her love for the black man. Desdemona had seen "Othello's visage in his mind." Her heart had become subdued even to the very quality of the man she had married despite her father's opinion that such marriage was "Against all rules of nature." To Othello, who himself saw people's visages in their minds, Desdemona was not only "gentle" but a "warrior." His love for his wife was not due, as he insists, to appetite; he wishes only to be "free and bounteous to her mind." He loved her whole character, which was capable of breaking with the conventional conception that intermarriage marks "foul disproportion."

But there remains an element of insecurity which Iago most astutely plays upon. Iago insinuates that a white Venetian woman cannot for long be faithful to a black Moor. As Margaret Webster puts the point in *Shakespeare Without Tears*: "It is very apparent, and vital to the play, that Othello himself was very conscious of these same considerations and quiveringly aware of what the judgment of the world would be upon his marriage. It is one of the most potent factors in his acceptance of the possibility of Desdemona's infidelity. And she herself loses much in the quality of her steadfastness and courage if it be supposed that she simply married against her father's wishes a man who chanced to be a little darker than his fellows, instead of daring a marriage which would cause universal condemnation among the ladies of polite society. To scamp this consideration in the play is to deprive Othello of his greatest weakness, Desdemona of her highest strength, Iago of his skill and judgment, Emilia of a powerful factor in her behavior both to her master and her mistress, and Venice itself of an arrogance in toleration which was one of the principal hallmarks of its civilizations—a civilization which frames first and last, the soaring emotions of the play."

In the present production this consideration is not "scamped" but placed in its right perspective and given its right emphasis. It is a play primarily of a vast human injustice. Othello's injustice to Desdemona is only a part of the great injustice which has been done to him and in which he himself has unwittingly collaborated. Iago is the evil instrument of that injustice, and it is highly significant that Iago is throughout the play a cynical and embittered hater of the black "thick lips." He must admit to himself, since this is the key to his strategy, that "The Moor is of free and open nature, that thinks men honest that but seem to be so." But recognizing for his own purposes Othello's virtues, he pours on him constantly the epithets that we associate with the poisoned minds of racists. To him Othello is an "erring barbarian," a "Barbary horse."

The treatment of Iago in the present production is excellent. He is not the cloven-hoofed villain of stage convention. When he appears with Othello, he is exasperatingly smooth, and there is little reason for the general to doubt that he is "honest." His motives require no dissertations. He hates Othello because Cassio was preferred to him in the matter of a military appointment. He is inordinately conscious of money, and he succeeds in putting Roderigo's in his own purse. He hates the nobility of the Moor as he despises his color. It is perfectly true, of course, that in a production where Iago overshadows Othello, one would feel the absence of a more detailed and profound motivation for his extravagant villainy. But this is only one of the proofs that Shakespeare did not intend Iago to steal the show from Othello, as he has done in so many inferior productions. Shakespeare's main effort is to explain Othello. The evil of Iago is more or less the given, the assumed, premise in the play; it is Othello who undergoes change, not Iago, and it is in Othello that we properly seek—and find—the basic psychological motivations of the drama.

In the conflict between Othello and Iago there is a gigantic contrast between the world of moral elevation and the world of moral nihilism. The one is devoted to principle and large purpose; for the other, a dynamo of calculating egotism, virtue is a fig. The one exalts love and duty; the other defines character as doing homage to oneself, lining one's own coat, serving one's "peculiar end." This mortal struggle of values is brilliantly defined by Robeson's Othello and Jose Ferrer as Iago.

Incapable of dissembling, the Othello we see is a man who genuinely expresses a tremendous range of human feeling. We see his powerful inward resentment when aspersions are cast on his color; the authoritative dignity with which he commands men to put up their swords; the towering indignation of his rebuke to Cassio. He has humor, as in his account of his wooing of Desdemona. Whether in a word or an embrace, his affection for Desdemona is sensitively registered. When his mind becomes racked with doubt and disillusionment, his contradictory emotions are expressed with subtle shading, yet simultaneously. He is neither the excessively restrained nor the excessively violent Othello of tradition. When he treats Desdemona as a strumpet, we see his tough exterior belied by his inner grief. There is terrific tension in the last scene when the world comes crashing down on him at the same time that he is flooded with understanding. And in all the scenes he speaks with a poetic resonance and depth of feeling that has simply never been heard before in our lifetime. Robeson does not act Othello; he is Othello.

Ferrer's Iago is a subtle and plastic performance. He is, as he should be, lithe, arrogant, cynical. He is an architect of hypocrisy, the conscious actor, even, as one feels, when he has only himself for an audience. He shrewdly communicates his delight in the success of his intrigue. We never for a moment question, as sometimes we do in reading the play, his ability to gull every character, adjusting himself to all temperaments and feeding on their weaknesses.

There are other fine performances. Margaret Webster's Emilia gives stature to that worldly but loyal and earnest companion of Desdemona. Uta Hagen's Desdemona is gentle, incorruptible, but a little too highly keyed. James Monks' Cassio projects the looseness and genial irresponsibility of Othello's lieutenant, but overplays, I think, his youthful glamour. An interesting portrayal of Roderigo by Jack Manning stresses his foppishness with humorous effects that delight the audience without jarring. Edith King is a buxom Bianca and Averell Harris an aggrieved Brabantio.

The designing and lighting by Robert Edmond Jones are appropriately simple, but they effectively suggest the dignity of the council chamber in Venice, the almost oriental splendor of Cyprus, and the tragic dimness of the bedroom scene. The Elizabethan balance between simple settings and splendid costume is properly maintained. The magnificent robes which Mr. Jones has designed for Robeson are in keeping with the great stature and gravity of the part. The use of the curtain to form an outer stage makes for speedy timing without making the modern playgoer too conscious of the artifice.

That Shakespeare was not of an age but for all time has never been demonstrated more movingly on the American stage. The combination of circumstances has been close to perfect. A great Negro artist as Othello; an English-born actor and Shakespearean student as director; a gifted artist born in Puerto Rico giving a subtle portrait as Iago—this is the very form and pressure of universality in our own day. For the masses of people in America and throughout the world who love and honor Paul Robeson there is matter for pride in this event. It has the scope and grandeur of a Shostakovich Victory Symphony. The product of years of aspiration, it comes into being in the midst of a people's war which it helps to sustain. We treasure the event. We mark it as a birthdate. We carry on from here, lifted by Paul Robeson to a height from which new and vast horizons of a creative people's culture endlessly unfold.

(1943)

James Agee

(1909–1955)

Laurence Olivier's Henry V

Poet, journalist, novelist, and screenwriter, James Agee was one of mid-century America's most gifted observers and storytellers. He was also one of its first major film critics, reviewing for both *Time* and *The Nation*. W. H. Auden, who did not care much for movies, nonetheless recognized the "permanent literary value" of Agee's film reviews, and no doubt spoke for many when he wrote of "looking forward all week to reading him again." Agee's three reviews of Olivier's *Henry V* in 1946 confirm his reputation. In the first of them, a rave in *Time*, Agee writes that Olivier succeeded at linking "the great past to the great present," having made the film "midway in England's most terrible war, within the shadows of Dunkirk." Writing nine months after the war's end, Agee went further, reminding readers (and Hollywood) that "no film of that war has yet said what they say so honestly or so well." Olivier's film spoke powerfully to Agee and he was not done with it yet, writing about it twice more, in July and August 1946, both times for *The Nation*. Agee, who had written elsewhere that movies held "the grandest prospect for a major popular art since Shakespeare's time," opts for cinema over theater: "the specific advantages of the screen are obvious, but no less important for that." Agee's archive, housed at the Harry Ransom Humanities Research Center at the University of Texas at Austin, contains his undated eleven-page outline for an adaptation of Shakespeare's *Macbeth*. It was never made. Agee died of a heart attack in a taxi in New York City in 1955, at the age of forty-five.

❧

April 8th, 1946

MASTERPIECE

THE movies have produced one of their rare great works of art.

When Laurence Olivier's magnificent screen production of Shakespeare's *Henry V* was first disclosed to a group of Oxford's

459

impassive Shakespeare pundits, there was only one murmur of dissent. A woman specialist insisted that all the war horses which take part in the Battle of Agincourt should have been stallions.

The film was given its U.S. premiére* this week (in Boston's Esquire Theater). This time, the horses engendered no complaint. At last there had been brought to the screen, with such sweetness, vigor, insight and beauty that it seemed to have been written yesterday, a play by the greatest dramatic poet who ever lived. It had never been done before.† For Laurence Olivier, 38 (who plays Henry and directed and produced the picture), the event meant new stature. For Shakespeare, it meant a new splendor in a new, vital medium. Exciting as was the artistic development of Laurence Olivier, last seen by U.S. cinemaddicts in films like *Rebecca* and *Wuthering Heights*, for his production of *Henry V* was even more exciting.

As Shakespeare wrote it, *The Chronicle History of Henry the Fifth* is an intensely masculine, simple, sanguine drama of kinghood and war. Its more eloquent theme is a young king's coming of age. Once an endearingly wild Prince of Wales, Henry V (at 28) had to prove his worthiness for the scepter by leading his army in war. He invaded France, England's longtime enemy. He captured Harfleur, then tried to withdraw his exhausted and vastly outnumbered army to Calais. The French confronted him at Agincourt. In one of Shakespeare's most stirring verbal sennets, Henry urged his soldiers on to incredible victory. English mobility (unarmored archers) and English firepower (the quick-

---

* Producer Filippo Del Giudice says the film will pay for itself in Great Britain (cost: almost $2,000,000). Paralleling Hollywood's bookkeeping on exports, he looks to the U.S. and elsewhere for profits. But United Artists, uneasy about the mass audience, is handling the film timidly. The plan: after opening in the most English and academic of U.S. cities, *Henry V* will place twice-a-day in all major cities at legit prices. Heavy play will be made for Mr. Gallup's estimated 15,000,000 who thinks most movies worthless. There will be special rates for colleges, etc. No date has been set for general release.

† *A Midsummer Night's Dream* and *Romeo and Juliet*, the two bravest attempts, were neither good cinema nor good Shakespeare.

shooting longbow) proved too much for the heavily armored French. Casualties (killed): English, 29; French, 10,000.* With victory came the courtly peacemaking at Rouen, and Henry's triumphant courtship of the French Princess Katherine.

There were important minor touches. In one of the most moving scenes in Shakespeare, Falstaff was killed off. To replace him, his pal, Pistol, the quintessential burlesque of the Elizabethan soul, was played far down to the groundlings. Because in writing *Henry V* Shakespeare was much hampered by the limitations of his stage, there was heavy work for the one-man Chorus, who, in persuasive and beautiful verbal movies, stirred his audience to imagine scenes and movement which the bare and static Elizabethan stage could not provide.

Olivier's *Henry V* frees Shakespeare from such Elizabethan limitations. The film runs two hours and 14 minutes. Seldom during that time does it fudge or fall short of the best that its author gave it. Almost continually, it invests the art of Shakespeare—and the art of cinema as well—with a new spaciousness, a new mobility, a new radiance. Sometimes, by courageous (but never revolutionary) cuts, rearrangements and interpolations, it improves on the original. Yet its brilliance is graceful, never self-assertive. It simply subserves, extends, illuminates and liberates Shakespeare's poem.

It begins with shots of 17th-Century London and Shakespeare's Globe Theater, where *Henry V* is being played. The florid acting of Olivier and his prelates and the Elizabethan audience's vociferous reactions are worth volumes of Shakespearean footnotes. For the invasion, the camera, beautifully assisted by the Chorus (Leslie Banks), dissolves in space through a marine backdrop to discover a massive set such as Shakespeare never dreamed of—and dissolves backward in time to the year 1415. Delicately as a photographic print in a chemical bath, there emerges the basic style of Shakespearean cinema.

*According to Shakespeare and medieval chroniclers, the English lost just 29. (Says Shakespeare's Duke of Exeter in magnificent understatement: "'Tis wonderful!") English historical estimates: English losses 500. French losses 7,000. French estimates: French losses 10,000. English 1,600.

Voice and gesture exchange Shakespeare's munificence for subtlety, but remain subtly stylized. Faces, by casting, by close-up and reaction, give Shakespeare's lines a limpid, intimate richness of interpretation which has never been available to the stage. One of the prime joys of the picture is the springwater freshness and immediacy of the lines, the lack of antiquarian culture-clogging. Especially as spoken by Olivier, the lines constantly combine the power of prose and the glory of poetry. Photographic perspectives are shallow, as in medieval painting. Most depths end in two-dimensional backdrops. Often as not, the brilliant Technicolor is deliberately anti-naturalistic. Voice, word, gesture, human beings, their bearing and costumes retain their dramatic salience and sovereignty. The result is a new cinema style.

Falstaff's death scene, for which the speeches were lifted bodily from *Henry IV,* Part 2, is boldly invented. The shrunken, heart-broken old companion of Henry's escapades (George Robey, famed British low comedian) hears again, obsessively, the terrible speech ("A man... so old and so profane. ...") in which the King casts him off. In this new context, for the first time perhaps, the piercing line, "The king has kill'd his heart," is given its full power. In the transition scene which takes the audience from Falstaff's death to the invasion of France, the Chorus makes a final appearance alone against the night sky, then recedes and fades as the movie takes over from him. In a flash of imagination, Britain's armada is disclosed through mist as the Chorus, already invisible, says: *Follow, follow....*

The French court, in fragility, elegance, spaciousness and color, is probably the most enchanting single set ever to appear on the screen. Almost every shot of the French court is like a pre-Renaissance painting. The French King (Harcourt Williams) is weak-minded and piteous as he was in history, if not in Shakespeare. There is one beautiful emblematic shot of his balding, pinkish pate, circled with the ironic gold of royalty.

The French Princess (Renee Asherson) has the backward-bending grace of a medieval statuette of the Virgin. Her reedy, birdlike exchange of French-English with her equally delightful duenna, Alice (Ivy St. Helier), is a vaudeville act exquisitely paced and played beyond anything that Shakespeare can have imagined. Her closing scene with Henry—balanced about equally between Olivier's extraordinarily deft delivery of his lines and her extraordinary deft pantomimic pointing of them—is a charming love scene.

The Battle of Agincourt is not realistic. Olivier took great care not to make it so. To find the "kind of poetic country" he wanted, and to avoid such chance anachronisms as air raids (the picture was made in Britain during the war), Olivier shot the battle sequence in Ireland.*

Making no attempt to over-research the actual fight, he reduced it to its salients—the proud cumbrousness of the armored French chevaliers, and Henry's outnumbered archers, cloth-clad in the humble colors of rural England. A wonderful epitomizing shot—three French noblemen drinking a battle-health in their saddles—is like the crest of the medieval wave. The mastering action of the battle, however, begins with a prodigious truckshot of the bannered, advancing French cavalry shifting from a walk to a full gallop, intercut with King Henry's sword, poised for signal, and his archers, bows drawn, waiting for it. The release—an arc of hundreds of arrows speeding with the twang of a gigantic guitar on their victorious way—is one of the most gratifying payoffs of suspense yet contrived.

But the most inspired part of Shakespeare's play deals with the night before the Battle of Agincourt. It is also the most inspired sequence in the film. Olivier opens it with a crepuscular shot of the doomed and exhausted English as they withdraw along a sunset stream to encamp for the night. This shot was made at dawn, at Denham (a miniature British Hollywood) against the shuddering

---

*On the estate of land-poor gentry who, perhaps in gratitude for the sudden prosperity the film brought them, named one of their donkeys for Olivier's wife, Cinemactress Vivien Leigh.

objection of the Technicolor expert. It is one of many things that Olivier and Cameraman Robert Krasker did with color which Technicolor tradition says must not or cannot be done.

The invisible Chorus begins the grandly evocative description of the night camps:

> Now entertain conjecture of a time
> When creeping murmur and the poring dark
> Fills the wide vessel of the universe.

The screen sustains this mood with a generalized shot of the opposed camps, their fires like humiliated starlight. There are no creeping murmurs, neighing steeds, crowing cocks, clanking armorers. Instead, William Walton's score, one of the few outstanding scores in movie history, furnishes subdued, musical metaphors. Midway through the Chorus, the film boldly breaks off to interpolate, to better effect, a scene in the French camp which in Shakespeare's version precedes it.

This scene itself also improves on Shakespeare. His Frenchmen, the night before their expected triumph, were shallow, frivolous and arrogant. By editing out a good deal of their foolishness, by flawless casting, directing and playing, and by a wonderfully paced appreciation of the dead hours of rural night, Olivier transforms the French into sleepy, over-confident, highly intelligent, highly sophisticated noblemen, subtly dis-unified, casually contemptuous of their Dauphin—an all but definitive embodiment of a civilization a little too ripe to survive.

The hypnotic Chorus resumes; the camera pans to the English camp and strolls, as if it were the wandering King himself, among the firelit tents.

And here poem and film link the great past to the great present. It is unlikely that anything on the subject has been written to excel Shakespeare's short study, in *Henry V*, of men stranded on the verge of death and disaster. The man who made this movie made it midway in England's most terrible war, within the shadows of Dunkirk. In appearance and in most of what they say, the three soldiers with whom Henry talks on the eve of Agincourt might just as well be soldiers of World War II. No film of that war has yet said what they say so honestly or so well.

Here again Olivier helped out Shakespeare. Shakespeare gave to a cynical soldier the great speech: *But if the cause be not good,* etc. Olivier puts it in the mouth of a slow-minded country boy (Brian Nissen). The boy's complete lack of cynicism, his youth, his eyes bright with sleepless danger, the peasant patience of his delivery, and his Devon repetition of the tolled word *die* as *doy*, lift this wonderful expression of common humanity caught in human war level with the greatness of the King.

Henry V is one of the great experiences in the history of motion pictures. It is not, to be sure, the greatest: the creation of new dramatic poetry is more important than the recreation of old. For such new poetry, movies offer the richest opportunity since Shakespeare's time, and some of them have made inspired use of the chance. But *Henry V* is a major achievement—this perfect marriage of great dramatic poetry with the greatest contemporary medium for expressing it.

Producer-Director Olivier is very earnest in his desire to share the honors of his production with those who helped him.

His friend Dallas Bower, a producer for BBC, was responsible for the idea of the production.

The Royal Navy had given Olivier leave to make *Demi-Paradise* (*Adventure for Two*) in the interest of Anglo-Russian relations, and extended it so that he could make *Henry V* "in the interests," says Olivier, "of Anglo-British relations."

Producer Filippo Del Giudice (who promoted Noel Coward's *In Which We Serve* on an original £15,000 shoestring) furnished some, and raised more, of the £465,000 (a little under $2,000,000) which *Henry V* cost.

Del Giudice did something more remarkable: he never interfered with Olivier's work; he never let him know that there were money difficulties. It was Del Giudice who suggested the excellent cameraman who had never worked in Technicolor before. He also suggested that Olivier should direct and produce the film as well as star in it. For those scenes in which Olivier played, his cutter,

Reginald Beck, took over the direction. Their collaboration resulted in a mere twenty-five per cent throwaway of film, instead of the usual British fifty per cent and Hollywood ninety per cent. Olivier and Alan Dent (the London *News-Chronicle*'s ace theater critic whose long suit is Shakespeare) teamed inextricably on the superb editing of Shakespeare's play. The final preparation of the shooting script was a team effort by all hands. But it was Olivier who called in Costume Designers Roger and Margaret Furse and Roger Ramsdell (an old Yaleman). It was Olivier who sought out William Walton, whom he regards as "the most promising composer in England." It was he who recruited all-important Art Directors Paul Sheriff and Carmen Dillon. He made use, in fact, of a good deal of talent which most professional moviemakers overlook. And within the profession, he respected professionals more than they usually respect each other.

It was chiefly Olivier who did the brilliant casting; he who gave the French court its more-than-Shakespearean character. Many of the most poetic ideas in cutting and transition were also his. Above all, his was the whole anti-naturalistic conception of the film—a true Shakespearean's recognition that man is greater, and nature less, than life.

The career of Laurence Olivier (pronounced O'lívvy yay) was decided at fifteen, when he played Katherine in a boys-school production of *The Taming of the Shrew*. When he announced that he wanted to go on the stage, his father, a rural Anglo-Catholic clergyman, did not groan: "Better that I should see you dead." Instead, he gave his endorsement and financial support. At seventeen, young Olivier enrolled at the Central School of Dramatic Art, which is second only to London's Royal Academy of Dramatic Art. At eighteen, he was able to tell the Oliviers' old housekeeper, who asked what Laurence did in his first professional engagement: "When you're sitting having your tea during the interval [intermission], and you hear the bell summoning you back to your seat, you'll know that my finger is on the bell."

Later, more substantial parts in plays like *Journey's End*, *The*

Green Bay Tree, No Time for Comedy proved Olivier to be one of the thoroughly good English actors. His performances as Hamlet, Sir Toby Belch, Macbeth, Henry V, Romeo, Iago, Coriolanus, Mercutio earned him a solid, if by no means preeminent, reputation as a Shakespearean actor—and gave him invaluable experience. He also picked up a good deal of experience, which he scarcely valued at all, acting intermittently in movies.

For years Olivier "just thought of movies as a quick way to earn money." In the '30s, his work with sincere, painstaking Director William Wyler made him realize that they can amount to a lot more. His fine performance as Heathcliff in *Wuthering Heights* first suggested that Olivier might be a great actor in the making. But Olivier was never really happy in Hollywood. He disliked the climate; he was homesick for the stage.

When England went to war, he planned, like his good friend Cinemactor David Niven, to join the air force. But he could not get out of his contract. While sweating it out, he took flying lessons and, in an unusually short time, piled up 200 hours.

In two years' service Olivier became a lieutenant in the Fleet Air Arm. He stepped unhurt out of a number of forced or crash landings, gave ground and gunnery instruction, never saw combat. But when he got back to work once more as an actor, theatrical London realized that a remarkable new artist had appeared. Olivier has no explanation for the change in himself except to say: "Maybe it's just that I've got older."

Now, as co-manager (with his friend, fellow flyer and fellow actor Ralph Richardson and with John Burrell) of London's Old Vic Theater, Olivier works at least ten hours a day. For recreation, he spends quiet evenings after work at the home of friends, listening to phonograph music (Mozart is a favorite). When possible, he runs up to his country home, the 15th-Century Notley Abbey in Buckinghamshire, where his second wife Vivien Leigh is convalescing from tuberculosis.

Next month Olivier and Richardson will bring the Old Vic troupe to Manhattan for six weeks of Sophocles, Shakespeare,

Sheridan and Chekhov. Later Olivier would like to film *Macbeth*, *Hamlet* and *Othello*. But he is in no hurry. He has not had enough plain rest to satisfy him since Britain went to war.

THE press on Laurence Olivier's production of Shakespeare's *Henry V* has been exceptionally warm and friendly, as seems no more than proper. Although the press is not to blame for it there is also a rumor, credited apparently by a good many, that it is the best movie ever made. Through some people I have talked with I gather that it is also possible for intelligent people to be disappointed, displeased, or even bored by the film. Indeed I will not be greatly surprised if a sort of highbrow underground develops, devoted to spoiling the fun of relatively easy-minded enthusiasts. Let me therefore first appease the more demanding among my readers, insofar as may be, by getting off my chest all I can possibly find to object to.

Henry V is by no means the best movie ever made; it is a recreation of an old dramatic poem, not the creation of a new one. Nor is it the best of Shakespeare's plays; it is merely a very good and vigorous and at times very moving and beautiful one which, among all his plays, is one of the most obviously amenable to movie treatment and which was for obvious reasons particularly germane at the time it was planned and made. The movie treatment, in turn, is by no means as adventurous as it might have been. No attempt is made to develop a movie style which might in poetic energy and originality work as a cinematic counterpart to the verse. The idea is, rather, to make everything on the screen and soundtrack serve the verse, as clearly and well and unobtrusively as possible. Within this relatively modest and, I think, very wise and admirable intention, moreover, the success is not complete.

Much as I like most things about the opening sequence, in the Globe Theater, and skillfully as I think it is used on the whole, to accustom many levels of the contemporary audience to Shakespeare's style and skill, I am sorry about the subtly patronizing way in which a good deal of it was done. We have a right to assume that the Elizabethan stage at its best was in its own terms as good as the theater or the screen can ever hope to be, and I wish this might have been suggested—as it is in flashes by Olivier—without even the faintest suggestion of *Murder in the Old Red Barn*, or of "life ran very high in those days." The gradual transference from theater to screen seems to me good or better than good in each single idea, but a little heavy and balky taken altogether, and in spite of shrewd editing and, within each single scene, exquisite pacing the movie is during its first hour or so almost as fitful and choppy as the play. I very greatly like the anti-naturalistic, two-and-a-half-dimensional effect that is got by obtunding shallow perspectives in painted drops, and these drops are very pretty and clever; but too many of them are pretty and clever in a soft, almost travel-poster way which to some extent conflicts with and lets down the foregrounds. The night sequence in the English camp might, I think, have been still better if it had taken more of its country-night poetic atmosphere straight from nature, and had wholly avoided the smell and look of a good, semi-naturalistic studio set. The shooting of the battle is fine in its main design; I have an idea that here again sharp naturalism and sharp detail would have improved it and would only have intensified its poetic quality. Shakespeare, after all, was exceedingly rangy in his diction; the movie diction of these good but lesser poets is a little too resolutely "poetic."

I personally enjoyed—and even heard and understood—nearly everything that was done by the comics and semi-comics—especially Robert Newton as Pistol—but well played as they mostly were, I'm not convinced that they survive three hundred years with enough vitality to make them honestly and generally amusing, without a sort of "cultured" over-generosity toward them which I rather dislike in any context and find particularly distasteful in humor. They were not up to giving the narration of Falstaff's death any of the dizzying blend of comedy and noble piteousness it has in the text, nor can I imagine any human beings who would be; and although the actress who played Mistress

Quickly gave her lines much tenderness and thought, she was, barring the Irish comic—with his unplayable role—the only embarrassing bit of amateurishness in the show.

I have, I must confess, a glimmer of the kind of unhappy premonition which sometimes signals a change of heart—a feeling that with many more seeings, and a good deal more remembrance, much that now seems highly satisfying, visually, will come to seem too much like conventional illustration to be quite so happy; and that a good deal of the casting, which now seems as nearly perfect as any I have ever seen in a film, and incomparably the best I have seen in a Shakespearian production, will seem perhaps no less good, so far as it goes, but a little predictable, even stodgy. I fear particularly that elements in Renée Asherson's performance as the French princess, which now seems to me pure enchantment, will in time look a little coarsely coy. But if this time ever comes I fear also that I will have lost a certain warmth of spirit, and capacity for delight, which this film requires of those who will enjoy it, and which it asks for, and inspires, with a kind of uninsistent geniality and grace which is practically unknown in twentieth century art, though it was part of the essence of Shakespeare's. I don't have the feeling that any extraordinary fresh creative force is at large in the film except that of Shakespeare, though the film itself swarms with the evidence of creative intelligence of a gentler and still highly honorable kind, and with evidence also of a quality of taste which is far too good and too sure of itself to need to scorn the great middle audience. It is not, I repeat, the most exciting or inspiring or original film I have seen. But I cannot think of any that seems to be more beautiful, more skillfully and charmingly achieved within its wisely ordered limits, or more thoroughly satisfying.

Such are my objections; I could with pleasure fill twenty times this space with a mere listing of specific excellence, without more than beginning to express my esteem for the film and its makers. But what little of that there will be room for will have to wait a couple of weeks.

August 3, 1946

It SEEMS impertinent to discuss even briefly the excellence of Laurence Olivier's production of Shakespeare's *Henry V* without saying a few words, at least, about the author. If Shakespeare had been no more gifted with words than, say, I am, the depth and liveliness of his interest in people and predicaments, and his incredible hardness, practicality, and resource as a craftsman and maker of moods, rhythms, and points, could still have made him almost his actual equal as a playwright. I had never realized this so well until I saw this production, in which every nail in sight is so cleanly driven in with one blow, and I could watch the film for all that Shakespeare gave it in these terms alone, and for all that in these terms alone is done with what he gave, with great pleasure and gratitude. But then too, of course, there is the language, of a brilliance, vigor, and absoluteness that make the craftsmanship and sometimes the people and their grandest emotions seem almost as negligibly pragmatic as a libretto beside an opera score. Some people, using I wonder what kind of dry ice for comfort, like to insist that *Henry V* is relatively uninteresting Shakespeare. This uninteresting poetry is such that after hearing it, in this production, I find it as hard to judge fairly even the best writing since Shakespeare as it is to see the objects in a room after looking into the sun.

The one great glory of the film is this language. The greatest credit I can assign to those who made the film is that they have loved and served the language so well. I don't feel that much of the delivery is inspired; it is merely so good, so right, that the words set loose in the graciously designed world of the screen, like so many uncaged birds, fully enjoy and take care of themselves. Neither of the grimmest Shakespearian vices, ancient or modern, is indulged: that is to say, none of the text is read in that human, down-to-earth, poetry-is-only-hopped-up-prose manner which is doubtless only proper when a charter subscriber to *PM* reads the Lerner editorial to his shop-wise fellow traveler; nor is any of it intoned in the nobler manner, as if by a spoiled deacon celebrating the Black Mass down a section of sewerpipe. Most of it is merely spoken by people who know and love poetry as poetry and have spent a lifetime learning how to speak it accordingly. Their voices, faces, and bodies are all in charge of a man who has selected them as shrewdly as a good orchestrator selects and blends his instruments; and he combines and directs them as a good conductor conducts an orchestral piece. It is, in fact, no surprise to learn that Mr. Olivier is fond of music; charming as it is to look at, the film is essentially less visual than musical.

I cannot compare it with many stage productions of Shakespeare; but so far as I can they were, by comparison, just so many slightly tired cultural summer-salads, now and then livened, thanks to an unkilled talent or an unkillable line, by an unexpected rose-petal or the sudden spasm of a rattlesnake: whereas this, down to the last fleeting bit of first-rate poetry in a minor character's mouth, was close to solid gold, almost every word given its own and its largest contextual value. Of course nothing prevents this kind of casting and playing on the stage, except talent and, more seriously, the money to buy enough talent and enough time to use it rightly in; and how often do you see anything to equal it on the Shakespearian stage? The specific advantages of the screen are obvious, but no less important for that. Microphones make possible a much more delicate and immediate use of the voice; reactions, in close-up, can color the lines more subtly and richly than on the stage. Thus it is possible, for instance, to get all the considerable excellence there is out of an aging player like Nicholas Hannen, who seemed weak in most scenes when, on the stage, he had to try to fill and dilate the whole Century Theater with unhappy majesty; and the exquisiteness of Renée Asherson's reactions to Olivier's spate of gallantry, in the wooing scene, did as much as he did toward making that scene, by no means the most inspired as writing, the crown of the film. When so much can be done, through proper understanding of these simple advantages, to open the beauties of poetry as relatively extroverted as this play, it is equally hard to imagine and to wait for the explorations that could be made of subtler, deeper poems like *Hamlet*, *Troilus and Cressida*, or *The Tempest*.

Speaking still of nothing except the skill with which the poetry is used in this film, I could go on far past the room I have. The sureness and seductive power of the pacing alone and its shifts and contrasts, in scene after scene, has seldom been equaled in a movie; the adjustments and relationships of tone are just as good. For just one example, the difference in tone between Olivier's almost schoolboyish "God-a-mercy" and his "Good old Knight," not long afterward, measures the King's growth in the time between with lovely strength, spaciousness, and cleanness; it earns as craftsmanship, the triumph of bringing off the equivalent to an "impossibly" delayed false-rhyme; and psychologically or dramatically, as it seems to me—though my guess may be far-fetched—it fully establishes the King's coming-of-age by raising honorable, brave, loyal, and dull old age (in Sir Thomas Erpingham) in the King's love and esteem to the level of any love he had ever felt for Falstaff.

Olivier does many other beautiful pieces of reading and playing. His blood-raising reply to the French Herald's ultimatum is not just that; it is a frank, bright exploitation of the moment for English ears, amusedly and desperately honored as such, in a still gallant and friendly way, by both Herald and King. His Crispin's Day oration is not just a brilliant bugle-blat: it is the calculated yet self-exceeding improvisation, at once self-enjoying and self-less, of a young and sleepless leader, rising to a situation wholly dangerous and glamorous, and wholly new to him. Only one of the many beauties of the speech as he gives it is the way in which the King seems now to exploit his sincerity, now to be possessed by it, riding like an unexpectedly mounting wave the astounding size of his sudden proud awareness of the country morning, of his moment in history, of his responsibility and competence, of being full-bloodedly alive, and of being about to die.

This kind of branching, nervous interpretive intelligence, so contemporary in quality except that it always keeps the main lines of its drive and meaning clear, never spiraling or strangling in awareness, is vivid in every way during all parts of the film.

It is tantalizing to be able to mention so few of the dozens of large and hundreds of small excellences which Mr. Olivier and his associates have developed to sustain Shakespeare's poem. They have done somewhere near all that talent, cultivation, taste, knowledgeability, love of one's work—every excellence, in fact, short of genius—can be expected to do; and that, the picture testifies, is a very great deal. Lacking space for anything further I would like to suggest that it be watched for all that it does in playing a hundred kinds of charming adventurousness against the incalculably responsive sounding-boards of tradition: for that is still, and will always be, a process essential in most, though not all, of the best kinds of art, and I have never before seen so much done with it in a moving picture. I am not a Tory, a monarchist, a Catholic, a medievalist, an Englishman, or, despite all the good that it engenders, a lover of war: but the beauty and power of this traditional exercise was such that, watching it, I wished I was, thought I was, and was proud of it. I was persuaded, and in part still am, that every time and place has since been in decline, save one, in which one Englishman used language better than anyone has before or since, or ever shall; and that nearly the best that our time can say for itself is that some of us are still capable of paying homage to the fact.

(1946)

Maurice Evans

(1901–1989)

Preface to G.I. Hamlet

Maurice Evans was born in England in 1901 and began acting professionally at the age of twenty-five. Over the course of the next decade he played leading Shakespeare roles, including Iago and Hamlet, before traveling to the United States and appearing in Broadway productions as Richard II, Falstaff, and Macbeth. Evans became an American citizen in 1941. A year later he was commissioned as an officer in the U.S. Army, where he was put in charge of an Entertainment Section in the Central Pacific, based in Hawaii. Over the next few years he managed to find and train a troupe of sixty soldier-actors, many of them veterans of combat, to perform musicals, variety shows, and stage plays. In 1944 Evans decided to stage a cut-down version of *Hamlet* for the troops, many of whom had never seen a Shakespeare play before. Most of those who saw his *Hamlet*, Evans writes, were either heading into combat or "staggering with fatigue and confusion after their first encounter with the enemy." Casting the women's roles was a special challenge, resolved when Evans enlisted the daughter of an army colonel to play Ophelia and persuaded his secretary to play Gertrude. Evans and his troupe had to scavenge where they could for props (ship lights from the sunken battleship *Oklahoma* were "liberated" for the stage lamps used in one scene). This was a heroic Hamlet with whom American soldiers could presumably identify. *G.I. Hamlet* opened in Honolulu in October 1944 and was seen by fifty thousand or so troops at over forty performances. After the war, the production was revived in December 1945 in New York City for a run of 147 performances, followed by a national tour. Having brought *Hamlet* to the troops, Evans subsequently brought Shakespeare to more American living rooms than anyone had ever done before, producing and starring in a half-dozen feature-length televised versions of the plays between 1953 and 1960.

O F the gallons of ink which have been spilt upon the topic of
Hamlet, the actors and stage producers are responsible for
a comparatively negligible quantity. Most of the torrent of word-
age already in existence has been unleashed by the academicians.
Every facet of Hamlet's character, each minutia of the play's intri-
cacies, has been discussed and discussed until it seems impossible
that the last word on the subject has not been said; yet here, once
more, the incredulous compositor is called upon to resurrect the
familiar letters for the title page: "The Tragedy of Hamlet, Prince
of Denmark." My apology, if one is needed, is that this little book
is a statement of a task actually *accomplished*, whereas its predecessors have in the main constituted theoretical approaches to the
task or criticisms of the finished product as seen through the eyes
of the reviewer. The acting version of *Hamlet* set forth in the pages
which follow is the diagram of a presentation of the play staged
under conditions which were imposed by the exigencies of the
moment—the moment being World War II and its immediate
aftermath. It was this production's principal claim to distinction
that, at a time when poets were suffering more than customary
neglect, it could nevertheless succeed in reaffirming the eternal
truth of Shakespeare's vision.

The accepted test of a classic is its readability by succeeding
generations despite the passage of time. The test of a classical play
(in terms of its sustained popularity in the theatre) is its capacity
to yield to the contemporary customs of play presentation no matter how these customs may alter with the development of new mechanical techniques or changes in styles of acting. One of the evidences of Shakespeare's great genius is that every age has found in
his thoughts a responsive echo and has been able to stage his plays
according to the fashion of the moment without departing materially from the original text or intention. Garrick played Hamlet
in a tiewig and Mrs. Siddons played Lady Macbeth in a sweeping
picture hat without in the least disturbing the sensibilities of their
audiences. The Victorian giants—Irving, Terry, and Booth—
interpreted the plays in the overdecorated and sententious fashion of their era and delighted their hearers. There is no such

thing as the oft-quoted "tradition" of presenting Shakespeare—only a timorous hesitation to depart from the manner of the immediate past. Because of the nature of their composition the old stock companies were guilty of perpetuating tradition for a time. The constant change of bill and interchange of actors made it convenient to adhere to a rigid formula for all of the stock plays in a company's repertoire. Thus when Mr. Booth became the visiting star in a score of provincial stock companies it was a foregone certainty that the Oshkosh Horatio would be in the identical spot for Hamlet's dying words as was the Mountain Bluff Horatio of the preceding week. Audiences became so accustomed to the details of stage business that it took a bold performer to risk any innovation. One reads in the *Theatrical Observer* of May 18, 1824, of the absurdity of Macready's being hissed by a member of the audience because he chose to retreat from the apparition of Banquo rather than advance upon it as had hitherto been customary.

To those of us who are called upon to make these departures from our predecessors the penalties are sometimes severe and the criticism scathing. Nevertheless it is my belief that if we are to prove ourselves worthy of retaining the envied honour of being one of Shakespeare's mouthpieces we may claim that distinction only so long as we speak in a voice understandable to our own time and bring vigour and originality to our interpretations.

The production outlined in this book became contemporary not of its own seeking but because of the conditions which existed at the time of its presentation. As officer in charge of troop entertainment in the Central Pacific Area during the war, I tried to leaven the otherwise giddy fare in which we and our friends in USO Camp Shows indulged with occasional productions of somewhat more substantial character. An experimental staging of *Macbeth* in 1943 encouraged us to try again the following year with *Hamlet*. Immediately we were faced with the problem of the play's length. A soldier could leave his post and be in the theatre by six-thirty but he had to be back in barracks for Lights Out at ten. Allowing time for transportation, this meant we were restricted to a total playing time of two hours and forty-five minutes, whereas the full text of *Hamlet* takes four hours to perform. A lot had to be sacrificed, but my soldier director, Sgt. George Schaefer, and I wielded the blue pencil with meticulous care. We strove to retain all the cardinal points of plot and character development while eliminating passages, odd lines, and even whole scenes in an effort to keep the play taut and swift. As one of the few actors in the world who has had the privilege of playing *Hamlet* in its entirety, as I did in 1937–38, it was a painful experience to sit, stop watch in hand, timing the passages which we felt could at a pinch be deleted, deducting the cuts so measured from the known playing time of the entirety, and finding with each calculation that we were still running over our limit. There was not much argument about sacrificing the lengthy references to the political background of the play, which occur in the first scene of the first act. In the Elizabethan playhouse the opening battlement scene was played in broad daylight, and it is understandable that the resulting visibility enabled the actors to hold their audience's attention with a political dissertation during the first ten minutes of the play without too much difficulty. Because of the generally held belief in the supernatural there was no need to employ theatrical devices to create the illusion of the ghost's appearance which immediately follows. But in our day the effectiveness of the ghost depends upon his materializing from the shadowy recesses of a dimly lit stage. In the intervals between his appearances, however, Marcellus and Horatio must wrestle in the semidarkness to project the long and intricate story of the Fortinbras, *père et fils*, and their relationship to the kingdom of Denmark. This is a feat which is well-nigh impossible for the actors concerned, and we felt that here, at least, was one justifiable omission. It naturally followed that in the succeeding scene Claudius' references to the Fortinbras theme also should be dropped, and some alternative means found of suggesting visually the threat of war which Shakespeare was stressing in these political speeches.

The rest of the cutting in the first act of our version adhered closely to the omissions customarily made in stage presentations, with the additional deletion of a line here and there which we thought might be dangerous for a soldier audience. "Something is rotten in the state of Denmark" could go, and good riddance to the inevitable but always misplaced laugh. It seemed wiser, too, to skip over the part of Ophelia's description of Hamlet's distraught appearance which includes "his knees knocking together." Otherwise our cutting was conservative. All the soliloquies remained intact and no major violence was done to the text in the first act. The Polonius-Reynaldo colloquy, usually omitted, was regretfully abbreviated by us; the long discussion among Hamlet, Rosencrantz, and Guildenstern about the travelling players was eliminated with a clear conscience, and it did not grieve me too much to attenuate the flamboyancy of the First Player on the subject of Hecuba.

When it came to dealing with the second act of our version, we knew it had to be compressed into a space of seventy minutes and we had a hundred and eighteen minutes of text asking to be played. The last half of *Hamlet* is so compact and so sweeping in its forward action that the greatest ingenuity was called for if we were to remain within the boundaries dictated by military necessity. Action and its frustration are the keynotes of the latter half of the tragedy; and at all costs these qualities had to be preserved. Most producers have elected to eliminate the plotting scene between Claudius and Laertes, creating, it seems to me, a disastrous gap in the final crescendo of the story of revenge. Productions of *Hamlet* that I have seen which have made this fatal omission left with me the impression that the play peters out towards the end. We were determined, therefore, to retain at least the nub of the Claudius-Laertes conspiracy, even though our allotted time forced us to tack it onto the end of Ophelia's mad scene. Comparison with the full text will reveal the considerable ingenuity with which the objective was achieved, but all our labours with the blue pencil could not compress the second act sufficiently. A final count showed that we were still a full fifteen minutes overtime. I reviewed the cuts in other acting versions and simply could not stomach them. Most of them left out the "How all occasions" soliloquy—an unthinkable omission in a performance before soldiers—and many of the valuable little scenes in the middle of the act where the play acquires almost a "cops and robbers" flavour. These are the episodes which bowl the play along with such terrific excitement, and somehow or other they had to be retained. It wasn't until I lighted on an old prompt script of David Garrick's *Hamlet* that I felt emboldened to follow his example and strike out altogether the graveyard scene. Not only did this give us the fifteen minutes that reprieved the other scenes which we considered more valuable, but it also removed from the play an inconsistency of which, probably, only those who have played Hamlet are fully aware. At the end of the graveyard scene Hamlet rushes from the stage, frenzied with grief over the death of Ophelia and shattered by his encounter with Laertes; yet he is required to re-enter only seven lines later, chatting blithely with Horatio about his adventures with the pirates on the high seas and his crafty disposal of Rosencrantz and Guildenstern. This sudden transition is so impossible to make with any kind of grace or conviction that I believe there are very real grounds for guessing that the graveyard scene was an addition to the original text, and that it was written in for some reason as simple as that Shakespeare had forgotten to include a part for the Globe's favourite comedian. The next to the last scene (Act II, Scene 8, in our version) was patently in the original, since it is the necessary introduction to the final episode; yet the conversation between Horatio and Hamlet that precedes Osric's entrance gives a definite feeling that the two friends have just met for the first time since Hamlet's return to Denmark and that Hamlet is impatient "to speak in thine ear words that will make thee dumb." Why such an outburst of information at this point when ample opportunity had presented itself during their stroll through the graveyard in the preceding scene? It seems most improbable that Hamlet would take time to exchange badinage with a sexton when matters of such urgency awaited impartment. That the whole graveyard scene was a Shakespearean afterthought may be merely an actor's hunch, but it was comforting to be bolstered by some argument besides the insistence of a bugle call. For those who objected to this theory, there was the additional argument that our warrior audiences had very fixed ideas about comedy and considered themselves authorities upon what was funny and what was not. I had seen too many renowned radio comedians lay the proverbial egg on too many occasions before Army audiences to believe that the gravediggers would arouse their risibilities. "Corny" was the epithet most dreaded by our visiting mirth makers, and "corny" indeed might our gravediggers be dubbed.

There were other and more potent factors to be considered than mere time saving, chief among them being the fact that we were proposing to present a classical play before spectators of whom the majority had never before experienced anything of the sort. We could not presume on their part any knowledge of the tragedy or any familiarity with the conventions with which it is usually associated. One of the bugbears of producing a classic in the professional theatre is that one can never start with a clean slate. There are comparisons with one's predecessors to be reckoned with, and prejudicial judgment formed often on the bare announcement that Mr. So-and-so is going to revise such and such a play. An actor assaying the part of Macbeth is courting disaster unless he is physically so constructed that he conforms to the popularly held belief that Macbeth was a colossus. He can argue eloquently that history shows that the worst of the world's troublemakers and dictators have been of moderate stature—like Napoleon, Mussolini, and Franco—and that there is no reason why the Scottish tyrant should not have been similarly proportioned. But no amount of eloquence will eradicate the preconceived notion of Macbeth's physical appearance. It becomes almost obligatory, too, for the professional producer to pay primary attention to the esoteric aspects of a classic at the expense, very often, of the basic values of the play. Nowhere is this truer than in the case of *Hamlet*. So familiar is the story to the habitual theatregoer that any emphasis on the theme of the play seems superfluous to the point of being ingenuous. Interest is centered, instead, on the finer shadings of interpretation, more particularly those executed by the actor playing the central character. Too often the net result is a performance which is all nuance and no fibre; and, while it may avoid making "the judicious grieve," it is doubtful whether it is intelligible to the uninitiated.

In our Army production we were mercifully free from the necessity of being supersubtle. In fact a performance which smacked of being "caviare to the general" would have defeated our desire to make the impact of the play clear and forceful. It was a refreshing experience to be producing a classic as though for the first time and to be able to put *Hamlet* on the stage without regard to someone's pet prejudice or theory. To us *Hamlet* had to be regarded as a brand-new script hot off the press, to be treated with no more reverence than any other play. If it was worth doing at all, it would have to be made intrinsically *entertaining*, a quality which one does not associate especially with a classic. Yet always there was the fact to be remembered that if *Hamlet* had endured as a theatre piece for over three hundred years the power to entertain must have been fundamental in its make-up since the beginning. Shakespeare, after all, was not consciously writing a classic, when he penned *Hamlet*, but was actually doctoring up an old play which fascinated him and which he must have known would meet the approval of his patrons at the Globe or Blackfriars. If it had achieved such popularity with a rough-and-tumble Elizabethan audience, it certainly should not be unacceptable to the far more literate audiences before whom we now had to play.

It was this consideration of the original presentations of the play on London's Thames-side which finally gave us the approach we were looking for. It occurred to us that there was a certain similarity between the conditions which prevailed in Shakespeare's day and those which we were about to encounter. He had his troubles with the groundlings in the pit and so might we. His audiences were seated on hard benches and so would ours be. His plays were given in theatres or inn yards open to the sky with street noises to punctuate the performances; some of our theatres would be open to the sky too, a sky interlaced with searchlights and tracer bullets, and in place of the street noises would be the rattle of anti-aircraft gun practice and peremptory words of command from a raucous top sergeant to dogfaces drilling in the courtyard below. What kind of a Hamlet would Burbage have played in the face of such conditions? In *Hamlet* Shakespeare was writing a thoroughly contemporary play, full of the manners of his own Renaissance times. As a poet, of course, his vision was timeless, but as a playwright, in this instance, he deliberately emphasized the modernity of the theme of the play in order to illustrate the universality of the tragedy. Unlike his method in *Antony and Cleopatra* and *Macbeth*, in which he took pains to create the illusion of locale, *Hamlet* is set in a royal court, the geography of which is merely hinted at, but a court, like Elizabeth's, in which diplomacy and intrigue are the rule and where the actors' Elizabethan clothing must have seemed appropriate and right. It would seem that Shakespeare wanted nothing to detract from Hamlet's having his feet firmly planted in the roots of human nature and representing a thoroughly normal man waging the eternal struggle of the individual against society. If such indeed was Shakespeare's intention, therein we had a pattern suited to our requirements.

He was a character in whom every G.I. would see himself vaguely reflected—a man compelled to champion his conception of right in a world threatened by the domination of evil; here was Shakespeare's play to be presented not as a chronicle of events happening in space but as a great drama in the Greek sense of the word—"the art of *Doing*." Action would be the keynote of our production, or, as Horatio sums up the plot in the play's last scene:

> "Of carnal, bloody, and unnatural acts,
> Of accidental judgments, casual slaughters,
> Of deaths put on by cunning and forc'd cause
> And, in this upshot, purposes mistook
> Fall'n on the inventors' heads."

In this approach one point was vastly in our favour. Our audiences were composed almost entirely of men on the eve of going into battle or those who were staggering with fatigue and confusion after their first encounter with the enemy. Each of them was in his own way a Hamlet, bewildered by the uninvited circumstances in which he found himself and groping for the moral justification and the physical courage demanded of him. If we could succeed in making the parallel of Hamlet's perplexities apparent, the significance of the play to our audience would be magnified. How to achieve this comparison without being obvious and vulgar was the problem. For more than a century Hamlet himself was depicted by actors within the same general framework, that of a princely philosopher so filled with fineness of feeling and poetic brooding that his being is incapable of wreaking the revenge urged by the ghost. Such a figure may have delighted past generations of playgoers, but it was too special, too abnormal, for our purpose; and would it, after all, have been any more acceptable to the Elizabethan audience than to ours? Shakespeare was by no means indifferent to the tastes and prejudices of his audiences; and it is a known fact that in his time learning and philosophy were considered the business of the clergy, more particularly the monks, and were not regarded as the attributes of the layman, least of all of one who was being cited as "the glass of fashion and the mould of form." Whenever Shakespeare *does* permit his heroes to indulge in philosophic or learned pursuits, it is to their disadvantage, as in *The Tempest* and *Measure for Measure*, or to their discomfiture as in *Love's Labour's Lost*. It does not seem reasonable to suppose that Hamlet was the one exception to Shakespeare's marked antipathy for the dreamer and that he would gainsay diametrically the virtues which his audience expected in their heroes.

More recently Hamlet the prince-philosopher has yielded to the Freudian portrait of a man whose will to act has been paralyzed by sudden nervous shock—the shock of his father's untimely death and his mother's "o'erhasty marriage" with Claudius. These events, it is argued, reduced Hamlet to a state of psychoneurosis, the principal symptom of which was a lethargic melancholia. Would this "Gloomy Dane," we were bound to ask ourselves, get a sympathetic hearing from our soldier audiences? In wartime a G.I. who brooded too much or who had too thin a skin to withstand "the whips and scorns of time" soon found himself behind the padded doors of a psychiatric ward and was referred to by his tougher comrades as a "Section 8-er." Though he may have been a subject of pity he was certainly not admired for his super-sensitivity, nor did his plight strike a responsive chord in the hearts of his buddies, who hated soldiering with equal intensity but whose stronger nervous systems stood the strain. It seemed fairly certain, therefore, that a study in abnormal psychology was the last approach for us. Using the same yardstick of audience-consideration, would Shakespeare himself or his auditors have accepted such a view of Hamlet? The Elizabethans employed the word "melancholy" in a sense quite different from modern-day usage, implying a physical disorder proceeding from frustrated passion and having outward manifestation in the form of violent behaviour. "Melancholy" did not paralyze the will, but enforced inaction was often considered the *origin* of the malady. Admitting this premise, the whole theory of Hamlet's innate incapacity to act falls to the ground, and in its place we have a normal man caught in the web of circumstance which denies him the *opportunity* to act; a man, in fact, not so very far removed from the average soldier in our audience, who knew himself trapped in a situation from which there was no escape.

In our desire to invest our production with the forthright qual-ities we believed must have been present when the play was acted originally, the obvious thing would have been to stage *Hamlet* in the Elizabethan manner on a bare stage and in the clothing of the period. In many ways this would have minimized our practical problems and relieved us of the monumental difficulties of gath-ering materials for scenery, costumes, and lighting on an Army outpost. But would such a production achieve the immediacy of impact that we were aiming for? The most startling productions of Shakespeare I have ever seen were the re-creations of the Eliza-bethan style of staging by William Poel in London some years back, but in spite of their authenticity and their blessed virtue of concentrating on play rather than on the scenery, they emphasized rather than minimized the consciousness of the play's antiquity. There is always something folksy and quaint about such produc-tions—an atmosphere which we wanted above all to avoid. The same would have been true if we had adopted the other easy way out and mounted the play in modern dress. The only thanks I would have received would have been from my overworked production staff. Nothing is more incongruous or self-defeating in its purpose than these productions in modern dress. A tuxedo-ed Hamlet is compelled to indulge in awkward devices to justify the sword that must be there for the killing of Polonius; a multitude of anachronisms distracts the audience's attention, and unless Shakespeare's greatest glory—his verse—is whittled down into colloquial prose, the whole thing takes on an air of pretentiousness that is far more foreign to the play than the most ornate period production.

Somewhere between the ancient and the modern we had to discover a style of production which would be consistent with the theme and would at the same time fulfill our aim of stressing its contemporary parallels. It would not be enough to design a vaguely palatial interior and put crowns on the King and Queen to indicate their station. This would inevitably thrust the play back into antiquity, inviting from the audience a detached regard for things happening long ago. I was sauntering one evening down one of Honolulu's streets (preposterously named Kalanianiole Avenue) pondering the problem, when an officer emerged from one of the houses, dressed in the full-dress uniform of a South American naval attaché. He was resplendent in high polished boots, silver sword, and a long flowing cape. Immediately I was struck with the oddity of the fact that, although here was as startling a period costume as one could possibly imagine, it did not seem in the least incongruous because of its military associations. I began to think of other uniforms, such as those worn at a levee at St. James's or Buckingham Palace today, and of how little they have changed over the years. Might not the comparative timelessness of uniforms be valuable to us and further our desire to remove the play from any specific period? Polonius could rightfully wear the knee breeches and swallowtail coat which are worn by the court chamberlain on state occasions to this day, and the courtiers in their dress uniforms could suggest the military character of Claudius' court while supplying the colour and richness which we wanted on the stage. Uniforms, too, could be worn by the guards in the first scene of the play and be so close in general design to a modern soldier's greatcoat and cap that one would think for the moment that the play was being played in present times. When it came to considering the Ghost's appearance, it followed that he, too, should be in uniform, probably that of a field marshal. His was the only instance where the choice of uniform forced us to cut references to clothes in the text; but since "He wore his beaver up" used to be a sure laugh with schoolboys, I was not sorry to see the line go, and was just as glad to be rid of the metallic armour which is apt to clank in a most unwraithlike manner. So the decision was made to give the play a military flavour, which we hoped would suggest visually the imminence of war, with which the kingdom of Denmark is threatened throughout the play, and emphasize for our soldier audience the immediacy of the happenings.

It was one thing to decide upon a style of clothing which would suit us but quite another to execute the idea under the stringent conditions which prevailed in our Pacific headquarters. In this gigantic organization we were a handful of sixty men, charged with the challenging assignment of supplying entertainment to the troops. Little by little we had melted the hearts of harassed supply officers and acquired at least a minimum of materials to work with, but they were the merest trickle as compared with our needs. It was hard, too, at times, to convince some of our superiors that there was any justification for the time, money, and labour which a production as ambitious as *Hamlet* demanded. If our play had dealt directly with some current topic related to the war, or contained instruction on military tactics, we would have had no difficulty in getting all we needed; but it was not easy to persuade "the brass" that in matters of troop morale the oblique approach was the most effective one. Other methods were tried and fell on deaf ears. A new branch of the service was formed to combat the indifference with which most of the Army regarded the ethics of the war. It was a matter of grave concern to the authorities at one stage of hostilities that our men had no spirit comparable to the fanatical faith of the Nazis and the Japs; in spite of all the attempts to whip up a bloodthirsty attitude, the men in the Pacific, at any rate, remained impervious to propaganda. It was really not surprising, nor was it seriously to their discredit. Most of them, after all, had been drafted into the Army and never became thoroughly adjusted to the loss of their personal freedom. For all the drilling and discipline, the American soldier remained very much an individual throughout the war, and the only way to get him to respond favourably was to treat him as an individual. This was the belief which governed our planning in the branch of the service to which our Entertainment Section was attached. By treating the soldier not as a moron, as was too often the case, but as an adult male who needed a little spiritual refreshment now and again, we believed we indirectly improved his efficiency as a fighting man. The intellectual desolation which was the companion of life in the Army was a deleterious factor, and it was the remedial aspects of our program which eventually became recognized. We were fortunate in our top commanders, Generals Delos Emmons and Robert C. Richardson, Jr., both of them humanistically inclined and sympathetic to the arts. With their approval we were allowed to construct a chain of theatres through the Central Pacific which housed the constant stream of entertainment of all sorts originating in our Section. Variety shows, concert groups, musical comedies, legitimate plays, and classics were included in our varied programme. Our detachment of sixty men, sometimes amplified by a hundred or so more on temporary loan, worked as hard as any combat soldiers; not only did they act in the plays, build the scenery, drive and repair the trucks, but they performed their regular military duties besides. A spirit existed in the Entertainment Section which was rare in the Army. The men were conscious of the privilege of being permitted to continue their civilian occupations under Army auspices and knew how much their efforts were appreciated by their less fortunate brothers-in-arms. Thus they could always be relied upon to co-operate to the fullest extent in promoting our ideas. In the case of *Hamlet*, enthusiasm ran high, and the imaginative direction of Sgt. George Schaefer, the costume department headed by Sgt. Paolo D'Anna, the scenic design by Sgt. Frederick Stover, and the musical composition by Pfc. Roger Adams, all had a unity which contributed greatly to the success of the production. Our audiences reacted with the kind of rapt attention which is every actor's dream; though, I must confess, I was somewhat startled by a G.I. at one performance who could not refrain from commenting on a line in the "To be or not to be" soliloquy: I had reached the point where Hamlet exclaims, "Thus conscience does make cowards of us all," when a voice, clearly audible to me on the stage, remarked, "Boy, you ain't kiddin'!" If we could draw such an involuntary exclamation from the typical G.I., or cause another to say, "They must have done a lot of re-writing to bring this up to date," it seemed pretty conclusive that our object had been achieved and that we had made *Hamlet* live for them.

The final phase in the history of the G.I. *Hamlet* had its origin in Hollywood. I was there on leave visiting friends on my way home from the Pacific after two and a half years. We had just emerged through the swinging doors of Romanoff's when the doorman handed me a note which said: "Welcome home—and bravo for what you've been doing. . . . Michael Todd." It wasn't until I returned to New York for the remainder of my leave that I acknowledged this gracious billet-doux. My letter released an avalanche of telegrams, telephone calls, and special deliveries from this energetic producer, whose acquaintance I had yet to have the pleasure of making. The upshot of it all was that, before I could catch my breath, VJ Day was upon us. I was suddenly translated into a civilian suit, and I had said yes to Mike Todd's proposal to present G.I. *Hamlet* on Broadway. New York responded by supporting the production for a run of 147 performances, a new record for the play, and on the road we were also received with great warmth and enthusiasm.

Whatever shortcomings there may have been in its execution, it is good to know from the reviewers and from audience reception that our idea came through clearly. We were seeking to be truthful to the temper of our own age and to restate Shakespeare's eternal verities in the spirit of these times. *Hamlet* is perhaps the Theatre's greatest heritage and we who are its servants hope we have served it well.

(1947)

Cole Porter

(1891–1964)

Brush Up Your Shakespeare

Cole Porter was a major composer and songwriter for both Hollywood and the Broadway stage. *Kiss Me, Kate*—a play within a play about a theater troupe staging a musical of *The Taming of the Shrew*—was probably his greatest hit and one of the most successful adaptations of Shakespeare of all time. It won the first Tony Award for best musical and ran for over a thousand performances in New York (W. H. Auden claimed that it was better than Shakespeare's original). The only genuinely Shakespearean lyrics in the adaptation appear in a pair of songs: "I Am Ashamed that Women Are So Simple" and "I've Come to Wive it Wealthily in Padua." One of the most popular of Porter's lyrics for the show—"Brush Up Your Shakespeare"—was written for a couple of gangsters waiting to collect a gambling debt, their knowledge of Shakespeare's plays acquired through "eight years in the prison library." The ironies and the tension between high and low culture here, full of rhymes that mangle Shakespeare's titles, delivered in an old waltz tempo, could not have been greater. Porter and his librettist Bella Spewack quickly realized that this bawdy song about using Shakespeare to win the ladies was "a 'boff' number—a show-stopper." It proved so popular that Porter added several encore verses.

∝

VERSE
The girls today in society
Go for classical poetry,
So to win their hearts one must quote with ease
Aeschylus and Euripides.
One must know Homer and, b'lieve me, Bo,
Sophocles, also Sappho-ho.
Unless you know Shelley and Keats and Pope,

Dainty debbies will call you a dope.
But the poet of them all
Who will start 'em simply ravin'
Is the poet people call
The bard of Stratford-on-Avon.

REFRAIN 1
Brush up your Shakespeare,
Start quoting him now.
Brush up your Shakespeare
And the women you will wow.
Just declaim a few lines from "Othella"
And they'll think you're a helluva fella.
If your blonde won't respond when you flatter 'er
Tell her what Tony told Cleopaterer,
If she fights when her clothes you are mussing,
What are clothes? "Much Ado About Nussing."
Brush up your Shakespeare
And they'll all kowtow.

REFRAIN 2
Brush up your Shakespeare,
Start quoting him now.
Brush up your Shakespeare
And the women you will wow.
With the wife of the British embessida
Try a crack out of "Troilus and Cressida,"
If she says she won't buy it or tike it
Make her tike it, what's more, "As You Like It."
If she says your behavior is heinous
Kick her right in the "Coriolanus."
Brush up your Shakespeare
And they'll all kowtow.

REFRAIN 3

Brush up your Shakespeare,
Start quoting him now.
Brush up your Shakespeare
And the women you will wow.
If you can't be a ham and do "Hamlet"
They will not give a damn or a damnlet.
Just recite an occasional sonnet
And your lap'll have "Honey" upon it.
When your baby is pleading for pleasure
Let her sample your "Measure for Measure."
Brush up your Shakespeare
And they'll all kowtow.

REFRAIN 4

Brush up your Shakespeare,
Start quoting him now.
Brush up your Shakespeare
And the women you will wow.
Better mention "The Merchant of Venice"
When her sweet pound o' flesh you would menace.
If her virtue, at first, she defends—well,
Just remind her that "All's Well That End's Well."
And if still she won't give you a bonus
You know what Venus got from Adonis!
Brush up your Shakespeare
And they'll all kowtow.

REFRAIN 5

Brush up your Shakespeare
Start quoting him now.
Brush up your Shakespeare
And the women you will wow.
If your goil is a Washington Heights dream
Treat the kid to "A Midsummer Night's Dream."
If she then wants an all-by-herself night

Let her rest ev'ry 'leventh or "Twelfth Night."
If because of your heat she gets huffy
Simply play on and "Lay on, Macduffy!"
Brush up your Shakespeare
And they'll all kowtow,
We trow, and they'll all kowtow.

GRAND FINALE
Brush up your Shakespeare,
Start quoting him now.
Brush up your Shakespeare
And the women you will wow.
So tonight just recite to your matey,
"Kiss me, Kate, kiss me, Kate, kiss me, Katey."
Brush up your Shakespeare
And they'll all kowtow.

(1948)

Hollis Alpert

(1916–2007)

The Abuse of Greatness

Hollywood has always been ambivalent about full-scale feature length Shakespeare films. From 1920 to 1950 the major studios only took a chance on three major Shakespeare ventures: Sam Taylor's *The Taming of the Shrew* (starring Mary Pickford and Douglas Fairbanks) in 1929, Max Reinhardt's *A Midsummer Night's Dream* in 1935, and Irving Thalberg and George Cukor's *Romeo and Juliet* in 1936. None were critical triumphs and the latter two were box office failures. In 1953 Joseph L. Mankiewicz and John Houseman persuaded MGM to bankroll a fourth attempt: a star-studded production of *Julius Caesar*. Hollis Alpert—biographer, novelist, and later co-founder of the National Society of Film Critics with Pauline Kael—reviewed the film in *The Saturday Review*, and was keenly aware in writing about this "political play" that "fifteen years ago there were different overtones to be gotten in the modern-dress 'black-shirt' version of the Mercury Theatre." The politics of this post-war film were blander and more cautious at a time when the House Committee on Un-American Activities was likely to read "anti-fascist" as "pro-communist." Mankiewicz, though including some anti-fascist elements in his film, found a more relevant analogy in General Eisenhower's triumph over the intellectual Adlai Stevenson in the 1952 presidential election. Togas replaced black-shirts and in place of an all-American cast and accents, British actors—most notably James Mason as Brutus and John Gielgud as Cassius—were brought in to act alongside a rising American star, Marlon Brando, fresh from his success in *A Streetcar Named Desire*, whose Antony, especially when declaiming "Friends, Romans, countrymen," was memorable. Despite its strong cast, Mankiewicz's *Julius Caesar* was only modestly successful at the box office and received mixed reviews; almost four decades would pass before Hollywood invested in Shakespeare again.

☙

"JULIUS CAESAR," a political play by William Shakespeare that has enough familiar lines to fill pages of Bartlett, and that has been dinned for Lord knows how long into the unwilling ears of countless high-school students, can only be supposed to have within it the powers of perpetual regeneration. M-G-M's new "Julius Caesar" would certainly seem to support this theory, and not only does it represent a clear-cut victory over the dull voices of high-school instructors and amateur intoners, but it firmly adapts the play, without the least sense of strain, into its motion-picture mold and, in the doing, gives it a gleaming new appearance. The marvelous poetry, oratory, and rhetoric of the play are apparent, almost as though heard for the first time; there are moments of shock and excitement that the contemporary drama never seems able to reach; one continually sees in it parallels to contemporary history, and prophetic lessons and warnings. That John Houseman, the producer, Joseph L. Mankiewicz, the director, and as accomplished a cast as one could wish could bring this pristine freshness and impact to a play three-and-a-half centuries old is the major accomplishment of the production. I will even go out on a limb and say that it seems to me to belong in the front rank of the great motion pictures.

We must get the inevitable comparisons to the "Hamlet" and "Henry V" of Laurence Olivier out of the way as soon as possible. Less consciously experimental, it seems to me superior to the Olivier "Hamlet," but not quite so gem-like and visually beautiful as the "Henry V." But they are, after all, three quite different plays, and as a result, three quite different movies. Shakespeare, for the movies, seems always to demand a certain refurbishing, perhaps less so for "Julius Caesar" than for "Hamlet," a most difficult movie nut to crack. What was demanded here was sensible cutting and sewing together of the gaps, and Houseman and Mankiewicz managed this job between them. There is not the slightest loss so far as I can see (unless one has memorized the entire play and thus misses certain favorite lines); there is, rather, a gain. The action proceeds with mounting foreboding and excitement, and in climactic scenes reaches a truly fervent pitch. Among scenes that will always be memorable are the brilliantly staged assassination of Caesar, Antony's oration to the mob, and the tent scene in which Cassius and Brutus have their gloomy clash of temperaments. Mankiewicz, who impresses more and more with his striking ability to get actors performing at their peaks, seems to have had the fullest sort of collaboration from John Gielgud, James Mason, and Marlon Brando. My impression is that in this movie we have the best Shakespearean acting yet seen on film, perhaps because of the virtuoso nature of the performances.

It may be a little unfair to single out one performance as dominating the play, but I was particularly struck by the Cassius of John Gielgud. Mr. Gielgud, of course, is probably the most accomplished Shakespearean actor of our day, but I was not fully prepared for the complexity he manages to give to the darkly brooding conspirator. While Brutus, I suppose, must be considered the "hero" of the piece, it is the character of Cassius that in Mr. Gielgud's handling gives off reflections most relevant to our own period. I kept seeing in him (perhaps fancifully) the prototype of the Marxist intellectual. And it is Cassius, after all, who shows most knowledge of the revolutionist's handbook. If his suggestion to dispose of Antony (Shakespeare has him urge this more than once) had been listened to by Brutus and the other conspirators we would not have had a play, for the overthrow of Caesar would have succeeded and there would have been no "counter-revolution." I'm not sure to what extent Mr. Mankiewicz emphasized these aspects in his direction, but some fifteen years ago there were different overtones to be gotten in the modern-dress "black-shirt" version of the Mercury Theatre—the last time, by the way, that the play was seen on the Broadway stage.

It is, however, evident that Mankiewicz has used the emphasis of the closeup more frequently on Gielgud than on any of the others. Mirrored on his face are the anger and the seething frustration, and also the envy that Caesar comments upon; he moves towards us as though possessed of an inner storm. The portrayal of these qualities makes his scenes—such as that with Brutus in the tent at Philippi—more vividly alive than I have seen them done before. You see in him not only the prophet and the organizer of revolution, but the possessor of the seeds of corruption that would seem inevitably to attend a bid for high power.

Perhaps because Cassius has been given this greater depth the simplicity and nobility of Brutus seem all the more emphasized, and James Mason gives him a luminous reading. Mason's acting career gained its first large impetus when he played Brutus nearly twenty years ago at the Gate Theatre in Dublin. It isn't accidental, then, that he should seem so completely at home in the role.

There must have been a good deal of worry in the minds of many as to whether Marlon Brando (who up to now has given the impression of always talking with his mouth full of little round stones) was capable, not only of clear and ringing speech, but of at least an approximation of the Shakespearean style Gielgud and Mason come by more or less naturally. I am happy to report that he turns in a magnificent Antony. His moments alone with the body of Caesar and his oration to the mob thronged before the Senate are quite stunning in their impact. Familiar phrases take on a new sound; even the hackeneyed ". . . lend me your ears," becomes an exhortation, "*Lend* me your ears!" Brando is, quite clearly, the very best of the younger American actors, and there is likely to be movement afoot to try him as Hamlet on the stage. His accomplishment here becomes all the more striking when one considers his inexperience with Shakespeare.

Since so much of the play is oratory, without the fuller differentiation of character in later plays, the mixture of accents (not at all obtrusive) is, I think, helpful. There is no jar when Brando exchanges phrases with Brutus, and again none when Edmond O'Brien enters as Casca. O'Brien, by the way, turns out to be a much better actor than one would have heretofore thought him to be. Louis Calhern's Caesar seems appropriate: the vanity, the susceptibility to flattery, the readiness to grasp total power are all neatly portrayed. The minor feminine roles might seem a concession to the box-office, for we find Calpurnia done by Greer Garson and Portia read by Deborah Kerr. It turns out, though, that they volunteered for their small roles, and they are quite good enough in them.

One decision Houseman and Mankiewicz had to make between them was whether to use color or black-and-white photography. The latter was chosen, obviously, because of the starker effect it gives. Another decision probably was to what extent the possibilities of spectacle were to be exploited. Here a sort of compromise seems to have resulted. Sets were built that were large, spacious, and more stylized than realistic. "Quo Vadis"-like views of ancient Rome have been avoided, but the mob scenes are of good size, numerically speaking. The dreary clanking on and off stage of participants in the Battle of Philippi has been completely avoided by the invention of a sort of ritualized battle sequence showing Antony's army ambushing the forces of Brutus and Cassius. My largest complaint is about the music that accompanies the action—it seems too much a matter of simple drum beats and the blare of trumpets, though on occasion the sounds do give a heightening effect.

I have heard all sorts of announcements about the way the movie will be shown; at present it seems scheduled for wide screen and stereophonic sound treatment, which was not the way I saw or heard it. In New York it will have a two-a-day, reserved-seat policy. That means the picture will be around for quite a while, but I wouldn't waste any time in getting tickets. Hollywood has given us our money's worth this time.

(1953)

Isaac Asimov

(1920–1992)

The Immortal Bard

Science fiction writer Isaac Asimov's most labored contribution to Shakespeare studies was his nearly fifteen-hundred-page *Asimov's Guide to Shakespeare*, published in 1970—a popular volume that was mercilessly attacked by professional scholars (to whom Asimov, stung, replied in an article entitled "Bill and I" that ran in *Fantasy and Science Fiction*). This collision between Shakespearean amateurs and experts (and by extension, between the belief that Shakespeare was fundamentally a popular entertainer like Asimov himself or else an elitist poet whose plays could only properly be understood by English professors) had been cannily anticipated by Asimov sixteen years earlier in his story "The Immortal Bard," first published in the May 1954 issue of *Universe Science Fiction*.

∽

"OH YES," said Dr. Phineas Welch, "I can bring back the spirits of the illustrious dead."

He was a little drunk, or maybe he wouldn't have said it. Of course, it was perfectly all right to get a little drunk at the annual Christmas party.

Scott Robertson, the school's young English instructor, adjusted his glasses and looked to right and left if to see they were overheard. "Really, Dr. Welch."

"I mean it. And not just the spirits. I bring back the bodies, too."

"I wouldn't have said it were possible," said Robertson primly.

"Why not? A simple matter of temporal transference."

"You mean time travel? But that's quite—uh—unusual."

"Not if you know how."

"Well, how, Dr. Welch?"

"Think I'm going to tell you?" asked the physicist gravely. He looked vaguely about for another drink and didn't find any. He said, "I brought quite a few back. Archimedes, Newton, Galileo. Poor fellows."

"Didn't they like it here? I should think they'd have been fascinated by our modern science," said Robertson. He was beginning to enjoy the conversation.

"Oh, they were. They were. Especially Archimedes. I thought he'd go mad with joy at first after I explained a little of it in some Greek I'd boned up on, but no—no——"

"What was wrong?"

"Just a different culture. They couldn't get used to our way of life. They got terribly lonely and frightened. I had to send them back."

"That's too bad."

"Yes. Great minds, but not flexible minds. Not universal. So I tried Shakespeare."

"*What?*" yelled Robertson. This was getting closer to home.

"Don't yell, my boy," said Welch. "It's bad manners."

"Did you say you brought back Shakespeare?"

"I did. I needed someone with a universal mind; someone who knew people well enough to be able to live with them centuries away from his own time. Shakespeare was the man. I've got his signature. As a memento, you know."

"On you?" asked Robertson, eyes bugging.

"Right here." Welch fumbled in one vest pocket after another. "Ah, here it is."

A little piece of pasteboard was passed to the instructor. On one side it said: "L. Klein & Sons, Wholesale Hardware." On the other side, in straggly script, was written, "Willm Shaksper."

A wild surmise filled Robertson. "What did he look like?"

"Not like his pictures. Bald and an ugly mustache. He spoke in a thick brogue. Of course, I did my best to please him with our times. I told him we thought highly of his plays and still put them on the boards. In fact, I said we thought they were the greatest pieces of literature in the English language, maybe in any language."

"Good. Good," said Robertson breathlessly.

"I said people had written volumes of commentaries on his plays. Naturally he wanted to see one and I got one for him from the library."

"And?"

"Oh, he was fascinated. Of course, he had trouble with the current idioms and references to events since 1600, but I helped out. Poor fellow. I don't think he ever expected such treatment. He kept saying, 'God ha' mercy! What cannot be racked from words in five centuries? One could wring, methinks, a flood from a damp clout!'"

"He wouldn't say that."

"Why not? He wrote his plays as quickly as he could. He said he had to on account of the deadlines. He wrote *Hamlet* in less than six months. The plot was an old one. He just polished it up."

"That's all they do to a telescope mirror. Just polish it up," said the English instructor indignantly.

The physicist disregarded him. He made out an untouched cocktail on the bar some feet away and sidled toward it. "I told the immortal bard that we even gave college courses in Shakespeare."

"I give one."

"I know. I enrolled him in your evening extension course. I never saw a man so eager to find out what posterity thought of him as poor Bill was. He worked hard at it."

"You enrolled William Shakespeare in my course?" mumbled Roberston. Even as an alcoholic fantasy, the thought staggered him. And *was* it an alcoholic fantasy? He was beginning to recall a bald man with a queer way of talking . . . .

"Not under his real name, of course," said Dr. Welch. "Never mind what he went under. It was a mistake, that's all. A big mistake. Poor fellow." He had the cocktail now and shook his head at it.

"Why was it a mistake? What happened?"

"I had to send him back to 1600," roared Welch indignantly. "How much humiliation do you think a man can stand?"

"What humiliation are you talking about?"

Dr. Welch tossed off the cocktail. "Why, you poor simpleton, you *flunked* him."

(1954)

John Berryman

(1914–1972)

Shakespeare's Last Word: Justice and Redemption

The poet John Berryman wrote enough on Shakespeare to fill a large book. Berryman had envisioned what he ultimately conceived of as a "large psychosocial critical biography" to be called *Shakespeare's Reality*, and he had even been awarded a fellowship from the National Endowment for the Humanities in 1971 to complete it, but the book remained unfinished when Berryman took his own life the following year. The scattered remains of his decades-long engagement with Shakespeare were gathered by John Haffenden and published in 1999 as *Berryman's Shakespeare*. Shakespeare's influence on Berryman's poetry—especially *Hamlet*, the Sonnets, and *Lear*—was pervasive, not surprising in a writer who observed that "nearly all pitch and accent is in Shakespeare somewhere, the body of language not revealing but creating passion." For all that he wrote and reflected on Shakespeare over the years, he only published one essay about him—"Shakespeare at Thirty"—during his lifetime. Yet Berryman was always able to finish and publish his poetry; *Homage to Mistress Bradstreet* as well as *Dream Songs* were completed hard on the heels of his most intensive periods of Shakespeare research, and were clearly shaped in complex ways by them. "Shakespeare's Last Word: Justice and Redemption," along with a brief companion piece, was posthumously published in 1976 in *The Freedom of the Poet*. Berryman turns his attention in this essay to Shakespeare's "most personal" and last solo-authored play, *The Tempest*. His friend and editor of that collection, Robert Giroux, guessed that it was written around 1962. John Haffenden, who reprinted it, concluded that it was finished by 1955, and I have followed his judgment here.

✧

THE dramatist's scene for *The Tempest* is an "vN-inhabited island" somewhere in the Mediterranean where live the exiled Duke of Milan, Prospero, his daughter Miranda, his slave

Caliban, and spirits, servants to him, of whom the chief is called Ariel. This, with the sea about, is his whole realm and he rules it by magic. By chance his enemies from Italy are delivered into the power of his art, punished with a storm and in other ways, and he regains his original kingdom. The play has sometimes been regarded as a comedy of revenge. But one is made to feel that, except in the interest of justice, Prospero does not much desire his original kingdom ("where Euery third thought shall be my graue"); he never even in the past really desired to rule or administer it: he was interested in *study*. It seems fair to regard him as an unwilling ruler in both the first and the last of the story's three periods of his sway; whether he must be thought of as an unwilling ruler also in the second period—that of the twelve years on the island culminating in the afternoon during which the action of the play occurs (from about two o'clock to about six)—is a question I postpone. Revenge, except as the agent of justice, does not quite name what happens. But revenge is an unsatisfactory characterization for a further reason. It is less striking that he punishes his enemies than that he forgives them, and more striking still is the hope that their natures are altered—most of their natures are altered—by their punishments and forgiveness—punishments, by the way, obviously symbolic: harmless shipwreck in a magic tempest, mental torture in a magic distraction. Yet what we have been saying has at once to be qualified in two ways. First, Prospero does absolutely rule—no other character in drama is so uncompromisingly in charge of all the presented events; and second, he does certainly not impress the spectator or reader as a naturally forgiving man. On the other hand, it is clear that he rules justly, or on behalf of justice; and he is concerned—as once with the education of Caliban—with the spiritual fate of his enemies. Let us take the play, tentatively, as a tragicomedy of justice and redemption, and look into a curious speech of Gonzalo's.

The unwilling visitors to the island are dispersed, you recall, in four places: Ferdinand alone to meet Prospero and Miranda, Stephano and Trinculo to meet Caliban, the sailors (with whom

we are not concerned) on the ship still, and last what we may call
the Court party—the King, Gonzalo, and the rest. Now Gonzalo's chief topic, considered as one for shipwrecked courtiers, is
a little surprising: how society ought to be organized, or disor-
ganized. "Had I plantation of this isle my Lord," he says (that is,
colonization)—

> I' th' Commonwealth I would (by contraries)
> Execute all things: For no kinde of Trafficke
> Would I admit: No name of Magistrate:
> Letters should not be knowne: Riches, pouerty,
> And vse of seruice, none: Contract, Succession,
> Borne, bound of Land, Tilth, Vineyard none:
> No vse of Mettall, Corne, or Wine, or Cyle:
> No occupation, all men idle, all:
> And Women too, but innocent and pure:
> No Soueraignty . . .
> All things in common Nature should produce
> Withour sweat or endeuour . . .
> . . . Nature should bring forth
> Of it owne kinde, all foyzen, all abundance
> To feed my innocent people . . .
> I would with such perfection gouerne Sir
> T 'Excell the Golden Age.

Now this view is satirized by the others as he develops it, and
Gonzalo concedes he spoke mockingly. But this is a respectable, or
distinguished rather, sixteenth-century European view of primitive social organization—the dramatist lifted half of it indeed,
almost uniquely for him, word for word nearly, from Montaigne's
essay on cannibals. Gonzalo, too, is linked with Prospero, not
only as the one notably good man among the Court party, but
as Prospero's saviour at the time of the usurpation; the Masque
of Ceres aims also at the Golden Age when "Spring came to you
at the farthest / In the very end of harvest"—that is, a winterless
age; and beyond some superficial resemblance between Gonzalo's

ironic description and Prospero's actual commonwealth on the island, they present of course radical and imposing differences, by which we may suppose the dramatist to be developing his theme. I take four of these differences.

Clusters of difference they really are, and may form a chain, but the first is absolute. "No Soueraignty," says Gonzalo, and Prospero is an autocrat. The nature of his sway can be suggested by a consideration of some features of his speech. Even among the grand rulers Shakespeare imagined, Prospero commands an utterance of incommensurable solemnity and majesty. When his daughter ventures a question, he answers, robed, erect:

> Know thus far forth,
> By accident most strange, bountifull *Fortune*
> (*Now* my deere Lady) hath mine enemies
> Brought to this shore: And by my prescience
> I finde my *Zenith* doth depend vpon
> A most auspicious starre, whose influence
> If now I court not, but omit, my fortunes
> Will euer after droope . . .

Birth, rule, age, wisdom do not by themselves account for the extremity of this tone; Prospero also is a magician, and sounds it. He speaks himself of his "dignity"; the transition, both in the courtiers and the drunkards, from levity to evil, is in this play an easy one. Then, his ceremonial elaboration is consistent with the most violent or expressive curtness—a curtness of which the next lines of this speech show an overbearing instance:

> Heere cease more questions,
> Thou art inclinde to sleepe, 'tis a good dulnesse,
> And giue it way: I know thou canst not chuse . . .

In the slowing of the final phrase we hear Miranda succumb; we feel the spell as real. The solemnity is executive.

Majesty, activity. Another feature of Prospero's speech worth signalizing is nakedly its power. Consider some lines from his final adjuration to his spirits—

> by whose ayde
> (Weake Masters though ye be) I have bedymn'd
> The Noone-tide Sun, call'd forth the mutenous windes,
> And twixt the green sea and the azured vault
> Set roaring warre . . .

This hair-raising language is thoughtful, not ornamental. He calls his assistants "weake" but acknowledges them "masters"; whose master he is. He bedimmed (a high-keyed word) the sun at the moment when that feat might be thought most difficult—a fancy borrowed from Ovid, who exaggerates it. Then he called forth (low or neutral key, as for calling dogs) winds that did not want to come (a figure for the reluctant Ariel); however, they come. Then a vast and blazing image: of the ocean and of heaven's arch, and of the space between them—and since a high "azured" is coming, plain "green" is vivid with "sea"; now, into this space, and between these great stages of nature, he "sets"—a detailed, local word, as if he were going to place a salt cellar there—he sets war, and before, or just as you learn "war," it "roars" at you.*

Sovereignty, then, as against Gonzalo's anarchy, and a sovereignty of which the hard characteristics, displayed in the style, are ritual solemnity, activity, all-mastering power. Prospero's sovereignty in the world of the play, the island, is founded upon power, and nothing else. His power is founded, however, and here we reach a second difference from Gonzalo's commonwealth, upon learning. "Letters should not be knowne." Prospero's learning— his magic art, his actual books—these are repeatedly insisted on; he even studies a good deal during the rather short course of the play, and in the end he has undertaken to drown his book. Prospero has also attended carefully, we learn, to the education of Miranda; and he and Miranda have taught Caliban what Caliban could be taught. Prospero, indeed, is a real pedant—this is one of the directions in which a risk was taken with the audience's sympathy for him.

---

* The word is taken over from the passage in Golding's *Ovid*, where its use is commonplace.

The ruler, in short, works. Everyone works under Prospero's commonwealth, he at ruling, Miranda at her education and Caliban's, Ariel and Caliban at tasks fitting their quality. This marks a third difference between Gonzalo's image of universal idleness and the island fact, and it is unusual in drama. The audience has been working itself all day (or the Elizabethan popular audience was exactly shirking work to attend the afternoon performance) and does not care to see people work on the stage. But much of this work, again, is done onstage, feeble indeed from a theatrical point of view, like the log-bearing. The sole visitor to the island with whom its ruler comes immediately into contact, Ferdinand, is put to work immediately. We must distinguish, of course, between on the one hand the unsuitable work done by Ferdinand, and Ariel's, and on the other hand, that done by Caliban. Ferdinand's is a test of character, imposed to determine the quality of his devotion to Miranda. Ariel's is on contract—another feature of society excluded by Gonzalo; it is performed partly out of gratitude to Prospero for having freed him from the pine, partly out of fear of the oak, and partly in reliance upon Prospero's promise to free him wholly in the end. And here we come first upon what anyone must feel is one of the play's dominant themes: the impending freedom of Ariel. The work done by these two is limited in term and teleological: it has an end, which is understood by the ruler—not necessarily by the subject (in Ferdinand's case not), but by the ruler. Caliban's labours are another matter.

A fourth difference between Gonzalo's description and Prospero's state let us describe as an error made by Gonzalo when he speaks of "my innocent people." Neither do most of the Court party, nor Stephano and Trinculo, illustrate any such conception of human nature as underlies this (ironic, to be sure) optimism; but them we will come to. On the island already exists a creature able to make mincemeat of Gonzalo's notion, or the later idea, consistent with it, of the Noble Savage. Caliban, however, who is certainly one of Shakespeare's most exquisite creations, crucial to this play, is as complicated as his parentage, and I am anxious not to oversimplify his character, which is at any rate triple. Upon his first appearance he is called "Thou Earth, thou," to Prospero's threats he answers only, "I must eat my dinner," and much of his talk presents nature in its earthiest form:

> I prethee let me bring thee where Crabs grow;
> And I with my long nayles will digge thee pig-nuts;
> Show thee a Jayes nest, and instruct thee how
> To snare the nimble Marazet: Ile bring thee
> To clustring Philbirts, and sometimes Ile get thee
> Young Scamels from the Rocke: Wilt thou goe with me?

Or

>   she will become thy bed, I warrent,
> And bring thee forth braue brood.

But it is clear that this is already very poetic, and the contrast between the tone of this last remark and Stephano's response to it ("Monster, I will kill this man") makes it clearer still that faculties far higher than those of the butler and jester have not been denied to Caliban. We are not wholly surprised when the poet places this in his mouth:

> Be not affeared [he says], the isle is full of noyses,
> Sounds, and sweet aires, that giue delight and hurt not:
> Sometimes a thousand twangling Instruments
> Will hum about mine eares; and sometime voices,
> That if I then had wak'd after long sleepe,
> Will make me sleepe again, and then in dreaming
> The clouds methought would open, and show riches
> Ready to drop vpon me, that when I wak'd
> I cride to dreame againe.

The gulf between him and his colleagues yawns again in Stephano's comment upon this:

> This will preue a braue kingdome to me, where I shall
> Haue my Musike for nothing.

But in Caliban's comment upon *this*—"When *Prospero* is destroye'd"—we are reminded of his third nature, or rather of the disposition that governs, for action and in the commonwealth, both his representative (or lower) and higher natures. This disposition (recognized by Caliban himself in "You taught me Language, and my profit on't, / Is, I know how to curse") is unregenerate and malicious, extending to designs of rape and murder, which require frustration, demand punishment, and make inevitable his status of slave. He is not master of himself, and therefore the freedom of Ariel is out of the question for him: he must be permanently mastered. One of his lines editors take as drunken nonsense. Caliban is fooling around with his name: "'Ban, 'Ban, Cacaliban." Shakespeare is not fooling around, however. "Ban" means *curse*, and the first two syllables of "Cacaliban" are suggestive: they suggest "cacodeman" (or devil)—a word the poet had applied twenty years before to Richard III, who is *also* deformed. Prospero finally, in Act IV, calls him "a devil." We may wonder whether Prospero's nature—in the dramatist's intention—has not been soured partly by his failure with the education of Caliban— "on whom my paines Humanely taken, all, all lost, quite lost . . ."

We are ready, perhaps, for a more detailed formulation. Sovereignty is implied by society. It should be based on power, and power should be based on learning. Work is necessary, and it should be work done on contract, with its end in view by the ruler, except where the subject is unable to enter into a contract because he cannot be depended upon to fulfill it; such cases exist, and are not incompatible with the possession of considerable and even elevated faculties otherwise than in the matter of self-mastery. Contract is strongest when triply based: on gratitude backward, present fear, and confident hope forward. Mutiny against a just ruler (such as Ariel's in prospect, Caliban's in practice) is the ultimate social crime and gives rise to or accompanies all other evil. Thus, there is no "freedom" upon this island at all. Even Miranda studies and educates Caliban and solaces Prospero. The ruler's work consists in: education (including unremitting self-education), the administration of justice (including punishment), and redemption. Before passing on to this third work of the ruler, of which we have said almost nothing, I want to notice one broad controlling design of justice dramatized.

A singular feature of the structure of *The Tempest* is that the catastrophe occurs in the opening scene, which delivers Prospero's enemies into his power. We do not at the time know this. We see only a storm at sea, rulers on board, a wreck. We learn it during the second scene, suspectingly and slow, then suddenly in the speech that I used to illustrate Prospero's solemnity. But meanwhile we have heard about another "sea-sorrow" twelve years before, of which the near-victims were Prospero and his daughter. Thus, the instant of full recognition of *what* has happened contains a full recognition of *why* it happened. Those tortured by the sea at first were innocent; those who caused that torture are guilty and are now tortured by the sea; justice exists. Deep in the play Ariel makes the vise-like pattern explicit:

> you three . . .
> Exposed vnto the Sea (which hath requit it)
> Him, and his innocent childe: for which foule deed,
> The Powres, delaying (not forgetting) haue
> Incens'd the Seas, and Shores, yea, all the Creatures
> Against your peace . . .

It is owing to this unexampled priority of the catastrophic action, as a German critic has pointed out, that imagery in *The Tempest* has not its normal Shakespearean function of foreshadowing but is used rather to recall, to remind of what has happened (and so, as well, of what it meant). I adduce two morose, disdainful instances of the way in which the persistent sea imagery is linked with the guilty men and with the conception of the ocean as an agent of retribution. When Anthonio is working the inert Sebastian toward the murder of his brother, Sebastian admits:

> I am standing water.
> ANTHONIO. Ile teach you how to flow.
> SEBASTIAN. Do so; to ebbe
>   Hereditary Sloth instructs me.

Here the water image is forced into a full sea image by "ebbe." The other, the most elaborate image perhaps in this play very scant in imagery, is declaimed by Prospero about the guilty men in Act V when he releases them from their distraction:

> Their understanding
> Begins to swell, and the approaching tide
> Will shortly fill the reasonable shore
> That now lyes foule, and muddy . . .

Here only the two abstract terms keep the subject in sight, all the rest being contemptuous metaphor; this is mercy with a *vengeance*.

Alonso is punished throughout in his grief for his son, and at last by Ariel's instruction is brought to despair:

> The thunder
> (That deepe and dreadfull Organ-Pipe) pronounc'd
> The name of *Prosper*: it did base my Trespasse—

that terrifying pun—and so thence to repentance. His enmity to Prospero was general, his crime against Milan general. With Prospero's brother an intenser course is necessary. Before he is punished, he is made (by temptation—the others' magic sleep) to re-enact his crime by persuading the dull Sebastian to the murder of *his* brother; and this persuasion has almost the tone of Iago—it is hardly comedic. Even the brutal fool Sebastian, when at last he sees Anthonio's drift, is moved to ask, "But for your conscience":

> ANTHONIO: Ay Sir: where lies that? If twere a kybe
> Twould put me to my slipper: But I feele not
> This Deity in my bosome: Twentie consciences
> That stand twist me, and *Millaine*, candied be they,
> And melt ere they mollest. Here lies your Brother,
> No better than the earth he lies vpon.
> If he *were* that which now hee's *like* (that's dead)
> Whom I with this obedient steele (three inches of it)
> Can lay to bed for euer: whiles you doing thus,

> To the perpetuall winke for aye might put
> *This* ancient Morsell: this Sir Prudence, who
> Should act vpbraid but course: for all the rest
> They'll take suggestion, as Cat laps milke,
> They'll tell the clocke to any businesse that
> We say befits the houre.

This enforced, hell-like recapitulation—it is the plotters who are lapping the poisoned milk set out—is *justice* with a vengeance. Are we drifting back to "revenge"? An element of vindictiveness disconcernible in Prospero ought not to make us lose our heads and see him as a vindictive rather than as a just man. Besides the twelve years of barbaric exile, take the nature of the crimes: intended murder and, far worse to an Elizabethan or Jacobean, usurpation and intended usurpation. The usurpation, moreover, had been, was to be, by worse rulers against better—self-deprecation is not one of Prospero's foibles—and his native state, Milan, thus became basely tributary. But I think we are bound to confess a sense that Prospero finally forgives his enemies rather from justice (the sense that they have suffered enough, and repent, and deserve his restored esteem) than from mercy. There exist touches of mercy; but even these are apt to be accompanied by *rational* resentment and rational, rather than emotional, redemptive operation:

> Thogh with their high wrongs I am strook to th' quick
> Yet, with my nobler reason, gainst my furie
> Doe I take part: The rarer Action is
> In *vertue*, then in vengeance . . .

And what reconciliation can be heard in this?—

> For you, most wicked sir, whom to call brother
> Would even infect my mouth, I do forgive
> Thy rankest fault . . .

—to which Shakespeare wisely gives Anthonio no reply. The general view taken of human nature here? Not high, not high. To see in the last plays, as recent critics do, a sort of ministry of reconciliation seems to me to sentimentalize them and falsify our experience of their reality. Everybody does by no means kiss and make up—not even in *The Winter's Tale*, which (as villianless) I should call the most charitable of them.

Now virtue for a ruler consists in the production of virtue in himself and his subjects—or, where it exists already, the encouragement, refinement, and maintenance of it, as in Prospero himself, in Miranda, in Ferdinand, in Gonzalo. But where it does not exist, it must be produced in whatever degree is practicable, according to the nature of the subject; and this brings us to the fates of Alonso, Anthonio, Sebastian, of Stephano and Trinculo, of Caliban.

Take the first group. Without insisting upon my term "redemption," I think we need not hesitate over the fact, which is that Alonso, Anthonio, and Sebastian are redeemed—reclaimed, ransomed, delivered, from their guilt, and by Prospero, in a sequence of deliberate operations. This makes the situation essentially different from the one in *As You Like It*, where, also, a duke is exiled by his brother to a sort of utopia, his daughter is with him, the usurper comes and is converted—there is even, also, a *second* wicked brother who comes and reforms. The imagination of this author used the same materials again and again, all down its mature working life; but it used them differently. The illuminating and nailing difference, between the conventional comedic reformations in the Forest of Arden and those on the enchanted island, is the thematic hammer in *The Tempest* of the word "free," the central word in the play. This is Shakespeare's word. It first appears as "Libertie," in Ariel's demand—which, with Prospero's promise, alluded to throughout and at last performed, is our metaphorical and dramatic instruction in the play's prime theme. But the constant words are "freedom," "free." Alonso, Anthonio (maybe), and Sebastian are set *free* from their old selves, from their guilt. Even Caliban, whose nature forestalls freedom, is freed, at any rate, from his illusions about Stephano and Trinculo, and undertakes in his final speech (one of Shakespeare's oddest and most attractive notes) to "be wise hereafter, / And seek for grace." How is it that Stephano and Trinculo have or can have no part in this general redemption?

Possibly it is because they are drunk. Amusingly as here their antics are handled, drunkenness is not much a comic topic in Shakespeare's mature plays—in *Hamlet*, *Othello*, *Measure for Measure*. The drunkenness of Stephano and Trinculo images their self-slavery and the moral stupidity that allows them to fall in with the suggestions of Caliban's malice. Their crime, too, like that of the men from the top of society, intends not murder only but usurpation—Stephano is to be King in Prospero's place. Irrational, self-set outside reason, they stand beyond the reach of the ruler's redemptive design. *They* think they are "free," of course, as Caliban imagines he is with his new master. "Freedome," he cries, "high-day, high-day freedome, freedome high-day, freedome." The catch sung by Stephano and Trinculo, adapting a proverb already employed in *Twelfth Night*, certainly embodies one of the dramatist's most daring and schematic ironies: "Flout 'em and cout 'em: and Skowt 'em and flout 'em / Thought is free."

The theme rules without irony the final line of the play, when Ariel hears at last:

> To the Elements
> Be free, and fare thou well . . .

and in the final line, the final word, of the epilogue, Prospero asks the audience to set *him* "free." Probably we are right to wonder whether Prospero *is* not himself in some way freed in the play or by its action. Prospero we have evidently to see in at least two characters; as the exile, injured and vindictive, and as the great Magician and Judge—God onstage—who rights the wrongs sustained by the exile (himself) and also redeems the exile's enemies, so far as their natures permit. Then clearly Prospero is set free, in both the rules: free from vindictiveness (strongly conveyed, the sense of this, in the fifth act) and from the sense of injustice, and free from his overwhelming power. Perhaps those men only who have exercised formidable power can feel fully what it means to wish to be free of it; but everyone understands both fatigue and the desire to be free of the responsibilities of power. But to be free of unruly and discreditable desire is the heart of the play's desire, and even in this does Prospero participate, released from the intoxications of hatred and might.

The scene, wonderful in production, where Ferdinand and Miranda are discovered "playing at Chesse," brings them, too, within the conclusion of this theme. Here is a game, as against the work they formerly did. No ordinary game: an exercise ancient, orderly, and intellectual. We remember Prospero's harsh adjuration to them *not*, before marriage, to

> Giue dalliance
> Too much the raigne; the strongest oaths, are
> To th' fire ith' blood . . .

and we *see* them holding in check their desires, and perhaps we remember Hamlet's crying

> Giue me that man
> That is not passions slaue, and I will weare him
> In my harts core, I in my hart of harts . . .

Nobody, I suppose, who had not himself *been* passion's slave could have made the longing envy in these lines so central in his most personal play and their sense so necessary in the design of his final play.

(1955)

Lord Buckley

(1906–1960)

Hipsters, Flipsters, and Finger-Poppin' Daddies

The traditions of Shakespearean burlesque and adaptation were alive and well in 1950s America, as exemplified in Lord Buckley's take on Mark Antony's funeral oration in "Hipsters, Flipsters, and Finger-Poppin' Daddies." The hard-living and now little-known Lord (Richard) Buckley, born in 1906, was both a throwback and ahead of his time, a bridge between American minstrel entertainers and the beats, comedians, singers, and rappers that followed in his wake. "Hipsters" was the title track of Buckley's 1955 RCA album, on which he recited these riffs to musical accompaniment. The instrumentalists included the great saxophonist Benny Carter (on clarinet), and the album anticipated Duke Ellington's iconic 1957 jazz reinterpretation of Shakespeare, *Such Sweet Thunder*. In addition to its parody of Antony's "Friends, Romans, countrymen" (a speech that Marlon Brando had recently popularized in Mankiewicz's film of *Julius Caesar*), Buckley's album updates another pair of familiar Shakespeare speeches: "Is This The Sticker?" (taking off on Macbeth's famous "Is this a dagger which I see before me?"), and "To Swing or Not to Swing," Hamlet's most famous soliloquy as rendered by a modern American hipster:

> Is it hipper for the wig to dig
> The flips and drags of the wheel of fortune
> Or to come on like Kinsey
> Against this mass mess
> And by this stance cover the action.

❧

Now you see in Hip Talk, they call William Shakespeare, "Willie the Shake!" You know why they call him "Willie the Shake"? Because, *HE SHOOK EVERYBODY!!* They gave this Cat five cents worth of ink, and a nickle's worth of paper, and he sat down and wrote up such a breeze, WHAMMMMM!!!

Everybody got off! Period! He was a hard, tight, tough Cat. Pen
in hand, he was a Mother Superior.

Now you remember when Mark and Cleo were swangin' up a
storm on that velvet-lined Nile barge, suckin' up a little Egyptian
whiskey with that wild incense flyin' all over the place and that
Buddha-headed moon pale Jazzmin colored flippin' the scene. It
was Romance City! Caesar meantime had split to Rome, went to
that big Jam Session and they sliced that poo' Cat up all over the
place. Naturally Mark has got to put Cleo down, this was a tight
move for him 'cause this Cleo was an early day Elizabeth Taylor.
This chick had more curves than the Santa Fe Railroad making
the Grand Canyon. But he had to split 'cause Caesar was his Main-
Day Buddy Cat and they were putting Caesar in the hole. "And
you know every Fox has got his Box."

The Roman Senate is jumpin' salty all over the place so Mark
the Spark showed on the scene, faced all the studs, wild and other
wise, and shook up the whole Scene! As he BLEW:

Hipsters, Flipsters, and Finger-Poppin' Daddies,
Knock me your lobes!
I came here to lay Caesar out,
Not to hip you to him.
The bad jazz that a cat blows,
Wails long after he's cut out.
The groovey, is often stashed with their frames,
So don't put Caesar down.

The swinging Brutus hath laid a story on you,
That Caesar was hooked for power.
If it were so, it was a sad drag,
And sadly hath the Caesar cat answered it.
Here, with a pass from Brutus and the other brass,
For Brutus is a worthy stud,
Yea, so are they all worthy studs.

I come to wail at Caesar's wake,
He was my buddy-cat, and he leveled with me.
Yet Brutus digs that he has eyes for power,
And Brutus is a solid cat.
It is true he hath returned with many freaks in chains,
And brought them home to Rome!
Yea, the booty was looty and hipped the treasury well!

Dost thou dig that this was Caesar's groove for the push?
When the cats with the empty kicks have copped out,
Yeah—, Caesar hath copped out too, and cried up a storm!
To be a world grabber, a stiffer riff must be blown.
Without bread, a stud can't even rule an ant hill.

Yet Brutus was swinging for the moon,
And Yea, Brutus is a worthy stud.
And all you cats were gassed on the Lupercal,
When he came on like a King freak.
Three times I laid the Kingly wig on him,
And thrice did he put it down.
Was this the move of a greedy hipster?
Yet Brutus said he dug the lick,
And Yea, a hipper cat hath never blown.

Some claim that Brutus's story was a drag,
But I dug the story was solid!
I came here to blow, now stay cool while I blow!
You dug him all the way once because you were hip that he was solid,
How can you now come on so square?
Now that he has cut out of this world?
City Hall has flipped, and swung to a drunken zoo!
And all of you cats have goofed to wig city!
Dig me hard, my ticker is in the coffin there with Caesar,
And Yea, I must stay cool, 'Til it flipeth back to me.

(1955)

Hyam Plutzik

(1911–1962)

Carlus

While serving in the U.S. military in England during World War II, Hyam Plutzik outlined and began writing an ambitious poem, *Horatio*, in which Hamlet's loyal friend struggles to fulfill his promise to "in this harsh world draw thy breath in pain / To tell my story." The two-thousand-line poem, sections of which appeared in print in the intervening years, was finally completed and published in 1961 and was a finalist for the Pulitzer Prize. The following year, at the age of fifty, Plutzik died of cancer. In "Carlus," a section of the poem first published in *The Yale Review*, forty-three years have passed since Hamlet's death. Horatio, now an old man, finds himself fending off the skeptical criticism of a pompous prime minister, Carlus, who, troubled by the political subversiveness of what Horatio is doing, tries to discourage him in his relentless and lifelong effort to clear Hamlet's name. This section of *Horatio* responds powerfully to Shakespeare's play, even as it speaks to the ominous political climate of Cold War America. Born in Brooklyn in 1911, Plutzik spoke only Yiddish, Hebrew, and Russian until the age of seven. He later attended Trinity College in Connecticut, then graduate school at Yale, and published three other volumes of poetry. The poet and critic Eric Ormsby wrote of Plutzik and his *Horatio* that he was "a marvelous poet whom Ted Hughes and others championed. He tried to recreate a credible Shakespearean voice in American verse but his success doomed his verse to obscurity."

❦

At Whitsuntide when the diminishing trumpet-call
Concluded the year's high audience and blessing,
And the throne, empty, looked down at a scattering multitude—
As I loitered, giving and taking hail and farewell,
Carlus, the Prime Minister, beckoned to me
With a fulsome smile that overstrained the occasion:

"Horatio, do come to my cabinet
To pass a quarter hour with an old old friend
And swallow, the spirit willing, a toast or three."

Since he took no wine, we sipped a candied water.
He stood at the window, regarding the issuing courtiers
In their red and purple vestments, upon the drawbridge,
And the ladies among them, gentle and beautiful.

"You and I, Horatio, are veterans"—
(He gave me the smile again and slapped my shoulder)—
"Have seen this often, yet does not the splendor still
Of royal prerogative stir your old heart,
As mine too—the Crown and its treasure of meaning
Delivered by God to secure our health and weal?
You, as one of His Majesty's truest liegemen,
Agree with me I know."

                              He sipped his drink.
I gave him a puzzled stare. He smiled once more.

"And that, my old friend, is why I am hurt
At these actions of yours that hint at a—lesser loyalty—"

I rose to my feet: "What! Do you presume—?"

"Eh, no offense! Sit down, my dear old friend.
Though I've lived this public life for forty years
I'm still, it seems, a fool at picking my words
(Where someone I love is concerned). Yet because I love you—
And only because—do I open my heart thus.
And because, as I said, I'm a master fool myself
(For who but a fool would become a politician?)
And know that breed of breast by personal pain,
My heart is forlorn, believe me, to see a friend—
Nay, more, a crony—make of himself a fool
As you have done by—"

                    "Go to the devil!" I cried.
"Will you quit that donkey's smile and that heeing and hawing?
I thought when you first spoke of a lapse of fealty
You were scheming to have my head. But no, I'm a 'fool'.
If to be a fool is now a capital crime
The world must soon become depopulated—
Except for its cows and horses. I admit the charge,
Being both mortal and human. But how, inform me,
Am I more of a fool than you?"

                                        He smiled again,
Sipping at the tasteless drink, and raised a finger.
"I am pleased you're not offended, so let me be frank.
I allude to your strange and dangerous infatuation
With the memory of that mad old Prince Hamlet—"

"Dangerous? Infatuate? What can you mean?
And how, may I ask, is the friendship you choose to mock at
Relevant or important to—?"

                            "Precisely!
It is important because of its unimportance."

"Ah, so you've read my grandmother's book of riddles!
And how do you like them?"

                            "Please be serious.
I shall not speak of the laughter behind your back—
A laughter, cousin, that's bad enough at Court,
But how much worse when the vulgar are in the secret?
Disguise yourself as a 'prentice or the Caliph of Bagdad,
Sit on a bench where the mean folk meet for guzzling,
And mention the Lord Horatio. Will you hear
Of the embassies to France, England and Italy,
Or services to the King at home in Denmark?
Or, instead, of a doting fellow constantly chattering

Of an ancient clown named Hamlet, whose like he is?
Then sidle up to the ear of a courtier
And whisper: 'Psst! there's old Horatio!
I'll bet you ten of the best that within the hour
He brings up his old Hamlet!' 'Done, if you give me
Three to one at least, for otherwise
We have no contest. Meanwhile, no leading remarks.
The slightest hint, and he's out with his favorite subject
Like a jack-in-the-box.' No, I shall not speak
On how this reflects on the good sense of His Majesty,
On my own good sense, on our basic judgment of men—
Since it is we (or our predecessors in council
Or on the throne) that have set you on your pedestal.
Who will concede us the wisdom of the good governor
If our ministers play the fool? Is this your loyalty?
So, by your 'unimportant' infatuation
You reveal an important lack, and fail to give
To weighty matters their true and rightful weight.
In sum, this loyalty to a dead pretender
Detracts from the love that must be given now
To a living king—"

                    "Tell me," I said at last,
"Has our lord the King concurred with you in this?"

"Do you mean, has he set his seal on a pompous document
With words of such a substance? No, my friend.
But, being his right arm, I know his sentiments—
Though let me assure you his love for you is warm—
As mine is too: which is my motive precisely
For driving myself to speak these painful words."

He sipped and smiled.

                    "Thank you, my lord Carlus,"
I said with a bow. "And I'm pleased that in your speaking

You've shown me once again, in all its splendor,
The oversimplification that's heart and liver
Of your talent and technique in government—"

"Ah, how glad I am you're not offended!"
He burst out with a laugh.

                              I cut him off.
"But I'm not yet the laughingstock of Denmark.
Nor need I preach a sermon on my deeds
Done with a humble heart for King and land,
Nor argue my allegiance. And if someone
Snickers behind my back some Wednesday noon
I shall not pause from building a monument
Of truth for a dear ghost that I revere.
And let me be a hundred times a clown—
Once for each piece of gold you say some simpleton
Bets on my words—if but I could establish
For a dead friend and prince, the truth—"

                                        "Horatio,
You drive me mad! What is this wild obsession
With a man who is dust these sixty or seventy years—"

"Forty-three years," I said.

                         "Well, have it so.
Such grief is *contra naturam*, against God
Who marks all men for death, both friend and foe.
History's nothing more than the chronicle
Of the death of friends. By Hercules, such dumps
Affront the Holy Ghost!"

                         A shudder shook me,
Which he mistook, and his voice lost its edge.
He rose and walked to the casement. The dark was sifting
Into the room.

Turning, with a shrug of the shoulder:
"Faw," he laughed, "but why do I irk myself
With your affairs? You reached the year of discretion
Somewhat before my time. And how should a pup
Presume to teach an older dog his catechism?
Perhaps it's because I'm puzzled—well, intrigued—
By this phenomenon. It throws a glove in my face
And challenges my wit. I pride myself
On being a judge of men; have studied the clockwork
That makes them stand or sit, be stupid or clever,
Hate or love. To what but this am I debtor
For these many years on the teetering pinnacle
Where a King's minister parries his enviers?
Say it's my business to know the current crop
Of humors, melancholies and obsessions—
Whatever's the fashion in bedlam or the court—
But yours, I must confess, is (how shall I phrase it?)
What the wisest of men declared as beyond the possible:
A new thing under the sun."

     "If so," I began—

"But," he blurted, "you persist in talking of 'truth'.
Your devotion's for truth's sake. What, pray, is truth?
What is this truth you would exhume from the grave?
I am a practical fellow. Truth to me
(Except, of course, for the doctrines of our religion)
Is what I can see—a fact, no more or less.
Recall that I was present at your drama,
A simple lad but nevertheless a bright one.
One of my dearest memories is your Hamlet
With spittle running down the ends of his mouth,
As he sat on the floor busily counting his toes
While the court looked on. . . . You think this a foul blow? . . .
Well, since we're bogged down in your endless subject,
What *are* the facts? That Hamlet killed a king.
What is the issue? That killing kings is wicked.

Judge Periwig could hale us twenty witnesses
Who saw the sword stuffed into Claudius
By a man they would swear they knew to be your Hamlet.
The rest is supposititious, a farrago
Of dreams and visions. You claim that Claudius
Had killed the older Hamlet? Proof! Proof!
Who saw it? What's his credibility?
A ghost? You were a sharp student of law.
Do you recall in the jurisprudence of Denmark
One single instance, back to the glorious days
When our ancestors painted their ears with ochre
And wore, for a bonnet, the horns of a bull, that a court
Admitted the testimony of a ghost,
Even at second remove? Who saw this spectre?
You and your friend the guard, What-you-may-call-him?
You swear it was old Hamlet and not a demon?
Do you swear indeed it was not some creature of Hamlet's
Tricked out in a ghostly disguise to further his ends?
And tell me what, with your own ears, you heard.
Ah, no one but Hamlet heard it?—at least he returned
From a whispered interview, all incoherent!
But later, hinting his secret to you alone
Urged you to watch the King as he sat at a play—
And if he blenched at the wrong moment—poof!"

Grinning, he lowered his voice. "Do let me whisper
A secret of state, on the good authority
Of my old aunt: When Claudius at the play
Rose and paled, it was only because that morning
He had physicked himself too much, and suddenly now
Was—called away to some urgent and—*privy* matter
That demanded action at once. . . . Come, no offense!
No, the only man who 'heard' the ghostly palaver
Was he who stood, or hoped, to profit the most
By his capable uncle's death, which he therefore schemed:
Hamlet himself, a disgruntled, ambitious fellow,

Of mysterious, changing moods, so unreliable
That, luckily for Denmark, the Electors
(Against the weight of primogeniture)
Had cast their vote on the more solid Claudius
When the elder Hamlet died."

                              The tepid liquid
Was low in the glass. He filled, he downed a draught,
And his lowered eyes met mine.

                              "And tell me, Carlus,
Do you believe all this?"

                              A gigantic laugh
Exploded in the still room. "You sly dog!
I thought (ha ha!) I had you neatly tied.
But that old (ha!) Horatio's no hound
To forget a trick. You ask: do I believe it?
I was about to say: 'Of course I don't!'
But that, though pleasantly paradoxical,
Doesn't quite match my measure. Rather say
The question of belief's irrelevant.
The nub of my little story is that it fits.
It's neat, takes some unpleasant circumstances
And explains them in a way that's best for Denmark,
And so (to skip some steps of schoolmen's logic)
Is true, if truth there is. No, cousin Horatio,
By this obsession of yours you tempt the populace
With impossible, dangerous dreams; you give them a sauce
That begins by tingling the palate harmlessly
But begets, by gradual increment, a thirst
Like that of a rabid dog. If you justify Hamlet
You strike a blow at the integrity
Of our dear land, and the body of its king;
Encourage the regicide who feeds on visions.
Once you convince the people that a fellow

Who thinks he sees a ghost may kill a king,
Then the cat's out of the bag, the rest is anarchy.
As the first minister of a powerful realm
It is my business to know the discontents,
The masterless anxieties, the irritants,
That gnaw at the heart of a nation—my concern
To see who fans these lusts and who abates them,
And (where is needful) take action. You have devoted
Too many days and nights to making possible—
Yea, plausible—at times, indeed, desirable—
That which must be beyond imagination.
If Claudius was a murderer, what of that?
Or Hamlet a saint? How are these statements meaningful?
These are the sort of 'truths' that live in a vacuum,
Which nature abhors. It is necessary for Denmark,
And the stability of Christendom,
Your happiness and mine, the courtier's, the peasant's,
That your Hamlet be a fool, a scoundrel, a murderer
Who was justly paid; yet better still, my friend
(For you have made too much of a dubious history,
And a princely madman too may poison the brain)
If he and his deeds are given a chance to sleep."

He suddenly pulled at the bell-cord: "Give me some light!
Lights! Lights!" A shiver went down my back.
"But how we babble on, eh, old fellow.
The sin of age. . . . I hear there's splendid hunting
Up at your northern place—at Forstness is it?
If I had the time! But these constant affairs and crises.
This very moment," he looked at the clock and arose,
"The King awaits me in his private office.
The Swedish matter. Fare you well, my brother."

I left at once by the southern gate. In the courtyard
The King was pacing his new Arab courser.
When he saw me, he dismounted, took both my hands,

Remarked on a grim sadness in my look,
Bemoaned my rare comings to the court.
For over an hour we paced, in easy talk.
When I took my leave, he kissed me on both cheeks.

(1960)

Mary McCarthy

(1912–1989)

General Macbeth

McCarthy writes that she "majored in Elizabethan literature" at Vassar, where she studied Shakespeare with Professor Helen Sandison and recalled that year-long course as "formative." Looking back in 1979, she told an interviewer that aside "from Christian doctrine, the thing that has most formed my cast of mind has probably been Shakespeare." Best known as a novelist, essayist, and social critic, early on in her career McCarthy was also a theater critic (writing about Orson Welles's productions of *Julius Caesar* and *Macbeth* in *Partisan Review*). Her reading of *Macbeth*, published in Harper's in 1962, turns received wisdom on its head. Rather than seeing Macbeth as a hero possessed of vision and imagination, McCarthy suggests instead that his tragedy resides in his literal-mindedness, that he is no more than a familiar "modern" and "bourgeois type," superstitious and credulous, the "eternal executive" whose "main concern throughout the play is . . . to get a good night's sleep," and whose savvy wife—who sees him for what he is, a shallow mix of "fear and ambition"—can barely mask her impatience and contempt for him. The moral: "ambition, fear, and a kind of stupidity make a deadly combination," one that McCarthy sees around her in modern-day leaders, all too willing to unloose "the potential destructiveness that was always there in Nature." In recasting the play in contemporary terms, McCarthy turns the domestic dynamics of the Macbeths into a familiar suburban story (akin to the marital dynamics of Richard Yates's *Revolutionary Road*, published in 1961), and the politics of the play into a mirror of the Cold War world. It is no surprise that her good friend Hannah Arendt, who came across "General Macbeth" in *Harper's* while she was at work on her own study of a banal and evil figure, Adolf Eichmann, wrote to McCarthy that "I fell greatly and enthusiastically in love with the Macbeth article."

H E is a general and has just won a battle; he enters the scene making a remark about the weather. "So foul and fair a day I have not seen." On this flat note Macbeth's character tone is set. "Terrible weather we're having." "The sun can't seem to make up its mind." "Is it hot/cold/wet enough for you?" A commonplace man who talks in commonplaces, a golfer, one might guess, on the Scottish fairways, Macbeth is the only Shakespeare hero who corresponds to a bourgeois type: a murderous Babbitt, let us say.

You might argue just the opposite, that Macbeth is over-imaginative, the prey of visions. It is true that he is impressionable. Banquo, when they come upon the witches, amuses himself at their expense, like a man of parts idly chaffing a fortune-teller. Macbeth, though, is deeply impressed. "Thane of Cawdor and King." He thinks this over aloud. "How can I be Thane of Cawdor when the Thane of Cawdor is alive?" When this mental stumbling-block has been cleared away for him (the Thane of Cawdor has received a death sentence), he turns his thoughts *sotto voce* to the next question. "How can I be King when Duncan is alive?" The answer comes back, "Kill him." It does fleetingly occur to Macbeth, as it would to most people, to leave matters alone and let destiny work it out. "If chance will have me King, why, chance may crown me, Without my stir." But this goes against his grain. A reflective man might wonder how fate would spin her plot, as the Virgin Mary must have wondered after the Angel Gabriel's visit. But Macbeth does not trust to fate, that is, to the unknown, the mystery of things; he trusts only to a known quantity—himself—to put the prophecy into action. In short, he has no faith, which requires imagination. He is literal-minded; that, in a word, is his tragedy.

It was not *his* idea, he could plead in self-defense, but the witches', that he should have the throne. *They* said it first. But the witches only voiced a thought that was already in his mind; after all, he was Duncan's cousin and close to the crown. And once the thought has been put into *words*, he is in a scrambling hurry. He cannot wait to get home to tell his wife about the promise; in his excitement, he puts it in a letter, which he sends on ahead, like a businessman briefing an associate on a piece of good news for the firm.

Lady Macbeth takes very little stock in the witches. She never pesters her husband, as most wives would, with questions about the Weird Sisters: "What did they say, exactly?" "How did they look?" "Are you sure?" She is less interested in "fate and metaphysical aid" than in the business at hand—how to nerve her husband to do what he wants to do. And later, when Macbeth announces that he is going out to consult the Weird Sisters again, she refrains from comment. As though she were keeping her opinion—"O proper stuff!"—to herself. Lady Macbeth is not superstitious. Macbeth is. This makes her repeatedly impatient with him, for Macbeth, like many men of his sort, is an old story to his wife. A tale full of sound and fury signifying nothing. Her contempt for him perhaps extends even to his ambition. "Wouldst not play false, And yet wouldst wrongly win." As though to say, "All right, if that's what you want, have the courage to get it." Lady Macbeth does not so much give the impression of coveting the crown herself as of being weary of watching Macbeth covet it. Macbeth, by the way, is her second husband, and either her first husband was a better man than he, which galls her, or he was just another general, another superstitious golfer, which would gall her too.

Superstition here is the opposite of reason on the one hand and of imagination on the other. Macbeth is credulous, in contrast to Lady Macbeth, to Banquo, and, later, to Malcolm, who sets the audience an example of the right way by mistrusting Macduff until he has submitted him to an empirical test. Believing and knowing are paired in Malcolm's mind; what he *knows* he believes. Macbeth's eagerness to believe is the companion of his lack of faith. If all works out right for him in this world, Macbeth says, he can take a chance on the next ("We'd jump the life to come"). Superstition whispers when true religion has been silenced, and Macbeth becomes a ready client for the patent medicines brewed by the jeering witches on the heath.

As in his first interview with them he is too quick to act literally on a dark saying, in the second he is too easily reassured. He will not be conquered till "great Birnam Wood to high Dunsinane Hill shall come against him." "Why, that can never happen!" he cries out in immediate relief, his brow clearing.

It never enters his mind to examine the saying more closely, test it, so to speak, for a double bottom, as was common in those days (Banquo even points this out to him) with prophetic utterances, which were known to be ambiguous and tricky. Any child knew that a prophecy often meant the reverse of what it seemed to say, and any man of imagination would ask himself how Birnam Wood *might* come to Dunsinane and take measures to prevent it, as King Laius took measures to prevent his own death by arranging to have the baby Oedipus killed. If Macbeth had thought it out, he could have had Birnam Wood chopped down and burned on the spot and the ashes dumped into the sea. True, the prophecy might still have turned against him (since destiny cannot be avoided and the appointment will be kept at Samarra), but that would have been another story, another tragedy, the tragedy of a clever man not clever enough to circumvent fate. Macbeth is not clever; he is taken in by surfaces, by appearance. He cannot think beyond the usual course of things. "None of woman born." All men, he says to himself, sagely, are born of women; Malcolm and Macduff are men; therefore I am safe. This logic leaves out of account the extraordinary: the man brought into the world by Caesarean section. In the same way, it leaves out of account the supernatural—the very forces he is trafficking with. He might be overcome by an angel or a demon, as well as by Macduff.

Yet this pedestrian general sees ghosts and imaginary daggers in the air. Lady Macbeth does not, and the tendency in her husband grates on her nerves; she is sick of his terrors and fancies. A practical woman, Lady Macbeth, more a partner than a wife, though Macbeth treats her with a trite domestic fondness—"Love," "Dearest love," "Dearest chuck," "Sweet remembrancer." These middle-aged, middle-class endearments, as though he called her "Honeybunch" or "Sweetheart," as well as the obligatory "Dear," are a master stroke of Shakespeare's and perfectly in keeping with the prosing about the weather, the heavy credulousness.

Naturally Macbeth is dominated by his wife. He is old Iron Pants in the field (as she bitterly reminds him), but at home *she* has to wear the pants; she has to unsex herself. No "chucks" or "dearests" escape her tightened lips, and yet she is more feeling, more human finally than Macbeth. She thinks of her father when she sees the old King asleep, and this natural thought will not let her kill him. Macbeth has to do it, just as the quailing husband of any modern virago is sent down to the basement to kill a rat or drown a set of kittens. An image of her father, irrelevant to her purpose, softens this monster woman; sleepwalking, she thinks of Lady Macduff. "The Thane of Fife had a wife. Where is she now?" Stronger than Macbeth, less suggestible, she is nevertheless imaginative, where he is not. She does not see ghosts and daggers; when she sleepwalks, it is simple reality that haunts her—the crime relived. "Yet, who would have thought the old man to have had so much blood in him?" Over and over, the epiphenomena of the crime present themselves to her dormant consciousness. This nightly reliving is not penitence but more terrible—remorse, the agenbite of the restless deed. Lady Macbeth's uncontrollable imagination drives her to put herself in the place of others—the wife of the Thane of Fife—and to recognize a kinship between all human kind: the pathos of old age in Duncan has made her think, "Why, he might be my father!" This sense of a natural bond between men opens her to contrition—sorrowing with. To ask whether, waking, she is "sorry" for what she has done is impertinent. She lives with it and it kills her.

Macbeth has no feeling for others, except envy, a common middle-class trait. He *envies* the murdered Duncan his rest, which is a strange way of looking at your victim. What he suffers on his own account after the crimes is simple panic. He is never contrite or remorseful; it is not the deed but a shadow of it, Banquo's spook, that appears to him. The "scruples" that agitate him before Duncan's murder are mere echoes of conventional opinion, of what might be *said* about his deed: that Duncan was his king, his cousin, and a guest under his roof. "I have bought golden opinions," he says to himself (note the verb), "from all sorts of people";

now these people may ask for their opinions back—a refund—if they suspect him of the murder. It is like a business firm's being reluctant to part with its "good will." The fact that Duncan was such a good king bothers him, and why? Because there will be universal grief at his death. But his chief "scruple" is even simpler. "If we should fail?" he says timidly to Lady Macbeth. Sweet chuck tells him that they will not. Yet once she has ceased to be effectual as a partner, Dearest love is an embarrassment. He has no time for her vapors. "Cure her of that," he orders the doctor on hearing that she is troubled by "fancies." Again the general is speaking.

The idea of Macbeth as a conscience-tormented man is a platitude as false as Macbeth himself. Macbeth has no conscience. His main concern throughout the play is that most selfish of all concerns: to get a good night's sleep. His invocation to sleep, while heartfelt, is perfectly conventional; sleep builds you up, enables you to start the day fresh. Thus the virtue of having a good conscience is seen by him in terms of bodily hygiene. Lady Macbeth shares these preoccupations. When he tells her he is going to see the witches, she remarks that he needs sleep.

Her wifely concern is mechanical and far from real solicitude. She is aware of Macbeth; she *knows* him (he does not know her at all, apparently), but she regards him coldly as a thing, a tool that must be oiled and polished. His soul-states do not interest her; her attention is narrowed on his morale, his public conduct, the shifting expressions of his face. But in a sense she is right, for there is nothing to Macbeth but fear and ambition, both of which he tries to hide, except from her. This naturally gives her a poor opinion of the inner man.

Why is it, though, that Lady Macbeth seems to us a monster while Macbeth does not? Partly because she is a woman and has "unsexed" herself, which makes her a monster by definition. Also because the very prospect of murder quickens an hysterical excitement in her, like the discovery of some object in a shop—a set of emeralds or a sable stole—which Macbeth can give her and which will be an "outlet" for all the repressed desires he cannot satisfy. She behaves as though Macbeth, through his weakness, will deprive her of self-realization; the unimpeded exercise of her will is the voluptuous end she seeks. That is why she makes naught of scruples, as inner brakes on her throbbing engines. Unlike Macbeth, she does not pretend to harbor a conscience, though this, on her part, by a curious turn, *is* a pretense, as the sleepwalking scene reveals. After the first crime, her will subsides, spent; the devil has brought her to climax and left her.

Macbeth is not a monster, like Richard III or Iago or Iachimo, though in the catalogue he might go for one because of the blackness of his deeds. But at the outset his deeds are only the wishes and fears of the average, undistinguished man translated into half-hearted action. Pure evil is a kind of transcendence that he does not aspire to. He only wants to be king and sleep the sleep of the just, undisturbed. He could never have been a good man, even if he had not met the witches; hence we cannot see him as a devil incarnate, for the devil is a fallen angel. Macbeth does not fall; if anything, he somewhat improves as the result of his career of crime. He throws off his dependency and thus achieves the "greatness" he mistakenly sought in the crown and scepter. He swells to vast proportions, having supped full with honors.

The isolation of Macbeth, which is at once a punishment and a tragic dignity or honor, takes place by stages and by deliberate choice; it begins when he does not tell Lady Macbeth that he has decided to kill Banquo and reaches its peak at Dunsinane, in the final action. Up to this time, though he has cut himself off from all human contacts, he is counting on the witches as allies. When he first hears the news that Macduff is not "of woman born," he is unmanned; everything he trusted (the literal word) has betrayed him, and he screams in terror, "I'll not fight with thee!" But Macduff's taunts make a hero of him; he cannot die like this, shamed. His death is his first true act of courage, though even here he has had to be pricked to it by mockery, Lady Macbeth's old spur. Nevertheless, weaned by his very crimes from a need for reassurance, nursed in a tyrant's solitude, he meets death on his own, without metaphysical aid. "Lay on, Macduff."

What is modern and bourgeois in Macbeth's character is his

wholly *social outlook*. He has no feeling for others, and yet until the end he is a vicarious creature, existing in his own eyes through what others may say of him, through what they tell him or promise him. This paradox is typical of the social being—at once a wolf out for himself and a sheep. Macbeth, moreover, is an expert buck-passer; he sees how others can be used. It is he, not Lady Macbeth, who thinks of smearing the drunken chamberlains with blood (though it is she, in the end, who carries it out), so that they shall be caught "red-handed" the next morning when Duncan's murder is discovered. At this idea he brightens; suddenly, he sees his way clear. It is the moment when at last he decides. The eternal executive, ready to fix responsibility on a subordinate, has seen the deed finally take a *recognizable* form. Now he can do it. And the crackerjack thought of killing the grooms afterward (dead men tell no tales—old adage) is again purely his own on-the-spot inspiration; no credit to Lady Macbeth.

It is the sort of thought that would have come to Hamlet's Uncle Claudius, another trepidant executive. Indeed, Macbeth is more like Claudius than like any other character in Shakespeare. Both are doting husbands; both rose to power by betraying their superior's trust; both are easily frightened and have difficulty saying their prayers. Macbeth's "Amen" sticks in his throat, he complains, and Claudius, on his knees, sighs that he cannot make what priests call a "good act of contrition." The desire to say his prayers like any pew-holder, quite regardless of his horrible crime, is merely a longing for respectability. Macbeth "repents" killing the grooms, but this is for public consumption. "O, yet I do repent me of my fury, That I did kill them." In fact, it is the one deed he does *not* repent (*i.e.*, doubt the wisdom of) either before or after. This hypocritical self-accusation, which is his sidelong way of announcing the embarrassing fact that he has just done away with the grooms, and his simulated grief at Duncan's murder ("All is but toys. Renown and grace is dead, The wine of life is drawn," etc.) are his basest moments in the play, as well as his boldest; here is nearly a magnificent monster.

The dramatic effect too is one of great boldness on Shakespeare's part. Macbeth is speaking pure Shakespearean poetry, but in his mouth, since we know he is lying, it turns into facile verse, Shakespearean poetry buskined. The same with "Here lay Duncan, His silver skin lac'd with his golden blood. . . ." If the image were given to Macduff, it would be uncontaminated poetry; from Macbeth it is "proper stuff"—fustian. This opens the perilous question of sincerity in the arts: is a line of verse altered for us by the sincerity of the one who speaks it? In short, is poetry relative to the circumstances or absolute? Or, more particularly, are Macbeth's soliloquies poetry, which they sound like, or something else? Did Shakespeare intend to make Macbeth a poet, like Hamlet, Lear, and Othello? In that case, how can Macbeth be an unimaginative mediocrity? My opinion is that Macbeth's soliloquies are not poetry but rhetoric. They are tirades. That is, they do not trace any pensive motion of the soul or heart but are a volley of words discharged. Macbeth is neither thinking nor feeling aloud; he is declaiming. Like so many unfeeling men, he has a facile emotionalism, which he turns on and off. Not that his fear is insincere, but his loss of control provides him with an excuse for histrionics.

These gibberings exasperate Lady Macbeth. "What do you mean?" she says coldly after she has listened to a short harangue on "Methought I heard a voice cry 'Sleep no more!'" It is an allowable question—what *does* he mean? And his funeral oration on *her*, if she could have heard it, would have brought her back to life to protest. "She should have died hereafter"—fine, that was the real Macbeth. But then, as if conscious of the proprieties, he at once begins on a series of bromides ("Tomorrow, and tomorrow . . .") that he seems to have had ready to hand for the occasion like a black mourning suit. All Macbeth's soliloquies have that ready-to-hand, if not hand-me-down, air, which is perhaps why they are given to school children to memorize, often with the result of making them hate Shakespeare. What children resent in these soliloquies is precisely their sententiousness—the sound they have of being already memorized from a copybook.

Macbeth's speeches often recall the Player's speech in *Hamlet*—

Shakespeare's example of how-not-to-do-it. He tears a passion to tatters. He has a rather Senecan rhetoric, the fustian of the time; in the dagger speech, for example, he works in Hecate, Tarquin, and the wolf—recherché embellishment for a man who is about to commit a real murder. His taste for hyperbole goes with a habit of euphuism, as when he calls the sea "the green one." And what of the remarkable line just preceding, "The multitudinous seas incarnadine," with its onomatopoeia of the crested waves rising in the t's and d's of "multitudinous" and subsiding in the long swell of the verb? This is sometimes cited as an example of pure poetry, which it would be in an anthology of isolated lines, but in the context, dramatically, it is splendid bombast, a kind of stuffing or padding.

The play between poetry and rhetoric, the *conversion* of poetry to declamation, is subtle and horrible in *Macbeth*. The sincere pent-up poet in Macbeth flashes out not in the soliloquies but when he howls at a servant. "The Devil damn thee black, thou cream-faced loon! Where got'st thou that goose look?" Elsewhere, the general's tropes are the gold braid of his dress uniform or the chasing of his armor. If an explanation is needed, you might say he learned to *use* words through long practice in haranguing his troops, whipping them and himself into battle frenzy. Up to recent times a fighting general, like a football coach, was an orator.

But it must be noted that it is not only Macbeth who rants. Nor is it only Macbeth who talks about the weather. The play is stormy with atmosphere—the screaming and shrieking of owls, the howling of winds. Nature herself is ranting, like the witches, and Night, black Hecate, is queen of the scene. Bats are flitting about; ravens and crows are hoarse; the house-martins' nests on the battlements of Macbeth's castle give a misleading promise of peace and gentle domesticity. "It will be rain tonight," says Banquo simply, looking at the sky (note the difference between this and Macbeth's pompous generality), and the First Murderer growls at him, striking, "Let it come down." The disorder of Nature, as so often in Shakespeare, presages and reflects the disorder of the body politic. Guilty Macbeth cannot sleep, but the night of

Duncan's murder, the whole house, as if guilty too, is restless; Malcolm and Donalbain talk and laugh in their sleep; the drunken porter, roused, plays that he is gatekeeper of hell.

Indeed, the whole action takes place in a kind of hell and is pitched to the demons' shriek of hyperbole. This would appear to be a peculiar setting for a study of the commonplace. But only at first sight. The fact that an ordinary philistine like Macbeth goes on the rampage and commits a series of murders is a sign that human nature, like Nature, is capable of any mischief if left to its "natural" self. The witches, unnatural beings, are Nature spirits, stirring their snake-filet and owl's wing, newt's eye and frog toe in a camp stew: earthy ingredients boil down to an unearthly broth. It is the same with the man Macbeth. Ordinary ambition, fear, and a kind of stupidity make a deadly combination. Macbeth, a self-made king, is not kingly, but just another Adam or Fall guy, with Eve at his elbow.

There is no play of Shakespeare's (I think) that contains the words "Nature" and "natural" so many times, and the "Nature" within the same speech can mean first something good and then something evil, as though it were a pun. Nature is two-sided, double-talking, like the witches. "Fair is foul and foul is fair," they cry, and Macbeth enters the play unconsciously echoing them, for he is never original but chock-full of the "milk of human kindness," which does not mean kindness in the modern sense but simply human "nature," human kind. The play is about Nature, and its blind echo, human nature.

Macbeth, in short, shows life in the cave. Without religion, animism rules the outer world, and without faith, the human soul is beset by hobgoblins. This at any rate was Shakespeare's opinion, to which modern history, with the return of the irrational in the Fascist nightmare and its fear of new specters in the form of Communism, Socialism, etc., lends support. It is a troubling thought that bloodstained Macbeth, of all Shakespeare's characters, should seem the most "modern," the only one you could transpose into contemporary battle dress or a sport shirt and slacks.

The contemporary Macbeth, a churchgoer, is indifferent to

religion, to the categorical imperative of any group of principles that may be held to stand above and govern human behavior. Like the old Macbeth, he'd gladly hazard the future life, not only for himself but for the rest of humanity: "Though palaces and pyramids do slope Their heads to their foundations; though the treasure Of Nature's germens tumble all together . . ." He listens to soothsayers and prophets and has been out on the heath and in the desert, putting questions to Nature on a grand scale, lest his rivals for power get ahead of him and Banquo's stock, instead of his, inherit the earth. Unloosing the potential destructiveness that was always there in Nature, as Shakespeare understood, the contemporary Macbeth, like the old one, is not even a monster, though he may yet breed monsters, thanks to his activities on the heath; he is timorous, unimaginative, and the prayer he would like to say most fervently is simply "Amen."

(1962)

Adrienne Rich

(1929–2012)

After Dark

A leading poet, critic, and feminist of the post-war years, Adrienne Rich restlessly explored the complex interplay of identity, privilege, gender, oppression, and tradition. Rich, for whom writing came to constitute "re-vision," thought it vital "not to pass on a tradition but to break its hold over us." Her work wrestles with the intersection of the political and the personal. Her deeply ambivalent relationship with her father, Arnold Rich, undoubtedly shadows her exploration of the relationship of Cordelia to the most patriarchal of all Shakespeare's fathers, King Lear; Rich would later write of her father in *Split at the Root* (1982) that "Arnold demanded absolute submission to his will." Rich is an incisive critic of Shakespeare, most visibly in her subtle revisions of the plays' language. In "After Dark," published in her early collection, *Necessities of Life* (1966), Prospero's words from *The Tempest*—"our revels now are ended"—are quietly changed to a daughter's "our struggles now are ended," while the title of her subsequent 1976 volume, *Of Woman Born*, deliberately lops off the initial "none" from where this phrase appears in *Macbeth*. In "After Dark," Rich also quotes but alters King Lear's words to Cordelia—"let's away to prison"—changing it to "let's away from prison." Tellingly, unlike Shakespeare's Lear, the father in her poem does not kneel and ask forgiveness, leaving open troubling questions of failed reconciliation and stifling legacy—familial and literary.

∞

I

You are falling asleep and I sit looking at you
old tree of life
old man whose death I wanted
I can't stir you up now.

Faintly a phonograph needle
whirs round in the last groove
eating my heart to dust.
That terrible record! how it played

down years, wherever I was
in foreign languages even
over and over, *I know you better*
than you know yourself   I know

you better than you know
yourself   I know
you   until, self-maimed,
I limped off, torn at the roots,

stopped singing a whole year,
got a new body, new breath,
got children, croaked for words,
forgot to listen

or read your *mene tekel* fading on the wall,
woke up one morning
and knew myself your daughter.
Blood is a sacred poison.

Now, unasked, you give ground.
We only want to stifle
what's stifling us already.
Alive now, root to crown, I'd give

—oh,—something—not to know
our struggles now are ended.
I seem to hold you, cupped
in my hands, and disappearing.

When your memory fails—
no more to scourge my inconsistencies—
the sashcords of the world fly loose.
A window crashes

suddenly down. I go to the woodbox
and take a stick of kindling
to prop the sash again.
I grow protective toward the world.

II

Now let's away from prison—
Underground seizures!
I used to huddle in the grave
I'd dug for you and bite

my tongue for fear it would babble
—Darling—
I thought they'd find me there
someday, sitting upright, shrunken,

my hair like roots and in my lap
a mess of broken pottery—
wasted libation—
and you embalmed beside me.

No, let's away. Even now
there's a walk between doomed elms
(whose like we shall not see much longer)
and something—grass and water—

and old dream-photograph.
I'll sit with you there and tease you
for wisdom, if you like,
waiting till the blunt barge

bumps along the shore.
Poppies burn in the twilight
like smudge pots.
I think you hardly see me

but—this is the dream now—
your fears blow out,
off, over the water.
At the last, your hand feels steady.

(1966)

Pauline Kael

(1919–2001)

Orson Welles: There Ain't No Way

Pauline Kael was one of the most controversial and influential American film critics. Her essay in *The New Republic* defending Welles and his 1966 film *Falstaff*—much maligned in the popular press—is one of her finest. Acknowledging the films technical flaws, she nonetheless insisted that he was "the one great creative force in American films in our time, the man who might have redeemed our movies from the general contempt in which they are (and for the most part, rightly) held." *Falstaff*, later retitled *Chimes at Midnight*, was Welles's last Shakespeare film, and for many his greatest. Welles himself said of it that "If I wanted to get into heaven on the basis of one movie, that's the one I'd offer up." His earlier, often brilliant and always underfunded efforts to film Shakespeare include *Macbeth* and *Othello*; his subsequent plans to play Shylock and Lear on film came to naught. The roots of *Chimes at Midnight* can be traced back at least to 1939, when Welles wrote and staged *Five Kings*, which wove together the plots of several of Shakespeare's history plays. *Chimes at Midnight* stands as a retrospective of Welles's own career as well as a reflection on Hollywood and post-war America. He put "old Jack Falstaff"—with whom he so clearly identified—at the heart of *Chimes at Midnight*, turning it into a lament for a lost era, a film, as he put it, about the betrayal of friendship and the "terrible price" that Prince Hal "must pay in exchange for power."

❧

WHAT MAKES movies a great popular art form is that certain artists can, at moments in their lives, reach out and unify the audience—educated and uneducated—in a shared response. The tragedy in the history of movies is that those who have this capacity are usually prevented from doing so. The mass audience gets its big empty movies full of meaningless action; the art-house audiences gets its studies of small action and large inaction loaded with meaning.

Almost everyone who cares about movies knows that Orson Welles is such an artist. Even audiences who don't know that Welles is a great *director* sense his largeness of talent from his presence as an actor. Audiences are alert to him, as they often were to John Barrymore, and later to Charles Laughton, as they sometimes are to Bette Davis, as they almost always are to Brando—actors too big for their roles, who play the clown, and not always in comedy but in roles that for an artist of intelligence can only be comedy. Like Brando, Welles is always being attacked for not having fulfilled his prodigious promise; but who has ever beaten the mass culture fly-by-night system of economics for long? What else could Welles do with his roles in *Black Magic* or *Prince of Foxes* or *The Black Rose* or *Trent's Last Case* but play them as comedy? Could one take such work seriously? The mediocre directors and the cynical hacks got money when he couldn't. His ironic playing is all that one remembers from those movies anyway; like Brando, he has the greatness to make effrontery a communicated, shared experience—which lesser artists had better not attempt. It takes large *latent* talent to tell the audience that you know that what you're doing isn't worth doing and still do it better than anyone else in the movie.

Waiting for a train in Grand Central station recently, I was standing next to a group of Negroes. To everything that they talked about, one of them—a young girl—said, "There ain't no way"; and it fit perfectly each time.

Orson Welles's *Falstaff* came and went so fast there was hardly time to tell people about it, but it should be back (it should be around forever) and it should be seen. It's blighted by economics and it will never reach the audience Welles might have and should have reached, because there just ain't no way. So many people—and with such complacent satisfaction, almost, one would say, delight—talk of how Welles has disappointed them, as if he had willfully thrown away his talent through that "lack of discipline" which is always brought in to explain failure. There is a widespread notion that a man who accomplishes a great deal is thus a "genius" who should be able to cut through all obstacles; and if he can't (and who can?), what he does is too far beneath what he should have done to be worth consideration. On the contrary, I think that the more gifted and imaginative a director, the greater the obstacles. It is the less imaginative director who has always flourished in the business world of movies—the "adaptable," reliable fellow who is more concerned to get the movie done than to do it his way, who, indeed, after a while has no way of his own, who is as anonymous as the director of *Prince of Foxes*. And the more determined a man is to do it his way or a new way, the more likelihood that this man (quickly labeled a "troublemaker" or "a difficult person" or "self-destructive" or "a man who makes problems for himself"—standard Hollywoodese for an artist and, of course, always true at some level, and the greater the artist, the more true it's likely to become) won't get the support he needs to complete the work his way. In the atmosphere of anxiety surrounding him, the producers may decide to "save" the project by removing him or adding to or subtracting from his work, or finally dumping the film without publicity or press screenings, consigning it to the lower half of double bills.

All these things have happened to Welles (*Citizen Kane* was not big enough at the box office and it caused trouble; he was not allowed to finish his next picture, *The Magnificent Ambersons*). Treatment of this sort, which usually marks the end of great movie careers, was for Welles the beginning. Most of these things have happened to men as pacific as Jean Renoir, whom few could accuse of being "undisciplined." (Renoir turned to writing a novel, his first, in 1966, when he could not raise money to make a movie, though the budget he required was less than half that allotted to movies made to be premiered on television.) And they are still happening to men in Hollywood like Sam Peckinpah. Such men are always blamed for the eventual failure of whatever remains of their work, while men who try for less have the successes (and are forgiven their routine failures because they didn't attempt anything the producers didn't understand). Joseph L. Mankiewicz's *Julius Caesar* was considered a success and Orson Welles's *Othello* a failure. The daring of doing Shakespeare at all was enough for Mankiewicz and his producer, John Houseman, who was to be ritualistically referred to as "the distinguished producer John Houseman" because of this film—not from his early theatre work with Orson Welles—much as George Schaefer is referred to as "the distinguished director" because of his specialty of embalming old war horses for television. Mankiewicz's luck held good on *Julius Casear*: it's perfectly suited to the small screen, where it recently appeared, while Welles's *Othello*—with its disastrous, imperfectly synchronized soundtrack—isn't even intelligible. How could it be? A movie shot over a period of four years with Welles dashing off periodically to act in movies like *The Black Rose* to earn the money to continue; and then, his cast scattered, trying to make a soundtrack, reading half the roles himself (not only Roderigo, but if my ear is to be trusted, parts of Iago, too), selecting long shots and shots with the actors' backs to the camera to conceal the sound problem. This, of course, looked like "affectation." And his splendid, flawed production—visually and emotionally a near-masterpiece—was a "failure." Earlier, working on a Republic Pictures budget (for Republic Pictures), Welles had shot his barbaric *Macbeth*—marred most by his own performance—in twenty-three days because "no one would give me any money for a further day's shooting."

In the early fifties, Welles as an actor was in top flamboyant form. Nobody seemed to enjoy the sheer physical delight of acting as much as he in roles like his Lord Mountdrago in *Three Cases of Murder*. Still very young, he played like a great ham of the old school—which was marvelous to watch in his Father Mapple in *Moby Dick* and in *The Roots of Heaven*. This lesser talent that he could live on was a corollary to his great talent. It was a demonstration of his love of (and prowess in) traditional theatre—like the way Vittorio De Sica (also an actor from adolescence) could go from being the romantic singing star of Italian musical comedy to make *Shoeshine* and then back again (he, too, to raise money for his own films) to playing in an ornate style, Gina's lawyer or Sophia's papa, a whole Barzini gallery of glory-ridden, mustachioed Italians. But Welles was beginning to turn into America's favorite grotesque. Like Barrymore and Laughton and Brando, he seemed to be developing an obsession with false noses, false faces. He had once, at least, played a role in his own face, Harry Lime in *The Third Man*, a role he had written for himself; by the sixties he was encased in makeup and his own fat—like a huge operatic version of W. C. Fields. Audiences laughed when he appeared on the screen. He didn't need to choose the role of Falstaff: it chose him.

When Welles went to Europe, he lost his single greatest asset as a movie director: his sound. (He had already lost the company that *talked* together, the Mercury players he had brought to Hollywood—Joseph Cotton, Agnes Moorehead, Everett Sloane, et al.—who were now working separately.) Welles had first skyrocketed to public attention on radio, and what he had brought to movies that was distinctively new was the radio sound—with an innovative use of overlapping dialogue—which was used for trick shock purposes, almost playfully, in *Citizen Kane*. But by the time of *The Magnificent Ambersons* he was using this technique for something deeper (the family bickering was startling in its almost surreal accuracy; the sound was of arguments overheard from childhood, with so many overtones they were almost mythic). Welles himself had a voice that seemed to carry its own echo chamber; somehow, in becoming the whiz kid of vocal effects, in simulating so many deep, impersonal voices, he had emptied his own voice of emotion, and when he spoke his credit at the end of *The Ambersons*, audiences laughed at the hollow voice (and perhaps at the comic justice of the *spoken* credit). Ironically, sound—the area of his greatest mastery—became his worst problem as he began to work with actors who didn't speak English and actors who did but weren't around when he needed them (for the postsynchronization which is standard practice in Europe, because the actors don't speak the same language, and is becoming standard here, too, because it saves shooting time). Welles compensated by developing greater visual virtuosity.

Yeats said "Rhetoric is heard, poetry overheard," and though I don't agree, I think I see what he means, and I think this assumption is involved in much of the rejection of a talent like Welles's. His work is often referred to as flashy and spectacular as if this also meant cheap and counterfeit. Welles is unabashedly theatrical in a period when much of the educated audience thinks theatrical flair vulgar, artistry intellectually respectable only when subtle, hidden. Welles has the approach of a *popular* artist: he glories in both verbal and visual rhetoric. He uses film *theatrically*— not stagily, but with theatrical bravado. He makes a show of the mechanics of film. He doesn't, if I may be forgiven the pun, hide his tracks. Movies gave him the world for a stage, and his is not the art that conceals art, but the showman's delight in the flourishes with which he pulls the rabbit from the hat. (This is why he was the wrong director for *The Trial*, where the poetry needed to be overheard.) I think that many people who enjoy those flourishes, who really love them—as I do—are so fearfully educated that they feel they must put them down. It's as if people said he's a mountebank, an actor showing off. But there's life in that kind of display: it's part of an earlier theatrical tradition that Welles carries over into film, it's what the theatre has lost, and it's what brought people to the movies.

Welles might have done for American talkies what D. W. Griffith did for the silent film. But when he lost his sound and his original, verbal wit, he seemed to lose his brashness, his youth, and some of his vitality. And he lost his American-ness; in Europe he had to learn a different, more exclusively visual language of film. An *enfant terrible* defeated ages fast. At fifty-one, Welles seems already the grand old master of film, because, of course, everybody knows that he'll never get in the position to do what he might have done. Governments and foundations will prattle on about excellence and American film companies will rush to sign up Englishmen and Europeans who have had a hit, hoping to snare that magic moneymaking gift. And tired transplanted

Europeans will go on making big, lousy American movies, getting financed because they once had a hit and maybe the magic will come back. And Welles—the one great creative force in American films in our time, the man who might have redeemed our movies from the general contempt in which they are (and for the most part, rightly) held—is, ironically, an expatriate director whose work thus reaches only the art-house audience. And he has been so crippled by the problems of working as he does, he's lucky to reach that. The distributors of *Falstaff* tested it out of town before risking Bosley Crowther's displeasure in New York.

You may want to walk out during the first twenty minutes of *Falstaff*. Although the words on the soundtrack are intelligible, the sound doesn't match the images. We hear the voices as if the speakers were close, but on the screen the figures may be a half mile away or turned from us at some angle that doesn't jibe with the voice. In the middle of a sentence an actor may walk away from us while the voice goes on. Often, for a second, we can't be sure who is supposed to be talking. And the cutting is maddening, designed as it is for camouflage—to keep us from seeing faces closely or from registering that mouths which should be open and moving are closed. Long shots and Shakespearean dialogue are a crazy mix. It's especially jarring because the casting is superb and the performance beautiful. It's not hard to take Shakespeare adapted and transformed by other cultures—like Kurosawa's *Throne of Blood*, a *Macbeth* almost as much related to Welles's as to Shakespeare's—but the words of Shakespeare slightly out of synch! This is as intolerable as those old prints of *Henry V* that the miserly distributors circulate—chewed up by generations of projection machines, crucial syllables lost in the splices. The editing rhythm of *Falstaff* is at war with the rhythm and comprehension of the language. Welles, avoiding the naturalistic use of the outdoors in which Shakespeare's dialogue sounds more stagey than on stage, has photographically stylized the Spanish locations, creating a theatrically darkened, slightly unrealistic world of angles and low beams and silhouettes. When this photographic style is shattered by the cuts necessary to conceal the dialogue problems, the camera angles seem unnecessarily exaggerated and pretentious. But then despite everything—the angles, the doubles in long shots, the editing that distracts us when we need to concentrate on the dialogue—the movie begins to be great. The readings in *Falstaff* are great even if they don't always go with the images, which are often great, too.

Welles has brought together the pieces of Falstaff that Shakespeare had strewn over the two parts of *Henry IV* and *The Merry Wives of Windsor*, with cuttings from *Henry V* and *Richard II*, and fastened them into place with narration from Holinshed's Chronicles (read by Ralph Richardson). Those of us who resisted our schoolteachers' best efforts to make us appreciate the comic genius of Shakespeare's fools and buffoons will not be surprised that Welles wasn't able to make Falstaff very funny: he's a great conception of a character, but the charades and practical jokes seem meant to be funnier than they are. This movie does, however, provide the best Shakespearean comic moment I can recall: garrulous Falstaff sitting with Shallow (Alan Webb) and Silence (Walter Chiari), rolling his eyes in irritation and impatience at Silence's stammer. But Welles's Falstaff isn't essentially comic; W. C. Fields's Micawber wasn't either: these actors, so funny when they're playing with their own personae in roles too small for them, are not so funny when they're trying to measure up. The carousing and roistering in the tavern doesn't seem like such great fun either, though Welles and the cast work very hard to convince us it is. Oddly, we never really see the friendship of Prince Hal—played extraordinarily well by Keith Baxter—and Falstaff; the lighter side in *Henry IV, Part I* is lost—probably well lost, though we must take it for granted in the film. What we see are the premonitions of the end: Hal taking part in games that have gone stale for him, preparing himself for his final rejection of his adopted father Falstaff in order to turn him into a worthy successor of his father the king. And we see what this does to Falstaff, the braggart with the heart of a child who expects to be forgiven everything, even what he knows to be unforgivable—his taking the credit away from Hal for the combat with Hotspur (Norman Rodway). Falstaff lacks judgment, which kings must have.

John Gielgud's Henry IV is the perfect contrast to Welles; Gielgud has never been so monkishly perfect in a movie. Welles could only get him for two weeks of the shooting and the make-shift of some of his scenes is obvious, but his performance gives the film the austerity it needs for the conflict in Hal to be dramatized. Gielgud's king is so refined—a skeleton too dignified for any flesh to cling to it, inhabited by a voice so modulated it is an exquisite spiritual whine. Merrie England? Falstaff at least provides a carcass to mourn over.

Welles as an actor had always been betrayed by his voice. It was too much and it was inexpressive; there was no warmth in it, no sense of a life lived. It was just an instrument that he played, and it seemed to be the key to something shallow and unfelt even in his best performances, and most fraudulent when he tried to make it tender. I remember that once, in *King Lear* on television, he hit a phrase and I thought his voice was emotionally right; it had beauty—and what a change it made in his acting! In *Falstaff* Welles seems to have grown into his voice; he's not too young for it anymore, and he's certainly big enough. And his emotions don't seem fake anymore; he's grown into them, too. He has the eyes for the role. Though his Falstaff is short on comedy, it's very rich, very full.

He has directed a sequence, the battle of Shrewsbury, which is unlike anything he has ever done, indeed unlike any battle ever done on the screen before. It ranks with the best of Griffith, John Ford, Eisenstein, Kurosawa—that is, with the best ever done. How can one sequence in this movie be so good? It has no dialogue and so he isn't handicapped: for the only time in the movie he can edit, not to cover gaps and defects but as an artist. The compositions suggest Uccello and the chilling ironic music is a death knell for all men in battle. The soldiers, plastered by the mud they fall in, are already monuments. It's the most brutally somber battle ever filmed. It does justice to Hotspur's great "O, Harry, thou hast robbed me of my youth."

Welles has filled the cast with box-office stars. Margaret Ruth-erford, Jeanne Moreau, Marina Vlady are all in it (though the girl I like best is little Beatrice Welles as the pageboy). And Falstaff is the most popular crowd-pleasing character in the work of the most enduringly popular writer who ever lived. Yet, because of technical defects due to poverty, Welles's finest Shakespearean production to date—another near-masterpiece, and this time so very close—cannot reach a large public. There ain't no way.

(1967)

John Houseman

(1902–1988)

FROM *Run-Through*

John Houseman was born in Romania, educated in England, and became a U.S. citizen in 1943, two decades after arriving in America. In the mid-1930s he became involved in the Federal Theatre Project, one of President Roosevelt's New Deal programs, run by the visionary Hallie Flanagan. Flanagan brought in Houseman to oversee the Negro Theatre Unit, based in New York City. Houseman in turn hired the young Orson Welles as a director, along with Virgil Thomson, Abe Feder, and Nat Karson, to work with Rose McClendon and other leading African American writers, musicians, and actors. One of their first productions, which premiered at Harlem's Lafayette Theatre on April 14, 1935, was *Macbeth*—set in the court of the autocratic Henri Christophe, a general who ruled Haiti in the early nineteenth century. The innovative production, with an all-black cast (including Jack Carter as Macbeth and Edna Thomas as Lady Macbeth), was like no *Macbeth* that had ever been staged. Because voodoo witch doctors were substituted for Shakespeare's Scottish witches, the production came to be known, and celebrated, as "Voodoo Macbeth." Over a hundred thousand playgoers saw the show when it subsequently toured the nation, from Hartford to Dallas. Houseman writes vividly about the making of "Voodoo Macbeth" in his book-length 1972 memoir, *Run-Through*, excerpted here. A four-minute clip of the production miraculously survives (available at youtube.com). Houseman was also involved in two other groundbreaking American productions of Shakespeare: Orson Welles's Mercury Theatre staging of *Julius Caesar* in 1937 and Joseph Mankiewicz's film of the same play in 1953. In the late 1950s he served as artistic director of the American Shakespeare Festival in Stratford, Connecticut.

❧

I HAD acceded to Orson's request that I stay away from early rehearsals of *Macbeth*. When I finally visited the Elks' Hall, what I heard and saw delighted but in no way astonished me. I had never seriously doubted the company's ability to speak Elizabethan blank verse when they encountered it under the right conditions and, though he had never staged a play except at school, I had complete faith in Welles's ability to direct them. We had chosen the cast together: Jack Carter, the creator of Crown in the original *Porgy*, was the Thane, with Edna Thomas as his murderous lady. For the Macduffs we had Maurice Ellis and Marie Young; J. Louis Johnson was the Porter, Canada Lee was Banquo and Eric Burroughs (a graduate of London's RADA) played Hecate, a composite figure of evil which Welles had assembled out of fragments of witches' lines and to whose sinister equipment he presently added a twelve-foot bullwhip. Our supernatural department was very strong at the Lafayette. In addition to the witches and sundry apparitions called for by the Bard, we had a troupe of African drummers commanded by Asadata Dafora Horton (later minister of culture of the Republic of Sierra Leone). Except for their leader, who had a flawless Oxford accent, they spoke little English: the star of the troupe, Abdul, an authentic witch doctor, seemed to know no language at all except magic. Their first act, after they had been cast in *Macbeth*, was to file a formal requisition for five live black goats. These were brought into the theatre by night and sacrificed, hugger-mugger, according to approved tribal ritual, before being stretched into resonant drum skins.

This supernatural atmosphere added to the excitement that was beginning to form around our production of *Macbeth*. By the end of February it had become the most debated subject in Harlem—one on which the entire future of the Negro Theatre Project was felt to depend. Partly, this had to do with the nature of the show—the first full-scale, professional Negro Shakespearean production in theatrical history. Partly it was the effect of sheer mass. For *Macbeth* had grown steadily with the months until it had become an undertaking of such magnitude that the whole project was beginning to sag under its weight. Backstage at the Lafeyette, to make room for the huge slabs of scenery and acres of painted backdrops that continued to arrive from the shops, *Conjur Man Dies* was gradually being edged down toward the footlights, to the fury of its director and cast. And, in the basement, the glow of hundreds of Karson's gorgeous uniforms, stiff with gold braid, the sheen of satin ball gowns and the gnarled and hairy horror of the witches' hides could not fail to arouse the envious resentment of members of the project's contemporary wing, who were confined to the realistic drabness of street clothes and denim. Soon, ugly rumors began to fly: someone had been told downtown by an authoritative source that *Macbeth* would never open; so much of the project's money had been spent by me on my boyfriend's folly that all future productions of the Negro unit had been canceled. And a stale but dangerous whispering campaign was revived: that what was being so secretly prepared was, in reality, a vast burlesque intended to ridicule the Negro in the eyes of the white world. As a result, Orson was attacked one night, as he was leaving rehearsal, by four alcoholic zealots determined to prevent this insult to their race.

Partly, too, there was the agitation generated by the show itself. Since the first day of rehearsal, from behind the locked doors of the Elks' Hall, waves of excitement had been radiating in ever-widening circles through the Harlem streets. These were created in part by Orson, whose demonic energy was transmitted first to his leading actors, then to his exhausted and bewildered but enthusiastic company and finally, through them, to the whole puzzled community. When the *Macbeth* troupe came out of hiding and began to rehearse, often all through the night, on the stage of the Lafayette, this sense of anxious anticipation continued to grow— especially after drummers, dancers and sound effects had been added and could be heard, like distant thunder, seeping through the walls of the theatre into Seventh Avenue and the surrounding streets.

Including his regular midtown radio jobs, to which he commuted by taxi (sometimes two or three times a day), Orson was now working about twenty hours of the twenty-four. When he was not drilling the company in mass scenes of battle, revelry or witch-craft, or rehearsing individually with the Macbeths and Macduffs, he was working with Virgil on music, Karson on costumes, Feder on lights or Asadata on voodoo.

It was during the preparation of *Macbeth* that Orson revealed his surprising capacity for collaboration. For all the mass of his own ego, he was able to apprehend other people's weakness and strength and to make creative use of them: he had a shrewd instinctive sense of when to bully or charm, when to be kind or savage—and he was seldom mistaken. With Feder, who was a garrulous masochist, Orson was abusive, sarcastic and loud. At light rehearsals he would set him impossible tasks, then howl at him, shamefully and continuously, before the exhausted company, who were so delighted to hear someone else (a white man especially) catching hell, that they persevered with their own stage maneuvers long after their normal span of patience had run out. As a result Orson completed his light rehearsals, preserved the morale of his troupe and retained Feder's professional devotion—if not his love. With Virgil Thomson it was less easy. For here Orson was dealing with a temperament, an intelligence and an attitude of a kind he had seldom encountered. Virgil was wary of the boy genius:

> You brought Orson to the flat where we were living on Fifty-ninth Street. We argued late one night and as an older man I tried to beat him down because I felt he was full of bluff and because his verbalization of what he wanted to do in the theatre was not entirely convincing. I argued hard and not always fairly against Orson and you told me later to stop it because he was a very, very good man in the theatre. You were the one that believed in him . . .

Then as they began to work together, things got easier.

> Orson was nearly always likable. He was never hateful or brutal with me, though I was a little terrified of his firmness. He was extremely professional and he knew exactly what he wanted. He knew it so well and so thoroughly that I, as an older musician with a certain amount of pride, would not write him original music. I would not humiliate myself to write so precisely on his demand. On the other hand, I respected his demands dramatically. So, as your employee, I gave him sound effects and ready-made

music—trumpet call, battle scenes and percussive scores where he wanted them—and, of course, the waltzes for the party scene.

Orson and I never quarreled—as you and he did; but we never really agreed. We used to take each other out to elaborate dinners; and it was I who taught him to drink white wine, and not whiskey, at rehearsals . . .

Another quite different set of problems arose during our collaboration with Asadata Dafora Horton and his troupe of African drummers. With the exception of Abdul, the witch doctor, who several times during rehearsals fell into deep and agitated trances from which not even his fellow witches could rouse him, our Gold Coast contingent was thoroughly professional, adaptable and eager to please—except in the matter of spells. One day, after Orson, Virgil and I had been auditioning their voodoo numbers, we complained to Asadata that his chants did not sound evil enough. Virgil, as usual, got right down to the point.

"Are those really voodoo?"

"Oh, yes. Yes, indeed, Sirs. That is absolutely real, authentic voodoo."

"They don't sound wicked enough."

"Sirs, I . . ."

"Sometimes for the theatre you have to exaggerate."

"I am sorry, Sirs. You can't be any more wicked than that!"

I stayed behind with Virgil and the drummers. As fellow musicians they argued for most of the afternoon. Finally Asadata admitted what those chants of his really were: they were strong spells intended to *ward off* the beriberi—not to induce it. He dared not give us the real thing, he explained. It might have worked.

Later, when we insisted, they did somewhat darken the tone of their incantations. For that reason I was unnerved when, one night, in the first witch scene, through the moaning and banging of drums, I quite distinctly heard, amid the incomprehensible sounds of Abdul's unknown tongue, the words "Meesta Welles" and "Meesta Houseman" several times repeated. I never told Orson, for he was ridiculously superstitious. Besides, he was haunted throughout rehearsals by the old English theatrical tradition that of all the plays in the canon, *Macbeth* is the most ill-fated and accident prone. (It was, in fact, the only play I ever did with him in which he neither sprained nor broke a limb nor otherwise incapacitated himself before or after its opening.)

The *Macbeth* troupe, including understudies, stage managers, cripples, children and dependents, finally numbered one hundred and thirty-seven. Orson led them with an authority that was extraordinary in a boy just out of his teens. He had the strength; but he also had the infinite and loving patience which, in my experience, distinguishes the great from the competent director. And he displayed a capacity for total concentration without which our whole perilous venture could never have been brought off. For this *Macbeth* troupe of ours was an amazing mishmash of amateurs and professionals, church members and radicals, sophisticates and wild ones, adherents of Father Divine and bushmen from Darkest Africa. It was one thing to handle them administratively and paternalistically as I did (firm but understanding, not always truthful but generally fair) and quite another to lead them creatively through unknown country during months of rehearsal in an atmosphere of gathering enervation and doubt. Orson kept them going by the sheer force of his personality. His energy was at all times greater than theirs; he was even more mercurial and less predictable than they were—driving and indolent, glum and gay, tender and violent, inflexibly severe and hopelessly indulgent. I once estimated that a quarter of his growing radio earnings, during *Macbeth*, went in loans and handouts to the company; another quarter was spent on the purchase of props and other necessities (including a severed head) held up by bureaucratic red tape; a third quarter went for meals and cabs; the rest was spent on the entertainment of Jack Carter.

Jack Carter was the most furious man I have ever known. Six foot four, elegant and malevolent in his bespoke shoes and his custom-made English suits, he had bright blue eyes and a skin so light that he could pass as white anywhere in the world, if he'd wanted to. He didn't. The son of one of the famed beauties from the original Floradora Sextet, born in a French chateau, unaware of his own Negro blood and brought up in the lap of European luxury, he had never heard of a race problem until he returned to America in his teens. What he then discovered made an outlaw of him; he became a pimp, a killer and finally an actor. As Crown in *Porgy* he scored a big personal success, which was soon threatened by bouts of misbehavior. His favorite diversion on tour was to register in a town's leading hotel, then invite his black friends, male and female, up to his room and fight till the blood flowed when they were denied admission. He had not worked much in recent years, but made a living somehow through his underworld connections in Harlem. His life was a nagging torment, not knowing whom he despised and hated most—his mother's people for submitting to humiliation or his father's for inflicting it.

When it became known that Jack had been cast for the part of Macbeth, in which he would be directed by a twenty-year-old white man, eyebrows were raised all over Harlem and people waited with mixed emotions for the outcome of their first encounter. If they hoped for mayhem, they were disappointed. From the moment at the first reading when Orson threw his arms around Jack, his eyes brimming with tears of gratitude and admiration, a close and passionate friendship had sprung up between these two giants who, together, measured close to thirteen feet. For four months they were seldom apart, driven by a need for each other's presence which caused Jack to appear at every *Macbeth* rehearsal, whether he had been called or not, and which sent them, when work was ended, at four or five in the morning, roaring together through the late-night spots and brothels of Harlem till it was time to rehearse again.

I never really knew how much of all this was director's strategy calculated to nurse a difficult leading man through opening night or how much it reflected a true and urgent affinity between these two troubled and dangerous men. (I used to wonder, sometimes, seeing Orson returning from these nocturnal forays, if they did not perhaps evoke some echo of those other long, wild nights which he had spent as a boy, with his father, in the red-light districts of the Mediterranean, Hong Kong and Singapore.) This curious intimacy proved of inestimable value to the project. In the state of anxiety and exhaustion which the company had reached by the beginning of April, Jack Carter's loyalty was a major factor in sustaining its morale. Not only was he above reproach in his own behavior, but he constituted himself Orson's champion with the company—scornful of its fatigue, quick to detect signs of revolt and to crush movements of disaffection.

This zeal sometimes got us into trouble. One night, not long before opening, around four in the morning, a minor mutiny broke out on stage. In sheer exhaustion, weighed down by the heavy uniforms in which they had been working for almost ten hours, the company exploded suddenly into open anger and refused to go on. First Eddy Perry, then I, then Orson—sweating and gray with fatigue—pleaded with them, explaining that, for technical reasons, certain stage movements must be fixed that night or not at all. They shook their heads and started to scatter. At that moment a tall figure, superb in full Napoleonic regalia, vaulted onto the parapet of Glamis Castle and began to harangue the rebellious troops. Jack was in a towering rage; he looked and sounded magnificent, full of the unrestrained fury which Orson had been trying to infuse into the last act of *Macbeth*. He told them he was tired too, for he had a bigger part than they did; they might have worked for nine hours but he had been rehearsing for thirteen—and, anyway, what was a little fatigue when the whole future of the Negro Theatre was at stake? Here was the chance they had never been given before; the opportunity for which they had never even dared to hope. If these men (Orson and I, Harry Hopkins and the President of the United States) were willing to risk their reputations on such a project—to work on it as Welles had done, night and day, month after month, on their behalf, when he could easily have been earning a fortune in radio, as they goddamn well knew—there was only one thing that they, as self-respecting Negro actors and human beings could do: follow him, unquestioningly, to the ends of the earth and stop screwing up his wonderful production with their fucking stupid complaints. If they were tired, let them rest after opening! Because if the opening was a bust and the production failed through their fault—they'd have the rest of their goddamn lives to rest in!

The company listened in silence. When he finished they began to pick up their props and to drift back into their positions; the mutiny was over; they were ready to rehearse till dawn or longer. It was then that the demon that drove him made it necessary for Jack Carter to add one more sentence to his oration.

"So get back to work!" he yelled. "You no-acting sons of bitches!"

In the brawl that followed, some scenery was smashed and a court lady was slightly injured when she was pushed off the stage. And no more work was done that night.

Finally, not an hour too soon, the end of rehearsals drew near for Orson Welles and his *Macbeth* company. April 14th (which also happened to be the first day of the national baseball season) was announced as our opening date: it promised the Harlem community an emotional release such as they had not known since the riots of 1935. Little else was talked about above 125th Street. The news that Haile Selassie's troops were in headlong flight before Mussolini's mechanized army and airforce made no stir at all in a week that was entirely monopolized by the activities of the Lafayette Theatre. Nor did the downtown press neglect us. A reporter named Bosley Crowther was sent north by *The New York Times* to report on this latest version of "the Bard's most slaughterous drama."

> Midnight was the time. It seems that twenty-four hours makes too short a day for the WPA's Negro Theatre and, with its house pretty well filled up by workmen during the day and the performances of *Conjur Man Dies* during the evening, the only time left for the final rehearsals of *Macbeth* has been from midnight on till dawn. Sounds fantastic, but it's true . . .
>
> This scout, upon arrival, discovered a goodsized crowd of Negroes milling around the back of the theatre. These were the Shakespearian thespians waiting to begin rehearsal. Not to them, however, but to John Houseman and Orson Welles, supervisor and director, respectively, of the Negro *Macbeth*, it was that this scout went for information. Why, he wanted to know, had they mustered the audacity to take the Bard for a ride? What sort of Thane of Cawdor would find himself in Haiti? Whither would Malcolm and Donalbain flee—to Jamaica or possibly Nassau?

Both Mr. Houseman and Mr. Welles were pleased to talk, brightly and intelligently, about their unusual creation. But they were also quite serious about it. "We were very anxious to do one of Shakespeare's dramas in the Negro Theatre," said Orson Welles, "and *Macbeth* seemed, in all respects, the most adaptable. The stormy career of Christophe, who became 'The Negro King of Haiti' and ended by killing himself when his cruelty led to a revolt, forms a striking parallel to the history of Macbeth. The costumes and settings of the production are therefore in the period of Haiti's grimmest turbulence. Place names have been altered with particular care to retain the rhythm to Shakespeare's lines. Malcolm and Donalbain don't flee to England but to 'the Coast . . . .'"

As to the company itself, they seemed as alert and enthusiastic as the day—or night—they started. The New Deal, not only in the theatre, but in Shakespeare, was meat and drink for them. And any actor who will rehearse from midnight until dawn, the rosy-fingered, must be interested in something more than a pay check. At least that's the way it looked to this scout.

Some of this excitement was spontaneous; some of it was induced and stimulated. Three days before opening, Harlem woke up to find *Macbeth* stenciled in luminous paint on every street corner from 125th to 140th—from Lexington to Broadway. The Tree of Hope, a gnarled relic that survived with difficulty on Seventh Avenue in front of the Lafayette Theatre and which was credited with magic properties of some sort, was festooned with garlands and bright-colored ribbons for luck. By April 10th every seat in the theatre (except those reserved for U.S. Government officials and the press) had been sold, sometimes twice over, as ticket scalpers became active in Harlem's fancier bars. A free preview, given two days before opening, drew three thousand more would-be spectators than the theatre could hold—necessitating the calling of a police emergency squad to disperse the crowd. From the downtown WPA press department came word that every first-string critic in town would attend. (One of them, tactfully, requested that he and his wife should be seated, if possible, "not next to Negroes.")

On opening night, just before dusk, the massed bands of the

Monarch Lodge of the Benevolent and Protective Order of Elks, in uniforms of light blue, scarlet and gold, began to march in two detachments through the streets of Harlem behind two huge, crimson banners that read:

MACBETH
by
William Shakespeare

By six-thirty they had converged before the theatre where they continued to play eighty-five strong, standing around the Tree of Hope, while ten thousand people milled around them and dozens of police, including two on horses, tried in vain to keep a way clear into the Lafayette. As reported in *The New York Times*: "All north-bound automobile traffic was stopped for more than an hour, while from trucks in the street, floodlights flared a circle of light into the lobby and cameramen took photographs of the arrival of celebrities." Later, someone wrote of "the flash of jewels, silk hats and ermine," but I was too nervous to notice and too anxious to get the curtain up before eight o'clock.

It rose, finally, following the customary overture, on a jungle set "luxuriant, savage and ominous with shadows," where the trees met in a great overhead arch of twisted trunks that suggested a gigantic, living skeleton. Within five minutes, amid the thunder of drums and the orgiastic howls and squeals of our voodoo celebrants, we knew that victory was ours.

> The Witches' scenes from *Macbeth* have always worried the life out of the polite, tragic stage; the grimaces of the hags and the garish make-believe of the flaming cauldron have bred more dis-enchantment than anything else that Shakespeare wrote. But ship the witches into the rank and fever-stricken jungle echoes, stuff a gleaming naked witch doctor into the cauldron, hold up Negro masks in the baleful light—and there you have a witches' scene that is logical and stunning and a triumph of the theatre art.*

---

* Brooks Atkinson in *The New York Times*, April 15, 1936, under the headline MACBETH OR HARLEM BOY GOES WRONG.

The next scene to stop the show was that of the Macbeths' royal reception immediately following the murder of Banquo: dozens of shimmering couples in their court finery swirling with wild abandon to the crashing rhythms of our Thomson-orchestrated nineteenth-century waltzes—then, suddenly, a wild, high, inhuman sound that froze them all in their tracks, followed by Macbeth's terrible cry as the spirit of Banquo, in the shape of a huge luminous death mask, suddenly appeared on the battlements to taunt him in the hour of his triumph.

For Birnam Wood, Central Park and half of Rockland County had been stripped of their burgeoning boughs, till the floor of the stage became a moving forest above which Macbeth, cornered at last on the highest platform of his castle, first shot down the "cream-faced loon" who brought him the news of Macduff's approach, then kicked him, for an eighteen-foot drop, into the courtyard below. It was here that the defiant hero vainly emptied his pistol into the body of the tall, dark, bearded man whose wife and children he had murdered and of whom he discovered, too late, as they closed for their final duel, that he had been "from the womb untimely ripped." A moment later, as Macbeth's head came sailing down from the battlements, a double cry rose from the stage—of jubilation from Macduff's army over the tyrant's death, and of triumph from the assembled members of the Negro Theatre Project's classical wing at the successful outcome of their long and agonizing ordeal.

> At the conclusion of the performance there were salvos of applause and countless curtain calls as bouquets of flowers were handed over the footlights to the leading players.

Here again, the clapping and cheering that filled the theatre for fifteen minutes had a double meaning: it was the natural enthusiasm of a delighted audience; it was also Harlem's explosion of relief at the project's final vindication after months of anxiety and doubt.

The notices the next morning were a joy to read: "As an experiment in Afro-American showmanship, *Macbeth* merited the excitement that fairly rocked the Lafayette Theatre last night," concluded *The New York Times*. Others wrote of "an Emperor Jones gone beautifully mad," of "the dark, sensual rhythms, the giant tropic fronds" and of "a tragedy of black ambition in a green jungle shot with such lights from heaven and hell as no other stage has seen." Arthur Pollock of the Brooklyn *Daily Eagle* commented on the "childlike austerity" of the performance: "With all their gusto, they play Shakespeare as though they were apt children who have just discovered and adore the old man."

There were reservations, of course. Atkinson, after rhapsodizing over our "fury and phantom splendor," questioned our company's grasp of poetic tragedy: "They speak the lines conscientiously, but they have left the poetry out of them." There were others, with preconceived notions of "poetic delivery" and "vocal passion," who complained of the very thing that Welles had gone to such pains to accomplish with his Negro cast: the elimination of the glib English Bensonian declamatory tradition of Shakespearean performance and a return to a simpler, more direct and rapid delivery of the dramatic verse.

Because the Negro *Macbeth*, before and after it opened, was a news event as well as a show, the most revealing reactions are to be found in reporters' rather than in critics' accounts. Martha Gellhorn, describing her visit to Harlem, saw at once that

> . . . these Negroes had taken Shakespeare to themselves and that *Macbeth* would remain in this audience's mind from now on, as a play about people living in a Haitian jungle, believing in voodoo, frightened and driven and opulent people, with shiny chocolate skins, who moved about the stage superbly, wearing costumes that belonged to them and suddenly belonged to the play. Macduff, in the battle scenes, wore a pair of epaulets a foot wide made of heavy red cord, complemented by a pair of satin-striped red and white breeches. Macbeth wore superb military costumes of canary yellow and emerald green and shining boots. Women came on and off the stage in salmon pink and purple. The impression was of a hot richness that I have almost never seen in the theatre or anywhere else.

The lines were spoken without Negro accent, but in those

beautiful voices made for singing; and the gestures were lavish, but not amateur or overdone. The audience sat and watched and listened as if this were a murder mystery by Edgar Wallace, only much more exciting.

Roi Otley, a militant Negro journalist, was less concerned with these picturesque aspects than with the racial significance of the production:

> The Negro has become weary of carrying the White Man's blackface burden in the theatre. In *Macbeth* he has been given the opportunity to discard the bandana and burnt-cork casting to play a universal character . . .
>
> From the point of view of the Community, Harlem witnessed a production in which the Negro was not lampooned or made the brunt of laughter. We attended the *Macbeth* showing, happy in the thought we wouldn't again be reminded, with all its vicious implications, that we were niggers.

Like all WPA productions, *Macbeth* was judged by standards that were not purely theatrical. Percy Hammond, dean of New York drama critics, representing the city's leading Republican journal, the *Herald Tribune*, wrote what was not so much of a review as an attack on the New Deal:

> The Negro Theatre, an offshoot of the Federal Government and one of Uncle Sam's experimental philanthropies, gave us, last night, an exhibition of deluxe boondoggling.

He went on to ridicule the whole idea of a popular theatre supported by government funds, citing the size of our cast, the brightness of our costumes and the loudness of our music as evidences of criminal extravagance and presumptuous folly. As an example of political polemic it was savage but eloquent; as a theatrical notice it was irrelevant and malignant. It did not surprise us, nor were we unduly disturbed. But there were some that were.

Early in the afternoon of April 15th, the day of the *Macbeth* reviews, Orson and I were formally visited in my office by Asadata Dafora Horton and his corps of African drummers, including

Abdul, the authentic witch doctor. They looked serious. Asadata was their spokesman. They were perplexed, he said, and desired guidance. He then produced a sheaf of clippings from which he detached the *Herald Tribune* review. He had read it to his men, he declared, and it was their opinion, and his, that the piece was an evil one. I agreed that it was.

"The work of an enemy?"

"The work of an enemy."

"He is a bad man?"

"A bad man."

Asadata nodded. His face was grim as he turned to his troupe, to Abdul in particular, and repeated what I had said. The men nodded, then silently withdrew. Excited by waves of praise and a line a block long at the box office, we quickly forgot both them and Percy Hammond. We stayed for that night's performance, which was better played and no less enthusiastically received than the first. We thanked the company, had a brief, violent personal row on the sidewalk over the *Times* notice in which my name had been coupled with Orson's as director, then went home to get some sleep.

It was reported to us by our disturbed house manager when we arrived at the theatre around noon of the next day that the basement had been filled, during the night, with unusual drumming and with chants more weird and horrible than anything that had been heard upon the stage. Orson and I looked at each other for an instant, then quickly away again, for in the afternoon paper which we had picked up on our way uptown was a brief item announcing the sudden illness of the well-known critic Percy Hammond. He died some days later—of pneumonia, it was said.

(1972)

Woody Allen

(b. 1935)

But Soft ... Real Soft

This story by Brooklyn-born comedian, filmmaker, and writer Woody Allen parodies the absurdities of the Shakespeare authorship controversy. Its title riffs on Romeo's famous line, "But soft, what light through yonder window breaks?" Allen would later write, direct, and star in another work that plays off of Shakespeare, his film *A Midsummer Night's Sex Comedy* (1982). "But Soft ... Real Soft" was first published in Allen's second collection of stories and plays, *Without Feathers*, in 1975.

∽

Ask the average man who wrote the plays entitled *Hamlet, Romeo and Juliet, King Lear,* and *Othello,* and in most cases he'll snap confidently back with, "The Immortal Bard of Stratford on Avon." Ask him about the authorship of the Shakespearean sonnets and see if you don't get the same illogical reply. Now put these questions to certain literary detectives who seem to crop up every now and again over the years, and don't be surprised if you get answers like Sir Francis Bacon, Ben Jonson, Queen Elizabeth and possibly even the Homestead Act.

The most recent of these theories is to be found in a book I have just read that attempts to prove conclusively that the real author of Shakespeare's works was Christopher Marlowe. The book makes a very convincing case, and when I got through reading it I was not sure if Shakespeare was Marlowe or Marlowe was Shakespeare or what. I know this, I would not have cashed checks for either one of them—and I like their work.

Now, in trying to keep the above mentioned theory in perspective, my first question is: if Marlowe wrote Shakespeare's works, who wrote Marlowe's? The answer to this lies in the fact that Shakespeare was married to a woman named Anne Hathaway.

This we know to be factual. However, under the new theory, it is actually Marlowe who was married to Anne Hathaway, a match which caused Shakespeare no end of grief, as they would not let him in the house.

One fateful day, in a jealous rage over who held the lower number in a bakery, Marlowe was slain—slain or whisked away in disguise to avoid charges of heresy, a most serious crime punishable by slaying or whisking away or both.

It was at this point that Marlowe's young wife took up the pen and continued to write the plays and sonnets we all know and avoid today. But allow me to clarify.

We all realize Shakespeare (Marlowe) borrowed his plots from the ancients (moderns); however, when the time came to return the plots to the ancients he had used them up and was forced to flee the country under the assumed name of William Bard (hence the term "immortal bard") in an effort to avoid debtor's prison (hence the term "debtor's prison"). Here Sir Francis Bacon enters into the picture. Bacon was an innovator of the times who was working on advanced concepts of refrigeration. Legend has it he died attempting to refrigerate a chicken. Apparently the chicken pushed first. In an effort to conceal Marlowe from Shakespeare, should they prove to be the same person, Bacon had adopted the fictitious name Alexander Pope, who in reality was Pope Alexander, head of the Roman Catholic Church and currently in exile owing to the invasion of Italy by the Bards, last of the nomadic hordes (the Bards give us the term "immortal bard"), and years before had galloped off to London, where Raleigh awaited death in the tower.

The mystery deepens for, as this goes on, Ben Jonson stages a mock funeral for Marlowe, convincing a minor poet to take his place for the burial. Ben Jonson is not to be confused with Samuel Johnson. He was Samuel Johnson. Samuel Johnson was not. Samuel Johnson was Samuel Pepys. Pepys was actually Raleigh, who had escaped from the tower to write *Paradise Lost* under the name of John Milton, a poet who because of blindness accidentally escaped to the tower and was hanged under the name of Jonathan Swift. This all becomes clearer when we realize that George Eliot was a woman.

Proceeding from this then, King Lear is not a play by Shakespeare but a satirical revue by Chaucer, originally titled "Nobody's Parfit," which contains in it a clue to the man who killed Marlowe, a man known around Elizabethan times (Elizabeth Barrett Browning) as Old Vic. Old Vic became more familiar to us later as Victor Hugo, who wrote *The Hunchback of Notre Dame*, which most students of literature feel is merely *Coriolanus* with a few obvious changes. (Say them both fast.)

We wonder then, was not Lewis Carroll caricaturing the whole situation when he wrote *Alice in Wonderland*? The March Hare was Shakespeare, the Mad Hatter, Marlowe, and the Dormouse, Bacon—or the Mad Hatter, Bacon, and the March Hare, Marlowe—or Carroll, Bacon, and the Dormouse, Marlowe—or Alice was Shakespeare—or Bacon—or Carroll was the Mad Hatter. A pity Carroll is not alive today to settle it. Or Bacon. Or Marlowe. Or Shakespeare. The point is, if you're going to move, notify your post office. Unless you don't give a hoot about posterity.

(1975)

Walter McDonald

(b. 1934)

Caliban in Blue

Born and raised in Lubbock, Texas, Walter McDonald served as a pilot and career officer in the U.S. Air Force from 1957 to 1971 and served a tour in Vietnam in 1969–70. He taught English at the U.S. Air Force Academy and while on active duty was sent by the Air Force to the University of Iowa, where he earned a doctorate in 1966 before returning to the Academy. He subsequently taught at Texas Tech. McDonald has said he "came to poetry late." He told an interviewer that after "some of my friends went off to Vietnam, and one was shot down, then another, I felt a need to say something to them, or about them. I could talk to their wives or widows, but I turned to poems when nothing else worked." McDonald has since published over twenty collections of poetry; his first, containing the following title poem, was *Caliban in Blue and Other Poems* (1976), primarily about flying, war, and loss. The poem's speaker shares the name of the Shakespearean character, son of the "blue-eyed hag" Sycorax, who unwillingly serves Prospero (who calls him "savage") in *The Tempest*. Caliban also worships his mother's god Setebos, and McDonald's speaker invokes that deity as well: "Skies even here / belong to Setebos: / calls it air power." The haunting poem, set against the disturbing ambiguities of Caliban's role in *The Tempest*, captures the "solitary masculine delight" as well as the "savage release" of the trained fighter pilot. The blue likely refers not only to the color of the sky, but also to the Air Force's service dress blue uniform.

❧

Off again,
thrusting up at scald
of copper in orient west
I climb into such blue skies.
Skies even here
belong to Setebos:

calls it air power.
Air power is peace power,
his motto catechizes
as we, diving, spout
flame from under,
off in one hell
of a roar.

His arms like radar
point the spot.
For this, I trained to salivate
and tingle, target-diving,
hand enfolding hard throttle
in solitary masculine delight.

Focused on cross hairs,
eyes glazing, hand triggers switches in
pulsing orgasm,
savage release;
pull out
and off we go again
thrusting deep
into the martial lascivious blue
of uncle's sky.

(1976)

Gloria Naylor

(b. 1950)

Cora Lee

Gloria Naylor's *The Women of Brewster Place: A Novel in Seven Stories* won a National Book Award in 1983 for best first novel. It describes the lives and hardships of seven African American women who live on the same ghetto street in an unnamed American city. "Cora Lee," the fifth of the novel's interlinked stories, recounts the troubled life of a woman who from an early age is obsessed with babies and all too quickly has seven of them. She is a single mother who loses interest in her children when they are no longer infants—and allows them to grow up neglected. The story, and Cora Lee's life, turns on a neighbor's invitation to see a local production of *A Midsummer Night's Dream* directed and performed by African Americans. The thrilling production is as potentially transformative for Cora Lee as it is for her children, one of whom asks her whether Shakespeare is black, and is told, optimistically, "Not yet." Naylor transmutes her own experience in this story: she lived for a few years in the early 1960s on West 119th Street in Harlem, two blocks from Morningside Park, and recalled in an interview how at that time her mother "took us over to see 'Shakespeare in the Park' and the play was *A Midsummer Night's Dream*." Naylor, while admiring Shakespeare's "courage to dream different worlds" and acknowledging that "he has consciously played a part in each of my works," also challenges many of the assumptions inherent in his plays, most visibly in her novel *Mama Day* (1988).

∾

> True, I talk of dreams,
> Which are the children of an idle brain
> Begot of nothing but vain fantasy

HER new baby doll. They placed the soft plastic and pink flannel in the little girl's lap, and she turned her moon-shaped eyes toward them in awed gratitude. It was so perfect and so small.

She trailed her fingertips along the smooth brown forehead and down into the bottom curve of the upturned nose. She gently lifted the dimpled arms and legs and then reverently placed them back. Slowly kissing the set painted mouth, she inhaled its new aroma while stroking the silken curled head and full cheeks. She circled her arms around the motionless body and squeezed, while with tightly closed eyes she waited breathlessly for the first trembling vibrations of its low, gravelly "Mama" to radiate through her breast. Her parents surrounded this annual ritual with full heavy laughter, patted the girl on the head, and returned to the other business of Christmas.

Cora Lee was an easy child to please. She asked for only this one thing each year, and although they supplied her over the years with the blocks, bicycles, books, and games they felt necessary for a growing child, she spent all of her time with her dolls—and they had to be baby dolls. She told them this with a silent rebellion the year they had decided she was now old enough for a teenaged Barbie doll; they had even sacrificed for an expensive set of foreign figurines with porcelain faces and real silk and lace mantillas, saris, and kimonos. The following week they found the dolls under her bed with the heads smashed in and the arms twisted out of their sockets.

That was when her father began to worry. Nonsense, her mother had replied. Wasn't he always saying that she was different from their other children? Well, all children were careless with their toys, and this only proved that she was just like the rest. But the woman stared around the room, thoughtfully fingering the broken pieces of china, while her daughter's assortment of diapered and bottled dolls stared back from their neat row with fixed smiles.

They reluctantly bowed in the face of her quiet reproach and soothed their bruised authority by giving her cheaper and cheaper baby dolls. But their laughter grew hollow and disquieting over Cora's Christmas ritual with the plastic and flannel because her body was now growing rounded and curved. Her father quickly averted his face and busied himself with the other children during the moments that her mother would first hand her the doll from under the tree. Yet a lump still formed in his throat from the lingering glimpse of her melted gratitude for the gift of dead plastic.

He put his foot down on her thirteenth Christmas. There would be no more dolls—of any kind. Let her go play like other children her age. But she does play like other children, her mother pleaded. She had secretly watched her daughter over the years for some missing space, some faintly visible sign in her schoolwork or activities that would explain the strange Christmas ritual, but there was none. She wasn't as bright as her brother, but her marks were a great deal better than her sister's, and she was certainly their most obedient child. Was he going to deny her child this one thing that made her happy? He silently turned from the anger that his seeming unreasonableness fixed on his wife's face, because there were no words for the shudder that went through his mind at the memory of the dead brown plastic resting on his daughter's protruding breasts.

In his guilt and bewilderment he spent more money on her that Christmas than on all the other children, but they still felt the quiet reproach in her spirit as she listlessly fingered the new sweaters, camera, and portable radio.

"That's okay, baby," her mother whispered in her ear, "you have lots of dolls in your room."

"But they don't smell and feel the same as the new ones." And the woman was startled by the depths of misery and loss reflected on the girl's dark brown face. She quickly pushed the image away from herself and still refused to believe that there was any need to worry. And it would be many months later before she recalled that image to her consciousness. It would return to her after her youngest daughter would approach her with the news one afternoon that Cora Lee had been doing nasty with the Murphy boy behind the basement steps. And she would call her older daughter to her and hear her recount with a painful innocence that it wasn't nasty, he had just promised to show her the thing that felt good in the dark—and it had felt good, Mother.

And she would then sadly and patiently give an explanation,

long overdue, that Cora Lee mustn't let the Murphy boy or any other boy show her the thing that felt good in the dark, because her body could now make babies and she wasn't old enough to be a mother. Did she understand? And as she would watch the disjointed mysteries of life connect up in her daughter's mind and hear her breathe out with enlightened wonder—"A real baby, Mother?"—the image of that Christmas would come smashing into her brain like a meat cleaver. It was then that she began to worry.

"Cora, Cora Lee!" The voice echoed shrilly up the air shaft. "I told ya to stop them goddamned children from jumping over my goddamned head all the goddamned day! Now I'm gonna call the police—do you hear me? The goddamned police!" And the window banged shut.

Cora Lee sighed slowly, turned her head from her soap opera, and looked around the disheveled living room at the howling and flying bodies that were throwing dingy school books at each other, jumping off of crippled furniture, and swinging on her sagging velveteen draperies.

"Y'all stop that now," she called out languidly. "You're giving Miss Sophie a nervous headache, and she said she's gonna call the cops." No one paid her any attention, and she turned back toward the television with a sigh, absentmindedly stroking the baby on her lap. What did these people on Brewster Place want from her anyway? Always complaining. If she let the kids go outside, they made too much noise in the halls. If they played in the streets, she didn't watch them closely enough. How could she do all that—be a hundred places at one time? It was enough just trying to keep this apartment together. Did she know little Brucie was going to climb the wall at the end of the block and fall and break his arm? The way they had carried on, you'd think she had pushed him off herself.

Bruce ran in front of the television, chasing one of his sisters and trying to hit her over the head with his dirty unraveling cast.

"Stop that, you're messing up the picture," she said irritably.

Now the doctors were saying that his arm wasn't mending right and she had to bring him back to have it reset. Always something —she must remember to look at the clinic card for his next appointment. Tuesday the something, she faintly recalled. She hoped it wasn't last Tuesday, or she would have to wait forever for a new appointment.

"I just don't know," she sighed aloud, shifted the baby into her arms, and got up to adjust the picture and change channels. She hated it when her two favorite stories came on at the same time; it was a pain to keep switching channels between Steve's murder trial and Jessica's secret abortion.

A rubber ball came hurling across the room and smacked the baby on the side of the head. It began screaming, and her eyes blazed around the room for the offender.

"All right, that's it!" she yelled, charging around the room, hitting randomly at whoever wasn't quick enough to dodge her swinging fists. "Now just get outside—I'm sick of you. Wait! Doesn't anyone have any homework?" She only threatened them with homework when they had pushed her to the end of her patience. She listened suspiciously to the mottled chorus of "nos" to her question, but couldn't gather the energy to sort through the confused pile of torn notebooks that lay scattered about the floor.

"Awful strange," she muttered darkly. "No one ever has any homework. When I was in school, we always got homework." But they had already headed for the door, knowing she had used up her ultimate weapon against them. "And we didn't get left back like you little dumb asses," she called out impotently to the slamming door. It had surprised her when Maybelline had gotten left back. Her oldest daughter had always liked school, and there were never any truant notices for her in the mailbox like there were for the others. Take her to the library, the teachers had said, encourage her to read. But the younger ones had torn and marked in her library books, and they made you pay for that. She couldn't afford to be paying for books all the time. And how was she expected to keep on top of them every minute? It was enough just trying to keep the apartment together. She underscored that thought by picking up a handful of discarded clothes and throwing them into a leaning chair. So now truant notices were coming for Maybelline, too.

"I just don't know," she sighed, and sat back down in front of the television. She gently examined the side of the baby's head to see if the ball had left a mark and kissed the tiny bruise. Why couldn't they just stay like this—so soft and easy to care for? How she had loved them this way. Taking the baby's hand in her mouth, she sucked at the small fingers and watched it giggle and try to reach for her nose. She poked her thumb into the dimpled cheek and lifted the child onto her breast so she could stroke its finely curled hair and inhale the mingled sweetness of mineral oil and talcum powder that lay in the creases of its neck. Oh, for them to stay like this, when they could be fed from her body so there were no welfare offices to sit in all day or food stamp lines to stand on, when she alone could be their substance and their world, when there were no neighbors or teachers or social workers to answer to about their actions. They stayed where you put them and were so easy to keep clean.

She'd spend hours washing, pressing, and folding the miniature clothes, blankets, and sheets. The left-hand corner of her bedroom which held the white wooden crib and dresser was dusted and mopped religiously. As she got on her hands and knees to wash the molding under the crib, the red and black sign in the clinic glared into her mind—GERMS ARE YOUR BABY'S ENEMIES—and she was constantly alert for any of them hidden in that left-hand corner. No, when her babies slept she made sure they went unmolested by those things painted on that clinic poster. There was no place for them to hide on that brown body that was bathed and oiled twice a day, or in the folds of the pastel flannel and percales that she personally scrubbed and sterilized, or between the bristles of the hair brushes that were boiled each week and replaced each month. She couldn't bear the thought of those ugly red things creeping into the soft, fragrant curls that she now buried her nose into.

She wondered at the change in the fine silky strands that

moved with the slightest force of her breath and raised to tickle
her nostrils when she inhaled. In a few years they would grow
tight and kinky and rough. She'd hate to touch them then, because
the child would cry when she yanked the comb through its matted
hair. And she would have to drag them from under the bed or
out of closets and have to thump them on the head constantly
to get them to sit still while she combed their hair. And if she
didn't, there would now be neighbors and teachers and a motley
assortment of relatives to complain about the linty, gnarled hair of
the babies who had grown beyond the world of her lap, growing
wild-eyed and dumb, coming home filthy from the streets with
rough corduroy, khaki, and denim that tattered faster than she
could mend, and with mouthfuls of rotten teeth, and scraped
limbs, and torn school books, and those damned truant notices
in her mailbox—dumb, just plain dumb.

"Are you gonna be a dumb-ass too?" she cooed at the baby.
"No, not Mama's baby. You're not gonna be like them."

There was no reason for them being like that—so difficult. She
had gone to school until her sophomore year, when she had her
first baby. And in those days you had to leave high school if you
were pregnant. She had intended to go back, but the babies just
seemed to keep coming—always welcome until they changed, and
then she just didn't understand them.

*Don't understand you, Cora Lee, just don't understand you. Hav-
ing all them babies year after year by God knows who. Only Sammy
and Maybelline got the same father. Daughter, what's wrong with
you? Sis, what's wrong with you? Case number 6348, what's wrong
with you?*

What was wrong with them? If they behaved better, people
wouldn't always be on her back. Maybe Sammy and Maybelline's
father would have stayed longer. She had really liked him. His
gold-capped teeth and glass eye had fascinated her, and she had
almost learned to cope with his peculiar ways. A pot of burnt
rice would mean a fractured jaw, or a wet bathroom floor a loose

tooth, but that had been their fault for keeping her so tied up she couldn't keep the house straight. But she still carried the scar under her left eye because of a baby's crying, and you couldn't stop a baby from crying. Babies had to cry sometimes, and so Sammy and Maybelline's father had to go. And then there was Brucie's father, who had promised to marry her and take her off Welfare, but who went out for a carton of milk and never came back. And then only the shadows—who came in the night and showed her the thing that felt good in the dark, and often left before the children awakened, which was so much better—there was no more waiting for a carton of milk that never came and no more bruised eyes because of a baby's crying. The thing that felt good in the dark would sometimes bring the new babies, and that's all she cared to know, since the shadows would often lie about their last names or their jobs or about not having wives. She had stopped listening, stopped caring to know. It was too much trouble, and it didn't matter because she had her babies. And shadows didn't give you fractured jaws or bruised eyes, there was no time for all that—in the dark—before the children awakened.

She turned her head toward the door and sighed when she heard the knock. Now what? It couldn't be the kids, once they were out she had to go down and scrape them from the streets unless they got too cold or hungry. Did that cranky old woman really call the cops? She opened the door and faced a tall pretty young girl with beaded hair, holding a struggling and cursing Sammy by the collar and a stack of papers in the other arm. The other children littered the hallway and stairs to watch their brother's ordeal.

"Mama, I ain't done nothing. Tell this shit face; I ain't done nothing."

"What a way to talk." She snatched him and flung him into the apartment. "Missy, I'm sorry. Did he steal something from you? He's always taking things and I've beat him about it but he still won't stop. I've told the little dumb-ass the teachers have threatened to send him to reform school." She turned toward her son. "Do you hear that—*reform school* you little . . ."

"No, wait, you've got it all wrong—it's not that!" The girl

shifted the papers in her arm uncomfortably. "He was downstairs eating out of one of the garbage cans and I thought you oughta know because, well, he might be hungry or something."

"Oh," Cora Lee seemed relieved, "I know he does that." She saw the girl's eyes widen slightly in disbelief. "He's looking for sweets. The dentist at the clinic said all his teeth are rotten so I won't give him anything sweet and he searches through garbage cans for them. I tried to make him stop but you can't be everywhere at once. I figure once he gets sick enough from that filthy habit, he'll stop by himself."

The girl was still staring at her. Cora went on, "Believe me, my kids get plenty to eat. I got two full books of food stamps I haven't used yet. I don't know why I bother to cook; they just mess over their food—always eating that damned candy. But I had to stop Sammy because the doctors said his gums were infected and I didn't want that spreading to the baby." Why was this girl looking at her so strangely? She probably thought she was lying. Sammy was really gonna get it for embarrassing her like this. "I was just about to cook dinner when you came to the door," she lied. She still had two more stories to watch before forcing herself to face the greasy sinkful of day-old dishes and pots that had to be cleared away before making dinner. "Okay, y'all," she called over the girl's shoulder, "come on in the house, it's almost time to eat."

Howls of protest and disbelief followed in the wake of her words and she ran out in the hall behind the retreating footsteps. "I said get your ass in this house!" she yelled. "Or you gonna be damned sorry!" The unaccustomed force in her voice stunned them into a reluctant obedience. They sulked past her into the apartment with a series of sucking teeth and "we never eat this earlys" that were not lost on the girl.

Cora smiled triumphantly at the girl and let out a long sigh. "You see what I mean—they're terrible. I just don't know."

"Yes," the girl looked down uneasily at her papers, "it must be difficult with so many. I'm sorry I had to meet you like this but I was coming by anyway." She looked up and slipped into a practiced monologue. "I'm Kiswana Browne and I live up on the sixth floor. I'm trying to start a tenants' association on this block. You know, all of these buildings are owned by one man and if we really pull together, we can put pressure on him to start fixing this place up. Once we get the association rolling we can even stage a rent strike and do the repairs ourselves. I'd like you to check off on this sheet all the things that are wrong with your apartment and then I'm going to take these forms and file them at the housing court."

Cora Lee listened to Kiswana's musical, clipped accent, looked at the designer jeans and striped silk blouse, and was surprised she had said that she lived in this building. What was she doing on a street like Brewster? She couldn't have been here very long or she would know there was nothing you could do about the way things were. That white man didn't care about what a bunch of black folks had to say, and these people weren't gonna stick together no way. They were too busy running around complaining, trying to make trouble for her instead of the landlord. It's a shame she's wasting her time because she seems like a nice girl.

"There's plenty wrong with this place, but this ain't gonna do no good."

"It will if we can get enough people to sign these forms. I've already been through four of the buildings and the response is really great. We'll be having our first meeting this Saturday at noon."

"I just don't know," Cora sighed and looked around her apartment. Kiswana openly followed her gaze and Cora Lee answered what she saw reflected in the girl's face. "You know, you can't keep nothing nice with these kids tearing up all the time. My sister gave me that living room set only six months ago and it was practically new."

"No, I know what you mean," Kiswana said a little too quickly as her eyes passed over the garbage spilling out of the kitchen can.

"You got kids then?"

"No, but my brother has two and he says they can really be a handful at times."

"Well, I got a lot more than that so you can imagine the hell I go through."

Kiswana jumped as they heard a loud crash and a scream coming from the corner of the room. Cora Lee turned around placidly and without moving called to the child tangled in the fallen curtain rods and drapery. "You happy now, Dorian? Huh? I told ya a million times to stop swinging on my curtains, so good for you!"

Kiswana pushed past her and went toward the screaming child. "Maybe he's hurt his head."

"Naw, he's always falling from something. He's got a head like a rock." Cora followed her to examine her curtains and see if they were torn. "He's just like his father—all those West Indians got hard heads." Well, at least, I guess he was West Indian, she thought, he had some kind of accent. "This curtain rod's totally gone." She glared down at the child Kiswana was cradling. "And I got no more money to replace it, so these drapes can just stay down for all I care."

Dorian had stopped crying and was feeling the colorful beads attached to Kiswana's braids.

"Leave her hair alone and get up and go in the other room."

Kiswana looked up at Cora alarmed. "There's a big knot coming up on the side of his head; maybe we should take him . . ."

"It'll go down," Cora said and went to the couch and picked up the baby. Kiswana was still holding Dorian and made no attempt to hide the disapproval on her face. "Look," Cora Lee said, "if I ran to the hospital every time one of these kids bumps their head or scrapes their knee, I'd spend the rest of my life in those emergency rooms. You just don't know—they're wild and disgusting and there's nothing you can do!" She rocked the baby energetically as if the motions of her body could build up a wall against the girl's silent condemnation.

Dorian tried to snatch one of the beads twisted in Kiswana's hair and she cried out in pain as he jumped from her lap with the end of a braid clenched in his fist. "Son-of-a . . . !" flew out of her mouth before she stopped herself and bit on her lip.

"See what I mean?" Cora almost smiled gratefully at Dorian as he raced around the door into the other room.

"You know," Kiswana got off her knees and brushed the dust

from her jeans, "they're probably that way from being cramped up in this apartment all the time. Kids need space to move around in."

"There's plenty of room in that school yard for them to play, but will they go to school? No. And the last time I let them go to the park somebody gave Sammy a reefer and when my mother found it in his pocket, I caught hell for that. So what am I supposed to do? I gotta keep them away from there or I'll end up with a bunch of junkies on my hands."

She saw out of the corner of her eye that *Another World* was going off. Aw shit! Now she wouldn't know until Monday if Rachel had divorced Mack because he'd become impotent after getting caught in that earthquake. Why didn't this girl just go home and stop minding her business.

"Look, I have your paper and I'll look it over, okay? But I got a million things to do right now so you can come back for it some other time." She knew she was being rude, but there were only three commercials left before *The Doctors* started.

"Oh, sure, I'm sorry; I didn't mean to keep you. You know, I wasn't trying to tell you how to raise your children or anything. It's just that . . ." She involuntarily glanced around the living room again.

"Yeah, I know," Cora said with one eye on the television, "it's just that I'm busy right now. You see, I got to get up . . ."

"And cook dinner," Kiswana said sadly.

"Yeah, right—dinner." And she went to open the door.

Kiswana seemed reluctant to move. "You know, there's a lot of good things that go on in the park too." She pulled a leaflet out of her pocketbook. "My boyfriend's gotten a grant from the city and he's putting on a black production of *A Midsummer Night's Dream* this weekend. Maybe you could come and bring the children," she offered, barely hopeful.

Cora looked begrudgingly at the flyer. "Abshu Ben-Jamal Productions," she mouthed slowly. "Hey, I know him—a big, dark fellow. Didn't he have a traveling puppet show last summer?"

"Yes, that's him." Kiswana smiled.

"Came around here with a truck or something and little danc-ing African dolls. I remember, the kids talked about it for weeks."

"You see," Kiswana hurried on encouraged, "they love things like that. Why don't you bring them tomorrow night?"

"I don't know," Cora sighed and looked at the leaflet. "This stuff here—Shakespeare and all that. It'll be too deep for them and they'll start acting up and embarrassing me in front of all those people."

"Oh, no—they'll love it," Kiswana insisted. "It's going to be funny and colorful and he's brought it up to date. There's music and dancing—he's going to have the actors do the Hustle around a maypole—and they slap each other five and all sorts of stuff like that. And it'll have fairies—all kids like stories with fairies and things in them; even if they don't understand every word, it'll be great for them. Please, try to come."

"Well, I'll see. Saturday is pretty busy for me. I have to clean up the baby's things and do the wash. Then there's so many of them to get ready. I don't know; I'll try."

"Look, I'm not doing much tomorrow. After the tenants' meet-ing. I'll come by early and help you with the kids. Then we can all go together. Okay? It'll be fun."

Aw dammit! She could hear the opening music to *The Doctors*. Anything to get rid of this girl. "Okay, I'll bring them, but you don't have to stop by. I'll manage alone; I'm used to it."

"No, I want to. It's no problem."

"Yeah, but they'll just show off if you're here. It'll be easier if I get them ready myself." She swung the door open.

"Okay, then I'll wait and stop by for you on my way out. How about six-thirty so we can get good seats?"

"Yeah, all right—six-thirty." And she opened the door a little wider.

Kiswana was elated and she cooed at the baby, "Hear that, sweetie? You're going to a play." She stroked the child under the chin. "She's a fine little thing. What's her name?"

Her attentions to the baby bought her a few more minutes of

Cora Lee's time. "Sonya Marie," she said and proudly hoisted the child up to be admired.

"She looks just like you." Kiswana took the baby and tickled her nose with the end of her braids.

"It's a shame you ain't got none of your own. You're good with kids."

"I don't have a husband, yet," Kiswana answered automatically, watching the baby laugh.

"So, neither do I." Cora shrugged her shoulders.

Kiswana looked up and added quickly, "Well, someday, maybe, but right now all I have is a studio."

"Babies don't take up much space. You just bring in a crib and a little chest and you're all set," Cora beamed.

"But babies grow up," Kiswana said softly and handed the child back to Cora with a puzzled smile.

Cora Lee shut the door and sat back down in front of the television, but Maggie's battle with the rare blood disease she'd contracted in Guatemala flickered by unnoticed. There was no longer any comfort in stroking the child on her lap. Kiswana's perfume, lingering in the air mixed with the odor of stale food and old dust, left her unsettled and she couldn't pinpoint exactly why. After a few restless moments, she laid the baby on the couch and went over to the stack of albums she kept on a corner table. She slowly flipped through the expensive studio poses of her babies. Dorian, Brucie, Sammy, Maybelline—Dierdre and Daphane (how pleased she had been that year to have two come at once). Her babies— all her babies—stared back at her, petrified under the yellowing plastic. She must get Sonya's pictures taken before it was too late.

But babies grow up

She looked at the hanging draperies, the broken furniture, the piles of litter in her living room. That girl probably thought that she was a bad mother. But she loved her babies! Her babies— her . . . She began to go through the albums again—Shakespeare, humph. Her class had gone to see Shakespeare when she was in junior high. She stared into Maybelline's brown, infant eyes—*We are such stuff as dreams are made on, and our little life is rounded with a sleep*—Where had that come from? Had the teacher made them memorize that from the play, "The Temple," or something it was called. She had loved school; she always went to school— not like them. Why didn't her babies go to school? She shook her head confusedly. No, babies didn't go to school. Sonya was her baby and she was too little for school. Sonya was never any trouble. Sonya . . .

But babies grow up

She slammed the album shut. That girl probably thought she didn't want to take her children to that play. Why shouldn't they go? It would be good for them. They needed things like Shakespeare and all that. They would do better in school and stop being so bad. They'd grow up to be like her sister and brother. Her brother had a good job in the post office and her sister lived in Linden Hills. She should have told that girl that—her sister was married to a man with his own business and a big house in Linden Hills. That would have shown her—coming in here with her fancy jeans and silk blouse, saying she was a bad mother. Yeah, she'd have her babies ready tomorrow.

Cora Lee went and turned off the television and decided to start dinner early after all.

"Why we gotta take a bath—Grandma's coming over?"

"No, you're going to a play." Cora Lee was changing the water in the tub for the third shift of children.

"I don't wanna go to no play," Dorian protested.

"Yes, you do," she said, stripping him and throwing him into the sudsy water. "And if you know what's good for you, you'll stay in that tub." She went through the door to find Brucie.

"Dierdre, you can't wear those socks—they got holes in them."

"But I always wear these to school."

"Well, you're not wearing them like that tonight—give 'em to me!" She took the socks from the girl, dragged Brucie into the tub, and went in search of a needle and thread.

The children followed her bewildering behavior with freshly combed and brushed heads. They had never seen their mother so active. The feeling had begun after breakfast when she took their plates from the table, washed and stacked them, and swept the kitchen floor before moving into the living room to leave it dusted and in some semblance of order, and then on to the bedrooms, where she had even changed their sheets—there was something in the air. It felt like Christmas or a visit from their grandparents, but neither of these was happening, so they exchanged troubled glances and moved cautiously about with only token protests to the stranger who had awakened them that morning.

Cora sorted feverishly through their clothes—washing, pressing, and mending. She couldn't believe they were in such a state. Trouser legs were ankle-high or frayed to distraction, dresses were ripped from the waist and unraveled at the hem, socks were missing entire toes or heels—when had all this happened? She patched and fussed, meshed and mated outfits until she was finally satisfied with the neatly buttoned bodies she assembled before her. She lined up the scoured faces, carefully parted hair, and oiled arms and legs on the couch, and forbid them to move.

When she opened the door for Kiswana, the girl was touched as she sensed the amount of effort that must have gone into the array of roughly patched trousers, ill-fitting shirts, and unevenly hemmed dresses that the woman proudly presented to her. She smiled warmly into Cora Lee's eyes. "Well, I see we're all set. Let's go." She took the two smallest hands in hers and they all trooped down the steps.

Cora flanked the group like a successful drill sergeant, and she made a point of personally addressing each neighbor that was standing on the stoop and along the outside railing, ignoring the openly surprised stares as they emerged from the building. Where could she be going with all them kids? The welfare office wasn't open. She was greeted with the friendly caution that women hold toward unmarried women who repeatedly have children—since they aren't having them by their own husbands, there is always the possibility they are having them by yours.

Mattie was coming up the block, wheeling a heavy shopping cart.

"Hi, Miss Mattie," Cora called out warmly. She sincerely liked Mattie because unlike the others, Mattie never found the time to do jury duty on other people's lives.

"Why, hello y'all. My don't we look nice. Where you going?"

"To the park—for Shakespeare." Cora emphasized the last word, extending her smile into a semicircle that covered the other listening ears.

"That's right nice. This the new baby? Ain't she pretty. You gonna have to stop this soon, Cora. You got a full load now," Mattie chided lightly.

"I know, Miss Mattie," Cora sighed. "But how you gonna stop?"

"Same way you started, child—only in reverse." The three women laughed.

"Sammy, help Miss Mattie up the steps with that cart and then meet us at the end of the alley." They were approaching the six-foot alley that lay between Mattie's building and the wall on Brewster Place.

"Naw, I can manage. I don't want him walking in that alley alone; it's getting dark. C. C. Baker and all them lowlifes be hanging around there, smoking that dope. I done called the police on 'em a hundred times, but they won't come for that."

Mattie and Kiswana spoke a few minutes about the new tenants' association getting the city to fence off the alley, and then the group moved on. They approached the park and then followed the huge red arrows painted under the green and black letters—A Midsummer Night's Dream—toward the center. Cora had come to the park prepared. She had a leather strap folded up in her bag and she placed herself in the middle of the row with the children seated on both sides of her so no one would be beyond the reach of her arm. Kiswana sat on the end, holding Sonya. They weren't going to cut up and embarrass her in front of these people. They would sit still and get this Shakespeare thing if she had to break their backs.

She looked around and didn't recognize anyone from Brewster so the blacks here probably came from Linden Hills, and over half of the people filtering in were white. This must really be something if they were coming. She straightened up on the rough bench, poked Brucie and Dorian, who were sitting on either side of her, and threw invisible threats to the left and right at the others. There would be no fidgeting and jumping up—show these people that they were used to things like this. She uncurled Brucie's collar and motioned to Daphane to close her legs and pull down her dress.

The evening light had turned into the color of faded navy blue blankets when the spotlights came on. Cora couldn't understand what the actors were saying, but she had never heard black people use such fine-sounding words, and they really seemed to know what they were talking about—no one was forgetting the lines or anything. She looked to see if she would have to sneak her strap out of her bag, but the children were surprisingly still, except for Dorian, and she only had to jab him twice because when they changed the set for the forest scenes, even he was awed. That girl was right—it was simply beautiful. Huge papier-mâché flora hung in varying shades of green splendor among sequin-dusted branches and rocks. The fairy people were dressed in gold and lavender gauze with satin trimming that glimmered under the colored spotlight. And the Lucite crowns worn on stage split the floodlights into a multitude of dancing, elongated diamonds.

At first Cora took her cues from the people around her and laughed when they did, but as the play gained momentum the evident slapstick quality in the situation drew its own humor. The fairy man had done something to the eyes of these people and everyone seemed to be chasing everyone else. First, that girl in brown liked that man and Cora laughed naturally as he hit and kicked her to keep her from following him because he was after the girl in white who was in love with someone else again. But after the fairy man messed with their eyes, the whole thing turned upside down and no one knew what was going on—not even the people in the play.

That fairy queen looked just like Maybelline. Maybelline could be doing this some day—standing on a stage, wearing pretty clothes, and saying fine things. That girl had probably gone to college for that. But Maybelline could go to college—she liked school.

"Mama," Brucie whispered, "am I gonna look like that? Is that what a dumb-ass looks like when it grows up?"

The character, Bottom, was prancing on the stage, wearing an ass's head.

Cora felt the guilt lining her mouth seep down to form a lump in her throat. "No, baby." She stroked his head. "Mama won't let you look like that."

"But isn't that man a dumb-ass, too? Don't they look . . ."

"Shhh, we'll talk about it later."

The next scene was blurred in front of her. Maybelline used to like school—why had she stopped? The image of the torn library books and unanswered truant notices replaced the tears in her eyes as they quietly rolled down her face.

School would be over in a few weeks, but all this truant non-sense had to stop. She would get up and walk them there person-ally if she had to—and summer school. How long had the teachers been saying that they needed summer school? And she would check homework—every night. And P.T.A. Sonya wouldn't be little forever—she'd have no more excuses for missing those meet-ings in the evening. Junior high; high school; college—none of them stayed little forever. And then on to good jobs in insurance companies and the post office, even doctors or lawyers. Yes, that's what would happen to her babies.

The play was approaching its last act, and all the people seemed to have thought they were sleeping. *I have had a most rare vision. I have had a dream, past the wit of man to say what dream it was* . . . In the last scene the cast invited the audience to come up on stage and join them in the wedding dance that was played to rock music. The children wanted to jump up and join them, but Cora held them back. "No, no, next time!" she said, not wanting their clothes to be seen under the bright lights. The participants from the audience sat down crosslegged on the stage and the little fairy man pranced between them:

> If we shadows have offended,
> Think but this, and all is mended:
> That you have but slumber'd here,
> While these visions did appear.
> And this weak and idle theme,
> No more yielding but a dream . . .

Cora applauded until her hands tingled, and felt a strange sense of emptiness now that it was over. Oh, if they would only do it again. She let the children jump around their seats and dance to the music that continued after the play was over. Cora went down the row to Kiswana and grabbed her hand.

"Thanks so much—it was wonderful."

Kiswana was slightly taken aback by this burst of emotion from the woman. "I knew you'd like it, and see how good the kids were."

"Oh, yes, it was great. I'm gonna bring them back again."

"Well, if things work out, he's planning to produce another one next year."

"We'll be here," Cora said emphatically, taking the baby from Kiswana. "Was she too much?"

"No, she's precious. Look, I'm not going back right now. I want to run and congratulate Abshu. You'll be okay?"

"Sure, and please tell him I thought it was wonderful."

"I will. See you later."

Cora and her family moved home through the moist summer night, and she smiled as the children chattered and tried to imitate some of the antics they had seen.

"Mama," Sammy pulled on her arm, "Shakespeare's black?"

"Not yet," she said softly, remembering she had beaten him for writing the rhymes on her bathroom walls.

The long walk had tired them so there were few protests about going to bed. No one questioned it when she sponged them down and put them each into bed with a kiss—this had been a night of wonders. Cora Lee took their clothes, folded them, and put them away.

She then went through her apartment, turning off the lights and breathing in hopeful echoes of order and peace that lay in the clean house. She entered her bedroom in the dark and the shadow, who had let himself in with his key, moved in the bed. He didn't ask where they had been and she didn't care to tell him. She went over and silently peeked in the crib at her sleeping daughter and let out a long sigh. Then she turned and firmly folded her evening like gold and lavender gauze deep within the creases of her dreams, and let her clothes drop to the floor.

(1982)

Dramatists Guild
Landmark Symposium

West Side Story

In 1985 the Dramatists Guild invited the four artists most responsible for the 1957 musical *West Side Story* to talk about how their show was created. This is a transcript of that conversation, published later that year. Leonard Bernstein had written the music, Jerome Robbins had choreographed and directed it, Stephen Sondheim had composed the lyrics, and Arthur Laurents had written the book, based on Shakespeare's *Romeo and Juliet*. While three decades after their show first opened their recollections necessarily differ at various points—Laurents calls it "Rashomon West Side Story"—their conversation, moderated by the playwright Terrence McNally, illuminates the collaborative efforts of these phenomenally talented (and at the time young) artists. We learn here that the musical, the idea for which emerged in the late 1940s, was originally imagined as *East Side Story*, the warring households Jewish and Christian, and the action taking place at the "Easter–Passover season." But that religious divide was no longer quite as explosive in the 1950s and that story, as Laurents points out, had already been staged on Broadway in the wildly successful *Abie's Irish Rose* in the 1920s. Their revision of Shakespeare's story of ill-fated lovers and social division turned into a more contemporary one about immigration, gang violence, and the clash between mainstream American and Latino cultures. It would prove to be the defining twentieth-century American adaptation of Shakespeare. The original production ran for 732 performances at the Winter Garden Theatre and went on to many revivals across America and around the world. It was also made into a popular film in 1961.

※

The musical "West Side Story" was the subject of a Dramatists Guild Landmark symposium at which the authors of its conception and choreography (Jerome Robbins, also its director), its book (Arthur Laurents), its lyrics (Stephen Sondheim) and its music (Leonard Bernstein) were on hand to tell an audience of dramatists how it was at the creation of this now-memorable hit. Their discussion was moderated by Vice President Terrence McNally, who as a member of the Guild's Projects Committee (Gretchen Cryer chairman, Sandra Schreiber director of special projects) was in large measure responsible for creating, inspiring and organizing the Landmark series. Here is the transcript of this session, edited with the approval of the participants. Questioners from the floor are not named but are identified by the letter "Q."

TERRENCE MCNALLY: It's hard to imagine what the musical theater would be like in 1985 without the efforts of the four gentlemen sitting here with me, the authors of *West Side Story*. In our theater community, they are held in great, great respect and much love. *West Side Story* is the one time these four extraordinary talents came together. I'd like to start with the germ of the idea, the first time somebody said, "Hey, there's a musical there," up through opening night in New York, in this case September 26, 1957, when *West Side Story* opened at the Winter Garden Theater.

JEROME ROBBINS: I don't remember the exact date—it was somewhere around 1949—a friend of mine was offered the role of Romeo. He said to me, "This part seems very passive, would you tell me what you think I should do with it." So I asked myself, "If I were to play this, how would I make it come to life?" I tried to imagine it in terms of today. That clicked in, and I said to myself, "There's a wonderful idea here." So I wrote a very brief outline and started looking for a producer and collaborators who'd be interested. This was not easy. Producers were not at all interested in doing it. Arthur and Lenny were interested, but not in getting together to work on it at that time, so we put it away.

Many years later, they were involved in another musical and

asked me to join them. I was not interested in *their* musical, but I did manage to say, "How about *Romeo and Juliet*?" I won them back to the subject, and that started our collaboration.

MCNALLY: Were Arthur and Lenny the first librettist and composer you approached?

ROBBINS: Oh, yes. During the long period we put the project aside, I wasn't actively seeking other collaborators, I thought these were the best people for the material. I stuck to trying to get these guys, and when they came back to me I had the bait to grab them.

MCNALLY: When did Steve come into the picture?

STEPHEN SONDHEIM: 1955. By the time I joined them, Arthur had a three-page outline.

ARTHUR LAURENTS: There should be a preface to all this. Several years ago, Harold Prince wrote his theatrical memoirs—rather prematurely, as it turned out. In them, he talked about producing *West Side Story*. The original producer, the one who stuck all the way, was Roger Stevens. Later, he was joined by Hal Prince and the late Bobby Griffith. I read Hal's recollections, and I phoned Steve and told him, "I don't think that's the way it happened." Steve agreed. My point is not that Hal's account was distorted, he was telling it the way he saw it. Today, each of us is going to tell it the way each of us remembers it. It's a sort of *Rashomon West Side Story*.

ROBBINS: I'm leaving out some details. Leland Heyward was interested in the idea for a while. Cheryl Crawford was interested up to the point where we all four auditioned the show to backers and raised not a cent. We offered it to Richard Rodgers at one point.

LAURENTS: Actually, we were turned down by every producer in the theater except Roger.

ROBBINS: No one should be shocked by that. A *fait accompli* is one thing, but it's not surprising that people said, "I don't understand what that's about" in the case of a work in the embryo stage that was quite radical in its time. They hadn't heard Lenny's score, they hadn't read the script, they certainly hadn't seen what was going to be danced. At that one audition we all got up there and did everything we could to make it happen.

SONDHEIM: We all performed.

LAURENTS: It was in a room in an apartment on the East River, no air conditioning and a lot of tugboats.

SONDHEIM: Windows open, and the sound of tugboats, which we subsequently used in the show.

MCNALLY: Lenny, part of the *West Side Story* lore is that you intended to do the lyrics yourself. Is that true?

LEONARD BERNSTEIN: This will be my contribution to *Rashomon*. All of us recall events slightly differently, and that's as it should be, because we are very subjective people in our objective way. In order to be objective on this occasion, we have to be somewhat subjective, because that's the only way we can tell our truths.

As I recall, the origins of *West Side Story* were indeed in 1949. Jerry called up and gave us this idea and said, "Come over and let me explain it to you." Arthur and I were quite excited by it. I remember that evening in Jerry's apartment as though it were yesterday *because* of the excitement. What was basically different from the way *West Side Story* turned out was that it was conceived as taking place on the *East* Side of New York. It was an East Side version of *Romeo and Juliet*, involving as the feuding parties Catholics and Jews at the Passover-Easter season with feelings in the streets running very high, with a certain amount of slugging and blood-letting. It seemed to match the Romeo story very well, except that this was not a family feud, but religion-oriented.

As a matter of fact, Arthur and I were so excited about it that Arthur wrote some sketched-out scenes, one of which was pretty complete.

LAURENTS: I remember absolutely none of this.

BERNSTEIN: I can tell you exactly where I was, I was in St. Louis, Missouri conducting that orchestra when I received the opening scene and an outline of the second scene. I was really excited.

LAURENTS: My reaction was, it was *Abie's Irish Rose*, and that's why we didn't go ahead with it. Lenny and I were involved with James M. Cain's *Serenade*. We brought it to Jerry, who said he wasn't interested. Jerry had come to us a couple of times in the intervening years, but what he did so effectively was knock out *Serenade* and start us thinking about *Romeo and Juliet*. Then, by some coincidence, Lenny and I were at the Beverly Hills pool, and Lenny said, "What about doing it about the chicanos?" In New York we had the Puerto Ricans, and at that time the papers were full of stories about juvenile delinquents and gangs. We got really excited and phoned Jerry, and that started the whole thing.

BERNSTEIN: We were sitting by the pool talking about other things. There was a copy of the Los Angeles *Times* in a nearby deck chair, with a headline which said "Gang Riots on Oliviera Street," about Mexicans and so-called Americans rioting against each other.

What worries me is that all this is really not answering Terrence's question about my originally writing the lyrics. I'm trying to get to it, but it takes a little doing.

Yes, when we began I had—madly—undertaken to do the lyrics as well as the music. In 1955, I was also working on another show, *Candide*; and then the *West Side Story* music turned out to be extraordinarily balletic—which I was very happy about—and turned out to be a tremendously greater amount of music than I had expected, ballet music, symphonic music, developmental music. For those two reasons, I realized that I couldn't do all that music, plus the lyrics, and do them well. Arthur mentioned that he'd heard of a young fellow named Stephen Sondheim sing some of his songs at a party . . .

SONDHEIM: A small correction: Arthur was auditioning people to write the songs for *Serenade*, and that's how he heard my songs, as an audition piece. And then, several months later, I ran into Arthur at a party . . .

LAURENTS: The opening night of *Isle of Goats* . . .

SONDHEIM: Correct. I asked Arthur what he was doing, and he told me he was beginning to work on this musical. I asked him who was doing the lyrics, and he said, "We don't have anybody because Comden and Green were supposed to do them, but they're in California and may be tied up with a movie contract. Would you like to come and play your songs for Leonard Bernstein?" I said "Sure," and the next day I met Lenny.

BERNSTEIN: I freaked out when Steve came in and sang his songs. From that moment to this, we've been loving colleagues and friends.

SONDHEIM: A week later we learned that the movie would keep Comden and Green in California, so I got the job.

ROBBINS: I'd like to talk a little bit about that period, because it was one of the most exciting I've ever had in the theater; the period of the collaboration, when we were feeding each other all the time. We would meet wherever we could, depending on our schedules. Arthur would come in with a scene, the others would say they could do a song on this material, I'd supply, "How about if we did this as a dance?" There was this wonderful, mutual exchange going on. We can talk here about details, "I did this, I did that," but the essence of it was what we gave to each other, took from each other, yielded to each other, surrendered, reworked, put back together again, all of those things. It was a very important and extraordinary time. The collaboration was most fruitful during that digestive period. I say that because we got turned down so much, and for so many reasons, that we kept going back to the script, or rather our play, saying, "That didn't work, I wonder why not, what didn't they like, let's take a look at it again."

I remember Richard Rodgers's contribution. We had a death scene for Maria—she was going to commit suicide or something, as in Shakespeare. He said, "She's dead already, after this all happens to her." So the walls we hit were helpful to us in a way, sending us back for another look. I'm glad we didn't get *West Side Story* on right away. Between the time we thought of it and finally did it, we did an immense amount of work on it.

BERNSTEIN: Amen to that. This was one of the most extraordinary collaborations of my life, perhaps *the* most, in that very sense of our nourishing one another. There was a generosity on everybody's part that I've rarely seen in the theater. For example, the song "Something's Coming" was a very late comer. We realized we needed a character-introduction kind of song for Tony. There was a marvellous introductory page in the script that Arthur had written, a kind of monologue, the essence of which became the lyric for this song. We raped Arthur's playwriting. I've never seen anyone so encouraging, let alone generous, urging us, "Yes, take it, take it, make it a song." Almost all the "Something's Coming" lyrics had been written as poetic prose by Arthur.

SONDHEIM: Arthur, do you remember it that way? As I remember it, the scene *ended* with the line "Something's coming."

LAURENTS: The main thing is what Jerry said, to an extraordinary degree. If I pushed myself, I could think of a moment when one or two of us were isolated, but in my memory it's the four of us together almost all the time. It's really true, without any consciousness of it we were all just high on the work and loving it.

BERNSTEIN: This is one of the shortest books of any major Broadway musical, a testimony to Arthur's particular generosity. He never said, "I'm sorry, that's got to be spoken, what's going to happen to my scene, my characters have to be developed"—none of that. He gave whenever he could.

LAURENTS: That's very sweet, but there was one place where I was too careless. We all hold certain set beliefs, and I've always believed that the climax of a musical should be musicalized. Well, the climax of *West Side Story* is *not* musicalized. It's a speech that I wrote as a dummy lyric for an aria for Maria, with flossy words about guns and bullets. It was supposed to be set to music, and it never was.

BERNSTEIN: Yes it was, and discarded, four or five times. It's not that I didn't try.

ROBBINS: We're all four talking about the creative processes because that was the incredibly exciting time, that's what the show came out of. This should be a lesson to future collaborators. At the time, it was a state of creative bliss combined with hard work. Much later, we all went our different ways, and years later we can start to pull it apart with each of us saying, "I did this" or "I did this." But at the time we weren't thinking about that, we were all of us just dedicated to making that show happen. There were pushes and pulls by everybody to get it to where it was.

Arthur had the hardest job of anybody converting a Shakespeare play into musical theater of today. Lenny, Steve and I had nothing to put our work against. Arthur had that text by Mr. William S all the time. We could make our poetry out of the music, the dancing, the song lyrics, but Arthur had the burden of making his text go along with *Romeo and Juliet* and still communicate some of the poetry, the argot, the drives and passions of the 1950s, while trying to match, somehow, the style we were creating as we went along.

SONDHEIM: The book is remarkable not only because it's so brief but because so much happens in it. *Romeo and Juliet* is, after all, a melodrama with something extraordinary happening in every scene, something that has to be set up and then has to pay off. On top of the flavor, there is the compactness of the plot. It's one thing that drives the show even when it isn't well sung or well danced—the plot is still exciting. It was when Shakespeare took it, and it was when Arthur adapted it.

MCNALLY: When you read it, the leanness of it is very impressive; also, a lot of the story is accomplished in the dance sequences.

BERNSTEIN: Another example of how closely we worked together was the prologue. Believe it or not, it originally had words. That extraordinarily instrumental music was sung. It didn't take us long to find out that wouldn't work. That was when Jerry took over and converted all that stuff into this remarkable thing now known as "the prologue to *West Side Story*," all dancing and movement. We all learned something from one another. We learned how to re-learn and to teach. It was an extraordinary exchange.

LAURENTS: I remember Jerry asking the most important question asked any time about anything in the theater: "What is it about?" One of the reasons why he is the most brilliant of all choreographers is that he knows a dance has to be *about* something, not just an abstract dance. When it's *about* something, no one knows better how to make it dance and move the story.

MCNALLY: Was this a fast show to write?

LAURENTS: It took us thirteen working months—we counted them up.

SONDHEIM: There was a six-month hiatus in there somewhere after I came aboard, when *Candide* came to life again after being dormant for a while, but it was nice to get away from *West Side Story* for a while and then come back to it fairly coldly.

MCNALLY: Were there big changes after you got to rehearsals?

SONDHEIM: It certainly changed less from the first preview in Washington to the opening in New York than any other show I've ever done, with the exception of *Sweeney Todd*, which also had almost no changes. We fiddled with the opening number in Washington, and Lenny and Jerry fiddled with a second-act ballet.

BERNSTEIN: We also fiddled with a couple of extra numbers that never got in.

SONDHEIM: Yes, but we'd been working on those in New York. On the way to the airport in Washington after a very nice run, I said rather ingenuously to Jerry, "Gee, this is my first show, and I wanted to the experience of sitting up until three o'clock in the morning in a smoke-filled room rewriting the second act." He looked at me in such anger and said, in effect, "Take that back, don't ever say that out loud. Until you've been through it, you don't know what it's like." I thought it would have been glamorous. I learned that Jerry was right, at two or three o'clock in hotel rooms in subsequent years. But the show was changed very little. It was what it was when it opened.

ROBBINS: We had eight weeks of rehearsals, the first time that was ever done. There was a large amount of dancing, a hell of a book to put on and a lot of song numbers to stage. I got permission from Equity to rehearse four weeks prior to the rest of the rehearsal period.

It also was a wonderfully exceptional cast. I was able to pull them into the reality of that show. As part of our collaboration, we had to sort out whether a specific actor was going to sing, or dance, or just act, and how to put him together with the rest of the show. We were very fortunate in getting the cast that we did, from a great dancer like Chita Rivera to someone like Larry Kert who had a wonderful voice and could do acrobatic things when we needed it.

BERNSTEIN: It was the hardest show to cast I've ever heard of. Everybody has either to be or seem to be a teenager, to sing a very difficult score, to act a very difficult role and dance very difficult dances. Everybody had to seem to be doing all of these things, so that Larry Kert and Carol Lawrence had to seem to be dancing as much as anybody else. Part of Jerry's magic was to make it seem that way. We were also very lucky to find people like Mickey Calin, who played Riff. He sang "Cool"—not like an operatic star, but the way it should be sung, I felt—and he was a fabulous dancer.

SONDHEIM: The casting went on for a period of six months. Cheryl Crawford held the property for quite a long time but dropped it two months before we were to go into rehearsals. The remaining two months we held auditions in Hal's and Bobby's office.

LAURENTS: Cheryl Crawford didn't like the book, she was on my back from the very beginning about the vocabulary of invented slang. She told me, "No place do they say 'That's how the cookie crumbles.'" She wanted it in very badly. I think maybe if I'd put it in she might have produced the show.

SONDHEIM: She said the essential reason she was withdrawing from the show was, she wanted us to explain why these kids were the way they were. We are making a poetic interpretation of a social situation, but she wanted it to be more realistic.

BERNSTEIN: Do you want to hear a real *Rashomon* comment? I remember her saying, "We have *had* this whole school of ash can realism." I can't have made that up.

LAURENTS: I have a letter from her saying she wanted to see how the neighborhood changes from immigrant Jews to Puerto Ricans and blacks.

ROBBINS: My version of Cheryl's withdrawal is very simple: she couldn't raise the money.

MCNALLY: *West Side Story* seemed to get a mixed reception in a lot of places including, later on, the critics.

BERNSTEIN: Well, the idea of a musical the first act of which ends with two corpses on the stage was reprehensible. Even the score itself . . . I remember Steve and I, poor bastards that we were, trying by ourselves at a piano to audition this score for Columbia Records, my record company. They said no, there's nothing in it anybody could sing, too depressing, too many tritones, too many words in the lyrics, too rangy—"Ma-ri-a"—nobody could sing notes like that, impossible. They turned it down. Later they changed their minds, but that was an afternoon Steve and I will never forget, I don't think there's any *Rashomon* about it. There was a tremendous animosity to the whole idea.

ROBBINS: Some of the people who helped make that show were the scene, costume and lighting designers who supported us and enhanced what we were doing. Oliver Smith's rumble set for the first-act finale was one of the most beautiful sets, creating the atmosphere for what we were doing before we even started. When Oliver first brought in his designs I became the old-fashioned person asking him, "Where's your close-in in one so we can work in one while you're changing the sets behind?" He said, "Well, we're not going to do that." I thought, "Wait a minute, what's happening, this is going to be a whole new game here." Part of the set was going up and downstage, and I wondered how we were going to get in and out, and how to set the lights. He solved all these problems for us and enhanced us with them. The same goes for Irene Sharaff's costumes and Jean Rosenthal's lighting.

SONDHEIM: About the set, when we got down to Washington there had been a mistake made—somebody hadn't gotten the right dimensions of the stage. When the bedroom set was rolled off in the second act to make room for the dream ballet which required a totally cleared, empty stage, about a third of it didn't roll off. The space at the National Theater was too small. I was afraid that we couldn't open, but Jerry said that we had fifteen hundred people coming Monday night, so we would just take a saw and saw it in half. He was affected more than anybody because, after all, this was the moment, the ballet, toward which he was building the entire scene and music—and here it just didn't work at all. He was totally cool. They got a saw and sawed the set in half, and on opening night half the bedroom went off one way and half the other.

ROBBINS: As I remember it, the set was supposed to go off, except Oliver designed it not to go off but to leave these arches showing on either side. I was furious inside, and I went to Oliver and said, "That set *has* to go off," I didn't get a saw out, but he solved the problem.

BERNSTEIN: I like the saw version better.

MCNALLY: Was *Romeo and Juliet* always a source you kept going back to for parallels?

BERNSTEIN: It was Jerry's source, and Jerry was our source.

ROBBINS: Remarkably, Arthur managed to follow that story as outlined in the Shakespeare play without the audience or critics realizing it. That was a real achievement. These scenes follow each other in a certain way in the long arc of the Shakespearean pattern, but everyone gets so caught up in our story that they don't refer back for similarities.

SONDHEIM: The hardest part—correct me if it was not—was how to find a contemporary, believable substitute for the philter, the potion part of Shakespeare's plot; how somebody takes poison and seems to be dead and then comes alive again. That's what led us eventually to the mad aria Arthur was talking about earlier.

LAURENTS: The thing I'm proudest of in telling the story is why she can't get the message through: because of prejudice. I think it's better than the original story.

BERNSTEIN: It was the point of the Shakespeare plot, if we can call it the Shakespeare plot, where we spent most of the time and had most of the sludge. Arthur was the most faithful, while others of us sometimes wondered, "Why do we have to stick to it at this point?"

While we're toasting absent friends and colleagues, mention should be made of Roger Stevens, because he saved us at the most critical moment, the moment just after Cheryl Crawford told the four of us we'd have to rewrite the whole thing. We all stood up and said goodbye, and left very gravely, all trusting in one another's fortitude. We walked to the corner of whatever street it was, and as we stood on the corner we all went to jelly: "What are we going to do now?" Arthur went into a phone booth and called Roger Stevens in London, collect, at a number he'd left with us in case we ran into trouble—and God knows, we were in trouble. Arthur came out of that phone booth and told us, "Roger says, whatever happens, keep working. He will guarantee everything somehow. Just don't worry about it." This was the life saver. I can never praise that man enough for that one moment when he gave us the strength to have the courage of our own somewhat shaken convictions.

SONDHEIM: Addenda to that: the Algonquin Hotel played a part. We went in there to have a drink. They wouldn't serve us because Arthur didn't have a tie on. Our entire lives had gone down the drain, and they wouldn't let us have a drink. We went next door to the Iroquois where we did indeed have a drink. My memory is that Arthur called from a phone booth there—to Germany.

LAURENTS: No, London.

SONDHEIM: Also, I got on the phone that night to Hal Prince and Bobby Griffith in Boston, where they were trying out *New*

Girl in Town. I told Hal our problem, and he said, "Why don't you send the material to Bobby and me?" I told him that a few years ago he'd said it wasn't for him. But he knew we'd worked on it, and he was anxious to get onto another show. We sent them what script we had, and within twenty-four hours they called to say they would do it.

It was well for Roger to be the centerpiece, but he had a number of things and couldn't have spent the next two months solely on us. And we had to get the show into rehearsal by a certain date, because Lenny was about to take over the Philharmonic. I think he left October 3, and we opened September 27—we just made it. Those of you who've been through this mill know how hard it is within two months to get the producer to accept the show, raise the money, finish the casting and go ahead and book theaters, particularly a show as unusual and peculiar as this one.

ROBBINS: Does anyone remember what the show cost?

SONDHEIM: $375,000?

LAURENTS: $350,000.

ROBBINS: That was a lot then, mostly caused by the long rehearsal period.

LAURENTS: I remember Bobby and Hal said that Irene's costumes would be too expensive. Jerry said, "How much can you budget?" and they said, "$65,000," and he said, "Irene will do it for that," and she did!

SONDHEIM: When Hal and Bobby came in on it, we all felt we had to make quick decisions and do whatever was required of us. We got very excited. With Cheryl, for all the enthusiasm, there was this feeling that we might not get into rehearsal on time. Suddenly there was this deadline right around the corner, only eight weeks away.

ROBBINS: We started rehearsals in a place called the Chester Hale Studio, which is now gone. It was on Fifty-sixth Street near Carnegie Hall in a loft above a garage. I'd need more space today, but in four weeks we managed to start on the book and stage some of the numbers. I had the assistance of Peter Gennaro as co-choreographer. He did most of "America" and the Sharks' dances in the dance hall competition, and he was very supportive all the way through.

I remember always being in a state of saying to myself, "Oh, it's moving, it's moving, something's happening, we're going on, not getting stuck." I don't remember getting stuck anywhere. We played around a lot with the marriage scene. It took us a lot of work to try to get that right.

LAURENTS: We made one change in rehearsal that was important. We switched the positions of "One Hand, One Heart" and "Tonight."

ROBBINS: What was wonderful about rehearsals was, we had the chance to try something, to move a number into a spot that turned out to be very exciting, even though in theory it wouldn't be.

SONDHEIM: In one instance we argued that a change didn't make logical sense. Jerry said, "but it makes theatrical sense," and he was absolutely right.

MCNALLY: Lenny, were you composing the dance music with Jerry, or were you composing it in advance?

BERNSTEIN: We worked closely together. I remember all my collaborations with Jerry in terms of one tactile bodily feeling: his hands on my shoulders—composing with his hands on my shoulders. This may be metaphorical, but it's the way I remember it. I can feel him standing behind me saying, "Four more beats there," or "No, that's too many," or "Yeah—that's it!"

ROBBINS: Or Lenny would play something and I'd take off right there in the room, telling him, "I can see this kind of movement, or that kind of movement."

I wrote a scenario for the second-act ballet, so that Lenny had that as a premise to start with. He would compose on that, and then we'd get together and he'd play it, and I'd say, "That sounds wonderful, let's have more of this or more of that."

BERNSTEIN: There was only one moment when I was really scared to play something. It was the "Cool" fugue. He liked it so much he freaked out. I was so happy.

MCNALLY: Steve, you're very fond of turning against some of the lyrics nowadays. Why didn't you then?

SONDHEIM: I was outvoted. I changed the lyric of "I Feel Pretty" after seeing the run-through in New York because I was ashamed of it. Later the others said they liked it better the way it was before, so I went home. I'm not fond of a lot of the *West Side Story* lyrics. To me, they seem very "written." I like "Something's Coming" and "Jet Song" because they have a kind of energy to them. The more contemplative lyrics I find very self-conscious and a mite pretentious every now and then. I hear a writer at work instead of a character.

MCNALLY: How about "Gee, Officer Krupke?"

SONDHEIM: There are some good jokes there. Parenthetically, Jerry staged it in three hours by the clock, three days before we went to Washington. Jerry had been staging everything else, and we kept reminding him that this was a comedy number, and he kept saying, "I'll get to it, I'll get to it." One afternoon he did it in almost no time at all. Maybe the ideas had been cooking, but the staging of "Krupke" is one of the most brilliantly inventive in one number I've ever seen.

ROBBINS: By the end of the rehearsal period you're really into the work, you know the actors, you know the scenes. It isn't like the first days of rehearsals when you're fishing around and going tentatively toward what you want. You're on course. It's like those numbers you write in rehearsal or out of town. By that time, the wheels are rolling, you are into the character, the mood, the energy. Also, I find I do a lot of my best work when I'm tired and have less tension inside of me.

SONDHEIM: One of my objections to "Gee, Officer Krupke" was always that I felt it was out of place in the second act. It should occur in the first act, and "Cool" should occur where "Krupke" is. Here is a group of kids running from a double murder, and for them to stop and do this comic number seemed to me to be out of place. I kept nudging Arthur and Jerry to reverse the two. We didn't, and of course "Krupke" works wonderfully in the second act, on the old Shakespearean drunken-porter principle. In the middle of a melodrama, you cut in with comedy. On the other hand, when Shakespeare does it, it's an irrelevant character. For the movie, the numbers were reversed and weren't nearly as effective, in my opinion. Again, there was theatrical truth in putting "Krupke" there, if not literal truth.

LAURENTS: I was the only one for it, and I sold it with the rather grandiose business about the porter scene in Shakespeare.

McNALLY: How were the reviews in Washington?

BERNSTEIN: Splendid.

LAURENTS: What I remember about Washington is the first preview. I was sitting in front of Jerry, and at some point we began to get a feeling, and Jerry began pounding me on the back, saying, "They like it, they like it!"

SONDHEIM: The only time "Something's Coming" ever stopped the show was that night. One of the things we did out of town was try to find another ending for "Something's Coming" because it never got that kind of a hand again, though it always worked. We kept writing high loud endings and low trail-off endings, and we finally just gave up. But Arthur's right, there was something about that night.

BERNSTEIN: It was an incredible night. It was August in Washington—horribly hot—and none of us knew whether anyone would listen to the show, or look at it, or stay in the theater. We'd had a lot of insults, a lot of warnings: "You're crazy," "Give it up," and so forth. At intermission I remember Justice Felix Frankfurter, the most distinguished man in Washington, in a wheelchair, in tears. And this was only intermission. It was an incredible hello, because we didn't know whether the show was even all right, let alone something special and deeply moving.

ROBBINS: Steve spoke about not being happy with some of the lyrics. I think probably we all look at that work now from this vantage point and think, "Oh, maybe I could have done this, or could have done that." The big point is, the show in its time was quite a radical change. When it's performed now, it doesn't look radical. The techniques, the subject matter, the values seem to be a matter of course in other shows. Sometimes when I see it now it looks a little old-fashioned to me.

MCNALLY: The boldness of the show was very much appreciated by the critics. In re-reading the reviews, the one thing that amazed me was the absence of mention of Steve's work. Walter Kerr and Brooks Atkinson talked about the score, the direction, the book, but they did not mention the name "Stephen Sondheim." I don't know who they thought wrote the lyrics.

LAURENTS: There's nothing amazing about that. Reviewers review reputation, not work.

BERNSTEIN: The most recent *West Side Story* I've seen was a couple of months ago in London. The reaction was terrific, and all the reviews mention Steve in the first paragraph, if that's any consolation. To me, Arthur is the one who doesn't get mentioned enough.

MCNALLY: You seem to have resisted making changes in *West Side Story*, though you've had plenty of opportunity to fiddle with it in the revivals and recordings.

BERNSTEIN: There are two big fiddles in the new recording. One is, I'm conducting the score for the first time ever, and the performers are all opera singers. I've always toyed with this idea. It can't be done on the stage, obviously. There is that built-in collision between dance and singing performance in the work. We were very, very lucky with this show, because in every production we've always found people against all odds, who formed casts and could do all the different things they had to do. But there is an ideal way of hearing "One Hand, One Heart," for example. I've always kept it in the back of my mind, feeling that maybe some day I could hear that song sung the way I've always wanted it to be sung, which is quite slow with real operatic voice control and quality. In some ways it's come true on this record, in which I also have a hand-picked orchestra and a fabulous cast.

That's fiddling, all right, but there are no changes of any sort in the orchestration, in which Sid Ramin and Irwin Kostal assisted me. Actually, they did more than assist, they executed the orchestration. After the others went home at two-thirty in the morning, we had pre-orchestration sessions in which I would indicate exactly what I wanted, note by note, in a shorthand that is intelligible only to orchestrators. They would come back with the score a couple of days later and have a final post-orchestration session at the same time as a pre-session on the next number coming up. So they really executed it in a way without which I couldn't have gotten the score finished.

MCNALLY: Was opening night in New York like opening night in Washington?

SONDHEIM: No, for the first half hour the audience was pretty dead, they'd heard this was a work of art—capital W, capital A— so they sat there like children in church until "America." At that point they realized it was a musical, and they were supposed to be having a good time. From then on it went very well.

BERNSTEIN: What I remember best from opening night was the set change from the quintet, which drew prolonged applause, into the remarkable rumble set that Jerry mentioned. The quintet applause was just beginning to dip as the set changed before your eyes. The whole wave rose again until it doubled the preceding applause. For me, this was one of the most magical moments in the theater. That's where I had the sense that we had a hit.

ROBBINS: We were talking about revivals over the years, as a director I discovered something fascinating. At the time we did the show, the cast understood the material very, very well, deeply and organically. It was part of the times. In the recent revival—and I don't mean to cast any slurs upon it—I found that the cast had rather middle-class attitudes. It was hard for them to understand the street, the turf, the toughness, the necessity to own something, the struggle on the street. I felt I could never get out of them a real understanding of the material from either an acting or a dancing point of view. The original cast knew what it was about and could react to it.

LAURENTS: The day of our first run-through for an audience, they came out on stage in colors they had chosen for Jets and Sharks and their girls. They did it on their own, by themselves, and it was very, very touching.

BERNSTEIN: My impression in London was that they were very understanding of the material, maybe they came to it later.

LAURENTS: They're having a social revolution in England now.

SONDHEIM: It helped that Jerry kept the Jets and the Sharks apart as groups separate during rehearsals, even having their meals as separate gangs. I thought it was pretentious, but of course it was perfect, because, without any animosity or hostility, there was a sense of each gang having its own individuality, so that you had two giant personalities onstage. And I believe this is the first show whose chorus had individual characterizations. Maybe one or two people would be characterized, like Agnes de Mille's The Girl Who Falls Down in *Oklahoma*, but in *West Side Story* each of the members of the chorus had a name and a personality and was cast accordingly. Everybody takes that for granted now, but in those days it was a startling notion.

ROBBINS: It was not only cast that way, the collaboration continued, because once we found the people we wanted, Arthur began to write a little for them and even shift lines around. The characters were formed during the rehearsal period, with Arthur being there to see what could happen and what could not happen.

I'd like to add one thing about the scene changes. In Washington, as we were leaving the theater, I happened to turn back as they were flying in the gym set, which had streamers at the corners. By turning my head at the fortunate moment, I saw those streamers come down. I ran to Oliver and asked him, "Can we make a whole curtain of that?", which we did. Without that accident happening, and Oliver being ready to collaborate on it, I don't think that transition going into the gym would have been half as good. You always have to keep your eyes open for the mistakes, because they can be great.

Q: Wasn't there some controversy over the number "America?"

SONDHEIM: I got a letter complaining about the one line "Island of tropical disease," outraged on behalf of Puerto Rico, claiming that we were making fun of Puerto Rico and being sarcastic about it. But I didn't change it.

BERNSTEIN: Opening night in Washington we had a telephone message from *La Prensa* saying that they'd heard about this song and we would be picketed when we came to New York unless we omitted or changed the song. They made particular reference to "Island of tropical diseases," telling us everybody knows Puerto Rico is free of disease. And it wasn't just that line they objected to. We were insulting not only Puerto Rico but the Puerto Ricans and all immigrants. They didn't hear "Nobody knows in America/ Puerto Rico's in America"—it's a little hard to hear at that tempo. We met that threat by doing nothing about it, not changing a syllable, and we were not picketed.

Q: Mr. Laurents, did you plan from the beginning to invent your own slang?

LAURENTS: Yes.

Q: Did you use bebop?

LAURENTS: No . . . now you can see why the book was so short.

Q: Does a difference between logical truth and theatrical truth often occur in shows?

SONDHEIM: It's happened to me a number of times, but never quite as startlingly as in *West Side Story*. That's where I learned that theatrical truth, theatrical time, has nothing to do with real truth, real time. Sometimes it's supplied by the director and sometimes by the writers, saying, "This is theatrical truth, even though . . ." Generally you try to make it true on both levels, because it's richer that way.

Q: It's generally conceded that *West Side Story* was a turning point in the American musical, with a lot of new ideas of form and subject. Does the panel have any additional thoughts about how the show changed the conventions of the musical theater? What did it make possible that had not been possible before?

SONDHEIM: Essentially, it's a blend of all the elements—music, book, lyrics, dance. More than subject matter, its innovation has to do with theatrical style. We were influenced by the movies— there was a fluidity in the staging which had a cinematic quality. Other shows have done that since. This show demonstrated one way a musical could be done. No show had ever been staged—I'm talking about the larger sense, not just Jerry's work—or conceived this way as a fluid piece which called on the poetic imagination of the audience. This is something that's taken for granted now. Prior to *West Side Story*, shows had been staged fairly stodgily, in the sense that you would do a scene in three, and then the curtain would come down, then there'd be a scene in one, and then a scene in three, and so forth. It's not exactly the first time that convention had been broken down—it was broken down a little in *South Pacific* and *Allegro*. But *West Side Story* has been the major influence.

BERNSTEIN: I agree with what Steve said, its influence went far beyond the subject matter. It has a kind of . . . if you want to be polite, you say bravery, if you want to be impolite, you say chutzpah . . . a kind of bravery in which we all fortified one another, to the point where we could try our utmost; not trying to break rules, not trying to go further—because you get nowhere trying to go further—but having the bravery to follow your instincts and follow one another's instincts in order to produce something new, something that has never been envisioned before. It's not so much what it's about, it's how bravely it's done.

ROBBINS: I don't like to theorize about how or if the show changed future musicals. For me what was important about *West Side Story* was in our *aspiration*. I wanted to find out at that time how far we, as "long-haired artists," could go in bringing our crafts and talents to a musical. Why did we have to do it separately and elsewhere? Why did Lenny have to write an opera, Arthur a play, me a ballet? Why couldn't we, in aspiration, try to bring our deepest talents together to the commercial theater in this work? That was the true *gesture* of the show.

LAURENTS: That's the whole point, we all had real respect for each other and, without doing it overtly, challenged each other to do our best. That's all we thought about—doing our best.

(1985)

Frank Rich

(b. 1949)

and Joseph Papp

(1921–1991)

The Shakespeare Marathon

In 1954, Joseph Papp founded in New York City the Shakespeare Workshop—now called the Public Theater—an organization that has done more than any other to promote the performance of Shakespeare in America. Papp believed that theater was a powerful social force and his goals from the outset were ambitious: Shakespeare productions that were devoted to nurturing American actors and directors and that reflected onstage the racial and cultural diversity of its audiences. A turning point came in 1959 when he battled and defeated the powerful parks commissioner of New York, Robert Moses, enabling Papp to stage Shakespeare in Central Park for free—a tradition that continues to this day. Over the past fifty years, many of America's most distinguished actors have graced that stage, including Meryl Streep, Kevin Kline, Raul Julia, Al Pacino, Christine Baranski, James Earl Jones, Anne Hathaway, George C. Scott, Colleen Dewhurst, Stacy Keach, Sam Waterston, Morgan Freeman, and F. Murray Abraham. Frank Rich served as the chief drama critic for the *New York Times* from 1980 to 1993. Like Papp, Rich loved the stage, and his memoir, *Ghost Light* (2000), describes the roots of his lifelong passion for theater. In 1987 Papp announced a new venture at the Public Theater: a Shakespeare Marathon that would give audiences a chance to see all of Shakespeare's plays over the next six years. Two years into that experiment Frank Rich crossed swords with Papp, writing a long piece in the *Times* that questioned the wisdom of this sprint through the canon. Papp took umbrage at this attack and the *Times* gave him ample space for a rebuttal. Papp died in 1991, two years before the successful completion of the Marathon.

Peaks and Valleys in Papp's Marathon

WHEN it comes to amassing culture, Americans like to collect the complete set. This is the impulse that leads us to sign up for the Book-of-the-Month Club when it offers every last volume of Will and Ariel Durant, or to dial an 800 number when Vincent Price beckons us from the depths of cable television to purchase recordings of all the world's great music on the installment plan. So it was no surprise that the public rushed to enlist in Joseph Papp's Shakespeare Marathon, as announced in an ad in these pages in November 1987. "For the first time in America, see *all* of Shakespeare!" read the headline. "All of William Shakespeare's 36 plays performed by most of America's finest actors!" Charter subscribers were promised a free "I've seen it all" T-shirt, as well as a glass of celebratory champagne with Mr. Papp, when the marathon reaches completion at the Public Theater on Sept. 15, 1993.

Always a shrewd impresario, Mr. Papp had once again succeeded at a task few of his peers in the theater would even attempt: selling Shakespeare to a broad public. Why does he bother? The reasons, by now well enshrined in New York City folklore, are not venal. An impoverished child of immigrant Brooklyn, Joseph Papirofsky discovered Shakespeare, and a liberating view of life and culture, in a Williamsburg public library. Out of that childhood came the mission that has propelled the New York Shakespeare Festival for over 30 years: Joseph Papp believes in Shakespeare, especially free Shakespeare, for a mass urban audience, particularly a student audience that might be spiritually transported from the same grinding poverty he experienced in his youth. The same principle that led Mr. Papp to battle Robert Moses over the right to present free Shakespeare in the park a generation ago is the one that informs most Festival activities today, the marathon included.

But if Mr. Papp produces Shakespeare in part as a civic cause—he expects New York's diverse ethnic mix to be reflected on stage no less than in the seats—he obviously loves Shakespeare's plays simply as theater. He has directed "Hamlet" more times (four) than many of his fellow producers have seen it. Before the marathon began, the Festival had produced every play in the canon save one ("Henry VIII") and most of them many times. Were it not for Mr. Papp, front-rank Shakespeare productions in New York might dwindle to the occasional star revival, like last season's unfortunate Glenda Jackson-Christopher Plummer "Macbeth," or the even more occasional Royal Shakespeare Company import. (So rare are imported R.S.C. Shakespeare productions these days—the last was the Terry Hands "Much Ado About Nothing" in 1984—that New Yorkers have lost touch with the whole generation of English actors and directors that has followed the Trevor Nunn era.)

Still, legitimate criticism of Mr. Papp persists. One can admire the producer's motives and calling without necessarily endorsing the results—which have been erratic. Might the worst Papp stagings be more counterproductive than no Shakespeare at all? It can be argued that the sexless and passionless "Romeo and Juliet" performed at the Public last spring—to take one example from the marathon—could serve as a form of aversion therapy for teen-agers who saw it; instead of being inspired to see more Shakespeare, a young audience subjected to a deadly "Romeo" might turn away from Shakespeare for good. Why, promotional expediency aside, is there a need for a marathon? Would it be more worthwhile to do some of Shakespeare's plays with deliberate care rather than to mount three dozen at a sprint simply so the culturally acquisitive can say "I've seen it all"?

Some of these questions are academic: the ill-starred "Romeo and Juliet" has come and gone; the marathon is here to stay, with the seventh production, "Love's Labour's Lost," scheduled to open Feb. 14. But one year and six plays into the 36-production cycle, it is neither too early nor too late to examine what the marathon has been so far and to imagine what it might yet become.

To date, the marathon has been so inconsistent that it seems to be swinging idly in and out of Mr. Papp's field of concentration. There have been good productions, in-between productions and barely nominal productions. There has been no unifying principle,

other than the rubric "Joseph Papp presents," to galvanize the entire enterprise, to make the marathon seem like an exciting journey for audience and company alike rather than merely a stunt—a
dash to the 1993 finish line.

When the marathon was first announced, Mr. Papp did state a
unifying plan. "Shakespeare was an actor," he told The New York
Times. "Everything was done by actors. I want to get away from
all the other ideas of the way Shakespeare is done, in which other
people have the main say." In other words, Mr. Papp seemed to be
rejecting the conceptualist directors—people he has employed
in the past, like Lee Breuer and Liviu Ciulei—who impose their
own idiosyncratic vision on Shakespeare, sometimes to the extent
of neglecting the performances (as was the case with the disap-
pointing pre-marathon Ciulei "Hamlet" starring Kevin Kline).
Mr. Papp further promised an "exclusively American company,"
which is consistent with his often expressed disdain for the more
etiolated traditions of British Shakespeare acting.

Fair enough. Yet in the marathon itself Mr. Papp has not
consistently applied his guiding principle—or demonstrated its
viability in those productions where it has been invoked. That
marathon's most embarrassing failure was a "Julius Caesar"
turned over to three heroic American actors of the kind Mr. Papp
admires: Al Pacino, Martin Sheen, Edward Herrmann. The director was Stuart Vaughan, who first directed the same play for Mr.
Papp 30 years ago. The production was straightforward, the stars
in theory well cast, but the slovenliness of the acting (Mr. Sheen
never departed from a monotone) and the low energy level of the
staging, even in fool-proof mob scenes, assassinated the play well
before its hero reached the Ides of March. While Mr. Vaughan's
subsequent "King John" in Central Park was better acted, its superior performances (by Kevin Conway and Moses Gunn) still
had to wage a losing battle against the mechanical, unimaginative
choreography of the rest of the production.

The other actor-oriented marathon productions have been
the "Romeo and Juliet"—directed by Les Waters, an Englishman
with a knack for contemporary political plays by Caryl Churchill

("Fen") and Keith Reddin ("Rum and Coke") and no experience in Shakespeare—and the summer's "Much Ado About Nothing," directed by the long-time Festival hand Gerald Freedman. In Kevin Kline and Blythe Danner, Mr. Freedman had a sublime Benedick and Beatrice; what's more, their teamwork suggested the presence of the strong directorial guidance that was missing in the all-star "Julius Caesar." Even so, the production suffered from an inconsistent supporting cast, an aimless transposition of era (does anyone remember that the clock was advanced to 1800, or why?) and a blurry tone when not focused on its leading players' "merry war." It didn't hurt the huge popularity of this "Much Ado" one bit that many of its performances were rained out by intermission, thereby sparing some happy audiences the washed-out Claudio and Hero machinations of the dimmer second half.

Given Mr. Papp's let's-return-Shakespeare-to-the-players-approach, it is startling that two of the most stimulating (and talked-about) marathon attractions, the first and the last of the six, were both highly stylized directors' visions that relied as much, if not more, on a production metaphor than on the actors or the play. A. J. Antoon's "Midsummer Night's Dream" was echt Papp Shakespeare—the voguish Papp satirized in "Forbidden Broadway"—brought to a high boil. Mr. Antoon, whose Teddy Roosevelt-era "Much Ado" (of 1972) remains one of the Festival's classics, switched the setting of "Dream" to turn-of-the-century Bahia, all the better to prompt a bossa nova musical beat, a racially diverse cast and a modern political conflict between the royalty of a colonial court and the indigenous spirits of a third-world rain forest. The performances may have been wildly variable, but the execution of the concept was so stylish and vibrant that the show sizzled even when Shakespeare played second banana to F. Murray Abraham's seeming impersonation (in the role of Bottom) of Mr. Papp himself.

"Coriolanus" was a stranger success. Not only was it directed by an English actor and playwright, Steven Berkoff—like Mr. Waters, admitted through a loophole, given Mr. Papp's professed desire for an "exclusively American company"—but it was also marked by a wholesale disregard for the text. Mr. Berkoff took large cuts, wrote lines of his own, and set the cast, led by a swaggering Christopher Walken, to boogeying about in the martial "West Side Story" style in which he directs his own plays in London. The result was a scabrous diatribe about the futility of politics—not Shakespeare's show exactly, but one that spoke to American audiences disillusioned by the election campaign. And despite the tyranny of the director's staging conceits, the acting was generally above the Shakespeare Festival average.

While "Coriolanus" may have aroused more interest in the marathon than any event since the first ad, it would be ridiculous to attempt to replicate it. Mr. Berkoff is sui generis; no one could imitate his style successfully, and that style is too rigid to be applied to many other, if any, Shakespeare plays. But Mr. Berkoff's "Coriolanus" proved a broader point—and the point is not that directors should have dictatorial stay, or that texts should be mutilated, or that Brechtian style is a must in Shakespearean production. Rather, "Coriolanus" demonstrated the importance of mating a play with a director who has a real passion for it, rather than merely doling out the marathon assignments haphazardly, as seems to happen half the time, to whichever Shakespeare Festival regular might be available. That Mr. Berkoff would have such a passion for "Coriolanus" was no surprise to anyone (including, one assumes, Mr. Papp) who had seen the director's own plays in England; his scripts often deal, in a contemporary working-class setting, with the relationship between the individual and the mob. "Coriolanus" was made for him.

Are there not other directors new to the Festival, in this country and abroad, who might be matched up with specific Shakespeare plays? Michael Maggio, of Chicago's Goodman Theater, did a Papp-style production this season—"Romeo and Juliet" set in Chicago's Italian-American enclave of the 1920's—that made better use of the frequent Festival actress Phoebe Cates than the marathon's own "Much Ado" did. One can imagine many other American directors fitting in well with the Shakespeare Festival,

and some unavailable in the marathon's first year are already
signed up (James Lapine, Mike Nichols), or about to be. But,
given Mr. Papp's powers of persuasion and his willingness to hire
English directors (if not actors), the list of possible directing re-
cruits could be wider ranging. Why not go after Ingmar Bergman,
whose recent "Hamlet" (seen in New York at the Brooklyn Academy of Music) gave equal due to a strong director's concept and its
cast, or Yukio Ninagawa, whose astonishing Kabuki "Medea" was
imported by Mr. Papp to Central Park two years ago, or Deborah
Warner, the young (age 29) Royal Shakespeare Company director who has shaken up the English theatrical establishment with
her new, intimate-scale approaches to "Titus Andronicus" and
"King John"?

While one can respect Mr. Papp's desire to give actors rather
than directors the primary voice in his productions, that dream
is difficult, if not impossible, to realize without forming a permanent acting company. Actors hired on a pick-up basis from play to
play bring their passion to bear on individual roles, not whole productions or seasons. However much talent Kevin Kline may lavish
on Benedick or Hamlet or Richard III, he can't single-handedly
bring the constantly changing companies surrounding him up to
his level. That's where a director comes in, from the first day of
casting to opening night.

The director may or may not tie a play to a strong conception,
like Mr. Antoon's "Dream" or Mr. Berkoff's "Coriolanus," but he
must have some compelling reason for doing a given work, and be
capable of firing up a cast with that compulsion. The failed marathon productions have been those without an animating impulse,
an inner drive—those that seem to have been put on for no other
reason than to fill the marathon's relentless march of scheduling
slots or to capitalize on the availability of this or that name actor.
These second-tier productions announce themselves to audiences
immediately; the viewer's heart sinks as soon as he sees bland sets
of the old Stratford, Connecticut, school and finds perfunctory
performances in small roles. The consistency of the mediocrity is
inevitable: a director who is merely putting the play up because

it is there communicates his dispassion to the entire production team, from the lightman to the lowliest bit player.

Were Mr. Papp never to produce another Shakespeare play, his legacy to Shakespeare production in the United States would still be incalculable. He has long since fought and won the war to prove that American actors of all types need not be second to the English in performing the canon; he has kept Shakespeare a constant in a New York theater that has changed radically in every other way during the three decades since free Shakespeare began. But the marathon, which so far has too frequently seemed like a mechanical winding down to the finish line of the Festival's mission, offers Mr. Papp the opportunity for a new beginning. It's his chance to build an audience for the next generation, to cap his career with a magical flourish worthy of Prospero. He will have succeeded if the "I've seen it all" crowd that gathers at the Public Theater on Sept. 15, 1993 has not relegated Shakespeare's complete plays to the dusty shelf of dutiful cultural collectibles but is instead as eager as Mr. Papp has always been to return to them again and again.

The Shakespeare Marathon: The Coach's View

The Shakespeare Marathon has been characterized in this newspaper ["Peaks and Valley in Papp's Marathon," by Frank Rich, Feb. 5] as an enterprise lacking a unifying vision and having no unifying principle other than "Joseph Papp presents." Needless to say, I consider such charges baseless and I resent them.

To build his case the critic begins by trotting out a heart-rending tale of my early years: "an impoverished child of immigrant Brooklyn, Joseph Papirofsky discovered Shakespeare, and a liberating view of life and culture, in a Williamsburg public library." "Grinding poverty," he suggests, is what did it. The facts, however, are much different. Poor, yes; impoverished, hardly. "Life and culture" was not discovered in a library, but at home, in the streets, at school and shul (synagogue), all places rich in culture.

There was music, both classical and jazz. I sang boy soprano in a Jewish choir, danced the Lindy Hop, read tales of adventure as well as poetry; played marbles after shul and won enough to pay for a five-cent Charlie Chaplin movie, harmonized at home with my father and brother and two sisters. And taste—the ability to distinguish a good ballplayer, dancer, actor, songwriter, marble player, hot dog or knish from a mediocre one—was ever present. Anything and everything was always being judged, compared, and commented on, and there was no need for sophisticated jargon. We all knew that Frank Sinatra was a better singer than Bing Crosby.

So it was not poverty that "informs most Festival activities today, the Marathon included." Clearly, the opposite is true. The inspiration for the creation of a theatrical home for American actors where they are given the opportunity to perform in the works of Shakespeare represents an esthetic stance informed, if you will, by the gorgeous concoction that is the rich cultural life of New York City's neighborhoods.

With the poverty-to-Shakespeare theory out of the way, we can move to our critic's fundamental objections to the Marathon. He begins with the all-encompassing query, known in my circles as the "Why don't you drop dead?" question: "Might the worst Papp stagings be more counterproductive than no Shakespeare at all?" Well, I find that question difficult to answer. How is anyone to foretell what will end up as "the worst stagings"? Our critic admits that the Marathon has produced, at the least, two unreservedly fine stagings. Yet the beginnings of one of them, "Coriolanus," did not augur well at all. In fact, that production so lacked one of the musts laid down by our critic for a successful undertaking, "mating a play with a director who has a real passion for it," that he would no doubt have vetoed this ill-born venture from the start.

For though our critic writes "that Mr. Berkoff would have such a passion for "Coriolanus" was no surprise to anyone," in fact Steven Berkoff had absolutely no outward passion for the play.

It was I, having seen his work in London and the United States over the years, who felt that Steven Berkoff was the man for the job. But he remained uncertain and later revealed to me that he had made numerous inquiries amongst his friends as to his being the proper director. After his colleagues and I overwhelmingly assured him that "Coriolanus" was right for him, he grudgingly accepted the assignment, though not until we had fought over the terms, at one stage nearly reaching the deal-breaking point.

Complicating the passion theory even more is the fact that Mr. Berkoff was performing in London and was unable to come to the United States to cast the play. At which point, with the assistance of Rosemarie Tichler, our casting director, I passionately set out to second-guess Maestro Berkoff by casting the show with Christopher Walken, Irene Worth, Keith David, and Paul Hecht in the leading roles.

Even the first week of rehearsals was so lacking in anything resembling passion that the concept of a set had yet to be found. There were, I admit, some passionate disagreements along the way, which caused the temporary departure of one of the leading actors, the costumer and the lighting designer. To an outsider, it would have appeared that "Coriolanus" was heading for a fiasco of unprecedented dimensions. And one must assume that our critic, had he the authority, would have called it quits at this impossible juncture. But the producer, trained through years of experience to discern any signs of life in what appears to be an irreversible catastrophe, was able both to detect and to keep faith with the spark of Berkoff's genius that finally caught fire in a production of unusual style and interest.

With poverty and passion out of the way, we now come to our critic's charge that I pass out directorial assignments haphazardly, "to whichever Shakespeare Festival regular might be available." A. J. Antoon, highly touted by our critic for his inventive production of "A Midsummer Night's Dream," is a Shakespeare Festival regular who "was available." Should the fact that he had directed plays for the Festival in the past have been a reason to exclude him from working again? Surely not. And I chose the play he was to direct, not haphazardly, but purposefully. And as it turned out, it was exactly the right Shakespeare for him.

The Shakespeare production most disliked by our critic, presiding over the Marathon like Marc Antony pricking the names of those slated for execution, was "Julius Caesar." Lest anyone be tempted to accept one man's definition of failure, I must remind the reader that "Julius Caesar" received some of the best reviews of the Marathon, not to mention numerous letters of praise. In one review, Al Pacino's Marc Antony was called superior to Brando's. And the most important test of success or failure, as we in the theater understand the term, is attendance. "Julius Caesar" sold out every performance of its run.

The weight of our critic's displeasure with this production fell on the backs of some of the leading actors, "the kind Mr. Papp admires." I certainly do admire Al Pacino, Martin Sheen, and Ed Herrmann. Who doesn't? Are they to be discarded, written off, because our critic took exception to their performance in a play of Shakespeare's?

If our critic was sincere that "a permanent acting company" is the answer to "actors hired on a pick-up basis from play to play," his unconstructive demeaning of the efforts put forth by three of America's finest actors is hardly the way to go. These actors, eager to grow in their work, put their reputations on the line, and took a sizable risk in appearing in a New York production, knowing what perfect targets they make for any journalistic marksman ready to shoot them down. If our critic was sincere, he would appreciate the courage these men showed and not vent his displeasure in a manner that can't help but discourage not only these actors but the many others who aspire to similar risks.

"Are there not other directors new to the Festival, in this country and abroad," our critic asks, "who might be matched up with specific Shakespeare plays?" What a question! He answers some of that himself. No complaints, it seems, about James Lapine, who is directing "The Winter's Tale," or Mike Nichols, hardly a festival regular, who will be directing "Othello." He fails to mention JoAnne Akalaitis, who is directing "Cymbeline." And since his article appeared, we have obtained commitments from Jerry Zaks, who will be directing "As You Like It", Harold Guskin, who will be directing "Twelfth Night" and Des McAnuff, who wants to direct "Macbeth." And that, believe me, is just the beginning.

Perhaps our critic's most insidious complaint comes when he asks, "Would it be more worthwhile to do some of Shakespeare's plays with deliberate care rather than mount three dozen at a sprint simply so the culturally acquisitive can say 'I've seen it all'?" Our critic knows full well that we do not and cannot mount 36 plays at a sprint. It's not possible. What is possible is working way ahead, getting commitments from the actors and directors we want, one, two, three years before the fact so that they can work out their film commitments. There is no sprinting. Only careful, prudent planning. As to the sentence's final twist, identifying the broad-based Shakespeare Marathon audience as some undesirable, rich, cultural elite, that is too far off the mark even to merit a reply.

But what of our critic's postulation that less is better, that using "deliberate care" will insure better productions, if not hits? Deliberate care is a constant process at the New York Shakespeare Festival. The notion that by engaging in a Marathon we are so harried and *fartootzt* we are unable to pay proper attention to the oncoming or ongoing production is untrue. We have many instances (over a 35-year period) of plays approached with the greatest and most deliberate care which failed to receive unanimous approval. On the other hand, we have literally thrown shows together which happen to have the right writer, director, and actors, all of whom combine to create a harmony and a chemistry that all the preparation in the world could not achieve. I'm not in favor of these situations, but the truth is, you cannot plan or predict them. Nobody knows what will finally make a show work until it does.

All that remains is dealing with the matter of the Marathon having no unifying vision, to answer what I presume is a provocative and rhetorical question but which I will address as though it were in earnest. "Why," our critic asks, "promotional expediency aside, is there a need for a Marathon?" Here once more is the "Why don't you drop dead?" question. After having thrown accolades at me for my deep and abiding interest in Shakespeare— "were Mr. Papp never to produce another Shakespeare play" (something our critic would no doubt find desirable) "his legacy to Shakespeare production in the United States would still be incalculable"—how could our critic then accuse me of embarking on such a monumental theatrical journey, spending inordinate sums of hard-to-raise money to produce six works of Shakespeare each year, staking my professional reputation on the results of such an effort, all for the sake of "promotional expediency"?

If our critic chooses to label in that manner my confidence in a strong audience reaction, my profound belief that the Marathon could capture the imagination of audiences new to Shakespeare and my hope that it could attract some of America's finest actors, directors and designers, I can come up with only one word to describe his thinking: cynicism. What is being promoted? And for what purposes? Is the Marathon proving to be helpful in raising money? It is not. Does the Marathon have even the remote possibility of paying for itself? Because of our small theaters at the Public, it does not. Even if part of the reason for launching the Marathon was to bring stronger attention to an institution that, lacking the basic underwriting of such companies as the Royal Shakespeare, struggles day in and day out to stay alive, how could such a huge effort by so many people over the course of six years be fundamentally inspired by "promotional expediency?"

Is there a "need" for a Marathon? Come on. We are living in a country where philistinism and violence ride high, where education, in the best sense of that word, is at a new low. Our critic speaks of my "mission," calls me a believer in "Shakespeare for a mass urban audience, particularly a student audience that might be spiritually transported from the same grinding poverty he experienced in his youth." But even the middle class needs a lift these days. The Marathon is an act of cultural affirmation. It proclaims Shakespeare alive. It opens up all kinds of possibilities for programs to reach our young people as well as the loyal elderly. It is doing that now. It is causing lots of people to read and reread the plays of Shakespeare. There is a destination, a road to follow, and thousands of people are on it. Is there a need for a Marathon? What a question!

(1989)

Sam Wanamaker

(1919–1993)

Address to the Royal Society of Arts

The seemingly quixotic and ultimately successful project to rebuild Shakespeare's Globe in Southwark, now one of the most iconic and important theaters in the world for performing Shakespeare, was the dream of an American: the actor and director Sam Wanamaker. A young Wanamaker had performed one of his first Shakespearean roles in an early replica of the Globe Theatre, built for the Great Lakes Exposition in Cleveland, Ohio, in 1936–37. When Wanamaker traveled to London in 1949 one of the first things he did was "search out the site of the Globe," which he "had the devil of a time finding." He was disappointed to find that "the only recognition of the site of the most important theatre of our Western civilization was a black plaque erected some time in the early part of the century." He thought it "extraordinary that the British had not tried to do something more meaningful," and twenty years later, after a successful career in film and theater in both America and Britain, he set about doing it himself, establishing the Shakespeare Globe Trust in 1970 and working tirelessly until the end of his life to secure the fundraising and research necessary to rebuild a replica of the Globe near its original site. Wanamaker delivered the following remarks about his project in 1989 upon being presented by the Royal Society of Arts with the Benjamin Franklin Medal honoring those "who have made profound efforts to forward Anglo-American understanding." He died of cancer in 1993, four years before the Globe Theatre was officially opened by the Queen.

❧

BENJAMIN FRANKLIN and I had certain things in common—both Americans, both associated with communication, both lived for long periods in London, both were given encouragement and support by the Earls of Bessborough, and both have been honoured by the Royal Society of Arts, Manufactures and Commerce.

To quote from his biography:

> Without my having made any application for that honor, they chose me to be a member and voted that I should be excused the customary payments which would have amounted to 26 guineas, and ever since have given me their transactions gratis. They also presented me with a Gold medal for the year 1753, the delivery of which was accompanied by a very handsome speech of the President, wherein I was highly honored.

We celebrated the 200th anniversary of Franklin's death last week and that of Shakespeare's 426th birth today. Appropriately, England's patron saint is also remembered this day—two figures both wrapped in mystery and myth representing the highest spiritual ideals and cultural achievements of the English people.

John Milton, another great English poet, wrote:

> What needs my Shakespeare for his honoured bones
> The labour of an age in piled stones?
> Or that his hallowed relics should be hid
> Under a star-y pointing pyramid?
> Dear son of memory, great heir of fame.
> Thou in our wonder and astonishment
> Hast built thyself a livelong monument.

This question goes to the heart of the matter. Is there a real need for another Shakespeare monument? Milton is probably right. In any case, the whole town of Stratford-upon-Avon is a kind of monument—his statue has a place of honour in Westminster Abbey; his plays are sometimes brilliantly performed in Britain and throughout the world.

Is there a need to mark the site where the Globe stood? There's been a plaque on a brewery wall there for nearly 80 years. Now with the exciting discovery of the actual foundations and their designation as a national monument, these must be—as with the earlier discovery of the Rose—fully excavated, conserved and put on display for future generations.

So where's the need?

As Milton points out, the need is not Shakespeare's. The need is *ours*—not for sentimental and romantic gestures; today, some say the world can ill-afford unproductive and unprofitable constructions, like the Albert Memorial or other such grand and wonderful follies—the cost in human toil of building 'star-y pointing' pyramids is no longer acceptable.

Nevertheless, mankind needs its touchstones—we need to stand where great men stood and where great events took place which changed our world and affected our lives—to give us a sense of what man can accomplish and, sadly, what he can destroy.

> All the world's a stage and all the men and women
> merely players.

It was on that Globe stage of the world that Elizabethan man began to see a further horizon, to understand himself and his neighbours better. Shakespeare held a mirror up to nature while at the same time creating an art form with a parade of his plays on that hallowed stage that has never been surpassed.

Shakespeare's adult and productive life was spent in London, apparently most of it in Southwark, on Bankside, close to his own Globe theatre. It was here that he wrote *Hamlet*, *Lear*, *Macbeth*, *Othello*, it was at the Globe that they were first staged, where he himself was a leading actor; it was on Bankside in Southwark Cathedral that he worshipped, buried his brother Edmond, and it was from there that he retired to Stratford.

Reconstructing a faithful replica which can now be based exactly on the recently excavated foundations nearby, is indeed a necessity for those countless students, teachers, scholars and practitioners of theatre arts who seek to recover the original form, shape and staging of his play, so as to illuminate them further and transmit them better for the enjoyment and pleasure of everyone who will read, teach, see and be moved, inspired and thrilled by this treasure trove of poetry, drama, tragedy and comedy of living, breathing, recognizable human beings with all our common strengths, passion and frailties.

Rebuilding the Globe is also necessary for the future prosperity and wellbeing of the people of London and especially of the people who live and work in Southwark.

For centuries Southwark was a 'ward-without'—with the only access to the City through the South gate of London Bridge topped by the warning array of gruesome heads of beheaded criminals. For hundreds of years it was the receptacle for thieves and vagabonds in the prisons of the Clink, the Counter and the Marshalsea where sometimes even playwrights and famous novelist's fathers were incarcerated, where the unwanted noxious industries of tanning, brewing and glue manufacture were relegated, where victims of the plague were dumped and where the poor, the unskilled and hard-working rivermen made their homes.

But also in Southwark, banished from the City, were the places of popular entertainment, the theatres, the brothels, bear- and bull-baiting, cockfighting and gambling, and all Elizabethan London flocked to Bankside.

Southwark's greatest heritage, to this day, is that the Globe, the Rose, the Swan and the Hope playhouses collectively produced the extraordinary Golden Age of English drama and poetry which has to this day never been surpassed. Apart from Shakespeare, Ben Johnson and Christopher Marlowe, many of the brilliant literary figures of English letters have been associated with Southwark, including Gower, Chaucer, Bunyan, Massinger, Fletcher, Oliver Goldsmith, Samuel Johnson and Dickens.

That heritage, crowned and burnished by the Globe restoration as the jewel in the reclamation of Shakespeare's London on Bankside, will reaffirm Southwark's identity and the pride of its people in their glorious history and bring, in its wake, a new prosperity, new jobs, an attractive new environment with places, once again, of entertainment and pleasure for the people who live, work, and visit there. It is surely destined to become a place of pilgrimage for people from the four corners of the world.

The reconstruction of the Globe must be perceived as the restoration of an historic building of national importance, as was the rebuilding of St Paul's Cathedral after the Great Fire of London.

Finally, for London and all of Britain, the creation of a new international centre of learning, together with the enhancement of an important piece of Britain's cultural heritage, is at least as necessary to its future wellbeing as are the millions of square feet of new offices being built in the race to retain London's status as the financial and cultural leader of Europe in the 21st century.

Without such new additions to its cultural life and environment, London is in danger of becoming a sterile, soulless, materialistic and uninviting metropolis. Can any Government of Britain be content to see a brilliant modern Globe completed in 1988 in the heart of Tokyo and not help to realise a faithful reconstruction of the *original* within yards of the actual site in the heart of London? Britain, the European Community, the Commonwealth, my own country, the largest English speaking nation of the world, and UNESCO must all recognise, reclaim and finally support The International Shakespeare Globe Centre and Shakespeare's London as a world heritage site.

Encouraging words and sympathetic gestures of support from the Ministers of Education, Environment, Tourism, and the Arts have been much appreciated. However, it is hoped that these expressions can be converted into bricks and timber, lathe and plaster, and the fire-proof thatch with which the original roof was clad. For other nations to follow, it must be demonstrated that Britain, Shakespeare's birthplace, and the apogee of its glorious English language and poetry at the Globe, must take the lead and help make possible the completion of this important international educational, cultural and visitor facility on its soil.

To this end, I have the pleasure to announce that since the beginning of the year, contributions and pledges in various denominations have been received from Japan, Australia, New Zealand, Canada and the United States. It gives me particular pleasure to announce also that the American, Mr Gordon P Getty, Chairman of the International Council, has offered to contribute 1 million to the project on condition that a further 9 million is assured from Britain and the rest of the world, which is the sum needed to complete the building of the Globe Theatre itself.

I gratefully accept this award on behalf of all those thousands from throughout the world who have made possible, against every obstacle, the start of construction of The International Shakespeare Globe Centre: Mr Samuel Scripps the first founder donor among several of whom are with us today; Sir David Orr, the indefatigable Chairman of the Shakespeare Globe Trust; American Board members Mr Herbert Mendel, Mr Marshall Wais, Mr Malcolm Kingston, Mr David Hulme; the Earl of Bessborough, Trustee; Mr Stephen Perry and Ann Ward, U.K. Board Members; Mrs Henny Gestetner, Mr Andrew Wadsworth, and, foremost among them, HRH Prince Philip, the Duke of Edinburgh, our valued Patron.

(1989)

Jane Smiley

(b. 1949)

Shakespeare in Iceland

Jane Smiley's sixth novel, *A Thousand Acres* (1991), which won a Pulitzer Prize and was made into a film, modernizes *King Lear*, relocating Shakespeare's plot and characters in the American Midwest. Five years after its publication, Smiley was invited to speak about the creative process that led to *A Thousand Acres* before a group of scholars at the World Congress of the International Shakespeare Association. Smiley traces a process that began with her resistant and disappointed reading of Shakespeare's *Lear* in high school, and her deepening understanding of that resistance as a female reader—"recasting the whole argument"—when studying the play at Vassar. Her talk is no less perceptive about the political, social, and environmental factors that subtly shaped her reworking of *Lear*, along with what was going on in her own life and world, the seeming accidents that led to her writing the novel. Hence her title, "Shakespeare in Iceland," for her immersion in Icelandic sagas for over a decade did much to shape her grasp of what was at stake for her, and in a way for Shakespeare as well, in the story.

❧

I would like to dedicate this talk to the memory of Harriet Hawkins, a former teacher of mine, who died last autumn, and who was, as many of you know, an erudite and avid Shakespeare enthusiast, and without whose influence I might never have written *A Thousand Acres*.

O VER the last few weeks, I've been privileged to enjoy one of the fruits of the literary life that Shakespeare himself seems not to have enjoyed, that is, reading academic papers that take seriously and thoughtfully my novel *A Thousand Acres*. Some writers might conceivably consider this a torment, but as a sometime academic myself, who wrote many English papers, I appreciate not only the thoughts that I have read, but also the habit of mind that ponders a work, finds connections within it and between it and other works, and in other ways is stimulated and moved by that work. This is especially gratifying in the case of *A Thousand Acres* because that novel grew out of a very similar mental process. In one sense, *A Thousand Acres* is my academic paper on *King Lear*, while in another sense, it is my production of the play.

What I would like to do today is use this interesting opportunity that I have had to close the loop between artistic production and cultural response to investigate the nature of composition, using *A Thousand Acres* as a case study, drawing on my memories and thoughts. Let me call this an "as if" biography. I am going to try to consider the composition process as if from the outside, asking whether how *A Thousand Acres* seemed to come together for me actually accounts for what seems to be in it, according to the various papers upon it that I have read. It is my hope that this case study might shed some light on modes of composition in general, an area that, as far as I know, isn't much investigated. Conversations of critics and scholars with artists don't seem to me to get to the heart of this matter, and for lack of time or lack of interest or lack of perspective, most writers don't write much about how writing comes about.

First, let me suggest an image of the mind working at its novelistic task. I see an organic machine mostly immersed in darkness, but partly revealed. The machine is organic because it is not metal, has not been constructed, but is machinelike, because it is orderly in its operations and predictable, when you know the principles by which it operates. It is these principles that are largely mysterious, because much of the machine, though present, is unseen and unknown even to the writer. The visible part is intellect, reason, and intention. But the larger part, lost in darkness, is made up of the body, the emotions, the remembered and the unremembered but still present, the DNA, the immediate environment, the passing currents of attention, dreams, half-thought thoughts, the impressions made by others. The organic machine of composition works twenty-four hours a day. It sucks in more than it puts out.

The writer is aware of its working, involves herself more or less closely with it depending on the time of day and other pleasures or obligations, but also relies upon it to go on working without her. I would like you to keep this image in mind as I touch on other elements of composition.

Of course, the novelist has many intentions for her novel, and one of these is a straightforward one—an intention to enter into a relationship with a reader during which both contemplate a subject and some characters together. In my experience, this sense of the reader's presence sometimes gets lost when the writer's mind is taken over by the characters during the act of composing, but every novelist understands that writing is essentially a social exchange and every writer to a greater or lesser degree brings a strategy for communicating to her side of the exchange. I stress this, because I feel that certain critical schools portray the writer as more or less unconscious, as if reading were a form of eavesdropping on the author's inner life. This sort of criticism demeans the writer's quest for technical mastery and the writer's talent for making artistic choices. I think when we say that so and so is a genius, we imply that the writing was done through them rather than by them, while for the writer the very exercise of technique, the choice to employ one image rather than another, or to cast a scene from the point of view of one character rather than another, is the central delight of composition.

And so, I had an intention in *A Thousand Acres* which grew out of something less rational, a response to the play. I wanted to communicate the ways in which I found the conventional reading of *King Lear* frustrating and wrong. Beginning with my first readings of the play in high school and continuing through college and graduate school, I had been cool to both Cordelia and Lear. While I understood and accepted how I should feel about them, he struck me as the sort of person, from beginning to end, that you would want to stay away from—selfish, demanding, humorless, self-pitying. Even when cast low by events, he seemed to hog the stage—his self-effacement a pose, his strategies for calling attention to himself myriad and completely successful. In all the productions I saw, no actor, not even my favorite, Olivier, could make him sympathetic to me. My acceptance of his tragedy was pro forma, the response of a good girl and a good student. I didn't like Cordelia, either. She seemed ungenerous and cold, a stickler for truth at the beginning, a stickler for form at the end. No amount of beauty in an actress warmed her up for me. On the other hand, the older sisters, figures of pure evil according to conventional wisdom, sounded familiar, especially in the scene where they talk between themselves about Lear's actions, and later, when they have to deal with his unruly knights. They were women, and the play seemed to be condemning them morally for the exact ways in which they expressed womanhood that I recognized. I was offended. Let me emphasize that these were visceral responses—semi-conscious "No's" that being a good student and a good girl didn't change. These responses made me find the play less enjoyable than my favorite Shakespeare plays—*Hamlet*, *Measure for Measure*, *Much Ado*. I felt an automatic resistance when people labelled *King Lear* Shakespeare's greatest tragedy, but I read my resistance as an idiosyncratic reaction, something not to mention in educated company—not exactly a failure in myself but more like a tiny tear in the social fabric that could be overlooked.

Responses, of course, are connected to some of the hidden parts of the machine, but let me speculate a bit more about mine to King Lear.

Perhaps I was unsympathetic to fathers in general because I didn't live with a father and had never been trained to accept the fatherly qualities that Lear represents—command, power, self-centeredness. Although my grandfather was quite patriarchal, and I spent a lot of time with him as a child, he was much more charming than Lear, and in all events, he was a grandfather. His power had been diminished already before I knew him and he had accepted that with grace. Also, as a resident of the American midwest, I found the extreme expression of emotion off-putting, which is not to say that in my family and among my friends extreme emotions were never expressed—they were, but afterwards we were ashamed of ourselves for saying rash things, hurting each other and threatening our relationships. When Lear, at the end, is ashamed of himself, I saw his shame not as transcendent, but only as what it should be. I didn't think he should get any extra credit for it, especially since he becomes no more considerate of Cordelia than he had been—he still overrules her desire to go "see these daughters and these sisters," still wants her all for himself, and she no longer has the strength to resist.

And so these responses to the play formed a beginning, but their realization as a novel was hardly assured. I was a lot more interested in other things.

Perhaps every writer is modeled by seminal texts. I certainly was. For me, the three books that formed my future writing were two novels, *Giants in the Earth*, by O. E. Rölvaag, which I read in eighth grade, and *David Copperfield*, which I read in ninth grade, and a science book, *The Web of Life*, which introduced me to the field of ecology, also in eighth grade. Each of these books, in its way, seemed entirely true to me at the time I read it. They were almost the first books I read that weren't series books for children. Though I remember very little of the style of the Rölvaag novel, I remember that the hardships endured by Per Hansa and his family, and the tragic outcome of their immigration to Minnesota, seemed absolutely right as a picture of the way the world worked—like the "westward ho" stories I was always seeing on TV but more honest in counting the costs of western settlement and predicting that the probable outcome would be terrifying rather than happy. I do remember the style of *David Copperfield*. Who doesn't? I was enchanted by it, but the real lesson of Dickens was the complexity and liveliness of the novel as a form. In David's novel, David is still the center of a swirl of other characters, uncountable for me at fourteen. And *The Web of Life* reinforced that sense I had of the variousness and interconnectedness of land, animals, plants, people, town and countryside, prairie and civilization. From these readings I came to Shakespeare, who fit right in. Each year, we read a Shakespeare play, starting with *Twelfth Night* in seventh grade, going through *A Midsummer Night's Dream*, *Julius Caesar*, *As You Like It*, *Hamlet*, and *King Lear*. What I liked at first was the treasury of names in the list of dramatis personae, and what I kept liking was the action and liveliness on the stage—everything was interconnected, plenty was happening. It was almost Dickensian. But, though fond, I remained unpossessed by Shakespeare. Things in Shakespeare plays were not quite dark enough to be right for me and there was too much talk. Drama was not going to be my natural form, either. I grew up in a family of storytellers, gossipers, natural narrators. We did not mimic voices or take parts or perform. We specialized in irony of tone. When I discovered the Icelandic sagas, I discovered us.

Here is another part of the authorial machine, the assimilation of the writer to a form. Perhaps the writer does choose, but it seems different from that to me, more like a taking in of the writer by the form, complete with a gentle sucking noise. Perhaps what I blamed Lear for was actually a feature of dramatic form that I was uncomfortable with—all the talk, especially talk about emotions which seemed simultaneously to trivialize and make self-indulgent and shrill the passions being expressed. Narrative gives more direct access to the inner life, allows the writer to reveal the disjuncture between what is felt and what appears, and to suggest emotions so powerful that their complete expression must fail, resulting in silence. Each form makes a psychological assertion. Neither assertion is precisely true or complete, which is why each form is a compromise and why both forms exist. At any rate, narrative and I assimilated each other, and I made a career plan.

I have often thought how neatly Virginia Woolf foretold my generation of writers in *A Room of One's Own*, for we of the SAT generation, from, say, the early 1960s on, were the first generation of girls for whom education was so normal that we took our career choices for granted. I went to Vassar, my boyfriend went to Yale; we thought that the fight for women's education was a historical matter, already won. When we discussed our futures we automatically discussed our work. Mine was to be writing novels and his was to be building the revolution. Everyone took my education seriously—my parents, my professors, my boyfriend, myself. I was surrounded by other girls whose educations were also taken seriously, taught by women who were scholars and writers, given access to books and libraries. If the plan was for us to get married and raise children, it was not communicated directly to us. The boys I knew were no more or less ambitious than I was, than the girls I knew. I stress this demographic detail because, of course, no woman can think about Shakespeare after Virginia Woolf without being aware of Woolf's figure of Judith Shakespeare. Every novel is, in part, a demographic demonstration of what is possible during a writer's lifetime, and as I get older, I realize with more modesty than I felt as an eighteen-year-old, that my path, that is, my automatic assumptions about my choices and intentions, was cleared by others. What I was doing seemed normal, not radical. What my boyfriend was doing seemed radical.

My career plan was straightforward—to read as many books as possible and to get as much praise for my own writing as possible. My only system was taste, and my tastes, as I mentioned above, were largely formed. In college I took courses almost entirely in English literature, from Old English to the beginning of the twentieth century. Courses at Vassar were almost all year-long courses, and so investigation of a subject was intensive. At Vassar I met Harriett Hawkins, to whom this talk is dedicated. She taught me freshman English for a year and then taught me Renaissance and Restoration drama. She was a wonderful teacher—compelling, enthusiastic, friendly, and supportive. I liked her and I felt that she liked me, so I showed her a few of my poems, which she reacted to with enthusiasm. It was in Harriett's class that I read *King Lear* with real seriousness for the first time, and where I became aware of how my reaction to the play did not conform to the standard interpretation of it. Harriett's was, simultaneously, a voice of authority, dispensing the conventional wisdom about the play, and also a woman's voice, slightly recasting the whole argument. I clearly remember what she had to say about Goneril and Regan, and I remember noticing what she said because she was a woman talking about women in a way that I do not remember what she had to say about *Everyman*, for example. I also continued to like big complex novels—*Pamela, Emma, Tom Jones*, the Russians. I got some praise for my writing. My education, in other words, moved smoothly forward.

The only things my boyfriend and I talked about were class warfare, racism, endangered species, whether Marxist analysis was appropriate to the history of the Merovingian period, in what ways literature and music were inherently political, and whether the workers actually wanted an alliance with the students. Another demographic detail—he was a member of the notorious Yale class of 1970, the first class that was predominately middle class and public school educated, whose admission was primarily based on merit examinations. I now think that the visceral reaction of my boyfriend and his friends in finding themselves in the bastion of privilege that was Yale University in 1966 was from the beginning to the end rage at finding what was behind those closed doors, that their forebears had been shut out of. My reaction, once I gained access to the facilities through him, was more goofy, more Virginia Woolfian—I saw what they had that I, even at Vassar, did not have, for example, William Blake's real works at the Beinecke library, compared to what we had, postcards. I was more amazed that they had them than I was angry that we did not. But I noted the difference. Politics had not been in my educational or career plan, but one thing I have noticed is the profound effect a young man with ideas can have upon a young woman with desire. He would say that I argued with him about every mote and dust particle. I would say that he changed and shaped my sense of the world from top to bottom. Of course, all of our discussions were juvenile, partial, half-baked. But they came at a significant moment for me, at a moment where sexual awakening and intellectual awakening coincided, and however right or wrong the conclusions we drew, what we learned did not later get unlearned. I now had a political consciousness. Soon feminism would flow into it, both as a response to feminist writing and as a recognition of the realities of my first experience of intimacy with a man.

I do not want to give into the temptation of chronology here, I want only to reflect for a moment on how certain things I did in my teens and twenties began to form the mold that *A Thousand Acres* was finally struck form in my forties.

Let's return to the organic machine, and shine a different light on it, seeing it now not as a solid object, but as a large, three-dimensional web, with filaments running everywhere, so numerous and variously connected that we can only follow a few of them out.

My boyfriend and I, now married, went to the University of Iowa, he in medieval history, I in nothing. I hadn't been accepted to the Writer's Workshop, and so found myself as graduate student wife making teddy bears in a factory. At the first party of medievalists in October of that year, I met a man named John C. McGalliard, who was teaching Old Norse. I had loved Old English in college, so I asked if I could join his class. He agreed, and I began rearranging my teddy bear schedule to accommodate Hrafnkels Saga. Here is where, in my life, Shakespeare set sail for Iceland.

While I was not possessed by Shakespeare as I was by the great English novelists, every writer of English has a relationship to him, both direct and indirect. English cannot be written without Shakespeare, or for that matter, read without Shakespeare. My officemate in grad school seriously considered Shakespeare to be an incarnation of the deity, and so every discussion of Shakespeare that we had, and there were many, proposed his universality. I took this as a question I had to answer but could not, as well as a characterization of what it meant to be a writer that I had to grapple with. If Shakespeare was not God, then he certainly was a writer, and therefore a model of what a writer should be—adept at comedy and tragedy and irony and characterization and poetry and prose, a person of wide-ranging interests and skillful at the illusion of expertise, lively and sober by turns, familiar with the full range of emotions, able to believably extrapolate from the quotidian life of a citizen to the epic life of a king or a queen. Why not, I felt, try for that? Why try for less? Shakespeare did not seem confessional, more investigative, a writer who used his instrument to explore the world and not himself. That's how I thought of him, anyway. So while I did not feel particularly close to the plays, as my officemate did, I did feel inspired by Shakespeare the writer as a model. Why in the world I felt I could dare to take this particular model I will never know; it is one of those filaments of the web that runs away into the darkness.

I read all of Njalssaga, word by painstaking word, line by translated line. Some of you lucky ones in the audience may be familiar with the Icelandic sagas. Of them, Njalssaga is the longest and grandest, detailing the ramifications of a marriage and an ever-widening feud while at the same time depicting the panorama of life in Iceland. The words of Njalssaga were so engraved on my brain by my translating process, that ten years later when I reread the saga in translation, I remember it almost line for line. I was not a good student of Old Norse, in that I never memorized grammar rules or vocabulary, and often relied on a more general sense of the burden of the prose than I should have. But the result of my lack of facility was that the sagas that I worked on dripped very slowly into my brain, and the images that they made there were ones that I pondered over and over.

In graduate school I also took a course in Shakespeare's problem plays from Miriam Gilbert, at the University of Iowa. I wrote a production paper in which I attempted to solve the problems of *Measure for Measure*, my favorite, most dark, cynical, and ironic play. I set my production in the medieval period, and a certain way of looking at Shakespeare, as a generation or two removed from the middle ages, opened up for me. I realized that I had always assumed that Shakespeare knew he was the great precursor, as if when he held out his arms, he could see all of English history and literature to come flowing from his fingertips. But now I imagined him looking backward, as I looked backward to him. When I returned to *King Lear* later on, this sense of Shakespeare attending to the mysterious past was important in my inspiration.

So far, I have talked a great deal about school, coursework, books. As I reveal these mundanities, I feel a little uneasy, even here, or perhaps especially here, in front of you. It sounds as though I read some books and kind of understood them, then wrote some books, straining mightily over any number of gnats.

I was no scholar of Shakespeare, even of Dickens, even of the Icelandic sagas. I was just a reader, and a slow one at that. When I
was studying Middle English for my Ph.D exams, I napped over
my work morning, noon, and night. It took me a week to read
Sir Gawain and the Green Knight. Some of what I learned about
the Middle Ages wasn't from sources at all, but from *The Seventh
Seal* and *Virgin Spring*. I was and am hardly the reader that Virginia Woolf was—perhaps, unlike Shakespeare, she was the model
who intimidated me. Even so, I read enough to form my notion
of what a writer does, a literary theory, and here it is. A writer is
first a reader, who enters the realm of literature and soon forms a
reciprocal relationship with it, work by work, and not only with
works she has read, but also with works she has not read, but
heard about or even just seen on the shelf. She carries with her
emotional, intellectual, spiritual, physical baggage, but she isn't
even, at first, seeking a form. At first she is seeking the most basic
ideas. In fact, until she finds a form, her mind is a blank, she has
no ideas at all. Later, there are some aborted, unimagined, failed
ideas. The specific forms each work takes, not just the novel, but
the novel *Pride and Prejudice*, for example, give her the very ideas
that she thinks are her own, but as soon as she has those ideas,
she has other slightly different ideas that are the fruit of her non-
Pride-and-Prejudice life. The relationship builds on itself, so that
more experience of forms creates more ideas, which whets the
appetite for more precisely suitable forms, that is a specific novel
that is not any novel that the novelist has ever read before. What
is available even to not very good scholars such as myself is the
passion of this reciprocal relationship. I cannot count the times
I have put down a book because I was too inspired by it to keep
reading. I could feel some sort of joy or power flowing from the
book to me, filling me with the yearning to write, which felt like a
desire to form something like clay or music. Most of these times, I
had nothing to write about, and so I took a few deep breaths and
picked up the book again. The writer in the realm of literature is
first and foremost a reader, or perhaps maybe a listener also, for
whom the giving back of the energy received from the text is an

almost physical need. Writing is a social act, a social response, an effort to make a connection, an act of love that is sometimes frankly libidinous, but other times friendly, sisterly, affectionate, or merely interested. The realm of literature excites these social feelings as much as the writer's associates do. But in addition to the possibility of connection, the writer is excited by technical mastery.

I have often noticed that I am less moved by my works than my readers are—that is, I pass through a phase where I am moved by the plight of the characters and into a longer or more interesting period where, whatever is happening to them and however bad it is, I am excited and pleased at the writing process. Once Mark Strand, the author of *Darker*, among other volumes of poetry, and I had a whale of a time laughing at how funny we found our work, though we were both known in general for gloom and doom. I later thought that it wasn't the work itself that we found funny, but the way the technical process delighted us. Writing a novel or a poem is playing a game, and it puts the writer in a similar mood to that of chess or baseball—serious and playful at the same time, a separate mental region. And so, in the realm of literature, the reciprocal relationship between the writer and the works is both emotional and technical, and at times one side is more exciting and at times the other side is more exciting. I always felt that I sensed this joy in technical mastery in Shakespeare's writing, a kind of click click of words and images and scenes and themes falling neatly, clearly, meaningfully into place. After I sensed it in his writing, I sought the same feeling in my own.

Although I didn't become famous until *A Thousand Acres*, the most important period of my life as a writer so far was the fourteen months, from May 1984 to July 1985, when I was writing my novel *The Greenlanders* and then my novella *The Age of Grief*. By then, I had been obsessively focused on writing and publishing novels for about seven years or so, since taking my degree from the Iowa Writer's Workshop and going on a Fulbright to Iceland. In Iceland I exchanged the sociable, coupled, communal life I had lived in Iowa City for a solitary one, my many companions and amusements for reading, reading, and only reading. I read, among others, *Anna Karenina*, *War and Peace*, *Madame Bovary*, *The Brothers Karamazov*, *The Grapes of Wrath*, Christina Stead's *The Man Who Loved Children*, every Icelandic saga translated into English, and two or three books by Halldór Laxness, including *Independent People*. I wrote some short stories and conceived my first two novels as well as *The Greenlanders*. By the spring of 1984 I had two children, had been married for six years, owned a house, had tenure in an academic job, and was otherwise firmly fixed in my writing and childcare routine. In June of 1984, I went to England, Denmark, and Greenland on a research trip. Before I left, I had sixty-eight awkward pages of my manuscript written. I got back on the first of July. By Labor Day I was up to 130, by Christmas, I was up to 385. I was thirty-five years old and dissatisfied with my marriage. Somehow connected to that but not was the fact that writing *The Greenlanders* was taking hold of me, seemingly from the outside. My characters were in part historically attested by the Icelandic chronicles, and they seemed to be coming through me onto the page from outside myself. Though I kept to my writing schedule of only a few hours each day, I was frantic with inspiration—filled with energy and interest in things, so gripped by narrative flow that I could go in and out of my novel at will. I thought of Shakespeare constantly. I was very aware of how old I was in comparison to him in 1600, when he was writing the great tragedies. I was convinced that what I was going through would be the only way a writer could do so much work in a short period. It was a *kind* of literary madness in the sense that the normal haphazard and contingent conditions of life had suddenly organized themselves, probably through the obscure agency of the id, into an entirely meaningful and fully realized symbolic universe. I was the concentrating point for the creation of *The Greenlanders*, and that was all that mattered, really. By 1 June I had about 720 pages, and when I finished, on Midsummer's Eve, I had over 1100. At the end, I was writing all day, twenty pages a day. In retrospect, a day's work seems to have lasted the usual two hours. After I finished *The Greenlanders*, I woke up the next morning, full of momentum, and for the next month wrote *The Age of Grief*, employing all the figurative, introspective language I had been storing up while writing in the plain style of *The Greenlanders*. Both works are for all practical purposes rough drafts, as I imagined Shakespeare's works from the first years of the seventeenth century were. I'll admit here that while I was writing *The Greenlanders*, I was convinced that it was my masterwork, and that the process I was going through was a necessary process for such a work. I also have to say that I didn't like it, that what it had done to my life, my routine, and my sense of myself appalled me, and I thought, though I loved *The Greenlanders* itself and still do, that I never wanted to go through that again, even for another masterwork. I learned my lesson, and the lesson was that literature wasn't everything, didn't deserve to be everything.

In studying Old Icelandic and in writing and researching *The Greenlanders*, I engaged for ten years or so with a distinctly premodern mind, as expressed in the stories and the style of the Icelandic sagas and the poetic Edda, and yet, because the sagas were written prose narratives about the social consequences of unrestrainable conflict in the polity, they were also strangely modern, strangely American. I always thought of Njalssaga as the great proto-American novel, halfway here in place and time. After I turned in *The Greenlanders*, I was still reeling from the experience of writing it—I thought about the characters and incidents daily for about three-and-a-half years, until they were driven out by the composition of *A Thousand Acres* during the fall of 1988. For the purposes of this paper, that means that almost every literary thought I had for something like fifteen years, from 1973 to 1988, was linked to or influenced by medieval Icelandic literature. Lear's heath, in my mind, was not in populous, voluble, green England, but in treeless, distant Iceland. The conflict between Lear and his daughters, primal and so quickly going out of control, so isolated and depopulated in feeling, seemed Germanic and even Nordic to me, by contrast to, let's say, the distinctly Italian feel of *Romeo and Juliet*. I had found medieval literature to be very close to its folkloric sources, so it was automatic for me to imagine Shakespeare cocking his ear backward when he was writing *King Lear*, probing the Germanic side of his English heritage rather than the Latin side.

Nevertheless, it took a few accidents to precipitate *A Thousand Acres*. One of these was a visit to McDonald's in Delhi, New York, in the summer of 1987. For some reason, that McDonald's was decorated with pictures of the Midwest, and the one in the booth we sat down in had a man standing in a barn in what seemed to be wheat country. While I was looking at the picture, I described, idly and briefly to my husband, the idea of rewriting *King Lear*. He said, "You could set it on a farm in Kansas," and I said, "I don't know anything about Kansas." Pooh. Dismissing him! Right around that time, I had a visit from the actress Glenn Close, who had enjoyed *The Age of Grief* and written me a note. Sometime late in the evening, after the children were in bed and we had already eaten and I was casting about for something to say, I began to describe a production of *King Lear*, or a movie, done as if from the older daughters' point of view, in which, of course, Miss Close would star. A good role for a woman. Though I was describing this in order to connect with her somehow, I didn't feel that I was successful in that, and I fell silent. Still, having my own *King Lear* was now more than a thought, though less than a project. That did not happen until the following March, when, for the first time since moving to Ames, I happened to drive with my husband to Minneapolis. As we were coming home in what we called "the iron season"—that is, everything frozen and dead and unattractive, I looked out the window somewhere around mile 170, and said, "You know, I could set that *King Lear* book around here. I know about this area." And there we were; as had happened to me with each book, a sight of the place where the novel was set caused the ideas and the characters to jell, as if all at once. *A Thousand Acres* was not a presence. The actual writing of it seemed more like a manageable detail than an effort of creation.

Three other threads that tied up for me in *A Thousand Acres* were feminism, environmentalism, and a vaguely Marxist materialism. No longer a student, I was now a teacher, and one course I

was assigned to teach was a course of world literature in translation for nonmajors. My reading list started with some parts of
Don Quixote, galloped apace through four centuries, and ended
with short stories by modern Latin American women writers. In
addition to literary works such as *Candide, Taras Bulba, Claudine
at School*, and *The Metamorphoses*, my class read and reported on
Fernand Braudel's three-volume history, *Civilization and Capitalism*. By the end of the semester, the students knew what capitalism
was and how the works we read expressed and critiqued it. By the
end of three semesters teaching this course, I had a much clearer
idea of how our times have evolved out of Shakespeare's times, and
how ideas and questions posed in his works have been answered
and modified by history. I developed a thought or two about the
intrusion of notions of ownership and commodification upon
familial and romantic relationships, and a thought or two about
the specificity, as opposed to universality, of western European
ideas of family order; of ownership and exploitation of land, resources, and the services of other human beings; of conflict, literary form, ego, power, gender, and the finality of death. Most of my
ideas were suggested by Braudel but realized through the literary
readings and our class discussions. While I was teaching this class,
I was writing *A Thousand Acres*.

In addition, I was living in Iowa. When my first husband was
accepted to graduate school, he was accepted by Iowa and Virginia. We discussed where he should go extremely briefly. Iowa
seemed nicer and more rural, somehow, and it was closer to Wyo-
ming, his home state. That was just about all we said about it. And
yet, of course, as it turned out, all sorts of agricultural issues and
environmental issues became a part of my daily life once I moved
to Iowa, lived in small towns, started reading the *Des Moines Register*, began to know people who lived on farms or had been raised
on farms. My absolutely first ecological concern when I got to
Iowa was to wonder, as a result of reading Barry Commoner's *The
Closing Circle*, whether the well water on the farm we were renting
was contaminated with nitrates, and whether, if I got pregnant,
I would be able to carry the baby to term. My second one was to

wonder how often over the years the bees who were living in our house had been poisoned with DDT. A lot of times, as it turned out. When we first moved there, I went for nature walks, but of course, the only place to walk was down the gravel road. Nature, as I had known it elsewhere, was missing, and large fields of crops had been put in its place.

And then there was feminism. Women's education made feminism inevitable. The rise of the Left ensured its almost immediate emergence. The outward flow of college women into work and family life disseminated it. When women of my generation became writers, editors, publishers, and literary critics, they could not help but express feminism because they could not help but express the right they felt to be doing what they were doing. And, I think, they couldn't help but express anger of same sort that the Yale class of 1970 expressed, not gratitude that they had been allowed in the gates, which I think is what those already inside thought we should express, but resentment at how long the gates had been barred, and how deluxe the accommodations inside the gates turned out to be.

When I looked out my car window at mile 170 and thought I might set my production of *King Lear* right there, these were the main ideas that fell together so suddenly and so completely. I had a global apprehension of the entire book which did not change significantly afterward, and I thought the book would be easy to write, but it wasn't. Of all my books it was the most difficult, and for that I blame Mr. Shakespeare.

After writing *The Greenlanders*, I rather prided myself on my cruelty to my characters. I was pleased at how readily I could sacrifice them to principle. Sudden, accidental death, for example, is a prominent feature of the Icelandic saga, often followed by the saga writer's remark, "And now he is out of this story." Boom, you're dead, doesn't matter how good or useful or interesting you are, that's life in the Middle Ages. And, I thought, in the modern period, too. Russell Banks once told me that it was his ambition to write the saddest novel ever written, in *Continental Drift*. I thought, that, except for *The Greenlanders*, he had succeeded. NO

REDEMPTION, the characteristic failure of artistic integrity of all western European authors. Every time you thought someone really great, like Tolstoy, was going to look straight down into the abyss, at the last minute, he stepped back—there was that little streak of light—even in Kafka, even, for God's sake, in Gogol. Only the Yiddish writers we read had the courage to fall at last into total darkness. The Yiddish writers and I. That was my claim to artistic respectability. I had read *King Lear* four or five times by the time I reread it to begin *A Thousand Acres*, and I had seen three productions of the play as well as Kurosawa's *Ran*. But I had never entered into a relationship with the play or the author like the one I entered into when I began writing through my version.

My intention was to stick as closely to the plot as I could, given one or two caveats. The first was that family battles in the twentieth-century rural midwest are more likely to be fought in the courts than with weapons—actual fighting with guns, say, would be too melodramatic. The second was that I wanted Goneril and Regan to live through to the end, so that they could reflect upon their experiences. That, too, I felt would be characteristic of life as we know it. The world population explosion shows us that survival has become the norm, survival even of terrible cataclysms like the genocide in Rwanda. Otherwise, though, I planned to play the game of following the storyline. When I began, I had a particular vision of Shakespeare—mentally healthy, passionate but also funny, smart, balanced, essentially good. A guy I could relate to. I thought that following his dramatic logic would be easy. And remember, I brought a suspicion of all that talk into the project, so I half wasn't listening to the particulars of what the characters were saying.

But I didn't find writing *A Thousand Acres* at all easy. Instead, I found myself, an author who had killed off hundreds of characters in *The Greenlanders* and ending a whole little world, recoiling from the cruelties of Shakespeare's twists and turns of plot. At first this wasn't conscious. I would be writing along, and discover that some plot point didn't quite fit, that is, that I had become confused, or that I didn't know how to progress the action. Then

I would read over what I had written, and compare it to the play, and discover that I had diverged slightly from what was happening in the play. I attributed this to lack of attentiveness on my part. But as the play progressed and the stakes got higher with each scene, I realized that what I was doing was avoiding the crueler judgments of the play upon its characters. Where Shakespeare had a character do something intentionally and coldly self-serving, I would resist it. But the plot was always the test, a puzzle that had to work out. The challenge was sticking to the plot but substituting what I considered a truer but what many would say was simply a more congenial view of human nature. As I followed him into the story, the Shakespeare that I thought I knew rapidly metamorphosed into a harsher, more alien, and more distant male figure. I felt very strongly our differences as a modern woman and a Renaissance man. At the root lay the question of the nature of evil. His view I read more and more as Machiavellian—cold, irreducible self-interest, unashamed, unsoftened by any sense of connection with others or of any common humanity. That these feelings should be present in a man of the Renaissance did not surprise me, but that they should be so forcibly expressed by the man who had also written *Much Ado*, *As You Like It*, even *Macbeth*, a treatise on the power of remorse, disturbed me because the cruelty of *King Lear* that I felt I was experiencing by rewriting it called into question all the softer and more humane insights of the other plays. Having to wrestle with his vision forced me to assert my own—not to knuckle under but to redouble my efforts to counter his characters' cold evil with my characters' hot passion, his characters' clear agenda of self-interest with my characters' ill-thought-out confusion. I could not allow his universality, but instead, as a rhetorical mode, had to counter it with assertions of the universality of my vision. My tool, the ace in my deck, was narrative form itself.

Drama privileges action over point of view. This privilege can sometimes be mitigated by asides, soliloquies, prologues, epilogues, and other devices, but for sheer relentless inescapable immersion in subjectivity and point of view, you can't beat narrative.

Narrative, in my opinion, always calls into question the validity of appearance, always proposes a difference between the public perception of events and their actual meaning. We see this all the time in our adversarial court system, where an event of apparent criminality has taken place, and the jury or the judge must decide which narrative of the event is more likely to be true. As the lawyer for Goneril and Regan, I proposed a different narrative of their motives and actions which cast doubts on the case Mr. Shakespeare was making for his client, King Lear. I made Goneril my star witness, and she told her story with care. I made sure that, insofar as I was able to swing it, she was an appealing witness as well—cautious, judicious, ambivalent, straightforward. I didn't, for example, dare to make Regan my star witness. She was too outspoken and full of spleen. The jury would have reacted negatively no matter whether what she had to say was true or not. The goal of the trial was not to try or condemn the father, but to gain an acquittal for the daughters. The desired verdict was not "innocent," but rather "not guilty," or at least, "not proven." One thing I learned from *Hamlet* is that none of us are innocent, but one thing I learned from narrative is that all of us have something to say in our own defense.

I would not say that I won the wrestling match with Mr. Shakespeare by any means. He exhausted my inventiveness, my theoretical underpinnings, my spirit. Where I had found writing *The Greenlanders* exhilarating though frightening, I found writing *A Thousand Acres* laborious. The work did not speed up as it went along, but rather slowed. When I was finished, I was both dissatisfied and at the end of my artistic rope. I felt that I was stopping rather than finishing. While I thought I had worked through the plot well enough, I knew that I had failed with Cornwall, who was so much a creature of his time and social class that he was not translatable at all; with Oswald, whose servility I could do nothing with; and to some degree with Cordelia, who just wouldn't talk to me. I thought I could solve these problems with another draft, but I didn't have another draft in me.

Even so, I felt that I had not given in to Mr. Shakespeare's alleged universality, but had, in fact, cut him down to size a little bit. I was happy to have made my case about what it means to be a father, what it means to be a daughter, about the asymmetry of power in patriarchal capitalist western European society, about the attempt to possess other persons as objects and to call that love. I knew that the mind of the reader-jury would be influenced by the order in which it encountered the two works. I hoped that the minds of adolescent girls would encounter *A Thousand Acres* first, and that it would serve them as a prophylactic against the guilt about proper daughterhood that I knew *King Lear* could induce.

At the same time, I pondered my new image of Shakespeare, and I thought of him doing just what I had done—wrestling with old material, given material, that is in some ways malleable and in other ways resistant. I thought about how all material, whether inherited or observed, has integrity. The author doesn't just do something with it, he or she also learns from it. The author's presuppositions and predispositions work on the material and are simultaneously transformed by it. I imagined Shakespeare wrestling with the "Leir" story and coming away a little dissatisfied, a little defeated, but hugely stimulated, just as I was. As I imagined that, I felt that I received a gift, an image of literary history, two mirrors facing each other in the present moment, reflecting infinitely backward into the past and infinitely forward into the future. I knew that the wrestling I had done had not been only with Shakespeare, but also with his nameless predecessors, who carried forward this question of the nature of evil from the earliest human times. Since to me the greatest joy of writing and reading is connecting, this sense of connection through Shakespeare with the distant past has been the loveliest reward of writing *A Thousand Acres*.

Once the novel was out of my hands, it entered into the publishing process and then into the hands of readers. My feeling about it was different from my feeling about *The Greenlanders*—I didn't live with the characters day after day, but instead lived with its success. The fact that *The Greenlanders* had had a devoted but narrow readership and had not made me famous meant that my private experience of it remained the most important one for me. In some sense I was its ideal reader as well as its author, and this bolstered the sense I had of it coming to me from the outside. *A Thousand Acres* was much different. As soon as I turned it in to the publisher it began becoming public. They began planning its promotion and I began talking officially about it. This, again, went right along with my sense of the novel while I was writing it—it was my production of *King Lear*, but hardly mine any more than any production belongs more than temporarily to any theater company. Since it had also exhausted me and I had found it difficult to write, I didn't exactly revel in its success—it wasn't dear to me. This sense of an impersonal relationship to the novel (though accompanied by a fondness for Ginny and Rose) was new and unlike what you might call the afterbirth of any of my previous novels. I therefore read with interest, but some detachment, the letters and papers that I began to get, analyzing various aspects of the novel, and it is to that response that I would now like to turn, as another way of regarding the composition of the novel.

I would say that the dozen or so analyses that I have read (this includes only papers written in the academic mode, not book reviews, which are a separate category) fall into three groups. The first of these discusses the novel in a way that I never thought of. An example would be the analysis I received not too long ago of my use of names in the novel. The writer considered "Zebulon," the county where the novel is set, "Ginny," and "Rose," the names of my main characters. I had chosen Zebulon for a concrete reason. Iowa has ninety-nine counties, and I did not want to pinpoint any of them, so I made an impossible geography and named it with the only Z word I could think of quickly, so that it would come after all the other counties (Wright is the last one in Iowa). I was surprised and gratified to learn that the land of Zebulon, in the Bible, is a land of Godless gloom, where the people of Israel have gone wrong. It fit nicely, but I hadn't thought of it. The same reader felt sure that I was likening Ginny to a jenny, or a female donkey, because it was her burden to carry the weight of the family history, and that in Rose's name, I was referring to Blake's line, "Oh, Rose, thou art sick!" I wish I had been! In my novel *Moo*, I found out only after publication that "Gift," the name of my villain, means "poison" in German. Gosh, I think, whenever I read one of those logical analyses that adds something to my understanding of the novel, I certainly am smart!

What I really think is only partially a fudge of the theoretical problem that these interpretations raise, and that is that since the novel exists in a cultural soup, it has references even to parts of the cultural soup that I am not conscious of but am possibly aware of on some level. The image of the sick rose was common in medieval literature, for example, and I did know what a jenny was. An author cannot use either the language or a wide array of images apart from their other appearances in the culture, and in many cases, as in this one, the work demonstrates a productive relationship to the culture that is partly independent of the conscious intentions of its author. The reader's analysis is neither right or wrong—it notes a true connection, but doesn't understand its source. There are in fact at least three logical systems at work in any piece of literature—there is the one that the author knowingly constructs, the one that the book makes in relationship to the rest of the culture, and the one that the reader constructs. These probably more or less overlap, but they are not identical. Recognition of these three separate incarnations of my work has helped me accept its independence, made me a bit more cautious as a reader, and also made me more accepting as a writer. I do think, though, that scholars need to be aware of all three incarnations in order to really understand a given work.

The second category is that of papers that seem to understand everything I tried to do, but don't go beyond that. These papers appeal to my pedagogical instincts—they please me because they make me feel that I was clear and cogent in my presentation. I also feel that the reader passed the test and understood what I put in there. If he or she liked it, so much the better. They gratify my ego, but they leave me feeling a little bad, as if the novel were only a simple communication, like a chart with names down one side and characteristics down the other, and all a good reader has to do is draw lines correctly from elements in one line to elements in the other. I suppose what I am saying is that these papers don't recognize and then reveal the darkened parts of the authorial machine outside consciousness and intention, and so there is nothing surprising in them, and therefore, nothing surprising in me.

The third group of papers takes more risks, and is, in my opinion, the sort of criticism I really like to read, both of me and of others. This group of papers is drawn to, and tries to come to terms with, the paradoxical other in the text. All my greatest reading experiences have had one thing in common, and that is that at some point I am made aware of how irreducibly different from me an author speaking through a given work truly is, and how completely alluring and marvelous it is to accept that difference. I am reading along, sensing the common humanity of author, narrator, characters, and me, and suddenly there is something entirely meet and fitting in the text that I would never have thought of, were I the author, and yet I understand and appreciate it. Dickens does this for me on almost every page, especially in my favorite of his, *Our Mutual Friend*. His style displays a way of organizing the world that is utterly alien from mine, yet perennially fascinating. I want to read and write criticism that explores how he came up with that style—that is the crux of Dickens for me.

I will say that in this group of papers, I have found a few where the writer of the paper seems resentful and antagonistic toward the otherness of the author—complaints of what the author should have been doing, how the novel might have been more to the taste of the critic, descriptions of mistakes and prescriptions of how to avoid them in the future, or even theories of how authors in general are severely wanting. But apart from these, I think that papers that openly acknowledge the literary paradox of otherness-simultaneous-with-kinship-or-affinity are getting at the heart of what I consider to be my experience as a reader who writes who reads who writes, the heart of why I started writing and keep writing, the literary mystery.

In closing, I would like to emphasize the tentative nature of the observations I've made here. The typical structure of scholarly and critical discourse is based on the presumption that the author's experience of the process and the text must be divined from the often fragmentary evidence. The freedom the death of the author gives his or her readers, I think, amply compensates for its inconvenience. At the same time, though, I am reminded of Freud's question, "What do women want?" Why, I have always thought, didn't he ask? One reason, perhaps, was that the women he might have asked could not have answered him in a language that he understood. In some ways, the language he used about women precluded an answer that he would have credited. Authors, too, have not developed a language for talking about what is going on inside them. For example, I have often felt that I could sense the physical effort of composing a novel, and that what it felt like was movement from one side of the brain to the other, back and forth, a form of physical exertion not unlike any other pleasurable but tiring exercise, though more subtle. Perhaps this is an actual perception of a physiological process, perhaps it is only an image, perhaps, with the brain, one gives rise to the other, or is the other. I haven't really discussed this with other authors because when we talk, it doesn't come up, or it sounds stupid to say it. I certainly have not discussed it with scholars, because no one has ever seemed interested. Additionally, the confessional mode is, of course, rhetorically, the trickiest of all modes, self-reflection the trickiest of all forms of observation. Nevertheless, I thank you for listening to these attempts I have been making to narrate the creation of *A Thousand Acres*, and I thank you for inviting me to think about it.

(1996)

Cynthia Ozick

(b. 1928)

Actors

The Jewish King Lear (1892) was written after brutal pogroms in Eastern Europe set in motion a massive wave of Jewish immigration to America. Jacob Gordin's adaptation of Shakespeare's tragedy spoke powerfully to an audience torn between old ways and new, traditional values and enlightenment ones. The play, which had its Lower East Side debut in 1892, was written as a star vehicle for Jacob Adler, one of the greatest actors of New York's Yiddish stage, and Adler played the part hundreds of times, even after suffering a debilitating stroke in 1920. The story goes that a playgoer was so caught up in the production, and so incensed at how Adler (as Lear) was mistreated by his daughters, that he made his way down the aisle and shouted to Adler that he should leave his heartless daughters and come home with him. Cynthia Ozick's short story "Actors" serves as a coda to that play and cultural tradition. Ozick, a major Jewish American novelist, essayist, and short story writer, briefly turned her attention to theater in the 1990s (in *Blue Light* and *The Shawl*, which was produced off-Broadway), and "Actors" dates from, and surely draws on, her experiences in what she describes in her essay "Old Hand as Novice" as the "delectable theatrical dark." "Actors," which captures both the timelessness of the story of *King Lear* as well as its particular meanings for both first and second generation American Jews in the twentieth century, was first published in the *New Yorker* in 1998; it subsequently appeared in a quartet of Ozick's stories, *Dictation*, in 2008.

∞

MATT SORLEY, born Mose Sadacca, was an actor. He was a character actor and (when they let him) a comedian. He had broad, swarthy, pliant cheeks, a reddish widow's peak that was both curly and balding, and very bright teeth as big and orderly as piano keys. His stage name had a vaguely Irish sound, but his origins were Sephardic. One grandfather was from Constantinople, the other from Alexandria. His parents could still manage a few words of the old Spanish spoken by the Jews who had fled the Inquisition, but Matt himself, brought up in Bensonhurst, Brooklyn, was purely a New Yorker. The Brooklyn that swarmed in his speech was useful to him. It got him parts.

Sometimes he was recognized in the street a day or so following his appearance on a television lawyer series he was occasionally on call for. These were serious, mostly one-shot parts requiring mature looks. The pressure was high. Clowning was out, even in rehearsals. Matt usually played the judge (three minutes on camera) or else the father of the murder victim (seven minutes). The good central roles went to much younger men with rich black hair and smooth flat bellies. When they stood up to speak in court, they carefully buttoned up their jackets. Matt could no longer easily button his. He was close to sixty and secretly melancholy. He lived on the Upper West Side in a rent-controlled apartment with a chronic leak under the bathroom sink. He had a reputation for arguing with directors; one director was in the habit of addressing him, rather nastily, as Mr. Surly.

His apartment was littered with dictionaries, phrase books, compendiums of scientific terms, collections of slang, encyclopedias of botany, mythology, history. Frances was the one with the steady income. She worked for a weekly crossword-puzzle magazine, and by every Friday had to have composed three new puzzles in ascending order of complexity. The job kept her confined and furious. She was unfit for deadlines and tension; she was myopic and suffered from eyestrain. Her neck was long, thin, and imperious, with a jumpy pulse at the side. Matt had met her, right out of Tulsa, almost twenty years ago on the tiny stage of one of those downstairs cellar theatres in the Village—the stage was only a clearing in a circle of chairs. It was a cabaret piece, with ballads and comic songs, and neither Matt nor Frances had much of a voice. This common deficiency passed for romance. They analyzed their mutual flaws endlessly over coffee in the grimy little café next door to the theatre. Because of sparse audiences, the run petered out after only two weeks, and the morning after the last show Matt and Frances walked down to City Hall and were married.

Frances never sang onstage again. Matt sometimes did, to get laughs. As long as Frances could stick to those Village cellars she was calm enough, but in any theatre north of Astor Place she faltered and felt a needlelike chill in her breasts and forgot her lines. And yet her brain was all storage. She knew words like "fenugreek," "kermís," "sponson," "gibberellin." She was angry at being imprisoned by such words. She lived, she said, behind bars; she was the captive of a grid. All day long she sat fitting letters into squares, scrambling the alphabet, inventing definitions made to resemble conundrums, shading in the unused squares. "Grid and bear it," she said bitterly, while Matt went out to take care of ordinary household things—buying milk, picking up his shirts from the laundry, taking his shoes to be resoled. Frances had given up acting for good. She didn't like being exposed like that, feeling nervous like that, shaking like that, the needles in her nipples, the numbness in her throat, the cramp in her bowel. Besides, she was embarrassed about being nearsighted and hated having to put in contact lenses to get through a performance. In the end she threw them in the trash. Offstage, away from audiences, she could wear her big round glasses in peace.

Frances resented being, most of the time, the only breadwinner. After four miscarriages she said she was glad they had no children, she couldn't imagine Matt as a father—he lacked gumption, he had no get-up-and-go. He thought it was demeaning to scout for work. He thought work ought to come to him because he was an artist. He defined himself as master of a Chaplinesque craft; he had been born into the line of an élite tradition. He scorned props and despised the way some actors relied on cigarettes to move them through a difficult scene, stopping in the middle of a speech to light up. It was false suspense, it was pedestrian. Matt was a purist. He was contemptuous of elaborately literal sets, rooms that looked like real rooms. He believed that a voice, the heel of a hand, a hesitation, the widening of a nostril could furnish a stage. Frances wanted Matt to hustle for jobs, she wanted him to network, bug his agent, follow up on casting calls. Matt could do none of these things. He was an actor, he said, not a goddam peddler.

It wasn't clear whether he was actually acting all the time (Frances liked to accuse him of this), yet, even on those commonplace daytime errands, there was something exaggerated and perversely open about him: an unpredictability leaped out and announced itself. He kidded with all the store help. At the Korean-owned vegetable stand, the young Mexican who was unpacking peppers and grapefruits hollered across to him, "Hey, Matt, you in a movie now?" For all its good will, this question hurt. It was four years since the last film offer, a bit part with Marlon Brando, whom Matt admired madly, though without envy. The part bought Matt and Frances a pair of down coats for winter, and a refrigerator equipped with an ice-cube dispenser. But what Matt really hoped for was getting back onstage. He wanted to be in a play.

At the shoe-repair place his new soles were waiting for him. The proprietor, an elderly Neapolitan, had chalked "*Attore*" across the bottom of Matt's well-worn slip-ons. Then he began his usual harangue: Matt should go into opera. "I wouldn't be any good at it," Matt said, as he always did, and flashed his big even teeth. Against the whine of the rotary brush he launched into "La donna è mobile." The shoemaker shut off his machine and bent his knees and clapped his hands and leaked tears down the accordion creases that fanned out from the corners of his eyes. It struck Matt just then that his friend Salvatore had the fairy-tale crouch of Geppetto, the father of Pinocchio; the thought encouraged him to roll up the legs of his pants and jig, still loudly singing. Salvatore hiccupped and roared and sobbed with laughter.

Sometimes Matt came into the shop just for a shine. The shoemaker never let him pay. It was Matt's trick to tell Frances (his awful deception, which made him ashamed) that he was headed downtown for an audition, and wouldn't it be a good idea to stop first to have his shoes buffed? The point was to leave a decent impression for next time, even if they didn't hire you this time. "Oh, for heaven's sake, buy some shoe polish and do it yourself," Frances advised, but not harshly; she was pleased about the audition.

Of course there wasn't any audition—or, if there was, Matt wasn't going to it. After Salvatore gave the last slap of his flannel cloth, Matt hung around, teasing and fooling, for half an hour or so, and then he walked over to the public library to catch up on the current magazines. He wasn't much of a reader, though in principle he revered literature and worshipped Shakespeare and Shaw and Oscar Wilde. He looked through *The Atlantic* and *Harper's* and *The New Yorker*, all of which he liked; *Partisan Review, Commentary*, magazines like that, were over his head.

Sitting in the library, desultorily turning pages, he felt himself a failure and an idler as well as a deceiver. He stared at his wristwatch. If he left this minute, if he hurried, he might still be on time to read for Lionel: he knew this director, knew he was old-fashioned and meanly slow—one reading was never enough. Matt guessed that Lionel was probably a bit of a dyslexic. He made you stand there and do your half of the dialogue again and again, sometimes three or four times, while he himself read the other half flatly, stumblingly. He did this whether he was seriously considering you or had already mentally dismissed you: his credo was fairness, a breather, another try. Or else he had a touch of sadism. Directors want to dominate you, shape you, turn you into whatever narrow idea they have in their skulls. To a director an actor is a puppet—Geppetto with Pinocchio. Matt loathed the ritual of the audition; it was humiliating. He was too much of a pro to be put through these things, his track record ought to speak for itself, and why didn't it? Especially with Lionel; they had both been in the business for years. Lionel, like everyone else, called it "the business." Matt never did.

He took off his watch and put it on the table. In another twenty minutes he could go home to Frances and fake it about the audition: it was the lead Lionel was after, the place was full of young guys, the whole thing was a misunderstanding. Lionel, believe it or not, had apologized for wasting Matt's time.

"Lionel apologized?" Frances said. Without her glasses on, she gave him one of her naked looks. It was a way she had of avoiding seeing him while drilling straight through him. It made him feel damaged.

"You never went," she said. "You never went near that audition."

"Yes, I did. I did go. That shit Lionel. Blew my whole day."

"Don't kid me. You didn't go. And Lionel's not a shit, he's been good to you. He gave you the uncle part in 'Navy Blues' only three years ago. I don't know why you insist on forgetting that."

"It was junk. Garbage. I'm sick of being the geezer in the last act."

"Be realistic. You're not twenty-five."

"What's realistic is if they give me access to my range."

And so on. This was how they quarreled, and Matt was pained by it: it wasn't as if Frances didn't understand how much he hated sucking up to directors, waiting for the verdict on his thickening fleshy arms, his round stomach, his falsely grinning face, his posture, his walk, even his voice. His voice he knew passed muster: it was like a yo-yo, he could command it to tighten or stretch, to torque or lift. And still he had to submit to scrutiny, to judgment, to prejudice, to whim. He hated having to be obsequious, even when it took the form of jolliness, of ersatz collegiality. He hated lying. His nose was growing from all the lies he told Frances.

On the other hand, what was acting if not lying? A good actor is a good impostor. A consummate actor is a consummate deceiver. Or put it otherwise: an actor is someone who falls into the deeps of self-forgetfulness. Or still otherwise: an actor is a puppeteer, with himself as puppet.

Matt frequently held forth in these trite ways—mostly to himself. When it came to philosophy, he didn't fool anybody, he wasn't an original.

"You got a call," Frances said.

"Who?" Matt said.

"You won't like who. You won't want to do it, it doesn't fit your range."

"For crying out loud," Matt said. "Who was it?"

"Somebody from Ted Silkowitz's. It's something Ted Silkowitz is doing. You won't like it," she said again.

"Silkowitz," Matt groaned. "The guy's still in diapers. He's sucking his thumb. What's he want with me?"

"That's it. He wants you and nobody else."

"Cut it out, Frances."

"See what I mean? I know you. I knew you'd react like that. You won't want to do it. You'll find some reason." She pulled a tissue from inside the sleeve of her sweater and began to breathe warm fog on her lenses. Then she rubbed them with the tissue. Matt was interested in bad eyesight—how it made people stand, the pitch of their shoulders and necks. It was the kind of problem he liked to get absorbed in. The stillness and also the movement. If acting was lying, it was at the same time mercilessly and mechanically truth-telling. Watching Frances push the earpieces of her glasses back into the thicket of her hair, Matt thought how pleasing that was, how quickly and artfully she did it. He could copy this motion exactly; he drew it with his tongue on the back of his teeth. If he looked hard enough, he could duplicate anything at all. Even his nostrils, even his genitals, had that power. His mind was mostly a secret from him—he couldn't run it, it ran him, but he was intimate with its nagging pushy heat.

"It's got something to do with Lear. Something about King Lear," Frances said. "But never mind, it's not for you. You wouldn't want to play a geezer."

"Lear? What d'you mean, Lear?"

"Something like that, I don't know. You're supposed to show up tomorrow morning. If you're interested," she added; he understood how sly she could be. "Eleven o'clock."

"Well, well," Matt said, "good thing I got my shoes shined." Not that he believed in miracles, but with Silkowitz anything was possible: the new breed, all sorts of surprises up their baby sleeves.

Silkowitz's building was off Eighth Avenue, up past the theatre district. The neighborhood was all bars, interspersed with dark little slots of Greek luncheonettes; there was a sex shop on the corner. Matt, in suit and tie, waited for the elevator to take him to Silkowitz's office, on the fifth floor. It turned out to be a cramped two-room suite: a front cubicle for the receptionist, a boy who couldn't have been more than nineteen, and a rear cubicle for the director. The door to Silkowitz's office was shut.

"Give him a minute. He's on the phone," the boy said. "We've run into a little problem with the writer."

"The writer?" Matt said stupidly.

"She died last night. After we called you about the Lear thing."

"I thought the writer died a long time ago."

"Well, it's not *that* Lear."

"Matt Sorley," Silkowitz yelled. "Come on in, let's have a look. You're the incarnation of my dream—I'm a big fan, I love your work. Hey, all you need is the Panama hat."

The hat crack was annoying; it meant that Silkowitz was familiar mainly with one of Matt's roles on that television lawyer show—it was his signature idiosyncrasy to wear a hat in court until the judge reprimanded him and made him take it off.

Matt said, "The writer's *dead*?"

"We've got ourselves a tragedy. Heart attack. Passed away in intensive care last night. Not that she's any sort of spring chicken. Marlene Miller-Weinstock, you know her?"

"So there's no play," Matt said: he was out of a job.

"Let me put it this way. There's no playwright, which is an entirely different thing."

"Never heard of her," Matt said.

"Right. Neither did I, until I got hold of this script. As far as I know she's written half a dozen novels. The kind that get published and then disappear. Never wrote a play before. Face it, novelists can't do plays anyhow."

"Oh, I don't know," Matt said. "Gorky, Sartre, Steinbeck, Galsworthy, Wilde." It came to him that Silkowitz had probably never read any of these old fellows from around the world. Not that

Matt had, either, but he was married to someone who had read them all.

"Right," Silkowitz conceded. "But you won't find Miller-Weinstock on that list. The point is what I got from this woman is raw. Raw but full of bounce. A big look at things."

Silkowitz was cocky in a style that was new to Matt. Lionel, for his arrogance, had an exaggerated courtly patience that ended by stretching out your misery; Lionel's shtick was to keep you in suspense. And Lionel had a comfortingly aging face, with a firm deep wadi slashed across his forehead, and a wen hidden in one eyebrow. Matt was used to Lionel—they were two old horses, they knew what to expect from each other. But here was Silkowitz with his baby face—he didn't look a lot older than that boy out there—and his low-hung childishly small teeth under a bumpy tract of exposed fat gums: here was Silkowitz mysteriously dancing around a questionable script by someone freshly deceased. The new breed, they didn't wait out an apprenticeship, it was drama school at Yale and then the abrupt ascent into authority, reputation, buzz. The sureness of this man, sweatshirt and jeans, pendant dangling from the neck, a silver ring on his thumb, hair as sleek and flowing as a girl's—the whole thick torso glowing with power. Still a kid, Silkowitz was already on his way to Lionel's league: he could make things happen. Ten years from now the scruffy office would be just as scruffy, just as out of the way, though presumably more spacious; the boy out front would end up a Hollywood agent, or else head out for the stock exchange in a navy blazer with brass buttons. Lionel left you feeling heavy, superfluous, a bit of an impediment. This Silkowitz, an enthusiast, charged you up: Matt had the sensation of an electric wire going up his spine, probing and poking his vertebrae.

"Look, it's a shock," Silkowitz said. "I don't feel good about it, but fact is I never met the woman. Today was supposed to be the day. Right this instant, actually. I figured first organize the geriatric ward, get the writer and the lead face to face. Well, no sweat, we've still got her draft and we've still got our lead."

"Lead," Matt said; but "geriatric," quip or no, left him sour.

"Right. The minute I set eyes on the script I knew you were the one. As a matter of fact," Silkowitz said, flashing a pair of clean pink palms, "I ran into Lionel the other night and he put me on to you."

These two statements struck Matt as contradictory, but he kept his mouth shut. He had his own scenario, Silkowitz scouting for an old actor and Lionel coming up with Matt: "Call Sorley. Touchy guy; takes offense at the drop of a hat, but one hundred per cent reliable. Learns his lines and shows up." Showing up being nine-tenths of talent.

Matt was businesslike. "So you intend to do the play without the writer."

"We don't need the writer. It's enough we've got the blueprint. As far as I'm concerned, theatre's a director's medium."

Oh, portentous: Silkowitz as infant lecturer. And full of himself. If he could do without the writer, maybe he could do without the actor?

Silkowitz handed Matt an envelope. "Photocopy of the script," he said. "Take it home. Read it. I'll call you, you'll come in again, we'll talk."

Matt hefted the envelope. Thick, not encouraging. In a way Silkowitz was right about novelists doing plays. They overwrite, they put in a character's entire psychology, from birth on: a straitjacket for an actor. The actor's job is to figure out the part, to feel it out. Feather on feather, tentative, gossamer. The first thing Matt did was take a black marking pen and cross out all the stage directions. That left just the dialogue, and the dialogue made him moan: monologues, soliloquies, speeches. Oratory!

"Never mind," Frances said. "Why should *you* care? It's work, you wanted to work."

"It's not that the idea's so bad. A version of a classic."

"So what's the problem?"

"I can't do it, that's the problem."

Naturally he couldn't do it. And he resented Silkowitz's demand that he trek all the way down to that sex-shop corner again—wasn't the telephone good enough? Silkowitz threw out the news that he couldn't proceed, he couldn't think, except in person: he was big on face to face. As if all that counted was his own temperament. With a touch of spite Matt was pleased to be ten minutes late.

A young woman was in the outer cubicle.

"He's waiting for you," she said. "He's finishing up his lunch."

Matt asked where the boy was.

Silkowitz licked a plastic spoon and heaved an empty yogurt cup into a wastebasket across the room. "Quit. Got a job as assistant stage manager in some Off Off. So, what d'you say?"

"The part's not for me. I could've told you this straight off on the phone. The character's ten years older than I am. Maybe fifteen."

"You've got plenty of time to grow a beard. It'll come in white."

"I don't know anything about the background here, it's not my milieu."

"The chance of a lifetime," Silkowitz argued. "Who gets to play Lear, for God's sake?"

Matt said heavily, bitterly, "Yeah. The Lear of Ellis Island. Just off the boat."

"That's the ticket," Silkowitz said. "Think of it as a history play."

Matt sat there while Silkowitz, with lit-up eyes, lectured. A history riff for sure. Fourth, fifth generation, steerage troubles long ago strained out of his blood—it was all a romance to little Teddy Silkowitz. Second Avenue down at Twelfth, the old Yiddish theatre, the old feverish plays. Weeping on the stage, weeping in all the rows. Miller-Weinstock ("May she rest in peace," Silkowitz put in) was the daughter of one of those pioneer performers of greenhorn drama; the old man, believe it or not, was still alive at ninety-six, a living fossil, an actual breathing known-to-be-extinct duck-billed dodo. That's where she got it from—from being his daughter. Those novels she turned out, maybe they were second-rate, who knows? Silkowitz didn't know—he'd scarcely looked at the handful of reviews she'd sent—and it didn't matter. What mattered was the heat that shot straight out of her script, like the heat smell of rusted radiators knocking in worn-out five-story tenements along Southern Boulevard in the thirties Bronx, or the whiff of summer ozone at the trolley-stop snarl at West Farms. It wasn't those Depression times that fired Silkowitz—it wasn't that sort of recapturing he was after. Matt was amazed—Matt who worshipped nuance, tendril, shadow, intimation, instinct, Matt who might jig for a shoemaker but delivered hints and shadings to the proscenium, Matt who despised exaggeration, caricature, going over the top, Matt for whom the stage was holy ground. . . . And what did little Teddy Silkowitz want?

"Reversal," Silkowitz said. "Time to change gears. The changing of the guard. Change, that's what! Where's the overtness, the overture, the passion, the emotion? For fifty, sixty years all we've had is mutters, muteness, tight lips, and, God damn it, you can't hear their voices, all that Actors Studio blather, the old religion, so-called inwardness, a bunch of Quakers waiting for Inner Light—obsolete! Dying, dead, finished! Listen, Matt, I'm talking heat, muscle, human anguish. Where's the theatrical *noise*? The big speeches and declamations? All these anemic monosyllabic washed-out two-handers with their impotent little climaxes. Matt, let me tell you my idea, and I tell it with respect, because I'm in the presence of an old-timer, and I want you to know I know my place. But we're in a new era now, and someone's got to make that clear—" Silkowitz's lantern eyes moved all around his cubicle; it seemed to Matt they could scald the paint off the walls. "This is what I'm for. Take it seriously. My idea is to restore the old lost art of melodrama. People call it melodrama to put it down, but what it is is open feeling, you see what I mean? And the chance came out of the blue! From the daughter of the genuine article!"

Matt said roughly (his roughness surprised him), "You've got the wrong customer."

"Look before you leap, pal. Don't try to pin that nostalgia stuff on me. The youthful heart throbbing for grandpa's world. That's what you figure, right?"

"Not exactly," Matt fibbed.

"That's not it, honest to God. It's the largeness—big feelings, big cries. Outcries! The old Yiddish theatre kept it up while it was dying out everywhere else. Killed by understatement. Killed by abbreviation, downplaying. Killed by sophistication, modernism, psychologizing, Stanislavsky, all those highbrow murders of the Greek chorus, you see what I mean? The Yiddish Medea. The Yiddish Macbeth! Matt, it was *big*!"

"As far as I'm concerned," Matt said, "the key word here is old-timer."

"There aren't many of your type around," Silkowitz admitted. "Look, I'm saying I really want to do this thing. The part's yours."

"A replay of the old country, that's my type? I was doing Eugene O'Neill before you were born."

"You've read the script, it's in regular English. American as apple pie. Lear on the Lower East Side! We can make that the Upper West Side. And those daughters—I've got some great women in mind. We can update everything, we can do what we want."

"Yeah, we don't have the writer to kick around." Matt looked down at his trouser cuffs. They were beginning to fray at the crease; he needed a new suit. "I'm not connected to any of that. My mother's father came from Turkey and spoke Ladino."

"A Spanish grandee, no kidding. I didn't realize. You look—"

"I know how I look," Matt broke in. "A retired pants presser." He wanted to play Ibsen, he wanted to play Shaw! Henry Higgins with Eliza. Something grand, aloof, cynical; he could do Brit talk beautifully.

Silkowitz pushed on. "Lionel says he's pretty sure you're free."

Free. The last time Matt was on a stage (television didn't count) was in Lionel's own junk play, a London import, where Matt, as the beloved missing uncle, turned up just before the final curtain. That was more than three years ago; by now four.

"I'll give it some thought," Matt said.

"It's a deal. Start growing the beard. There's only one thing. A bit of homework you need to do."

"Don't worry," Matt said. "I know how the plot goes. Regan and Goneril and Cordelia. I read it in high school."

But it wasn't Shakespeare Silkowitz had in mind: it was Eli

Miller the nonagenarian. Silkowitz had the old fellow's address at a "senior residence." Probably the daughter had mentioned its name, and Silkowitz had ordered his underling—the boy, or maybe the girl—to look it up. It was called the Home for the Elderly Children of Israel, and it was up near the Cloisters.

"Those places give me the creeps," Matt complained to Frances. "The smell of pee and the zombie stare."

"It doesn't have to be like that. They have activities and things. They have social directors. At that age maybe they go for blue material, you never know."

"Sure," Matt said. "The borscht belt revived and unbuckled. You better come with me."

"What's the point of that? Silkowitz wants you to get the feel of the old days. In Tulsa we didn't *have* the old days."

"Suppose the guy doesn't speak English? I mean just in case. Then I'm helpless."

So Frances went along; Tulsa notwithstanding, she knew some attenuated strands of household Yiddish. She was a demon at languages anyhow; she liked to speckle her tougher crosswords with "*cri de cœur,*" "*Mitleid,*" "*situación difícil.*" She had once studied ancient Greek and Esperanto.

A mild January had turned venomous. The air slammed their foreheads like a frozen truncheon. Bundled in their down coats, they waited for a bus. Icicles hung from its undercarriage, dripping black sludge. The long trip through afternoon dusk took them to what seemed like a promontory; standing in the driveway of the Home for the Elderly Children of Israel, they felt like a pair of hawks surveying rivers and roads and inch-tall buildings. "'The Magic Mountain,'" Frances muttered as they left the reception desk and headed down the corridor to Room 1-A: Eli Miller's digs.

No one was there.

"Let's trespass," Frances said. Matt followed her in. The place was overheated; in two minutes he had gone from chill to sweat. He was glad Frances had come. At times she was capable of unexpected aggressiveness. He saw it now and then as she worked at her grids, her lists of synonyms, her trickster definitions. Her hidden life inside those little squares gave off an electric ferocity. She was prowling all around 1-A as if it was one of her boxes waiting to be solved. The room was cryptic enough: what was it like to be so circumscribed—a single dresser crowded with tubes and medicines, a sagging armchair upholstered in balding plush, a bed for dry bones—knowing it to be your last stop before the grave? The bed looked more like a banquet table, very high, with fat carved legs; it was covered all over with a sort of wrinkly cloak, heavy maroon velvet tasselled at the corners—a royal drapery that might have been snatched from the boudoir of a noblewoman of the Tsar's court. A child's footstool stood at the bedside.

"He must be a little guy," Frances said. "When you get old you start to shrink."

"Old-timer," Matt spat out. "Can you imagine? That's what he called me actually."

"Who did?"

"That twerp Silkowitz."

Frances ignored this. "Get a look at that bedspread or whatever it is. I'd swear a piece of theatre curtain. And the bed! Stage furniture. Good God, has he read all this stuff?"

Every spot not occupied by the dresser, the chair, and the bed was tumbled with books. There were no shelves. The books rose up from the floorboards in wobbly stacks, with narrow aisles between. Some had fallen and lay open like wings, their pages pulled from their spines.

"German, Russian, Hebrew, Yiddish. A complete set of Dickens. Look," Frances said. "'Moby-Dick'!"

"In the atrium they told me visitors," said a voice in the doorway. It was the brassy monotone of the almost-deaf, a horn bereft of music. Frances hiked up her glasses and wiped her right hand on her coat: "Moby-Dick" was veiled in grime.

"Mr. Miller?" Matt said.

"Bereaved, sir. Eli Miller is bereaved."

"I heard about your daughter. I'm so sorry," Matt said; but if this was going to be a conversation, he hardly knew how to get hold of it.

The old man was short, with thick shoulders and the head of a monk. Or else it was Ben-Gurion's head: a circle of naked scalp, shiny as glass, and all around it a billowing ring of pearl-white hair, charged with static electricity. His cheeks were a waterfall of rubbery creases. One little eye peeped out from the flow, dangerously blue. The other was sealed into its socket. You might call him ancient, but you couldn't call him frail. He looked like a butcher. He looked like a man who even now could take an axe to a bull.

He went straight to the stepstool, picked it up, and tossed it into the corridor; it made a brutal clatter.

"When I go out they put in trash. I tell them, Eli Miller requires no ladders!" With the yell of the deaf he turned to Frances: "She was a woman your age. What, you're fifty? Your father, he's living?"

"He died years ago," Frances said. Her age was private; a sore point.

"Naturally. This is natural, the father should not survive the child. A very unhappy individual, my daughter. Divorced. The husband flies away to Alaska and she's got her rotten heart. A shame, against nature—Eli Miller, the heart and lungs of an elephant! Better a world filled with widows than divorced." He curled his thick butcher's arms around Frances's coat collar. "Madam, my wife if you could see her you would be dumbstruck. She had unusually large eyes and with a little darkening of the eyelids they became larger. Big and black like olives. Thirty-two years she's gone. She had a voice they could hear it from the second balcony, rear row."

Matt caught Frances's look: it was plain she was writing the old fellow off. *Not plugged in*, Frances was signalling, *nobody home upstairs, lost his marbles*. Matt decided to trust the better possibility: a bereaved father has a right to some indulgence.

"There's real interest in your daughter's play," he began; he spoke evenly, reasonably.

"An ambitious woman. Talent not so strong. Whoever has Eli

Miller for a father will be ambitious. Eli Miller's talent, this is another dimension. What you see there"—he waved all around 1-A—"are remnants. Fragments and vestiges! 'The Bewildered Bridegroom,' 1924!" He pinched a bit of the maroon velvet bedspread and fingered its golden tassel. "From the hem of Esther Borodovsky's dress hung twenty-five like this! And four hundred books on the walls of Dr. Borodovsky! That's how we used to do it, no stinginess! And who do you think played the Bridegroom? Eli Miller! The McKinley Square Theatre, Boston Road and 169th, they don't forget such nights, whoever was there they remember!"

Matt asked, "You know your daughter wrote a play? She told you?"

"And not only the Bridegroom! Othello, Macbeth, Polonius. Polonius the great philosopher, very serious, very wise. Jacob Adler's Shylock, an emperor! Thomashefsky, Schwartz, Carnovsky!"

"Matt," Frances whispered, "I want to leave *now*."

Matt said slowly, "You daughter's play is getting produced. I'm *in* it. I'm an actor."

The old man ejected a laugh. His dentures struck like a pair of cymbals; the corona of his magnetic hair danced. "Actor, actor, call yourself what you want, only watch what you say in front of Eli Miller! My daughter, first it's *romanen*, now it's a play! Not only is the daughter taken before the father but also the daughter is mediocre. Always mediocre. She cannot ascend to the father! Eli Miller the pinnacle! The daughter climbs and falls. Mediocre!"

"Matt, let's go," Frances growled.

"And this one?" Again the old man embraced her; Frances recoiled. "This one is also in it?"

"Here," Matt said, and handed Eli Miller one of Teddy Silkowitz's cards. "If you want to know more, here's the director." He stopped; he thought better of what he was about to say. But he said it anyway: "He admires your daughter's work."

"Eli Miller's Polonius, in the highest literary Yiddish, sir! Standing ovations and bravo every night. Every matinée. Three matinées a week, that's how it was. Bravo bravo. By the time she's born, my daughter, it's after the war, 1948, it's finishing up, it's practically gone. Gone—the whole thing! After Hitler, who has a heart for tragedy on a stage? Anyhow no more actors, only movie stars. Please, sir, do me a favor and name me no names, what is it, who is it, who remembers? But Eli Miller and Esther Borodovsky, also Dr. Borodovsky, whoever was there they remember!"

"With or without you," Frances warned, "I'm going."

Matt hung on. "Your daughter's play," he said, "is out of respect for all that. For everything you feel."

"What are you saying? I know what she is! My daughter, all her life she figures one thing, to take away Eli Miller's soul. This is why God makes her mediocre, this is why God gives her a rotten heart, this is why God buries the daughter before the father!"

They left him with tears running out of the one blue eye.

"I think you incited him," Frances said. "You just went ahead and provoked him." They were huddled in the bus shelter, out of the wind. It was five o'clock and already night.

Matt said, "An old actor, maybe he was acting."

"Are you kidding?" Frances said; hunched inside the bulk of her coat, she was shivering.

"You're always telling me *I* do that."

"Do what?"

"Act all the time."

"Oh, for Pete's sake," Frances said. "Why did you make me come anyhow? My toes are numb."

Late in February, on a day of falling snow, rehearsals began. Silkowitz had rented a cellar in a renovated old factory building in the West Forties, in sight of the highway and the river. The space had a stage at one end and at the other a sort of stockade surrounding a toilet that occasionally backed up. The ceiling groaned and shuddered. A far-off piano thumped out distracting rhythms: there was a dance studio directly overhead. The cast was smaller than Matt had expected—the three female roles had been reduced to two. Silkowitz had spent the last month reviewing the script, and was still not satisfied. No sooner did Matt learn the movements of a scene than the director had second thoughts and rearranged the blocking. To Matt's surprise, the boy who had been in Silkowitz's office was there, presiding over a notebook; Silkowitz had brought him back to be stage manager. Matt calculated that the kid had six weeks' experience.

Silkowitz had put himself in charge of secrets. Each rehearsal session felt like a cabal from which the actors were excluded. Strangers came and went, carrying portfolios. Silkowitz never introduced any of them. "This is going to be a tight job, nothing extraneous. I believe in collaboration with all my heart, but just remember that collaboration runs through me," he announced. And another time: "My intention is to clot the curds." It was a tyranny that outstripped even Lionel's. The veneer was on the shabby side, but there was a stubborn complacency beneath. Matt, who had his own ideas and liked to cavil, was disinclined to argue with Silkowitz. The director would stop him mid-sentence to murmur against a wall with one of those coming and going unknowns: it was a discussion of the set, or some question about the lighting; or there would be a cassette to listen to. The house was already booked, Silkowitz reported—a two-hundred-and-ninety-nine-seater west of Union Square—and he had nailed down a pair of invisible backers, whom he did not name. Silkowitz had a reputation for working fast: what seemed important yesterday no longer mattered today. He scarcely listened when Matt began to tell about the visit to Eli Miller. "Good, good," he replied, "right," and turned away to look over someone's swatch of cloth. It was as if he had never insisted on the journey to the Home for the Elderly Children of Israel.

At the end of each day's rehearsal, the director sat on the edge of the stage and drew the actors around him in a half-circle and gave them his notes. And then came the daily exhortation: what he wanted from them all, he said, was more passion, more susceptibility. He wanted them to be drinking metaphorical poison; he wanted them to pour out blood and bile and bitter gall.

"Especially you, Matt. You're under-playing again. Forget that less-is-more business, it's crap! More energy! We've got to hear the thunderclap."

Matt's throat hurt. He was teaching himself to howl. He had

abandoned all his customary techniques: his vocal cords seemed perplexed by these new uses. He felt his chest fill with a curious darkness. In the morning, before taking the subway down to rehearsal, he tramped through the blackening snow to the public library and found a warm spot near a radiator and fell into "King Lear," the original. He saw how those selfish women were stripping the old guy to the bone—no wonder he howls!

He was heading back to the subway when it occurred to him that it was weeks since he had stepped into the shoe-repair shop.

Salvatore did not know him.

"Hey, Salvatore!" Matt called in that stagy roar Silkowitz liked, and attempted an abbreviated version of his little comic jig. But in his clumsy buckled-up snow boots he could only stamp.

Salvatore said over the noise of his machines, "You got shoes to fix, Mister?"

"What the matter with *you*?" Matt said.

"*Il attore!*"

The trouble was the beard, the shoemaker said. Who could see it was his friend Matteo? What was the beard *for*? Had he gone into opera after all? With the beard he looked one hundred years old. This frightened Matt. Just as Silkowitz had predicted, Matt's whiskers had grown in stark white: he was passing for an old-timer in earnest.

And it was true: in a way he *had* gone into opera. Marlene Miller-Weinstock's primal voices still reverberated, even with Silkowitz's changes. His changes were logistical: he had moved the locale, updated the era, and accommodated the names of the characters to contemporary ears. Marlene Miller-Weinstock's play was a kind of thirties costume drama, and Silkowitz had modernized it. That was all. The speeches were largely unaltered. Grandiloquence! There were no insinuations or intimations, none of those shrewd hesitations that Matt loved to linger over. His gods were ellipsis and inference. Hers were bombast and excitation. Matt's particular skill was in filling in the silent spaces: he did it with his whole elastic face, and in the stance of his legs—a skeptical tilt of knee, an ironical angle of heel. But Marlene Miller-Weinstock's arias left no room for any play of suggestion or uncertainty. Fury ruled; fury and conviction and a relentless and fiery truth. It came to Matt that fury *was* truth; it amazed him that this could be so. His actor's credo had always been the opposite: glimmer and inkling are truth, hint and intuition are truth; nuance is essence. What Marlene Miller-Weinstock was after was malevolence, rage, even madness: vehemence straight out; shrieks blasted from the whirlwind's bowel. She was all storm. In the gale's wild din— inside all that howling—Matt was learning how to hear the steady blows of some interior cannon. The booms were loud and regular: it was his own heartbeat.

Those two women with him on that dusty little ill-lit stage—he felt apart from them, he saw them as moving shadows of himself. He felt apart from the men, one of whom he had worked with before, under Lionel's direction. And in the darkened margins of the place, on folding chairs along the wall, here was the boy with his notebook, and Silkowitz next to him, faintly panting, kicking his foot up and down as if marching to an unheard band. But Matt had pushed through a vestibule of embarrassment (it was shame over being made to howl) into some solitary chamber, carpeted and tapestried; it was as if he had broken through a membrane, a lung, behind which a sudden altar crouched, covered with Eli Miller's heavy tasselled bedspread. In this chamber Matt listened to his heartbeat. He understood that it wasn't Silkowitz who had led him here. Silkowitz was a literalist, a sentimentalist, a theorist—one of these, or all. Mainly he was flashy. Silkowitz's bets were on the future. He had nothing to do with this voluptuous clamor, Matt inside the gonging of his own rib cage, alone and very large; terrifyingly huge there on that dusty ill-lit stage. Marlene Miller-Weinstock had drawn him in. Or her father had. Inside his howl, Matt was beginning to believe the father's accusation: the daughter had taken hold of the father in order to copy his soul.

Silkowitz was pleased. "You've got it together," he told Matt. "Stick with Matt," he said to the others. He praised Matt for being everywhere at once, like a rushing ghost; for looking into the women's eyes with a powerful intimacy beyond naturalism; for what he called "symbolic stature" and "integration into the scene." All this puzzled Matt. He hated the lingo. It wasn't what he was feeling, it wasn't what he was doing. He had no consciousness of being part of a company. He wasn't serving the company, whatever Silkowitz might think. He was in pursuit of his grand howl. He wanted to go on living inside it. When rehearsals were over he kept to himself and hurried to the subway.

Ten days before the opening, Silkowitz moved the cast to the theatre. It was a converted movie house; the stage was undersized but workable. To get to the men's dressing room you had to go through a narrow airless tunnel with great rusted pipes sweating overhead. The place was active, swarming. The boy with the notebook kept on checking his lists and schedules; he seemed professional enough. Wires crisscrossed the floor. Taped music travelled in phantom waves between scenes. Big wooden shapes materialized, pushed back and forth along the apron. Silkowitz had a hand in everything, running from corner to corner, his long girlish hair rippling, the silver thumb ring reddening in the light of the "Exit" sign whenever he glided past it.

Frances had decided to attend these final days of rehearsal. Silkowitz made no objection. She came hauling a tote bag, and settled into the next-to-last row, laying out her dictionaries and references and pencils on the seats around her. She worked quietly, but Matt knew she was attentive and worried. He was indifferent to her inspections and judgments; he was concentrating on his howl. She mocked it as rant, but it didn't trouble her that Matt had departed from his usual style—he was doing his job, he was giving the director what he wanted. What it meant was a paycheck. And by now Matt couldn't claim, either, that Silkowitz was egging him on. The director was taking in whatever Matt was emitting. He was emitting a sea of lamentation. Frances dumped her papers back into the tote and listened. Matt was standing downstage, alone, in profile, leaning forward like a sail in a wind, or like the last leaf of a wintry tree. He looked wintry himself. It was the day's concluding run-through; the rest of the cast had left. Matt was doing his solo scene near the end of the second act. His big belly had mostly sunk. Lately he had no appetite. He was never hungry. His beard had lengthened raggedly; a brownish-yellowish tinge showed at the tips. He seemed mesmerized, suffering. He was staring ahead, into the dark of the wings.

He turned to Silkowitz. "Someone's out there," he said.

"There shouldn't be," Silkowitz said. "Lily's kid's sick, she went home. And anyhow her cue brings her in the other way. Is that electrician still working back there?" he called to the boy with the notebook.

"Everyone's gone," the boy called back.

Matt said hoarsely, "I thought I saw someone." He had let his hair grow down to meet the beard. His eyes were birdlike, ringed with creases.

"O.K., call it a day. You're not the only one who's dead tired," Silkowitz said. "Go get some sleep."

On the way to the subway, Frances beside him, Matt brooded. "There was a guy out there. He was coming from the men's toilet, I saw him."

"It's the neighborhood. Some creep wandered in."

"He was there yesterday, too. In the middle of that same speech. I think someone's hiding out."

"Where? In the men's toilet?"

"Ever since we got to the theatre. I saw him the first day."

"You never said anything."

"I wasn't sure he was there."

He was sorry he had spoken at all. It was not something he wanted to discuss with Frances. She had ridiculed his howl; she told him it was rant, he was only ranting. The ignorance, the obtuseness! He seized, dissolved, metamorphosed. His howl had altered him: the throat widens and becomes a highway for spectres, the lungs an echo chamber for apparitions. His howl had floated him far above Frances, far above Silkowitz. Silkowitz and Lionel, what did it matter? They were the same, interchangeable, tummlers and barkers, different styles, what did it matter? Silkowitz was attracted to boldness and color, voices as noisy as an old music hall; he was as helpless as Frances to uncover what lay in the cave of the howl. As for the actors, Matt saw them as automatons; he was alone, alone. Except for the man who was hiding out, lurking, gazing.

"My God, Matt," Frances exploded, "you're hallucinating all over the place. It's enough you've started to *look* the part, you don't have to go crazy on top of it. Don't expect me there again, I'm keeping away. I've got my deadlines anyhow."

That night her grids sprouted "urus," "muleta," "athanor," "stammel," "nystagmic," "mugient." She worked into the dawn and kept her head down. Occasionally she stopped to polish her lenses. Matt knew her to be inexorably logical.

The day before dress rehearsal, Matt brought his shoes in for a shine. Salvatore seemed wary. Matteo, he said, no longer looked one hundred years old; he looked two hundred.

"You know," Matt said carefully—he had to whisper now to preserve his howl—"there's something better than opera."

Salvatore said there was nothing better than opera. What could be better than opera? For the first time he let Matt pay for his shine.

Dress rehearsal went well, though a little too speedily. The man in the wings had not returned. Silkowitz sat with the cast and gave his last notes. He did not address Matt. Odors of coffee and pastries wafted, and with unexpected lust Matt devoured a bagel spread with cream cheese. He understood himself to be in possession of a deep tranquillity. All around him there was nervous buffoonery, witticisms, unaccountable silliness; it was fruition, it was anticipation. The director joined in, told jokes, teased, traded anecdotes and rumors. A journalist, a red-haired woman from the *Times*, arrived to interview Silkowitz. He had hired an industrious publicist; there had been many such journalists. This one had just come from speaking to Lionel, she said, to cover the story from another angle: how, for instance, a more traditional director might view the goings on down near Union Square. Lionel had responded coolly: he was a minimalist; he repudiated what he took to be Teddy Silkowitz's gaudy postmodern experimentalism. Would he show up at the opening? No, he thought not.

"He'll be here," Silkowitz told the interviewer. The little party was breaking up. "And don't I know what's bugging him. He used to do this sort of thing himself. He was a child actor at the old Grand Theatre downtown."

"Oh, come on. Lionel's an Anglophile."

"I read up on it," Silkowitz assured her. "In 1933 he played the boy Shloymele in 'Mirele Efros.' God forbid anybody should find out."

The cast, packing up to go home, laughed; wasn't this one of Silkowitz's show-biz gags? But Matt was still contemplating the man in the wings. He had worked himself up to unhealthy visions. It was likely that Frances was right; at least she was sensible. Someone had sneaked in from the street. A homeless fellow sniffing out a warm corner to spend the night. A drunk in need of a toilet. Or else a stagehand pilfering cigarettes on the sly. A banner, a rope, an anything, swaying in the narrow wind that blew through a crack in the rafters. Backstage—deserted at the end of a day, inhabited by the crawling dark.

On the other hand, he knew who it was; he knew. It was the old guy. It was Eli Miller, come down on the M-4 bus from his velvet-curtained bed in the Home for the Elderly Children of Israel.

Lionel would keep his word. He would stay away. Matt had his own thoughts about this, on a different track from Silkowitz's. Matt as Lear! Or a kind of Lear. Lionel had never given Matt the lead in anything; he was eating crow. Naturally he wouldn't put in an appearance. Thanks to Marlene Miller-Weinstock— swallowing her father's life, vomiting out a semblance of Lear—it was a case of Matt's having the last laugh.

In the clouded dressing-room mirror, preparing during intermission for the second act, he thickened his eyebrows with paint and white gum and spilled too much powder all over his beard—the excesses and accidents of opening night. He stepped out of his newly polished shoes to stand on bare feet and then pulled on his costume: a tattered monkish robe. Sackcloth. A tremor shook his lip. He examined the figure in the mirror. It was himself, his own horrifying head. He resembled what he remembered of Job—

diseased, cut down, humiliated. The shoemaker if he could see him would add another hundred years.

The first act had survived the risks. Silkowitz had all along worried that the audience, rocked by the unfamiliar theatricality—the loudness, the broadness, the brazenness, the bigness—would presume something farcical. He was in fear of the first lone laugh. A shock in the serpent's tail pulses through to its tongue. An audience is a single beast, a great vibrating integer, a shifting amoeba without a nucleus. One snicker anywhere in its body can set off convulsions everywhere, from the orchestra to the balcony. Such were the director's sermons, recounting the perils ahead; Matt habitually shut out these platitudes. And more from that cornucopia—think of yourselves, Silkowitz lectured them all, as ancient Greek players on stilts, heavily, boldly masked; the old plays of Athens and the old plays of Second Avenue are blood cousins, kin to kin. Power and passion! Passion and power!

Were they pulling it off? During the whole first act, a breathing silence.

Sweating, panting his minor pant, Silkowitz came into the dressing room. Matt turned his back. A transgression. An invasion. Where now was that sacred stricture about the inviolability of an actor's concentration in the middle of a performance, didn't that fool Silkowitz know better? A rip in the brain. Matt was getting ready to lock it up—his brain; he was goading it into isolation, into that secret chamber, all tapestried and tasselled. He was getting ready to enter his howl, and here was Silkowitz, sweating, panting, superfluous, what was he doing here, the fool?

"Your wife said to give you this." Silkowitz handed Matt a folded paper. He recognized it as a sheet from the little spiral pad Frances always carried in her pocketbook. It was her word-collector.

"Not now. I don't want this now." The fool!

"She insisted," Silkowitz said, and slid away. He looked afraid; for the first time he looked respectful. Matt felt his own force; his howl was already in his throat. What was Frances up to? Transgression, invasion!

He read "metamerism," "oribi," "glyptic," "enatic"—all in Frances's compact orderly fountain-pen print. But an inch below, in rapid pencil: "*Be advised. I saw him. He's here.*"

She had chosen her seat herself, in the next-to-last row, an aerie from which to spot the reviewers and eavesdrop on the murmurs, the sighs, the whispers. She meant to spy, to search out who was and wasn't there. Aha: then Lionel was there. He was in the audience. He had turned up after all—out of rivalry. Out of jealousy. Because of the buzz. To get the lay of Silkowitz's land. An old director looking in on a young one: age, fear, displacement. They were saying Lionel was past it; they were saying little Teddy Silkowitz, working on a shoestring out of a dinky cell over a sex shop, was cutting-edge. So Lionel was out there, Lionel who made Matt audition, who humiliated him, who stuck him with the geezer role, a bit part in the last scene of a half-baked London import.

As flies to wanton boys are we to the gods; they kill us for their sport.

Unaccommodated man is no more but such a poor, bare, fork'd animal as thou art.

Lear on the heath—now let Lionel learn what a geezer role could be, and Matt in it!

Lionel wasn't out there. He would not come for Silkowitz; he would not come for Matt. Matt understood this. It was someone else Frances had seen.

He made his second-act entrance. The set was abstract, filled with those cloth-wrapped wooden free forms that signified the city. Silkowitz had brought the heath to upper Broadway. But no one laughed, no one coughed. It was Lear all the same, daughter-betrayed, in a storm, half mad, sported with by the gods, a poor, bare, forked animal, homeless, shoeless, crying in the gutters of a city street on a snowy night. The fake snow drifted down. Matt's throat let out its unholy howl; it spewed out old forgotten exiles, old lost cities, Constantinople, Alexandria, kingdoms abandoned, refugees ragged and driven, distant ash heaps, daughters unborn, Frances's wasted eggs and empty uterus, the wild, roaring cannon of a human heartbeat.

A noise in the audience. Confusion; another noise. Matt moved downstage, blinded, and tried to peer through the lights. A black silhouette was thudding up the middle aisle, shrieking. Three stairs led upward to the apron; up thudded the silhouette. It was Eli Miller in a threadbare cape, waving a walking stick.

"This is not the way! This is not the way!" Eli Miller yelled, and slammed his stick down again and again on the floor of the stage. "Liars, thieves, corruption! In the mother tongue, with sincerity, not from a charlatan like this!" He thudded toward Matt; his breath was close. It smelled of farina. Matt saw the one blue eye, the one dead eye.

"Jacob Adler, *he* could show you! Not like this! Take Eli Miller's word for it, this is not the way! You weren't there, you didn't see, you didn't hear!" With his old butcher's arm he raised his stick. "People," he called, "listen to Eli Miller, they're leading you by the nose here, it's charlatanism! Pollution! Nobody remembers! Ladies and gentlemen, my daughter, she wasn't born yet, mediocre! Eli Miller is telling you, this is not the way!"

Back he came to Matt. "You, you call yourself an actor? You with the rotten voice? Jacob Adler, this was a thunder, a rotten voice is not a thunder! Maurice Schwartz, the Yiddish Art Theatre, right around the corner it used to be, there they did everything beautiful, Gordin, even Herzl once, Hirschbein, Leivick, Ibsen, Molière. Lear! And whoever was there, whoever saw Jacob Adler's Lear, what they saw was not of this earth!"

In a tide of laughter the audience stood up and clapped—a volcano of applause. The laughter surged. Silkowitz ran up on the stage and hauled the old man off, his cape dithering behind him, his stick in the air, crying Lear, Lear. Matt was still loitering there in his bare feet, watching the wavering cape and the bobbing stick when the curtain fell and hid him in the dark. Many in the audience, Frances informed him later, laughed until they wept.

(1998)

BJ Ward

(b. 1967)

Daily Grind

BJ Ward, poet, essayist, and teacher, is the author of three volumes of
poetry, *17 Love Poems with No Despair*, *Landing in New Jersey with Soft
Hands*, and *Gravedigger's Birthday*, in which "Daily Grind"—a poem
that explores what it might mean to make rereading Act 5 of *Othello* part
of one's daily life—first appeared. His poem is reprinted in the collection
In a Fine Frenzy: Poets Respond to Shakespeare (2005).

✎

  A man awakes every morning
and instead of reading the newspaper
reads Act V of Othello.
He sips his coffee and is content
that this is the news he needs
as his wife looks on helplessly.
The first week she thought it a phase,
his reading this and glaring at her throughout,
the first month an obsession,
the first year a quirkiness in his character,
and now it's just normal behavior,
this mood setting in over the sliced bananas,
so she tries to make herself beautiful
to appease his drastic taste.
And every morning, as he shaves
the stubble from his face, he questions everything—
his employees, his best friend's loyalty,
the women in his wife's canasta club,
and most especially the wife herself
as she puts on lipstick in the mirror next to him
just before he leaves. This is how he begins

each day of his life—as he tightens the tie
around his neck, he remembers the ending,
goes over it word by word in his head,
the complex drama of his every morning
always unfolded on the kitchen table,
a secret Iago come to light with every sunrise
breaking through his window, the syllables
of betrayal and suicide always echoing
as he waits for his car pool, just under his lips
even as he pecks his wife goodbye.

(2002)

Jen Bervin

(b. 1972)

FROM *NETS*

The title of Bervin's book embodies the principle at work in these poems, in which letters or words of the original are highlighted, netting new and unexpected meanings: "THE SON**NETS** OF WILLIAM SHAKE-SPEARE." In a note at the end of a volume that reimagines 60 of Shakespeare's 154 sonnets, Bervin, who works at the intersection of poetry and the visual arts, describes how she "stripped Shakespeare's sonnets bare to the 'nets' to make the space of the poems open, porous, possible—a divergent elsewhere." She adds that when "we write poems, the history of poetry is with us, pre-inscribed in the white of the page; when we read or write poems, we do it with or against this palimpsest." Bervin thus discovers deeper and unexpected meanings or resonances in a way that recalls what T. S. Eliot wrote of Shakespeare's contemporary John Webster: he "saw the skull beneath the skin." One of the most haunting revisions of Shakespeare's originals is Net 64, which highlights in that sonnet language that foreshadows the destruction of the Twin Towers on September 11, 2001: "I have seen . . . towers . . . down-razed . . . loss . . . loss."

63

Against my love shall be as **I am** now
With Time's injurious hand crushed and o'er worn;
When hours have drained his blood and filled his brow
With lines and wrinkles; when his youthful morn
Hath travelled on to age's steepy night,
And all those beauties whereof now he's king
Are **vanishing or vanished** out of sight,
Stealing away the treasure of his spring;
For such a time do I now fortify

Against confounding age's cruel knife,
That he shall never cut from memory
My sweet love's beauty, though my lover's life:
   His beauty shall **in these black lines** be seen,
   And they shall live, and he in them still green.

64

When **I have seen** by Time's fell hand defaced
The rich proud cost of outworn buried age,
When sometime lofty **towers** I see **down-razed**,
And brass eternal slave to mortal rage;
When I have seen the hungry ocean gain
Advantage on the kingdom of the shore,
And the firm soil win of the wat'ry main,
Increasing store with **loss** and **loss** with store;
When I have seen such interchange of state,
Or state itself confounded to decay,
Ruin hath taught me thus to ruminate—
That Time will come and take my love away.
   This thought is as a death, which cannot choose
   But weep to have that which it fears to lose.

93

So shall I live, supposing thou art true,
Like a deceived husband; so love's face
May still seem love to me, though altered new,
Thy looks with me, thy heart in other place.
For there can live no **hatred in** thine eye,
Therefore in that I cannot know thy change.
In many's looks, **the** false **heart's history**
Is writ in moods and frowns and wrinkles **strange**,
But heaven in thy creation did decree
That in thy face sweet love should ever dwell;

Whate'er thy thoughts or thy heart's workings be,
Thy looks should nothing thence but sweetness tell.
How like Eve's apple doth thy beauty grow,
if thy sweet virtue answer not thy show!

130

My mistress' eyes are nothing like the sun;
Coral is far more red than her lips' red;
If snow be white, why then her breasts are dun;
If hairs be wires, black wires grow on her head.
I have seen roses damasked, red and white,
But **no such roses** see I in her cheeks,
And in some perfumes is there more delight
Than in the breath that from my mistress reeks.
I love to hear her speak, yet well I know
That music hath a far more pleasing sound.
I grant I never saw a goddess go;
My mistress when she walks, treads on the ground:
And yet, by heaven, I think my love as rare
As any she belied with false compare.

(2004)

SOURCES AND
ACKNOWLEDGMENTS

INDEX

Sources and Acknowledgments

Care has been taken to find and acknowledge all owners of copyrighted materials included in this volume. If an owner has been unintentionally omitted, acknowledgement will gladly be made in future printings.

Anonymous, "The Pausing American Loyalist," *The Middlesex Journal, and Evening Advertiser*, January 27–30, 1776.

Jonathan M. Sewall, "Epilogue to Coriolanus," *Miscellaneous Poems* (Portsmouth, NH: William Treadwell, 1801).

Peter Markoe, "The Tragic Genius of Shakespeare; An Ode," *Miscellaneous Poems* (Philadelphia: W. Prichard and P. Hall, 1787).

John Adams to John Quincy Adams, January 20, 1805. The Adams Family Papers, Massachusetts Historical Society, Boston. Used by permission.

Washington Irving, "Stratford-on-Avon." *Washington Irving: History, Tales & Sketches*, ed. James W. Tuttleton (New York: The Library of America, 1983).

Charles Sprague, "Prize Ode," *The Port Folio*, Vol. 17, ed. John E. Hall (Philadelphia: Harrison Hall, 1824).

John Quincy Adams, "The Character of Desdemona," in James Henry Hackett, *Notes, Criticisms, and Correspondence upon Shakespeare's Plays and Actors* (New York: Carleton, 1863).

Edgar Allan Poe, "Hazlitt's *Characters of Shakspeare*," in *Edgar Allen Poe: Essays and Reviews*, ed. G. R. Thompson (New York: The Library of America, 1984).

J.M.W. [Jessie Meriton White?], "First Impressions of Miss Cushman's 'Romeo,'" *The People's Journal*, Vol. 2, ed. John Saunders (London: People's Journal Office, 1847).

Maungwudaus, "Indians of North America," transcribed in James Mc-Manaway, "Shakespeare in the United States," *PMLA* 79, 1964. Used by permission of the Modern Language Association of America.

Anonymous, *Account of the Terrific and Fatal Riot at the New-York Astor Place Opera House* (New York: H. M. Ranney, 1849).

Ralph Waldo Emerson, "Shakespeare; or, the Poet," in *Ralph Waldo Emerson: Essays and Lectures*, ed. Joel Porte (New York: The Library of America, 1983).

Herman Melville, "Hawthorne and His Mosses," in *Herman Melville: Pierre, Israel Potter, The Piazza Tales, The Confidence-Man, Uncollected Prose, Billy Budd*, ed. Harrison Hayford (New York: The Library of America, 1984).

William Wells Brown, "Ira Aldridge," in *The Black Man: His Antecedents, His Genius, and His Achievements* (New York: Thomas Hamilton, 1862).

Nathaniel Hawthorne, "Recollections of a Gifted Woman," in *Our Old Home: A Series of English Sketches*, (Boston: Ticknor & Fields, 1863).

Emily Dickinson, "Drama's Vitallest Expression is the Common Day," *The Poems of Emily Dickinson*, Volume II, ed. R. W. Franklin (Cambridge, MA: The Belknap Press, 1998). Used by permission of the publishers and the Trustees of Amherst College. Copyright © 1998 by the President and Fellows of Harvard College. Copyright © 1951, 1955, 1979, 1983 by the President and Fellows of Harvard College.

Henry Timrod, "Address Delivered at the Opening of the New Theatre at Richmond," in *The Poems of Henry Timrod*, ed. Paul H. Hayne (New York: E. J. Hale & Son, 1873).

Abraham Lincoln to James H. Hackett, August 17, 1863. In *Abraham Lincoln: Speeches and Writings 1859–1865*, ed. Don E. Fehrenbacher (New York: The Library of America, 1989). Used by permission of the Abraham Lincoln Association.

Mark Twain, "The Killing of Julius Cæsar 'Localized,'" in *Mark Twain: Collected Tales, Sketches, Speeches, & Essays 1852–1890*, ed. Louis J. Budd (New York: The Library of America, 1992). Used by permission of the University of California Press.

Oliver Wendell Holmes, "Shakespeare. Tercentennial Celebration. April 23, 1864," in *Songs of Many Seasons* (Boston: James R. Osgood and Company, 1875).

John Wilkes Booth, "Letter to Editors of the *National Intelligencer*," *The Washington Evening Star*, December 7, 1881.

Herman Melville, "'The Coming Storm,'" in *The Writings of Herman Melville: Published Poems,* ed. Robert Ryan et al. Copyright © 2009 by Northwestern University Press and the Newberry Library. Used by permission. All rights reserved. See also *American Poetry: The Nineteenth Century,* Vol. 2, ed. John Hollander (New York: The Library of America, 1993).

G.W.H. Griffin, *"Shylock," A Burlesque* (New York: Samuel French, [1867?]).

Mary Preston, "Othello," in *Studies in Shakspere. A Book of Essays* (Philadelphia: Claxton, Remsen & Haffelfinger, 1869).

Frederick Wadsworth Loring, "In the Old Churchyard at Fredericksburg," *The Atlantic Monthly*, September 1870.

Walt Whitman, "What Lurks behind Shakspere's Historical Plays?" In *Walt Whitman: Poetry and Prose*, ed. Justin Kaplan (New York: The Library of America, 1982).

William Winter, "The Art of Edwin Booth: Hamlet," *The American Stage: Writing on Theater from Washington Irving to Tony Kushner*, ed. Laurence Senelick (New York: The Library of America, 2010).

William Dean Howells, "Shakespeare," in *My Literary Passions* (New York: Harper & Brothers Publishers, 1895).

Willa Cather, FROM Between the Acts, *Nebraska State Journal*, April 29, 1894; "Antony and Cleopatra," in *The American Stage*, ed. Laurence Senelick (New York: The Library of America, 2010).

Henry Cabot Lodge, "Shakespeare's Americanisms," *Harper's New Monthly Magazine*, Vol. 90, January 1895.

Jane Addams, "A Modern Lear," *The Survey*, Vol. 29, November 2, 1912.

Belle Marshall Locke, *The Hiartville Shakespeare Club: A Farce in One Act* (Philadelphia: Penn Pub. Co., 1920).

Henry James, "The Birthplace," *Henry James: Complete Stories 1898–1910*, ed. Denis Donoghue (New York: The Library of America, 1996).

Mark Twain, "Autobiographical Dictation, January 11, 1909." *Unpublished manuscripts*, by Mark Twain, copyright © 2001 by the Mark Twain Foundation. All rights reserved. Used by permission of the University of California Press and the Mark Twain Papers, Bancroft Library.

George Santayana, "Shakespeare: Made in America," *The New Republic*, Vol. 2, No. 17, February 27, 1915.

Robert Frost, "'Out, Out—'", *The Poetry of Robert Frost*, edited by Edward Connery Lathem, copyright © 1916, 1969 by Henry Holt and Company, LLC. Copyright © 1944 by Robert Frost. Used by permission of Henry Holt and Company, LLC. All rights reserved. See also *Robert Frost: Collected Poems, Prose, & Plays*, ed. Richard Poirier and Mark Richardson (New York: The Library of America, 1995).

Charlotte Perkins Gilman, "Shakespeare's Heroines as Human Beings," *The New York Times*, March 5, 1916.

Charles Mills Gayley, "Heart of the Race," in *A Book of Homage to Shakespeare*, ed. Israel Gollancz (Oxford: Oxford University Press, 1916).

T. S. Eliot, "Hamlet and His Problems," *The Athenæum*, No. 4665, September 26, 1919.

William Carlos Williams, "To Mark Antony in Heaven," in *The Collected Poems of William Carlos Williams*, Vol. 1, ed. A. Walton Litz and Christopher MacGowan (New York: New Directions, 1986). Copyright © 1938 by New Directions Publishing Corp. and Carcanet Press Limited.

Lorenz Hart and Morrie Ryskin, "Shakespeares of 1922," in *The Complete Lyrics of Lorenz Hart,* ed. Dorothy Hart and Robert Kimball (New York: Knopf, 1986).

Stark Young, "The Tragedy of Hamlet," in *The American Stage*, ed. Laurence Senelick (New York: The Library of America, 2010).

George F. Whicher, "Shakespeare for America," *The Atlantic Monthly* 147, June 1931. Copyright © 2013. Used by permission of *The Atlantic*.

Joseph Quincy Adams, "Shakespeare and American Culture," *The Spinning Wheel* 12:9–10, June–July 1932.

James Thurber, "The Macbeth Murder Mystery," *My World And Welcome To It*. Copyright © 1942 by Rosemary A. Thurber. Used by arrangement with Rosemary A. Thurber and The Barbara Hogenson Agency, Inc. All rights reserved. See also *James Thurber: Writings & Drawings*, ed. Garrison Keillor (New York: The Library of America, 1996).

Sidney B. Whipple, "New 'Julius Caesar' at Mercury Theater," *New York World-Telegram*, November 12, 1937; "Beauties of 'Caesar' Impressive," *New York World-Telegram*, November 15, 1937.

Toshio Mori, "Japanese Hamlet," in *The Chauvinist and Other Stories* (Los Angeles: Asian American Studies Center, University of California, Los Angeles, 1979). Used by permission of the Asian American Studies Center, University of California at Los Angeles.

Langston Hughes, "Shakespeare in Harlem," *The Collected Poems of Langston Hughes*, edited by Arnold Rampersad with David Roessel, Associate Editor, copyright © 1994 by the Estate of Langston Hughes. Used by permission of Alfred A. Knopf, an imprint of the Knopf Doubleday Publishing Group, a division of Random House LLC. All rights reserved.

Samuel Sillen, "Paul Robeson's Othello," *The New Masses,* November 2, 1943.

James Agee, "Laurence Olivier's Henry V," *Time*, April 8, 1964 and *The Nation*, July 20, 1946 and August 3, 1946 in *James Agee: Film Writing and Selected Journalism*, ed. Michael Sragow (New York: The Library of America, 2005). Used by permission of Time Inc. and *The Nation*.

Maurice Evans, "Preface to *G. I. Hamlet,*" in *Maurice Evans's G. I. Production of 'Hamlet'* (Garden City, New York: Doubleday & Co., Inc, 1947). Copyright © 1947 by Maurice Evans. Used by permission of Random House, Inc.

Cole Porter, "Brush Up Your Shakespeare," *Kiss Me, Kate* (1948). Published 1949. Words and music by Cole Porter. Copyright © 1949 by Cole Porter. Copyright renewed. Assigned to John F. Wharton, Trustee of the Cole Porter Musical & Literary Property Trusts. Chappell & Co., Inc., Publisher. International Copyright Secured. Used by permission. All rights reserved. See also *Cole Porter: Selected Lyrics*, ed. Robert Kimball (New York: American Poets Project, 2006).

Hollis Alpert, "The Abuse of Greatness," *The Saturday Review*, June 6, 1953.

Isaac Asimov, "The Immortal Bard," *Earth is Room Enough: Science Fiction Tales of Our Own Planet* (Garden City, NY: Doubleday & Company, 1957). Copyright © 1953 by Palmer Publications. Used by permission of Doubleday, an imprint of the Knopf Doubleday Publishing Group, a division of Random House LLC. All rights reserved.

John Berryman, "Shakespeare's Last Word: Justice and Redemption," in *The Freedom of the Poet* (New York: Farrar, Straus, & Giroux). Copyright © 1976, renewed 1993 by Kate Berryman. Used by permission of Farrar, Straus and Giroux, LLC.

Lord Buckley, "Hipsters, Flipsters, and Finger-Poppin' Daddies," *Hiparama of the Classics* (San Francisco: City Lights Books, 1960). Copyright © 1960 by Lord Buckley. Used by permission of City Lights Books.

Hyam Plutzik, "Carlus" (from *Horatio*), *The Yale Review* 50, December 1960. Copyright © 1960 Blackwell Publishing Ltd. Used by permission of Blackwell Publishing Ltd.

Mary McCarthy, "General Macbeth," in *The Writing on the Wall, and Other Literary Essays* (New York: Harcourt, Brace, and World, Inc., 1970). Used by permission of the Mary McCarthy Literary Estate.

Adrienne Rich, "After Dark," *Necessities of Life: Poems, 1962–1965* (New York: W. W. Norton & Company, 1966). Copyright © 1993 by Adrienne Rich. Copyright © 1966 by W. W. Norton & Company, Inc. Used by permission of W. W. Norton & Company, Inc.

Pauline Kael, "Orson Welles: There Ain't No Way," *The Age of Movies: Selected Writings of Pauline Kael*, ed. Sanford Schwartz (New York: The Library of America, 2011).

John Houseman, from *Run-Through: A Memoir* (New York: Simon & Schuster, 1972).

Woody Allen, "But Soft . . . Real Soft," *Without Feathers* (New York: Random House, 1975). Copyright © 1975 by Woody Allen. Used by permission of Random House, Inc.

Walter McDonald, "Caliban in Blue," *Caliban in Blue and Other Poems* (Lubbock: Texas Tech Press, 1976). Used by permission of Texas Tech University Press.

Gloria Naylor, "Cora Lee," *The Women of Brewster Place* (New York: Viking Penguin, 1982). Copyright © 1980, 1982 by Gloria Naylor. Used by permission of Viking Penguin, a division of Penguin Group (USA) Inc.

Leonard Bernstein, Arthur Laurents, Jerome Robbins, and Stephen Sondheim, moderated by Terrence McNally, "Landmark Symposium: *West Side Story*," *Dramatists Guild Quarterly*, Vol. 22, Autumn 1985. Used by permission of the Dramatists Guild of America, Inc.

Frank Rich, "Peaks and Valley's in Papp's Marathon," *The New York Times*, February 5, 1989. Copyright © 1989 by *The New York Times*. All rights reserved. Used by permission and protected by the copyright laws of the United States. The printing, copying, redistribution, or retransmission of this content without express written permission is prohibited.

Joseph Papp, "The Shakespeare Marathon: The Coach's View," *The New York Times*, February 19, 1989. Used by permission of the Estate of Joseph Papp.

Sam Wanamaker, "Address to the Royal Society of Arts," Globe Theatre archives, 1989. Used by permission of Shakespeare's Globe.

Jane Smiley, "Shakespeare in Iceland," *Shakespeare and the Twentieth Century: The Selected Proceedings of the International Shakespeare Association World Congress, Los Angeles 1996*, ed. Jonathan Bate, Jill L. Levenson, and Dieter Mehl (Newark: University of Delaware Press, 1998). Used by permission of Associated University Presses.

Cynthia Ozick, "Actors," *The New Yorker*, October 5, 1998. Copyright © 2008 by Cynthia Ozick. Used by permission of Houghton Mifflin Harcourt Publishing Company. All rights reserved.

BJ Ward, "Daily Grind," in *Gravedigger's Birthday: Poems* (Berkeley, CA: North Atlantic Books, 2002). Copyright © 2002 by BJ Ward. Used by permission of North Atlantic Books.

Jen Bervin, from *NETS* (Brooklyn: Ugly Duckling Presse, 2004). Used by permission of Ugly Duckling Presse.

Illustrations

1. Ira Aldridge as Othello circa 1854, by S. Bühler. Used by permission of the Folger Shakespeare Library.
2. Maungwudaus circa 1844–65, by W. K. Sherwood. Courtesy of the Library and Archives Canada/W. K. Sherwood.
3. Charlotte Cushman as Romeo circa 1846, by Thomas Fairland after Margaret Gillies. Used by permission of the Folger Shakespeare Library.
4. Riot at the Astor Place Opera House, 1849. Courtesy of the Library of Congress, Prints & Photographs Division.
5. Booth brothers in Shakespeare's *Julius Caesar*, 1864. Courtesy of John Hay Library, Brown University.
6. Jacob Adler as Shylock, by the Byron Company. Used by permission of the Folger Shakespeare Library.
7. John Barrymore as Hamlet, 1922, by Frank W. Bergmann. Used by permission of the Folger Shakespeare Library.
8. "Voodoo Macbeth" at Harlem's Lafayette Theatre, 1936. Works Progress Administration. Courtesy of the Library of Congress, Federal Theatre Project Collection, Music Division.
9. Cinna the Poet in Orson Welles's 1937 *Julius Caesar* at the Mercury Theatre. Courtesy of Photofest, Inc.
10. Paul Robeson as Othello, 1943. U.S. Farm Security Administration/Office of War Information. Courtesy of the Library of Congress, Prints & Photographs Division.
11. Patricia Morison in *Kiss Me, Kate*, 1948, by Ralph Morse. Courtesy of Time & Life Pictures/Getty Images.
12. Marlon Brando as Antony in *Julius Caesar*, 1953. © Metro-Goldwyn-Mayer Pictures/Sunset Boulevard/Corbis.
13. *West Side Story* playbill, 1957. Courtesy of Photofest, Inc.
14. Orson Welles as Falstaff, 1966, by the John Kobal Foundation. Courtesy of Getty Images.
15. Reconstruction of the Globe Theater at the Great Lakes Exposition circa 1936–37. Courtesy of the Cleveland Public Library Photograph Collection.
16. Joseph Papp at the Delacorte Theater, 1961, by George Joseph. Copyright © George Joseph/The New York Public Library.

I am grateful for the help of a number of friends and colleagues: Mary Cregan, Andrew Delbanco, Michael Dobson, Anne Edelstein, Stephen Enniss, David Scott Kastan, Theodore B. Leinwand, Richard McCoy, Gail Kern Paster, Ross Posnock, Alden and Virginia Vaughan, H. Aram Veeser, Michael Witmore, and Georgianna Ziegler. Working with the extraordinary team of scholars and editors at The Library of America has been a wonderful experience; I am especially grateful for the sage advice of my publisher, Max Rudin, as well as for the insights and contributions of Geoffrey O'Brien, Stefanie Peters, and Brian McCarthy. I am also indebted to the outstanding staff at the Folger Shakespeare Library, the New York Public Library, and Columbia University Libraries. My greatest debt is to the terrific students, from whom I have learned so much, in my undergraduate and graduate seminars at Columbia on 'Shakespeare in America.'

James Shapiro

Index

*This book is set in 11 point Adobe Garamond Premier Pro, a
face designed for digital composition by Robert Slimbach and based
on the sixteenth-century fonts of Claude Garamond and Robert Granjon.
The paper is acid-free lightweight opaque and meets the requirements for
permanence of the American National Standards Institute. The
binding material is Brillianta, a woven rayon cloth made
by Van Heek-Scholco Textielfabrieken, Holland.
Composition by David Bullen Design.
Printing and binding by Edwards
Brothers Malloy, Ann Arbor.*

THE LIBRARY OF AMERICA SERIES

The Library of America fosters appreciation and pride in America's literary heritage by publishing, and keeping permanently in print, authoritative editions of America's best and most significant writing. An independent nonprofit organization, it was founded in 1979 with seed funding from the National Endowment for the Humanities and the Ford Foundation.

To subscribe to the series or to order individual copies, please visit www.loa.org or call (800) 964.5778.

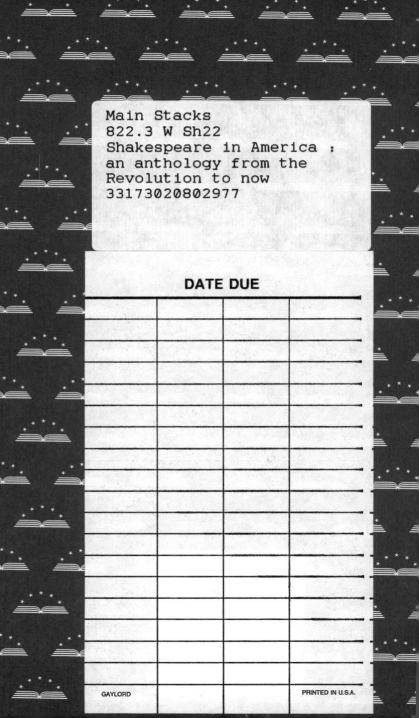

DATE DUE

GAYLORD   PRINTED IN U.S.A.